# Beginning ASP Databases

## John Kauffman

**with**
**Kevin Spencer**
**Thearon Willis**

Wrox Press Ltd. ®

# Beginning ASP Databases

Reprinted:    April 2000

Published by Wrox Press Ltd, Arden House, 1102 Warwick Road, Acocks Green,
Birmingham, B27 6BH, UK
Printed in the United States
ISBN 1-861002-7-26

# Trademark Acknowledgements

# Credits

**Authors**
John Kauffman
Kevin Spencer
Thearon Willis

**Additional Material**
Chris Blexrud
David Buser
David Sussman
Chris Ullman

**Technical Reviewers**
Burt Abreu
Chris Blexrud
David Buser
Charles Caison Jnr
Robert Chang
Michael Corning
Steve Danielson
Marco Gregorini
Scott Haley
Rob Hebron
Jon Jenkins
Manohar Kamath
Pieter Reint Siegers Kort
Robert MacDonald
Sam MacDonald
Dave Navarro Sr
Geoff Pennington
John Timney
David Williams

**Managing Editor**
Joanna Mason

**Development Editor**
Sarah Bowers

**Technical Editors**
Joanna Mason
Dianne Parker
Andrew Polshaw

**Design/Layout**
Tom Bartlett
Mark Burdett
Jonathan Jones
John McNulty
William Fallon
David Boyce

**Figures**
David Boyce
William Fallon

**Cover**
Chris Morris

**Index**
Alessandro Ansa

# About the Authors

## John Kauffman

John Kauffman was born in Philadelphia, the son of a chemist and a nurse. John's family of six shared daily brain teasers and annual camping forays that covered most of the 50 United States. After jobs weeding strawberry patches, bussing tables, running spotlights for rock and roll concerts, touring North America with a drum and bugle corps, prematurely leaving three colleges, stuffing voles for a mammologist, packing boxes of rat poison, tarring roofs, delivering drapes in New York City, laboring in a candy factory, teaching canoeing, driving a forklift, studying tiger beetles in the Chihuahua desert, managing a picture framing factory, coaching a youth yacht racing team and volunteering as a human guinea pig for medical research, John (to the great relief of all around him) earned a pair of degrees in the sciences from The Pennsylvania State University and appeared to settle down. He then conducted research for Hershey Foods in the genetics of the cacao tree and the molecular biology of chocolate production. Subsequently he moved to Rockefeller University where he identified, cloned and sequenced DNA regions which control the day and night biochemical cycles of plants.

But science didn't hold a candle to a woman he met in 1985 and married. Since then he has followed Liz in her career as a diplomat across four continents. They moved to Tanzania in 1986 and John began work with computers and business management in an assistance program for subsistence-level farmers. In 1990 they moved to Taiwan and then mainland China where John provided software training services to multi-national corporations and the diplomatic community in Beijing, Hong Kong, Shanghai and Sichuan. During the graduation banquet for one course he was honored by his students with a special entree of snake bile, frog skin and turtle meats.

John and Liz performed their most significant genetics experiments in 1988 and 1990 with the production of their children Sylvia and John. Growing up in Africa and China, they are doing well hashing through another generation's worth of brain teasers and camping trips.

John now divides his freelance consulting time evenly between teaching, writing and programming, primarily in the areas of Visual Basic, Word macros, Access and Access Programming, and ASP. John is available for contract training in Asia, Europe and North America by contacting Training@Kauffmans.org.

*This book is dedicated my parents in appreciation of their tremendous effort raising my siblings and me: to my father, who spent so much of his time helping us to understand science and mathematics; and to my mother, who invested so much of herself in facilitating our far-reaching interests in science, music and business. But their greatest gift was helping us to understand how other people think, feel and learn, and to value what others have to say. That gift is the key to my success. It is my parents' lessons that allow me to listen to my students and clients, then work with them to achieve their goals.*

## Kevin Spencer

I started programming in C in the early '90's and wrote a number of shareware programs for DOS, most of which were Door programs for BBSs. In the process, I learned to construct relational databases in C, and later worked with Microsoft Visual FoxPro and Access. As Internet Database Connectivity technologies began to emerge from Microsoft, I learned them as well, and several years ago, started my business, "Site Design by TAKempis," which specializes in Internet Database application programming with ASP/ADO. Microsoft awarded me the MVP award in 1997. I have written articles about Microsoft FrontPage and ASP/ADO for several online magazines, including Wrox's ASP Today.

## Thearon Willis

A senior consultant with 19 years of IT experience, Thearon is currently a consultant for an International Insurance company providing Web programming services. His Web development tools of choice are ASP, Dynamic HTML, Visual Basic and SQL Server. Thearon lives in Charlotte, North Carolina with his wife and daughter.

*To my wife Margie for her patience and understanding while I write yet another book, I love you very much.*

Setup cannot install system files or update shared files if the files are in use. Before co
any open applications.

WARNING: This program is protected by copyright law and international treaties.

You may install Microsoft Data Access 2.1 on a single computer. Some Microsoft products
with additional rights, which are stated in the End User License Agreement included with y

Please take a moment to read the End User License Agreement now. It contains all of the te
conditions that pertain to this software product. By choosing to continue, you indicate accept
these terms.

Continue                                          Exit Setup

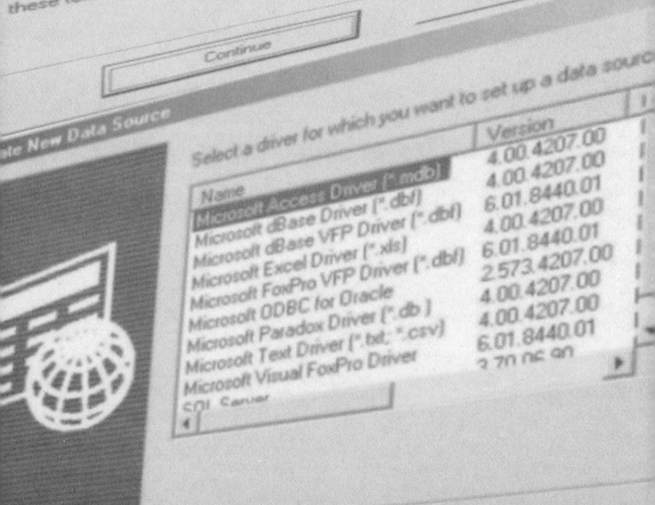

te New Data Source

Select a driver for which you want to set up a data sourc

| Name | Version |
| --- | --- |
| Microsoft Access Driver (*.mdb) | 4.00.4207.00 |
| Microsoft dBase Driver (*.dbf) | 4.00.4207.00 |
| Microsoft dBase VFP Driver (*.dbf) | 6.01.8440.01 |
| Microsoft Excel Driver (*.xls) | 4.00.4207.00 |
| Microsoft FoxPro VFP Driver (*.dbf) | 6.01.8440.01 |
| Microsoft ODBC for Oracle | 2.573.4207.00 |
| Microsoft Paradox Driver (*.db ) | 4.00.4207.00 |
| Microsoft Text Driver (*.txt; *.csv) | 4.00.4207.00 |
| Microsoft Visual FoxPro Driver | 6.01.8440.01 |
| SQL Server | 3.70.06.90 |

Cancel

# Table of Contents

# Chapter 5: More Uses for Simple Recordsets                159

# Chapter 6: Connections                                   187

## Chapter 7: Behind the Scenes of ADO 223

# Chapter 8: Recordset Parameters 255

## Chapter 13: Command Object

# Chapter 15: Irregular Data                                        597

# Chapter 16: ADO Tips and Tricks                                   625

# Chapter 17: Performance Testing and Performance Improvements 651

# Appendix G: VBScript Reference   789

Setup cannot install system files or update shared files if the files are in use. Before co
any open applications.

WARNING: This program is protected by copyright law and international treaties.

You may install Microsoft Data Access 2.1 on a single computer. Some Microsoft products
with additional rights, which are stated in the End User License Agreement included with yo

Please take a moment to read the End User License Agreement now. It contains all of the te
conditions that pertain to this software product. By choosing to continue, you indicate accepta
these terms.

Exit Setup

Continue

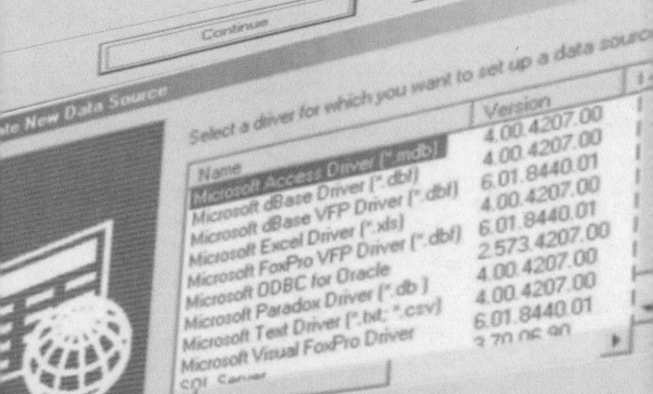

e New Data Source

Select a driver for which you want to set up a data sourc

| Name | Version |
|------|---------|
| Microsoft Access Driver (*.mdb) | 4.00.4207.00 |
| Microsoft dBase Driver (*.dbf) | 4.00.4207.00 |
| Microsoft dBase VFP Driver (*.dbf) | 6.01.8440.01 |
| Microsoft Excel Driver (*.xls) | 4.00.4207.00 |
| Microsoft FoxPro VFP Driver (*.dbf) | 6.01.8440.01 |
| Microsoft ODBC for Oracle | 2.573.4207.00 |
| Microsoft Paradox Driver (*.db ) | 4.00.4207.00 |
| Microsoft Text Driver (*.txt; *.csv) | 4.00.4207.00 |
| Microsoft Visual FoxPro Driver | 6.01.8440.01 |
| SQL Server | 2.70.06.90 |

Cancel

# Introduction

Microsoft created Active Server Pages (ASP) to sew together a group of technologies for creating modern web sites, which can intelligently interact with the user at the front end and with servers and datastores at the back end. Among these technologies is ActiveX Data Objects (ADO), which allows easy, powerful and robust control of technologies that access datastores. This book explains the theory and practice of using ADO with ASP by presenting numerous examples, exercises, lists of common errors and quizzes. The emphasis is on the author's proven teaching techniques and the presentation of the most commonly used features of ADO in ASP. If you read each chapter and do the exercises you will have a portfolio of several dozen data-intensive web pages of increasing complexity – a fine return on your investment.

## What Is This Book About?

This book explains, demonstrates and applies techniques that lie at the intersection of the two great tools of the Information Age. One tool, the database, is relatively old. The other, the World Wide Web, is quite new. ASP and ADO together provide the ability to combine these two to maximum effect.

Even the most computer-illiterate managers realize that business as we know it today could not exist without databases to hold information on customers, orders, inventory, accounts, payroll and every other facet of commercial activity. Many of the great advances in productivity since 1960 have been possible because of the speed and accuracy that databases provide for business information. However, until recently there has not been a convenient way to provide universal access to this information. For example, it was difficult for a worker while on a trip to Buenos Aires to register her overtime hours with the payroll department back at headquarters in Orlando.

The newer technology is the World Wide Web, a universal (well, planetary) method of exchanging and viewing information. Since the explosion of Web access that started in the mid-1990s, virtually all computer users are now able to view the information offered on the Internet. However, it has not always been easy to provide customized pages, designed to display database information specifically useful to an individual user. For example, a person interested in buying a boat saw a static page with a generic picture of the boat; it was difficult for a web programmer to create a dynamic page displaying an image of the boat, configured with the sailor's specific requests regarding sail plan, colors and deck fittings.

ASP and ADO make it relatively easy to bring together these two great information technologies of our time, to provide the capacity to use the data of business through the Web. With ASP-ADO the traveling technician can now use any computer in any country, with any browser connected to the web, to send in her overtime hours directly to her company's payroll database. The sailor can not only see his prospective purchase in the color and sail plan of his desires, but docked in front of palm trees or pine trees depending on his zip code, with a list of the dealers nearest to the sailor and the dealers' current inventories. The web page can even suggest the next more expensive yacht if it is still within the financial grasp of an average citizen in the sailor's zip code.

# Why Is This Book Different?

There are many books that present the ideas of ASP and a dozen more that focus on ADO. Some are quite advanced and assume an existing knowledge of other techniques. But to date no other book has been written with the intention of coaching beginners through their first uses of ADO on ASP pages.

The first word in the title of this book is *Beginning*, thus setting the tone for the tome. The theory is covered, but then there are also copious examples for you to study. An important role of any teacher is to select *which* out of all the software's features to teach, and in what order. Considerable effort has been made in this book to present material in the best way for it to be learned; not alphabetically or divided by object or according to historical precedent. In this book we start by stating a business goal, then present the minimum techniques to achieve that goal. After we have the basics working we add on the most commonly used parameters to enhance that technique.

## Written By An Experienced Teacher

In many ASP books the code is simply demonstrated, and the assumption is that the reader can learn why code was written just by looking at the final result. I think that is a big jump for most beginners. Although I am also a programmer, I am primarily a teacher, with over a thousand students in classrooms and on-line ASP courses. I keep a notebook of students' questions and where students make mistakes in exercises. This body of knowledge is wrapped up and presented in this book in ways that are most useful for the classroom or home-student.

My goal is not to write the book that presents the most depth or breadth of ASP and ADO solutions. Rather, my goal is to do the best job of explaining how to build your first fifty pages using ADO with ASP. After you master this book and go on you will find additional ways to perform tasks and additional features in the software. But those discoveries are for the future. The purpose of this book is to focus your attention on what you must learn to get started and to insulate you from the sea of non-essential material which can overwhelm a beginner.

## Exercises

Each chapter ends with one or more exercises. Keep your solutions on file as they can become a good portfolio when you apply for a job or make a presentation to a client. Furthermore, you know the code works and you can cut and paste it into the pages of future sites.

## Quizzes

It is only the poor students that groan about quizzes. Most of my pupils are glad to check their own mastery of the material and find places where they may have missed a point. These questions are specifically written as a check on the topics where students usually make mistakes. In the early chapters there is a focus on understanding confusing vocabulary or tricky theory while in the later chapters the questions involve troubleshooting code.

## Detailed Code Dissection

**Try It Out**

### How It Works

The chapters in this book are sprinkled with mini-exercises called *Try It Outs*. Each one states an objective and then follows that with the answer in code and a screen shot. Immediately following is a *How It Works* section that dissects the code line-by line and explains the syntax, choice of techniques, purpose of variables, etc.

## More Explanations

There is far more explanation of code in this book than in many other books. My assumption is that if you understand some code and read the explanation you will confirm your thinking. If you don't understand some code then the explanation will straighten it out for you. Many professional programmers will snort that some of these explanations are not needed, the ideas are trivial. But students give the same paragraphs great comments, *"This was the first time this syntax was explained carefully and thoroughly enough for me to really get it."*

I also understand that not everybody (including myself) reads books from cover to cover. Sometimes I explain a vital idea more than once if there are two places where I think folks might jump into the middle of the book. Feel free to skip over things you already know. In many chapters I've noted when we are covering topics that may be familiar to some readers so at these places I've tried to give you a note on where you could skip to, to get right into the more advanced material.

## Lists of Common Errors

Another feature that sets this book apart from others is the focus on troubleshooting problems you may encounter. I've included many lists of common errors drawn from my records of students' failed pages. I suggest that you read through them prior to starting to code a page to give yourself a reminder of problem spots. If your page works then give yourself a pat on the back. But if your page fails then try checking your code against each item on the list. I'll bet in at least 80% of the cases you'll find your problem.

## Clarifications

In almost every class on ASP the same questions arise. I have answered many of these in additions to the main text. These can clarify how the same word is used with more than one meaning, provide help on topics that the main text assumes you already understand, or explain alternative ways of doing a task.

## Useful Examples

When selecting a book at the shop (or on-line) I look closely at the examples. Can I re-use them in my business? If the examples are artificial and produce nothing more then *"Hello world!"* I put the book back on the shelf. This book gives you solutions to real-world problems. I use a database to support the membership of a sailors' organization and web pages to achieve the expected goals of such a club, such as providing up to date information and registering boats. You can use the examples in this book to solve problems or perform tasks that you might be faced with.

# Who is this Book For?

The programming community generated a tremendous response to Beginning ASP 2.0. We thank you. We fitted two chapters and one case study on data access into that book but didn't have room for the dozen more chapters that I wanted. So here it is, the logical next step to Beginning ASP 2.0 for those of you who plan to connect your sites to datastores.

This book is also well suited to people from the database community who now want to implement their solutions with a Web interface. These folks have plenty of experience with database programming, but want to translate that knowledge into ADO solutions in ASP pages.

Many web designers are from non-programming backgrounds, with an education in graphics design or word processing. These people can benefit from the book by learning how to take their visually appealing sites and giving them the business power of database connectivity. Folks in this group would probably do well to study the Beg ASP book first.

Lastly, I get students who are interested in computers but are not sure what to study. I predict that there will be strong growth in demand for programmers comfortable with ADO and ASP, so building a portfolio of ASP pages can only help your resume.

# What Software Do You Need?

In order to practice writing web pages you need four types of software. First is a browser. Actually, most web designers have several browsers so they can test their pages on both Internet Explorer and Netscape and for the last few versions of each.

Second, you need a page editor. This can be as simple as Notepad or as powerful as Visual InterDev. The simpler editors such as FrontPage do a fine job with HTML but lack tools to speed the development of database connections.

Third, you need software to hold and serve your pages. This software must be capable of processing the ASP scripts, so your two main choices are IIS running on NT, or PWS running on Windows 95/98 or NT Workstation. This topic is discussed in detail in chapter 2. In short, if you have permission to test pages on a site with ASP capability then you are all set. If not, you can set up a Personal Web Server (PWS) on your own Windows machine and do just about everything in this book.

Fourth, you will need some type of database management software. In this book we mostly use Access because most people have it or can easily get it and set it up. Since Access databases are file-based, they are very easy to download from the WROX site, make backups, and make changes by flipping into the Access software. The second database management system we use in the book is MS SQL Server, mainly to illustrate differences when moving to full-powered systems for deployment.

# What Knowledge Is Assumed?

Three skill sets are needed before studying the concepts of this book. The first is to be comfortable with the basics of HTML. You should have built many static pages by now using tags such as <FONT>. Furthermore, this book covers many pages of code that build tables and gather information from forms. All of this is generated, of course, using ASP pages. A surprisingly high percent of the failed pages from my students is caused by simple HTML mistakes. Granted, some of those tags must be built from difficult concatenations, but students should be able to spot <TABLE> and <FORM> tag errors in finished pages. These topics are covered well in Beginning Active Server Pages (ISBN 1-861001-34-7). If you have no problems understanding the demonstrations and exercises in chapters 3, 5 and 10 of Beg ASP then you are ready to study implementing ADO in ASP. It is not important which page editor you use. I find Microsoft's Visual Interdev to be the best, but Allaire's HomeSite, Adobe PageMill and others are fine and even Notepad will do.

Second, this book will only be accessible to those who have some experience with programming. The scripting languages (VBScript or JScript) hold together the ASP and ADO objects. This book uses VBScript so you will be particularly well-prepared if you have worked in the VB family such as AccessVBA, Word macros or VB itself.

Third, a basic understanding of database theory is an advantage in learning from this book. We provide some example databases for this book, available for download, which are discussed in Appendices A to C. These appendices describe the structure of the databases, however you should be familiar with terms such as tables, fields and queries, and understand the basic half dozen data types. We explain the basics of SQL over a couple chapters, so no prior knowledge is required of SQL statements. In this book we use Access and Microsoft SQL server, but ADO can connect to almost any relational or non-relational database.

To summarize: to get the most from a course in ASP pages using ADO, prospective students should have some experience with:

- ❑ HTML and ASP
- ❑ Any programming language
- ❑ Any database management system

If students are smart, they can learn one of these on the fly, but if they lack two or all three then they should do some prerequisite work first.

# How Is This Book Organized?

The chapters of this book roughly fall into five groups. The first group provides background material, including help in understanding when an ASP and ADO solution is suitable for you (chapter 1) and how to set up various configurations of ASP-enabled servers and operating systems (chapter 2). We have paid particular attention to addressing the many problems that can arise when installing PWS.

The second group leads you through read-only recordsets starting with simple recordsets that are essentially a snapshot of a table (chapter 3). Having mastered that, we study selection and sorting of records using SQL (chapter 4). We finish off this section by exploring how to use these read-only recordsets to solve a series of business situations (chapter 5).

By the third section we delve into the underpinnings of how ADO works with ASP. We start with switching our work to explicit connection and native OLDB providers (chapter 6). A theoretical chapter follows explaining the flow of information up and down through the software layers (chapter 7). We finish the section with a closer look at the parameters for the Recordset Open method (chapter 8).

You can only bill clients half an invoice for reading data. In the next section we study the modification of data. Chapter 9 covers techniques using the methods of ADO without SQL. Handling SQL statements to modify data is explored in chapter 10. This section closes with applying those modification techniques to cookies (chapter 11). At this point we take the time to examine the Errors collection, and discuss error handling in chapter 12. From here we look at the ways that ADO offers to work with queries using the Command object, in chapter 13. Once you have worked with the Command object you can then pass parameters into and out of stored procedures as described and demonstrated in chapter 14.

The last section addresses common questions from my students. Modern web sites go way beyond text to include various types of irregular data as covered in chapter 15. Having kept a list of common students mistakes, it was easy to write chapter 16 on tips and tricks, which lists some common toe-stubbers and how to avoid them. And last, for a beginners book, is a discussion of how to improve server performance in chapter 17.

# Where To Find The Code

We provide the source code for all the code examples in this book for download from our web site, together with the Access databases used in the examples. All the code for the book is contained in one zip file. When you extract the code on your machine, the zip file will create a folder for each chapter with the relevant code.

To download the code navigate to http://www.wrox.com and click on the Download link on the menu bar at the top of the page. This will take you to a page where you should select Beginning ASP Databases from the dropdown list available and click the Download Source Code button. You can then select to download from our US or our UK site.

The code samples are completely free, however you will need to register on the Wrox site. If you have already registered, you will be prompted for your password, otherwise you will be asked to register during the download process – we've tried to make registration as quick and simple as possible.

# Conventions

We have used a number of different styles of text and layout in the book to help differentiate between the different kinds of information. Here are examples of the styles we use and an explanation of what they mean:

*Advice, hints, and background information comes indented and italicized, like this.*

> **Important information comes in boxes like this.**

❑  Bullets are also indented, and appear with a little box marking each new bullet point, like this.

**Important Words** are in a bold type font.

Words that appear on the screen in menus like the <u>F</u>ile or <u>W</u>indow are in a similar font to the one that you see on screen.

Keys that you press on the keyboard, like *Ctrl* and *Enter*, are in italics.

Code has several fonts. If it's a word that we're talking about in the text, for example when discussing the `For...Next` loop, it's in a fixed width font. If it's a block of code that you can type in as a program and run, then it's also in a gray box:

```
Set oCars = CreateObject("WCCCars.Cars")
Set recCars = oCars.GetAll(RegistryRestore("Showroom", "Not Set"))
```

Sometimes you'll see code in a mixture of styles, like this:

```
If IsMissing(ConnectionString) Then
    varConn = RegistryRestore("Showroom", "Not Set")
Else
    varConn = ConnectionString
End If
```

The code with a white background is code we've already looked at and that we don't wish to examine further.

These formats are designed to make sure that you know what it is you're looking at. We hope they make life easier.

# Tell Us What You Think

We've worked hard on this book to make it useful. We've tried to understand what you're willing to exchange your hard-earned money for, and we've tried to make the book live up to your expectations.

Please let us know what you think about this book. Tell us what we did wrong, and what we did right. This isn't just marketing flannel: we really do huddle around the e-mail to find out what you think. If you don't believe it, then send us a note. We'll answer, and we'll take whatever you say on board for future editions. The easiest way is to use e-mail:

feedback@wrox.com

You can also find more details about Wrox Press on our web site. There, you'll find the code from our latest books, sneak previews of forthcoming titles, and information about the authors and editors. You can order Wrox titles directly from the site, or find out where your nearest local bookstore with Wrox titles is located.

## Customer Support

If you find a mistake, please have a look at the errata page for this book on our Web site first. If you can't find an answer there, tell us about the problem and we'll do everything we can to answer promptly! Just send us an e-mail (with the title and ISBN of the book, and the page number you're referring to), at:

support@wrox.com

Setup cannot install system files or update shared files if the files are in use. Before co
any open applications.

WARNING: This program is protected by copyright law and international treaties.

You may install Microsoft Data Access 2.1 on a single computer. Some Microsoft products
with additional rights, which are stated in the End User Licence Agreement included with y

Please take a moment to read the End User License Agreement now. It contains all of the te
conditions that pertain to this software product. By choosing to continue, you indicate accepta
these terms.

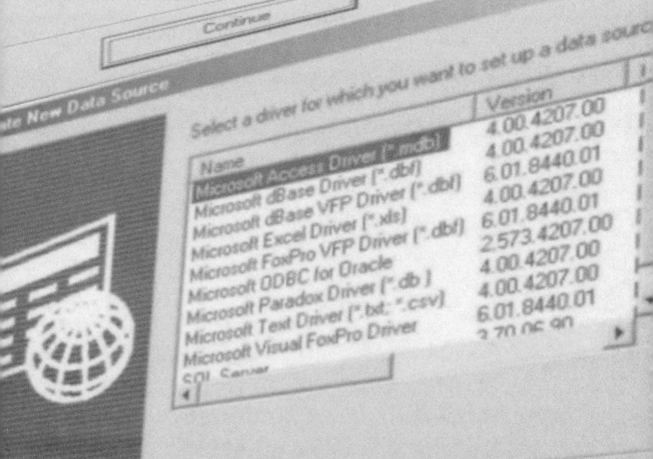

te New Data Source

Select a driver for which you want to set up a data sourc

| Name | Version |
| --- | --- |
| Microsoft Access Driver (*.mdb) | 4.00.4207.00 |
| Microsoft dBase Driver (*.dbf) | 4.00.4207.00 |
| Microsoft dBase VFP Driver (*.dbf) | 6.01.8440.01 |
| Microsoft Excel Driver (*.xls) | 4.00.4207.00 |
| Microsoft FoxPro VFP Driver (*.dbf) | 6.01.8440.01 |
| Microsoft ODBC for Oracle | 2.573.4207.00 |
| Microsoft Paradox Driver (*.db ) | 4.00.4207.00 |
| Microsoft Text Driver (*.txt; *.csv) | 4.00.4207.00 |
| Microsoft Visual FoxPro Driver | 6.01.8440.01 |
| SQL Server | 2.70.06.90 |

Cancel

# Why Use ASP and ADO to Put Your Database on the Web?

In your experience of programming Active Server Pages, you've probably created a variety of pages. Some of the tasks these pages can perform might include counting the number of visitors that use your site, checking to see if the user has visited your site before and customizing the information on the page accordingly. You may have taken user particulars in forms and passed this data from page to page. However, without belittling your achievements thus far, have you actually provided any "real" content? By real content, I mean the sales report that's several inches thick and changes on a day to day basis and lies festering on your desk; or at home the analysis of your baseball team's latest dismal run with statistics to back it up!

In business when your information changes day to day, and you've got customers buying items and inventories that need replenishing, how often are you going to update your page - once a month, once a week or once a day? And where is that information coming from? Is it a document, a spreadsheet, a database or even all three? How can you link this information into your web pages and keep it current? What happens if your airline reservation system is still showing available seats on a flight that sold out last Tuesday? Your customers aren't going to be too pleased. . .

What you need to do when you create your dynamic pages using Active Server Pages (ASP) is to be able to connect to your text file or database to drag up and display the information, so that when somebody views your page, they're viewing the current state of the database. Every time you make an amendment in your database, it should be instantly reflected on your web site, without the need for you to change a single line of HTML. Wouldn't that make life easy? Fortunately for you, that's what ASP is best at and it provides you with access to a whole set of components for doing just this. They are known as the ActiveX Data Objects or ADO for short. ADO brings together the power of databases with the universality of the Web. This chapter discusses what ASP and ADO can do together as well as the several limitations to the technologies. We're going to look at:

- ❑ A quick reminder of what ASP does
- ❑ Databases and Data Stores
- ❑ What ODBC is
- ❑ What OLE-DB and ADO are and the relationship between the two
- ❑ ASP and ADO in action together
- ❑ A series of explanations and questions to help you decide on whether to implement ASP and ADO as your solutions

# Business Impact of Dynamic Web Pages

ASP and ADO bring together these two great information technologies of our time to provide the capacity to use the data of business through the Web. With ASP the traveling technician can now use any computer in any country with any browser connected to the web, to send in their overtime hours directly and use ADO to connect to their company's payroll database. The sailor can not only see his prospective purchase in the color and sail plan of his desires, but docked in front of palm trees or pine trees depending on his zip code, with a list of the dealers nearest to the sailor and the dealers' current inventories. The web page can even suggest the next more expensive yacht if it is still within the financial grasp of an average citizen in the sailor's zip code.

ASP and ADO offer the business world the ability to gather orders and requests from virtually anyone in the world, and process that data directly into the business database systems that control the production and delivery of the product. The customer request process is without any requirement other than Internet access. Whether your prospective customer is on a Macintosh in Sudan, an NEC in Fukuoka or a Dell in Savannah, you can use Active Server Pages. And because of ADO, the output to your database is also without prejudice, with connections available to virtually every type of database.

# Active Server Pages Overview

This book explains, demonstrates, and applies the techniques that lie at the intersection of the two great tools of the Information Age. One tool, the database, is relatively old. The other, the World Wide Web, is quite new. ASP with the power of ADO provides the ability to combine these tools and has emerged as the Microsoft Solution for web databases over the past few years. You should already be familiar with ASP, but we'll remind ourselves briefly of its structure before we see how ADO fits in.

ASP has a short history since version 1.0 was announced in July of 1996. ASP 1.0 beta hit the streets in November 1996 and the final product was released on December 12th, 1996. ASP 1.0 was available in the Windows NT3 Service pack 3 as part of IIS 3, and for a short while it was also available as a separate freely downloadable extension for IIS 2.

The current (as of mid-1999) version of ASP is 2.0, which was first released in the NT 4 Option Pack of December 1997. ASP 2.0 is part of IIS 4.0, which in turn is part of the NT 4.0 Option Pack. The components of NT4, including IIS/ASP, are built into NT4.0 distributed after mid-1998. The next version of ASP will be 3.0, which we expect to be part of IIS 5, shipping with the server-capable versions of Windows 2000. The primary changes in the late betas have been movement of the error functions to their own object, and movement of transactions into COM+.

ASP is actually an extension to your web server that allows server-side scripting. At the same time it also provides a compendium of objects and components, which manage interaction between the web server and the browser. These 'objects' can be manipulated by scripting languages:

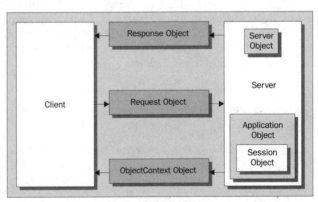

## Active Server Objects

There are six Active Server objects, each of which deals with a specific aspect of interactivity:

- ❑  `Request`
- ❑  `Response`
- ❑  `Server`
- ❑  `Application`
- ❑  `Session`
- ❑  `ObjectContext`

You probably don't need much reminding about what they all do. The `Request` object is used to deal with a request that a user might make of a site or application. The 'request' might be made in the form of input from an HTML form. The `Response` object is used to deal with the server's response back to the browser.

The `Application` and `Session` objects are used to manage information about the application that is currently running and the unique instances (versions) of the application, which individual users run, known as sessions. The `ObjectContext` object is used with Microsoft Transaction Server. However, it's the `Server` object that will be concerning us mostly. It's used to provide several commonly used functions, such as setting timeout properties for scripts and converting text into HTML or URLs, by far the most important is its ability to create new objects or components.

So where does ADO come into all of this? ADO provides its own set of objects that can be created via the `CreateObject` method of the `Server` object. Using this method, you can then use ADO to read records, move records, add or alter records and even delete records in your database. Before we look at ADO we need to consider quickly the events and technologies that have brought databases to where they are now.

# Databases in the Modern World

We use the model of relational databases first devised by Dr E.F. Codd in 1970 to store information. This model forms the foundation of any commercial database package, such as Access, SQL Server, Oracle, Informix, DB2, Sybase, the list is endless. In relational databases, items of data are stored in **tables**, which are logical groupings of **records**. So, for example, there would be a record for each customer in an airline reservation system database of everybody who booked a flight with that airline. Each customer's record would have items of information stored in a table, such as their name, address, method of payment, date of flight, airport and flight destination stored in separate **fields**. For every customer you would want to know the same details, but this information would be unique to each customer. Each customer would need to be identified individually so each record would require a unique identifier, known as a **key**. The key can then be used to cross reference information stored in other tables in the same database.

As every vendor uses the relational database model for their own database packages, it is possible to **query** any database and retrieve information in a generic way. The method for doing this is by using a language for creating queries — or asking questions if you like — of the database. The language is **Structured Query Language**, or its more familiar name **SQL** (pronounced **SeQueL**). You'll need to learn a little SQL to use in your ASP pages and there's a quick tour later in this book. The good news is that you can use practically the same SQL query to retrieve information from an Access 2000 database as you can from a SQL Server database or from an Oracle database.

# ODBC

That's not to say that the information stored in each database is stored in the same format by each vendor, that would be too much to ask. But all you're interested in at the end of the day is the data contained within the database and how to get hold of it. That's what we're going to talk about now: how to get the information you want.

We'll consider a more straightforward example first, that of word-processors. Each word-processor has a different format for saving what are essentially text-based files. They might have different fonts, colors and margins, but the bottom line is the *information* that you're interested in within a document is the *text* and this is universal. So, you can't use Notepad to open a Word document and expect to find a readable document, even though they both basically store text in files. If you opened the Word document containing this chapter for example, this is what you would see:

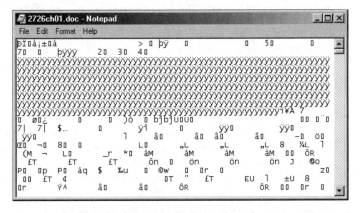

This makes sense to Word, because these symbols are representations of instructions on how to display the text in a certain style, but of course it's complete gobbledygook to you. But you're probably thinking if you saved it first as a .txt file and then viewed it in Notepad, you'd get something far more like the original chapter, and indeed you would:

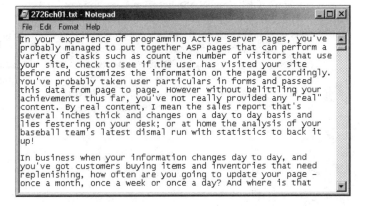

With databases it's the same, each vendor has their own proprietary formatting and undoubtedly opening up an Access database in SQL Server, if the operating system would even allow you to do such a thing, wouldn't yield an instructive set of results. Yet there are plenty of times when you'd want access from one database, to information or data stored in another type of database.

So with word-processors, we've demonstrated a way of getting at the basic information, the text, but how would you get the basic *information* from a database, the *data* — regardless of whether your data is held on Access, SQL Server, Oracle etc? The answer is you can go through an interface, which will allow you to view just the data held in a different type of database. This is known as **Open Database Connectivity** or **ODBC** for short.

ODBC is a standard, created in 1992 and predominantly supported by Microsoft, which allows you to add ODBC statements to a program to access information held in a database. There are a variety of **ODBC drivers** available, which allow you access to information held in a database of one type from a database package of another type. Indeed ODBC is implemented for nearly every type of database. It's aim is to allow a 'nirvana' of **universal data access**, where everybody can get at the information they want without having to worry about the method of data storage.

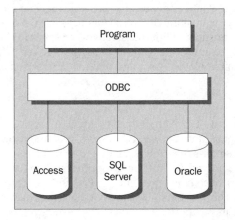

This has important ramifications for our plan of connecting web pages to databases. If you can use ODBC with your web server, then it should be a relatively easy task to get the basic data out of the database and onto our web page, regardless of what database the data is actually stored in.

# Databases on the Web Before ADO

In fact you should be thinking, if databases have been around for decades and there has been a common method for accessing data in different types of databases that has been around since 1992, then how come they haven't been put on the Web before now? The answer is they have. The most common method for doing this before ADO made its dramatic entrance, was to use **CGI** (the **Common Gateway Interface**) together with ODBC. In fact the majority of dynamic pages that use databases on the Web are probably still created using CGI.

The CGI method involved you sending a request to your web server for a normal HTML web page. Somewhere within that web page would be a call to a CGI application. It would be typical in forms for instance, where you wanted to store the user details in the database:

```
<HTML>
<HEAD>
</HEAD>
<BODY>

<H3>To subscribe to our email list, you must enter your details here:</H3>
<FORM ACTION="/cgi-bin/maillist.pl" METHOD=GET>
<P>Name: <INPUT TYPE="text" NAME="name"></P>
<P>Address: <INPUT TYPE="text" NAME="address"></P>
<P>Phone: <INPUT TYPE="text" NAME="phone"></P>
<P>Email: <INPUT TYPE="text" NAME="email"></P>
<INPUT TYPE="submit">
<INPUT TYPE="reset">
</FORM>
</BODY>
</HTML>
```

The server would then execute the CGI application and it would return a stream of text and HTML to the server. The CGI application would either be an executable file, or a file in another language known as a script. CGI scripts could come in many different languages such as Perl, C, C++, Tcl and Python. The scripts are used to control the flow of information between the HTML and the database. The web server itself would use ODBC to communicate with the database. The server would use the output it received from the database to assemble a 'new' web page, and then this web page would be returned to the browser.

So why isn't this a book about CGI? Although still very widely used, CGI has several disadvantages. One is that it adds another level of indirection to the client-server interaction, as the server is forced to call a CGI program. Secondly, the code that CGI receives and transmits isn't easily manipulated by a lot of programming languages, and you're forced to use a programming language that has good communication and text handling facilities. Such languages, such as Perl and C++, tend to be among the more complex programming languages. Third is that CGI often isn't the fastest method of accessing databases. So it's not surprising that other arguably 'superior' methods have been developed in the meanwhile.

# The Way Ahead: Data Stores

First you should note that databases aren't the only receptacle for storing information. We need to recognize that not all data is contained in databases. The 150 page sales report sitting on your desk is probably a spreadsheet that's been printed out. When your boss emails you demanding the latest sales figures, you can probably summarize them all within an email, or if it's a bit bigger, a Word document. Clearly these aren't all databases, so we need a more widely embracing term which encompasses all of these sources. From now on we will start using the term, **data store**.

## *What is OLE-DB?*

Here is where we hit another shortcoming. ODBC is fine so long as you only want to access data in a database but what if you want to access data in all types of data stores? ODBC on its own clearly isn't enough. In 1997, Microsoft provided a new specification for an interface called OLE-DB, and put in a lot of work to ensure that it was faster and easier to use than ODBC.

OLE-DB allows a program to access information in any type of data store; not just databases, but also spreadsheets, graphs, emails and so on. Eventually OLE-DB should be able to replace ODBC, but for now it sits on top of ODBC and allows you to use your existing ODBC drivers. The OLE-DB equivalent of an ODBC driver is known as a **provider**. A provider is simply something that provides data. Providers are not the same as drivers. There are many more ODBC drivers available than OLE-DB providers so if you wished to access information in a database, then you will most probably have to use OLEDB and ODBC together. There is an OLE-DB provider for ODBC, which then allows you to use the ODBC driver for that specific database. The following diagram should give you an idea of how this all works:

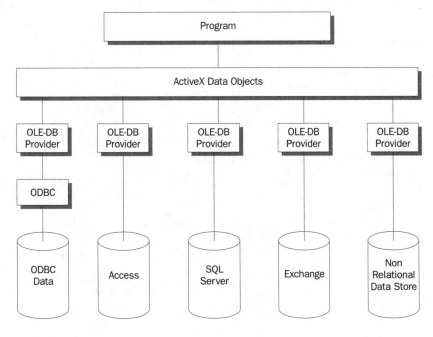

So by now, you've probably forgotten completely about ADO, which is the very reason for our digression in the first place. Well, despite OLE-DB being easier to use than ODBC, it's still not exactly a breeze to understand and can only be manipulated using very few programming languages, one of those being C++. If you know that then fine, but for the rest of us mere mortals a wrapper has been created, that not only hides a lot of the low level intricacies from the user, but also allows other languages, such as scripting languages to manipulate the data stores. This wrapper is **ActiveX Data Objects** or **ADO** for short. ADO itself is a COM (Microsoft's Component Object Model) component, and therefore can be used in any COM compliant language. While not platform independent, it is language independent, so ADO can be controlled via any number of languages such as C++, Visual Basic, Java or JavaScript and VBScript.

ADO is designed to give a single method for accessing data to everybody. To this end ADO provides a hierarchical series of objects or **object model**, which can be accessed in your chosen programming language.

## The ADO Object Model

The term object model should be familiar to you now - ASP has an object model, IE4 has one and ADO is no different. An object model is a representation of the relationships between each of the objects involved. It shows which objects need to be created before other objects or collections are created. These objects each handle a specific section of the interaction between the web page and the database.

We'll be introducing each ADO object in detail as we go through the book. For the moment, we'll just take a brief overview of the structure of ADO. There are three main objects on which the ADO object model is built:

❑   the Connection object
❑   the Command object
❑   the Recordset object

Let's take a look at the structure now:

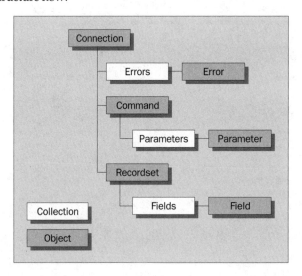

You'll notice that in addition to these three main objects there are also four collections available. Each collection in ADO contains an object of the same name that can only exist as part of a collection. So the Fields collection has a Field object and the Errors Collection has an Errors object and so on.

You may also notice that the ADO object model is more hierarchical than the ASP object model, in that one of the objects, the Connection object, contains the other two. However, it is possible for instances of the Recordset and Command objects to exist separately without requiring an instance of the Connection object, and we'll see this as we go through the book. In chapter three we'll be starting off with the most straightforward way of reading data from the database, using the Recordset object.

> *ADO 2.5 makes the addition of another two objects, the Record object and the Stream object, which are used to deal with nodes and the contents of nodes. As we don't wish to confuse the issue by adding another two objects, which many readers won't have access to unless they have Windows 2000 on their desktops, we won't be discussing these objects further.*

Here's a quick summary of what each object and collection does.

### The Connection Object

The Connection object is used to make a connection to the data store. Once a connection to the data store has been established, it can be reused as many times as you want in your code, as you'll see in subsequent chapters. Although you need a connection before you can get at your information inside a database, you don't actually have to use the Connection object to create the connection. Both the Command and Recordset objects can create connections independently.

### The Command Object

The Command object is there to run commands against the database. These commands are not actually in ASP script, but in SQL (Structured Query Language). The commands are used to typically return information from the database although you can use SQL to add new records, even new tables and delete information within the database. SQL doesn't have programs, but uses **queries** instead which are usually only a few lines long. These queries can be created beforehand and stored separately.

### The Recordset Object

The Recordset object is the most used object in ADO, and as a result has the most properties and methods. It's used to hold information about the **recordsets** that we create.

> *A recordset is, very pedantically speaking, a set of records. It can be some or all of the records in our database.*

The Recordset object can be used to both view and alter your databases. You can use it to find particular records, move through your database a record at a time, delete records, restrict views of sensitive information to certain users, sort records into numerical or alphabetic order and finally update old records.

The ability to create recordsets, or rather our own personal view of the database, is undoubtedly one of the most useful aspects of ADO, which we'll look at in much greater detail in chapter 3.

### The Fields Collection

The Fields collection contains information about a particular field in a recordset, it can be used with pre-existing recordsets or it can be used with recordsets that you create yourself.

### The Errors Collection

This is another self-explanatory collection, when your program can't achieve its intention, or encounters an unexpected condition, it will return an error, or a number of errors.

There are two other collections, which don't require any detailed explanation at this point:

❑ Parameters Collection — this is used to pass extra information to queries used by the Command object.

❑ Properties Collection — this can exist for each of our three main objects, Connection, Command and Recordset. It contains information that is specific to that object.

# What ASP and ADO Can Do

So having had a look individually at what ASP and ADO are, and where they fit into the general scheme of things, it's time to look at what these two technologies can do when linked together. In fact the list of what they can't do is probably shorter. Anything you can use a database for, you can pretty much put into a web page:

Here's just a few examples to think about:

❑ An online reference of movies, actors, directors, producers etc ever created. You put in the name of the film and immediately you can pull up details of all the actors, right down to the walk-ons in scene two or the people who were shot in the opening scene.

❑ A music seller application, which allows you to select CDs for your shopping basket, gets details off you, totals up your order and then when you post your final order for the CDs, emails confirmation of the order.

❑ A set of news forums, where developers can post queries and information about the latest developments in computing and browse the forums by subject or date looking for particular bits of information.

❑ An online dictionary of all HTML tags and attributes which lets a user lookup whether a certain tag is supported by a particular browser and in which versions of HTML that tag is legal (if any), together with one line code examples.

Now these examples might sound very wide-ranging and diverse but they have been all implemented inside one company's boundaries, and if you go on to the http://www.wrox.com site and looked hard enough, you'd find each of these examples in different places on the web site.

# ASP and ADO Examples

At the end of this book we'll be looking at a case study which will draw together everything we've learned so far. The case study will be based on the Sailors database – this is an example database which we'll be using for many of the examples in this book. It is described in Appendix A and is available for download from the Wrox website. The Sailors database stores information about people who race sailing boats, together with some personal information, their professional rating, and a ranking depending on how many races they have won. In addition, information is stored about the boats themselves, including name and class, and the yacht clubs which organize the races.

The case study consists of an ASP application which uses ADO to access the data in the database, and allows the user to perform tasks such as registering their boat in the database. We'll be covering everything we need to put this application together as we go through the book. To illustrate ADO however, we can look now at two pages within our Sailors database example, first to see the site before the introduction of a database and then to see how the pages can be improved by the addition of ASP and ADO.

## *Sailor's Home Page With Just HTML*

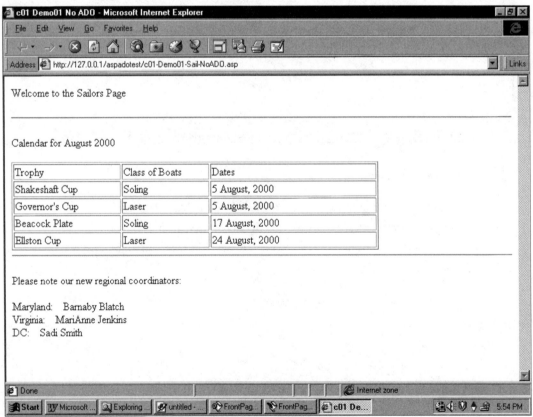

## Sailors Home Page with ASP and ADO added

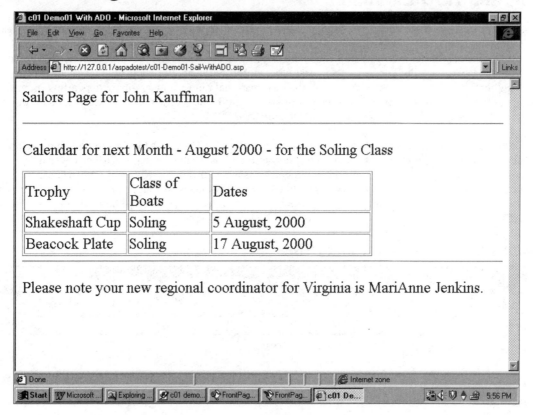

The main improvements are:

- ❑ Information gathered in forms can immediately be added to a database
- ❑ We can store special notes, and display them only to users from given domains
- ❑ Information gathered from users can be fed into other software for automated responses

## *Membership page with just HTML*

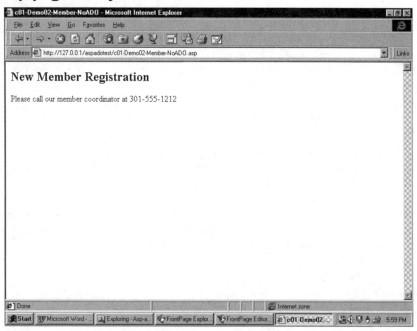

## *Membership Page with ASP and ADO added*

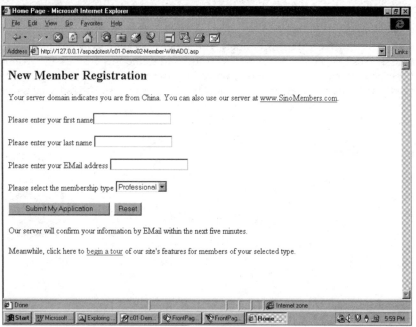

The main improvements are:

❑   ASP can store and then allow us to look up personal information about each visitor. For example, the user name is pulled from the 'people' table and used in the first line of the page.

❑   Each sailor owns a boat of a particular class or type – for example, a Laser or a Soling. Assuming the user is only interested in races for his type of boat, we can check the owner's class (contained in the 'people' table) and list only those regattas of interest to this particular visitor.

❑   Our site's visitors may register a desire for certain size fonts – particularly those of us who are aging baby-boomers with failing eyesight! This preference can be stored in the 'people' table and used to set style tags.

❑   Instead of wasting valuable page-space with a list of all of the new representatives, we can display *just* the coordinator information relevant to this visitor's area. Again, this is based on a look-up using ASP and ADO.

For the moment, if you want to have a look at a running example of ASP and ADO, you can refer back to the Wrox website. The music seller application we mentioned earlier provides a very good foundation for demonstrating the kind of thing that is ultimately achievable with ASP and ADO. To walk through the application looking at how ASP and ADO are being used, follow the steps below.

*You can find full details of the music seller application in Professional JavaScript (Wrox Press ISBN 1-861-002-70-X) where the code is discussed in detail.*

## Try It Out – A Tour Through an Application that uses ASP and ADO

This particular application is the solution for a company that sells music compact discs and wanted an online store through which to sell their products. The application allows customers to be able to browse their electronic shelves based on music genre. With such large amounts of stock and with large turnovers, the product lists and categories cannot be hardwired in to the HTML pages, so the pages have to be created on the fly and the addition of new products and categories has to be reflected automatically in the HTML.

**1.** Start up the browser and go to the URL http://webdev.wrox.co.uk/books/2726 and under the run the samples heading, select the E-Commerce Application link.

The first page is actually generated by ASP, one of the requirements of the system was that the categories can't be hard-coded, so we use ADO to scan a table of Categories and provide a link for each separate category. Also the dropdown listbox in the top right hand corner of the screen is filled by ADO, which once again has to provide the list of categories.

**2.** Click on the Rock category. The stock seems rather sparse, so the database is a little empty currently, and consequently there isn't much choice...

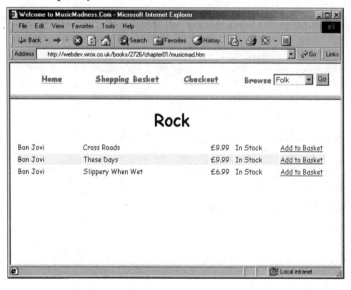

However this doesn't detract from our main point that once again this page is an ASP constructed using ADO to access the database. On this page, the application uses ADO to search the database for every item in stock that comes under the rock category and compiles a table of entries, together with a link to the shopping basket.

From here you can click on items to add them to your shopping basket and ultimately buy your CD. We won't follow through all these steps here, but hopefully you can see that at nearly every stage during the application there is some interaction with the database.

So now you've seen ASP and ADO in action, but we've not really examined in any detail the strengths and shortcoming of ASP and ADO technologies. Indeed they might not be suitable for your business, and in the next section we try and give a neutral overview of why you might or might not use them.

# Why use Server-Side Solutions?

ASP code is usually executed on the server. The code you write will produce a final page in pure HTML and send it out over the internet to the browser, there is no requirement from ASP or ADO for a specific browser software or version of browser software. This means that there is no programming code sent to the client. Client side scripts can be included on ASP pages, but they are not required in order to use ASP and ADO. Information can be obtained from the user by using the standard HTML techniques of form tags and scanning the request string.

ASP and ADO server-side solutions are fundamentally different than client-side scripts written in JavaScript or VBScript or applets written in Java. Client-side solutions send the actual scripting code out to the browser. The browser must then have the proper software (and perhaps version of the software) in order to execute the browser-side script. The execution of that script uses browser CPU time rather than server CPU time.

# What Server-Side Solutions Mean in Business Terms

You and I as programmers can understand the technical advantages of server-side scripting, but to make money from it we will also have to convince the people holding the purse strings. Let's look at some of the benefits and drawbacks of server-side solutions.

## Benefits

We can list four main advantages of using server-side scripting:

- universal readability
- protection of source code
- availability of specialized resources
- easier debugging

We'll look at each of these in a bit more detail.

### Universal readability

Every browser ever made can read HTML, since that is the definition of a browser. Therefore, every browser ever made can read the output of ASP, as ASP's usual output is pure HTML text and tags. There is no requirement that browsers be capable of interpreting various and competing types of client side scripts. Of course if you *want* to include browser-side scripts then ASP can send those out as well.

> *There are different specifications of HTML but all browsers will use the most recent as laid down by the W3 consortium. Different browsers may also use their own proprietary tags, but if you avoid these then all browsers should understand your HTML. You can get information on the latest specification from* www.w3.org.

### Protection of Source code

Server side processing uses data gathered from the browser plus rules on the server to produce a result that is sent back out to the browser. Note that it is the result (not the rules) that are sent to the client. Contrast that to client-side processing where your business rules are sent to the browser and there combine with user input to calculate answers. One problem with client-side processing is that interested parties can read the business rules from the browser page.

For example, you may want to give users a life insurance price quotation based on age, smoking habits, height, weight and amount of exercise. But you don't want everyone in the world to be able to see the way you calculate the quotation. ASP can get the data from the user, perform the calculation within the safety of your server, and then send only the answer out to the browser. A client-side solution would send the equation out to the browser, gather the user input, and perform the calculation at the browser. Your competitor, if crafty enough, could figure out the algorithms upon which you base your quotations.

### Availability of Specialized Resources

ASP can integrate with specialized software on the server. Perhaps there are business algorithms compiled from C++ that are used in calculating quotations. This software only has to exist at one location, the server, rather than be distributed to every browser.

### Easier debugging

Pages which include browser-side scripts must be tested on browsers. There are currently a half dozen major and lots of minor browsers in use, so debugging can become a nightmare. With a server-side solution like ASP/ADO, the target is to put out good HTML. Once that is achieved, any browser can read it.

## Drawbacks

There are, as always, some trade-offs when you use server-side scripting. The two principal problems are:

- ❑ multiple trips to the server
- ❑ increased server load

### Multiple Trips

There is a cost that is paid for processing on the server side. The price is that usually an additional trip must be made when a calculation is performed. For example in our life-insurance quotation, we would have to first present the user with a page that gathers the information, then send that to the server. The calculations are performed on the server and then the answer is sent back to the browser for display. If a businesswoman wants to get quotes for herself and her husband she will have to send the data across the Internet to the server twice (once for her and once for her husband) and the replies are sent back twice. In a client-side solution she could type in data for as many people as she wants without returning to the server, because the equation would be sitting on her machine ready to be reused as desired.

### Increased Server Load

As the traffic on your site increases, so will the processing load on your web server. For instance, if you run an ASP script with a particular welcome for every user who comes to your site, you could end up needing some very impressive hardware when your site becomes more popular. In a worst-case scenario, your web server could even crash under a sudden influx of visitors. Capacity planning, according to your hardware set-up, can cater for the growth of your site.

Overall, like many solutions in life, the optimum is a combination of server- and client-side scripting. Tasks such as data validation or quick and simple calculations are probably best carried out on the browser. The results of those browser-side scripts can then be sent up to the server to be handle the tasks of interfacing with data stores or the calculation of complex or confidential formulae. The following table summarizes the pros and cons of server- and client-side scripting.

| Issue | Server-Side (ASP-ADO) | Client Side Techniques (Java, Jscript, client-side VBScript) |
| --- | --- | --- |
| Universality of Browsers | Universal (although older browsers may not support cookies) | It is not possible to guarantee that all browsers support a particular language, or all features of that language |
| Exposure of Code | Not exposed | Exposed |
| Data Transfer between Browser and Server | One or two trips per calculation | One trip then allows unlimited calculations on that browser |
| Debugging | Single objective is good HTML, so easier to debug | Objective is to run well on any of dozens of browsers, so the debugging task is larger |
| Additional Resources | Additional resources such as optimized code, datastores or additional hardware can be added at one location, the server | Deployment of specialized code must occur to all visitors |
| Server Load | Far higher load requires better hardware | Computing is distributed out to the browsers |

### Benefit or Problem? ASP and ADO are Microsoft Solutions

This may seem like stating the obvious, but the very fact that these are Microsoft solutions restrict the number of platforms you can run them on. Microsoft don't have a great record of supporting UNIX platforms and when you consider the fact that the world's most popular web server, Apache, still runs over 50% of the worlds web sites (figures available at http://www.netcraft.com) and until relatively recently only ran on UNIX based platforms, you'll see it has restrictions. Also you still can't run ASP on Apache, except with third party products and even then it's not supported on every platform.

On the plus side, Microsoft offers many free or inexpensive support materials, such as white papers, seminars, and the on-line knowledge base at http://www.support.microsoft.com. Since Microsoft is the giant of the field, it attracts the lion's share of programmers, testers, users and authors. There are dozens of independent web sites devoted to ASP and ADO, and even more in the germane field of VB programming.

But what if these free resources can't solve your problem? You have several options. You can hire independent programmers and troubleshooters with experience in ASP-ADO. Many of these folks are Microsoft Solution Providers – which means they have passed a series of examinations about MS products. If that fails you can pay Microsoft's staff for per-incident troubleshooting. Alternatively you can try the many newsgroups available.

# Alternative Web Servers with ASP

There are now two companies who provide ASP as an add-on to web servers other than Microsoft.

### Chili!Soft

Chili!Soft, at http://www.ChiliSoft.com, has offered a solution for hosts that do not use IIS as their web server, or NT as their host, but still want to use ASP. Chili!ASP provides a functional and syntactic equivalent of Microsoft's IIS+ASP, including each of the five intrinsic objects, the FileSystem and BrowsCap objects, and ADO, as well as support for custom COM and Java objects. At the time of writing Chili!ASP does not support some of the additional components such as the AdRotator, ContentRotator, Tools, MyInfo, and NextLink component; but that situation may change in the future.

This solution is available, as of writing, for Apache, Netscape and Lotus web servers running on the Unix boxes Solaris and AIX, as well as Lotus, Netscape, O'Reilly and Apache web servers on Windows NT. Since Chili!ASP interfaces with the API of the web server there is no performance penalty, making it a logical choice for IT shops where web programmers want to code with ASP–ADO but there is a commitment to non-Microsoft platforms.

### HalcyonSoft

Halcyon Software provides a product called Instant ASP which runs as a Java servlet on your web server and provides ASP support. It's available from http://www.halcyonsoft.com. However it requires you to have the Java Development Kit (JDK) already loaded on your web server for it to work. There is a free Developer's version of Instant ASP available from their web site, the full version retailed at $495 at the time of writing. The free developer version has all features enabled and is only limited by the number of concurrent users you are allowed to have on the server at any one time. The JDK has to be downloaded separately from Sun Microsystems web site at http://www.sun.com.

## Alternatives to ASP

There are a lot of alternatives to using ASP and ADO, and we haven't the time and space to consider all of them. Besides, if you've bought this book, then you're hopefully interested in using ASP and ADO! If you want to do some comparisons then you might find some of the information in this section helpful.

### CGI

This is the longest established way of doing things and has been considered earlier in the chapter.

### Java Server Pages

JavaServer Pages (JSP) is a new technology that allows you to combine markup (HTML or XML) with Java code to dynamically generate web-pages. The JSP specification is implemented by several web servers, and plug ins are available which allow you to use JSP with IIS 4.0. One of the main advantages of JSP is the portability of code between different servers. More details can be found in the JSP FAQ at http://www.esperanto.org.nz/jsp/jspfaq.html.

### ColdFusion

ColdFusion (www.allaire.com/products/ColdFusion) also enables servers to access data as the server builds an HTML page. Like ASP, ColdFusion pages are readable by any browser. However, Cold Fusion utilizes a proprietary set of tags which are processed by the Cold Fusion Server software. This server software can run on multiple platforms, including Microsoft IIS, Netscape Enterprise Server, and Unix/Apache. The major difference is that whereas ASP-ADO solutions are built primarily with VBScript and objects, Cold Fusion utilizes the tags, which encapsulate functionality. Cold Fusion lacks some of the internal ASP objects, however it sports its own set of solutions to common problems, including access to ADO functionality.

### PHP

PHP is a server-side scripting language for creating dynamic Web pages. When a visitor opens the page, the server processes the PHP commands and then sends the results to the visitor's browser, just as with ASP or ColdFusion. Unlike ASP or ColdFusion, however, PHP is Open Source and cross-platform. PHP runs on Windows NT and many Unix versions, and it can be built as an Apache module and as a binary that can run as a CGI. When built as an Apache module, PHP is especially lightweight and speedy. Without any process creation overhead, it can return results quickly, and it doesn't require the tuning of mod_perl to keep your server's memory image small.

In addition to manipulating the content of your pages, PHP can also send HTTP headers. You can set cookies, manage authentication, and redirect users. It offers excellent connectivity to many databases (and ODBC), and integration with various external libraries that let you do everything from generating PDF documents to parsing XML.

PHP goes right into your Web pages, so there's no need for a special development environment or IDE. You start a block of PHP code with <?php and end it with ?>. (You can also configure PHP to use ASP-style <% %> tags or even <SCRIPT LANGUAGE="php"></SCRIPT>.) The PHP engine processes everything between those tags.

PHP's language syntax is similar to C and Perl. You don't have to declare variables before you use them, and it's easy to create arrays and hashes (associative arrays). PHP even has some rudimentary object-oriented features, providing a helpful way to organize and encapsulate your code.

Although PHP runs fastest embedded in Apache, there are instructions on the PHP Web site for seamless setup with Microsoft IIS and Netscape Enterprise Server. If you don't already have a copy of PHP, you can download it at http://www.php3.net. You'll also find a manual that documents all of PHP's functions and features.

# Take Home Points: A Summary Of Terminology

Before we close this chapter, we're going to do a quick run through of some of the new terms and technologies in this section, and before you go on you must be comfortable with them.

**Common Gateway Interface (CGI)** - The oldest and still most popular way of doing web databases.

**Active Server Pages (ASP)** – A technology which facilitates processing of code within a web page prior to sending the page to the requesting browser.

**ODBC** – An early industry standard for universal data access. Difficult for programmers, but ODBC is implemented for almost all databases.

**OLE-DB** – Microsoft's technology to replace ODBC which improves data access across the internet and from sources other than traditional relational databases such as email and textfiles.

**ADO** – Microsoft's technology to ease and improve scripting access to ODBC and OLEDB. The scripting is usually VBscript or Jscript when using ASP and ADO.

So an ADO data connection can be summarized as using ADO technology to control ODBC or OLEDB (or both) interfaces to the data stores.

# Summary

The combination IIS – ASP – ADO is one of several options for enabling databases on the Web. ASP is the technology that allows programmers to use functions, variables and control structures to build a web page at the moment it is requested by a browser. With these tools, we can bring to bear programming techniques for building HTML pages to perform tasks, such as building different pages for different days of the week, using input from the user to return personalized information, or redirecting the browser to one of several other pages. In addition, ASP supports the use of pre-built components that allow the programmer to easily add features such as rotation of advertisements or modification of formatting to accommodate the limitations of the requesting browser type. One of the strengths of ASP is that it lets the programmer build standard HTML pages, which are then readable on any browser. There is no requirement that the user have any particular type or version of browser installed.

ADO is a separate specification that allows universal access to data stores. It acts as a wrapper for the OLE-DB specification. It enables ASP (as well as many programming languages) to read and write to data stores. This function can be as simple as reading out the membership status of a user. On a more complicated level we can use a cookie from the browser to automatically look up a user's preferences. We can even gather information from the user using standard HTML/ASP techniques, then use ADO to open a database and store the information therein. ADO is able to work with data stores of many types. Access, SQL Server, Excel, Foxpro and text files are the options from Microsoft, but ADO works just as well with Oracle, Sybase, db2 and many other database management systems.

ASP – ADO solutions sit on the server thus reducing the complexity of accommodating multiple browser types. However, the load on the server can become overwhelming in a high-traffic site. Pure UNIX shops can deploy Chili!ASP or Instant ASP from HalcyonSoft to enable ASP-ADO on non-NT platforms. CGI running on Apache and using PerlScript really is the main alternative, but ColdFusion and other new third party products offer a range of solutions. We've tried to provide a balanced overview under which circumstances you might use ASP and ADO as your preferred solution. In the next chapter we look at how to set up ASP and ADO.

# Exercises

Rate your requirements for your web site in the light of three factors: flexibility, complexity, uniqueness. Poll the people who will be working on your web pages for their background in writing ASP, JavaScript, VBScript, VB, C++, and Java.

Visit the following web sites:

| | |
|---|---|
| Microsoft | www.microsoft.com/workshop/c- frame.htm#/workshop/server/default.asp |
| Chili | www.ChiliSoft.com |
| ColdFusion | www.allaire.com/products/ColdFusion/index.cfm |
| HalcyonSoft | www.halcyonsoft.com |

# Chapter One Quiz

1.   What are the two major scripting languages supported by ASP?

2.   Which scripting language is used in this book?

3.   If your site will be hosted on a Unix server, what are your options for using ASP/ADO?

4.   Compare and contrast server-side and client-side scripting.

5.   Which browsers are compatible with ASP-ADO?

6.   Which databases can be used with an ASP-ADO solution?

# Chapter One Quiz Answers

1. VBScript and JScript

2. VBScript

3. Chili!ASP and Halcyon Software's IASP

4. Server side scripting is more secure and more universally usable, but generally requires two trips for a calculation. Client side scripting requires specific browsers and exposes business rules to the public, but can run many calculations after one trip to the server. In addition, if you want to run client-side script you must make sure the browser will support it – for example client-side VBScript is supported by Internet Explorer but not by Netscape.

5. Every browser ever made that supports HTML and images.

6. Currently, almost all databases including MS SQL Server, MS Access, DB2, Oracle, Sybase – in fact any database with an ODBC driver, and some further data stores such as MS Index Server.

Welcome to the Microsoft...

Setup cannot install system files or update shared files if the files are in use. Before co...
any open applications.

Please take a moment to read the End User License Agreement now. It contains all of the te...
conditions that pertain to this software product. By choosing to continue, you indicate accepta...
these terms.

| Continue | Exit Setup |

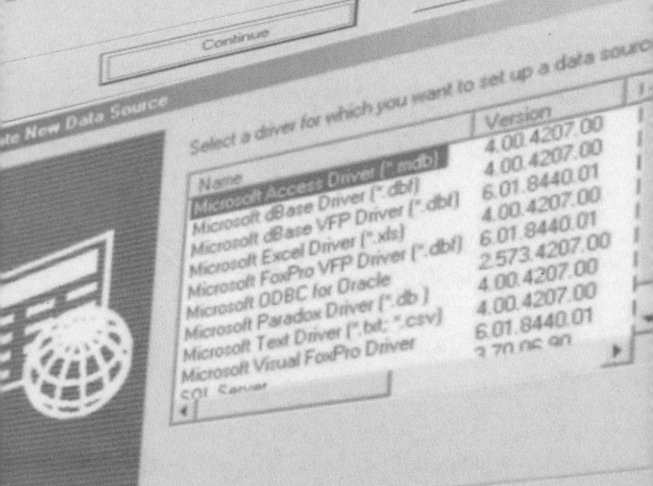

...te New Data Source

Select a driver for which you want to set up a data sourc...

| Name | Version | |
|---|---|---|
| Microsoft Access Driver (*.mdb) | 4.00.4207.00 | |
| Microsoft dBase Driver (*.dbf) | 4.00.4207.00 | |
| Microsoft dBase VFP Driver (*.dbf) | 6.01.8440.01 | |
| Microsoft Excel Driver (*.xls) | 4.00.4207.00 | |
| Microsoft FoxPro VFP Driver (*.dbf) | 6.01.8440.01 | |
| Microsoft ODBC for Oracle | 2.573.4207.00 | |
| Microsoft Paradox Driver (*.db ) | 4.00.4207.00 | |
| Microsoft Text Driver (*.txt; *.csv) | 4.00.4207.00 | |
| Microsoft Visual FoxPro Driver | 6.01.8440.01 | |
| SQL Server | 3.70.06.90 | |

| | | Cancel |

# Setting Up ASP and ADO

*"It took the human species some 4,000 years of experimenting before we hurled the first man-made object up 100 miles into orbit. But then in the next 15 years, men traveled 250,000 miles to the moon and sent a probe 3 million miles to leave our solar system. You see, sometimes it is the very first step of a project that is, by far, the most difficult."*

The first step you should make in using ASP and ADO is to get the software working properly. Before you can start programming databases in ASP, there are three steps that need to take place.

❑ Your web server, together with ASP, needs to be correctly installed

❑ ADO needs to be installed

❑ You need to set up a Data Source Name for the database with which you're going to be working

These deceptively simple tasks can often take a lot of time and effort. This chapter is about getting each of these three steps right.

There are three common configurations: NT/IIS, Win 2000/IIS and Windows9x/PWS. Each of these is discussed in detail, as well as lists of common problems and solutions. We will also go through the steps needed to create an ODBC Data Source Name (DSN) to assist in connecting to data stores.

Most people do not experience many problems setting up IIS and ASP on NT or Windows 2000. However, it is my experience that many students have a tough time getting PWS operating correctly on Win9x machines. We start this chapter with a review of some terminology and concepts, and then we run through the steps of setting up IIS on NT and Windows 2000, as well as PWS on Win9x. As setting up PWS has proved persistently problematic for novices, we have devoted a lot of space to troubleshooting the most commonly occurring problems. We continue with a look at the installation of ADO and finish with details on setting up DSNs. In order, the topics we'll cover are:

❑ An overview of the components and options used in installation

❑ Installing IIS on NT

❑ Installing IIS on Windows 2000

❑ Installing PWS on Win 9x

### Chapter 2

❑ Installing an up to date version of ADO

❑ Troubleshooting the most commonly occurring problems on PWS install

❑ Setting up a Data Source Name

❑ Testing your installation to see that it all works correctly

Once you've set up ASP, ADO and a DSN, you'll be ready to start programming.

# Overview of Components and Options

If this is your first time setting up ASP you may find some of the terminology confusing. The following are not official, all-inclusive definitions, but rather explanations for the purposes of getting ASP up and running.

❑ **Windows NT** – An MS operating system, the two main flavors being NT Workstation for desktops, which is an ideal development environment, and NT Server, which is designed to control the domain once the site is deployed. The latter is widely used to support commercial web sites.

❑ **Windows 95 and 98** (Win9x) – Microsoft operating systems designed for personal use. These versions of Windows are not as stable as NT and thus unsuitable for deployed sites.

❑ **Windows 2000** – Microsoft's next generation of operating system that forms the next upgrade for both NT and Win9x users alike. The Workstation version is geared more for personal users, the Server version is for developers.

❑ **Internet Information Server (IIS)** – An optional service for Windows NT Server to provide web site functionality. The most common MS solution for a web site is IIS running on NT Server.

❑ **Personal Web Server (PWS)** – A web server from Microsoft that is generally used by one person for development purposes locally on a personal OS like WIN 95/8 or NT Workstation. PWS is primarily for a web developer to test pages without connecting via a LAN or TCP/IP to a NT/IIS/ASP server. PWS can be used as a server for a small deployed site, but with severe restrictions, such as only allowing 5 concurrent users.

So here is the quick summary of operating systems and web servers: IIS is the web server which runs on NT Server and Windows 2000 and can handle commercial-scale deployment. PWS is a web server that runs on Win9x and NT Workstation, and is designed for small-scale deployment on one machine for the purpose of developing web sites. In other words:

❑ NT Server/Win2000 Server/IIS/ASP for deployment for public use

❑ Win9x (or WinNT Workstation or Win2000 Workstation)/PWS/ASP for local web developer use at design time

In fact, most web developers will have the optimal situation of both configurations installed; the PWS for development off-line or under Win9x OS and then the IIS/NT or Win 2000 for deployment to the public.

# Server Support for ASP

One of the most common, and important, questions is in regard to what servers are needed to support ASP. The answers frequently determine whether ASP is even considered as an option.

## Technical Facts about Server Support for ASP

ASP was designed by Microsoft to run as part of IIS, which runs on NT Server. Although you can run ASP scripts under PWS, without NT, this is only really suitable for development and testing. Before considering implementation of ASP solutions you must check that your production site is (or will be) running NT Server version 4 or later. (An early version of ASP, 1.5, ran on NT 3.51 without IIS but neither of those are any longer recommended). Not only must the server be NT, but IIS must be installed as the web server. In addition the server administrator must load the ASP option. Lastly, to implement the sort of functionality we discuss in this book, you must load ADO. ADO version 2.1 is available from SQL Server 7.0 and Service Pack 5a for SQL Server 6.5, or by download from the Microsoft website as part of MDAC (Microsoft Data Access Components). ADO version 1.5 in the NT4 option pack is less robust and less powerful, and this book is geared toward ADO 2.1. We'll discuss this in more depth further on.

Be careful about conflicts with legacy software. If an existing application requires an older version of an ADO or ODBC driver, then you may find it impossible to run your ASP pages containing ADO. Considering the current inexpensive price of hardware and the fact that servers are frequently upgraded for other reasons, you may find the cheapest solution to accommodating legacy software is to keep the existing server to run the legacy application, and add a new server which is configured for the current versions of NT, ASP and ADO.

If you are hosting with a service, as opposed to in-house, you will need to check that your hosting contract includes support for ASP and ADO. Some hosts make additional charges for this service, or only make it available in certain price plans. Another variation in hosting tariffs is to have an ASP-ADO service only available to clients that lease an entire server for their site. An additional issue to discuss with your host are the permissions on the database. The anonymous user (IUSR) needs to have read and write permissions on the directory in which the DB is stored. This causes some security problems if the database is stored in the same area as the general pages.

# Installing IIS on NT Server

Microsoft has provided relatively smooth installation procedures for setting up IIS/ASP on NT Servers. The basic steps are to obtain the software as a part of the NT 4 Option Pack, then run `Setup.exe`.

## Sources

ASP is available as part of IIS which is in the Windows NT 4.0 Option Pack. That is available from TechNet or the MSDN disks, or can be downloaded (about 30 Mb) from `http://www.microsoft.com/ntserver/nts/downloads/recommended/NT4OptPk/default.asp`.

> *Be sure to use the latest Option Pack since earlier versions were buggy. The NT4 option pack CD has also been in NT 4.0 shrink-wrap boxes sold since early 1998.*

## Installing IIS and ASP

**1.** Install Windows NT 4.0 Service Pack 3 server version 4.0. Unless you are setting up a new server specifically for your site, this has probably already been done. First stop all services which may be using ODBC, including SQL Server and Access:

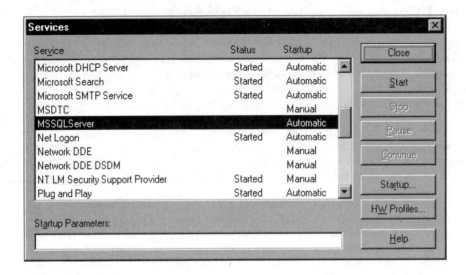

**2.** Service Pack 3 is required in order to install the Option Pack. Service packs are generally available at `http://www.microsoft.com/ntserver/nts/downloads/default.asp`.

**3.** Install IE version 4.01 or 5.0. IE should be installed at this point to meet the requirements of the NT 4.0 Option Pack.

**4.** Install the NT 4.0 Option Pack. The Option Pack contains the IIS software as well as the ASP engine (note that IIS4 requires MTS2, also installed). Choosing the typical installation provides all of the components necessary to run ASP and ADO on NT, as well as some additional components which are not required to run ASP-ADO. If you choose the custom installation, ensure that the following components are selected:

❑ Internet Service Manager (subcomponent of Internet Information Server) – this is the plugin to the Microsoft Management Console (discussed below) that enables administration of IIS 4.0.

❑ World Wide Web Server (subcomponent of Internet Information Server) – this is the core component of IIS.

❑ Data Sources (subcomponent of Microsoft Data Access Components 1.5) – these are the drivers and providers for accessing common data sources, such as SQL Server, Oracle, and Access.

❑ MDAC (subcomponent of Microsoft Data Access Components 1.5) – these are the ADO core components as well as OLE DB and ODBC files. We'll be looking at how to install ADO 2.1 further on in the chapter.

❑ Microsoft Management Console – also known as the MMC, this program is the shell from which administrative functions are performed. Microsoft intends to move all management functions (i.e. for NT, SQL Server, etc) to MMC.

❑ NT Option Pack Common Files – contains the core components of the Option Pack.

❑ Transaction Server Core Components (subcomponent of Transaction Server) – contains the core components of Transaction Server, which is required for IIS.

Use the **Select Components** dialog box to select and deselect components:

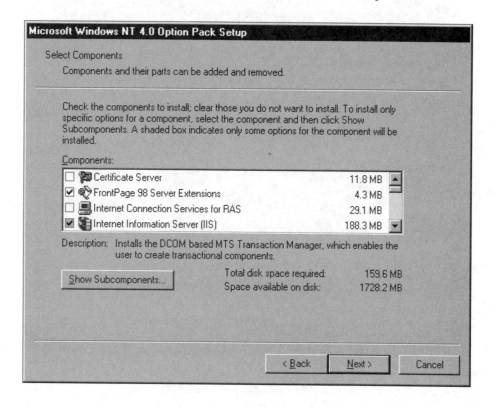

You can access the subcomponents of a particular component by selecting a component and clicking Show Subcomponents. The subcomponents dialog will appear:

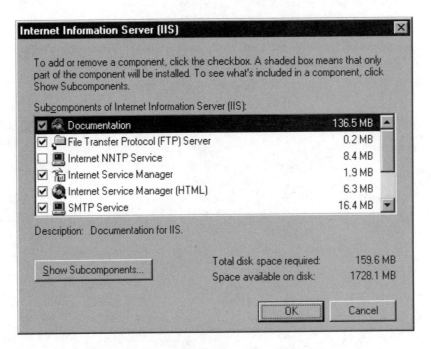

5. After you have selected your components and target directories, choose local for Microsoft Transaction Server's administration account.

6. Install NT 4.0 Service Pack 4 available at http://www.microsoft.com/ntserver/nts/downloads/default.asp

7. Install NT Service Pack 5. Run the latest MDAC service pack. At the time of writing, that was MDAC 2.1 Service Pack 1 (6 Mb) available at http://support.microsoft.com/support/ntserver/content/servicepacks/sp4 _central_40.asp, or from Visual Studio Service Pack 3.

8. Search the source CD for the files Adovbs.inc and AdoJavas.inc (for VBScript and JScript, respectively) and copy them into the root of your web site or to another folder where you will be able to access them for the ADO constants. They are commonly put into the Program Files\common files\system\ado directory.

**9.** You can now open up the Microsoft Management Console and find the IIS folder. Expand the folder, then expand the computer icon with the asterisk next to it. You should see something similar to the following screen:

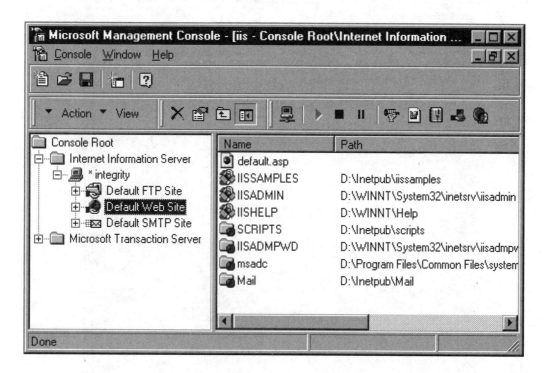

**10.** Right mouse click Default Web Site and open Properties. Under the Documents tab add
`Default.asp` or any other page names that should act as defaults. You will also want to
reorder those documents to fit your requirements – typically that would be with
`Default.asp` first.

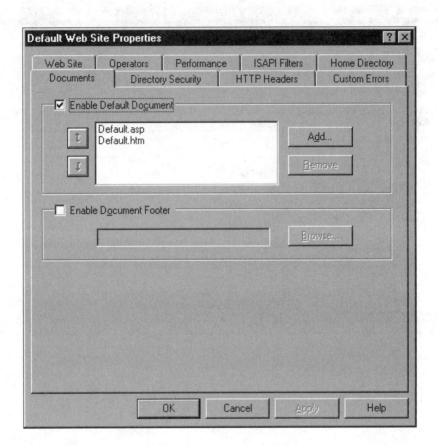

**11.** Staying within the Properties dialog, switch to the Home Directory tab and check that Permissions is set to Script:

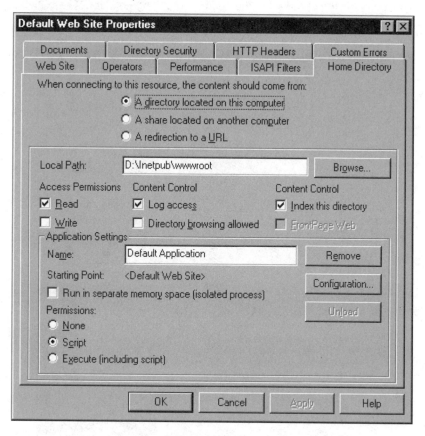

Your ASP set up on NT with IIS should now be complete.

# Installing IIS and ASP on Windows 2000 (Workstation or Server)

With Windows 2000 you might find that you don't have to do anything as IIS 5.0 is installed as part of Windows 2000. If you're not already running IIS 5.0, then you'll find that it's one of the many components available on the CD-ROM. We'll see now how you can check to see whether it's already up and running, or if it requires installing.

## Do I need to install it at all?

1. Go to the Control Panel and select the Add/Remove Programs icon. The following dialog will appear, displaying a list of your currently installed programs:

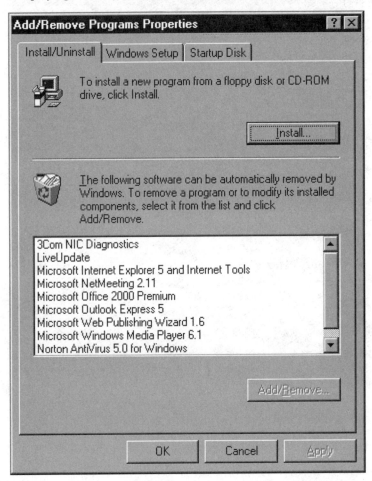

2.  Select the Add/Remove Windows Components icon on the left side of the dialog, to get to the
    screen that allows you to install new Windows components.

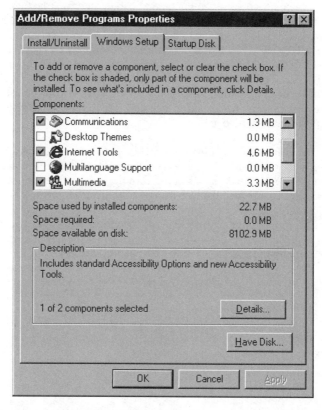

3.  Locate the Internet Information Services (IIS) entry in the dialog and check to see whether it is
    ticked or not. Unless you specified it during the custom install, most likely the check box will
    be cleared.

4.  If it is cleared, then select it and click on Next to load Internet Information Services 5.0 and
    Active Server Pages. It will take a few minutes to complete.

5.  If it is checked, then you won't need to install the component as it is already present on your
    machine, in which case you probably don't need to change anything, and you can click on
    Cancel to finish the whole process.

### How It Works

Once it has finished loading, it will automatically start web services running for you. You'll find that
Internet Information Services installs most of its bits and pieces on your hard drive under the InetPub
directory.

# Installing PWS on Win 9x

Many people develop their sites directly on the target host. In other words, they use FrontPage or another editor which can copy the page from the host to the editor, perform changes, then copy the page back to the host where the revised version is visible to the world. The copying is typically done using FTP software such as WS_FTP (`www.ipswitch.com`), although some editors such as FrontPage and Visual InterDev avoid FTP by using HTTP and a server-side extension to achieve the same transfer. When the web designer wants to check the result, she looks at the page using a browser with the URL of the web host. Note that this browser examination requires a working TCP/IP connection between the page designer and the site host. In other words, if the web designer is not connected to the target host via a network, she cannot edit or view the page.

Microsoft offers an alternative to developing on the deployed site — a Personal Web Server, or PWS. The Personal Web Server is very similar to the web server that hosts the site: it can receive requests, find the appropriate page, run scripts, connect to data and return the page. However, the PWS resides in the memory of the Windows PC on which the web designer is working. During development the memory of the designer's desktop PC contains three elements – the page editor, the browser, and the PWS – while the site (or a copy of it) sits on the designer's hard drive. When the web designer opens or saves a page in her editor it is from and to the local hard drive. When she views the changes, the browser sends the request to the part of memory (actually the process) running PWS, and PWS serves up the page to the browser.

PC running Windows 95 or 98

You can also work locally on one machine with NT Server and IIS installed. However, because NT Server is designed for larger-scale commercial use, it is a more resource-hungry product, and a more powerful PC is required than for just Windows 95 or 98. It is very convenient to be able to install PWS on your normal home PC.

Note that there is no need for any external connection cables; the TCP/IP connection is set up within the machine. The web designer can grab her laptop, sail out to the middle of the bay and drop anchor. Without any telephone connection she can design in her editor and view in her browser any page of her site. When she returns to shore she can then transfer (by FTP or HTTP) new or changed pages from her local drive to the real site on the host.

*Naturally if you are on a LAN with your server you can work across your 100BaseT line rather than a dial-up connection. This is the common solution for companies that do their own hosting. Of course that does not solve mobility, but it is much faster than a modem to an external host.*

The main strength of PWS is that it provides a convenient and inexpensive development environment, without the need for powerful hardware. A copy of the site can be made to a local machine and then worked upon without the possibility of damaging the real site during development. Saving and viewing sites on a local drive enables the developer to review progress without having to repeatedly transfer files. At the end of development all the code must be transferred by FTP or HTTP, but that one-time transfer is less expensive in terms of time and resources than repeated transfers.

It is important to separate the development copies of pages from the deployed versions. Pages changed on PWS can be tested under various browsers prior to being revealed to the world. You will be uploading the perfect page rather than making a series of incremental changes that are, during development, being viewed by visitors.

PWS can actually work as a server for a low-budget situation. PWS lacks the reliability of NT Server/IIS, although an improvement would be to run it on NT Workstation instead of Win9x. Furthermore, you will not be able to scale your domain beyond the single server. But for a limited load over an intranet, PWS might give acceptable service considering its price advantage over NT Server/IIS.

Lastly, if you keep a duplicate of your site on PWS, you have a complete site ready to upload to a new host, should your host's servers go down or its finances go belly up. Although this insurance works well for the pages, you may not have all of your data on your PWS machine. Developers with large data stores generally keep only a subset on their PWS machine for testing.

Once PWS is installed (see later in this chapter) you will have two new addressing techniques to understand. First is that your personal web server will be at the TCP/IP address 127.0.0.1. Sites you develop can be accessed from your browser by providing the URL of 127.0.0.1/MySiteName/MyPageName.asp. The second location is of the physical file. Whereas on NT/IIS your files are in the folder named InetPub, in PWS they are in C:\WebShare\WWWRoot\MySiteName\MyPages. The files for pages can be seen using Windows Explorer, as well as copied or renamed. Keep in mind that manipulations of page files can cause a site to become out of synchrony with some editors or site management software. It is safer to perform file management tasks for a site using the explorer features of your page editing software, such as VID or FrontPage.

# Sources of PWS

The current version (as of mid-1999) of PWS is version 4.0, which was first released in NT4 Option Pack of Dec 1997 as part of IIS 4.0. It is available from several sources, as follows.

## VID

Microsoft's Visual InterDev version 6.0 includes PWS. It can be installed at the time VID is set up or can be installed afterwards as an option from a custom set-up.

## Win98

The Win98 CD contains a folder named **Add-Ons/PWS**. Within that folder is a Setup.exe for PWS. My students who have installed PWS from the Win98 CD onto a Win98 OS seem to have less problems than students who use other sources.

## FP

Front Page, Front Page97 and FrontPage98 included PWS, however in different flavors.

> *The early releases of Front Page had a program named HTTPD which was sold as Front Page Server. The function was the same as PWS, but it was an entirely different set of code and did not run ASP.*

FP 97 contained PWS 1.0 and FP 98 contains PWS 4.0, the current incarnation of PWS.

## Download

Microsoft offers PWS as a download, but with a strange nomenclature. When you go to http://www.microsoft.com/windows/ie/pws you will see that there is the WinNT option pack for NT and a WinNT option pack for Win95. If you run the Windows NT Option Pack on a Windows9x machine, the option pack will recognize that this is not an NT OS and will install PWS instead of IIS.

"Wait A Minute! Run the Windows NT Option Pack on Windows9x?" Many students have a hard time believing that one possible technique to install PWS was to run the NT Option Pack on their Windows 9x machines. But it does work and is the recommended method.

## OFFICE 2000 Premium and Professional Editions

Pre-release information is that Microsoft will offer PWS on the Premium and Professional editions of Office 2000, that is those that include FrontPage.

## Which Source to Use?

I have found that students have the fewest problems when installing PWS on Win98 from the Win98 CD. The second least-problematic source seems to be the NT download which is good for Win95 as well as Win98. Another strategy with minimum complaints has been the installation from NT 4 Option pack onto NT workstation. Folks that are installing from VID and FrontPage CD-ROMs seem to have the most problems. I also suggest that if students are considering moving from Win95 to Win98 or WinNT, they do so prior to attempting to install PWS.

### Install Steps for PWS From Win98CD to Windows98

This is the safest option for installing PWS, in my experience, but is only possible if using Win98. The steps are as follows:

1. Ensure that the Windows 98 CD is in the drive.

2. Go to Start | Run...

3. Type x:\add-ons\pws\setup.exe where x: is the letter of your CD-ROM drive.

**4.** You will be greeted with a splash screen similar to the following:

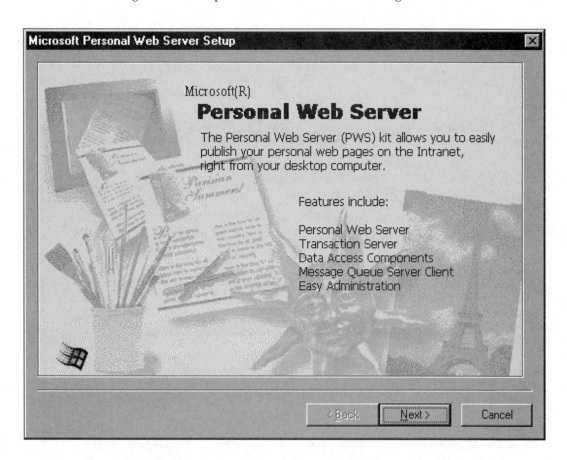

**5.** For most users, the typical install will work fine. If you choose to do a custom install, then ensure that the following components are selected:

❑ Common Program Files

❑ MDAC 1.5

❑ Personal Web Server

❑ Transaction Server

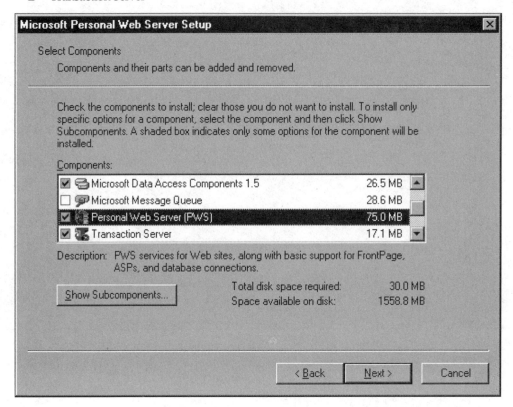

**6.** You will then be prompted for your default web publishing home directory.

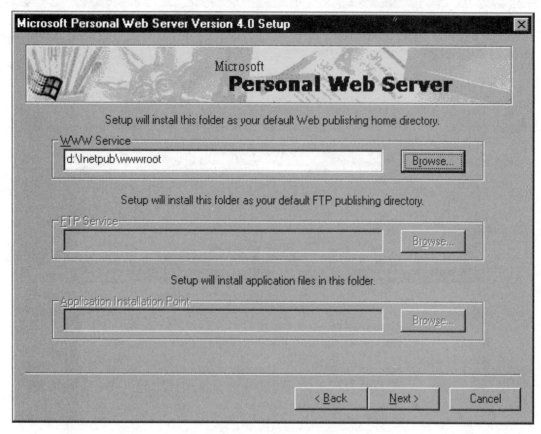

**7.** Leave the default install folder as it is for Transaction Server. The installation program will install the required files. Reboot your computer and it's all done.

## Install Steps Using Downloaded NT Option Pack onto Win95

This is the best option for Win95. However, keep in mind that a much higher percentage of my students have had problems with PWS on Win95 than PWS on Win98. If you are considering upgrading to Win98 I suggest you do it prior to installing PWS.

1. Close all applications.

2. Download WinNT Option Pack for Win95 from
   `http://www.microsoft.com/windows/ie/pws` using the link at the bottom of the page.

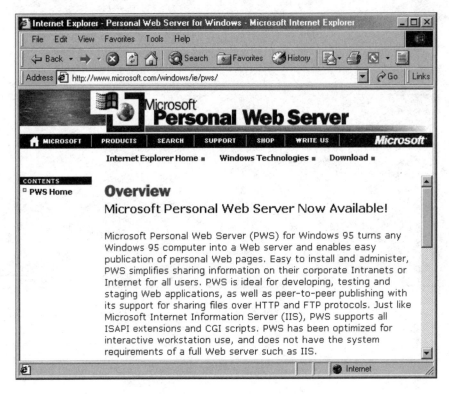

**3.** Select Option 1 of the the Download options, and then on the next page select the operating system you are running on. On the next page click on `download.exe` for the site nearest to you.

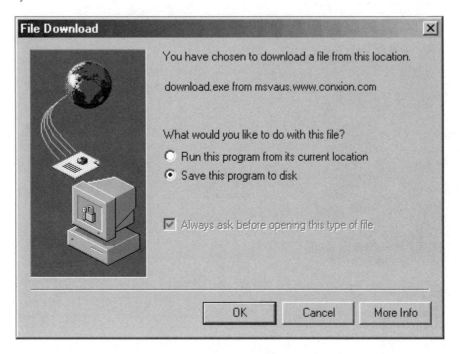

**4.** Save the program to disk.

**5.** Select Start | Run on `download.exe` and the wizard will first ask you to agree to the licensing terms, and then present you with the following screen:

**6.** Choose to download only, as, if the install option quits halfway through, it can possibly mess up your machine's configuration.

**7.** Click Next and choose x86: Windows 95 for the operating system and click Next.

**8.** Choose the Typical Installation and click Next.

**9.** Choose a location on your hard drive of where to download the pack to, and click Next.

**10.** Choose a location from where to download the pack.

**11.** Accept the verification certificate that appears and then the option pack will download.

**12.** Finally Start | Run the newly downloaded `setup.exe` and the setup is then same as the previous install from step 4.

# Typical Problems of PWS on Win9x

Over the years I have helped many students to get PWS running. In turn, many experts have passed their knowledge on to me. Here are our solutions to the most common problems.

## First, Be Sure You are Testing Correctly

Many times I have been asked to give a hand troubleshooting an ASP install. It appears that ASP is not working correctly, but I find that the problem is in the test page. I suggest that you test with a page from the ASP RoadMap (more later) or else the simple test file we'll look at a little further on in this chapter. If you are using your own test page and have problems, then check for the following common errors:

❑ File name does not end in .asp or the test page is misspelled in the browser address.

❑ Incorrect path for the page.

❑ VBScript is missing the delimiters <%%> or <SCRIPT> tags.

❑ VBScript has errors in syntax

❑ Check that PWS is running by either looking for its symbol in the tray or by Start | Programs | Microsoft Personal Web Server | Personal Web Manager and seeing the Stop button displayed.

❑ Also, on a few occasions when I created a page after PWS was running, I needed to stop and restart before PWS could find the page.

## Opening an ASP Page Launches Visual Interdev, FrontPage or PhotoShop

When trying to load a local (127.0.0.1) ASP page, Windows opens up Adobe Photoshop or VID instead. Regular .htm or .html pages view fine in the browser. In other cases the browser will load the ASP page, but also start Photoshop. This usually does not happen when viewing .asp pages sitting on a non-local host.

### Solution

The problem here is that there is a support file for Photoshop that has the .asp extension. We want to change the association for .asp to our editor. You can change the association by starting Windows Explorer then clicking on the menu View | Options | Win95-FileTypes | Win98-FileOptions. Click on ActiveServerDocument | Edit | Actions-Edit and set this to the same as the file type of Internet Document Set.

If there is no Active Server Document file type listed, then you need to find what file type is currently assigned to .asp and change it to be associated with your browser. Unfortunately Windows does not offer an alphabetical list of extensions, so do this:

1. Add a New Type.

2. Give it Description=test and Associated Extension = .ASP and click OK to save.

3. Windows will respond that .ASP is already taken by *xxx*. Make a note of the *xxx* file type and click OK to exit the error message.

**4.** Click Cancel to exit the Add New File Type dialog box.

**5.** Find and select the *xxx* file type in the list of files types.

**6.** Click Edit and change as follows:

❑ Description of Type = Active Server Document

❑ Content Type = text/asp

❑ Default Extension for Current Type = .asp

**7.** Under Actions = Edit:

❑ Enter your location of IE software, for example
"C:\PROGRA~1\INTERN~1\iexplore.exe".

❑ Click the icon for .asp files in a Photoshop.sep table.

In some cases the above will not work because Windows does not let you create the new file type. You will have to first delete the old association by hand in the registry as follows.

**1.** Start | Run | Regedit

**2.** Select HKEY_CLASSES_ROOT

**3.** Select the .asp folder

**4.** Find the key that has the PhotoShop.SepTablesFile value in it

**5.** Delete the data (not the key itself, just the text in it)

**6.** Now you can create the file type as described above

## IE Connects to Internet Even When Page is Local on PWS

After some installs, IE4 wants to connect to the Internet even when the page is sitting locally on PWS. This defeats one of the main advantages of PWS – the ability to work off-line. I observe this problem only in IE, not Netscape, and more frequently from students that install PWS from VID 6 CDs.

### Solution 1

You can control how IE looks for pages. For IE 3 go to View | Internet Options | Connection. The choices are Connect to the Internet using a modem and Connect to the Internet using Local Area Network. Once the LAN option is selected IE will no longer dial-up to find a page. However, whenever you do want to access a page by dial-up, you will have to do so by connecting before requesting the page. IE 4 and 5 have the same feature under Tools | Connections – select the option for Never dial a connection.

### Solution 2 (a variant of solution 1)

Install a network card as well as the modem. The NIC can just have a BNC terminator on it, it does not have to be physically attached to anything. Bind TCP/IP to the NIC card. Then set IE to connect by LAN. However, like solution 1, you still have to dial manually when you want the internet.

### Solution 3

Use the URL `http://localhost/MySite/MyPage.ASP`. If you just use `MySite/MyPage.asp` or `MyPage.asp`, IE connects to the Internet just in case the page is not found locally.

### Solution 4

When IE displays the dial-up connection screen, don't click Cancel or close the window. Just press Alt+Tab or click on the IE window to change the focus back to IE.

## Loss of FTP Message

If PWS version 1 is installed and then you install PWS version 4, you get a message "The Microsoft FTP service is no longer supported. If you click OK to continue the installation, FTP will be removed. Otherwise click Cancel to exit setup." This means you will lose the server-side FTP capability which was part of PWS 1 but not PWS 4. This is not a problem since you can still transfer files by using FrontPage with File | Publish, or you can install FTP software such as WS_FTP from `www.Ipswitch.com`.

## NotePad Adds a .txt Extension

Notepad may add `.txt` to the end of each page so you get, for example, `MyPage.asp.txt`. Then VBScript does not execute since PWS or IIS is looking at an extension of `.txt` instead of `.asp`.

### Solution 1

When naming your file select File Type *.* All Files. Name your file with its name and extension, for example `MyPage.asp`. Notepad will not add a `.txt` extension.

### Solution 2

Rename your file using Windows Explorer after saving it. If you are FTPing your files up to a server, do the rename before the FTP operation.

### Solution 3

When typing in the name of a file put double quotes around it. Then Notepad will save it exactly as typed.

### Solution 4

Change the way Notepad saves names on files. There are two ways of doing this:

1.  Open Windows Explorer and click on View | Options. Uncheck Hide File Extensions for registered types.

2.  On the desktop open My Computer, and click on View | Folder Options. Choose the View tab and uncheck Hide file extensions for known file types.

## IE Erroneously Changes the URL type

In some set-ups of IE, when you type `http://MyComputer/MySite/MyPage.asp` IE automatically adds `.com`. So, it becomes `http://www.MyComputer.com/MySite/Mypage.asp`, which causes a "file not found" message.

### Solution

Open IE and select View | Internet Options | Advanced | Browsing. Uncheck Use Autocomplete.

In Internet Explorer 5 you can find the same information under a different path: click Tools | Internet Options and select the Advanced tab. You will need to uncheck Use inline AutoComplete for Web addresses.

## Installation Error Message: Requires 32 bit TCP/IP Networking or Missing WinSock

When running the Personal Web Server `setup.exe` file on Win9x, you may get a message WinSock 2 is required to run this setup utility. Please click OK. Alternatively, you may find that on first running Front Page after installing PWS you get an error message along the lines of FrontPage requires 32 bit TCP/IP networking… not installed. These are both caused by PWS not being able to see a Dynamic Host Configuration Protocol.

### Solution 1

Both of these problems can be solved by Start | Settings | Control Panel | Network | Add | Protocol. Add the Microsoft TCP/IP protocol & bind to a dial-up networking adapter. Save and reboot. Adding the TCP stack will provide not only TCP/IP but also the WinSock.

### Solution 2

Sometimes the version of Winsock causes this problem. You must revert to WinSock version 1.1, then run the Windows Sockets 2 update.

1. Restore Windows Sockets 1.1 with Start | Run `C:\YourWindowsDirectory\ws2bakup\ws2bakup.bat`. If you get a sharing violation message, strike a key to abort. Repeat this step until the batch file has finished running.

2. Restart the computer in MS-DOS mode.

3. Enter `c:\YourWindowsDirectory\ws2bakup\ws2bakup.bat` and ignore the any errors about updating the registry

4. Enter `exit` to leave DOS mode and restart Windows.

5. Download the `W95ws2Setup.exe` file from the following Microsoft URL and save in your *Temp* folder: `http://www.microsoft.com/windows/downloads/contents/updates/`.

6. Click Start | Run and execute `c:\Temp\W95ws2Setup.exe`.

7. When the Windows Sockets 2 Setup program has finished running, restart the computer. You will now have Windows Sockets 2 installed.

## *PWS Install Can't see IE 4.01*

Install of PWS requires IE4.01 or higher. In some cases, particularly with the FrontPage 98 PWS and Windows 95, there is an error message that setup cannot continue because setup requires IE4.01, even though IE4.01 is installed and working.

### Solution

There are multiple problems with installing the NT4 download version over the FP98 version with Win 95. The first option would be to upgrade the OS to Win98 and use the PWS on the Win98 CD. In addition this problem is usually solved if you have run the IE4.01 Service Pack 1 or upgrade to IE5.

## *Synchronizing Default Pages*

Every site must have a page set as the default page. FrontPage uses `Default` ( `.htm`, `.html` or `.asp` all work the same). Other web servers (perhaps the one on your host) use `Index.xxx`. When you create a site using FrontPage you may get a default page that is not recognized by your host.

### Temporary Solution

Change the name of your file before uploading to your ISP. When using PWS on your local machine, your home page is `default.htm`. Before FTPing the site to your ISP, change the filename or make a copy of it with the correct default name for your host such as `Index.html`.

### Solution 1

Change the name of your PWS default file name to match your host's default file name:

1. Start PWS (if it doesn't start automatically)

2. Right mouse click on the PWS icon in the Windows tray

3. Select Administer

4. Select WWW Administration

5. Click the Directories tab, then scroll to the very bottom of the page

6. Enable Default Document should be checked on

7. Change the Default Document to the name specified by your host

8. Close the Internet Services Administrator

*With NT4 Service Pack 4, Option Pack 4, PWS, double click on the PWS icon on the taskbar. In the left pane select Advanced, then pick up with step 6 above.*

If PWS is running when you make the change you may have to stop and restart PWS for the change to take effect. Assuming that PWS is running:

1. Right mouse click on the PWS icon in the Windows tray

2. Select Properties

3. Click on the Startup tab

4. Click on STOP, wait for the message to change to "The server is stopped"

5. Click on Start, wait for the message to change to "The server is running"

6. Close the Personal Web Server Properties dialog box

### Solution 2

If replacing the name of the home page doesn't work, try adding it. You can set "Default Document" = Default.asp, Index.asp. Note that multiple names are separated by a comma.

### Solution 3

You can create a file that is named according to your host's requirements but that redirects visitors to your actual home page. This may be your best bet if you don't have control of the server.

The following code is put in a small file named Default.htm:

```
<HTML><HEAD>
<TITLE>Redirect Default.htm to Index.asp</TITLE>
<META HTTP-EQUIV="REFRESH" CONTENT="0; URL=index.asp">
<BODY></BODY></HTML>
```

In this case the file is named according to the host requirement Default.htm and redirects to your home, named Index.asp. Note that this will have to go in every directory where your host expects to see Default.htm. There is a performance hit for this solution as the server must open two files instead of one.

Of the above solutions, I recommend modifying your PWS to accept the default file accepted by your host. This only has to be done once and you will not suffer a performance penalty.

## MTS registry not installed

At the end of some installations there is a message that the Microsoft Transaction Server was not installed. Although MTS is required with IIS it is not required for PWS. This message can be ignored and PWS will run ASP fine.

## More Troubles and Troubleshooting

If you encounter other problems, there are newsgroups that discuss PWS install issues. Several can be found at msnews.microsoft.com and others at news.conitech.com. You can find additional groups at http://www.dejanews.com/, or by performing a search for "PWS".

### ASP Roadmap

Microsoft has adopted an unconventional approach to the help file for ASP. Rather than the classic Help dialog with Contents, Index and Find, Microsoft has set up the help and examples as a web site called the Active Server Pages Roadmap, which can be viewed by your browser. Of course there is a glitch here: if ASP isn't already set up properly you will look like a dog chasing its tail when you try to read the ASP-based roadmap for help. But for help with post-install issues this site includes several major areas:

- Release notes for ASP
- Tutorials on ASP
- Tutorials and sample code for VBScript and JScript
- An examples site for the fictitious *Adventure Works* company
- Reference pages for Components, including ADO

Although the interface requires yet another acclimatization period (just when we were comfortable with Win help), the roadmap provides a good sample of a web site.

The ASP Roadmap can be installed when you install PWS, and then from the desktop click on Start | Programs | Microsoft Personal Web Server | ActiveServerPages RoadMap. Alternatively, you can start your browser and then open `http://yourserver/iasdocs/aspdocs/roadmap.asp`.

The roadmap has several areas of particular interest for programmers of ASP. If you are going to use the sample database, be sure to read the *About Adventure Works* sections for setting up the SQL database. You may want to take a break from this book and go through two sections:

- Tutorial Overview
- Module 2 on ActiveX Server Components, Lesson 3 – Using Database Access Components

# Installing ADO on IIS/NT/Win 2000 or Win9x/PWS

I have talked at length about installing ASP, but what about ADO? ADO is a part of **MDAC** (Microsoft Data Access Components). There have been several different versions of ADO to date, and it's important that you have an up to date one. The version numbering of MDAC reflects the version numbering of ADO, so MDAC 2.0 contains ADO 2.0 etc. The examples in this book require you to have *at least* ADO 2.0 or a more recent version. Now there's a good chance that you don't actually know which version of ADO you have on your machine, so here's a quick potted history to help you determine which version you have:

- IIS 3 and ASP 1.0 come with ADO 1.0
- IIS 4/PWS 4.0 (aka the NT Option Pack 4.0) come with ASP 2.0 but only ADO 1.5
- Windows 98 comes with PWS 4.0, ASP 2.0 and ADO 1.5
- Visual Studio 6 comes with ADO 2.0
- Office 2000 and IE5 come with ADO 2.1
- Windows 2000 comes with ASP 3.0 and ADO 2.5

You should be able to work out which version of ADO you have from this. If you have an up to date version of ADO (such as with IE5) and have since installed software that contains an older version of ADO, don't worry as the latest version won't be affected. So people who have installed IE5 followed by PWS 4.0 won't suddenly revert to ADO 1.5.

So if you don't have one of Office 2000, IE5, Windows 2000 or Visual Studio, and haven't downloaded the MDAC separately, then you will need to do so.

> **The version of MDAC that is included as part of the NT4 Option Pack, only contains ADO 1.5 and doesn't contain all of the features of ADO 2.x. PWS 4.0 also uses MDAC 1.5, which is automatically installed from the Win98 CD. If you try and run examples in this book on ADO 1.5 you might find that they don't work as intended.**

The MDAC service packs are available at `http://www.microsoft.com/data/download.htm`.

## Installing ADO

**1.** Go to `http://www.microsoft.com/data/download.htm` and then download the most recent version of MDAC.

**2.** Run the `mdac_typ.exe` and after it has installed a few bits and pieces you will get to the following screen to begin setup:

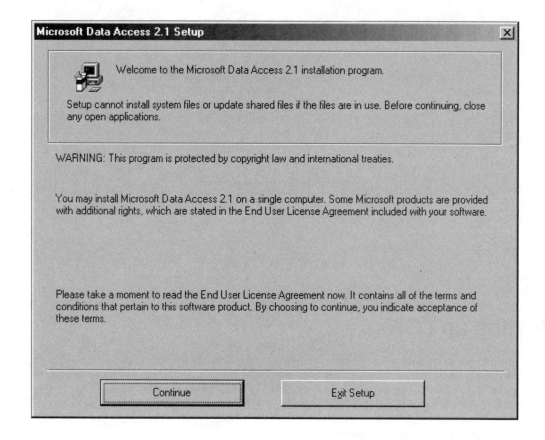

**3.** Press **Continue** and you get to the following screen:

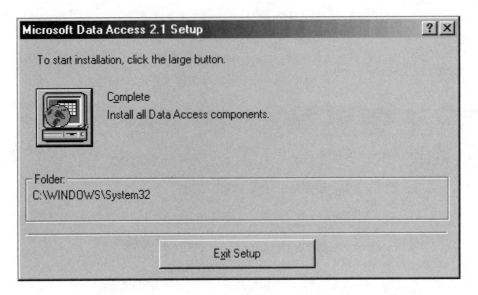

**4.** Click the large button to finish ADO's installation.

That's all there is to it, but before you can conveniently start accessing databases within your web pages, there's still one more task.

# Setting up DSNs

In order to use a database most conveniently we must set up an ODBC Data Source Name (DSN). There are ways to avoid DSNs, but most of this book demonstrates techniques that use them. In Chapter 6 on connections we also discuss faster and more efficient ways to connect to data by using native OLEDB providers. A DSN holds four or five pieces of information in either a file or as a registry setting:

❑ Its own name, that is the name of the DSN

❑ The datafile (or the server and provider for SQL or Oracle) to which it points

❑ Pointers to the drivers to connect to the data file

❑ UserID and Password to pass through to the data store

❑ Additional information needed for connection to specific datastores

DSNs are set up by a person with access to the system settings of the server machine. In the case of a desktop that is anyone with physical access. In the case of an NT server that would be a Systems Administrator. The DSN can be created either physically at the server or by remote software. Generally the web designer is not going to have access to a NT server. In most of my work I have had to send a request to the Systems Administrator to create a DSN for me.

DSNs come in three types: **User, System** and **File**. User DSNs are limited to the person who created them. Users logging in will not see the DSN of other users. System DSNs are stored in the registry and are available to all users on the local machine, including NT services and the IUSR account used by PWS and IIS. File DSNs hold the same information but as a text file rather then in the registry. In all of the examples in this book we use System DSNs.

# Steps to Create a DSN for an Access Database

First create the database. Even if it is not in its final form, you will need at least one table and a few records so you can test it. You must also know the type of database, that is whether it is Access, SQL or another DBMS type. With Access the database is a file with a .mdb extension.

1.  Create a new DSN by clicking through Start | Settings | ControlPanel | 32bit ODBC (or ODBC). You will see tabs for the three types of DSNs, as well as some other options. Click on the System DSN tab.

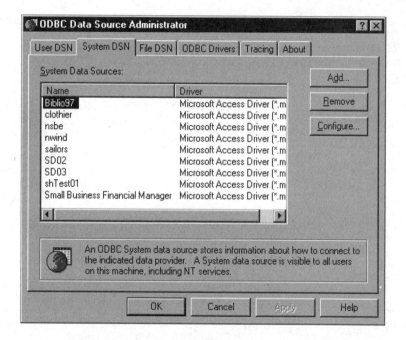

*These screen shots will vary slightly between versions of ODBC. On Windows 2000 the ODBC administrator is held in the Control Panel under Administrative tools and then Data Stores(ODBC).*

**2.** Click on Add and then the driver you want to use for your database. In our case this is Access.

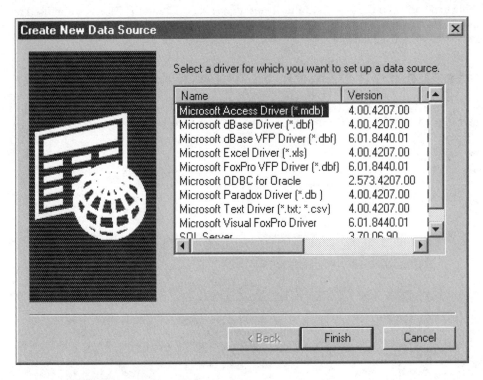

**3.** The DSN wizard then goes in different directions depending on the driver selected. In this case, using Access, the wizard asks you to name the DSN.

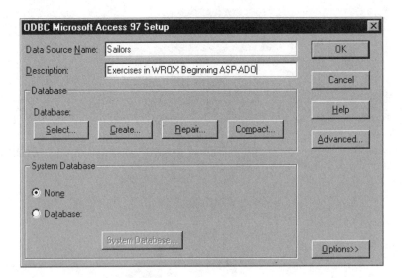

**4.** Last, you must identify which database the DSN should point to by clicking on the Select button then browsing to your database and selecting it.

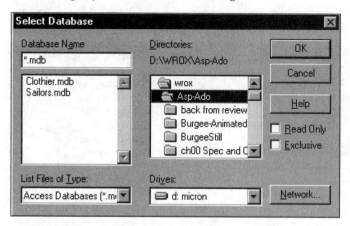

## Steps to Create a DSN for a SQL Datastore

There are a few pieces of information required before creating a DSN for a DBMS such as SQL Server. At the minimum, we need to know the following, usually available from your Database Administrator (DBA):

- ❑ network address of your database server
- ❑ network type of your database server (Named Pipes, TCP/IP, etc.)
- ❑ the security method of your server (NT or SQL Server)
- ❑ a valid login and password for the server
- ❑ the name of the database within the server

With this information in hand, we can create a SQL Server DSN.

## Creating a SQL Server DSN

1.  First, we must open the ODBC control panel. Then, click on the System DSN tab. Note that the screens below are particular to ODBC 3.5; your version may vary slightly.

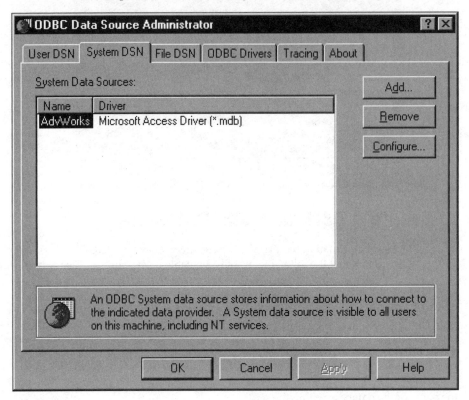

**2.** Click the Add... button to create a new System DSN. You will see the following dialog:

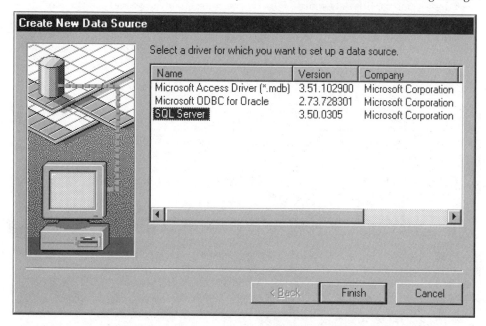

**3.** Select SQL Server from the list. Then click Finish. If SQL Server is not present in this list, you must reinstall MDAC. You will then be presented with the SQL Server DSN dialog.

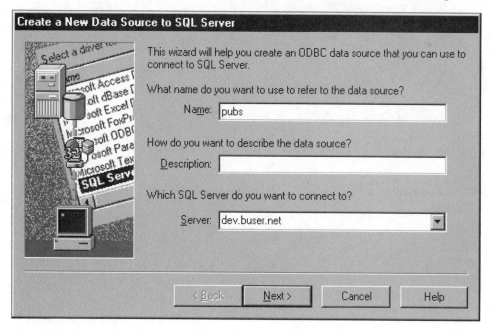

**4.** In this dialog, enter the name you will use for this data source. Next, you can enter a description for this data source. Finally, you must enter the network address of the SQL Server you are connecting to. If the database is located on the local machine, then you can choose (local) from the dropdown box. Otherwise, your safest bet is usually to enter the Internet address or IP address of the server. Again, this information should be available from your DBA.

*When naming data sources you will often use the name of the database you will be working in. The DSN name does not have to be the same as the source, so use any name that has meaning for you; but avoiding spaces and characters other than letters and numbers as this will make life a little easier later when coding.*

**5.** Click **Next** after you have entered this information. You will then be presented with the following entry screen.

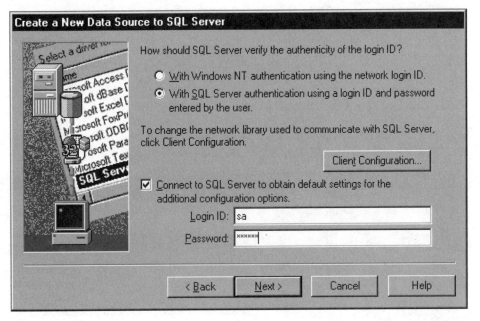

**6.** Depending on the security method used by your DBA, select NT or SQL Server authentication type.

**7.** Next, click the check box next to Connect to SQL Server ... This will provide the DSN with login information necessary for testing the connection when we are finished. Note that if you are using SQL Server authentication, you must enter your login ID and password here. If this is a database you have just set up with no security for a test environment, you can use the system administrator (sa) account with no password. Note that using this powerful account unsecured on a permanent basis is definitely NOT recommended!

**8.** Getting to the Client Configuration button, if the database server is on the local machine, you will probably not need to use this button. Otherwise, if your server is using a network type other than Named Pipes, you will need to click this button to change the default network used to connect to the database. Once the Client Configuration Utility is open, click the Net Library tab. Then, select the proper network type from the Default Network drop-down box. Click Done to return to the DSN setup dialog.

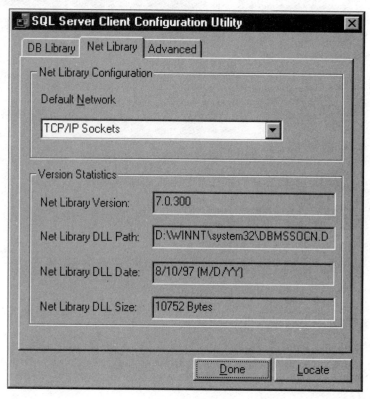

9. Click Next and the DSN setup dialog will attempt to connect to your database server.

*Note that if you changed the default network type in the Client Configuration utility, you will have to cancel the DSN setup dialog and start the process over again. However, you only have to set the default network once, and the setting will be persistent for future database connections.*

10. The next screen will present the opportunity to set the default database for this DSN. Click the dropdown box to find the database you want to use. Go ahead and leave all of the other settings as their defaults.

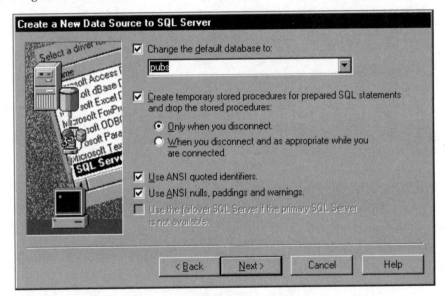

11. Click Next again, and leave the defaults as they are on this screen.

12. Click Next a final time, then click Finish.

13. At this point, you have the opportunity to test the DSN by clicking the Test Data Source button. If you get a failure message, go back and check your entries, and double check with your DBA to ensure that you are using the proper settings.

Provided all goes well, you will have a new entry in your Data Sources list, with SQL Server listed as the driver in your ODBC list as follows.

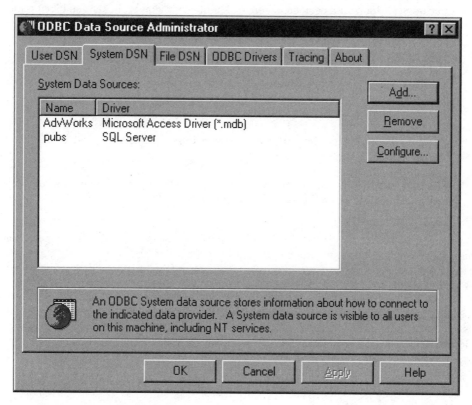

## A Practical Tip on Thinking Ahead

Generally you will not have the rights or access to set up a DSN on your server. That is fine during working hours, when you can go to the System Administrator, compliment him on his fine taste in music, then ask him for the favor of setting up a DSN for your database.

But what about when you are working on a project at midnight and the System Administrator is not available? If you are using Access there is a work-around. Before you get in a pickle, talk to your host server's System Administrator about setting up several DSNs for you with dummy databases and an FTP account for the directory where the databases are stored. Then, whenever you need a DSN for a database, you just FTP in the real database and replace the dummy. Then you can use the name of the pre-set DSN, which will now point to your real database rather than the dummy.

Again, let me make clear that this trick will never work with real-world multi-user data stores like SQL and Oracle. But as a student learning ASP and ADO it is great to be able to flip a new Access .mdb file onto the server at any time without kowtowing to the SysAdmins.

Here are the specific steps:

1. Lube up SysAdmin with beer, etc. - you are about to ask a favor. Better yet, lube up the SysAdmin's boss.

2. Make a few simple small databases in Access. Keep them real small: one table, one record.

3. Give the databases to the SysAdmin and ask him or her to make a folder on the server and copy into that new folder the databases. My SysAdmin has a folder named `C:\InetPubs\Kauffman\Databases`.

4. Ask your server systems admin to make a DSN pointing to each of the databases, naming them `YourName01`, `YourName02` and `YourName03`

5. Ask your SysAdmin for an FTP account with write/delete rights to the folders holding the small databases. Try not to lose the UserID and password.

When you need to use a DSN, just FTP your real database into the database folder, replacing the small database. Refer to that database in your VBScript using the existing DSN (e.g. `YourName01`). Before you write too many ASP-ADO pages using "`YourName01`," ask the Systems Administrator to set up a new DSN with a proper name.

Another way to avoid this problem is to use native OLEDB providers which can contain all of the necessary information in the connection string. See more on this in Chapter 6 which discusses connections. An additional alternative is to create a file DSN as explained by Manohar Kamath at `http://www.kamath.com/tutorial/filedsn.asp`.

# Is it all working?

To perform this test all you need to do is try and view the sample database that should have just been set up. We'll create a page on your server that does this and try viewing it in a browser.

## Useful Code Sample – Getting a Test Page Working

**1.** Either download the page `testsailor.asp` from the Wrox site or type the following text into a blank file in Notepad and save it as `testsailor.asp`:

```
<%@Language=VBScript%>
<HTML>
<HEAD>
<TITLE>Home Page</TITLE>
</HEAD>
<BODY>
<P>This line from HTML</P>
<HR>
<P>Next line from ASP will work<BR>
if ASP extensions installed correctly:<BR>
<%
  Response.Write "<B>From ASP</B>"
%>
<HR>
<P>Next line from ADO will work if a DSN named sailors has been set<BR>
for the example database which is named SAILORS.MDB.</P>
<%
  Set oRS=Server.CreateObject("ADODB.recordset")
  oRS.open "SELECT * FROM People", "DSN=sailors"
  oRS.MoveFirst
  Response.Write "<B>" & oRS("PeopleNameLast") & "</B>"
%>
<HR>
Finished test page</P>
</BODY>
</HTML>
```

> **Close Notepad and then check in Windows Explorer that the extension has not been changed.**

**2.** Transfer the file to the root of your web site and view the page in your browser using the HTTP://address:

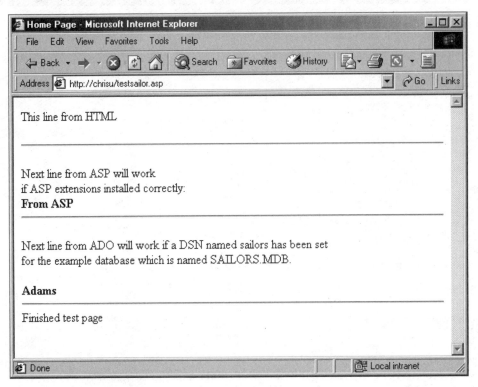

### Common Errors with the Test Page

Before you mail tech support at Wrox, please browse this list and check to see that none of these errors match up with anything you are experiencing.

- ❑ The page does not have an extension of .asp
- ❑ The DSN has not been set up
- ❑ The DSN was set up as a UserDSN or FileDSN instead of the proper SystemDSN
- ❑ The DSN has a name other than sailors – you will need to change this in the script to the name of your DSN
- ❑ Ensure that you are addressing the page by http://... and not by C:\...
- ❑ Be sure that the page is copied into the root of a working site
- ❑ Be very careful with punctuation on lines 12, 13 and 15
- ❑ Do not leave out one or more of the ASP delimiters: <% and %>
- ❑ Check that script or execute permissions are enabled on the folder holding the page

If all of the above are ruled out you can question:

❑ Is the server NT version 3 or above?

❑ Is IIS or PWS installed?

❑ Are the ASP extensions installed?

If you see the page, then you've accomplished everything you need to in this chapter.

# Summary

The official steps for setting up an ASP-enabled web server are to obtain the software and run the setup.exe. In reality, that works pretty well for installing IIS on Windows NT or Windows 2000, or for installing PWS from the Windows98 CD ROM onto Win98. However, when working with other sources of PWS, or whenever you work with Win95, there may be problems. Keep in mind that the path of fewest problems is to upgrade to Win98.

ADO comes from the Microsoft Data Access Components, (which form part of the NT4 Option Pack) and has its own service packs. You need to have at least version 2.0 downloaded to be able to use this book.

Finally, the establishment of Data Source Names enables easier access to databases. These can be set up in either NT or PWS using the ODBC wizard from the Control Panel.

# Exercises

These exercises use one or both of the two sample databases available from the WROX website at
http://webdev.wrox.co/uk. The structures of the databases are described in Appendix A for
Sailors.mdb and Appendix B for Clothier.mdb.

1. Take a look at the location for setting the files that PWS will look for as homepages.

2. Create a DSN pointing to the Sailor.mdb

3. Create a DSN pointing to the Clothier.mdb

# Quiz

1. Which type of DSN is normally used with PWS?

2. Describe the purpose of PWS.

3. You create a few pages on PWS. What must you do in order to display those pages to your
   boss on the company Intranet?

4. You want to see the list of pages of a new web site created using PWS. They are on your hard
   drive, but in what folder?

5. Where can you find PWS on the Windows98 CD ROM?

6. How do you install the "ADO" part of ASP-ADO?

7. I want to install PWS on my Win95 machine, but I only have the WindowsNT OptionPack.
   What should I do?

# Quiz Answers

**1.** System DSN

**2.** To allow the hosting of a single web site from a Win 9x or NT Workstation machine, usually for the purpose of modifying the site locally.

**3.** Transfer the pages to your host server. This can be done in two ways. First is that some HTML editors, such as FrontPage, have a facility to "publish" a site to another server. The second method is to FTP the files to the server. You must also be sure that the appropriate drivers are on the host server.

**4.** This varies from machine to machine, but you can start by looking in
`C:\webshare\wwwroot\MySite`

**5.** `D:\ add-ons\PWS\SetUp.exe`

**6.** ADO capability comes with MDAC which is part of the WindowsNT4 Option Pack or can be downloaded separately. MDAC has its own series of service packs, check with Microsoft for the latest.

**7.** You are doing fine. When the WindowsNT4 Option Pack is run on a Win95 machine the Option Pack recognizes the OS and just installs the PWS version for Win95.

Welcome to the Microsoft Data...

Setup cannot install system files or update shared files if the files are in use. Before c... any open applications.

WARNING: This program is protected by copyright law and international treaties.

You may install Microsoft Data Access 2.1 on a single computer. Some Microsoft products with additional rights, which are stated in the End User License Agreement included with y...

Please take a moment to read the End User License Agreement now. It contains all of the te... conditions that pertain to this software product. By choosing to continue, you indicate accept... these terms.

Continue

Exit Setup

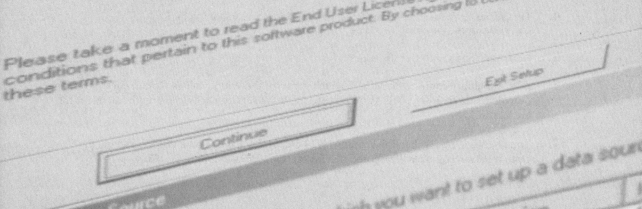

New Data Source

Select a driver for which you want to set up a data sourc...

| Name | Version |
|------|---------|
| Microsoft Access Driver (*.mdb) | 4.00.4207.00 |
| Microsoft dBase Driver (*.dbf) | 4.00.4207.00 |
| Microsoft dBase VFP Driver (*.dbf) | 6.01.8440.01 |
| Microsoft Excel Driver (*.xls) | 4.00.4207.00 |
| Microsoft FoxPro VFP Driver (*.dbf) | 6.01.8440.01 |
| Microsoft ODBC for Oracle | 2.573.4207.00 |
| Microsoft Paradox Driver (*.db ) | 4.00.4207.00 |
| Microsoft Text Driver (*.txt; *.csv) | 4.00.4207.00 |
| Microsoft Visual FoxPro Driver | 6.01.8440.01 |
| SQL Server | 2.70.06.90 |

Cancel

# Simple Recordsets - Reading Data

So you've decided that ASP-ADO is the solution for your situation, and you've learned how to set it up. Now you're ready to begin using ASP-ADO to access and manipulate data within web pages. This chapter discusses the simplest situation – the simple task of **reading** the data. Although we are only reading the data, we can still use it in several ways. Not only can we write it to the page; we can also use the data in variables, expressions and as the arguments for other functions.

Then we look at some of the techniques and problems with presenting the data that we read in an HMTL table. Last, even though VBScript implements only parts of Object Oriented Programming, we'll include a few paragraphs to provide an overview of the aspects of OOP that are available.

## Preparing to use Simple Recordsets

One of my sailing coaches emphasized that yacht races are won or lost long before the day of the race. Regattas are won during the months of preparation and training prior to the starting gun. Fortunately, ADO does not require many weeks of practicing tacks and jibes in the cold rain; you just have to consider the following three issues:

- ❑  Creating a DSN
- ❑  Having the correct user identification, password and permissions
- ❑  Understanding the structure of the database

## Step 1 - Create a DSN

In Chapter 2 we talked about creating an ODBC Data Source which is referred to by a DSN – this is typically performed by a systems administrator or other operator with access to the server. To review: the DSN contains the information necessary to make a physical connection into the database. This information may include database name, path, server name, user ID, password, driver name and other parameters. These pieces of information are wrapped up in a DSN, which is given a name. You need to get the name of your DSN from your systems administrator prior to using ASP-ADO.

If you are working on PWS you have access to the settings of your Windows OS and can set your own DSN (also discussed in Chapter 2), by selecting Start | Control Panel | 32 bit ODBC and following the steps of the wizard. In my development work I keep two copies of the database – one on my development machine using PWS and one on the server.

*In Chapter 6, we will talk about how to make a connection without a DSN.*

## Step 2 - User Identification and Password

I'm frequently approached by people seeking help with ADO, only to find that the problem is not with their ADO code, but that they do not have access rights to the database they're trying to use. Even if you're only going to request a simple recordset, you need to meet the security requirements of the database. Generally this means that you present a User Identification (UserID) and a password (pwd). Security can be established at various levels, but you will need to get this information from the owner or systems administrator of the database.

## Step 3 - Understand the Structure of the Database

Another obvious (but frequently overlooked) point of preparation is understanding the structure of the database. ADO will always produce errors if your commands don't use the exact spelling of the tables, queries, views and fields. A more subtle but equally deadly error arises when commands to the database conflict with its relationships between tables. In Chapter 5 we'll look at a technique for finding out the names of the fields, but you still have to know the names of the tables. The structures of the databases used in this book are provided in Appendices A through C.

### Common Errors in preparation:

- ❑ Incorrect spelling of DSN
- ❑ DSN no longer exists, or name has been changed
- ❑ The DSN will not work if the file is moved to another location after the DSN is created (applies to Access and Excel files)
- ❑ DSN is of User or File type rather than a System DSN
- ❑ UserID or password is misspelled or incorrect
- ❑ Names of fields or tables are incorrectly known by plural or singular (e.g. Author instead of Authors)
- ❑ Type (number/text/date) of fields is not known correctly

# Syntax for Simple Recordsets

Once you have properly prepared for using ADO, creating the simplest recordsets only requires three lines of code. Here's a first example: suppose we have a DSN by the name of Contacts, which contains a table called People. We can access this data with the following three lines of code:

```
Dim oRSp
Set oRSp = Server.CreateObject("ADODB.recordset")
oRSp.open "People", "DSN=Contacts"
```

Additionally, if there is database security enabled, we can specify our security details as we create the recordset. For example, suppose our User ID for accessing the database is AlbertE, and our password is emc2. We can pass these additional parameters as follows:

```
Dim oRSp
Set oRSp = Server.CreateObject("ADODB.recordset")
oRSp.open "People", "DSN=Contacts;uid=AlbertE;pwd=emc2"
```

*Connection drivers (see Chapter 6 on Connections) vary in their nomenclature for identifying users. The code in this section of the book is illustrating the syntax for ODBC for JET and SQL, that is* `uid=AlbertE`*. If you are using the native OLEDB drivers for SQL you would use* `UserID=AlbertE`*.*

Let's look more closely to understand what's happening in these three lines of code:

❑ The first line, above, dimensions a variable (that is, it reserves the name `oRSp`). Although in VB proper we try to dim variables with a specific type, in VBScript all variables are variants. In fact, this line is not mandatory in VBScript; however, as the ASP debugging tools become more robust (more like Visual Basic), dimensioning your variables and objects will help you to catch errors. Various programmers name their variables and objects in various ways, and in this book we'll use the convention of prefixing the name of any object with a lower case `o`. Since this object will be a recordset, we'll follow that with the `RS`. Before long you will be working with multiple recordsets on a page, so it's worth using a few other characters in your variable name to indicate what data this particular Recordset will hold. In this case I used a `p`, since this recordset will be filled with records of people.

❑ The second line creates a `Recordset` object and the `oRSp` object is turned into a pointer to this object. Now `oRSp` can hold all of the properties, react to the events and execute the methods of a recordset from the library called ADODB. This process is called **instantiation** (see *Notes on Objects* at the end of this chapter). The action is performed by the `CreateObject` method of ASP's `Server` object. The `CreateObject` method needs one parameter – the name of the class to use as a model. We specify the class library (in this case, ADODB) and the class within that library (in this case, Recordset). Once you create this new object, you have all of the capabilities that Microsoft built into the original tool (in this case, the ability to access data).

❑ The third line uses the `Recordset` object's `Open` method to make data available to you. Note the syntax: we're calling the `Open` method of the object called `oRSp`, so we write `oRSp.Open`. In order to carry out its task, the `Open` method requires two parameters.

*So it only takes us three lines of ADO code to open a recordset and prepare it for reading. However, keep in mind that this uses OOP. Under the covers lies all of the low-level code required to prepare the recordset (and believe me, that is plenty of code) – it's already been written by Microsoft and encapsulated in the* `Recordset` *object of the* ADODB *library.*

Before we go on, there is an additional line of code that will make your life easier. Although good debugging tools are still in the future, you can start your VBScript with the following line.

```
Option Explicit
```

This directive will allow VID to check your code and if you mis-type a variable you will get an error warning at design time. However, use of `Option Explicit` then requires that you `Dim` all variables prior to use.

Once we have established the recordset (Dim, Set, RS.Open) we can then access the data in the recordset. A given piece of data is utilized by stating the recordset and the field name as follows:

```
ORSp("PeopleNameFirst")
```

This will return the data in the `PeopleNameFirst` field of the current record. This is like a function in that a value is returned, and that value must go somewhere or be used somehow. We will discuss the four most common ways of using data in the following sections. But first let me share a list of the most common mistakes I have observed in code from my ASP-ADO students.

### Common Mistakes When Creating Recordsets and Using Recordset Data:

❑ (Most frequent of all) students forget that the RS("*field*") construct returns data. That data must go somewhere; as the argument for a `Response.Write`, or into a variable or used as a test expression. But you can never have a naked RS("*field*") sitting on a line.

❑ Leaving out the `Response.Write`.

❑ Misspelling the `Response.Write`.

❑ Putting double quotes around the entire `oRSp("PeopleNameFirst")`.

❑ Leaving out the double quotes or parentheses.

❑ Wrong RS name or wrong field name.

❑ Misspelled field name (very common error).

❑ A closed recordset is closed. Don't try to use it or close it again.

❑ The recordset is empty (End of File- and Beginning of File- are both true).

# Writing Data to the HTML Page

To write the data on the page:

```
Response.Write oRSp("PeopleNameFirst")
```

The above code examples would be used within a section of ASP, that is within the `<% %>`, to put the data onto the page. Keep in mind that there is also the ASP shortcut to drop a `Response.Write` into a section of HTML as shown below:

```
Welcome, <%=ORSp("PeopleNameFirst")%> to our page.
```

Microsoft now recommends a syntax that explicitly states the `Value` property to return. Although this is not yet common, stating this default property improves speed and robustness. An example follows.

```
Response.Write oRSp("PeopleNameFirst").Value
```

*The most common mistakes of the VBScript Response.Write Shortcut are:*

- ❑ Forgetting the equals sign
- ❑ Typing in "Response.Write"
- ❑ Forgetting the <% and %>
- ❑ Wrong RS name or wrong Field name
- ❑ Misspelled field name (very common error)

# Stuffing Data into a Variable

Sometimes we don't need the data to go directly to the page, in which case we can save the information into a variable. For example, we may need to perform some string manipulation or validation prior to building the page.

```
VarNameFirst = ORSp("PeopleNameFirst")
```

The code on the above line stores the data into a variable for later use. This must be performed within ASP delimiters, since HTML lacks the capacity to use variables.

*The most common mistakes are:*

- ❑ Attempting to perform this operation in HTML, outside of ASP
- ❑ Wrong RS name or wrong field name
- ❑ Misspelled field name (very common error)

# Using Data in an Expression

Data retrieved by ADO can be used directly in an expression. The pseudo-code listings below show examples:

```
If ORSp("NameFirst")="Enrico" then
  ' code for Enrico
End If
```

In the above code we use the data in a field of the current record of the oRSp recordset as the text to compare against the word "Enrico." A similar test is performed in the code below to determine if it is time to end the looping.

```
Do while NOT oRSp("NameFirst")="Enrico"
  ' code for people OTHER then Enrico
  oRSp.MoveNext
Loop
```

```
If oRSp("Member") then
  ' code for members
Else
  ' code for non-members
End If
```

In our last case we switch to retrieving data from a different field. The member field was established (at the time the database was designed) as of type True/False. Therefore it will return a value of true or false, which can be directly used as a whole expression. If the database contains true the code for members will be run.

***The most common mistakes are:***

❑ Attempting to perform this operation in HTML, outside of ASP

❑ Leaving the comparison sign (= or > or <) out of the expression

❑ Writing expressions where the two sides of the comparison sign are of two different data types. For example, "Joe" should not be compared to "2"

❑ Wrong RS name or wrong field name

❑ Misspelled field name (very common error)

❑ Errors in upper/lower case for data stores that are case sensitive

❑ Quotes around numerical values

# Using Data as an Argument in a Function

Data read by ASP-ADO can be used as an argument for another function. For example:

```
VarNameFirstLetter = Left(oRSp("PeopleNameFirst"),1)

VarPassword = lCase(oRSp("PeopleNameFirst"))

VarSpaceLocation = instr (oRSp("PeopleNameFirst")," ")
```

Although the above works, many coding shops prefer that you first read the data into a local variable. It is easier to read and maintain code without all of the quotes and parentheses.

***The most common mistakes are:***

❑ Attempting to perform this operation in HTML, outside of ASP

❑ Providing data from ASP-ADO which is of the wrong type for the argument

❑ Wrong RS name or wrong field name

❑ Misspelled field name (very common error)

❑ Not writing test code to handle a request that returns a NULL

## Try It Out – Using Recordset Data

We'll create a page that opens a recordset based on the `items` table of the Clothier database (see Appendix B for the source and structure of this database). From that recordset, we'll perform four tasks:

❑ Writing the name of the first item on the page

❑ Putting the type of the first item into a variable and then printing that variable to the page

❑ Using an `If..Then` structure so that items with less than 10 to a box show the warning "Small Box"

❑ Printing the price of the first item (using the Format function to make it with two decimal places only)

The following listing shows the code to generate the required page. All of the code for the examples can be found in file `C03 all T10.asp`. We will display sections of the code for each example.

```
<%
dim oRSi
set oRSi=Server.CreateObject("ADODB.recordset")
oRSi.open "items", "DSN=clothier"
oRSi.MoveFirst

Response.Write "Next line is a simple write of data:<BR>"
Response.Write oRSi("ItemName") & "<BR><BR>"

Response.Write "Next line is writing a variable that holds the data:<BR>"
dim varItemName
varItemName = oRSi("ItemType")
Response.Write varItemName & "<BR><BR>"

Response.Write "Next line is deciding what to write based on an If...Then using the _
          data:<BR>"
If oRSi("ItemQtyPerBox")<10 then
  Response.Write "Small Box<BR><BR>"
Else
  Response.Write "Large Box<BR><BR>"
End If

Response.Write "Next line uses the data as an argument for a function:<BR>"
Response.Write UCase(oRSi("ItemDepartment")) & "<BR><BR>"
%>
```

Your page should appear as shown:

**Chapter 3 Simple Recordsets**
**Try It Out - Using RecordSet Data**

Next line is a simple write of data:
Paltinum

Next line is writing a variable that holds the data:
shirt

Next line is deciding what to write based on an If...Then using the data:
Small Box

Next line uses the data as an argument for a function:
MENSFORMAL

**87**

### How It Works - Using Recordset Data

The first few lines in the next listing create the recordset. A recordset will open with the pointer at record one, so in this simple case there is actually no need for the `MoveFirst` method. On the other hand, if a recordset has been opened earlier and been in use, you would want to use `MoveFirst` so you are sure you are at BOF.

```
<%
dim oRSi
set oRSi=Server.CreateObject("ADODB.recordset")
oRSi.open "items", "DSN=clothier"
oRSi.MoveFirst
```

In our first section we merely need to print the data which is returned from the recordset, as follows:

```
Response.Write "Next line is a simple write of data:<BR>"
Response.Write oRSi("ItemName") & "<BR><BR>"
```

But we can also put data into a variable which can be used later, in the following case to write to the page:

```
Response.Write "Next line is writing a variable that holds the data:<BR>"
dim varItemName
varItemName = oRSi("ItemType")
Response.Write varItemName & "<BR><BR>"
```

As we can see in the next listing, you can use data without printing it to the page. Below we use it in a test to determine which of two messages to write to the page:

```
Response.Write "Next line is deciding what to write based on an If...Then using the _
        data:<BR>"
If oRSi("ItemQtyPerBox")<10 then
  Response.Write "Small Box<BR><BR>"
Else
  Response.Write "Large Box<BR><BR>"
End If
```

Another option is to use the data returned from the recordset as an argument in a function. Below we use the name of the department of the item as the argument for the Upper Case function.

```
Response.Write "Next line uses the data as an argument for a function:<BR>"
Response.Write ucase(oRSi("ItemDepartment")) & "<BR><BR>"
%>
```

# Which Record?

In the last section we discussed obtaining data from fields. But which record was providing the data? Were we on the first record, the last or somewhere in between? Later we will open recordsets with only one record, and we will also study how to find a specific record, but for now we need to understand which record we are on.

The first two methods to learn when shifting the focus, or pointer, from one record to another are simple.

```
oRSp.MoveFirst

oRSp.MoveNext
```

oRS.MoveFirst jumps the cursor to the first record. If we then request data from a field we will get the data from the first record. MoveNext jumps the pointer down to the next record of the recordset. By doing a series of MoveNext commands we can work our way through the entire record set.

Note that in most tables you can *not* assume that when you open a recordset you will be on the first record. In fact, you cannot be sure that you know what the first record is. You may think that the first record is determined by the alphabetical order of the PeopleNameLast field, but the records may have actually been entered into the database in chronological order and therefore the first person to be entered is the oldest record, even if her last name is Zyminski. Therefore, you should generally use a RS.MoveFirst prior to starting a walk through the data.

## Try It Out - Moving Through Three Records

In this example we'll write a script that produces a page that lists the first three vendors from the Clothier database. For this exercise we can assume that there will be at least three vendors in the database.

```
<TITLE>2726-03-SimpleRS TIO Move Through 3 Records</TITLE>
</HEAD><BODY>
<H1>Chapter 3 Simple Recordsets</h1>
<H3>Try It Out - Moving Through Three Records</H3>
<%
dim oRSv
set oRSv=Server.CreateObject("ADODB.recordset")
oRSv.open "vendors", "DSN=clothier"
oRSv.MoveFirst

Response.Write "Next line walks through the first 3 records:<BR>"
Response.Write oRSv("VendorName") & ", "
oRSv.MoveNext
Response.Write oRSv("VendorName") & ", "
oRSv.MoveNext
Response.Write oRSv("VendorName")
oRSv.MoveNext
oRSv.close
set oRSv=nothing
%></BODY></HTML>
```

The above code produces the following screen.

### How It Works - Moving Through Three Records

The first few lines, below, create the recordset, this time from the Vendors table and thus with the object named oRSv.

```
<H3>Try It Out - Moving Through Three Records</H3>
<%
dim oRSv
set oRSv=Server.CreateObject("ADODB.recordset")
oRSv.open "vendors", "DSN=clothier"
```

In order to be sure we are starting at the beginning we must use the following line:

```
oRSv.MoveFirst
```

Now we can write the data from the first record along with a following comma and space. Then we move to the next record and print its data, on then once again for the third record.

```
Response.Write "Next line walks through the first 3 records:<BR>"
Response.Write oRSv("VendorName") & ", "
oRSv.MoveNext
Response.Write oRSv("VendorName") & ", "
oRSv.MoveNext
Response.Write oRSv("VendorName")
oRSv.MoveNext
oRSv.close
set oRSv=nothing
%>
```

Of course we will soon learn to do this by looping.

### A Note on Moving Through Recordsets

Note here that different types of recordsets support different types of methods. We have been using the simplest of recordsets and by default that means that the pointer can only go forward through the data or back all the way to the start. Here are the key points to remember about the default cursor type of the recordset that we've used here:

❑ You can use the `MoveFirst` method, as well as `MoveNext` and `MoveLast`

❑ You can use these methods multiple times on one recordset. However, once you have walked through a recordset (using `MoveNext`), you can't go through it again without first calling `MoveFirst`

❑ You *cannot* use `MovePrevious`, bookmarks or other types of moving methods

❑ The `RecordCount` property lacks meaning with the default cursor

In Chapter 8 we will discuss using parameters to create recordsets enabled with other movement methods.

# Building Tables with Data

Very frequently your client will want to place data into an HTML table, for display on the browser. To review some HTML, let me state the three basic rules of table tags:

❑ Begin and end the entire table with `<TABLE BORDER="1">` and `</TABLE>`

❑ Begin and end each row with `<TR>` and `</TR>`

❑ Begin and end each cell with `<TD>` and `</TD>`

Using the double quotes for the border value ensures universal readability. However, many common browsers do not require them.

To build tables that display our data, we need to mix HTML table tags into the data that ADO returns. The most basic table contains only one row (one record or one name) and two columns, as follows. This is artificially easy, but a good way to start:

```
<%
dim oRSst
Set oRSst=Server.CreateObject("ADODB.recordset")
oRSst.open "People", "DSN=Sailors"
Response.Write "<TABLE BORDER='1'>"
Response.Write "<TR>"
Response.Write "<TD>"
Response.Write oRSst("PeopleNameFirst")
Response.Write "</TD>"
Response.Write "<TD>"
Response.Write oRSst("PeopleNameLast")
Response.Write "</TD>"
Response.Write "</TR>"
Response.Write "</TABLE>"
%>
```

The code sample above lays out the logic very explicitly. In the following listing we condense this to fewer lines of code. Keep in mind that this is still the same very simple 1-row, 2-column table:

```
<%
dim oRSst2
Set oRSst2=Server.CreateObject("ADODB.recordset")
oRSst2.open "People", "DSN=Sailors"

Response.Write "<TABLE BORDER='1'><TR><TD>"
Response.Write oRSst2("PeopleNameFirst")
Response.Write "</TD><TD>"
Response.Write oRSst2("PeopleNameLast")
Response.Write "</TD></TR></TABLE>"
%>
```

We can also use the Response.Write shortcut to further condense the code that generates this table, as follows. However, it is general good practice not to code your ASPs this way, as separating your server-side scripting, rather than keeping it all together in the same place, degrades performance.

```
<%
dim oRSst3
Set oRSst3=Server.CreateObject("ADODB.recordset")
oRSst3.open "People", "DSN=Sailors"
%>

<TABLE BORDER="1">
<TR><TD><%=oRSst3("PeopleNameFirst")%></TD>
<TD><%=oRSst3("PeopleNameLast")%></TD></TR>
</TABLE>
```

# Building Tables with For...Next Loops

It is rare that you or your client will be satisfied with a one-row table! Tables usually present data on many records. We will explore that technique first with a table that produces three rows as a result of putting the code for a row within a For...Next loop in the code below. Of course, we can only loop within ASP, so we will have to forget about the Response.Write shortcut used above; instead we'll revert to writing the HTML tags from within ASP, and using Response.Write explicitly:

```
<%
dim iRowCounter
dim oRSfn
set oRSfn=Server.CreateObject("ADODB.recordset")
oRSfn.open "People", "DSN=Sailors"
oRSfn.MoveFirst
Response.Write "<TABLE BORDER='1'>"
For iRowCounter=1 to 3
  Response.Write "<TR><TD>" & oRSfn("PeopleNameFirst") & "</TD>"
  Response.Write "<TD>" & oRSfn("PeopleNameLast") & "</TD></TR>"
  oRSfn.MoveNext
Next
Response.Write "</TABLE>"
%>
```

Note in the above listing that we have to be sure that the table tags are outside of the loop but that the rows and cell tags are inside the loop. For the purposes of this demo we are assuming that there are at least three records; in the real world that would be a dangerous assumption.

***The common errors on the above code include:***

- ❑ (the usual problems in creating recordsets)
- ❑ Putting the `<TABLE>` or `</TABLE>` inside the loop
- ❑ Leaving out `</TABLE>`
- ❑ Putting more than one `<TR>` or `</TR>` in a row
- ❑ Forgetting to include the `.MoveNext` line within the loop
- ❑ Trying to retrieve more records than are available in the database
- ❑ In later sections of the book we discuss even faster and more eloquent ways to build a table

## Try It Out - Building a Table of the First Five Clothing Items

Let's use the Clothier database again, to create a table that shows the Name and department of the first five items.

```
<TITLE>2726-03-SimpleRS TIO Building a Table of the First Five Clothing Items</TITLE>
</HEAD>
<BODY>
<H1>Chapter 3 Simple Recordsets<BR>
Try It Out - <BR>
Building a Table of <BR>
the First Five Clothing Items</h1>
<%
dim oRSc
dim iRowCounter
set oRSc=Server.CreateObject("ADODB.recordset")
oRSc.open "items", "DSN=clothier"
oRSc.MoveFirst

Response.Write "<TABLE BORDER='1'>"
For iRowCounter = 1 to 5
   Response.Write "<TR><TD>" & oRSc("ItemName") & "</TD>"
   Response.Write "<TD>" & oRSc("ItemDepartment") & "</TD></TR>"
   oRSc.MoveNext
next
%>
</TABLE></BODY></html>
```

The above code produces the following screen.

File   Edit   View   Go   Favorites   Help

Address  http://127.0.0.1/2726/2726-03-Simple-TIO-Table%20of%205.asp

# Chapter 3 Simple Recordsets
# Try It Out -
# Building a Table of
# the First Five Clothing Items

| Paltinum | MensFormal |
| Gloss | MensFormal |
| Gloss Trousers | MensSport |
| Beatrice | WomensSport |
| Stepping Out | WomensSport |

### How It Works - Building a Table of the First Five Clothing Items

The following lines create the recordset and ensure that we are positioned at the first record:

```
dim oRSc
dim iRowCounter
set oRSc=Server.CreateObject("ADODB.recordset")
oRSc.open "items", "DSN=clothier"
oRSc.MoveFirst
```

Then we begin to write the table to the web page. First, we write the <TABLE> tag, which belongs *outside* the loop:

```
Response.Write "<TABLE BORDER='1'>"
```

Now we can loop through the first five records. Note that, like all For...Next loops, we need a counter to keep track of the number of loops that have been performed. In each loop we write the open row tag <TR> then the tags and data for the two cells in the two columns:

```
For iRowCounter = 1 to 5
  Response.Write "<TR><TD>" & oRSc("ItemName") & "</TD>"
  Response.Write "<TD>" & oRSc("ItemDepartment") & "</TD></TR>"
  oRSc.MoveNext
next
%>
```

And then we place the table close tag outside of the loop as follows.

```
</TABLE>
</BODY></html>
```

# Reading All of the Records (with EOF)

By building a table that displays the first five records of a recordset, we get some idea of the techniques and practice of using the HTML codes for tables. However, most of the time you will have no idea of how many records are in your recordset – so you won't know how many times to repeat the loop. ADO provides a way to test whether you are at the end of the records, and thus should stop building rows. The property to use is called **EOF** (which is short for 'End Of File'). The recordset object's EOF property evaluates to True after you have moved beyond the last row. Take a look at the following test:

```
Do while NOT oRSp.EOF
  Response.Write oRSp("PeopleNameLast") & "<BR>"
  oRSp.MoveNext
Loop
```

The above code is a little tricky to understand if you have never used this construction before, so refill the coffee cup and follow this closely:

The way the DO WHILE works, in general, is that before each cycle of the loop ASP-ADO checks the test expression on the DO WHILE line. If the test is True, ASP-ADO will perform the loop again.

But we are using the value of the EOF property of oRSp as the test object. rs.EOF is False when we are still in the data and True when we are done with the records. That is the opposite of what we want for the DO WHILE. We want to continue looping when the rs.EOF is False (we are in the middle of records) and we want to stop looping when EOF is True (at the end of records).

VBScript provides us with the word NOT to reverse the value of the rs.EOF. Now when rs.EOF returns a False (in middle of records) NOT changes that into a True and the loop is performed again. When the rs.EOF is set to True (at end of records), NOT turns that into a False and the looping stops.

Remember that every loop must have a way to end. In this case we include the rs.MoveNext line to tell ADO's cursor to go to the next record. Eventually ASP-ADO will move beyond the last record and then the rs.EOF will turn to true. Our test will "NOT" that True into a False and end the loop right there at the end of the records.

### Common Errors

- ❏ Leaving the "RS." off RS.EOF
- ❏ Leaving RS.MoveNext out of the loop
- ❏ Leaving out the "NOT" from the expression
- ❏ Putting <TABLE> inside the loop
- ❏ Leaving out </TABLE>

In this example we'll build a table that lists the first and last names of all of the sailors in the `People` table of the Sailors database.

```
<%
dim oRSeof
set oRSeof=Server.CreateObject("ADODB.recordset")
oRSEOF.Open "PEople", "DSN=sailors"
oRSeof.MoveFirst
Response.Write "<TABLE BORDER='1'>"
Do while NOT oRSeof.EOF
   Response.Write "<TR><TD>" & oRSeof("PeopleNameFirst") & "</TD>"
   Response.Write "<TD>" & oRSeof("PeopleNameLast") & "</TD></TR>"
   oRSeof.MoveNext
Loop
Response.Write "</TABLE>"
%>
```

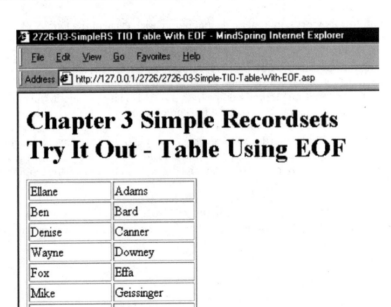

**Chapter 3 Simple Recordsets**
**Try It Out - Table Using EOF**

| | |
|---|---|
| Ellane | Adams |
| Ben | Bard |
| Denise | Canner |
| Wayne | Downey |
| Fox | Effa |
| Mike | Geissinger |
| Bjorn | Helemenson |
| Ibaria | Ipiotos |
| Helmut | Juvas |
| John | Kauffman |

### How It Works - Table Building with EOF

The first few lines create the recordset.

```
<%
dim oRSeof
set oRSeof=Server.CreateObject("ADODB.recordset")
oRSEOF.Open "People", "DSN=sailors"
```

Then with the following line we ensure that we are on the first record, followed by the tag to start the table:

```
oRSeof.MoveFirst
Response.Write "<TABLE BORDER='1'>"
```

Now we begin the loop. We want to loop if the opposite (NOT) of rs.EOF is true. In other words when EOF is False (not yet at end of records, or in other words not yet beyond the last record) we want ASP-ADO to see that as true and do another loop. When EOF is True (we are now done with the records, or in other words, beyond the last record) then we want ASP-ADO to see that as false and stop cycling.

```
Do while NOT oRSeof.EOF
```

Within each cycle we will build a row. That means start with the <TR> tag. Then add three items for each cell: <TD>, data and </TD>. At the end of the row we put in a </TR>:

```
  Response.Write "<TR><TD>" & oRSeof("PeopleNameFirst") & "</TD>"
  Response.Write "<TD>" & oRSeof("PeopleNameLast") & "</TD></TR>"
```

Without the next line ASP-ADO will cycle forever, writing more rows of the information for sailor number one. We must instruct our code to move down to the next sailor record after building the table row.

```
  oRSeof.MoveNext
```

*Will Bad Loops Cycle Forever?*

*We've all done it; forget to put in the .MoveNext and run the page, causing an infinite loop. The server is working away, perhaps putting up thousands of duplicate lines and we suddenly realize our mistake. At this point you have several options. First, understand that ASP scripts time out after about 2 minutes. If you are running a page on a remote host you can stop your browser, correct the problem and then revisit the page. If you are running PWS you can speed things up by Start/Programs/MS Personal Web Server/Personal Web Manager/Stop. Then start it again.*

That is it for the loop, and we write the table closing tag to the page.

```
Loop
Response.Write "</TABLE>"
%>
```

## Try It Out – Sailors Table with EOF and a Counter

Now we can improve on the last code listing by adding a numbering column and a note on the number of sailors at the bottom. Later we will learn the use of the recordcount property, but for now we will use a counter variable.

```
<%
dim oRSeofc
set oRSeofc=Server.CreateObject("ADODB.recordset")
oRSEOFc.Open "People", "DSN=sailors"
oRSeofc.MoveFirst
Response.Write "<TABLE BORDER='1'>"
Dim PersonCounter
PersonCounter = 0
Do while NOT oRSeofc.EOF
   PersonCounter =PersonCounter + 1
   Response.Write "<TR><TD>" & PersonCounter & "</TD>"
   Response.Write "<TD>" & oRSeofc("PeopleNameFirst") & "</TD>"
   Response.Write "<TD>" & oRSeofc("PeopleNameLast") & "</TD></TR>"
   oRSeofc.MoveNext
Loop
Response.Write "</TABLE><BR>"
Response.Write PersonCounter & " Sailors in this list"
 %>
```

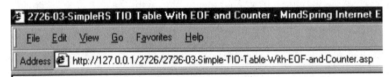

2726-03-SimpleRS TIO Table With EOF and Counter - MindSpring Internet E

File  Edit  View  Go  Favorites  Help

Address  http://127.0.0.1/2726/2726-03-Simple-TIO-Table-With-EOF-and-Counter.asp

# Chapter 3 Simple Recordsets
# Try It Out -
# Table Using EOF
# and a Counter

| | | |
|---|---|---|
| 1 | Ellane | Adams |
| 2 | Ben | Bard |
| 3 | Denise | Canner |
| 4 | Wayne | Downey |
| 5 | Fox | Effa |
| 6 | Mike | Geissinger |
| 7 | Bjorn | Helemenson |

### How it Works - Sailors Table with EOF and a Counter

The set up of the recordset is the same as the last code listing, but now we dim another variable for the purpose of keeping count of the people and initialize that to zero:

```
Dim PersonCounter
PersonCounter = 0
```

Now when we do our loops we start by increasing that `PersonCounter` by 1 and printing that in its own cell. Then we finish off the row as before.

```
Do while NOT oRSeofc.EOF
  PersonCounter =PersonCounter + 1
  Response.Write "<TR><TD>" & PersonCounter & "</TD>"
  Response.Write "<TD>" & oRSeofc("PeopleNameFirst") & "</TD>"
  Response.Write "<TD>" & oRSeofc("PeopleNameLast") & "</TD></TR>"
  oRSeofc.MoveNext
Loop
Response.Write "</TABLE>"
%>
```

# A Trap With Recordsets and Tables

## Table Warping by NULLS

Sometimes fields of a record contain no data or a NULL. A person may not have a phone number, or a member is registered with a title and last name but no first name. HTML tables will not automatically give you an empty cell to represent NULL data. Instead, many browsers will close up the empty space by shifting cells to the left to fill the gap. For example the cell that contains the Last Name gets shifted under the First Name heading, and all the rest of the row is similarly thrown off and a hole is generated all the way into the right column. Again, this is not a problem for all browsers, IE 4 and 5 heal this type of error well.

The shortest solution is to always concatenate an   before the data in your cells. This code will create a space before the data. Even if there is no data, the non-breaking space will hold the cell open. For example:

```
  Response.Write "<TD> " & oRSp("NameFirst") & "</TD>"
```

Although this trick solves the missing cell problem, it generates no small amount of angst in students. In the lines above we are using the ampersand for the same purpose, but in two different types of syntax. The first ampersand is for HTML, it is telling the browser to add in a non-breaking space after the <TD>. The second ampersand is for VBScript, telling it to concatenate another term (the data in the `NameFirst` field) to its `Response.Write` string.

The first ampersand must go to the page so the browser can see it, therefore it must be within the double quotes. It will be printed on the page by ASP, and then go out to the network. The browser will interpret that into a non-breaking space and remove the   (also known as an entity name) from the user's view.

The second ampersand will be used by ASP to build the string <TD> John for Response.Write to put on the page. As that string is built, ASP removes the ampersand, it is never seen by HTML. That second ampersand must go outside the double quotes. The third ampersand is of the same type as the second.

This code can also be re-arranged to put the   after the data which will preserve left-aligned columns, as follows.

```
Response.Write "<TD>" & oRSp("NameFirst") & " </TD>"
```

A less obtrusive technique is to insert the non-breaking space only if there is no data, as shown in the following code:

```
If IsNull(oRSp("NameFirst")) Then
  Response.Write " "
Else
  Response.Write oRSp("NameFirst")
End If
```

# A Note on Moving in Recordsets

By default, when you open a simple recordset it is a forward only cursor. That means for walking through the records you have just two options:

- ❑ MoveFirst
- ❑ MoveNext

You can only go forward through the recordset. After you go through the recordset once you must use rs.MoveFirst prior to being able to go through the recordset again. There is frequently confusion from my students that you only get one pass through the recordset. But as long as after each pass you do a Move.First, you can pass through many times. But you can never back up through the records or jump ahead over records.

# Summary

The most basic technique for reading data from a database can be accomplished in three lines, plus the lines to write the data to the page. The first line, Dim, sets aside a variable name, the second, Set, makes an instance of the Recordset object, and the third uses the Open method to fill the object with a recordset.

Once filled, we can move down through the records of the recordset writing data to the page. Writing to the page is frequently done within an HTML table, which requires shifting back and forth between HTML tags and ASP-ADO data. When writing code you must be careful of a few traps including collapsed HTML cells from missing data.

# Exercises

These exercises use one of the two sample databases available from the Wrox Press website, at http://webdev.wrox.co.uk/books/2726. Appendices A and B contain a description of the structure of (respectively) the Sailors database and the Clothier database.

**1.** Use Sailor.mdb to create a list of sailors with one sailor per line (no table).

**2.** Use Sailor.mdb to create a table of all of the boats.

**3.** Use Sailor.mdb to make a list of the yacht clubs; not in a table but separated by horizontal lines.

# Exercises – Answers

Note: answers are also presented in C01-Exercise.asp available from the Wrox site.

**1.** The code for this excercise is as follows:

```
<H1>Chapter 3 Simple Recordsets</h1>
<H3>Exercise 1 Use Sailors.mdb to create a list of sailors with one sailor per
line</H3>
<%
dim oRSp
Set oRSp=Server.CreateObject("ADODB.recordset")
oRSp.open "People", "DSN=sailors"
do while not oRSp.EOF
   Response.Write oRSp("PeopleNameFirst") & " "
   Response.Write oRSp("PeopleNameLast") & "<BR>"
   oRSp.movenext
loop
%>
```

The result of running our code is as shown:

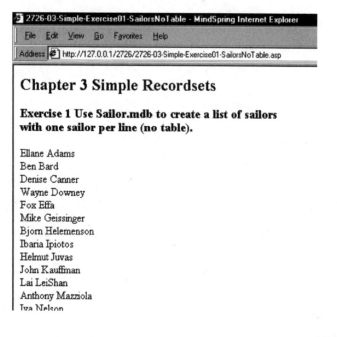

101

**2.** Here is the code:

```
<H1>Chapter 3 Simple Recordsets</h1>
<H3>Exercise 2 Use Sailors.mdb to create a table of all the boats</H3>
<TABLE BORDER="1">
<%
dim oRSb
Set oRSb=Server.CreateObject("ADODB.recordset")
oRSb.open "Boats", "DSN=sailors"
do while not oRSb.EOF
   Response.Write "<TR><TD>" & oRSb("BoatName") & "</TD>"
   Response.Write "<TD>" & oRSb("BoatClass") & "</TD></TR>"
   oRSb.movenext
loop
oRSb.close
set oRSb=nothing
%>
</TABLE>
```

This is the result:

**Chapter 3 Simple Recordsets**

**Exercise 2 Use Sailor.mdb to create a table of all of the boats.**

| | |
|---|---|
| Lyric | Laser |
| BlackBall | Laser |
| No Excuse to Lose | Laser |
| No Excuse Two Lose | Laser |
| White Lightning | Soling |
| Teal | Soling |
| TGV | Soling |
| BB3 | Soling |
| Nuts and Bolts | Soling |

**3.** Our solution is coded as follows:

```
<H1>Chapter 3 Simple Recordsets</h1>
<H3>Exercise 3 Use Sailors.mdb to make a list of the yacht clubs; not in a table</H3>
<%
dim oRSyc
Set oRSyc=Server.CreateObject("ADODB.recordset")
oRSyc.open "Clubs", "DSN=sailors"
do while not oRSyc.EOF
  Response.Write "<hr>" & oRSyc("ClubName") & "</TD>"
  oRSyc.movenext
loop
Response.Write "<hr>"
oRSyc.close
set oRSyc=nothing
%>
```

The code produces this screen:

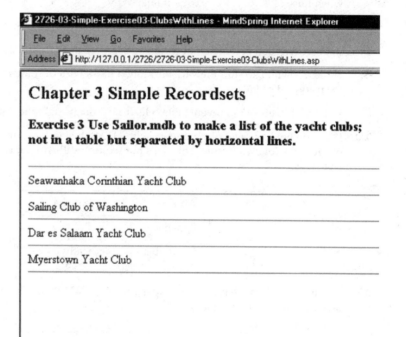

**Chapter 3 Simple Recordsets**

**Exercise 3 Use Sailor.mdb to make a list of the yacht clubs; not in a table but separated by horizontal lines.**

Seawanhaka Corinthian Yacht Club

Sailing Club of Washington

Dar es Salaam Yacht Club

Myerstown Yacht Club

# Quiz

1. What is the difference between the `Dim oRS` and `Set oRS` commands?

2. What punctuation (combination of parentheses, quotes, commas, periods, etc.) is used with the server's `CreateObject` method?

3. What is the syntax to write on the page the data of the field named "SSN" from the recordset oRS6?

4. What is the syntax to use if you have a section of HTML text and want to put into the middle of it the field named "SSN" from the recordset oRS6?

5. I've opened a recordset using the simple method but want to print it out in reverse order. But when I use `oRS.MovePrevious` it fails. Why?

6. Name three steps that should be performed prior to using ASP-ADO.

7. In the connection parameter, how do you separate the `DSN`, the `userID` and the `password`?

8. Write the syntax to stuff the variable named `sSSN` with the data in the field named "SSN" from the recordset oRS6.

9. What HTML text will prevent table cells from "collapsing" when NULL data is encountered?

10. If you do not have a lot of experience with HTML tables, try writing the tags and text to produce the following table. This does not require ASP-ADO, it is for practice with HTML table tags.

| 1 | Apples | Amelia |
| 2 | Bananas | Bob |
| 3 | Cucumber | Cathy |

11. Again, if you do not have a lot of experience with HTML tables, try writing the tags and text to produce the following table.

| 1 | Apples | Amelia |
| 2 | | Bob |
| 3 | Cucumber | Cathy |

# Quiz Answers

**1.** Dim sets aside space in memory and reserves the word oRS as a variable name. Set assigns to this variable a reference to an object that is instantiated using the CreateObject method.

**2.** Server.CreateObject("ADODB.recordset")
Period between *Server* and *CreateObject*
Period between ObjectType and class
ObjectType and class are inside double quotes which is within parentheses.

**3.**

```
<%
Response.Write oRS6("SSN").Value
%>
```

**4.**

```
We recorded you with SSN <%=oRS6("SSN").Value%>
```

**5.** Recordsets opened in the simple way of this chapter are forward-only. More flexible recordsets will be discussed in a later chapter.

**6.** Set up the DSN
Familiarize yourself with the database structure
Know a valid UserID and its valid password

**7.** With a semicolon (adding a space makes it easier to read and does not create problems)

```
ORS.Open "SourceTable", "DSN=MyDSNName; uid=MyUserID; pwd=MyPassword"
```

**8.**

```
sSSN = oRS6("SSN").value
```
or
```
sSSN = oRS6("SSN")
```

**9.**  

**10.**

```
<TABLE BORDER=1>
  <TR>
    <TD>1</TD>
    <TD>Apples</TD>
    <TD>Amelia</TD>
  </TR>
  <TR>
    <TD>2</TD>
    <TD>Bananas</TD>
    <TD>Bob</TD>
  </TR>
  <TR>
    <TD>3</TD>
    <TD>Cucumber</TD>
    <TD>Cathy</TD>
  </TR>
</TABLE>
```

By eliminating some spaces and carriage returns from the above we can build:

```
<TABLE BORDER=1>
<TR><TD>1</TD><TD>Apples</TD><TD>Amelia</TD></TR>
<TR><TD>2</TD><TD>Bananas</TD><TD>Bob</TD></TR>
<TR><TD>3</TD><TD>Cucumber</TD><TD>Cathy</TD></TR>
</TABLE>
```

**11.** In this case we have to be careful not to allow the collapse of the cell which formerly held banana by retaining the `<TD></TD>` for the old banana cell and filling it with  

```
<TABLE BORDER=1>
<TR><TD>1</TD><TD>Apples</TD><TD>Amelia</TD></TR>
<TR><TD>2</TD><TD> </TD><TD>Bob</TD></TR>
<TR><TD>3</TD><TD>Cucumber</TD><TD>Cathy</TD></TR>
</TABLE>
```

Setup cannot install system files or update shared files if the files are in use. Before c
any open applications.

WARNING: This program is protected by copyright law and international treaties.

You may install Microsoft Data Access 2.1 on a single computer. Some Microsoft products
with additional rights, which are stated in the End User License Agreement included with p

Please take a moment to read the End User License Agreement now. It contains all of the te
conditions that pertain to this software product. By choosing to continue, you indicate accep
these terms.

Continue

Exit Setup

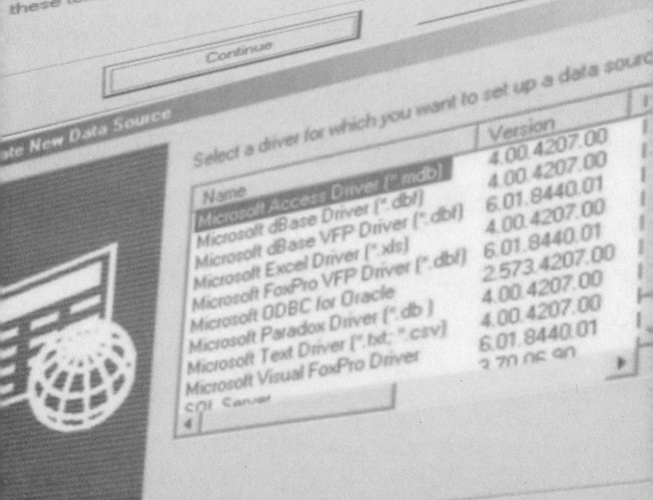

te New Data Source

Select a driver for which you want to set up a data sourc

| Name | Version |
| --- | --- |
| Microsoft Access Driver (*.mdb) | 4.00.4207.00 |
| Microsoft dBase Driver (*.dbf) | 4.00.4207.00 |
| Microsoft dBase VFP Driver (*.dbf) | 6.01.8440.01 |
| Microsoft Excel Driver (*.xls) | 4.00.4207.00 |
| Microsoft FoxPro VFP Driver (*.dbf) | 6.01.8440.01 |
| Microsoft ODBC for Oracle | 2.573.4207.00 |
| Microsoft Paradox Driver (*.db ) | 4.00.4207.00 |
| Microsoft Text Driver (*.txt; *.csv) | 4.00.4207.00 |
| Microsoft Visual FoxPro Driver | 6.01.8440.01 |
| SQL Server | 3.70.06.90 |

Cancel

# Basic SQL for ADO Recordsets

*Mateo Ricci, the 16th century Jesuit Missionary, commented that the Classical Chinese Language was tremendously difficult to learn, but that the years spent in its mastery were of benefit to society in that they diminished the "youthful licentiousness" to which young men would otherwise be inclined.*

Much of the communication between ASP-ADO and the database is conducted by the Structured Query Language (SQL). This chapter covers the fundamentals of **reading** data through the use of **SQL** statements. (SQL for *changing* and *adding* data is covered in Chapter 10.) In addition to the syntax of SQL statements, this chapter discusses specifically how to build those statements using ASP. The chapter ends by addressing the complexities added by using data gathered from forms or server functions.

*If you are already familiar with SQL statements, you may want to skip the first part of this chapter and move directly to the SQL Syntax Section.*

## Introduction to SQL

SQL is a way to communicate with databases. In this sense, communicate means:

❑   reading data from a datastore

❑   writing data to a datastore

❑   changing data in a datatstore without ever reading it out

❑   changing the structure or schema of the datastore itself

In this chapter we will focus on the first of these functions. The basic strategy is to create a SQL statement, somewhat like an English sentence, then instruct ADO to carry out the statement against the database. Whatever instructions are in the SQL statement will be performed on the data. It is quite similar to you writing up a request to have a cabinet built, then giving that request to a cabinet maker to build it.

Most SQL statements are of three types:

❑ SQL statements that *read* data, perhaps with some ordering or selecting

❑ SQL statements that *change* the data, such as adding a new record

❑ SQL statements that *change the structure* of a database, such as adding a new field or table

As you can see, the second two types carry out an action that changes the database. The first type merely reads from the database without changing the data or structure.

SQL has become a universal language for creating database instructions, used almost uniformly across many database platforms. The way that the SQL statement is executed will vary, but the statements themselves follow a standard syntax. This means two things for you:

❑ If you work with databases you will probably have to learn to write SQL statements

❑ Your knowledge of SQL statements can be applied to many database platforms, and not just using ADO

## Flavors of SQL

The term SQL refers to an industry standard. There are many database platforms that offer a way to write and execute SQL statements; the most common include PL/SQL (Oracle), T-SQL (SQL Server, Sybase), Access SQL, and ANSI SQL (the standard). ADO can take any of these statements and pass them down to the driver or provider to be applied to the datastore. In this book we will use the SQL flavor for Access.

> There is a very good explanation of SQL flavor issues in John Connell's "Beginning Visual Basic 6 Database Programming" (ISBN 1-861001-06-1), pages 343-344.

Please keep in mind that this chapter explains basic SQL to cover most common ASP-ADO objectives and is neither exhaustive nor appropriate for every situation. Learn the techniques of this chapter, then you will have a good frame of reference for studying future SQL books such as Instant SQL Programming from Wrox Press (ISBN 1-874416-50-8).

# SQL Syntax

SQL has always had the objective of being somewhat English-like in its statements. In a sense this is an inheritance from the thinking of the folks that gave us COBOL. But one does not have to go far with databases before realizing that some of these requests are so fiendishly complex that our spoken languages have difficulty handling the logic. One of my database mentors, Norm Eaddy, always impressed me with his ability to construct English sentences that were able to contain the whole logic of even very complex database objectives.

# General Syntax Rules of SQL

The general syntax of SQL to build a sentence-like statement consists, like written English, of several clauses. Each **clause** begins with a SQL **keyword** followed by **arguments**. The generic form of the most basic of SQL statements makes available all the records and all the fields from a *source*, like a table, as follows.

```
SELECT FieldsList FROM Source;
```

For example, this most basic SQL statement can be used to retrieve a recordset containing all of the records and fields from the People table:

```
SELECT * FROM People;
```

> *A recordset is a group of records derived from a datastore. That subset can range in number from zero to all the records, depending on some criteria or the set maximum size for the recordset. Furthermore, the records can be sorted or left in the order in which they are stored in the datastore.*
>
> *In some circles a recordset is also called a cursor. This, of course, creates great confusion with the concept of a cursor as a pointer to a given record.*

In this statement, the keyword SELECT starts the first clause and indicates that we want to read data. The keyword FROM starts the second clause, which indicates from which table to gather the data. Each keyword in this example is followed by an argument; the asterisk indicates all fields, and the word People indicates the name of the table to be read. Note that the asterisk is like the DOS wildcard, representing all of something, in this case all of the fields. The semicolon at the end of the statement indicates the end of the SQL statement. Although in theory it is optional I suggest you always use it, particularly with Access SQL.

# Using SQL Statements to Open Recordsets

To review, in the past chapter you opened recordsets with something like:

```
oRs.Open "People", "DSN=Sailors"
```

Note that the recordset was filled with all records and all fields from the People table. Furthermore, there was no selecting or sorting available. This shortcoming is precisely what the SQL statements will overcome. One way to use SQL statements with VBScript is to put them into the source parameter of the Rs.Open method, as shown in this example:

```
oRs.Open "SELECT * FROM People;", "DSN=Sailors"
```

The syntax is quite simple. Instead of specifying the source for the recordset as an entire table, we specify the source as the result of a SQL statement. Although that is a trivial difference now, we will soon build SQL statements that will allow far more control over the recordset than simply naming tables. Note that the statement is in quotes, just like the name of the table was, and that the semicolon that ends SQL statements stays within those quotes.

## Try It Out - Using a SQL Statement with Rs.Open

The following code creates a page that lists the names of the classes of boats from the Sailors database. The code can be found in `2726-04-TIO-01-Basic.asp`:

```
<HTML>
<HEAD>
<TITLE>Chapter 4 - Basic SQL TIO 1-4</TITLE>
</HEAD>
<BODY>
<H2>Chapter 4 - Basic SQL for ADO Recordsets</H2>
<P>Try It Out #1 - Using a SQL Statement with Rs.Open</P>
<%
  Dim oRSbc
  Set oRSbc=Server.CreateObject("ADODB.Recordset")
  oRSbc.Open "SELECT * FROM BoatClass;", "DSN=Sailors"
  oRSbc.MoveFirst
  Do While NOT oRSbc.EOF
    Response.Write oRSbc("ClassName") & ", "
    oRSbc.MoveNext
  Loop
  oRSbc.Close
  Set oRSbc=nothing
%>
</BODY>
</HTML>
```

This code produces the following:

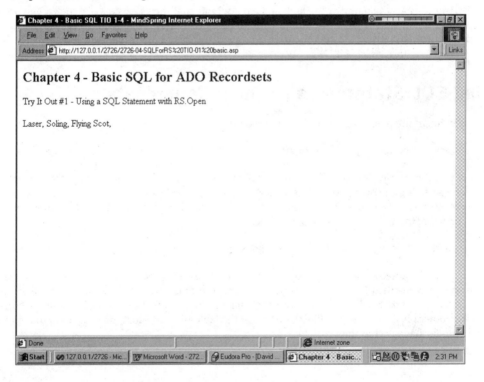

### How It Works: Using a SQL Statement with Rs.Open

The first few lines are basic HTML to display the page headings. The next few lines, below, create a `Recordset` object:

```
<TITLE>Chapter 4 - Basic SQL TIO 1-4</TITLE>
<P>Try It Out #1 - Using a SQL Statement with Rs.Open</P>
<%
  Dim oRSbc
  Set oRSbc=Server.CreateObject("ADODB.Recordset")
```

But now when we open the object we don't specify the table name, rather we provide a SQL statement.

```
  oRSbc.Open "SELECT * FROM BoatClass;", "DSN=Sailors"
```

Now, I'll readily agree, the statement `SELECT * FROM BoatClass;` produces the same result as the table name `BoatClass`. But we will shortly be elaborating on that SQL statement. The rest of the code, below, should be trivial for you by now, as it was explained in Chapter 3.

```
  oRSbc.MoveFirst
  Do While NOT oRSbc.EOF
    Response.Write oRSbc("ClassName") & ", "
    oRSbc.MoveNext
  Loop
  oRSbc.Close
  Set oRSbc=nothing
%>
</BODY>
</HTML>
```

# Solving the Elephantine SQL Statement Problem

SQL statements frequently extend to hundreds of characters in length. This creates three problems. First, you will get unwanted word-wrapping or the need for horizontal screen scroll. Second is that the statement becomes virtually impossible to read because of the number of concatenations. Third is that we can easily exceed the number of characters that are allowed in a single VBScript statement.

To solve this problem we build long SQL statements in a variable prior to the time we need them. We write the first clause and put it into the variable. Then we add on the next clause to the existing text in that same variable. This process is repeated until the whole SQL statement is contained in the variable. The process of appending text at the end of existing text is called concatenation, and it is performed by VBScript when it reads the ampersand (&).

For example, we can apply this process to the simple SQL statement from earlier. The first level is to move the SQL statement out of the `Recordset.Open` line and into a variable. Instead of:

```
Rs.Open "SELECT * FROM People;", "DSN=Sailors"
```

We use:

```
sSQL = "SELECT * FROM People;"
Rs.Open  sSQL, "DSN=Sailors"
```

We can use any name for the variable: I use s for string and then SQL to indicate what is in this string variable. You will see other programmers use SQLTemp, SQLText, strSQL, or even just plain sql.

Now that we have separated the building of the SQL statement from the execution, we can use multiple lines to build a large and complex SQL statement:

```
sSQL = "SELECT * "
sSQL = sSQL & " FROM People;"
Rs.Open sSQL, "DSN=Sailors"
```

In the above code, the first line puts the text string "SELECT *" into the variable. Line two then adds the additional string of "FROM People;" to whatever is already in sSQL. After executing line 2, the variable sSQL contains the string SELECT * FROM People;. This process can go on for many lines. When updating or adding records we may have ten or twenty lines concatenating data into our sSQL variable, which is then executed by a RecordSet.Open operation.

Keep in mind that building large statements by multiple appends to a variable is memory-intensive. When performance is paramount you can extend a line in VBScript using the underscore character, like the following:

```
SQL = "SELECT * " & _
        "FROM People;"
```

Be aware of the following common errors when building SQL statements:

❑    When you use the variable sSQL in the Rs.Open line it should not be within quotes.

❑    Remember that the first line starts with a simple sSQL= whereas all subsequent lines begin with sSQL=sSQL &.

❑    Be careful to include the required spaces for SQL syntax, especially when the space comes at the beginning or end of a line. An extra space around keywords won't hurt.

# SELECT Statements

The first SQL statement to learn gathers a set of records for us to read. It was introduced earlier as the archetype for syntax study.

```
SELECT * FROM People;
```

The keyword SELECT means read from the database; do not change the data or structure, just read from it. The asterisk is a wildcard that means "everything" and thus indicates to read all of the fields. Following the asterisk is the keyword FROM which is followed by the table from which we want the records to be read. Put in simple English, the above statement reads into the recordset all of the fields from all of the records of the People table.

However, in many cases we do not need all of the fields. We can specify which fields we want to read by substituting the field names for the asterisk. This feature can speed up our code since the server will not have to manage a lot of fields that will not be used. If we only need the sailors' names we can use the code below:

```
SELECT PeopleNameFirst, PeopleNameLast FROM People;
```

This returns all the records, but only the data within the two named fields. The fields can be listed in any order, but they must be separated by commas. You may not put a comma after the last field name. And although it seems obvious, I have seen many people specify only one or two fields in a SQL statement but then try to use data from additional fields later in the code. That won't work, because those additional fields have never been put into the recordset. Some of my students react by always requesting * for all fields. But that can lead to some huge performance penalties, as the server reads out scores of fields when only a few are needed. Another common error occurs when words in the SQL statement are not separated by spaces. It is easy to leave out the space at the beginning or end of the fragments created for concatenation.

Some common errors to watch out for when using SELECT statements are listed here:

❑ Misspelled keywords SELECT or FROM

❑ Misspelled or incorrect table name

❑ Misspelled field names

❑ Incorrect field names (for example, in this database of sailors, the field holding the sailors' name may be called Skipper rather than Name)

❑ In the first example, there is no punctuation (commas, quotes or parentheses)

❑ There should be a comma between multiple field names

❑ There should *not* be a comma after the last field name

❑ You must include in the SQL statement all of the fields that you intend to use, and avoid including any you won't use

## Try It Out - SELECT With a Limited Number of Fields

Try making a page which makes a table of the boats and their class, like the one shown below. Since you only need two fields, limit your SQL statement.

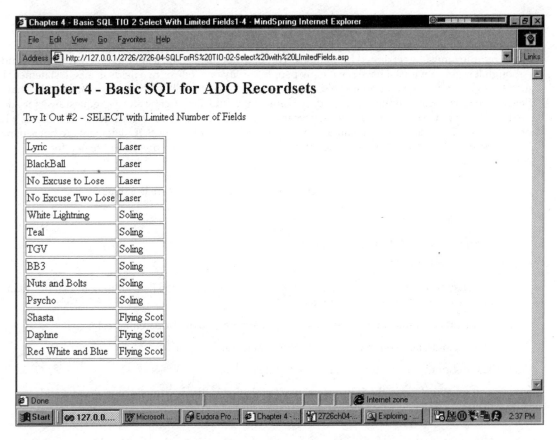

This page can be created using the following code, available in file `2726-04-SQLForRS TIO-02-Select with LimitedFields.asp`:

```
<HTML>
<HEAD>
<TITLE>Chapter 4 - Basic SQL TIO 2 Select With Limited Fields1-4</TITLE>
</HEAD>
<BODY>
<H2>Chapter 4 - Basic SQL for ADO Recordsets</H2>
<P>Try It Out #2 - SELECT with Limited Number of Fields</P>
<%
  Dim oRSbn
  Set oRSbn=Server.CreateObject("ADODB.Recordset")
  sqltext = "SELECT BoatName, BoatClass FROM Boats;"
  oRSbn.Open sqltext, "DSN=Sailors"
  oRSbn.MoveFirst
  Response.Write "<TABLE BORDER=1>"
  Do While NOT oRSbn.EOF
    Response.Write "<TR><TD>" & oRSbn("BoatName") & "</TD>"
    Response.Write "<TD>" & oRSbn("BoatClass") & "</TD></TR>"
    oRSbn.MoveNext
```

```
       Loop
       Response.Write "</TABLE>"
       oRSbn.Close
       Set oRSbn=nothing
%>
</BODY>
</HTML>
```

### How It Works: SELECT With a Limited Number of Fields

In this code, there is a key line in the SQL statement that is different from the previous listings:

```
sqltext = "SELECT BoatName, BoatClass FROM Boats;"
```

Instead of using an asterisk to pull into the recordset all of the fields from the Boats table, we only retrieve two fields: BoatName and BoatClass.

# ORDER BY Clause

In the two examples above, we accepted the order of records as they were in the table. Data in tables could be in any order, SQL doesn't guarantee any order for records stored in a table. Usually records are arranged chronologically; as new records come in they are added to the bottom of the table. This is rarely of use to humans, who like to process information in some sort of alphabetic or numeric order. SQL provides this service with the ORDER BY clause, shown in the following:

```
SELECT * FROM People ORDER BY PeopleNameLast;
```

And what if there are several Ms Tackmeisters? The following statement, in the case of several same last names, will revert to first names to solve the ordering.

```
SELECT * FROM People ORDER BY PeopleNameLast, PeopleNameFirst;
```

By default SQL will order in ascending order, i.e. small to large numbers, A to Z, early dates to later dates. You can, if you wish, make that more clear by adding the SQL keyword ASC after the field on which to sort. However, in some cases we want to sort from Z to A, or from the largest number to the smallest, in which case we add the word DESC (for descending) after the field. For example, to arrange a list for seating from youngest to oldest we order on the Date of Birth field, as follows:

```
SELECT * FROM People ORDER BY PeopleDOB DESC;
```

> *Ascending, when referring to dates, means from 1900 to 2000, so specifying DESC with the Date of Birth field will order with the youngest person first.*

More likely for the seating chart we would only be using a few fields, so we would combine the techniques of the last section (limiting fields) and this section (ORDER BY) to get:

```
SELECT PeopleNameFirst, PeopleNameLast FROM People ORDER BY PeopleDOB DESC,
PeopleNameLast;
```

The last example brings up an interesting point. You do not have to include in the results a field to be used in the ORDER BY clause. We are ordering by DOB, but we are not getting the data from the PeopleDOB field back in our recordset.

Note the following common errors encountered with SQL ORDER BY clauses:

❑ Second fields in the ORDER BY clause are only consulted in the case of a tie in the first field.

❑ When adding additional fields for tie-breakers they must be separated by a comma.

❑ There is no comma after the last field in the ORDER BY clause.

❑ Sorting on a field (column) that was not included in the SELECT clause.

❑ Logical error of sorting in the wrong order.

❑ Reverse order should be specified by DESC, not DESCENDING.

## Try It Out - ORDERing

Make a page with an HTML table from the Clothier database. The table lists items and their prices from the most expensive down to the cheapest. This is shown in the screenshot:

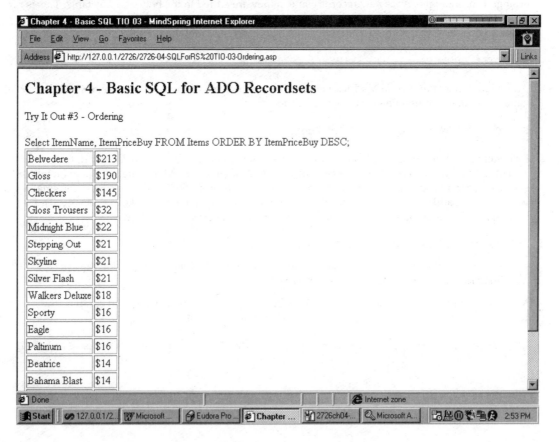

The above page was generated by the following code, which can be found in `2726-04-SQLForRS TIO-03-Ordering.asp`:

```
<HTML>
<HEAD>
<TITLE>Chapter 4 - Basic SQL TIO 03</TITLE>
</HEAD>
<BODY>
<H2>Chapter 4 - Basic SQL for ADO Recordsets</H2>
<P>Try It Out #3 - Ordering</P>
<%
  Dim oRSco
  Set oRSco=Server.CreateObject("ADODB.Recordset")
  sqltext = "SELECT ItemName, ItemPriceBuy "
  sqltext = sqltext & " FROM Items ORDER BY ItemPriceBuy DESC;"
  Response.Write "<FONT COLOR=brown>" & sqltext & "</FONT>"
  oRSco.Open sqltext, "DSN=Clothier"
  oRSco.MoveFirst
  Response.Write "<TABLE BORDER=1>"
  Do While NOT oRSco.EOF
     Response.Write "<TR><TD>" & oRSco("ItemName") & "</TD>"
     Response.Write "<TD>$" & oRSco("ItemPriceBuy") & "</TD></TR>"
     oRSco.MoveNext
  Loop
  Response.Write "</TABLE>"
  oRSco.Close
  Set oRSco=nothing
%>
</BODY>
</HTML>
```

### How It Works: ORDERing

The only lines that are new to us are the following two, which create the SQL statement. Note that we are only loading two fields into the recordset. In addition note that we order by `ItemPriceBuy`, in descending order.

```
sqltext = "SELECT ItemName, ItemPriceBuy "
sqltext = sqltext & " FROM Items ORDER BY ItemPriceBuy DESC;"
```

The following line is included to help you see the SQL and its result on the page. This is good for testing, but would be commented out prior to delivery to the client.

```
Response.Write "<FONT COLOR=brown>" & sqltext & "</FONT>"
```

If you are wondering about getting the dollar sign, look at the following line.

```
Response.Write "<TD>$" & oRSco("ItemPriceBuy") & "</TD></TR>"
```

# WHERE Clause

The above techniques, SELECT and ORDER BY, determine which fields are returned and in what order, but you get all of the records. Your client may only want the boats in the Laser class or only want the sailors who are over 45 years old. SQL offers the WHERE clause, which is similar to the words Criteria, Filter or Selection in various other database systems.

# Simple WHERE Clause

If we are generating a list for only those sailors of intermediate skill, then we will want to limit the records to people with a value of 2 in the `PeopleProfessionalClass` field:

```
SELECT * FROM People WHERE PeopleProfessionalClass=2;
```

Notice that the keyword `WHERE` is followed by a test. The test generally is composed of three parts:

❑   a field name (in this case `PeopleProfessionalClass`)

❑   a comparison operator (in this case an equals)

❑   a value (in this case 2)

This is the first case in our study of SQL in which we are presenting a value. Up to now all of the words in the SQL statement were either keywords, like `SELECT`, or else names from the database, such as `People` and `BoatClass`. But when using `WHERE`, we will want to add values such as `45` or `Laser`. There are three common types of values, and you must present them to SQL encased in characters as follows:

❑   **text string** values must be entered within quotes. It is an important fact that SQL doesn't care whether the text is within single or double quotes, but we will present text within single quotes.

❑   **date** values must be entered within # signs, such as `#07/08/1929#`. This is true when using Access, other databases have their own conventions. A more generic system when using ODBC, is to use the format `{d '1929-07-09'}`, this will be converted into the correct syntax for the database. Here we will stick with Access as our database provider.

❑   **number** values are entered naked.

Note the numeric comparison operators that we can use:

| | |
|---|---|
| Equal to | = |
| Greater than | > |
| Less than | < |
| Greater than or equal to | >= |
| Less than or equal to | <= |
| Not equal to | <> |

For example, if we are generating a seating chart from the `People` table for the Old Salts Club (those born before 1950) then we will want to use a `WHERE` clause to limit the records:

```
SELECT * FROM People WHERE PeopleDOB < #01/01/1950#
```

When using these, think carefully about the "cusp cases", in other words those data that will be the same as the value. For example, what about the case where you want to divide people into two groups according to whether they were born before or after 05/05/1995 and one guy was born right on that day? I suggest you run tests with the smallest datum you expect, the largest datum you expect, a datum exactly equal to the values, and then with several data just above and below the value you are using. Be extra careful with dates since they start and end at midnight.

# Using WHERE to Find One Record

A common objective for the WHERE clause is to find a specific record. If we were looking for a Mr Hogbreath we would write the following:

```
SELECT * FROM People WHERE PeopleNameLast='hogbreath';
```

which should return one record only; the one with the data for the swine herder. But there may be more than one Hogbreath in the database. Your code will be more robust if you can base the WHERE clause on an autonumbered, unique ID such as PeopleID. We will see this technique later in the chapter.

In Access we can use the equals sign for comparing text, but note that the search is case sensitive. For other text comparisons we use the LIKE or NOT LIKE comparison operators. For example, to find all the records where the sailor belongs to the Hogbreath family:

```
SELECT * FROM People WHERE PeopleLastName LIKE 'hogbreath'
```

You can also use the IS NOT operator to eliminate NULL values, for example:

```
SELECT * FROM People WHERE PeopleClubCode IS NOT NULL
```

If using wildcards with a WHERE clause, note that in Access the wildcard character is *, but in other databases it may be different (in SQL Server % is used). For example, the following will find all the sailors whose surname begins with Hog.

```
SELECT * FROM People WHERE PeopleLastName LIKE 'hog%'
```

# WHERE with BETWEEN...AND

WHERE statements become more powerful when you can specify a range of values. SQL offers the BETWEEN...AND keywords, which must be used as a pair. In VBScript the definition of BETWEEN is inclusive of the upper and lower values. For example, there are four divisions of athletes in regattas:

❏  Youth, for sailors born after 1982

❏  Open, for sailors born in 1956 through 1982

❏  Masters, for sailors born in 1945 through 1981 and

❏  Grand Masters, for sailors born prior to 1945.

The race committee would want to generate a page with four tables, each listing the competitors for one division. The SQL statements for each table would be (in the year 2000):

```
sSQLYouth = "SELECT * FROM People WHERE PeopleDOB>=#01/01/1982#;"

sSQLOpen = "SELECT * FROM People WHERE PeopleDOB BETWEEN #01/01/1956# AND_
12/31/1981#;"

sSQLMaster = "SELECT * FROM People WHERE PeopleDOB BETWEEN #01/01/1945# AND_
#12/31/1956#;"

sSQLGrandM = "SELECT * FROM People WHERE PeopleDOB<=#12/31/1944#;"
```

Be aware of the following common errors when using BETWEEN . . . AND:

❑   Leaving a number unallocated to a division

❑   Overlapping divisions

❑   Leaving out the word AND - this SQL construct must use both of the keywords BETWEEN...AND

❑   BETWEEN...AND is not used for text, only numbers, currency and dates

# WHERE with IN

But what if we have a list of words that we want to match, rather than a range of numbers? In this case we use the SQL keyword IN. For example, in the Canadian National Championship the sailors are divided into three divisions: East, Central and West. We would create and execute three SQL statements to build three tables, one for each division.

```
sSQLWest = "SELECT * FROM People WHERE State IN('BC','YT','NT','AB');"

sSQLCentral = "SELECT * FROM People WHERE State IN('SK','MB','ON','QC');"

sSQLEast = "SELECT * FROM People WHERE State IN('NF','NB','NS','PE');"
```

## Try It Out - List Sailors in Two Clubs Only

In preparation for a match race between two clubs, the organizers ask you to make a page of just the sailors in the Dares Salaam Yacht Club (DSYC) and the Sailing Club of Washington (SCOW), similar to the following:

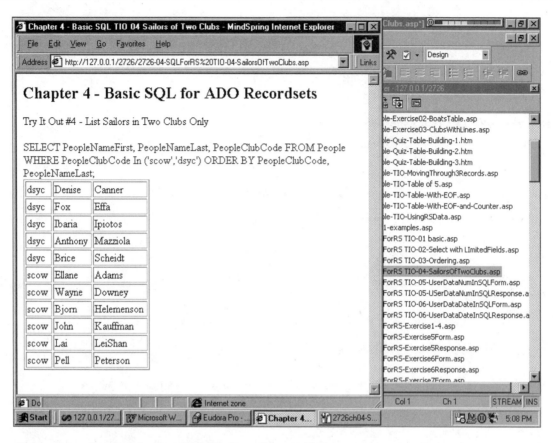

This page can be created using the following code, provided as `2726-04-SQLForRS TIO-04-SailorsOfTwoClubs.asp`:

```
<HTML>
<HEAD>
<TITLE>Chapter 4 - Basic SQL TIO 04 Sailors of Two Clubs</TITLE>
</HEAD>
<BODY>
<H2>Chapter 4 - Basic SQL for ADO Recordsets</H2>
<P>Try It Out #4 - List Sailors in Two Clubs Only</P>
<%
  Dim oRStc
  Set oRStc=Server.CreateObject("ADODB.Recordset")
  sqlText = "SELECT PeopleNameFirst, PeopleNameLast, PeopleClubCode "
  sqlText = sqlText & " FROM People "
  sqlText = sqlText & " WHERE PeopleClubCode IN ('scow','dsyc') "
  sqlText = sqlText & " ORDER BY PeopleClubCode, PeopleNameLast;"
  Response.Write "<FONT COLOR=brown>" & sqlText & "</FONT>"
  oRStc.Open sqlText, "DSN=Sailors"
  Response.Write "<TABLE BORDER=1>"
  Do While NOT oRStc.EOF
    Response.Write "<TR><TD>" & oRStc("PeopleClubCode") & " </TD>"
    Response.Write "<TD>" & oRStc("PeopleNameFirst") & " </TD>"
    Response.Write "<TD>" & oRStc("PeopleNameLast") & " </TD></TR>"
    oRStc.MoveNext
```

```
   Loop
   Response.Write "</TABLE>"
   oRStc.Close
   Set oRStc=nothing
%>
</P>
</BODY>
</HTML>
```

### How It Works: List Two Sailors in Two Clubs Only

We start with the normal code to create a recordset, this time naming it oRStc for two clubs:

```
<%
  Dim oRStc
  Set oRStc=Server.CreateObject("ADODB.Recordset")
```

In the WHERE clause below we see the syntax to only return records where the sailor's club is one of the following: dsyc or scow.

```
  sqlText = "SELECT PeopleNameFirst, PeopleNameLast, PeopleClubCode "
  sqlText = sqlText & " FROM People "
  sqlText = sqlText & " WHERE PeopleClubCode IN ('scow','dsyc') "
  sqlText = sqlText & " ORDER BY PeopleClubCode, PeopleNameLast;"
```

The following line shows you the SQL for reference; it would be taken out before deployment.

```
  Response.Write "<FONT COLOR=brown>" & sqlText & "</FONT>"
  oRStc.Open sqlText, "DSN=Sailors"
```

And then we write the table, in this case writing the table tags from within ASP.

```
  Response.Write "<TABLE BORDER=1>"
  Do While NOT oRStc.EOF
     Response.Write "<TR><TD>" & oRStc("PeopleClubCode") & " </TD>"
     Response.Write "<TD>" & oRStc("PeopleNameFirst") & " </TD>"
     Response.Write "<TD>" & oRStc("PeopleNameLast") & " </TD></TR>"
     oRStc.MoveNext
  Loop
  Response.Write "</TABLE>"
  oRStc.Close
  Set oRStc=nothing
%>
```

A variation is to write the expression in the Do statement, using the reverse logic, by telling VBScript to keep performing the task until the property EOF becomes true, as follows:

```
  Do Until oRStc.EOF
```

# WHERE with Logical Operators

More complex WHERE clauses can be built using combinations of the logical operators AND, OR, and NOT.

```
SELECT * FROM People WHERE (PeopleDOB < #01/01/1950# OR PeopleProfessionalClass =2)_
AND (PeopleNameLast LIKE 'Hogbreath')
```

This will find all records for any member of the Hogbreath family who was either born before 1950 or who is an intermediate sailor. Note the use of parentheses to group together the clauses. By moving them around the results will be totally different. For example, the following statement will select intermediate ranking Hogbreaths of any age plus any other sailors who were born before 1950.

```
SELECT * FROM People WHERE (PeopleDOB < #01/01/1950#) OR (PeopleProfessionalClass =2_
AND PeopleNameLast LIKE 'Hogbreath')
```

# Building SQL Statements with a Query Grid

You are blessed to be learning SQL in these modern times. In the past we had to laboriously build all SQL statements by hand. It was the worst of times, fraught with misplaced commas, misspelled field names, missed deadlines and clients reduced to tears. But since the advent of the MS query grid it is the best of times. Rather than typing (or in my case typo-ing) the SQL statement, we can build it with a drag and drop visual interface.

You are probably familiar with the query building tool in Microsoft Access, SQL Server, VB6 or Visual InterDev. In Access you can access the tool by clicking Start in the database window, click on the Query tab, then New Query and select the Design View.

> *If you are already comfortable with the query grid, then just look at step five below. If you are new to the query grid then read steps one to four as well.*

The query building grid window has a top pane which holds tables, and a bottom pane which is a grid. Once the query is built in this visual form you have several options for viewing and running the query. You use the query builder to make SQL statements in five steps.

**1.** First, you add tables to the top pane by clicking on Query | ShowTables. Drag and drop the table(s) that you want to use in the SQL statement up on to the top pane. Note that you can also add queries, since there is no problem building a query on a query. The act of dragging a table onto the upper pane defines the argument for the FROM clause of the SQL. Once you have added the table of interest, close the box listing the tables.

**2.** The second step is to drag and drop fields from the tables down to the top row of the grid. This act defines which fields will be arguments after the SELECT keyword of the SQL statement. For example if we wanted a SQL statement like:

```
SELECT PeopleNameLast, PeopleNameFirst FROM People;
```

We would produce the following grid, saved as qDemoQueryGrid:

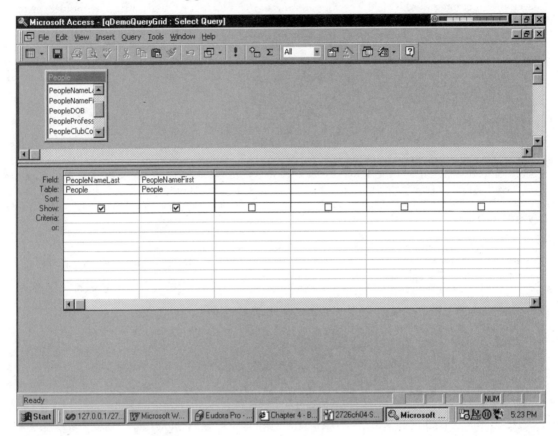

**3.** The third step is adding, sorting, or selecting options. Sorting can be either ascending or descending, as set in the Sort row. Note that when you click in the Sort cell under a field you get a drop-down box - no need to type anything in. Specifying Ascending or Descending in the Sort row is the act that creates the ORDER BY clause of the SQL statement. If you do not want all rows to be included in the recordset, then you must add a test to the Criteria line. For example, we could type 2 for the criteria of the column for PeopleProfessionalClass. The criteria row creates the test for the WHERE clause in the SQL statement. If we wanted the following SQL statement:

```
SELECT PeopleNameLast, PeopleNameFirst, PeopleProfessionalClass FROM People_
WHERE PeopleProfessionalClass=2 ORDER BY PeopleNameLast;
```

We would create the grid as follows:

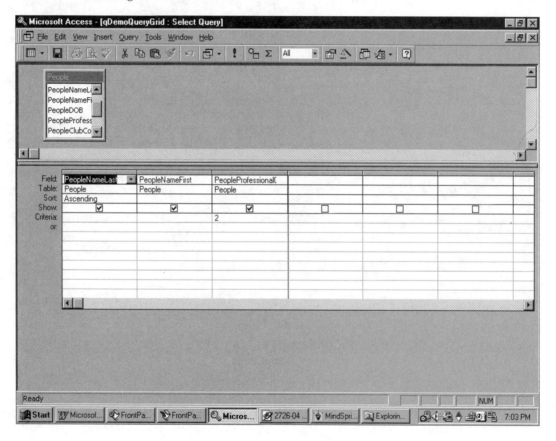

**4.** The fourth step is to test the query. By clicking on Query | Run we see the results of the query. This alone is a tremendous benefit since we can test without spending time setting the query into a Rs.Open operation and making trips back and forth to the server. As long as you have a local copy of the database, you can do very rapid SQL statement testing. After running the query, your window will change to:

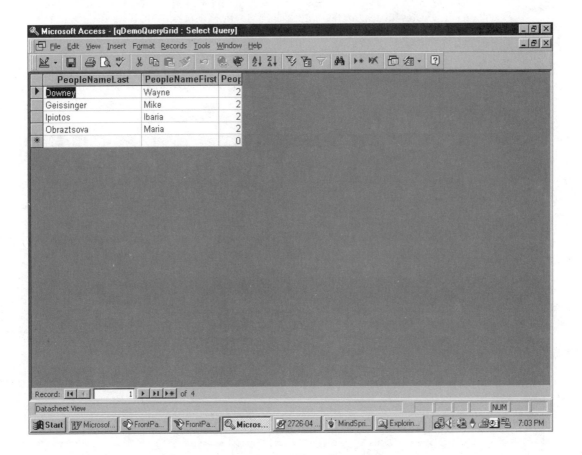

**5.** The fifth and last step is the most exciting. All of the time that you were doing visual development with drag and drop, Access was interpreting it into SQL statements. If you click on View | SQL View, you will see the SQL statement built as per the grid you created.

For example, the grid we've just seen will produce the following view:

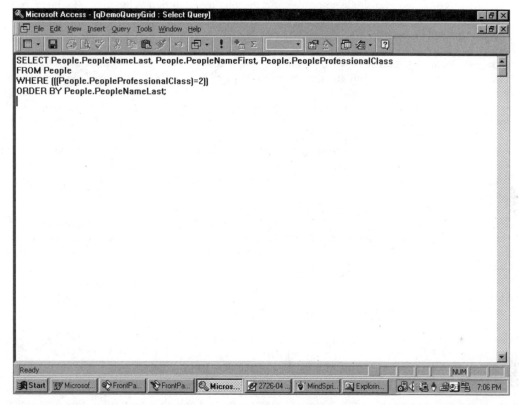

The SQL statements built by Access are not exactly the same as we have built in this chapter, in fact they are better. Access is more meticulous in that it specifies the source of each field by putting the source table before the name of the field. In addition, it encapsulates the expression of the WHERE clause in parenthesis. These improvements make the statement harder to read, but more robust as you scale up through increasingly complex SQL statements.

In the SQL view you can select the entire statement with Control+A and then copy with Ctrl+C. Switch back to your ASP editor and paste in the code. In many cases you will then have to divide the code up over several lines and concatenate them into a SQL text variable. Be very careful in that process to not lose the spaces that surround keywords or the commas that separate items in a list.

# JOIN Queries – A Marriage of Tables

Now, there are times when you are going to want to select fields from more than one table at a time. This happens most often when the tables are *related* – that is, they share a common field. For example, I have done several employment services web sites, where there is an `employers` table, and a `jobs` table. There may be many jobs posted by a single employer, and the jobs are identified as belonging to the employer by the employer's number field – an AutoNumber field in the `employers` table. The related, or *foreign key* field, in the `jobs` table, is called `password`.

When two tables are related in this way, they have a **one-to-many** relationship, sometimes called a parent/child relationship, probably the most common type of relationship in *relational* databases. There are many uses for these types of relationships, such as *referential integrity* – the prevention of errors occurring when records are altered or deleted. The best example I can give of this is, what happens when you delete an employer record? Now you've got a bunch of jobs with no employer. These are what are called *orphaned* records. The parent record in the employer table has died (alas!), and they are now taking up useless space. When you create a relationship with 'cascade update' and/or 'cascade delete' referential integrity, these changes are cascaded to the child table automatically. Kill the parent, and you kill all the children. Update the parent record, and the corresponding fields in the child records are updated automatically.

There are actually many types of relationships, and I don't want to go into a detailed explanation of them all here (after all, this is a discussion of SQL statements). And similarly, there are many kinds of JOINs. There are Equi-JOINs, Non-Equi-JOINs, INNER JOINs, OUTER JOINs, LEFT and RIGHT JOINs, LEFT and RIGHT INNER and OUTER JOINs...

What is a JOIN? It is, simply put, the marriage of two or more tables. It is a query that creates a table from one or more records in each of the tables. Let's take a look at the following example:

```
SELECT jobs.number AS number,jobs.category AS category,jobs.title AS title, _
 jobs.password AS password,_
 employers.contname AS contname,employers.email AS email FROM employers_
 INNER JOIN jobs ON employers.number = jobs.password
```

Believe it or not, this is actually a rather simple JOIN query. It is probably the most common type as well. Let's take a look under the hood.

Since you're selecting fields from two tables, you have to indicate which table each field comes from. This is done by naming the table, and adding a period before the field name in the fields list. Note the AS operator (SELECT jobs.number AS number...). This creates a new name for the resulting field. I've *aliased* the fields (assigned a new name), because they are no longer the fields they were in the first place; they are new fields in a new recordset. When they are referred to in the ASP-ADO code in the page, they will be referred to by their aliases.

Then comes the JOIN: (...FROM employers INNER JOIN jobs ON employers.number = jobs.password). What does this do? Well, remember when I said that the two tables shared a common field (employers.number and jobs.password)? This common field is used to JOIN the tables together. What it does is tell the database that it wants to put the jobs fields together with the employers fields that have the same employer number.

Let's take a look at two examples from both tables (just the significant fields):

Jobs Table

| Number | Category | Password | Title |
| --- | --- | --- | --- |
| 1 | Administrative | 1 | Office Manager |
| 2 | Computer Related | 1 | Programmer |
| 3 | Engineering | 1 | Drafting |
| 4 | Sales | 2 | Computer Sales |
| 5 | Engineering | 2 | Drafting |
| 6 | Administrative | 2 | Secretary |

Employers Table

| Number | ContName | Email |
| --- | --- | --- |
| 1 | Joe Blow | joe@eats.com |
| 2 | Ted Sputnik | ted@sput.com |

The query puts these two tables together into one recordset:

| Number | Category | Title | Password | ContName | Email |
| --- | --- | --- | --- | --- | --- |
| 1 | Admin | Office Manager | 1 | Joe Blow | joe@eats.com |
| 2 | Computer Related | Programmer | 1 | Joe Blow | joe@eats.com |
| 3 | Engineering | Drafting | 1 | Joe Blow | joe@eats.com |
| 4 | Sales | Computer Sales | 2 | Ted Sputnik | ted@sput.com |
| 5 | Engineering | Drafting | 2 | Ted Sputnik | ted@sput.com |
| 6 | Admin | Secretary | 2 | Ted Sputnik | ted@sput.com |

Okay, okay, I hear you. "How do I know whether to do an inner, outer, right, left, ...join?" Good question. In fact, the rules vary slightly from one database to another. What I recommend is using the Access Query Designer to get your basic syntax. Visually draw the query, selecting the tables and the fields you want, and selecting the fields you want to use as `JOIN` fields. Then copy and paste the SQL into your code. Once you've got the tough part (`...FROM employers INNER JOIN on employer.number = jobs.password`, for example), you can tweak the rest of it, adding fields, a `WHERE` condition if you need one, etc.

I will get to the WHERE condition in a bit. But since you asked, here's an example of the same JOIN query with a WHERE condition, just so you can get a taste:

```
SELECT jobs.number AS number,jobs.category AS category,jobs.title AS title, _
jobs.password AS password,_
  employers.contname AS contname,employers.email AS email FROM employers_
  INNER JOIN jobs ON employers.number = jobs.password WHERE jobs.approved = 'TRUE'
```

There's a lot more to joining than we have space for here, so it might be worth getting yourself a good SQL reference, such as the previously mentioned Wrox Press book, and use the Access Query Designer or the Visual Data Tools in Visual Studio!

# Incorporating Data from HTML Forms into SQL Statements

So far, all of the SQL statements that we have studied consisted entirely of text which we typed into VBScript at design time. But in the real world we may want to use information gathered from the user. For example, we could present an HTML form that asks for a city, then return all of the events for that city.

There are plenty of good books on HTML forms - my favorite is Instant HTML Programmer's Reference by Steve Wright (ISBN 1-861000-76-6), Chapter 7. (This book is out of print – if you can't get hold of it, then a suitable alternative is a book of the same name, ISBN 1-861001-56-8, co-written with Alex Homer.) You can see the exact HTML syntax there, but here is a quick synopsis of the theory, enough for you to understand how to utilize in SQL the data from a visitor's input.

- ❑ Data is collected in a page with an HTML form. This page does not have to be a VBScript page since it does not do the processing. In my programming, these pages always have the word Form at the end of their name.

- ❑ Form pages have a submit button and an ACTION argument which is an URL. When the submit button is clicked, the browser automatically requests (opens) the URL of the ACTION argument, and passes to that page the data the user entered. In my practice, I always name these pages requested by forms with a Response at the end of the name.

- ❑ The data entered by the user is sent back to the server. Each field of the form has a name, followed by an equals sign and the value the user entered.

- ❑ The response page can obtain that data and stuff it into a variable using the following syntax:

```
varName = Request.Querystring("FormFieldName")
```

- ❑ The data in the variable can now be used in an SQL statement.

The above points are simplified. The biggest difference you may encounter is that some forms use a POST action and some use the GET action. The differences are covered in the HTML texts. We will use both in this book, so keep in mind that in the response page, POST requires the use of Request.Form, whereas GET requires Request.QueryString.

Again, if this is completely new to you, practice a few simple Form - Response pages before trying to integrate the data into SQL. You can also follow some of the annotated exercises in Beginning Active Server Pages 2.0 (ISBN 1-861001-34-7), Chapter 3.

## Definition of Hard Coded

In general we can provide data to a line of code in one of two ways. The first way is to type it in at design time. This will always be the same, regardless of interactions at runtime. For example, if we always send prizes to the first five people on the list, then we can put the number five into code. This is called **hard-coding**.

The second source of data is from a variable which is stuffed each time the program runs. If we give away a varying number of prizes each day, then we must get the number at run time and put that into the code. I don't know of alternative lingo for this option, no-one says *soft coded*. I usually say *by variable, in code, dynamic* or *live data*.

## Working with User-Entered Numbers in SQL Statements

Once we have the user data from the form in a variable, we can use it in a SQL statement. The most common case is looking up a user's information. It is easier to use a number than it is to use text, so let us start with that.

## Try It Out - User Data in SQL Statements

Make a page for a sailor to enter her SailorID number, then get back her data such as name, DOB and professional class. Keep in mind that this is a two-page project. The first page (form page) asks for the ID number in an HTML form, the second (response page) picks up the information, puts it in the WHERE clause of a SQL statement, executes the statement to get a recordset containing one record, then shows the data to the page. The completed pages should look like the following. First, the form page:

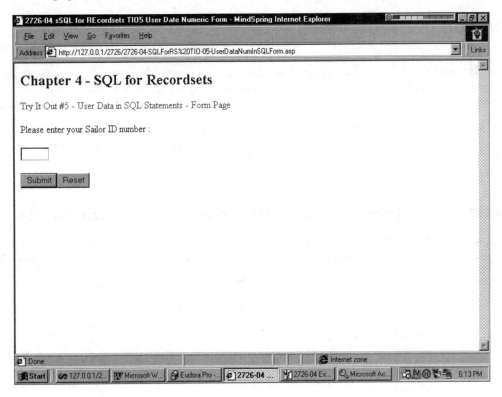

Then the response page; in this example the user entered ID number 11.

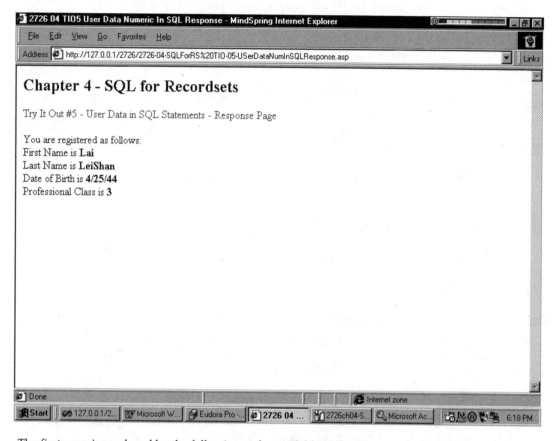

The first page is produced by the following code, available in the file named C04-UserDataInSQLForm.asp:

```
<HTML>
<HEAD>
<TITLE>c04 User Data In SQL Form</TITLE>
</HEAD>
<BODY>
<H2>Chapter 4 - SQL for Recordsets</H2>
<P><FONT SIZE="3" COLOR="green">Try It Out #5 - User Data in SQL Statements - Form
Page</FONT></P>
<FORM METHOD="post" ACTION="2726-04-SQLForRS-TIO5-USerDataNumInSQLResponse.asp">
<P>Please enter your Sailor ID number :</P>
<P><INPUT TYPE="text" NAME="SailorID" SIZE="5"></P>
<P><INPUT TYPE="submit" VALUE="Submit"><INPUT TYPE="reset" VALUE="Reset"></P>
</FORM>
</BODY>
</HTML>
```

The second page is produced by the following code, which can be found in a file named `2726-04-SQLForRS-TIO5-USerDataNumInSQLResponse.asp`:

```
<HTML>
<HEAD>
<TITLE>c04 User Data In SQL Response</TITLE>
</HEAD>
<BODY>
<H2>Chapter 4 - SQL for Recordsets</H2>
<P><FONT SIZE="3" COLOR="green">Try It Out #5 - User Data in SQL Statements - Response
Page</FONT></P>
<%
  varSailorID= Request.Form("SailorID")
  'Response.Write varsailorid 'for testing
  Dim oRSp
  Set oRSp=Server.CreateObject("ADODB.Recordset")
  sqltext="SELECT * FROM People "
  sqltext=sqltext& " WHERE PeopleID=" & varSailorID & ";"
  oRSp.Open sqltext, "DSN=Sailors"
%>
<P>You are registered as follows:<BR>
First Name is <B><%=oRSp("PeopleNameFirst")%></B><BR>
Last Name is <B><%=oRSp("PeopleNameLast")%></B><BR>
Date of Birth is <B><%=oRSp("PeopleDOB")%></B><BR>
Professional Class is <B><%=oRSp("PeopleProfessionalClass")%></B><BR>
</P>
</BODY>
</HTML>
```

### How It Works: User Data in SQL Statements - The Form Page

The form page picks up the information from the user. There are two key points. The first is on the following line. In the ACTION argument you must specify the page that will be picking up the user information and putting it into the SQL statement.

```
<FORM METHOD="post" ACTION="c04-UserDataInSQLResponse.asp">
```

Second is that you must remember the name you give to the text input field on the form that will hold the user data, in this case SailorID as on the following line.

```
<P><INPUT TYPE="text" NAME="SailorID" SIZE="5"></P>
```

My sharper students frequently ask why this page is named with an .asp extension. They are right in that there is no requirement for scripting in the form page. However, most sites have ASP-dependent elements standardized throughout all pages of the site, such as cookies or session variables. I find it easier to give all the pages in such a site an .asp extension right from the start. Then when those elements are added to the page there is no need to go back and change the name and all the hyperlinks to the site.

### The Response Page

The response page offers us more of a challenge. First, we must pull the user data out of the request and get it into a variable as in the following code. The variable can have any name, but the text at the end of the line must match the name you gave to the form field back on the form page. Many students get this wrong, so let me repeat: the text which is in the double quotes of the varSailorID= Request.Form("SailorID") must match the name attribute of the text-type input box name on the form page, which is in the <INPUT TYPE=text NAME="SailorID">.

Next we have to use that data in the WHERE clause of the SQL statement. This is done by concatenating the variable into the hard coded part of the SQL string. Compare the following two lines:

Hard coded:

```
sqltext="SELECT * FROM People WHERE PeopleID=5;"
```

Live data:

```
sqltext="SELECT * FROM People WHERE PeopleID=" & varSailorID & ";"
```

When the code executes, VBScript will swap out varSailorID and substitute whatever number the variable contains. The variable was filled with the number that the user typed in the HTML form page. After VBScript swaps in the number, it excises the ampersands and quotes to leave us with the same SQL statement as the hard coded version.

A performance improvement would be to change the output by adding the exact property we want from the field, as discussed in Chapter 3. This eliminates a lookup within the object.

```
<P>You are registered as follows:<BR>
First Name is <B><%=oRSp("PeopleNameFirst").value%></B><BR>
Last Name is <B><%=oRSp("PeopleNameLast").value%></B><BR>
Date of Birth is <B><%=oRSp("PeopleDOB").value%></B><BR>
Professional Class is <B><%=oRSp("PeopleProfessionalClass").value%></B><BR>
```

# Working with User-Entered Text and Dates in SQL Statements

Back at the beginning of the chapter, I laid out the rules for user-entered data. Numbers are entered in a SQL statement naked, but text must be surrounded by quotes, and dates by # signs. The pound signs (hash marks) are no problem, but the quotes can give VBScript trouble. Consider the following line:

```
sqlText = "SELECT * FROM People WHERE PeopleNameLast = "kauffman";"
```

The problem is that VBScript will put into the variable sqlText the characters starting at the first double quotes and going up to the next double quotes, which would be:

```
SELECT * FROM People WHERE PeopleNameLast =
```

To a human there is a premature ending to the statement because it treats the first quotes around the name as the second quotes around the string. Then VBScript looks at the next characters, kauffman, realizes that this is not a keyword, and returns an error message. The SQL statement is never built.

Fortunately, most SQLs prefer a single quote around text. Equally fortunate is that VBScript does not recognize a single quote as encompassing text, VBScript treats a single quote the same as any other character. So we will be successful if we change the SQL statement to the following:

```
sqlText = "SELECT * FROM People WHERE PeopleNameLast = 'kauffman';"
```

Or, if we have data coming from a form, we can construct the SQL as follows:

```
sqlText= "SELECT * FROM People "
sqlText= sqlText & " WHERE PeopleNameLast ='" & varName & "';"
```

Let us look at the code above quite carefully, since this is where students frequently make mistakes. And, as mentioned before, you can often catch these problems by having the SQL statement displayed on the page (using `Response.Write`) during development time. Review the following points:

❏ The first line is no different from what we have discussed before.

❏ The second line contains four terms (or *sections* or *string values*) that are put together by VBScript at the points of the ampersands.

❏ The last character in the second term (just after the equals sign) is a single quote. When VBScript concatenates, this will be the quote SQL requires before a text value.

❏ The last term consists of a single quote that SQL requires after text values, and the SQL-closing semicolon.

When VBScript puts it all together it looks the same as in the last example, where we hard coded 'kauffman'. In fact, there is no reason to ever put text in double quotes.

The technique is similar for dates. If we received two dates from a form and want to make a list of people born between those dates, we would write it as in the following example.

## Try It Out - User Data of Date Type in a SQL Statement

Create a form which asks the user to type in a start and an end date. Use that information in a response page that shows a table of all the sailors born between the two dates.

The form page looks like this:

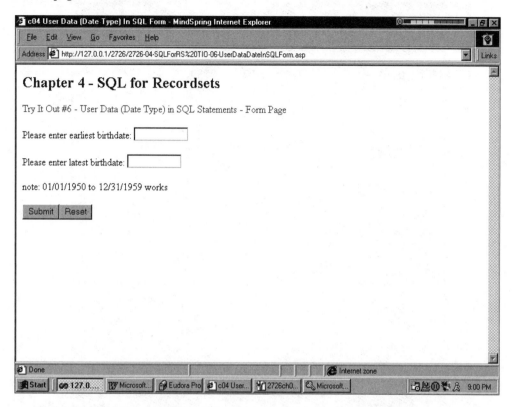

It is generated by the following code, saved in the file `2726-04-SQLForRS-TIO6-UserDataDateInSQLForm.asp`:

```
<HTML>
<HEAD>
<TITLE>c04 User Data (Date Type) In SQL Form</TITLE>
</HEAD><BODY>
<H2>Chapter 4 - SQL for Recordsets</H2>
<P><FONT SIZE="3" COLOR="green">Try It Out #6 - User Data (Date Type) in SQL
Statements Form Page</FONT></P>
<FORM METHOD="post" ACTION=" 2726-04-SQLForRS-TIO6-UserDataDateInSQLResponse.asp">
<P>Please enter earliest birthdate: <INPUT TYPE="text" NAME="DOBStart"></P>
<P>Please enter latest birthdate: <INPUT TYPE="text" NAME="DOBEnd"></P>
<P>note: 01/01/1950 to 12/31/1959 works</P>
<P><INPUT TYPE="submit" VALUE="Submit">
<INPUT TYPE="reset" VALUE="Reset"></P>
</FORM></BODY>
</HTML>
```

If the user enters dates to represent the decade of the 1950s then the response page is as follows.

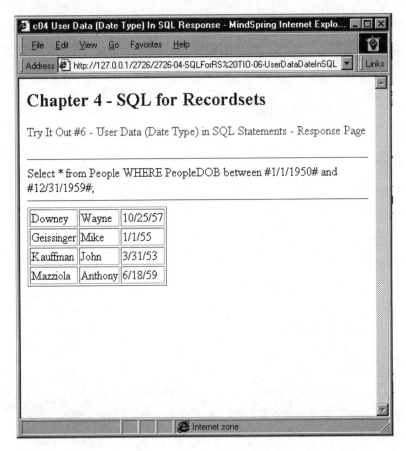

The above page is produced by the following code, available as file `2726-04-SQLForRS-TIO6-UserDataDateInSQLResponse.asp`:

```
<HTML>
<HEAD>
<TITLE>c04 User Data (Date Type) In SQL Response</TITLE>
</HEAD>
<BODY>
<H2>Chapter 4 - SQL for Recordsets</H2>
<P><FONT SIZE="3" COLOR="green">Try It Out #6 - User Data (Date Type) in SQL
Statements Response Page</FONT></P>
<%
  varDOBStart = Request.Form("DOBStart")
  varDOBEnd = Request.Form("DOBEnd")
  Dim oRSp
  Set oRSp=Server.CreateObject("ADODB.Recordset")
  sqltext="SELECT * FROM People "
  sqltext=sqltext & " WHERE PeopleDOB BETWEEN "
  sqltext=sqltext & "#" & varDOBStart
  sqltext=sqltext & "# AND #" & varDOBEnd & "#;"
  Response.Write "<HR>" & sqltext & "<HR>"
  oRSp.Open sqltext, "DSN=Sailors"
  Response.Write "<TABLE BORDER=1>"
```

```
  Do While NOT oRSp.EOF
    Response.Write "<TR><TD>" & oRSp("PeopleNameLast") & "</TD>"
    Response.Write "<TD>" & oRSp("PeopleNameFirst") & "</TD>"
    Response.Write "<TD>" & oRSp("PeopleDOB") & "</TD></TR>"
    oRSp.MoveNext
  Loop
  Response.Write "</TABLE>"
%>
</BODY>
</HTML>
```

### How It Works: User Data of Date Type in a SQL Statement - The Form Page

In the form page we just have to remember two concepts. First, we must give the name of our response page as the URL in the ACTION attribute of the FORM tag as below.

```
<FORM METHOD="post" ACTION="c04-UserDataDateInSQLResponse.asp">
```

Second, we must remember the names that we give to the input fields, in this case DOBStart and DOBEnd, so we can use them in the response page.

```
<P>Please enter earliest birthdate: <INPUT TYPE="text" NAME="DOBStart"></P>
<P>Please enter latest birthdate: <INPUT TYPE="text" NAME="DOBEnd"></P>
```

### The Response Page

In the response page we start by pulling the data out of the Request object, specifying the names we gave to the fields in the form page.

```
varDOBStart = Request.Form("DOBStart")
varDOBEnd = Request.Form("DOBEnd")
```

Then we can use the contents of those variables to build a SQL statement by concatenation. Remember that within a SQL statement we must encase the date values in # signs, as follows. Look carefully at how, at the beginning of the fourth line, we add both the # sign to follow the start date and the # sign to precede the end date.

```
sqltext="SELECT * FROM People "
sqltext=sqltext & " WHERE PeopleDOB BETWEEN "
sqltext=sqltext & "#" & varDOBStart
sqltext=sqltext & "# AND #" & varDOBEnd & "#;"
```

We could improve the final appearance of that page by adding a clause to sort the names according to date of birth, as follows:

```
sqltext="SELECT * FROM People "
sqltext=sqltext & " WHERE PeopleDOB BETWEEN"
sqltext=sqltext & "#" & varDOBStart
sqltext=sqltext & "# AND #" & varDOBEnd & "#"
sqltext=sqltext & " ORDER BY PeopleDOB;"
```

Note that in this case we are simplifying the code surrounding dates, by assuming that we are working with Access or MS SQL Server, and that we are working in the USA.

# Troubleshooting SQL Statements

Much of the time in my ASP-ADO classes is spent on troubleshooting SQL statements. The errors can be at one or more of three levels:

- errors in the ASP code which builds the SQL statements
- errors in the syntax of the SQL statement once it is assembled
- errors in what SQL is asking the data server to do

This section provides a series of techniques that I use to solve students' problems. Note that I am not focused here on the problems themselves, rather what to do to be able to get our attention to the point of the problem. For each troubleshooting technique, I present what it looks like before troubleshooting, then what it looks like in troubleshooting mode. Finally, unless speed is more important than maintenance, I suggest you leave some troubleshooting tools behind as comments. Where applicable, these are shown in the after troubleshooting listing.

## Response.Write the SQL Statement

The first step I usually take when solving problems with VBScript pages and SQL statements is to Response.Write the SQL statement to the page. It can be difficult to figure out what is actually being built by concatenation, but if you can see the result then many problems will become obvious.

Before troubleshooting:

```
VarNameLast=Request.Querystring("NameLast")
sSQL= "SELECT * FROMPeople WHERE PeopleNameLast='Adams';"
oRs.Open sSQL, "DSN=Sailors"
```

In troubleshooting mode we add a Response.Write. In more complex SQL statements, an erroneous statement can cause trouble (for example it could change all of the records to the wrong date). So, until done troubleshooting, I also usually comment out the line that executes the SQL. This will be expanded on in the next section.

```
VarNameLast=Request.Querystring("NameLast")
sSQL= "SELECT * FROMPeople WHERE PeopleNameLast='Adams';"
Response.Write sSQL
'oRs.Open sSQL, "DSN=Sailors"
```

An improvement is to set off the statement with a couple of horizontal lines so that it is easier to see on the page. If I am building several SQL statements on a page, I also add a short reminder to myself:

```
VarNameLast=Request.Querystring("NameLast")
sSQL= "SELECT * FROMPeople WHERE PeopleNameLast='Adams';"
Response.Write "<HR>SQL for finding Adams:<BR>" & sSQL & "<HR>"
'oRs.Open sSQL, "DSN=Sailors"
```

This produces a page like many of the Try-It-Outs in this chapter, where you could see the SQL statement near the top of the page. The problem in this case is a missing space between FROM and People. After troubleshooting, I usually just rem (comment out) the Response.Write-SQL statement, so that it is there if I ever need to do some quick troubleshooting again. Furthermore, when I read through the code, the commented line gives me a note about what this SQL is supposed to do:

```
VarNameLast=Request.Querystring("NameLast")
sSQL= "SELECT * FROM People WHERE PeopleNameLast='Adams';"
'Response.Write "<HR>SQL for finding Adams:<BR>" & sSQL & "<HR>"
oRs.Open sSQL, "DSN=Sailors"
```

Two improvements to this idea may help you. First is to write to the page the contents variables that are used in the SQL statement. Second is to add a line after oRs.Open to Response.Write the oRs.Source. That will put out the exact SQL statement that the recordset received, after all concatenation, insertion of variable data, and any other machinations.

# Comment Out the Line that Executes the SQL

We generally focus on the SQL statement when troubleshooting, since that is the trickiest part of the page, but the problem could be elsewhere. One troubleshooting technique is to comment out the line that executes the SQL statement (usually Rs.Open). If the trouble persists above the Rs.Open-SQL statement line, we know it was not from executing the SQL.

*Commenting out is a way to prevent a line of code from being performed, but not erasing it. By adding an apostrophe at the beginning of the line you turn a working line of code into a non-executing comment. The apostrophe is an abbreviation for 'rem' so this is sometimes called 'remming' a line, from the concept of turning it into a remark. To put the code back into action, just remove the apostrophe.*

*Remmed lines can be left in pages and delivered to the client. They are frequently re-used, when pages are changed or maintained, and therefore have to undergo a second period of troubleshooting.*

Before troubleshooting:

```
<%
  Dim oRSt
  Set oRSt=Server.CreateObject("ADODB.Recordset")
  oRSt.Open "SELECT * FROM People;", "DSN=Sailors"
  Response.Write oRSt("PeopleNameLast")
  oRSt.Close
  Set oRSt=Nothing
%>
```

In troubleshooting mode, note the apostrophe prior to the `Rs.Open` line:

```
<%
  Dim oRSt
  Set oRSt=Server.CreateObject("ADODB.Recordset")
  'oRSt.Open "SELECT * FROM People;", "DSN=Sailors"
  Response.Write oRSt("PeopleNameLast")
  oRSt.Close
  Set oRSt=Nothing
%>
```

# Add a Response.End and Walk Through the Code

In a large page we may want to focus our analysis on just the first section. After ASP sets up the initial part of the page we want ASP to stop, and just send the page out to our browser as it is at that point. This capability is provided by the `Response.End` command.

Before troubleshooting:

```
<%
  Dim oRSt
  Set oRSt=Server.CreateObject("ADODB.Recordset")
  sqlText = "SELECT PeopleNameFirst, PeopleNameLast FROM People ORDER BY PeopleDOB;"
  oRSt.Open sqlText, "DSN=Sailors"
  Response.Write oRSt("PeopleNameLast")
  oRSt.Close
  Set oRSt=Nothing
%>
```

In troubleshooting mode, note the new `Response.End` line:

```
<%
  Dim oRSt
  Set oRSt=Server.CreateObject("ADODB.Recordset")
  Response.End
  sqlText = "SELECT PeopleNameFirst, PeopleNameLast FROM People ORDER BY PeopleDOB;"
  oRSt.Open sqlText, "DSN=Sailors"
  Response.Write oRSt("PeopleNameLast")
  oRSt.Close
  Set oRSt=Nothing
%>
```

If the above code does not produce any errors, then try moving the `Response.End` down a line, as below.

```
<%
  Dim oRSt
  Set oRSt=Server.CreateObject("ADODB.Recordset")
  sqlText = "SELECT PeopleNameFirst, PeopleNameLast FROM People ORDER BY PeopleDOB;"
  oRSt.Open sqlText, "DSN=Sailors"
  Response.End
  Response.Write oRSt("PeopleNameLast")
  oRSt.Close
  Set oRSt=Nothing
%>
```

Continue moving the `Response.End` line down until the code bombs. Then there's a good chance that the problem is just above that `Response.End` line. However, there is an important exception. There are two kinds of mistakes you could make in your SQL. The first is that you could make an error in the VBScript building the text, for example leaving the double quotes off the end of a line. That type of error will bomb on the line with the mistake. The other error is to build SQL statements with the wrong syntax. In that case, it will bomb on the line that attempts to execute the bad SQL, not the line that actually built the error.

## Type (or Rebuild on a Query Grid) the SQL Statement Elsewhere and Compare to the Original

It is easy to look at a problem for so long that you become 'blind' to the error, especially when you are under pressure. If a problem seems unsolvable, try recreating the SQL statement independently of what already exists. Either go to a new screen and type up the statement, or go to a new, clean grid and rebuild it. If the new one works, then compare the new to the old and look for differences.

## When Fixing, Save the Original

When working on complex SQL code it is easy to twist around with 'fixes' until you've solved some things but created other problems. You can preserve your baseline by making a copy of the SQL statement and commenting out the old version. Then work on fixing the copy. Or even copy the section to a clean page to work on it independently of the other features of the failed page. If you ever get too convoluted in the solution, you can see the point from whence you started. This works particularly well with the technique of simplifying the statement covered next.

Before troubleshooting:

```
VarNameLast=Request.Querystring("NameLast")
sSQL= "SELECT * FROMPeople WHERE PeopleNameLast='Adams';"
Rs.Open sSQL, "DSN=Sailors"
```

In troubleshooting mode we first copy the original and comment out the original.

```
VarNameLast=Request.Querystring("NameLast")
'sSQL= "SELECT * FROMPeople WHERE PeopleNameLast='Adams';"
sSQL= "SELECT * FROMPeople WHERE PeopleNameLast='Adams';"
Response.Write sSQL
'Rs.Open sSQL, "DSN=Sailors"
```

Now we can begin changing the syntax of the copy to fix the problem.

## Write a Simpler Statement and See if it Works, then Add Clauses

Long SQL statements provide plenty of places to go wrong. If the error is not obvious when you see the statement printed to the page, then try substituting a simpler statement. Make a copy of the original, as discussed above, and comment out the original. Then distill it down to just the following:

```
SELECT * FROM Table;
```

If that works, add in the fields you are looking for:

```
SELECT PeopleNameLast, PeopleNameFirst FROM Table
```

If that works, then add in the ORDER BY and then the WHERE clauses. At some point the SQL will break, and then you know exactly where the offending code is located.

Before troubleshooting:

```
sqltext="SELECT PeopleNameLast, PeopleNameFirst "
sqltext=sqltext & " FROM People "
sqltext=sqltext & " WHERE PeopleDOB BETWEEN"
sqltext=sqltext & "#" & varDOBStart
sqltext=sqltext & "# AND #" & varDOBEnd & "'#;"
```

In troubleshooting mode — level one:

```
sqltext="SELECT * FROM People;"
```

In troubleshooting mode — level two:

```
sqltext="SELECT PeopleNameLast, PeopleNameFirst "
sqltext=sqltext & " FROM People;"
```

In troubleshooting mode — level three. Here I do a bit of changing of the WHERE expression, in order to add in the dates one at a time.

```
sqltext="SELECT PeopleNameLast, PeopleNameFirst "
sqltext=sqltext & " FROM People "
sqltext=sqltext & " WHERE PeopleDOB ="
sqltext=sqltext & "#" & varDOBStart & "#;"
```

In troubleshooting mode — level four. Since all of the above constructs worked, we can be sure that it has to be in the last bit, and sure enough the following code fails. I've accidentally typed an apostrophe before the last # sign.

```
sqltext="SELECT PeopleNameLast, PeopleNameFirst "
sqltext=sqltext & " FROM People "
sqltext=sqltext & " WHERE PeopleDOB BETWEEN"
sqltext=sqltext & "#" & varDOBStart
sqltext=sqltext & "# AND #" & varDOBEnd & "'#;"
```

The last line of the SQL builder, after fixing the problem, is as shown:

```
sqltext=sqltext & "# AND #" & varDOBEnd & "#;"
```

# Hard Code the Variable Information

To review, if we are getting data from a form and then using it in SQL, there are four basic steps where we could fail:

- ❑ Gathering the information on the form
- ❑ Stuffing data from the form into the variable
- ❑ Building the SQL
- ❑ Executing the SQL

When I am called to a student's PC and the problem is not obvious, I first like to divide the problem in half. I hard code the variable into the SQL, then we are just testing the SQL statement structure and the Rs.Open. If that works, then we know that the failure must be upstream, where we gather data or stuff the data from the request into the variable.

Before troubleshooting:

```
VarNameLast=Request.Querystring("NameLast")
sSQL=SELECT * FROM People WHERE PeopleNameLast='" & varNameLast & "';"
Rs.Open sSQL, "DSN=Sailors"
```

In troubleshooting mode, with variables hard coded, we can identify whether the problem is with the form and stuffing variables, or whether it is later on in the SQL statement and Rs.Open.

```
' rem this line VarNameLast=Request.Querystring("NameLast")
sSQL=SELECT * FROM People WHERE PeopleNameLast='Bertrand';"
Rs.Open sSQL, "DSN=Sailors"
```

# Is there Data to be Returned?

More than once I have been asked to help a student whose code did not return data. I sweated over that code and came to the conclusion that it must work, only to find out that the student did not have data in the database yet, or no data matched what we were seeking. For example, one time a student failed at trying to list all the people born in 1946. I worked on it for five minutes, then ten, even got to pulling on my beard and scratching my bald spot for all I was worth. But I never could get the data to show up. I sure felt like a fool when I finally looked at the data and noticed that none of the records had a birth date of 1946.

If you can use other database management software on your datastore, such as Access or the MS SQL Server interface, you can Response.Write the SQL statement to your page, copy it off the browser page and run the same statement in an Access query. If no data is returned, then either the SQL statement contains a logical error, or there is no data matching that SQL statement.

If you don't get an error message, then SQL probably did what it was told to do. If the result is not what you expect, you should be looking hard at what it is that you do expect. For example, you may write a SQL statement that orders a recordset by last name, and then you check it with a print of the first record's last name. You will frequently get nothing on the page, because if there is one record with nothing in the last name field, that will show up first in the ordering. When you print the last name of the first record you will be printing nothing, even though the SQL worked perfectly.

The troubleshooting technique to deploy here is to check the data as directly as possible. I try (when I remember) to start by identifying a record by eye in the table, perhaps even printing some or all of its data. I then go back to my VBScript page and try to bring out that specific record.

A second technique is to look at your data in more than one way. Instead of printing just the first record's last name, try printing the first five records or several fields of the first record. Also, try printing a field that you know for sure must have data – in other words the primary key.

## Low Tech Solutions

An astute colleague added two suggestions of a completely different nature. First is to walk away from the page for a few minutes. Stretch your muscles, get a drink, go breathe some fresh air. It's amazing how many problems become easily solvable while you are out taking a break. He also mentioned that when stymied, you can show the code to a colleague for another opinion.

# Summary

SQL is a near-universal method of giving instructions to relational databases. This chapter covered SQL statements that read data from a database. We specify which fields we want to use immediately after the keyword SELECT. The next clause contains the keyword FROM and a source (usually a table). Sorting is performed with the next keyword, ORDER BY. We can work with a limited set of records by using the WHERE clause.

Building SQL statements in VBScript is an art because of a fundamental conflict. We must meet the SQL rules but not violate the VBScript rules. SQL requires particular characters to encapsulate text (quotes) and dates (# sign). When concatenating a SQL string, it is important to use single quotes around the text for SQL, and double quotes to indicate to VBScript the beginning and end of strings.

Troubleshooting VBScript that generates SQL statements requires practice, but several techniques can help. Preventing execution of some code and substituting simpler structures will help to point to the trouble. Lastly, be sure that the code, even if written perfectly, will return the result you expect.

# Exercises

These exercises all use the Clothier database discussed in Appendix B.

1. Create a page that lists the vendors in alphabetical order.

2. Create a page that lists all of the items from vendor number 4.

3. Create a page that lists all of the items from vendor number 4, listed in order of release date.

4. Create a page that lists only items that are under $25 each, ordered from the most expensive items down to the least expensive.

5. Create a form and response, so that the response lists all of the clothing items that are supplied by a given vendor number. The vendor number will be entered by the user in the form page.

6. Create a form page that asks the user for a price, then a response page that lists the items that are within ten dollars (above or below) of that price. List the items from most expensive to least expensive.

7. Create a form that asks for a date, then a response page that lists the items released before that date. Order the list by vendor number, from 4 down to 1 and, within vendor, alphabetically by item name.

# Exercises Answers

The code for the first four exercises can be found in `2726-04-SQLForRS-Exercise1-4.asp`.

**1.** Create a page that lists the vendors in alphabetical order.

```
<HTML>
<HEAD>
<TITLE>Chapter 04 SQL for Recordsets Exercises 1 to 4</TITLE>
</HEAD>
<BODY>
<H2>Chapter Four - SQL for Simple Recordsets - Exercises 1 to 4</H2>
<FONT COLOR="#0000FF" SIZE="3"><B><I>
<P>Create page that lists the vendors in alphabetical order</I></B></FONT> </P>
<%
  Dim oRSv
  Set oRSv = Server.CreateObject("ADODB.Recordset")
  sqlText="SELECT * FROM Vendors ORDER BY VendorName;"
  oRSv.Open sqltext, "DSN=Clothier"
  Do While NOT oRSv.EOF
    Response.Write oRSv("VendorName") & "<BR>"
    oRSv.MoveNext
  Loop
  oRSv.Close
  Set oRSv = nothing
%>
</BODY>
</HTML>
```

**2.** Create a page that lists all of the items from vendor number 4.

```
<HTML>
<HEAD>
<TITLE>Chapter 04 SQL for Recordsets Exercises 1 to 4</TITLE>
</HEAD>
<BODY>
<H2>Chapter Four - SQL for Simple Recordsets - Exercises 1 to 4</H2>
<FONT COLOR="#0000FF" SIZE="3"><B><I>
<P>Create a page that lists all of the items FROM vendor number
4</B></I></FONT></P><BR>
<%
  Dim oRSi1
  Set oRSi1 = Server.CreateObject("ADODB.Recordset")
  sqlText="SELECT ItemName, ItemVendor FROM Items WHERE ItemVendor=4;"
  oRSi1.Open sqltext, "DSN=Clothier"
  Do While NOT oRSi1.EOF
    Response.Write oRSi1("ItemName") & " (vendor number " & oRSi1("ItemVendor") & _
        ")<BR>"
    oRSi1.MoveNext
  Loop
  oRSi1.Close
  Set oRSi1 = Nothing
%>
</BODY>
</HTML>
```

**3.** Create a page that lists all of the items from vendor number 4, listed in order of release date.

```
<HTML>
<HEAD>
<TITLE>Chapter 04 SQL for Recordsets Exercises 1 to 4</TITLE>
</HEAD>
<BODY>
<H2>Chapter Four - SQL for Simple Recordsets - Exercises 1 to 4</H2>
<FONT COLOR="#0000FF" SIZE="3"><B><I>
<P>Create a page that lists all of the items FROM vendor number 4 listed in order of
 release date.</B></I></FONT></P><BR>
<%
  Dim oRSi4
  Set oRSi4 = Server.CreateObject("ADODB.Recordset")
  sqlText="SELECT * FROM Items "
  sqlText=sqlText & " WHERE ItemVendor=4 "
  sqlText=sqlText & " ORDER BY ItemDateRelease;"
  oRSi4.Open sqltext, "DSN=Clothier"
  Do While NOT oRSi4.EOF
    Response.Write oRSi4("ItemName") & " (vendor number " & oRSi4("ItemVendor") & ") "
    Response.Write " for release on " & oRSi4("ItemDateRelease") & "<BR>"
    oRSi4.MoveNext
  Loop
  oRSi4.Close
  Set oRSi4= Nothing
%>
</BODY>
</HTML>
```

**4.** Create a page that lists only items that are under $25 each, ordered from the $25 items down to the least expensive.

```
<HTML>
<HEAD> .
<TITLE>Chapter 04 SQL for Recordsets Exercises 1 to 4</TITLE>
</HEAD>
<BODY>
<H2>Chapter Four - SQL for Simple Recordsets - Exercises 1 to 4</H2>
<FONT COLOR="#0000FF" SIZE="3"><B><I>
<P>Create a page that lists only items that are under$25 each, ordered FROM the
 $25 items down to the least expensive</B></I></FONT></P><BR>
<%
  Dim oRS25
  Set oRS25 = Server.CreateObject("ADODB.Recordset")
  sqlText="SELECT ItemName, ItemPriceBuy FROM Items "
  sqlText=sqlText & " WHERE ItemPriceBuy<25"
  sqlText=sqlText & " ORDER BY ItemPriceBuy DESC;"
  oRS25.Open sqltext, "DSN=Clothier"
  Do While NOT oRS25.EOF
    Response.Write oRS25("ItemName") & " priced at $" & oRS25("ItemPriceBuy") & "<BR>"
    oRS25.MoveNext
  Loop
  oRS25.Close
  Set oRS25= Nothing
%>
</BODY>
</HTML>
```

**5.** Create a form and response so the response lists all of the clothing items that are supplied by a given vendor number. The vendor number will be entered by the user in the form page. The code is given in `2726-04-SQLForRS-Exercise5Form.asp`:

```
<HTML>
<HEAD>
<TITLE>Chapter 04 SQL for Recordsets Exercise 5 Form</TITLE>
</HEAD>
<BODY>
<H2>Chapter Four - SQL for Simple Recordsets - Exercise 5 - Form</H2>
<FONT COLOR="#0000FF" SIZE="3"><B><I>
<P>Create a form and response so the response lists all of the clothing items that are
supplied by a given vendor number. The vendor number will be entered by the user in
the form page.</I></B></FONT></P>
<FORM METHOD="post" ACTION="2726-04-SQLForRS-Exercise5Response.asp">
<P>Please enter the Number of the Vendor<BR>
(Vendor numbers are 1 to 4 inclusive)</P>
<P><INPUT TYPE="text" NAME="VendorNumber" SIZE="6"></P>
<P><INPUT TYPE="submit" VALUE="Submit" NAME="B1">
<INPUT TYPE="reset" VALUE="Reset" NAME="B2"></P>
</FORM>
</BODY>
</HTML>
```

and `2726-04-SQLForRS-Exercise5Response.asp`:

```
<HTML>
<HEAD>
<TITLE>Chapter 04 SQL for Recordsets Exercises 1 to 4</TITLE>
</HEAD>
<BODY>
<H2>Chapter Four - SQL for Simple Recordsets - Exercise 5 - Response</H2>
<B><I><FONT COLOR="#0000FF" SIZE="3"><B><I>
<P>Create a form and response so the response lists all of the clothing items that are
supplied by a given vendor number. The vendor number will be entered by the user in
the form page.</I></B></FONT></P>
<%
  'this is the response page
  varVendorNum = Request.Form("VendorNumber")
  Dim oRSiv
  Set oRSiv = Server.CreateObject("ADODB.Recordset")
  sqlText="SELECT * FROM Items "
  sqlText=sqlText & "WHERE ItemVendor=" & varVendorNum & ";"
  oRSiv.Open sqlText, "DSN=Clothier"
  Do While NOT oRSiv.EOF
    Response.Write oRSiv("ItemName") & "<BR>"
    oRSiv.MoveNext
  Loop
  oRSiv.Close
  Set oRSiv= Nothing
%>
</BODY>
</HTML>
```

**6.** Create a form page that asks the user for a price, then a response page that lists the items that are within ten dollars (above or below) of that price. List the items from most expensive to least expensive. The code below can also be found in `2726-04-SQLForRS-Exercise6Form.asp`:

```
<HTML>
<HEAD>
<TITLE>Chapter 04 SQL for Recordsets Exercise 6 Form</TITLE>
</HEAD>
<BODY>
<H2>Chapter Four - SQL for Simple Recordsets - Exercise 6 - Form</H2>
<FONT COLOR="#0000FF" SIZE="3"><B><I>
<P>Create a form page that asks the user for a price, then a response page that lists
the items that are within ten dollars (above or below) of that price. List the items
from most expensive to least expensive.</I></B></FONT></P>
<FORM METHOD="post" ACTION="2726-04-SQLForRS-Exercise6Response.asp">
<P>Please enter your target price<BR>
(good  numbers are 20 to 40 inclusive)</P>
<P><INPUT TYPE="text" NAME="PriceTarget" SIZE="6"></P>
<P><INPUT TYPE="submit" VALUE="Submit" NAME="B1">
<INPUT TYPE="reset" VALUE="Reset" NAME="B2"></P>
</FORM>
</BODY>
</HTML>
```

and the following code is in `2726-04-SQLForRS-Exercise6Response.asp`:

```
<HTML>
<HEAD>
<TITLE>Chapter 04 SQL for Recordsets Exercise 6 response</TITLE>
</HEAD>
<BODY>
<H2>Chapter Four - SQL for Simple Recordsets - Exercise 6 - Response</H2>
<FONT COLOR="#0000FF" SIZE="3"><B><I>
<P>Create a form page that asks the user for a price, then a response page that lists
the items that are within ten dollars (above or below) of that price. List the items
from most expensive to least expensive.</I></B></FONT></P>
<P><BR>
<%
  'this is the response page
  'this can be done in less lines of code
  'but this way is easier to read
  varPriceTarget = Request.Form("PriceTarget")
  varPriceHigh = varPriceTarget + 10
  varPriceLow = varPriceTarget - 10
  Response.Write "Your target price is $" & varPriceTarget & ", which means "
  Response.Write "an acceptable price range FROM $" & varPriceLow
  Response.Write " to $" & varPriceHigh & ".<BR><BR>"
  Dim oRSiv
  Set oRSiv = Server.CreateObject("ADODB.Recordset")
  sqlText="SELECT ItemName, ItemPriceBuy FROM Items "
  sqlText=sqlText & " WHERE ItemPriceBuy BETWEEN "
  sqlText=sqlText & varPriceLow & " AND " & varPriceHigh
  sqlText=sqlText & " ORDER BY itemPriceBuy DESC;"
  'Response.Write sqltext
  oRSiv.Open sqltext, "DSN=Clothier"
  Do While NOT oRSiv.EOF
    Response.Write oRSiv("ItemName") & " priced at $" & oRSiv("ItemPriceBuy") & "<BR>"
    oRSiv.MoveNext
  Loop
```

```
  oRSiv.Close
  Set oRSiv= Nothing
%>
</P>
</BODY>
</HTML>
```

**7.** Create a form that asks for a date, then a response page that lists the items released before that date. Order the list by vendor number, from 4 down to 1, and within vendor number, alphabetically by item name. The form page code is in `2726-04-SQLForRS-Exercise7Form.asp`:

```
<HTML>
<HEAD>
<TITLE>Chapter 04 SQL for Recordsets Exercise 7 Form</TITLE>
</HEAD>
<BODY>
<H2>Chapter Four - SQL for Simple Recordsets - Exercise 7 - Form</H2>
<FONT COLOR="#0000FF" SIZE="3"><B><I>
<P>Create a form that asks for a date, then a response page that lists the items
released before that date. Order the list by vendor number from 4 down to 1 and within
vendor number alphabetically by item name.</I></B></FONT></P>
<FORM METHOD="POST" ACTION="2726-04-SQLForRS-Exercise7Response.asp">
<P>Please enter the release date of interest<BR>
(good dates to try are 01/01/99 to 12/31/99 inclusive)</P>
<P><INPUT TYPE="text" NAME="DateLast" SIZE="10"></P>
<P><INPUT TYPE="submit" VALUE="Submit" NAME="B1">
<INPUT TYPE="reset" VALUE="Reset" NAME="B2"></P>
</FORM>
</BODY>
</HTML>
```

and code for the response page is in `2726-04-SQLForRS-Exercise7Response.asp`:

```
<HTML>
<HEAD>
<TITLE>Chapter 04 SQL for Recordsets Exercise 7 Response</TITLE>
</HEAD>
<BODY>
<H2>Chapter Four - SQL for Simple Recordsets - Exercise 7 - Response</H2>
<FONT COLOR="#0000FF" SIZE="3"><B><I>
<P>Create a form that asks for a date, then a response page that lists the items
released before that date. Order the list by vendor number from 4 down to 1 and within
vendor number alphabetically by item name.</I></B></FONT></P>
<P><BR>
<%
  'this is the response page
  varDateLast = Request.Form("DateLast")
  Dim oRSiv
  Set oRSiv = Server.CreateObject("ADODB.Recordset")
  sqlText="SELECT ItemName, ItemDateRelease, ItemPriceBuy, ItemVendor FROM Items "
  sqlText=sqlText & " WHERE ItemDateRelease<#" & varDateLast & "# "
  sqlText=sqlText & " ORDER BY itemVendor DESC, ItemName;"
  'Response.Write sqltext
  oRSiv.Open sqltext, "DSN=Clothier"
  Do While NOT oRSiv.EOF
     Response.Write oRSiv("ItemName")' & " priced at $" & oRSiv("ItemPriceBuy")
     Response.Write " FROM vendor #" & oRSiv("ItemVendor")
     Response.Write " for release on " & oRSiv("ItemDateRelease") & "<BR>"
     oRSiv.MoveNext
```

```
   Loop
   oRSiv.Close
   Set oRSiv= Nothing
%>
</P>
</BODY>
</HTML>
```

# Quiz

1. My SQL returns the fields that I want and orders the records correctly. But I'm getting all of the records. I want only some of the records. How should I change the SQL?

2. What is wrong with the following SQL statement applied to the Sailors database?

```
SELECT PeopleNameFirst PeopleNameLast FROM People ORDER BY PeopleDOB;
```

3. How can you change data with a SQL SELECT command?

4. What does the asterisk do in the following SQL statement?

```
SELECT * FROM People WHERE PeopleNameLast = 'canner';
```

5. What is the error in the following SQL statement?

```
SELECT * FROM People WHERE PeopleNameFirst = John;
```

6. What is the error in the following SQL statement?

```
SELECT * FROM People WHERE ItemPrice <#25.00#;
```

7. What keyword must always be used with the keyword BETWEEN?

8. Explain the purpose of each of the last six characters of this line of code:

```
Sqltext = "SELECT * FROM People WHERE PeopleNameFirst = '" & varNameFirst & "';"
```

9. What is the error in the following code?

```
SqlText = "SELECT PeopleNameLast, PeopleNameFirst"
SqlText = SqlText & "FROM People ORDER BY PeopleNameLast;"
```

10. What is a JOIN query?

# Quiz Answers

**1.** Add a WHERE clause.

**2.** Lacks commas between fields. Should be:

```
SELECT PeopleNameFirst, PeopleNameLast FROM People ORDER BY PeopleDOB;
```

**3.** With SQL alone, you cannot, because SELECT is only for reading data. However, in later chapters we will learn non-SQL (ADO recordset) methods to change data. We will also cover, in Chapter 10, how to modify data using SQL commands other than SELECT.

**4.** Indicates that you want all of the fields from the People table.

**5.** Text values, such as John, need to be surrounded by single quotes, otherwise the SQL server will think that John is a field name and will not be able to find it. The following line is correct:

```
SELECT * FROM People WHERE PeopleNameFirst = 'John';
```

**6.** Numeric values should be naked. The # sign is for dates. Should be:

```
SELECT * FROM People WHERE ItemPrice <25.00;
```

**7.** AND, for example: WHERE ItemPrice BETWEEN 25 AND 20;

**8.**

| | |
|---|---|
| & | tells VBScript there is another string to concatenate |
| (space) | makes code easier to read |
| " | indicates to VBScript the beginning of the literal text to be concatenated |
| ' | a literal character that will form the ending of the string containing the first name |
| ; | a literal character that indicates to SQL the end of the SQL statement |
| " | indicates to VBScript the end of the literal string holding the single quote and the semicolon |

**9.** When the two lines are concatenated you will have a missing space before FROM as follows

```
SELECT PeopleNameLast, PeopleNameFirstFROM People ORDER BY PeopleNameLast;
```

To correct the problem add a space after `First` at the end of line one or before `FROM` at the beginning of line two. You can add both to be sure, as follows:

```
SqlTExt = "SELECT PeopleNameLast, PeopleNameFirst "
SqlTExt = SqlTExt & " FROM People ORDER BY PeopleNameLast;"
```

**10.** A `JOIN` query takes fields from two or more tables and combines them into a single table.

Welcome to the Microsoft D...

Setup cannot install system files or update shared files if the files are in use. Before c...
any open applications.

Exit Setup

Continue

te New Data Source

Select a driver for which you want to set up a data sourc...

| Name | Version | |
|---|---|---|
| Microsoft Access Driver (*.mdb) | 4.00.4207.00 | |
| Microsoft dBase Driver (*.dbf) | 4.00.4207.00 | |
| Microsoft dBase VFP Driver (*.dbf) | 6.01.8440.01 | |
| Microsoft Excel Driver (*.xls) | 4.00.4207.00 | |
| Microsoft FoxPro VFP Driver (*.dbf) | 6.01.8440.01 | |
| Microsoft ODBC for Oracle | 2.573.4207.00 | |
| Microsoft Paradox Driver (*.db ) | 4.00.4207.00 | |
| Microsoft Text Driver (*.txt; *.csv) | 4.00.4207.00 | |
| Microsoft Visual FoxPro Driver | 6.01.8440.01 | |
| SQL Server | 2.70.06.90 | |

Finish

Cancel

# More Uses for Simple Recordsets

## Introduction

There are many business problems that can be solved with nothing more than a simple recordset. In the last chapter we created half a dozen recordsets, and used them to get data for trivial ASP pages. Prior to going on to learn about more complicated recordsets, I want to demonstrate applying the basic techniques to some more useful business applications. This chapter will lead you through creating pages that you can show to your boss, and will allow you to already justify the cost of the book.

For this chapter, I will define a simple recordset as one that uses no more then the syntax introduced in Chapters 3 and 4, in other words it uses:

- ❏ no explicitly defined connection or command objects (these will covered in later chapters)
- ❏ only the first two recordset Open parameters (source and connection)
- ❏ only SQL SELECT statements

Therefore, with these constraints, there are some limitations to consider for this chapter:

- ❏ Simple recordsets are inefficient if you are using more than two recordsets on a page, and they are all hitting the same database.
- ❏ The recordset will only go through the records in the forward direction.
- ❏ Once you have gone through the records from first to last, you can only go through them again if you first reset the pointer to the beginning of the recordset, by using MoveFirst. You can go through as many times as you want, but you must reset before each trip.
- ❏ You cannot pass parameters to queries.
- ❏ You cannot edit, add to, or delete data.

Once you've read the whole book, these constraints will not apply, but let's keep it simple for the time being.

In this chapter we'll be looking at:

❑ filling list boxes

❑ obtaining the field names from an unfamiliar database

❑ different methods for creating tables

# Filling a List Box

One of the most common requests from students is how to fill a list box of an HTML form with records from a database. For example, we can ask the viewer to select one class of boat for which she wants information. The list of classes is ever changing, but is always available from the BoatClass table of the Sailors database.

To perform this task you must clearly understand the HTML tags for list boxes. The following code shows how to set a list box in HTML without using ASP or ADO.

```
<FORM METHOD="Get" ACTION="ClassRegisterResponse.asp">
<SELECT NAME="lstClasses" SIZE="1">
<OPTION SELECTED VALUE="Laser">Laser</OPTION>
<OPTION VALUE="FlyingScot">FlyingScot</OPTION>
<OPTION VALUE="Soling">Soling</OPTION>
</SELECT>
<P><INPUT TYPE="submit"> </P>
</FORM>
```

In the first line, we have the normal HTML form code; either the Post or Get method is fine, and remember to name your response page with a .asp extension if it will contain script.

Within the form there may be tags such as INPUT TYPE = text or INPUT TYPE = checkbox, but in this case we want to set up the list box with the <SELECT> and </SELECT> tags. Within these tags, we will have one line of code for each item that will be in the list box. These lines of code contain four required parts and one optional part. For example, the required parts:

```
<OPTION VALUE="Soling">Soling</OPTION>
```

The line above starts with the <OPTION> tag, which has one argument, VALUE. This is assigned the piece of data that will be returned when this option is selected. After the value, we have plain text, which is what will appear to the user in the box. The line is finished with the </OPTION> tag. There is an additional attribute, SELECTED, which can be added in the option tag to give a default selection, as in the choice for FlyingScot below:

```
<FORM METHOD="Get" ACTION="ClassRegisterResponse.asp">
<SELECT NAME="lstClasses" SIZE="1">
<OPTION SELECTED VALUE="Laser" >Laser</OPTION>
<OPTION VALUE="FlyingScot" SELECTED >FlyingScot</OPTION>
<OPTION VALUE="Soling" >Soling</OPTION>
</SELECT>
<P><INPUT TYPE="submit"> </P>
</FORM>
```

Remember:

❑ The text is what is shown to the user

❑ The value is what is sent back to the server

❑ The value is assigned its variable name from the NAME attribute of the <SELECT> tag (in this case lstClasses).

The code above, when given the usual HTML headings and endings, produces a list box, hard wired in HTML. The result is as shown:

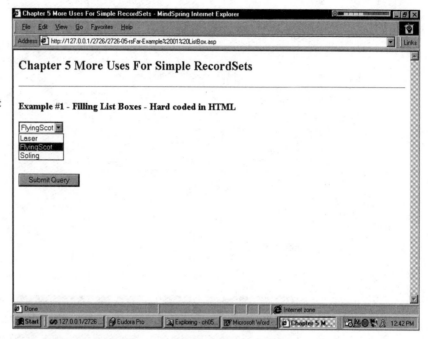

If we selected one class and clicked on submit, even though we have not yet made a response page, we would see on the URL line that the value is returned to the server.

Now, how can we take that HTML form list box syntax, and populate the options from a database rather than using the hard coding method as above? There are two steps: first create the recordset, then read it into the list box, as we'll see in the next example. Keep in mind that the list of classes is held in the ClassName field of the table called BoatClass.

## Try It Out - Boat List Box

Create a page which offers the names of the boat classes in a drop-down list box. For now, we will not program the action page of the form. You can find the code for the example here, in file `2726-05-MoreRS-TIO-01-ListBox boat.asp`:

```
<HTML>
<HEAD>
<TITLE>Chapter 5 More Uses For Simple Recordsets</TITLE>
</HEAD>
<BODY>
<H2>Chapter 5 More Uses For Simple Recordsets</H2>
<P>Try It Out #1 List of Boat Classes</P><BR>
<%
  Dim oRScl
  Set oRScl=Server.CreateObject("ADODB.Recordset")
  oRScl.Open "BoatClass", "DSN=Sailors"
  oRScl.MoveFirst
%>
<FORM METHOD="get" ACTION="ClassRegisterResponse.asp">
<P><SELECT NAME="lstClasses" SIZE="1">
<%
  Do While NOT oRScl.EOF
    Response.Write "<OPTION VALUE='" & oRScl("className") & "'>"
    Response.Write oRScl("className") & "</OPTION>"
    oRScl.MoveNext
  Loop
  oRScl.Close
  Set oRScl=nothing
%>
</SELECT> </P>
<P><INPUT TYPE="submit"> </P>
</FORM>
</BODY>
</HTML>
```

The result should look like this:

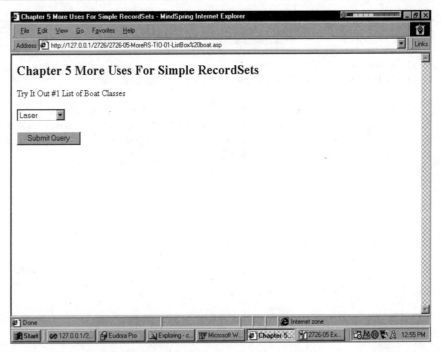

### How It Works: Boat List Box

The first section of VBScript sets up the recordset as we have done many times before. The table of interest to us is called BoatClass and it is in the DSN named Sailors. I'm naming my object oRScl to differentiate it from other recordsets we may set up on the page; the cl reminds me that this recordset is for the class list.

```
<H2>Filling List Boxes - Options from ASP-ADO</H2>
<%
  Dim oRScl
  Set oRScl=Server.CreateObject("ADODB.Recordset")
  oRScl.Open "BoatClass", "DSN=Sailors"
  oRScl.MoveFirst
%>
```

In the following section of code we switch back to HTML, and set up the FORM and SELECT tags.

```
<FORM METHOD="get" ACTION="ClassRegisterResponse.asp">
<P><SELECT NAME="lstClasses" SIZE="1">
```

Now in the code below we put the choices into the list box. We must switch back to VBScript because we want to loop and retrieve data using ADO. There are three Response.Write lines within the loop. The first sets the OPTION tag, and concatenates in the data from ClassName as the value attribute. The punctuation here is a little tricky. Some browsers are fussy about having quotes around values if there is more than one word in the value, but in that case they accept single or double quotes. Single quotes are a lot easier to provide from VBScript, so we include one in the text on either side of the oRScl("ClassName"). The second Response.Write picks up the ClassName again, and uses it for the text that will be shown to the user. The last line writes out the option close tag. As with almost all recordset loops, we include within the loop a line advancing us to the next recordset.

```
<%
  Do While NOT oRScl.EOF
    Response.Write "<OPTION VALUE='" & oRScl("ClassName") & "'>"
    Response.Write oRScl("ClassName")
    Response.Write "</OPTION>"
    oRScl.MoveNext
  Loop
```

To improve server performance we want to close any recordsets and objects that are no longer used, as in the following lines:

```
  oRScl.Close
  Set oRScl=nothing
%>
```

Now that we are done looping through the list box choices, we can leave ASP for the simpler HTML, to close up the list box and the form:

```
</SELECT></P>
<P><INPUT TYPE="submit"> </P>
</FORM>
```

Some common errors that you need to look out for when populating list boxes are:

- Can't see the errors that are generated when filling the list box, so you must look at the source code from the browser (usually View | Source)
- Forgetting the .MoveNext
- Forgetting the oRScl before the EOF

# Fields Collection

So far in this book, we have enjoyed the luxury of having the database structure available for our inspection. It isn't always that way in the real world. Sometimes you will be expected to write VBScript to hit a database for which you know the DSN and table name but not the field names. Perhaps you get an error as follows:

ADODB.Recordset error '800a0cc1'    Item not found in this collection.

This indicates that the name of the field is actually different from what you thought.

ADO offers the fields collection for you to get a list of the fields directly from the database. To use the fields collection, you first open the recordset, then refer to objRS.Fields. Specifically, you refer to a given field as ObjRS.Fields("FieldName"). Of course, we are trying to solve the problem of unknown names, so there is an alternative reference, which is ObjRS.Fields (#). In other words, you can refer to fields in a generic manner, as field 0, field 1, etc.

In addition, ADO provides a means to quickly get a count of the number of fields in a recordset, by using:

```
VarNumber = ObjRS.Fields.Count
```

## Try It Out - Fields

Create a page that will provide the fields of the `People` table of the Sailors database. The result should look like the following:

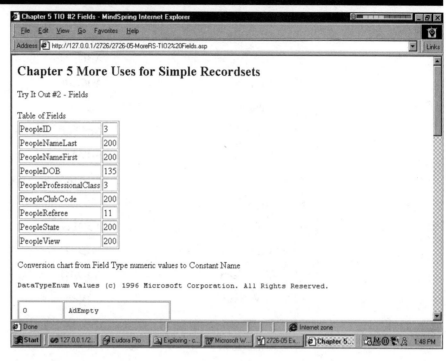

The above screen is produced by the code below, which is available in file `2726-05-TI02 Fields.asp`:

```
<HTML>
<HEAD>
<TITLE>Chapter 5 TIO #2 Fields</TITLE>
</HEAD>
<BODY>
<H2>Chapter 5 More Uses for Simple Recordsets</H2>
<P>Try It Out #2 - Fields</P>
<%
  Set rs=Server.CreateObject("ADODB.Recordset")
  rs.Open "people", "DSN=Sailors"
  Response.Write "<TABLE BORDER=1> Table of Fields"
  For Each ofield in rs.Fields
    Response.Write "<TR><TD>" & ofield.name & "</TD>"
    Response.Write "<TD>" & ofield.type & "</TD></TR>"
  Next
  Response.Write "</TABLE>"
%>
</BODY>
</HTML>
```

**165**

Moreover, if you download this file from the Wrox site you get a simple table that translates constants for field data types, as below.

| 0 | AdEmpty | 20 | AdBigInt |
|---|---|---|---|
| 2 | AdSmallInt | 21 | AdUnsignedBigInt |
| 3 | AdInteger | 72 | AdGUID |
| 4 | AdSingle | 128 | AdBinary |
| 5 | AdDouble | 129 | AdChar |
| 6 | AdCurrency | 130 | AdWChar |
| 7 | AdDate | 131 | AdNumeric |
| 8 | AdBSTR | 132 | AdUserDefined |
| 9 | AdIDispatch | 133 | AdDBDate |
| 10 | AdError | 134 | AdDBTime |
| 11 | AdBoolean | 135 | AdDBTimeStamp |
| 12 | AdVariant | 200 | AdVarChar |
| 13 | AdIUnknown | 201 | AdLongVarChar |
| 14 | AdDecimal | 202 | AdVarWChar |
| 16 | AdTinyInt | 203 | AdLongVarWChar |
| 17 | AdUnsignedTinyInt | 204 | AdVarBinary |
| 18 | AdUnsignedSmallInt | 205 | AdLongVarBinary |
| 19 | AdUnsignedInt | | |

### How It Works: Fields

After creating the recordset, we establish a For...Each loop through the fields collection of a recordset made from the People table. Note that in the Response.Write lines we must use the same reference to the fields (ofield) as we made in the counter variable of the For...Each line.

```
For Each ofield in rs.Fields
  Response.Write "<TR><TD>" & ofield.name & "</TD>"
  Response.Write "<TD>" & ofield.type & "</TD></TR>"
Next
%>
```

# Making a Table Procedure

In the last example, we used the fields collection to elucidate the field names. But even if we know the names, we may be interested in using them without having to type them all into the page, for example in the heading row of a table. In fact, it would be nice not to have to type anything to make a table. We would like to write a table procedure once, which could then be used every time we needed to build a table on the page.

In the following code we create a procedure, which has two arguments:

- ❑ A source string such as a table name or a SQL statement
- ❑ A DSN name

With that data, the procedure builds the table. And once we have the procedure working, you can cut and paste it into any other page. Even easier, you can do an HTML include.

Build a procedure that produces a table, and then test it with several tables. The result of running our code is shown below:

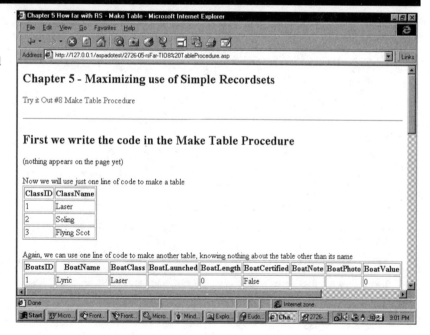

**167**

The code which produces this page can be found in `2726-05-MoreRs-TIO-03-TableProcedure.asp`:

```
<HTML>
<HEAD>
<TITLE>Chapter 5 MoreRS TIO 03 Table Procedure</TITLE>
</HEAD>
<BODY>
<H2>Chapter 5 - More Uses for Simple Recordsets</H2>
<H3>Try it Out #3 Make Table Procedure</H3>
<BR>
<H3>First we write the code in the Make Table Procedure</H3>
<P>(nothing appears on the page yet)
<%
  'Procedure to create a table
  Sub MakeTable(SourceIn,dsnIn)
    Dim oRSmt
    Set oRSmt=Server.CreateObject("ADODB.Recordset")
    oRSmt.Open SourceIn, "DSN=" & dsnIn
    oRSmt.MoveFirst
    Response.Write "<TABLE BORDER=1><TR>"
    For Each Field in oRSmt.Fields
      Response.Write "<TH>" & Field.name & "</TH>"
    Next
    'Response.End
    Do While NOT oRSmt.EOF
      Response.Write "<TR>"
      For each objField in oRSmt.fields
        Response.Write "<TD>" & objField.value & " </TD>"
      Next
      oRSmt.MoveNext
      Response.Write "</TR>"
    Loop
    Response.Write "</TABLE>"
    oRSmt.Close
    Set oRSmt=nothing
  End Sub
%>
</P>
<H3>Now we will use just one line of code to make a table</H3>
<%call MakeTable("BoatClass;","sailors")%></P>

<H3>Again, we can use one line of code to make another table, knowing nothing about
the table other than its name</H3>

<%call MakeTable("Boats;","sailors")%></P>

<H3>If we know something about the fields we can make a table based on a SQL
statement, with just one line of code</H3>

<%call MakeTable("SELECT * FROM People WHERE PeopleID=5;","sailors")%></P>

<H3>If we change the number of fields we collect in the SQL, the table maker adjusts
the number of columns automatically</H3>

<%call MakeTable("SELECT PeopleNameFirst, PeopleNameLast FROM
  People;","sailors")%></P>

</BODY>
</HTML>
```

### *How It Works: Table Procedure*

First, we must write the procedure. Keep in mind that these lines will not be run until they are called by later code. The procedure includes all lines between `Sub...` and `End Sub`. Also, as we review sub procedures, recall from your study so far of ASP, that words placed in parentheses after the sub name will become arguments or parameters holding data, which is passed into the sub when it is called.

We start by creating the recordset. Normally in the `rs.Open` method we provide two arguments, the source and the DSN. In this case, we don't want to hard code these arguments; rather we will get them passed as arguments from the code that calls the procedure. `SourceIn` could hold a table name like `People`, or a SQL statement like `SELECT PeopleNameLast FROM People WHERE PeopleID=5`. Regardless of its shape, it is placed into the `rs.Open` line. Likewise with the DSN, but in this case we must place the characters `DSN=` in front of it.

```
<%
  'Procedure to create a table
  Sub MakeTable(SourceIn,dsnIn)
    Dim oRSmt
    Set oRSmt=Server.CreateObject("ADODB.Recordset")
    oRSmt.Open SourceIn, "DSN=" & dsnIn
```

Now we move to the first record and start to create the table:

```
    oRSmt.MoveFirst
    Response.Write "<TABLE BORDER=1><TR>"
```

To make our table more useful we will put the field names in the first row to make headers. However, at design time we have no idea about the field names or the quantity of fields. Remember, we are writing this code to work with any table or DSN, so instead of hard coding the file names we use the `For Each...Next` construct to go through each field in the record set. Note that this does not go through each field in the table, only those that were returned in the `rs.Open`. Therefore, if our source only returned two fields, we will only go through two fields here. By the way, `<TH>` and `</TH>` tell the browser to treat this cell as a header cell, which usually means bold typeface.

```
    For Each Field in oRSmt.Fields
      Response.Write "<TH>" & Field.name & "</TH>"
    Next
```

Now that the header row is set up we can add the data rows. You already have experience with looping through the records. The `Do... Loop` was so useful because we did not have to know how many records there were in the recordset, as VBScript would just keep going until it hit the `rs.EOF` condition.

Now, we also need to loop through the fields, to build and fill the cells with data, going across the row. But this time we want to write to the page the *value* of the field for the current record, not the *name* of the field like we did in the header row. We can use a `For Each` loop, because VBScript can step through the fields from the information ADO provides in the recordset.

If you have never constructed a table this way before, it is worth thinking about how the loop-in-a-loop works. The header row is already created, so we just concentrate on the data rows here. The first row starts with the first iteration of the outer (Do While) loop, which puts the row-starting tag <TR> on the page. Then the inner (For Each...Next) loop runs once to make the first cell, then again to make the next cell to the right. The inner loop repeats again and again as it builds cells, going from left to right across the first row, with each cell getting filled by the data from the next field in the list. When VBScript gets to the end of the field list, it stops the inner loop and stops adding cells to the right end of the row. The outer loop finishes its task of ending the row with the </TR> tag, and then starts over for row two. In the end, the *outer* loop will have run once for each data *row*, and the *inner* loop will have run once for each *cell* in the table. Moreover, the beauty of the code is that it works without any hard coded values for the number of rows, the number of fields, or the field names. Keep in mind that we can use any name for the variable that represents the members of the fields collection. I've used objFields but it will work fine with objElvisLivesOnMars, as long as you use the same name in the Response.Write line that puts the value on the page.

```
Do While NOT oRSmt.EOF
   Response.Write "<TR>"
   For Each objField in oRSmt.fields
      Response.Write "<TD>" & objField.value & " </TD>"
   Next
   oRSmt.MoveNext
   Response.Write"</TR>"
Loop
```

Now, let us reap the benefits of our investment in the labor of building this procedure. In the next few lines, we build four tables with only one line of code for each. That line needs only to call the MakeTable procedure, and provide the procedure with two arguments. The first is a table name or SQL statement for a source (which will be stuffed into SourceIn upon receipt). The second is the DSN. I have included notes on the four tables within the code itself.

```
<P>Now we will use just one line of code to make a table<BR>
<%call MakeTable("BoatClass;","sailors")%></P>

<P>Again, we can use one line of code to make another table, knowing nothing about the
table other than its name<BR>
<%call MakeTable("Boats;","sailors")%></P>

<P>If we know something about the fields we can make a table based on a SQL statement,
with just one line of code<BR>
<%call MakeTable("SELECT * FROM People WHERE PeopleID=5;","sailors")%></P>

<P>If we change the number of fields we collect in the SQL, the table maker adjusts
the number of columns automatically<BR>
<%call MakeTable("SELECT PeopleNameFirst, PeopleNameLast FROM
People;","sailors")%></P>
</BODY></HTML>
```

# Writing Tables With the GetString Method

Obviously, many programmers will need to create tables using the data of a recordset. The designers of ADO have expedited this task by creating the `GetString` method of the `Recordset` object. In short, `GetString` mines each piece of data out of the recordset, and then surrounds the data with the HTML tags that you would have typed by hand. It then gives you that whole package of data and tags in a long string, which you can `Response.Write` onto the page. About all you have to do is add the `<TABLE>` tags before and after the string, and you have a complete table.

What does `GetString` need in the way of parameters in order to do this task?

- ❏ A string of tags to put in between the cells (ColumnDelimiter)
- ❏ A string of tags to put after each record to tell the browser to begin a new row (RowDelimiter)
- ❏ A string to put in a cell for which there is missing data

With this information, `GetString` will create an internal string variable and begin putting text into it. It reads into the variable the first field of the first record, and then appends the ColumnDelimiter string to it. `GetString` then picks up the second field of the first record, and appends the cell separator again. When it gets to the last field of the first record, it appends the row separator string and goes through all of the fields of that record. If there is missing data, `GetString` will put the missing data string in between the cell separators.

Let us analyze an example using the most basic syntax, as follows.

```
'Create a recordset called oRS

Response.Write "<TABLE BORDER=1><TR><TD>"
Response.Write oRS.GetString(adClipString, _
   1,"</TD><TD>","</TD></TR><TR><TD>"," ")
Response.Write "</TD></TR></TABLE>"
```

The initial two parameters are throwaways in most cases. The first is a StringFormat code. There is only one available now (`adClipString`) so it is the default, and in fact can be left out. Future versions of ADO will have XML support for this parameter. The second parameter indicates the number of records to include in the output string. You almost always want all of the records of the recordset, so you can leave this at its default (-1) by leaving it blank. If you do leave out the first two parameters, you should keep their comma placeholders as shown in the code below. If you forget, you will know you have made this mistake when you get a type mismatch error, resulting from ADO getting a string instead of the default numerical code for the first parameter.

```
Response.Write oRS.GetString(,,"</TD><TD>","</TD></TR><TR><TD>"," ")
```

The third parameter is the ColumnDelimiter that ADO will add to the string between every pair of field data. For now forget about the first cell. When this column delimiter goes between the second and third cells, we want `GetString` to put in a `</TD>` tag to close the second cell, and then a `<TD>` tag to open the third cell. Note that this is backwards to what you might think.

The fourth parameter, the RowDelimiter, is also reversed from what you might think at first. Furthermore, this string must deal with limiting the last and first cells of each row as well as delimiting the rows themselves. Note that `GetString` does not put a column delimiter and a row delimiter at the end of a row; only the RowDelimiter. We use a string with `</TD>` to close off the last cell of the row.

**171**

Keep in mind that GetString works on the whole recordset and nothing but the recordset. So if you have opened the recordset with a request for all fields, then all fields will appear in the string and be put in the table. There is no opportunity to select or filter once GetString performs its task. Likewise with records: once you have created the recordset, GetString will include all of the records as they are ordered in the recordset. Students also make mistakes on the flip side, thinking that GetString will draw data directly from the table.

The last issue is the pair of command lines that set up the table. A common error is to think that GetString gives you the whole table. Sorry, but you've got to do a bit yourself! GetString places neither a column delimiter nor a row delimiter before the first cell of the table, nor after the last cell. Thus, before writing the GetString, we normally have a line that creates tags for opening a table, starting the first row, opening and initiating the first cell. Likewise we reverse the process at the end, closing the last cell, the last row and finally the table.

### Common Errors when Using GetString

Note these common errors encountered with the GetString method:

- ❑ GetString method by itself without a place to direct its output (e.g. Response.Write)
- ❑ Reversing the tags in the ColumnDelimiter or RowDelimiter – the closing tag goes first
- ❑ Leaving out the <TABLE> tag
- ❑ Leaving out the initial row open and cell open tags
- ❑ Leaving out the final cell close and row close tags
- ❑ Using GetString without creating a recordset
- ❑ Using GetString against a connection or command object rather than a recordset
- ❑ Typo in the strings for parameters
- ❑ Forgetting to put all three of the string parameters in double quotes
- ❑ Leaving out the first two parameters but not leaving in the comma space holders
- ❑ Expectation that GetString will return only some of the fields or rows in the recordset.
- ❑ Expectation that GetString will return all of the records of a source table rather than all of the records of a recordset
- ❑ Expectation that GetString will put a ColumnDelimiter as well as a RowDelimiter after each record

## Try It Out - Tables by GetString

Create a page that uses the `GetString` method to build a table of boats, showing their number, name, and class only. The code can be found in `2726-05-MoreRS-TIO-04-GetStringTable.asp`:

```
<HTML>
<HEAD>
<TITLE>Chapter_05_MoreRS_TIO_4_GetString_Table_of_Three_Columns</TITLE>
</HEAD>
<BODY>
<H2>Chapter 05 More With Recordsets</H2>
<H3>Try It Out #4 GetString Table With 3 Columns</H3>
<%
  Set oRSmt=Server.CreateObject("ADODB.Recordset")
  txtSQL = "SELECT BoatsID, BoatName, BoatClass FROM Boats;"
  oRSmt.Open txtSQL, "DSN=Sailors"
  oRSmt.MoveFirst
  Response.Write "<TABLE BORDER=1><TR><TD>"
  Response.Write oRSmt.GetString(,,"</TD><TD>","</TD></TR><TR><TD>"," ")
  Response.Write "</TD></TR></TABLE>"
  oRSmt.Close
  Set oRSmt=nothing
%>
</BODY>
</HTML>
```

The code produces the screen here.

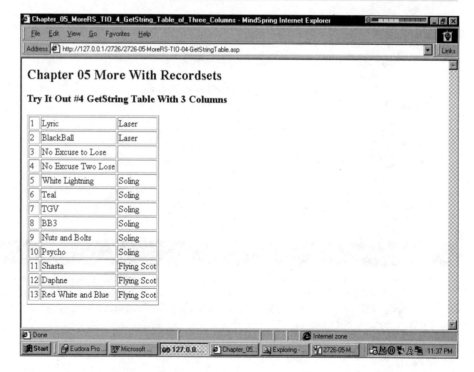

### How It Works: Tables By GetString

We start the core code by opening the recordset. But keep in mind that we cannot select fields to display in the `GetString` method, so we must do that in the SQL statement which opens the recordset, as below:

```
<HTML>
<HEAD>
<TITLE>Chapter_05_MoreRS_TIO_4_GetString_Table_of_Three_Columns</TITLE>
</HEAD>
<BODY>
<H2>Chapter 05 More With Recordsets</H2>
<H3>Try It Out #4 GetString Table With 3 Columns</H3>
<%
  Set oRSmt=Server.CreateObject("ADODB.Recordset")
  txtSQL = "SELECT BoatsID, BoatName, BoatClass FROM Boats;"
  oRSmt.Open txtSQL, "DSN=Sailors"
  oRSmt.MoveFirst
```

Now we write the table, row, and cell tags, which must be done "by hand" since `GetString` does not splice tags before the first cell:

```
  Response.Write "<TABLE BORDER=1><TR><TD>"
```

Next we perform the `GetString`, using the plain vanilla ColumnDelimiters and RowDelimiters, and a non-breaking space for missing data.

```
  Response.Write oRSmt.GetString(,,"</TD><TD>","</TD></TR><TR><TD>"," ")
```

We finish off the table with tags to close the last cell, close the last record's row, and finally the table itself. The page finishes with a clean up of the `Recordset` object:

```
  Response.Write "</TD></TR></TABLE>"
  oRSmt.Close
  Set oRSmt=nothing
%></BODY></HTML>
```

I suggest that you back up your database, then use your database management software (Access, SQL Server, etc.) to delete some of the data from the `BoatsClass` field of the `Boats` table, so you can test the last parameter of your `GetString`.

## Try It Out – Two Improvements

What if we are asked to make two improvements to the page? First, the customer wants the words "-unknown-" to appear if there is missing data. Second, they have asked for all data to be centered in the cells. Both of these requests can be met by changing the ColumnDelimiter and NullExpression strings of the `GetString` parameters, as follows:

```
<HTML>
<HEAD>
<TITLE>Chapter_05_MoreRS_TIO_4_GetString_Table_of_Three_Columns</TITLE>
</HEAD>
<BODY>
<H2>Chapter 05 More With Recordsets</H2>
<H3>Try It Out #4 GetString Table With 3 Columns</H3>
<%
```

```
Set oRSmt=Server.CreateObject("ADODB.Recordset")
txtSQL = "SELECT BoatsID, BoatName, BoatClass FROM Boats;"
oRSmt.Open txtSQL, "DSN=Sailors"
oRSmt.MoveFirst
Response.Write "<TABLE BORDER=1><TR><TD ALIGN=center>"
Response.Write oRSmt.GetString(,,"</TD><TD ALIGN=center>","</TD></TR><TR>",& _
                               "<TD ALIGN=CENTER>" , "-unknown-")
Response.Write "</TD></TR></TABLE>"
oRSmt.Close
Set oRSmt=nothing
%>
</BODY>
</HTML>
```

Note below that `GetString` now adds a `<TD>` tag, with the `ALIGN=center` attribute, to the beginning of each cell. We must also change the tag in the first line below, in order to have the initial cell centered. The missing data is now noted with a different character string, which `GetString` copies from the last parameter of the second line below:

```
Response.Write "<TABLE BORDER=1><TR><TD Align=center>"
Response.Write oRSmt.GetString(,,"</TD><TD Align=center>","</TD></TR><TR><TD>",& _
  = "-unknown-")
```

If you delete `BoatClass` data for the "No Excuse..." boats in the `Boats` table, you will get a screen as follows:

# Summary

In the last three chapters we discussed the basics of creating a recordset using VBScript to control ADO in ASP. To date we have only discussed *displaying* the contents, not editing, adding or deleting. But even with just this one tool, we can apply clever programming and the suite of HTML tags to solve many business objectives. ADO recordsets are perfectly suited for providing the choices of a drop-down list box. We also covered code that would allow you to gather information about a recordset's scheme, such as the field names, for use at design time. Lastly, we turned to two improvements for building tables. The first is a procedure that can be used to build any table from a one-line call in the body of the code. The second way we looked at was to build tables from the very easy but limited method of GetString. In the next few chapters we will go beyond reading data and begin to actually change it.

# Exercises

**1.** Create a procedure that builds tables based on a source and DSN passed to the procedure. But do not display the first field, since that is usually an autonumbered ID field. Try it out on two tables from the Clothier database, *vendors* and *items*, to get a page as follows:

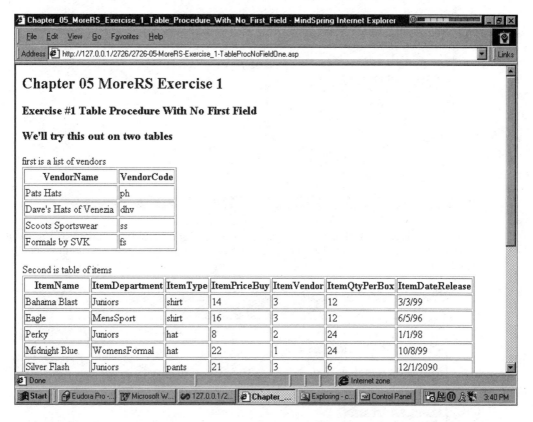

**2.** Your clothier sales staff would like to be able to print to hard copy, from the browser, a page with a table of all the items. They want an extra, empty, column on the left edge of the table, for customers to check off items to order. The page they sketched is similar to the one overleaf.

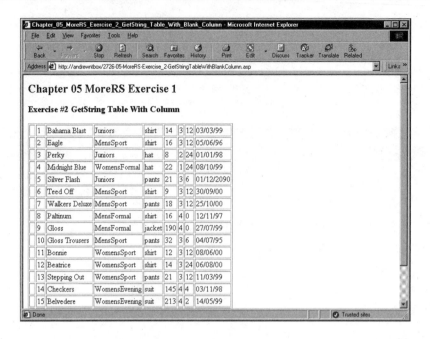

**3.** Build a form page which asks the user to select a vendor from a drop-down list. Then write a response page that lists all the items from that vendor. The form page should look like the following:

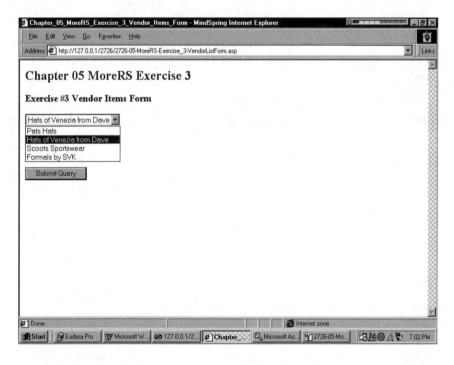

If the user selects **Hats of Venezia** from Dave, the response page should look like the following:

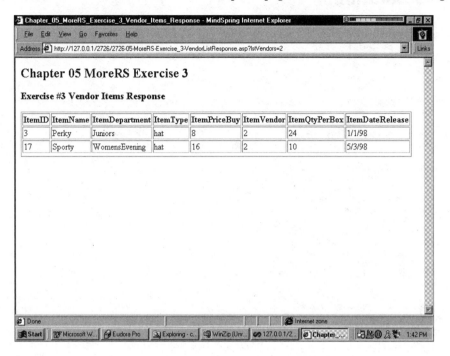

# Exercise Solutions

**1.** The code below can be found in file `2726-05-MoreRS-Exercise_1-TableProcNoFieldOne.asp`:

```
<HTML>
<HEAD>
<TITLE>Chapter_05_MoreRS_Exercise_1_Table_Procedure_With_No_First_Field</TITLE>
</HEAD>
<BODY>
<H2>Chapter 05 MoreRS Exercise 1</H2>
<H3>Exercise #1 Table Procedure With No First Field</H3>
<%
  'Procedure to create a table
  Sub MakeTable(SourceIn,dsnIn)
    Dim oRSmt
    Set oRSmt=Server.CreateObject("ADODB.Recordset")
    oRSmt.Open SourceIn, "DSN=" & dsnIn
    oRSmt.MoveFirst

    Response.Write "<TABLE BORDER=1><TR>"
    ' Create the header row
    For iFieldHeader=1 to oRSmt.Fields.Count-1
      Response.Write "<TH>" & oRSmt.Fields(iFieldHeader).name & "</TH>"
    Next

    ' Create the record rows
    oRSmt.MoveFirst
    Do While NOT oRSmt.EOF
      Response.Write "<TR>"
      For iFieldCounter=1 to oRSmt.Fields.Count-1
        Response.Write "<TD>" & oRSmt.Fields(iFieldCounter).Value & " </TD>"
      Next
      oRSmt.MoveNext
      Response.Write "</TR>"
    Loop
    Response.Write "</TABLE>"
    oRSmt.Close
    Set oRSmt=nothing
  End Sub
%>
<H3>We'll try this out on two tables</H3>
first is a list of vendors
<%call MakeTable("Vendors;","Clothier")%></P>
Second is table of items
<%call MakeTable("Items;","Clothier")%></P>
</BODY>
</HTML>
```

The essence of the solution is in solving how to not show the first field. Remember that we must do that for both the header row and data rows, but the solutions are basically the same, as follows:

```
For iFieldHeader=1 to oRSmt.Fields.Count-1
  Response.Write "<TH>" & oRSmt.Fields(iFieldHeader).name & "</TH>"
Next
```

In the examples and the Try It Outs in this chapter, we wanted to put all the fields of the database table into the HTML page table. But in this exercise we want to leave out one of those. Therefore we cannot use the For Each...Next since that cycles through *all* of the fields. So instead we use a simpler For... Next. But we have to tell VBScript how many loops. The fields are numbered (indexed) in the fields collection starting with the number 0. So we start the loop with our counter (named iFieldHeader) at number 1. The ending is a little trickier since we don't know how many fields are in the collection. We can get that number from oRSmt.Fields.Count. But since the count is one-based, and the indexing is zero-based, we must subtract one from the count to give us the correct number of the last loop.

**2.** The code below can be downloaded as file `2726-05-MoreRS-Exercise_2-GetStringTableWithBlankColumn.asp`:

```
<HTML>
<HEAD>
<TITLE>Chapter_05_MoreRS_Exercise_2_GetString_Table_With_Blank_Column</TITLE>
</HEAD>
<BODY>
<H2>Chapter 05 MoreRS Exercise 1</H2>
<H3>Exercise #2 GetString Table With Column</H3>
<%
   Set oRSmt=Server.CreateObject("ADODB.Recordset")
   oRSmt.Open "items", "DSN=clothier"
   oRSmt.MoveFirst

   Response.Write "<TABLE BORDER=1><TR><TD>  </TD><TD>"
   strRowDivider = "</TD></TR><TR><TD>  </TD><TD>"
   Response.Write oRSmt.GetString(,,"</TD><TD>",strRowDivider," ")
   Response.Write "</TD></TR></TABLE>"
   oRSmt.Close
   Set oRSmt=nothing
%></BODY>
</HTML>
```

The trick here is to get the extra column by adding a full column's worth of tags into each RowDelimiter. Since that string gets rather long, I have set it up in a variable named strRowDivider, which I then plug in as the fourth parameter in the lines below. Note that any modification to rows or columns must also be written into tags, created before the GetString for the start of the first row and first cell, also shown below.

```
   Response.Write "<TABLE BORDER=1><TR><TD>  </TD><TD>"
   strRowDivider = "</TD></TR><TR><TD>  </TD><TD>"
   Response.Write oRSmt.GetString(,,"</TD><TD>",strRowDivider," ")
```

**3.** The code for this exercise is split into two files, first the form page and then the response page.

This form page, in file `2726-05-MoreRS-Exercise_3-VendorListForm.asp`, will pull a recordset from the `Vendors` table:

```
<HTML>
<HEAD>
<TITLE>Chapter_05_MoreRS_Exercise_3_Vendor_Items_Form</TITLE>
</HEAD>
<BODY>
<H2>Chapter 05 MoreRS Exercise 3</H2>
<H3>Exercise #3 Vendor Items Form</H3>
<%
  Dim oRSv
  Set oRSv=Server.CreateObject("ADODB.Recordset")
  oRSv.Open "Vendors", "DSN=clothier"
  oRSv.MoveFirst
%>

<FORM METHOD="get" ACTION="2726-05-MoreRS-Exercise_3-VendorListResponse.asp"><P>
<SELECT NAME="lstVendors" SIZE="1">
<%
  Do While NOT oRSv.EOF
    Response.Write "<OPTION VALUE='" & oRSv("VendorID") & "'>"
    Response.Write oRSv("VendorName") & "</OPTION>"
    oRSv.MoveNext
  Loop
  oRSv.Close
  Set oRSv=nothing
%>
</SELECT></P><BR><BR><BR>
<P><INPUT TYPE="submit"></P>
</FORM>
</BODY>
</HTML>
```

Nothing tricky in the above code, but remember that for the form we want records from the `vendor` table. In the response page we will reap records from the `items` table. Also note that we put the `vendorID` into each option's `VALUE` attribute, since that is what the response will see. We put the vendor's name into the `NAME` attribute so that users can recognize what they are selecting.

The response page uses the `vendorID`, selected in the `WHERE` clause of a `SELECT` statement, against the `items` table, as follows. Code is in file `2726-05-MoreRS-Exercise_3-VendorListResponse.asp`:

```
<HTML>
<HEAD>
<TITLE>Chapter_05_MoreRS_Exercise_3_Vendor_Items_Response</TITLE>
</HEAD>
<BODY>
<H2>Chapter 05 MoreRS Exercise 3</H2>
<H3>Exercise #3 Vendor Items Response</H3>
<%
  Dim vVendor
  vVendor = Request.QueryString("lstVendors")

  Dim oRSi
  Set oRSi=Server.CreateObject("ADODB.Recordset")
  SQLtxt = "SELECT * FROM Items WHERE ItemVendor = " & vVendor & ";"
  oRSi.Open sqltxt, "DSN=clothier"
  oRSi.MoveFirst
```

```
Response.Write "<TABLE BORDER=1><TR>"
  ' Header row
  For Each oHeader in oRSi.Fields
    Response.Write "<TH>" & oHeader.name & "</TH>"
  Next
  Response.Write "</TR><TR><TD>"
  ' Data rows
  Response.Write oRSi.GetString(,,"</TD><TD>","</TD></TR><TR><TD>")
  Response.Write "</TD></TR></TABLE>"
  oRSi.Close
  Set oRSi=nothing
%>
</BODY>
</HTML>
```

In the response page we store the vendorID (not name) in a variable, since that is what is held in a field of the items table (there is no vendor name field in the items table). We set up a header row, then use the Getstring method to fill in the data rows.

# Quiz

**1.** What is the error in the following code?

```
Dim oRSsp
Set oRSsp=Server.CreateObject("ADODB.Recordset")
sqlText = "SELECT * FROM People "
sqlText = sqlText & "WHERE PeopleID=" & varSailorID & ";"
oRSsp.Open "People", "DSN=Sailors"
```

**2.** Which of the following are correct for identifying a field name in a recordset?

Rs.Fields(0)

Rs.Fields"0"

Rs.Fields.0

Rs.Fields("0")

Rs.Fields"*Name*"

Rs.Fields(*Name*)

Rs.Fields("*Name*")

Rs.Fields"(name)"

**3.** What is the problem in the following code?

```
For Each CountFields in oRSmt.Fields
    Response.Write "<TH>" & Field(CountFields).name & "</TH>"
Next
```

# Quiz Answers

**1.** The programmer built a beautiful SQL statement, but then did not use it in the `oRSsp.Open` line. The `oRSsp.Open` will work, but will return all of the records in `People`, rather than the one record matching the `SailorID`, as would happen if the SQL was actually implemented.

**2.** Rs.Fields(0) and Rs.Fields("Name"). In addition, if *Name* was a variable and not an actual field name, then Rs.Fields(Name) would work.

The logic is at two levels. At the higher level, we are presenting an argument to the collection of fields. All arguments, for example:

| | |
|---|---|
| Methods | `Server.CreateObject ("ADODB.Recordset")` |
| Functions | `lCase (string)` |
| Procedures | `call Closer ("John")` |

are encased in parentheses. So, supplying an argument to identify a field in a collection is no different. Whether text or a number, it must go into parentheses.

At the inner level, there is a difference between the field names and field numbers. Field names are literal - that is a string of characters to be processed by matching and filtering. They could be of any combination of characters, and therefore we must clearly delimit the beginning and end for VBScript, by presenting them within quotes. This is the same as passing string data into a SQL statement.

Field numbers, however, represent an identifier, which is intrinsic to ADO. We only have to supply the naked number. In most cases it is better to use the fieldname, since that allows easier maintenance of the code. The time to use numbers is when you are using the statements within a loop, and need to refer to the field by the number of the loop iteration.

**3.** When using `For...Next` or `For Each...Next`, you create your own variable for counting, and `CountFields` would be a good name. But within the loop we must then refer to that variable name. The correct code follows:

```
For Each CountFields in oRSmt.Fields
  Response.Write "<TH>" & CountFields.name & "</TH>"
Next
```

Setup cannot install system files or update shared files if the files are in use. Before co
any open applications.

WARNING: This program is protected by copyright law and international treaties.

You may install Microsoft Data Access 2.1 on a single computer. Some Microsoft products
with additional rights, which are stated in the End User License Agreement included with yo

Please take a moment to read the End User License Agreement now. It contains all of the ter
conditions that pertain to this software product. By choosing to continue, you indicate accepta
these terms.

Continue

Exit Setup

# Connections

*"The toe bone's connected to the foot bone and the foot bone's connected to the ankle bone and the ankle bone's connected to the leg bone and leg bone's connected..."*

In previous chapters we have focused on the recordset, allowing ADO to create the required background steps automatically. We now begin several chapters that discuss and practice the techniques to control the processes that make a recordset possible. In this chapter we start with learning how to specify aspects of the connection and how to create multiple recordsets from one connection. At the end of the chapter we master how to use a connection to derive information about the structure of the database.

## Introduction

Although we have accomplished many tasks with recordsets over the last few chapters, there are even more powerful techniques ahead. In this chapter we discuss controlling the nature of the connection between ADO and the datastore. Our intention is to improve a site by increasing the speed of some pages and by enabling additional capabilities lacking from our early techniques.

## Why Use Connection Objects?

ADO contains two objects which surround and enable the recordset; the Command object and the Connection object. We will start with the Connection object in this chapter since it is more fundamental, easier to understand, and easier to use.

The Connection object provides the link between ADO and a specific database. It holds three types of information:

- ❑ which database
- ❑ the protocol (driver and/or provider) to communicate with that kind of database
- ❑ the user name and the user's password.

Once a `Connection` object is used explicitly (see next section) the following tools are added to your ADO kit:

❑ Multiple uses of one connection

❑ Ability to divulge information about the structure of the database

❑ Use of transactions

❑ Ease in handling errors

The first two items will be covered in depth in this chapter. The third item, transactions, is a larger topic and outside the scope of this book. The advantages of `Connection` objects when handling errors is discussed in Chapter 13.

*You can learn more on Transactions from Professional Visual Basic 6 MTS Programming by Matthew Bortniker and James Connard (Wrox Press, ISBN 1-861002-44-0).*

# Implicit and Explicit Connections

When we create a recordset with the following line, we focus our attention on the resulting recordset.

```
oRS.Open "People", "DSN=Sailors"
```

However, a recordset cannot exist without a connection. Up until now we have just viewed the two parameters listed above as our way of identifying and retrieving from a database. But ADO observes that the program code is not creating a connection and so ADO creates a connection for you using the information of the source and connection parameters.

When ADO creates a connection for us, it is considered an *implicit* connection. ADO implicit connections use default values and you will have no further control over the result. In addition, ADO will make a new implicit connection for each recordset you create without specifying a `Connection` object. Because of this you can end up with several implicit connections created on the same page and pointing to the same data source.

An alternative is for you to take control of the process and *explicitly* create a connection. An explicit connection requires you to create a `Connection` object in the program code. In return for your effort you will have more control in both creating and using the `Connection` object.

In summary, it is important to understand that when you use a recordset there must be a connection. You can create a `Connection` object (explicit) or let ADO create a connection behind the scenes (implicit), but a connection will be there.

# Making Connections

The technique for making an explicit connections usually requires three steps: a DIM and SET to create the Connection object, then opening that object with three pieces of information:

❑   which database

❑   the connection provider

❑   User ID and password.

All three of the above pieces of information can be extracted from a DSN or can be provided individually. Once the Connection object is open we can then use it as the source of data for opening the recordset. When using a Connection object the Recordset.Open syntax changes slightly as we will see below.

# Syntax

The simplest connection only requires three lines of code (two if you don't bother to Dim the object).

```
dim oConn
set oConn=Server.CreateObject ("ADODB.connection")
oConn.open "DSN=Sailors"
```

The first line above reserves the name, with the prefix *o* standing for an object. Other programmers use *con* for connection, *dat* for data or the generic *obj* for object. The second line instantiates the Connection object so that oConn now has available all of the events, methods and properties of a Connection object.

The last line carries out the Open method, which actually creates the connection to the database. We provide as a parameter the name of a DSN. As we learned in Chapter 2, the DSN itself has three parts: a name, a designation of a provider, and a database. The Open method of a Connection object uses the ODBC or OLEDB provider designated in the DSN as the protocol for the link, and that link is to the database name stored in the DSN.

Typically you would then want to use this connection as the basis for a recordset, so to continue the above code we would write:

```
dim oConn
set oConn=Server.CreateObject ("ADODB.connection")
oConn.open "DSN=Sailors"

dim oRS
set oRS=Server.CreateObject("ADODB.recordset")
oRS.Open "People", oConn
Response.Write oRS("PeopleNameFirst")
```

If the database has a security scheme of:

> User ID = "Gallileo"
>
> Password = "rocks2fall"

we would embellish the connection's Open method as follows.

```
oConn.open "DSN=Sailors; UserID=Gallileo; pwd=rocks2fall"
```

Moreover, since we usually know ahead of time that we will be working with both a Connection and Recordset object, we would arrange the code as:

```
dim oConn
dim oRS
set oConn=Server.CreateObject("ADODB.connection")
set oRS=Server.CreateObject("ADODB.recordset")

oConn.open "DSN=Sailors; UserID=Gallileo; pwd=rocks2fall"

oRS.Open "People", oConn
Response.Write oRS("PeopleNameFirst")
```

### Common Errors:

- ❑ The library/class is "ADODB.Connection", not "ADODB.ConnectionObject"

- ❑ Misspelling or typos in the syntax Server.CreateObject

- ❑ You must be consistent in your use of the object name

- ❑ The DSN must exist and must still point to a valid datastore

- ❑ If you use more than one connection, you must keep the names straight when using them on the rest of the page

## Try It Out - Making an Explicit Connection

Use an explicit connection to get data for a list of all of the sailors who are of Professional class 1.

Here's what your code should produce:

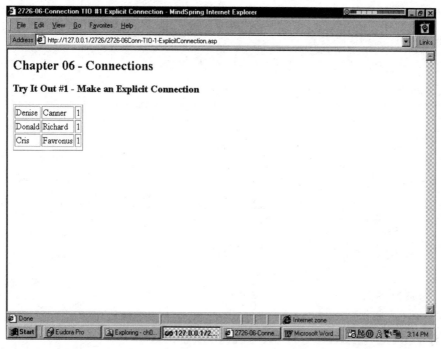

Here's the example code, available in file `2726-06Conn-T10-1-ExplicitConnection.asp`, shown without HTML beginning and ending tags:

```
<H2>Chapter 06 - Connections  </H2>
<H3>Try It Out #1 - Make an Explicit Connection </H3>
<%
dim  oConn
dim oRS
set oConn=Server.CreateObject("ADODB.connection")
set ors=Server.CreateObject("ADODB.recordset")
oConn.Open "DSN=sailors"
sqltext = "SELECT PeopleNameFirst, PeopleNameLast, PeopleProfessionalClass "
sqltext = sqltext & " FROM People WHERE PeopleProfessionalClass=1;"
oRS.Open sqltext, oConn

Response.Write "<TABLE BORDER=1><TR><TD>"
Response.Write oRS.GetString(,-1,"</TD><TD>","</TD></TR><TR><TD>"," ")
Response.Write "</TD></TR></TABLE>"
oRs.Close
Set oRs = nothing
oConn.Close
Set oConn = nothing
%>
```

### How It Works - Making an Explicit Connection

Whereas in earlier chapters we focused on just the `Recordset` object, below we start with code that prepares us to use both a recordset and an explicit `Connection` object.

```
<H2>Chapter 06 - Connections  </H2>
<H3>Try It Out #1 - Make an Explicit Connection </H3>
<%
dim  oConn
dim oRS
set oConn=Server.CreateObject("ADODB.connection")
set ors=Server.CreateObject("ADODB.recordset")
```

Next we open the `Connection` object, build our SQL statement and then open the `Recordset` object. Note how the parameter of the DSN has moved from the second parameter of the `RecordSet.Open` statement (as in previous chapters) to the first parameter of `Conn.Open`.

```
oConn.Open "DSN=sailors"
sqltext = "SELECT PeopleNameFirst, PeopleNameLast, PeopleProfessionalClass "
sqltext = sqltext & " FROM People WHERE PeopleProfessionalClass=1;"
oRS.Open sqltext, oConn
```

The remainder of the code is no different than if we used an implicit connection. If `RecordSet.GetString` throws you, check back to the last section of chapter five.

```
Response.Write "<TABLE BORDER=1><TR><TD>"
Response.Write oRS.GetString(,-1,"</TD><TD>","</TD></TR><TR><TD>"," ")
Response.Write "</TD></TR></TABLE>"
close oRS
set oRS=nothing
%>
```

# Multiple RecordSets on One Connection

The last Try-It-Out did not actually get us any further than if we had just set and opened a recordset. But a benefit comes when we want to open multiple recordsets from one connection. Rather than burning up server time creating multiple connections, we can do all of the recordsets through one explicit connection. There is no special syntax, we just open the `Connection` object then open each of the recordsets with the same `Connection` object as the second parameter.

## Try It Out - Multiple Recordsets

Our sailing association would like a page presenting the names and professional classes of the sailors. The sailors of each class should be listed in their own table.

We can perform this using one `Connection` object but three different recordsets to create the three tables. Your code should produce something similar to this:

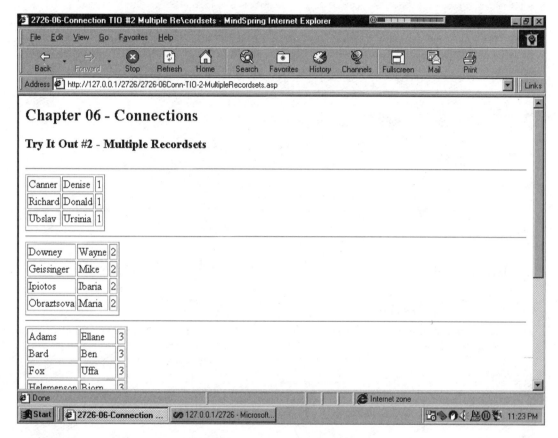

Here is the example code, again shown without the HTML start and end code, taken from file `2726-06Conn-T10-2-MultipleRecordsets.asp`:

```
<H2>Chapter 06 - Connections  </H2>
<H3>Try It Out #2 - Multiple Recordsets </H3>
<%
dim oConn
set oConn=Server.CreateObject("ADODB.connection")
oConn.Open "DSN=sailors"

dim oRS1
set oRS1=Server.CreateObject("ADODB.recordset")

sqltext = "SELECT PeopleNameFirst, PeopleNameLast, PeopleProfessionalClass "
sqltext = sqltext & " FROM People WHERE PeopleProfessionalClass=1;"

oRS1.Open sqltext, oConn
```

```
Response.Write "<HR>"
Response.Write "<TABLE BORDER=1><TR><TD>"
Response.Write ors1.GetString(,-1,"</TD><TD>","</TD></TR><TR><TD>"," ")
Response.Write "</TD></TR></TABLE>"
oRS1.Close
set oRS1=Nothing
dim oRS2
set oRS2=Server.CreateObject("ADODB.recordset")

sqltext = "SELECT PeopleNameFirst, PeopleNameLast, PeopleProfessionalClass "
sqltext = sqltext & " FROM People WHERE PeopleProfessionalClass=2;"
oRS2.Open sqltext, oConn

Response.Write "<HR>"
Response.Write "<TABLE BORDER=1><TR><TD>"
Response.Write ors2.GetString(,-1,"</TD><TD>","</TD></TR><TR><TD>"," ")
Response.Write "</TD></TR></TABLE>"
oRS2.Close
set oRS2=nothing

dim oRS3
set oRS3=Server.CreateObject("ADODB.recordset")

sqltext = "SELECT PeopleNameFirst, PeopleNameLast, PeopleProfessionalClass "
sqltext = sqltext & " FROM People WHERE PeopleProfessionalClass=3;"
oRS3.Open sqltext, oConn

Response.Write "<HR>"
Response.Write "<TABLE BORDER=1><TR><TD>"
Response.Write ors3.GetString(,-1,"</TD><TD>","</TD></TR><TR><TD>"," ")
Response.Write "</TD></TR></TABLE>"
oRS3.Close
set oRS3=nothing

oConn.Close
set oConn=nothing
%>
```

### How It Works – Multiple Recordsets

We start the same as the last Try-It-Out by setting up the Connection object, but this time we do not immediately dive into the recordset, because there will be three of them.

```
<H2>Chapter 06 - Connections  </H2>
<H3>Try It Out #2 - Multiple Recordsets </H3>
<%
dim  oConn
set oConn=Server.CreateObject("ADODB.connection")
oConn.Open "DSN=sailors"
```

Now we set up the first recordset and use it to build the table of sailors of professional class 1. Note that at the end we close the recordset but not the connection.

```
set oRS1=Server.CreateObject("ADODB.recordset")
dim oRS1
sqltext = "SELECT PeopleNameFirst, PeopleNameLast, PeopleProfessionalClass "
sqltext = sqltext & " FROM People WHERE PeopleProfessionalClass=1;"

oRS1.Open sqltext, oConn
Response.Write "<HR>"
Response.Write "<TABLE BORDER=1><TR><TD>"
Response.Write ors1.GetString(,-1,"</TD><TD>","</TD></TR><TR><TD>"," ")
Response.Write "</TD></TR></TABLE>"

oRS1.Close
set oRS1=nothing
```

Now we can do the same again just changing the name of the recordset and the WHERE clause of the SQL statement so we build the table for sailors in class 2. The second parameter of oRS2 is the same as for oRS1 since the purpose of the exercise is to avoid creating multiple connections. Again, the recordset is closed but not the Connection object.

```
set oRS2=Server.CreateObject("ADODB.recordset")
dim oRS2
sqltext = "SELECT PeopleNameFirst, PeopleNameLast, PeopleProfessionalClass "
sqltext = sqltext & " FROM People WHERE PeopleProfessionalClass=2;"
oRS2.Open sqltext, oConn
Response.Write "<HR>"
Response.Write "<TABLE BORDER=1><TR><TD>"
Response.Write ors2.GetString(,-1,"</TD><TD>","</TD></TR><TR><TD>"," ")
Response.Write "</TD></TR></TABLE>"
oRS2.Close
set oRS2=nothing
```

The third table is done the same way as the last (not shown). Now that we are done hitting the connection with our third and last recordset, we can put it to rest.

```
' (code for third table similar to first and second)

oConn.Close
set oConn=nothing
%>
```

# Alternative Types of Connections

The normal and easiest way to connect to a database is by a DSN. However there are several cases where you may want to use a different technique. The first is if a DSN is not available, and the second is if you want to bypass the OLEDB layer and go directly to the ODBC driver. A third, and probably the most important, is when you want to use a Native OLEDB Provider directly without ODBC.

## DSN-less

One of the useful points about a DSN is that it wraps up two important pieces of information in one package: the type of driver and the name and location of the database. But also remember that we make a DSN through the operating system. Now in some cases you may be able to get physical or remote access to the server and set a DSN, however DSNs must usually be made by the Server System Administrator, not by you the programmer. What can you do if you need to use ADO but do not have a DSN? You can create a DSN-less connection.

*In the examples in this section we will be talking mainly about Access, as this is our primary example database for this book. The name of the database file and the question of uploading a database don't apply to other databases such as SQL Server.*

> If your data store already resides on the server you need to know its name and location. If you are going to use a new database file, for instance from Access, you will have to transfer it, generally using FTP.

In essence, we provide on the `Connection.Open` line the information that is held in a DSN:

```
set oConn=Server.CreateObject("ADODB.connection")
oConn.Open "DRIVER={Microsoft Access Driver (*.mdb)}; _
                          DBQ=D:\WROX\ASP-ADO\Sailors.mdb"
ors1.open "SELECT * FROM People", oConn
```

In the above code the `oConn.Open` line is different than in the past because instead of using a DSN we use a DSN-less connection. We provide the `Open` method with two pieces of information within one parameter: the type of driver and the file specification of the database. You can go wrong with this code in a number of ways. First, the argument for `oConn.Open` must all be on one line. In the above code the line is split due to the width of this book's page, but in your code it should all be on one line.

> *By the time you build up some VBScript statements you will have long line of code. You can deal with it in one of three ways:*
>
> *First, in your editor you can just leave it on a long line. We can't do that in the book because physical paper does not have horizontal scrolling.*
> *Second, you can break the line with an underscore, as shown in the previous code.*
> *Last, you can create the statement parameters in string variables, much as we used to build long SQL statements. For example the above code would be:*
> > *vConnString = "DRIVER={Microsoft Access Driver (*.mdb)};"*
> > *vConnString = VConnString & "DBQ=D:\WROX\ASP-ADO\Sailors.mdb"*
> > *oConn.Open vConnString*

Second, you must be absolutely scrupulous about the punctuation of that long `oConn.Open` parameter. Note that:

- ❑ the entire argument is within one set of double quotes
- ❑ the driver is within braces
- ❑ the allowable file extensions are within parentheses
- ❑ the two parameters are separated by a semi colon

Third, you must know the exact file specification (name, path and extension) of the database.

The argument for that `Open` line can get long, and so ADO has made the connection information a property of the `Connection` object, and thus easier to work with as in the following code:

```
set oConn=Server.CreateObject("ADODB.connection")
oConn.connectionstring = "DRIVER={Microsoft Access Driver (*.mdb)} _
  ;DBQ=D:\WROX\ASP-ADO\Sailors.mdb"
oConn.Open
```

Be sure not to fill the connection string property prior to creating the object. You can make a SQL string whenever you want, but in this case you are putting the string into a property of the object and so the object must be created first. Reversing these lines gives you a VBScript error '800a01a8' for a missing Connection object on the line that tries to fill the connection string.

Also as we learned with long SQL strings, the ConnectionString property can be filled in several steps, as follows. If you have any problems with this technique the first troubleshooting step is to print the connection string to the page as seen in the commented-out artifact of development shown in the second last line below.

```
set oConn=Server.CreateObject("ADODB.connection")
oConn.connectionstring = "DRIVER={Microsoft Access Driver (*.mdb)}"
oConn.connectionstring = oConn.connectionstring & ";DBQ=D:\WROX\ASP-ADO\Sailors.mdb"
' Response.Write "<HR>" & oConnConnectionString & "<HR>"
oConn.Open
```

### Common Errors of DSN-Less connections:

- ❏  Misspelling of driver

- ❏  Errors in the parentheses and brackets when specifying the driver

- ❏  Errors in the semicolon of the driver

- ❏  Database location is incorrect

- ❏  Connection string must be on one line, both parts are within one set of quotes, separated by semicolon

- ❏  Path and driver must be correct

- ❏  The Connection object must be used as second argument when opening the recordset

A DSN-Less connection with Access is impossible if you don't know the path of the database. Here is a frequent configuration, but this must be confirmed by your Systems Administrator:
D:\InetPub\SiteName\Databases\DatabaseName

### Try It Out- DSN-Less Connection

Make a table containing the first and last name of the sailors of professional class 2 without the use of a DSN. We know the following facts about the database:

- ❏  It was created using MS Access 8 (from MS Office97)

- ❏  It is located in C:\My_Documents\ASPADO (this will be different on your machine)

- ❏  The name of the database is Sailors3.mdb

Here is the example code, taken from `2726-06Conn-T10-4-DSNLess.asp`, minus the HTML start and end tags:

```
<H2>Chapter 06 - Connections </H2>
<H3>Try It Out #4 DSN-Less Connection </H3>
<%
dim oConn
dim oRS
dim strSource

set oConn=Server.CreateObject("ADODB.connection")
set ors=Server.CreateObject("ADODB.recordset")
strSource = "Driver={Microsoft Access Driver (*.mdb)}"
strSource = strSource & "; DBQ=C:\My Documents\ASPADO\Sailors3.mdb"
oConn.ConnectionString = strSource
oConn.Open

sqltext = "SELECT PeopleNameFirst, PeopleNameLast, PeopleProfessionalClass "
sqltext = sqltext & " FROM People WHERE PeopleProfessionalClass=2;"
oRS.Open sqltext, oConn

Response.Write "<TABLE BORDER=1><TR><TD>"
Response.Write oRS.GetString(,-1,"</TD><TD>","</TD></TR><TR><TD>"," ")
Response.Write "</TD></TR></TABLE>"

oRS.Close
Set oRS=nothing
oConn.close
Set oConn=nothing
%>
```

The above code produces the following page:

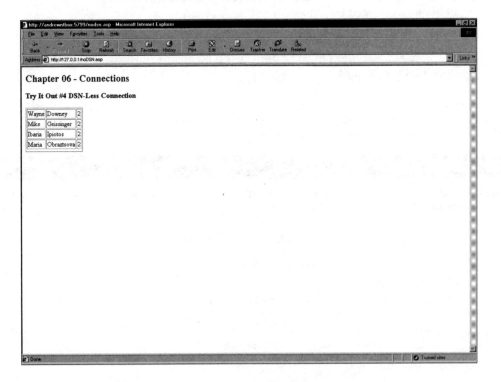

### *How It Works – DSN-Less Connections*

We start with the typical foundations, but note the preparation of a variable named `strSource` which will hold the information that will be used to establish the DSN-Less connection.

```
<H2>Chapter 06 - Connections  </H2>
 <H3>Try It Out #4 DSN-Less Connection </H3>
<%
dim  oConn
dim oRS
dim strSource

set oConn=Server.CreateObject("ADODB.connection")
set ors=Server.CreateObject("ADODB.recordset")
```

Now in the code below we fill that `strSource` variable with two pieces of information separated by a semicolon. The first datum is the provider, the exact syntax for which we got from the table on the previous page. The second datum is the location and name of the database. The string contents of that variable are then put into the `ConnectionString` property of the oConn. Now we can open the connection with a simple `OConn.Open` devoid of arguments since the data needed is sitting in the oConn `ConnectionString` property.

```
strSource = "Driver={Microsoft Access Driver (*.mdb)}"
strSource = strSource & "; DBQ=C:\My Documents\ASPADO\Sailors3.mdb"
oConn.ConnectionString = strSource
oConn.Open
```

As my professor of differential equations would have said, "The remainder of the solution is trivial." We just create a recordset from the connection and run that through a loop to print each record to the page.

```
sqltext = "SELECT PeopleNameFirst, PeopleNameLast, PeopleProfessionalClass "
sqltext = sqltext & " FROM People WHERE PeopleProfessionalClass=2;"
oRS.Open sqltext, oConn

Response.Write "<TABLE BORDER=1><TR><TD>"
Response.Write oRS.GetString(,-1,"</TD><TD>","</TD></TR><TR><TD>"," ")
Response.Write "</TD></TR></TABLE>"
```

As always, your server will run faster if you tidy up the objects after use.

```
oRS.Close
Set oRS=nothing
oConn.close
Set oConn=nothing
%>
```

# Native OLEDB Providers

As we discussed above and in more detail in chapter 7, OLEDB sits above ODBC. ODBC, the granddaddy of standardization in data access, is widely used. However, it is clear that the future will be in OLEDB, so database software designers are developing OLEDB native providers. In other words the model will be ADO to OLEDB to datastore, without the ODBC layer.

This doesn't mean to say that ODBC is dead and buried. There are still plenty of people using it, and still plenty of reasons for ODBC. Databases for which there are no OLEDB Providers still have to be accessed through ODBC, and this includes many legacy systems. However, the future is clearly aligned with OLEDB.

When talking about OLEDB it's often easy to confuse the terms Provider and Driver. The diagram below should make this clear:

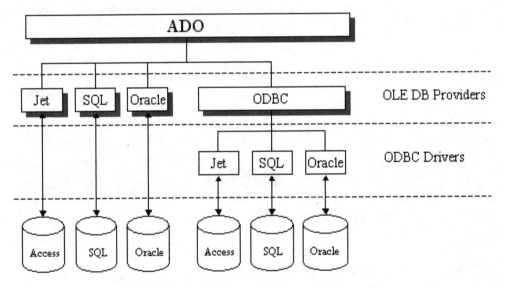

Here you can see that the Providers are related to OLEDB, and the Drivers are related to OLEDB and ADO. It's clear that without going through ODBC you will get better performance, simply due to there being one layer fewer. What's not obvious from the diagram though, is that the OLEDB Provider for ODBC has to work with all ODBC Drivers, and therefore it has less knowledge of the actual data provider. This means that the OLEDB Provider for ODBC may have less functionality than the native OLEDB Provider.

For Web programmers OLEDB is far superior to any other database access technology because it's been built partly with the Web in mind. Normally, we don't interact directly with OLEDB, but with ADO as we have been doing so far. ADO, as has been previously described, is a layer that sits between ASP (or another programming language) and OLEDB. In simple terms, ADO takes our scripting commands and translates them into the more difficult language that OLEDB can understand. ADO is easy to use, and allows data to be accessed easily from a variety of data stores. The list of OLEDB Providers currently shipped with the current release of ADO (2.1) is shown below:

- **Jet 4.0**, for Microsoft Access databases. This allows access to standard Access databases, including linked tables. ADO 2.0 shipped with the Jet 3.5 Provider.

- **Directory Services**, for resource data stores, such as Active Directory. This will become more important when Windows 2000 is available, as the Directory Service will allow access to user information, as well as network devices.

- **Index Server**, for Microsoft Index Server. This will be particularly useful as web sites grow, as the indexed data will be available.

- **Site Server Search**, for Microsoft Site Server. Again for use with web sites, especially large complex sites, where Site Server is used to maintain them.

- **ODBC Drivers**, for existing ODBC Drivers. This ensures that legacy data is not omitted as part of the drive forward.

- **Oracle**, for Oracle databases. Connection to Oracle has never been particularly easy with Microsoft products in the past, but a native driver will simplify access to existing Oracle data stores.

- **SQL Server**, for Microsoft SQL Server, to allow access to data stored in SQL Server.

- **Data Shape**, for hierarchical recordsets. This allows creation of master/detail type recordsets, which allow drilling down into detailed data.

- **Persisted Recordset**, for locally saved recordsets, and recordset marshalling. Topics which are beyond the scope of this book.

- **OLAP**, for accessing On Line Analytical Processing data stores.

- **Internet Publishing**, for accessing web resources that support Microsoft FrontPage Server Extensions or Distributed Authoring and Versioning (DAV). For more information on DAV check out the WebDAV Working Group home page at `http://www.ics.uci.edu/~ejw/authoring/`.

- **Remoting Provider**, for connecting to data providers on remote machines.

This is just the list of standard providers supplied by Microsoft; other vendors are actively creating their own. For example, a company called ISG (`www.isg.co.il`) provides an OLEDB provider that allows connection to multiple data stores at the same time. Oracle provides an OLEDB provider, which they claim is better than Microsoft's Oracle provider, and most other database suppliers have OLEDB providers for their databases.

One question that often gets asked is whether to use ODBC or the native providers, and there's a simple answer. If there's a native OLEDB provider, then use it. Not only will it give you better performance and functionality, but also it will continue to be developed, as OLEDB is an important part of Microsoft's data access future.

If you've already been using the OLEDB Provider for ODBC and want to switch to a native provider, then don't worry, as it's very simple. All you have to do is change the connection string. For example, the connection string for Access is like this:

```
strSource = "Provider=Microsoft.Jet.OLEDB.3.51"
strSource = strSource & "; Data Source=C:\My Documents\ASPADO\Sailors3.mdb"
oConn.ConnectionString = strSource
oConn.Open
```

Not much different from the DSN-less ODBC connection string is it? The first difference is that you specify the Provider and not the Driver (remember Providers are for OLEDB and Drivers for ODBC). The second difference is that you do not use a DSN.

*If you've got Office 2000 or ADO 2.1 installed, you can use Microsoft.Jet.OLEDB.4.0 for the provider name, as this is the latest version.*

Once you've switched from ODBC to OLEDB your program should work in exactly the same way. That's the beauty of ADO - you can chop and change your providers, often without changing your code.

## Try It Out– Native OLEDB Connection

Write a page that lists the names of the boats. The output should be similar to this:

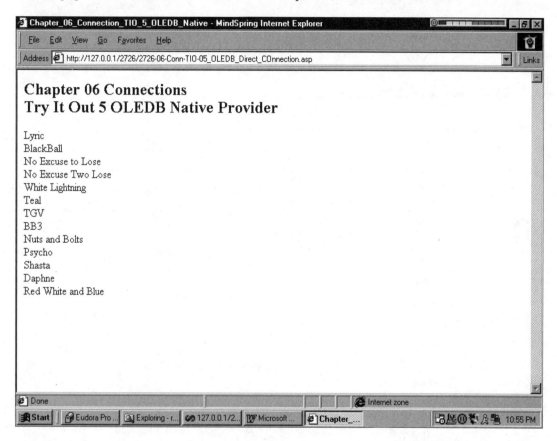

The above page is created by the following code lifted from `2726-06Conn-T10-5-NativeOLEDB.asp`:

```
<HTML>
<HEAD>
<TITLE>Chapter_06_Connection_TIO_5_OLEDB_Native</TITLE>
</HEAD>

<BODY>
<H2>Chapter 06 Connections <BR>
Try It Out 5 OLEDB Native Provider </H2>

<%
Dim oConn
Dim oRS
Dim vCS
Dim sqltxt

set oConn=Server.CreateObject("ADODB.connection")
vCS = "Provider=Microsoft.Jet.OLEDB.3.51"
vCS = vCS & "; Data Source=C:\My Documents\WROX\ASP-ADO\Sailors.mdb"
oConn.connectionstring = vCS
oConn.Open
```

```
set oRS = Server.CreateObject("ADODB.recordset")
sqltxt = "SELECT BoatName FROM Boats;"
oRS.Open sqltxt,oConn
Do until oRS.EOF
  Response.Write oRS("BoatName") & "<BR>"
  oRS.MoveNext
Loop  'each boat record
%>

</BODY>
</HTML>
```

### How It Works – Native OLEDB Connection

We start with the basics of the page

```
<HTML>
<HEAD>
<TITLE>Chapter_06_Connection_TIO_5_OLEDB_Native</TITLE>
</HEAD>

<BODY>
<H2>Chapter 06 Connections <BR>
Try It Out 5 OLEDB Native Provider </H2>

<%
```

Then we set up some variables

```
Dim oConn
Dim oRS
Dim vCS
Dim sqltxt
```

Now it starts to get more interesting. Instead of using the default ODBC driver we use the Microsoft OLEDB direct provider

```
set oConn=Server.CreateObject("ADODB.connection")
vCS = "Provider=Microsoft.Jet.OLEDB.3.51"
vCS = vCS & "; Data Source=C:\My Documents\WROX\ASP-ADO\Sailors.mdb"
oConn.connectionstring = vCS
oConn.Open
```

Once the connection is opened we use it the same as our earlier connections, as follows:

```
set oRS = Server.CreateObject("ADODB.recordset")
sqltxt = "SELECT BoatName FROM Boats;"
oRS.Open sqltxt,oConn
Do until oRS.EOF
  Response.Write oRS("BoatName") & "<BR>"
  oRS.MoveNext
Loop  'each boat record
%>

</BODY>
</HTML>
```

After you finish the chapter and know how to read the connection properties you may want to return to this code and add a table of connection properties as follows:

```
Loop  'each boat record
```

```
Response.Write "<TABLE BORDER=1 ><TR><TD>"
dim iCountProps
iCountProps = 0
for each item in oConn.Properties
  iCountProps = iCountProps + 1
  Response.Write "<TR><TD>" & iCountProps & "</TD>"
  Response.Write "<TD>" & item.name  & "</TD>"
  Response.Write "<TD>" & item.value & "</TD></TR>"
Next
Response.Write "</TABLE>"
%>
```

```
</BODY>
</HTML>
```

(For this extra section you can try swapping in and out the different connection strings and then observing the connection properties that are numbered 27-29 and 48 in this table).

# Connection Pooling

In some business situations, you will have many visitors extracting information from one database. In fact, they will each be requesting the creation of the exact same connection. For example, if you were running a lottery from your basement, you would have thousands of bettors checking today's lucky number from your database of daily winners.

The act of setting up the same connection for each of these requests would be very time consuming for the server. To overcome this drag, NT offers a feature called Connection Pooling. When a requester closes a connection by using Set oConn=Nothing, the connection is no longer available to that requester. However, the connection is still held open by ADO, albeit unassigned to a requestor. Whenever a connection request comes in, NT will automatically check to see if there is already a connection of that type and if so NT uses the existing connection rather than expend the time and memory to create a new one. The connection is kept available by ADO for a defined length of time, by default 60 seconds. The quantitative benefits of connection pooling are discussed in chapter 17 on performance issues.

It is important to understand that ADO will use a pooled connection only if there is a perfect match between the new request and the one that originally created the pool. The exact match extends, of course, to the UserID and Password. There is no advantage at all to connection pooling if each request is earmarked with a different UserID and Password. For example, if our bettors had to log on with a name and password, then each of their requests would create a new connection.

If your Connection Pooling is turned off, you can turn it on or off in two ways. First, to turn it on you can change the IIS server registry setting for StartConnectionPool to 1. Second is to turn connection pooling off on an individual basis by inserting the following line into the ASP code:

```
oConn.Properties("OLE DB Services") = -2
```

# Viewing and Changing Connection Properties

There are close to a hundred properties of a connection. We have discussed the most important here, but you may encounter particular cases where you need to create a more specific connection. The `Properties` collection exists because the designers of ADO knew that they could not anticipate and include in ADO every attribute that every combination of driver, provider, and datastore might have. The `Properties` collection makes available those data store attributes that are not available through other ADO object properties. This means that the properties exposed by a connection are dependent upon the type of database, driver, and/or provider used.

The first step is to understand how to view exactly what properties your `Connection` object exposes by default. You can learn more about working with collections by studying the code we used to write the `Fields` collection in Chapter 5. For now, you can use the following code:

## Try It Out - Connection Properties List

This code is taken, without HTML start and end tags, from `2726-06Conn-T10-6-ConnPropList.asp`:

```
<%
dim oConn
set oConn=Server.CreateObject("ADODB.connection")
oConn.Open "DSN=sailors"
%>

<TABLE BORDER=1 ><TR><TD WIDTH = 10%>Number</TD>
<TD WIDTH = 70%>Name</TD><TD WIDTH = 20%>Value</TD></TR>

<%
dim iCountProps
iCountProps = 0
for each item in oConn.Properties
  iCountProps = iCountProps + 1
  Response.Write "<TR><TD>" & iCountProps & "</TD>"
  Response.Write "<TD>" & item.name  & "</TD>"
  Response.Write "<TD>" & item.value & "</TD></TR>"
Next
%>

</TABLE>
```

If you want to make a change to a given property you use its name as shown in the result of the above code, with the following syntax. Note that the double quotes allow you to type in the property name exactly as listed in the output of the above code.

```
oConn.Properties("Property Name") = value
```

For example, we've just mentioned turning off connection pooling for a particular connection. You can confirm the exact name of the property from the For Each Properties loop, then set the property with the following code. That is, of course, if your combination of datastore and driver or provider supports this feature.

```
oConn.Properties("OLE DB Services")=-2
```

# Elucidating Schema

Most of this chapter was on creating connections to prepare for using recordsets. There are also a few design-time objectives that can be met with the `Connection` object itself. Since the `Connection` object is bound to the database, we can get some information about how it is structured.

## An Introduction to Schema

Frequently we know less about our database than we would like. In the best of all worlds we would have designed the database ourselves and thus be intimately acquainted with its details (and foibles). But most worlds aren't perfect, so you frequently work with a database designed by another person and are stuck with one of the following situations:

❑   Your boss or customer admits she knows little if anything about the database structure.

❑   Your boss or customer states he knows all about the database structure, but some or all of that knowledge is wrong.

Unless you are absolutely sure about the structure of the database, I suggest that you spend one of your first hours on the project to do some investigations using the following techniques.

> *I will warn you that although obtaining the schema isn't complex, it does require thinking about some vocabulary and syntax in a different way than we have to date. I find that many students have to pause and really concentrate on these ideas in order to get the syntax correct.*

The terminology can be a little confusing at first. The *Schema* is considered to be a set of data describing the *structure* of the database. This set of data can be opened and examined in the same way as the data itself. When we open the schema the structural data is put into a recordset for our use. Even though we have used the term *recordset* up to now for a container of data, it is important to keep in mind that when studying schema the recordset holds information about the structure of the database, not the data of the database.

There are three sets of parameters to understand when obtaining schema information.

❑   Which schema to return: tables, fields, etc.

❑   Which values from within the schema: Field Name, field type, etc.

❑   Translation of values into English words: 3 = Integer data type

Furthermore, the syntax is odd because we actually use the `SET` command to create the object from the Schema. In the rest of the book we instantiate recordsets with the Server.CreateObject method using the ADOVBS library, but in this section we `SET` recordsets from the `Connection.OpenSchema` method using one of the keywords for schema which we will list below.

A last point of confusion is that when you begin to examine the schema you will come across more information about the database than you ever knew existed. For example, an Access database in which you created two tables will suddenly have six more tables with unrecognizable names. Don't worry, the information you want will be available and the extra information can be filtered out by your mind. Human minds have been separating the wheat from the chaff for thousands of years; they adapted well from grain to code.

# Schema Technique

Working with schema requires many constants, so we want the Microsoft ADOVBS file included. In addition to the first line of code below, don't forget to find the file on your drive by Start | Find | File | adovbs.inc | OK, and then copy it into the root of your site (frequently it is in \inetpub\iissamples\ISSamples, but yours could be elsewhere). The next few lines of the technique create a new connection. There is nothing new so far.

```
<!--#include file="ADOvbs.inc"-->
<%
dim  oConn
set oConn=Server.CreateObject("ADODB.connection")
oConn.Open "DSN=sailors"
```

Now in the code below we create a fundamentally different recordset from anything we have done before. We do *not* do a Set oRS=Server.CreateObject("ADODB.recordset") like we have in the last chapters. We actually instantiate the recordset from the result of the OpenSchema method of the Connection object. Take a look at the syntax twice; we are using the OpenSchema method of the Connection object rather than the usual CreateObject method.

```
set oRS=oConn.OpenSchema(adSchemaTables)
```

We do not have to open this recordset, it is already filled with the information from the above command. The data will be in records and fields, with each record being a table and each field data about the table. For example we can see a list of table names with the following code.

```
oRS.MoveFirst
while not oRS.EOF
   Response.Write ors("Table_Name") & "<BR>"
   oRS.movenext
Wend
```

## Try It Out- Schema

Make a list of all of the field names and sizes in the Sailors database. The schema we want to use is adSchemaColumns and that will contain fields for Table_Name, Column_Name, and Character_Maximum_Length. The code for this example is in 2726-06Conn-TI0-7-Schema.asp, and is shown below without the HTML start and end tags:

```
<H3>Try It Out #7 - Schema </H3>
<!--#include file="ADOvbs.inc"-->

<%
dim  oConn
dim  oRS

set oConn=Server.CreateObject("ADODB.connection")
oConn.Open "DSN=sailors"
set oRS=oConn.OpenSchema(adSchemaColumns)
```

```
Response.Write "Columns from Sailors" & "<BR><BR>"
Response.Write "<TABLE BORDER='1'>"
Response.Write "<TH>Table Source</TH><TH>Column Name</TH><TH>Max Width (text fields)"

while not oRS.EOF
  Response.Write "<TR><TD>" & ors("Table_Name") & " </TD>"
  Response.Write "<TD>" & ors("Column_Name") & " </TD>"
  Response.Write "<TD>" & ors("Character_Maximum_Length") & " </TD></TR>"
  oRS.movenext
Wend

Response.Write "</TABLE>"

set oRS=nothing
set oConn=nothing
%>
```

The above code produces the following screen:

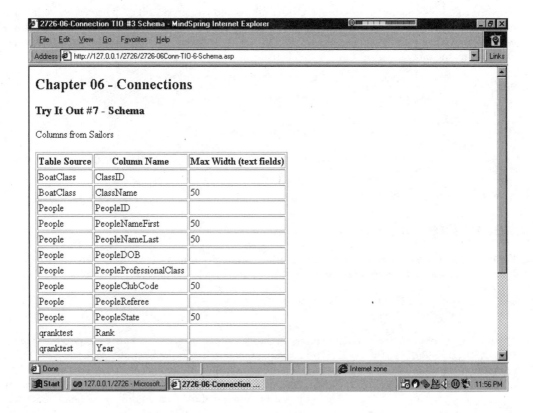

### How It Works – Schema

We start with some basic housekeeping, foremost of which is to get that ADOVBS file included. We then create a connection to the database of interest.

```
<H3>Try It Out #7 - Schema </H3>
<!--#include file="ADOvbs.inc"-->
<%
dim  oConn
set oConn=Server.CreateObject("ADODB.connection")
oConn.Open "DSN=sailors"
```

Next we use the trickiest line, where we set a recordset using the result of an OpenSchema method on the Connection object. In this case we need information on columns so we use the adSchemaColumns argument.

```
set oRS=oConn.OpenSchema(adSchemaColumns)
```

Now the oRS holds all the information on the columns and we can read it off by referring to the field names. The   is an HTML code which we concatenate on the end of each cell so that the browser will insert a (non-breaking) space to insure that the cell will appear (albeit empty) when there is no data. Don't forget the oRS.MoveNext so we don't create an endless loop.

```
Response.Write "Columns from Sailors" & "<BR><BR>"
Response.Write "<TABLE BORDER='1'>"
Response.Write "<TH>Table Source</TH><TH>Column Name</TH><TH>Max Width (text
fields)</TH>"
while not oRS.EOF
  Response.Write "<TR><TD>" & ors("Table_Name") & " </TD>"
  Response.Write "<TD>" & ors("Column_Name") & " </TD>"
  Response.Write "<TD>" & ors("Character_Maximum_Length") & " </TD></TR>"
  oRS.movenext
Wend
Response.Write "</TABLE>"
```

# Schema Arguments

For the above Try-It-Out, we were obtaining information on columns. However, there is far more information about a database that we can find by using other arguments, as in the following two lines.

```
set oRS=oConn.OpenSchema(adSchemaTables)
Response.Write oRS("Table_Name")
```

The total list of options covers over 30 pages in the *ADO Programmers Reference* by David Sussman (Wrox Press, ISBN 0-861001-83-5) so I will summarize the most useful and most universal here. Note that not all parameters are available for all providers, but the four options I discuss here work for both OLEDB and ODBC providers for Jet (Access) and Microsoft SQL server. The left two columns are the constant or number to use in the set oRS line. The right column is a list of most commonly used field names for use in the Response.Write statement. If you use the constants, remember to include the ADOvbs.inc file in the root folder of your site, and also to include the include tag located as follows:

```
<BODY>
<!--#include file="ADOvbs.inc"-->
<%
```

| Schema Query Type - as word | Schema Query Type - as number | Most Useful Value Names |
| --- | --- | --- |
| adSchemaTables | 20 | Table_Name |
| | | Column_Name |
| | | Column_Default |
| | | Data_Type |
| | | Character_Maximum_Length |
| | | Description |
| adSchemaColumns | 4 | |
| adSchemaIndexes | 12 | Table_Name |
| | | Index_Name |
| | | Description |

Listing Queries entails even trickier syntax. If you are using MS SQL Server you can get all of your queries from:

| AdSchemaProcedures (this type lists the queries in an Access .mdb) | 16 | Procedure_Name |
| --- | --- | --- |
| | | Procedure_Definition |
| | | Description |

But if you are using Access (Jet) with the default provider, you have to harvest the information in two listings:

| Select Queries | adSchemaProcedures (this type lists the queries in an Access .mdb) | 16 | Procedure_Name |
| --- | --- | --- | --- |
| | | | Procedure_Definition |
| | | | Description |
| Queries that change data (Update, Delete, etc.) | adSchemaViews | 23 | |

**211**

And finally, if you are using Access (Jet) with the ODBC provider, you set up the queries by using the adSchemaTables and select for the records with a Table_Type = View, as in the following code – being sure to use an uppercase VIEW in the expression.

```
set oRS=oConn.OpenSchema(adSchemaTables)
Response.Write "List Jet queries by using adSchemaTables"
Response.Write "and only show Table_Type = 'views'" & "<BR><BR>"
oRS.MoveFirst
while not oRS.EOF
  If oRS("Table_Type")="VIEW" then
    Response.Write ors("Table_Name") & " "
    Response.Write ors("Table_Type") & "<BR>"
  end if
  oRS.movenext
Wend
```

Code that asks for the data type returns a number. The next table converts those codes for the most common types. The other conversions can be found in the adovbs.inc file.

| | |
|---|---|
| adInteger | 3 |
| adSingle | 4 |
| adDouble | 5 |
| adCurrency | 6 |
| adDate | 7 |
| adBoolean | 11 |
| adVariant | 12 |
| adBinary | 128 |
| adChar | 129 |
| adNumeric | 131 |
| adDBDate | 133 |
| adDBTime | 134 |
| adDBTimeStamp | 135 |

If you find that viewing the systems tables (MSysACESS, MSysModules, etc.) is distracting, you can use the following code to prevent their display.

```
set oRS=oConn.OpenSchema(adSchemaTables)
while not oRS.EOF
  If oRS("Table_Type")="SYSTEM TABLE" then
    'skip display
  Else
    Response.Write ors("Table_Name") & "<BR>"
  End IF
  oRS.movenext
Wend
```

### Common Errors with Schema:

- ❏ Trying to fill a recordset with schema by using `RecordSet.Open` instead of `Set Recordset=Connection.OpenSchema`
- ❏ Putting an "`ADODB.recordset`" as an argument for `Connection.OpenSchema`
- ❏ Using the constants (such as `adSchemaTables`) but forgetting to include the `ADOVBS.inc` file in the root of the site and put an include file line in your HTML prior to entering the script.
- ❏ Using the wrong schema to obtain the information of interest
- ❏ Using the wrong fieldname
- ❏ Leaving out the `ors.MoveNext` in the loop to read out the recordset

# Summary

Although you can let ASP/ADO automatically create connections for your recordsets (implicit connections), it is more useful to create the connections yourself (explicitly). Explicit connections conserve resources by allowing more than one recordset to be created from a connection. Furthermore, using explicit connections allows the use of specific providers and identifying a data source without a DSN. Lastly, you can use the connection's `Schema` methods to derive information about the structure of a database.

# Exercises

**1.** Create a page which lists the names of the vendors from the Clothier database in four ways:

first with an implicit connection to the Clothier DSN
second with an explicit connection to the Clothier DSN
third with a DSN-less connection using the same ODBC driver
fourth with the Microsoft Jet Native OLEDB provider

Recall that the Clothier DSN uses the Microsoft Access Driver, `odbcjt32.dll`.

Your code could produce something like this:

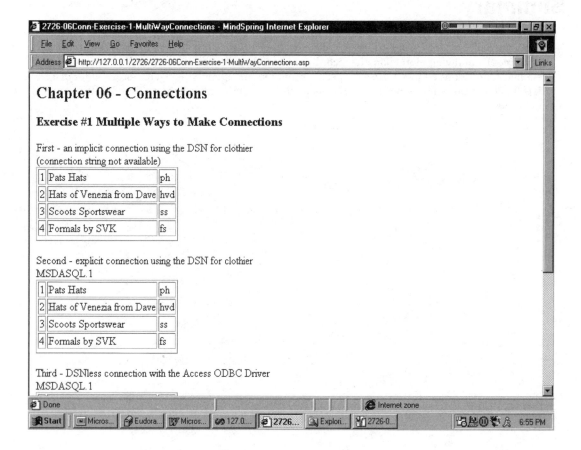

**2.** List on a page the names of all the tables in the Clothier Database. Do not include system tables such as MsysObjects. The result will be very simple, as follows:

# Exercise Answers

These exercises use one or both of the two sample databases available from the WROX website. The structures of the databases are described in Appendix A for `Sailors.mdb` and Appendix B for `Clothier.mdb`.

**1.** Create a page which lists the names of the vendors from the Clothier database, with first with an implicit connection to the Clothier DSN, second an explicit connection to the Clothier DSN, third a DSN-less connection using the same ODBC driver, and fourth with the Microsoft Jet Native OLEDB provider.

You can find this example code in the file `2726-06Conn-Exercise-1-MultiWaysConnection.asp`.

```
<%@ Language=VBScript %>
<HTML><HEAD>
<META NAME="GENERATOR" Content="Microsoft Visual Studio 6.0">
<TITLE>2726-06Conn-Exercise-1-MultiWayConnections</TITLE>
</HEAD><BODY>
<!--#include file="ADOvbs.inc"-->
<H2>Chapter 06 - Connections </H2>
<H3>Exercise #1 Multiple Ways to Make Connections</H3>
<%
'This snippet sets up the strings to build tables"
Dim vCol,vRow
vCol = "</TD><TD>"
vRow = "</TD></TR><TR><TD>"
%>

First - an implicit connection using the DSN for clothier<BR>
<%
Dim oRS1
set oRS1=Server.CreateObject("ADODB.recordset")
Response.Write "(connection string not available)"
oRS1.Open "Vendors", "DSN=clothier"
Response.Write "<TABLE BORDER=1><TR><TD>"
Response.write oRS1.GetString(,-1,vCol,vRow," ")
Response.Write "</TD></TR></TABLE>"
oRS1.close
set oRS1=nothing
%>
<BR>
Second - explicit connection using the DSN for clothier<BR>
<%
Dim oConn2
Dim oRS2
set oCOnn2 = Server.CreateObject("ADODB.Connection")
set oRS2=Server.CreateObject("ADODB.recordset")
oConn2.Open "DSN=Clothier"
Response.Write oConn2.provider
oRS2.Open "Vendors", oConn2,adOpenForwardOnly,adLockReadOnly
Response.Write "<TABLE BORDER=1><TR><TD>"
Response.write oRS2.GetString(,-1,vCol,vRow," ")
Response.Write "</TD></TR></TABLE>"
oRS2.close
set oRS2=nothing
oCOnn2.close
set oCOnn2=nothing
%>
```

```
<BR>
Third - DSNless connection with the Access ODBC Driver<BR>
<%
Dim oConn3
Dim oRS3
Dim vSource
set oConn3 = Server.CreateObject("ADODB.Connection")
set oRS3=Server.CreateObject("ADODB.recordset")

vSource = "Driver={Microsoft Access Driver (*.mdb)}"
vSource = vSource & "; DBQ=C:\Clothier.mdb"
oConn3.ConnectionString = vSource
oConn3.Open
Response.Write oConn3.provider
oRS3.Open "Vendors", oConn3,adOpenForwardOnly,adLockReadOnly
Response.Write "<TABLE BORDER=1><TR><TD>"
Response.write oRS3.GetString(,-1,vCol,vRow," ")
Response.Write "</TD></TR></TABLE>"
oRS3.close
set oRS3=nothing
oCOnn3.close
set oConn3=nothing
%>
<BR>
Fourth - Native OLDDB Provider<BR>
<%
dim  oConn4
dim oRS4
Dim vP   'Provider String
set oConn4=Server.CreateObject("ADODB.connection")
set oRS4=Server.CreateObject("ADODB.recordset")

vP = "Provider=Microsoft.Jet.OLEDB.3.51; "
vP = vP & "Data Source = C:\clothier.mdb"
oConn4.ConnectionString = vP
oConn4.Open
Response.Write oConn4.provider

oRS4.ActiveConnection = oConn4
oRS4.Open "vendors"
Response.Write "<TABLE BORDER=1><TR><TD>"
Response.write oRS4.GetString(,-1,vCol,vRow," ")
Response.Write "</TD></TR></TABLE>"
oRS4.close
set oRS4=nothing
oCOnn4.close
set oCOnn4=nothing
%>
</BODY></HTML>
```

**2.** List on a page the names of all the tables in the Clothier Database. Do not include system tables such as `MsysObjects`.

You can find the code for this example in the file `2726-06Conn-Exercise-2-ClothierSchema.asp`.

```
<%@ Language=VBScript %>
<HTML>
<HEAD>
<META NAME="GENERATOR" Content="Microsoft Visual Studio 6.0">
<TITLE>2726-06Conn-Exercise-2-Clothier-Schema</TITLE>
</HEAD>
<BODY>
<!--#include file="ADOvbs.inc"-->
<H2>Chapter 06 - Connections </H2>
<H3>Exercise #2 Clothier Schema</H3>

<%
dim oConn
set oConn=Server.CreateObject("ADODB.connection")
oConn.Open "DSN=Clothier"
set oRS=oConn.OpenSchema(adSchemaTables)
Response.Write "<BR><HR>Tables in Clothier.mdb" & "<BR><BR>"
while not oRS.EOF
  If left(ors("Table_Name"),4)<>"MSys" then
        Response.Write ors("Table_Name") & "<br>"
  End IF
  oRS.movenext
Wend
set oRS=nothing
set oConn=nothing
%>
</BODY>
</HTML>
```

Two places in the above code tend to be pitfalls for students. The first is that the `oRS` is not `Set` to an ADODB recordset, rather the schema in the following line:

```
set oRS=oConn.OpenSchema(adSchemaTables)
```

The other issue is getting rid of the system table names. The `If.. Then` prevents the writing of any table names that begin with the characters `Msys`.

# Chapter 6 Quiz

**1.** Why will the following code create an error?

```
dim oConn
dim oRS
set oConn=Server.CreateObject("ADODB.connection")
set oRS=Server.CreateObject("ADODB.recordset")
oRS.Open "People", oConn
oConn.open "DSN=Sailors"
Response.Write oRS("PeopleNameFirst")
```

**2.** What do you need to know prior to setting up an Access DSN-less connection?

**3.** What is the advantage to multiple recordsets on one connection?

**4.** How do you turn on Connection Pooling?

**5.** Will a DSN still work if the database to which it is connected is updated?

**6.** Why does the following code fail?

```
dim  oConn
dim oRS
dim strSource
set oConn=Server.CreateObject("ADODB.connection")
set ors=Server.CreateObject("ADODB.recordset")
strSource = "Driver={Microsoft Access Driver (*.mdb)}"
strSource = strSource & "DBQ=C:\My Documents\ASPADO\Sailors3.mdb"
oConn.ConnectionString = strSource
oConn.Open
sqltext = "SELECT PeopleNameFirst, PeopleNameLast, PeopleProfessionalClass "
sqltext = sqltext & " FROM People WHERE PeopleProfessionalClass=2;"
oRS.Open sqltext, oConn
```

# Chapter 6 Quiz Answers

**1.** The code attempts to open a recordset before the connection is created. The correct order of code is below:

```
dim oConn
dim oRS
set oConn=Server.CreateObject("ADODB.connection")
set oRS=Server.CreateObject("ADODB.recordset")
oConn.open "DSN=Sailors"
oRS.Open "People", oConn
Response.Write oRS("PeopleNameFirst")
```

**2.** File Specification of the .MDB file, including the server drive letter, path file name and file extension (MDB).
The type of data provider or drive that you want to use.

**3.** Since the server can use one connection to support the multiple recordsets, there is less load on the server, including:
Conservation of server memory
Conservation of server time

**4.** In the IIS server registry: change the setting for `StartConnectionPool` to 1
With `VBScript` in ASP, use the statement: `oConn.Properties("OLE DB Services") = -2`

**5.** Yes. You can use SQL statements to modify the structure (schema) of a database and the DSN is still valid.

**6.** The connection string lacks the semicolon and space between the Driver and DBQ specifications. It should be as follows.

```
strSource = "Driver={Microsoft Access Driver (*.mdb)}"
strSource = strSource & "; DBQ=C:\My Documents\ASPADO\Sailors3.mdb"
```

Or as follows:

```
strSource = "Driver={Microsoft Access Driver (*.mdb)}; "
strSource = strSource & "DBQ=C:\My Documents\ASPADO\Sailors3.mdb"
```

Welcome to the Microsoft...

Setup cannot install system files or update shared files if the files are in use. Before c... any open applications.

Egit Setup

Continue

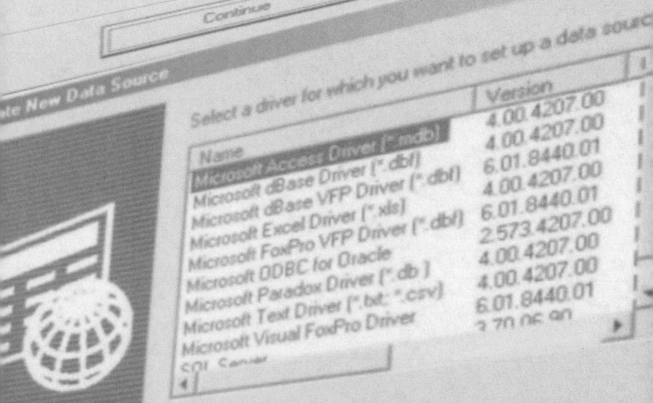

te New Data Source

Select a driver for which you want to set up a data sourc

| Name | Version |
|------|---------|
| Microsoft Access Driver (*.mdb) | 4.00.4207.00 |
| Microsoft dBase Driver (*.dbf) | 4.00.4207.00 |
| Microsoft dBase VFP Driver (*.dbf) | 6.01.8440.01 |
| Microsoft Excel Driver (*.xls) | 4.00.4207.00 |
| Microsoft FoxPro VFP Driver (*.dbf) | 6.01.8440.01 |
| Microsoft ODBC for Oracle | 2.573.4207.00 |
| Microsoft Paradox Driver (*.db ) | 4.00.4207.00 |
| Microsoft Text Driver (*.txt; *.csv) | 4.00.4207.00 |
| Microsoft Visual FoxPro Driver | 6.01.8440.01 |
| SQL Server | 3.70.06.90 |

Cancel

# Behind the Scenes of ADO

## Introduction

People are always asking me what went wrong with their ASP/ADO application. My favorite questions always go along the lines of "My ASP page doesn't work. What's wrong?" You know, if you went to a doctor and told him "I don't feel good. What's the matter with me?" he wouldn't have a clue. If you went to a mechanic and said "My car doesn't work. What's wrong with it?" he would probably laugh at you. There are 2 major aspects of troubleshooting ASP/ADO: symptoms, and a knowledge of the process. There are a lot of "links" in the "ASP/ADO chain." If you don't know what they are, even knowing what the symptoms are isn't going to help you much.

In this chapter we are going to take a look "under the hood" of ASP/ADO. We're going to discuss briefly what the various links in the ASP/ADO chain are, examine each one briefly, and show how they are inter-related.

Finally, we'll deal with common error messages, and we'll even create a few of our own, just to familiarize ourselves with them. We will talk about identifying the source of the problem, via the error message itself or the symptoms. We'll talk about some ways of getting those "invisible" problems to become "visible." And we'll discuss troubleshooting in general, along with some tips and tricks.

## The Components

An ASP/ADO Internet database application is one complex piece of work. It may seem that way to you already, but it will seem even more so by the time we're finished! Thankfully, most of the complexity of it is concealed from you and, in particular, from the users of your application. After all, one of the most important jobs of a programmer is to make his/her application "user friendly," which means making it simple to use, and hiding the intricacy of it from the user. The simpler it is on the *outside*, the more complex and difficult it is to program from the *inside*, because the programming is doing most of the work for the user.

This hidden complexity, however, is a two-edged sword. While it makes it *relatively* easy to work with databases, it also hides the problem areas when they occur. This can make the debugging process difficult at best. Knowing what these hidden components are is a good place to start. So let's take a look under the hood of the ASP/ADO chain. You should already be familiar with most of these, but we'll recap them briefly.

# ASP (Active Server Pages)

First, I want to examine the ASP chain in itself. As we know, ASP (**A**ctive **S**erver **P**ages), developed by Microsoft, is a *server-side scripting environment* that enables you to combine HTML, server-side scripting, and COM (**C**omponent **O**bject **M**odel) objects, to create interactive, **dynamic** web applications relatively easily. What do I mean by dynamic? I mean changeable. An HTML page is a **static** (unchangeable) document. While an HTML page may have some elements in it that can "play with" the appearance of the page, it is still the same data, the same HTML, the same scripting in the browser. When a request is sent from the browser to the web server for an HTML page, the web server simply pulls the file from its location on the server, and serves it to the browser. When a request for an ASP page is sent to the web server, the web server pulls the file from its location on the server, and feeds it to the **ASP Engine** (ASP.DLL) on the server. The ASP Engine then executes the scripting on the page and returns the dynamically-created HTML to the server, which in turn, streams it to the browser.

Consider the following illustration:

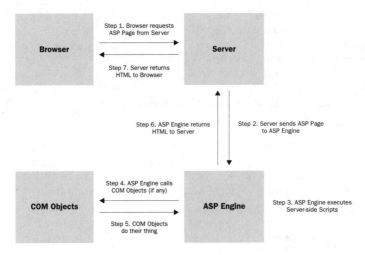

Here's the long version: The browser requests an ASP page from the server, either by URL (typed in, or hyperlink) or form input. The server sees the `.asp` extension, and sends the ASP page (file) to the ASP Engine on the server. The ASP Engine reads the file, which usually contains a mixture of server-side scripting and HTML, although it doesn't *have* to have server-side scripting *or* HTML (it can have one or the other alone).

As the ASP Engine reads the file, whenever it comes to server-side script, it executes it. Whenever it comes to HTML, it outputs it (back to the server). The process can involve a good bit of alternating back and forth between the server-side scripting and HTML in the page and, of course, you have some loops that contain a mixture of scripting and HTML. Any HTML inside the loop gets output every time the loop is executed.

Now here's what makes ASP so cool: ASP scripts can call (invoke *instances* of) COM objects stored on the server. COM objects are DLLs (**D**ynamic **L**ink **L**ibraries). They are a sort of pre-packaged programming that is bundled up into neat little packets which can be executed from within another program. Microsoft developed the Component Object Model, and it has become a software industry standard, because these objects can be used by any application, regardless of the language it was written in. Think of a COM object as a tool, of sorts. The application grabs the tool whenever it needs it, then puts it back on the shelf, where it can be used again by any application that needs it. In fact, more than one application can use these COM objects at any moment in time. What is actually happening is that a copy of the COM object is made (called an *instance*), and it is assigned its own *handle* (an identifier, like a name), which identifies who is using it.

There are all sorts of COM objects. Some are built right into the web server. Others can be *registered* (installed) on the web server. And what makes them so convenient is that the programming code to use them is built right into the object, in its *object model*. If you're not familiar with Object-Oriented Programming, let's just say that most of the functionality (or coding) is hidden from the application calling the object. In other words, let's compare a COM object to a car. The car has an engine, an electrical system, and a whole host of other parts that make it go. But you don't have to know how the engine works to drive the car. All you have to know is how to start and stop the engine, make it go forwards and backwards, use the steering wheel and brakes, and a few other things. The rest of it is unimportant to you, the driver.

The server-side scripts in the ASP page can often call these COM objects, and the COM objects will do their thing, sometimes returning HTML to the ASP Engine to be output to the server, and sometimes doing other things that are basically invisible to the browser.

As the HTML is output by the ASP Engine to the server, the server outputs the HTML in a stream to the browser. The result is the page seen by the browser. Because this page can look entirely different, depending on the results of the server-side scripting, it is called a *dynamically* generated page.

> *This has nothing to do with "Dynamic HTML" (or DHTML). Dynamic HMTL code is static! It produces a page which can change its appearance in the browser, but the HTML code for the page is always the same (static).*

# ADO (ActiveX Data Objects)

Again, as you should by now know, **A**ctiveX **D**ata **O**bjects is another Microsoft-developed technology for working with databases. ActiveX is synonymous with COM. ActiveX objects are a special kind of COM object developed specifically for the Internet. Therefore, as you can see, ADO is a collection of COM objects that you can use with ASP. It comes pre-packaged with IIS (Internet Information Server) and Microsoft PWS (Personal Web Server).

ADO is what is known as an **application-level** programming interface for database programming. It doesn't interact with databases directly, but instead interacts with a **system-level** programming interface called **OLE DB**.

Consider the following illustration:

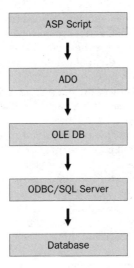

Perhaps now the complexity of the situation is becoming a bit more clear! As you can see, at the top level of the chain we have ASP. In fact, ADO can be used by a wide variety of applications, including ASP scripting and stand-alone applications written in C++ or Visual Basic, for example, and within databases themselves, in stored procedures, modules, etc.

When an instance of an ADO object (such as a `Connection` or `RecordSet`) is created, ADO interacts with OLE DB to communicate with the **provider**. A provider is a component such as a SQL-compliant database, indexed-sequential file, spreadsheet, etc. You will occasionally see error messages concerning providers. For example, you may see an error message indicating that the provider does not support a certain kind of `recordset`.

ADO is what is known as a **consumer**. A consumer is a component that *consumes* (uses) OLE DB data. Let's briefly review ODBC and OLE DB.

# ODBC (Open Database Connectivity)

Most often, you're going to be connecting to a database, such as Access or SQL Server, via ODBC. You can, however, connect directly to a SQL Server database without using ODBC. Later, we will discuss connecting to databases in various ways, but first let's look at ODBC.

ODBC is an international standard developed by Microsoft for manipulating relational data using SQL (Structured Query Language) among a wide variety of data sources. SQL was *not* developed by Microsoft (surprise, surprise!). It was developed a number of years ago by IBM. However, it took Microsoft to make it really useful by developing a technology that could make use of this language to interact with virtually any kind of database.

The idea of ODBC is for one database-type application to be able to interact with data stored in any other ODBC-compliant application, without having to use the interface provided by the application which stored the data. With ODBC, you can connect an Access database to a Visual FoxPro database, for example, and work with the data in the Visual FoxPro database through Access.

This is all done using **ODBC drivers**, which are DLLs containing the native code of the data source. An application simply uses the open standard of the ODBC programming interface to talk to the driver, sending SQL statements to the driver, and receiving data back from the driver, in the form of return values, cursors containing data, etc.

Usually, the driver is accessed through a System DSN (**D**ata **S**ource **N**ame), which is the way most often recommended by Microsoft. Remember, we set up DSNs for the Sailors and Clothier databases back in Chapter 2. However, you can also create DSN-less connections, as well as File DSNs. In most cases, however, ODBC is what is used to make the connection and interact with the data source.

# OLE DB

OLE DB is Microsoft's system-level programming interface to manage data across the organization. It is an open specification designed to build on the success of ODBC by providing an open standard for accessing all types of data. ODBC was designed to interact with *relational* databases. OLE DB can access both *relational* and *non-relational* information sources, including ODBC sources, Mainframe ISAM/VSAM and hierarchical databases, e-mail and file system stores, text, graphical, and geographical data, custom business objects, etc.

OLE DB is a collection of COM interfaces encapsulating various database management system **services**. A service is a component that extends the functionality of data providers, by providing interfaces not natively supported by the datastore. A cursor engine, for example, can provide a scrollable (movement forwards and backwards) cursor (synonymous with RecordSet), where the datasource may just provide a forward-only cursor.

ADO has three core objects, which are all discussed in greater detail elsewhere in this book:

**Connection**: The Connection object is what it sounds like. It contains all of the information needed for an ADO application to connect with a data source, such as the System DSN, user ID and password, and any additional parameters needed to specify what kind of connection is being made. In addition, it provides a number of methods for executing various functions, such as executing a command, conducting transactions, closing the connection, etc.

**Command**: The ADO Command object provides the SQL statement or Stored Procedure name, along with any parameters, and all related information regarding the command being sent to the data source.

**RecordSet**: The RecordSet is a cursor, which can contain the data returned by a query, as well as *metadata*, that is, information about the fields storing the data, such as data type, length, etc. The RecordSet has many properties and methods, and is most useful for working with data.

OLE DB has four core objects:

1. **Data Source**: The Data Source contains data and functions for working with the data provider (such as an Access or SQL Server database). It contains information about the location and type of data provider being used, user ID and password information, and functions for initializing the connection between the application and the data source.

2. **Session**: The Session object defines the transactional scope (what elements are involved, where it starts and stops, etc.) of the work done within a connection.

3. **Command**: The Command object contains the functions for invoking the execution of data-definition or data-manipulation commands, such as SQL statements.

4. **Rowset**: The Rowset is the container for the data.

As you can see, the relationship between the ADO objects and the OLE DB objects is very close, and this is because the OLE DB objects are encapsulated by the ADO objects. The Connection object of ADO combines the encapsulation of the OLE DB Data Source and Session objects. The ADO Command object encapsulates the OLE DB Command object. And the ADO RecordSet object encapsulates the OLE DB Rowset object. This is summarized below:

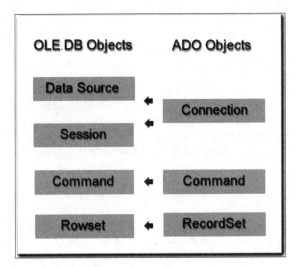

# RDS (Remote Data Services)

RDS is a technology developed by Microsoft that allows an ADO RecordSet to be used across one of three protocols: HTTP, HTTPS (an encrypted HTTP connection), and DCOM (Distributed **COM**). RDS allows data stores to be accessed across the web, rather than having to have all of the files on a local network. It was specifically developed for the use of Internet, web-based clients (such as ASP pages on a web server), but can be used in any application using one of these three protocols

# MDAC (Microsoft Data Access Components)

MDAC is the combination of ADO, ODBC, OLE DB, and RDS, as well as various ODBC drivers and OLE DB Data Providers. It also includes (in the later versions) extensions to both OLE DB and ADO, such as On-Line Analytical Processing, and Multi-Dimensional Data. The **MDAC Distribution** is an executable file which installs all of these on your computer. As at the time of writing, the latest MDAC Distribution is version 2.1, which is available for free download from the Microsoft web site, at `http://www.microsoft.com/msdownload/uda/mdac21/mdac_typ21.asp`.

# The Process

Okay, now that we've examined each of the components in the process, and discussed how each one behaves, let's summarize the process and talk about some particulars.

## Play By Play

Let's take a look at some ADO code and analyze the chain of events that is happening. The following code opens a connection to the `profile.mdb` database and gets records from it. It simply moves through the records one at a time, then closes the `RecordSet` and `Connection`:

```
<%
  ' ** Create and open the Connection
  Set cn = Server.CreatObject("ADODB.Connection")
  cn.Open "DSN=profile;"

  ' ** Execute the SQL Command, returning a RecordSet
  Set rs = cn.Execute("SELECT * FROM profile")

  ' ** Loop through the RecordSet, one record at a time
  While NOT rs.EOF
    rs.MoveNext
  Wend

  ' ** Clean up
  rs.Close
  cn.Close
  Set rs = Nothing
  Set cn = Nothing
%>
```

Here's what is happening:

```
Set cn = Server.CreateObject("ADODB.Connection")
```

The first line of the code creates an instance of the ADO `Connection` object and assigns it to the object variable cn. So, what is going on there?

Since the page has an an .asp extension, the web server feeds it to the ASP Engine on the server. The ASP Engine reads the first line of code and creates an ADO `Connection` object. ADODB is the parent object of ADO. All ADO objects, properties, and methods belong to the ADODB object model. ADO connects with OLE DB and accesses the OLE DB `Data Source` and `Session` objects, encapsulating them in its `Connection` object.

```
cn.Open "DSN=profile;"
```

The second line of code uses the `Connection` object's `Open` method to establish a connection with a System DSN named "profile". As you can see, this is done with a single line of ASP/ADO code. ADO takes this line of code and performs a variety of OLE DB functions with it, transparently. OLE DB talks to the ODBC Driver Manager and establishes a connection to the data source (profile.mdb).

```
Set rs = cn.Execute("SELECT * FROM profile")
```

The third line of code uses the `Connection` object's `Execute` method to return a `recordset`. Again, ADO performs a variety of OLE DB functions with this single line of code: initializes an OLE DB `Rowset` object, creates an ADO `RecordSet` object, and associates the `RecordSet` with the OLE DB `Rowset`. Then it initializes an OLE DB `Command` object, creates an ADO `Command` object, associates the ADO `Command` object with the OLE DB `Command` object, and executes the command ("SELECT * FROM profile"), filling the `Rowset`/`RecordSet` with the data returned by the provider.

```
While NOT rs.EOF
   rs.MoveNext
Wend
```

Here's a VBScript `While` loop. The loop is ASP/VBScript, but each time the loop is executed, ADO/OLE DB methods are being executed. The loop begins with a check of the recordset's `EOF` property. Again, this is cascaded down from the ASP Engine to the ADO DLL, which talks to OLE DB, which performs the actual processes, accessing the data source via ODBC, and reporting back up through the "chain of command" to the script.

```
rs.Close
cn.Close
Set rs = Nothing
Set cn = Nothing
```

Again, the same kinds of things are going on. When the `recordset` is closed, the OLE DB `Rowset` is closed, performing a variety of cleanup operations on it. The `Connection` is closed, and this tells OLE DB to terminate the Session with the data source, and perform all of its `Connection` object cleanup processes. Finally, all objects are destroyed, freeing up processor and memory capability.

# To Sum It Up

The idea of Universal Data Access is wonderful, but the process is quite complex, as there are so many kinds of data sources, and each one behaves in a different way. Even the SQL language varies from provider to provider. In order to achieve this remarkable goal, two highly complex and intelligent programming interfaces (OLE DB and ODBC) were created.

OLE DB and ODBC can be used by a large variety of programming interfaces. Because the scope of an ASP web application is limited to a specific set of functions, ADO was developed to speed up and simplify the development process. Each ADO object, property, method, or collection encapsulates all of the OLE DB objects, properties, and methods necessary to perform what ADO is designed to do. In a very real sense, ADO is to OLE DB what Visual Basic, C++, or other high-level programming languages are to Assembler. While the number of ADO objects, properties, methods, and collections may seem formidable, it is dwarfed by the number of objects, properties, and methods of OLE DB.

Of course, you can see from the number of objects in the ASP/ADO chain just why ADO consumes so much processor overhead. There are a whole lot of links in that chain, and the underlying technologies (OLE DB and ODBC) are highly complex, as they are capable of interacting with virtually *any* kind of data source.

# Troubleshooting ASP/ADO

If you remember the illustration of the ASP/ADO chain, you can see that there are five basic levels of technology involved in any ASP/ADO operation: ASP, ADO, OLE DB, ODBC, and the data source itself. In fact, four of them are completely invisible to you. Even if you use the ASP Script Debuggers available today, you are never going to get below the top level (ASP). So, how do we identify the source of a problem in an ASP/ADO web application?

Fortunately, ASP has an error reporting mechanism that streams out an error message to the browser, indicating

❑ The technology reporting the error

❑ The error number

❑ The error message itself

❑ What line in the ASP script the error occurred on

Here's a typical error message page from a browser:

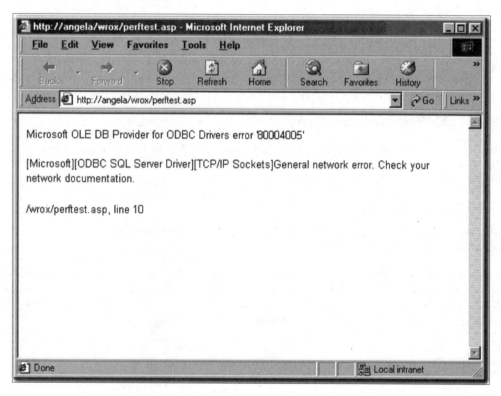

Note that we can see four of the five technologies involved in the process, mentioned right in the error message: OLE DB, ODBC, SQL Server (the data source), and ASP. How did I get this error? I just opened a perfectly good ASP/ADO page that connects to a local SQL Server database. Unfortunately, SQL Server wasn't running at the time! Note that, depending on your operating system and setup, your error messages may differ slightly from this, in appearance and wording. However, all of the basic elements will be there.

The first line of the message indicates who is sending the message: "OLE DB Provider for ODBC Drivers". It also includes the error number (which is practically irrelevant – that's why they include the error message text itself!). The second line of the message indicates at what level the error occurred: "SQL Server Driver" (the SQL Server ODBC driver). It also includes the text of the error message that was reported by the ODBC driver: "General Network Error. Check your network documentation". The third line (the second line is wrapped due to the size of the window) indicates the ASP page that caused the error, and the line number where the processing of the code stopped, due to the error.

# Common ASP/ADO Errors

The following is a list of the most common error messages, and what they indicate:

[Microsoft][ODBC Driver Manager] Data source name not found and no default driver specified

This error occurs when you have specified a DSN in your connection string, and the DSN you have specified doesn't exist. There are two common reasons why you might get this error. Either you have forgotten to create (or to get your hosting service to create) a DSN, or you have misspelled the DSN name in the connection string.

[Microsoft][ODBC Microsoft Access Driver] Could not find file '(unknown)'.

This error occurs when the DSN is pointing to a database that doesn't exist at the location specified in the DSN. It occurs most often when using Access, or other file-based databases. It can also occur when using a File DSN instead of a System DSN. Always use a System DSN with file-based databases.

ADODB.Field error '800a0bcd'

Either BOF or EOF is True, or the current record has been deleted; the operation requested by the application requires a current record.

This occurs when you attempt to work with data in a field in a recordset, and there is no current record. It occurs most frequently when you forget to check for EOF after performing a SELECT statement, and the SELECT statement returns no records. It can also occur if you have been moving through a recordset without checking for EOF, and you move past the end of the recordset, then attempt to work with data in a field.

[Microsoft][ODBC Microsoft Access Driver] Too few parameters. Expected 1.

This error occurs most frequently when you have misspelled some part of your SQL statement, for example, a field name in a table. When the ODBC driver attempts to execute the SQL statement, the database thinks that the misspelled field name is the name of a parameter, because it doesn't recognize the name.

### ADODB.Fields error '800a0cc1'

ADO could not find the object in the collection corresponding to the name or ordinal reference requested by the application.

This error generally indicates one of two things. You may have misspelled a field name that was selected in a query, and attempted to work with that field. You may have left the field out of your SELECT statement's fields list, and then attempted to work with it.

### Microsoft OLE DB Provider for ODBC Drivers error '80040e24'

The rowset does not support fetching backwards

This error occurs when attempting to use any cursor movement method (such as MoveLast, MovePrevious, or MoveFirst) other than MoveNext, when using a Forward Only cursor type. (Actually, you can use MoveFirst without any problems if the cursor is located on the first record, but why would you want to?). The Forward Only cursor type is the default ADO cursor type for recordsets. If you want to move forwards and backwards in the recordset, you must first set the CursorType property of the recordset, before opening it. If you open the recordset using the Connection object's, or the Command object's Execute method, you will always get a Forward Only cursor.

### ADODB.Recordset error '800a0e78'

The operation requested by the application is not allowed if the object is closed.

This error occurs usually in long scripts with a lot of nested loops, nested function calls, and such, and in scripts which open and close more than one recordset. It happens when you attempt to close a recordset that is already closed. If your code gets too complex, and in some special cases, you may want to check the state of the recordset before attempting to close it. You can do this by checking the State property of the recordset. For example:

```
<!--#INCLUDE FILE="adovbs.inc" -->
<! -- Note: The adovbs.inc file includes the constant definitions for all of the
enumerated constants in ADO. Using the constant names rather than the numeric values
makes it much easier to work with them -- >
<%
  If rs.State = adStateOpen then rs.Close
%>
```

You can also check for adStateClosed if you need to. These states apply to both RecordSet and Connection Objects. Note that I used an INCLUDE statement, including adovbs.inc. This include file contains the enumeration constants for all of ADO.

[Microsoft][ODBC Microsoft Access Driver] Data type mismatch in criteria expression.

This error occurs most often when you do not use the correct punctuation in your WHERE clause. In the WHERE clause, data types of literal values are defined by the kind of delimiters that you place around them. To recap from chapter 4, the rules are similar for Access and SQL Server, with a couple of exceptions:

**Access:**

- ❑ **numeric** (includes money and yes/no fields) – no delimiters (3.14 for example)
- ❑ **date-time** – "#" (#1/1/1999# for example)
- ❑ **text** – single quotes ('joe@eats.com' for example)

**SQL Server:**

- ❑ **numeric** (includes money and bit fields) – no delimiters (3.14 for example)
- ❑ **date-time** – single quotes ('1/1/1999' for example)
- ❑ **text** – single quotes ('joe@eats.com' for example

[Microsoft][ODBC Microsoft Access Driver] Syntax error (missing operator) in query expression 'lname LIKE 'O'Hara".

This error occurs when you are using single quotes in your SQL Query string. It often happens when you are getting form input from a user, and the user types in a string with a single quote, or several single quotes (as in my example, where I used the name "O'Hara"). Single quotes are string delimiters in ODBC and Transact-SQL (SQL Server).

ODBC (and Transact-SQL) does have an answer for this, though. When you double up your single quotes, it indicates to the ODBC driver (or SQL Server) that you are referring to a literal single quote, not a string delimiter. Sometimes double quotes (") can cause a problem too. I use a function to convert the data before putting it into the SQL statement, when it is text data:

```
Function newstr(str)
  newstr = Replace(Replace(str, "'", "''"), CHR(34) , "&quot;")
End Function
```

This function uses the VBScript Replace() function to replace single quotes with double single quotes, and double quotes with HTML encoding for double quotes. Why HTML encoding? Because the data will be eventually displayed in a web page. The "&quot;" will be displayed as double quotes. CHR() is the VBScript function for getting a character value from the ASCII numeric value of a character. I use it with the double quotes because the double quote is a string delimiter in VBScript. If I were to use """, it would generate an error. 34 is the value of the double quote character (").

Here's an example of the function at work:

```
<%
  Function newstr(str)
    newstr = Replace(Replace(str, "'", "''"), CHR(34), "&quot;")
  End Function
```

```
Dim lname

Set cn = Server.CreateObject("ADODB.Connection")
cn.Open "DSN=profile;"

lname = newstr(Request.Form("lname"))
strSQL = "SELECT * FROM profile WHERE lname LIKE '" & lname & "'"
Set rs = cn.Execute(strSQL)

' ** remaining code here
%>
```

[Microsoft][ODBC Microsoft Access Driver] Cannot update. Database or object is read-only.

You will see some version of this error when attempting to INSERT or UPDATE records in your Access (or other file-based) database. It usually indicates that the "IUSER_<machine name>" User account (the anonymous IIS user account) doesn't have change permission on the folder containing the database file on the server. This is something that the Network Administrator for the server has to set.

It can also indicate that security settings in the database itself may be preventing the INSERT or UPDATE, in an Access database, for example. This is something you can check for yourself.

[Microsoft][ODBC Microsoft SQL Server Driver][TCP/IP Sockets] Logon Failed()

This error occurs when a bad user name/password combination is used to access the SQL Server. It is most often associated with your connection string. You may have misspelled the user name and/or password. The user login may not exist on the SQL Server. Or, the login may not have been assigned the correct permissions for the tables in the database.

[Microsoft][ODBC SQL Server Driver][SQL Server]String or binary data would be truncated.

This is an error you will not see with Access. It occurs when you attempt to insert or update a record, and the length of the data exceeds the maximum length of the field. Access will blithely truncate the data and insert it, with no problem. SQL Server will not. The solution for this is to use good form validation to make sure that the length of the data is not longer than the length of the field. And although Access will accept and truncate data that is too long, it's still a good idea to use form validation with Access, so that the user will not enter too much data, and end up with only part of it inserted.

A note about form validation: you can do form validation either using JavaScript on the client side, or ASP VBScript on the server side. I prefer and recommend using client-side JavaScript form validation for the purpose of saving processor and memory overhead on the server, as well as reducing network traffic.

[Microsoft][ODBC Microsoft Access Driver] Field 'profile.fname' cannot be a zero-length string.

When you design an Access database, one of the properties of a text field is whether it allows or disallows zero-length strings. This is a different property from the REQUIRED property. Access and SQL Server both share the quality of having fields which allow NULL values. In addition, Access can require that a string contain some data. When you set the REQUIRED property of a field, you are saying that the value can not be NULL. In other words, you must put something into the field when you add a new record. When you disallow zero-length strings, you are requiring that a string of one or more characters be entered into the field. Here is what the error message looks like if you don't include a field that doesn't allow NULL values in an INSERT statement:

[Microsoft][ODBC Microsoft Access Driver] The field 'profile.fname' cannot contain a Null value because the Required property for this field is set to True. Enter a value in this field.

The ALLOW ZERO-LENGTH STRING property is set to NO by default. For the zero-length field error, there are two solutions:

❑ When you design the table, set the ALLOW ZERO-LENGTH STRING property to NO.

❑ Use form validation when necessary, to make sure that the form field is not left blank.

The solution to the null value error is to make sure to include the field in your INSERT statement. Example:

```
strSQL = INSERT INTO profile (fname) VALUES ('" & Request.Form("fname") & "')"
```

[Microsoft][ODBC Microsoft Access Driver] Syntax error in INSERT INTO statement

This error can occur in both Access and SQL Server web applications. Most often it is because one of your fields has a name that is a **reserved word**. A reserved word is a word that the database uses to identify some function or constant internally. For example, if you name a field "Date" in Access, and use the following SQL statement, you will get that error:

```
INSERT INTO profile (lname, date) VALUES ('Kevin', #03/19/56#)
```

There are two possible solutions:

❑ Avoid using reserved words for field names.

❑ If you have no control over this, enclose the field name in square brackets ("[date]" for example) whenever you reference it in your SQL statement. This indicates to the database that it is a field or table name, and not a reserved word reference.

A similar error can occur when you name fields with spaces in the name ("first name" for example). the solutions are basically the same. You can either avoid using spaces in your field names, or enclose references to those fields in square brackets ("[first name]" for example).

# Debugging Techniques

Debugging is possibly one third to one half of the work that is involved in programming. The more complex a web application (or any kind of application, for that matter), the more time you're going to need in the debugging process. Writing an application that works is only half the battle. Writing one that *always* works is quite another story!

Why is this? If you can remember Art Linkletter, (then you're probably over 40 too!) he used to say "Children say the darndest things." Well, I have a saying too: "People *do* the darndest things." A good application has programming to handle virtually any kind of user error. It's one thing to write code that does what it's supposed to, when the user does what they're supposed to. It's quite another (and quite necessary) to write code that does what it's supposed to when people *don't* do what they're supposed to!

So, there are two aspects to writing solid code: one is to get the bugs out of your application, so that it works properly. The second is to figure out what can possibly go wrong, and write code that anticipates and handles user error and problems in the "pipeline". This often involves deliberately trying to mess up the application in a number of ways. If you succeed, then you know that you've got to build in some sort of safety net. That's why beta software is released: the software developer is getting volunteers to test the program on a variety of platforms, and getting a large enough group of people to make every kind of user error imaginable. The beta testers report problems back to the software developer, and the software developer builds in fixes for the problems.

We've discussed that four fifths of the ASP/ADO chain is invisible and for the most part inaccessible. We've mentioned that even if you have an ASP Script Debugger, such as the debugger that comes with Microsoft Visual InterDev, you will only be able to see the ASP/ADO VBScript code, and not any of the underlying processes. So, the biggest challenge facing you is going to be making the invisible visible.

As we've mentioned, ASP has a built-in device for helping you get started: the error page. This gives a number of clues as to what went wrong. It gives you a URL and a line number to start from. But this is just the beginning. We're now going to discuss a number of techniques that you can use to get a look at those hidden processes. To do this, we will use `searchprofiles.asp`, and make some modifications to the page that will generate some errors in different circumstances. The code for `searchprofiles.asp` is below. To perform the exercises we're going to do, make a copy of this and modify it as you go:

```
<%
' ** This page is used for both an initial search page, and a search results page.
' ** As such, the code contains a number of conditional statements to determine
' ** which of these it is, and what code to execute.

' ** globally used Connection String
cstring = "DSN=profile"

' ** You can set the maximum number of records per page using this variable
maxrecords = 20

' ** variables to hold form values
Dim email
Dim lname
Dim city
Dim state
Dim country
Dim showresults
Dim results
Dim title
Dim url

' ** Function to determine a URL for viewing profiles of the names displayed
' ** It can be used for administrative purposes, if you know the password
' ** and how to use it in the form

Function geturl(master, e)
   If master = TRUE then
      geturl = "default.asp?mode=pword&email=" & e
   Else
      geturl = "viewprofile.asp?email=" & e & "&mode=view"
   End If
End Function

' ** Function to format the names displayed on the page
```

```
Function getname(l,f,h,u)
  name = ""
  If u = TRUE Then
    If h = "" Then h = "Hey You!"
    getname = h
  Else
    If f = "" Then
      name = "???"
    Else
      name = f
    End If
    If l = "" Then
      name = name & " ???"
    Else
      name = name & " " & l
    End If
    getname = name
  End If
End Function

' ** results determines whether any records were returned by a query (if any)
results = TRUE
' ** showresults determines whether this is the initial search page or a results
' ** page
showresults = FALSE

' ** gets the values from the form (if any)
lname = Request.Form("lname")
city = Request.Form("city")
state = Request.Form("state")
country = Request.Form("country")
email = Request.Form("email")

' ** if the word "webmaster" was typed into the city field of the form
' ** then the user is the webmaster, and URLs for viewing the profiles
' ** of the individuals will pull up an editable profile
If city = "webmaster" Then
  city = ""
  lname = "Any"
  Session("webmaster") = TRUE
End If

' ** "lname" is a drop-down list box. If the form was submitted
' ** then it will always have a value. This is used to determine
' ** whether a form was submitted. If so, then a query is built
' ** from the contents of the form, and the query is executed.
If lname <> "" Then

  ' ** "title" is used to display a dynamically-created title,
  ' ** indicating whether this is the initial search form
  ' ** or a search results page
  title = " - Results"
  showresults = TRUE
  email = Request.Form("email")
  Set cn = Server.CreateObject("ADODB.Connection")

  ' ** Since we're limiting the number of records returned, we will have to
  ' ** explicitly create our RecordSet, and set the MaxRecords property of it.
  ' ** We will also be using the RecordSet's Open method to execute the query.
  Set rs = Server.CreateObject("ADODB.RecordSet")
  cn.Open cstring
  rs.MaxRecords = maxrecords
  rs.ActiveConnection = cn

  ' ** Here we begin to build the query by conditionally concatenating values from
  ' ** the form into a query string named "strSQL"
  strSQL = "SELECT lname, fname, handle, usehandle, email " &_
  "FROM profile WHERE (email > '" & email & "')"
```

```
   ' ** The condition for the drop-down list box ("lname") is whether or not
   ' ** the value is "Any" (the first selection)
   If (lname <> "Any") Then
     strSQL = strSQL & " AND (lname = '" & lname & "')"
   End If

   ' ** Conditions for including text boxes are whether they contain any value
   If city <> "" Then
     strSQL = strSQL & " AND (city LIKE '%" & city & "%')"
   End If
   If state <> "" Then
     strSQL = strSQL & " AND (state LIKE '%" & state & "%')"
   End If
   If country <> "" Then
     strSQL = strSQL & " AND (country LIKE '%" & country & "%')"
   End If

   ' ** Since the "email" field in the table is uniquely valued, we will ORDER BY
   ' ** that field, and get the value of the last email in the RecordSet, to pass
   ' ** to the next page.
   strSQL = strSQL & " ORDER BY email"
   rs.Open strSQL

   ' ** We check for EOF here, because of the dual nature of the page. If the
   ' ** RecordSet is empty, we set the value of the "results" variable to FALSE.
   If rs.EOF Then
     results = FALSE
     rs.Close
     cn.Close
     Set rs = Nothing
     Set cn = Nothing
   End If
  End If
%>

<HTML>

<HEAD>
<STYLE><!--a:hover{color:rgb(255,0,0); text-decoration: none }a{ text-decoration:
none; font-family: Arial, Helvetica; font-weight: bold  }//.--></STYLE>
<TITLE>Search Profiles<%=title%></TITLE>
</HEAD>

<BODY BGCOLOR="#FFFFFF" TEXT="#000000" LINK="#0000FF" vLINK="#008080" aLINK="#FF0000"
BACKGROUND="images/backgrounds/takback.jpg">
<!-- #INCLUDE FILE="_private/header.inc" -->

<P ALIGN="center"><FONT FACE="Arial" SIZE="4" COLOR="#8000FF"><STRONG>Search
Profiles<%=title%></STRONG></FONT></P>

<TABLE BORDER="0">
<TR>
<TD VALIGN="top"><STRONG><FONT FACE="Arial" SIZE="2"><A HREF="Default.asp">Enter
Your Profile</A><BR>
<A HREF="passprofile.asp">Edit Your Profile</A></FONT></STRONG><BR>
<!--#INCLUDE FILE="books.inc" -->     </TD>
<TD VALIGN="top" ALIGN="center">

<%
  If showresults = TRUE Then
    If results = FALSE Then
%>
```

```
        <P><FONT FACE="Arial" SIZE="2" COLOR="#FF0000"><STRONG>
No Profiles matched your criteria. Please try again.</STRONG></FONT></P>
<%
    Else
%>
        <P><STRONG><FONT FACE="Arial" SIZE="2">The following Profiles matched your
criteria. Click on the name to view the profile, or click on the Email Address to
send email.</FONT></STRONG></P>
        <TABLE BORDER="1" WIDTH="100%" borderCOLOR="#00FFFF" cellspacing="0">
        <TR>
        <TD WIDTH="50%"><FONT FACE="Arial" SIZE="2"
COLOR="#8000FF"><STRONG>Name</STRONG></FONT></TD>
        <TD WIDTH="50%"><FONT FACE="Arial" SIZE="2" COLOR="#8000FF"><STRONG>Email
Address</STRONG>
        </FONT></TD>
        </TR>
<%
    ' ** This is the loop for displaying the results of a search
    x = 0

    ' ** we use both methods to check for the end of the list of records. The reason
    ' ** for this is that depending on the version of MDAC installed on the server,
    ' ** the maxrecords property of the RecordSet may or may not be supported by the
    ' ** provider. This is for maximum cross-platform compatibility.

    While (NOT rs.EOF) AND (x < maxrecords)
%>
        <TR>
        <TD WIDTH="50%"> <FONT FACE="Arial" SIZE="2"><a
        HREF="
<%
        =geturl(Session("webmaster"), rs("email").value)%>"><%=getname(rs("lname")_
            .value,rs("fname").value, rs("handle").value, rs("usehandle")_
            .value)%></A></FONT> </TD>
        <TD WIDTH="50%"> <FONT FACE="Arial" SIZE="2"><A HREF_
            ="mailto:<%=rs("email")%>"><%=rs("email")%></A></FONT>
        </TD>
        </TR>
<%
    x = x + 1

    ' ** The value of the email address is obtained each time through the loop.
    ' ** When the loop is ended, the value will be the last one in the RecordSet.
    ' ** It will be passed on in a hidden form field if there are more records.
    email = rs("email").value
    rs.MoveNext
    Wend

%>
        </TABLE>
<%

    rs.Close
    cn.Close
    Set rs = Nothing
    Set cn = Nothing

    ' ** If x is equal to maxrecords, then there are probably more records. The
    ' ** values of the
    ' ** form fields will be passed in hidden form fields to the next page (this
    ' ** same page).
    If x = maxrecords Then
%>
```

```
                    <FORM METHOD="POST" ACTION="searchprofiles.asp">
                    <INPUT TYPE="hidden" NAME="city" VALUE="<%=city%>"><INPUT TYPE="hidden"
NAME="country"
                    VALUE="<%=country%>"><INPUT TYPE="hidden" NAME="email"
VALUE="<%=email%>"><INPUT
                    TYPE="hidden" NAME="lname" VALUE="<%=lname%>"><INPUT TYPE="hidden"
NAME="state"
                    VALUE="<%=state%>"><P><INPUT TYPE="submit" VALUE="Next <%=maxrecords%>
Matching Records"
                    NAME="B1"></P>
                    </FORM>

                <%Else%>
                    <P ALIGN="center"><FONT FACE="Arial" SIZE="2">End of List</FONT></P>
                    <P><%End If
                End If
            End If%> </P>
    <P><STRONG><FONT FACE="Arial" SIZE="2">Please use the form below to search for
Profiles:</FONT></STRONG></P>

    <FORM METHOD="POST" ACTION="searchprofiles.asp">
    <TABLE BORDER="0">
    <TR>
    <TD ALIGN="right"><STRONG><FONT FACE="Arial" SIZE="2">Last Name:
</FONT></STRONG></TD>
    <TD><%

    ' ** This is a loop to populate the "lname" drop-down list box with all the last
    ' ** names in the database
    Set cn = Server.CreateObject("ADODB.Connection")
    cn.Open cstring
    strSQL = "SELECT lname FROM profile GROUP BY lname ORDER BY lname"
    Set rs = cn.Execute(strSQL)
%>
<P><SELECT NAME="lname" SIZE="1">
<OPTION VALUE="Any">Any</OPTION>
<%While NOT rs.EOF%>                <OPTION
VALUE="<%=rs("lname")%>"><%=rs("lname")%></OPTION>

<%
    rs.MoveNext
Wend
rs.Close
cn.Close
Set rs = Nothing
Set cn = Nothing
%></SELECT><BR>
<FONT FACE="Arial" SIZE="1">All last names in the database appear here.</FONT></TD>
</TR>
<TR>
<TD ALIGN="right"><STRONG><FONT FACE="Arial" SIZE="2">City: </FONT></STRONG></TD>
<TD><INPUT TYPE="text" NAME="city" SIZE="20"><FONT FACE="Arial" SIZE="1"><BR>
(Returns records <em>containing</em> what you type in)</FONT></TD>
</TR>
<TR>
<TD ALIGN="right"><STRONG><FONT FACE="Arial" SIZE="2">State: </FONT></STRONG></TD>
<TD><INPUT TYPE="text" NAME="state" SIZE="20"><FONT FACE="Arial" SIZE="1"><BR>
(Returns records <em>containing</em> what you type in)</FONT></TD>
</TR>
<TR>
<TD ALIGN="right"><STRONG><FONT FACE="Arial" SIZE="2">Country: </FONT></STRONG></TD>
<TD><INPUT TYPE="text" NAME="country" SIZE="20"><FONT FACE="Arial" SIZE="1"><BR>
(Returns records <em>containing</em> what you type in)</FONT></TD>
</TR>
<TR>
```

```
<TD ALIGN="right"></TD>
<TD><STRONG><FONT FACE="Arial" SIZE="2"><INPUT TYPE="submit" VALUE="Search"
NAME="B1"></FONT></STRONG><INPUT
TYPE="reset" VALUE="Reset" NAME="B2"></TD>
</TR>
</TABLE>
</FORM>

<!-- #INCLUDE FILE="_private/footer.inc" -->

</BODY>
</HTML>
```

# Viewing the SQL

Many times, you may have a long SQL statement, made by concatenating together a lot of values. If something goes wrong, chances are you're not going to have a clue as to what the problem is, because the line number indicated by the error message is the line which executes the SQL statement, not any of the lines of code in which the SQL statement is built, which is where the error actually resides. Worse yet, your SQL statement might be getting values from a form in a previous page, and of course, the problem may lie in the value of one of those form fields. So, how do we quickly identify the problem?

The first thing to keep in mind is that you want to put your SQL statement into a variable. (I always use strSQL as the variable name for my query string.) That way, the variable value can be accessed later.

What we do is to remark out the line of code that executes the SQL statement, and any subsequent lines of code that might throw up an error (due to the SQL statement not having been executed). Then we add code to display the value of the query string (the variable strSQL in this case).

## Try it out – Viewing the SQL

This is going to be a series of exercises in which we will view the SQL query for searchprofiles.asp under several different circumstances.

The first one is simple. Find the <BODY> tag in your code, and add the following line of ASP code immediately after it:

```
<P><%=strSQL%></P>
```

The section of code will now look like this:

```
<BODY BGCOLOR="#FFFFFF" TEXT="#000000" LINK="#0000FF" vLINK="#008080" aLINK="#FF0000"
BACKGROUND="images/backgrounds/takback.jpg">
<P><%=strSQL%></P>
<!-- #INCLUDE FILE="_private/header.inc" -->
```

Now save the file and view it in your browser, via http (e.g. http://mycomputername/profile/searchprofiles.asp). Of course, you should have the include files as well (header.inc, footer.inc, and books.inc). They are part of the profile web, which can be downloaded from the Wrox web site.

When you view it, at first it will not show anything apart from the form fields for the search. Why? Because there is no query string created when you first come to the page. The query is created when you search. So, now what you want to do is to search the database. Leave all the search fields blank, and the dropdown list as Any. This creates a search for all records. Submit the form, and view the page again. This time it should look like this:

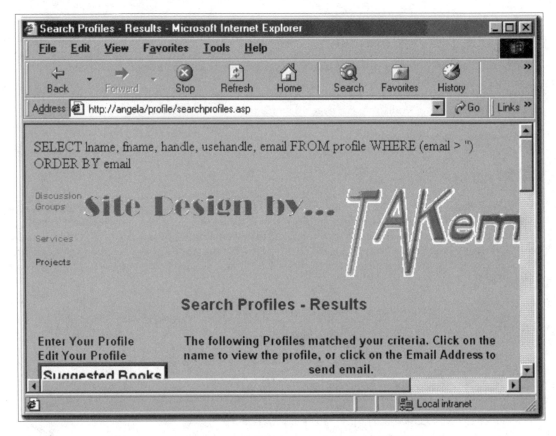

Now you can see the query on the page, as it was formatted by the ASP/ADO code:

SELECT lname, fname, handle, usehandle, email FROM profile WHERE (email > '') ORDER BY email

As you can see, none of the form fields were used in the query. The email value is blank, because there was no email form field value sent to the page. When a form field doesn't exist, the value in the Request.Form collection resolves to "" (an empty string).

The second exercise is going to be a bit more difficult because, as you can see, there are some operations done with the recordset before the HTML in the page:

```
rs.Open strSQL

' ** We check for EOF here, because of the dual nature of the page. If the RecordSet
' ** is empty, we set the value of the "results" variable to FALSE.
If rs.EOF Then
  results = FALSE
```

```
      rs.Close
      cn.Close
      Set rs = Nothing
      Set cn = Nothing
    End If
End If
%>
```

If an error occurs, no recordset will exist, and errors will occur before any HTML (including the SQL statement) is sent to the browser. So, what we need to do is to comment out all of the recordset operations that occur before the HTML. This will cause errors to occur *in* the HTML, but they will occur *after* the code that streams out the query string to the browser, which is the objective of what we're trying to do.

Okay, so how do we generate the error? Well, we play with the value of one of the form fields. Take a look at the following revised code from the page, in which the form field values are put into variables:

```
lname = Request.Form("lname")
city = Request.Form("city")
state = Request.Form("state")
country = Request.Form("country")
email = Request.Form("email")
```

If you remember, the section on common error codes discussed single quotes in strings. I mentioned a function called `newstr()` that converts single quotes to double single quotes. I didn't use it in this page because there are no states, countries, or e-mail addresses containing single quotes, and I'm pretty sure there aren't any cities either. So, all we need to do to blow up this application is to enter a value in one of the search boxes that has a single quote in it. Enter Oh'Hara in the state field, and this is what the results look like:

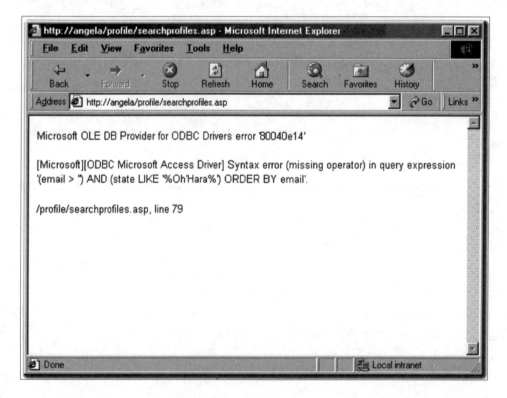

Now, if we want to diagnose the problem, and we want to display the query string in the page, we're going to have to stop any errors occurring in the code above the HTML. However, we still want to run the diagnostic with the same data, in order to find out what went wrong. So, the first thing we do is look at the line number: 79. Of course, this is the line which reads rs.Open strSQL. We know there's nothing wrong with that. The problem is in the SQL somewhere. So, we comment out that line. *But*, we also have to comment out any lines that deal with the values in the recordset, because we haven't opened one yet. So, we will comment out the remaining lines of code that do these things:

```
'   rs.Open strSQL

'   ** We check for EOF here, because of the dual nature of the page. If the RecordSet
'   ** is empty, we set the value of the "results" variable to FALSE.
'   If rs.EOF Then
'      results = FALSE
'      rs.Close
'      cn.Close
'      Set rs = Nothing
'      Set cn = Nothing
'   End If
End If
%>
```

> Always make sure when commenting out code, that if you comment out an If statement, you also comment out the End If statement that follows it!

Now we run the test and we see this instead:

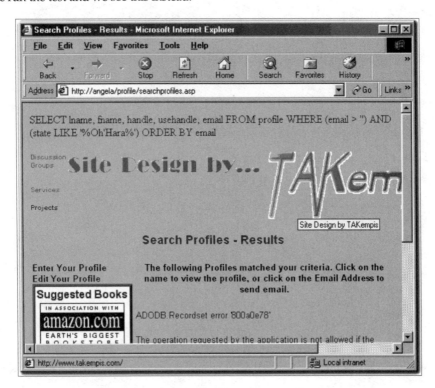

I've shown a little bit more below the SQL statement, to show you the error message that occurs later in the HTML, when the recordset is being accessed. It's not really important that the code isn't working properly at this point; the main thing is to get a look at the SQL statement.

Now, if this were a real-world situation, we'd look at the SQL statement, and the error that we previously received, and we'd say to ourselves "Aha! Looks like I need to handle those single quotes." So we'd add in the function that I described in the earlier section on common error Messages. Let's do that now:

First, we add the function to the function declarations, just under the variable declarations:

```
' ** variables to hold form values
Dim email
Dim lname
Dim city
Dim state
Dim country
Dim showresults
Dim results
Dim title
Dim url

Function newstr(str)
  newstr = Replace(Replace(str, "'", "''"), CHR(34), "&quot;")
End Function
```

Next, we use the function to get the string values from the form fields:

```
lname = newstr(Request.Form("lname"))
city = newstr(Request.Form("city"))
state = newstr(Request.Form("state"))
country = newstr(Request.Form("country"))
email = newstr(Request.Form("email"))
```

Finally, we remove the remarks from the code that blocked the opening of the recordset. We want to see if it works, after all!

When we run it again, we get what we're looking for:

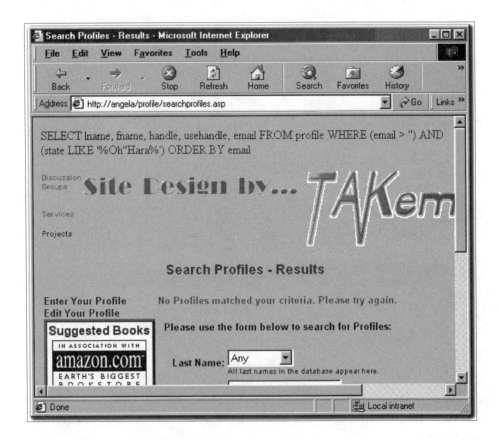

# Viewing Variable Values

You can use similar techniques to view the values of variables in your code. You just use the = operator and the variable name in your code, in a single ASP tag at the top of the page, just before the body (e.g. `<%=strSQL%>`) or, if necessary, you can put a tag into the code at any point in the page. The = operator is a shorthand code for `Response.Write`, and it can be used any time as long as only one line containing that code is in a scripting block. For example, if you wanted to test the value of something in a loop, you could put in code that displays the value of that thing every time the loop is processed.

## Try it out – Adding a Variable Viewer to the Results Table

There is a loop in our sample page that displays every matching record from a search. Let's add a table row to the loop that displays the value of several variables. In the following section of code, add the new code:

```
While (NOT rs.EOF) AND (x < maxrecords)%>
  <TR>
  <TD WIDTH="50%"> <FONT FACE="Arial" SIZE="2"><A
HREF="<%=geturl(Session("webmaster"),_
                rs("email").value)%>"><%=getname(rs("lname").value,rs("fname").value,_
                rs("handle").value, rs("usehandle").value)%></A></FONT> </TD>
  <TD WIDTH="50%"> <FONT FACE="Arial" SIZE="2"><A HREF=
"mailto:<%=rs("email")%>"><%=rs("email")%></A></FONT>
  </TD>
  </TR>
  <TR>
  <TD WIDTH="50%"> <FONT FACE="Arial" SIZE="2">Email = <%=rs("email")%>
</FONT></TD>
  <TD WIDTH="50%"> <FONT FACE="Arial" SIZE="2">x = <%=x%> </FONT></TD>
  </TR>
```

This adds a second table row to the loop. Now, run a search using no criteria (to return all records). Your results should look something like this:

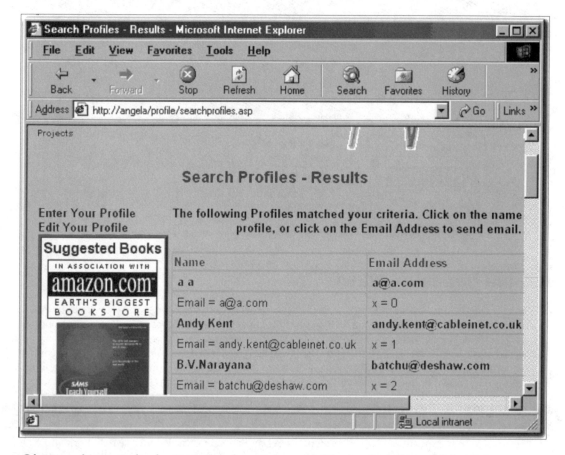

Of course, this particular demonstration doesn't show anything particularly useful, but it does demonstrate the technique.

# Erroneous Non-Errors

A final word about debugging: sometimes you won't get an error message. Instead, everything seems to run smoothly, but you don't get the results you expect. It's important to test-run your pages, and make sure that you are getting the right results. If you're not, check out your code. This particular aspect of debugging is difficult to master, because there is no clue provided as to where the error is occurring.

You can often use some of the techniques I've described above, such as viewing variable values at various points along the way, to get a look at what's going on in your pages. And judicious use of commenting in your code can help you when you write particularly complex applications and pages.

# Sabotaging Your Application

An important aspect to debugging is to test-run your application in pieces, and attempt to "blow it up" in as many a number of ways and as creatively as you can. Enter text in numeric form fields. Use single quotes in your strings. Fill in dates wrong. Leave required fields blank. Put spaces in fields where data is required. Do everything you're not supposed to do. Corrupt that data if you can. You can be sure that at some point, your users will!

A typical mistake of programmers is to forget, or hurry through this vital step in development. You know what should go into those form fields. You know how you should navigate through the system. And you're not a hacker. Let's not forget about hackers, and security issues. For example, using the GET method for a form in a password page (instead of the POST method) will send the password in the URL string, right out where anyone can see it. But your inclination during the design phase is likely to be to use the application as it's supposed to be used. Now you're going to want to do the exact opposite.

The more you practice the art of self-sabotage, the less you are going to have to fix when the application goes online in the real world. Fixing bugs in a production application is a very high-priority job, and can really cramp your schedule!

# Summary

In this chapter we've examined the ASP/ADO chain from top (ASP) to bottom (data provider). We've seen that ASP communicates with the data source by creating instances of ADO objects. We've seen that ADO encapsulates OLE DB, and enables us to talk to the complex technology of OLE DB, with a relatively simple language. We've followed the chain to the ODBC level, and discussed how ODBC works, and the various ways of using it to connect to a data source. We've talked about the merits of System DSNs, File DSNs, and DSN-less connections. We came to the conclusion that when working with file-based databases, such as Access, a System DSN is the best way to go. We also mentioned that with SQL Server, a DSN-less connection is probably the best way to go. We've talked about MDAC (Microsoft Data Access Components), and where to get the latest installation.

We've examined common ADO error messages, and what each one indicates. We've discussed the various solutions to these errors.

Finally, we've examined some handy troubleshooting techniques, such as viewing the SQL, viewing variable values, and how to view the changing values of variables inside loops. We've looked at the built-in ADO errors collection, and how to use it in a web application. We've shown some examples of these techniques, using `searchprofiles.asp` as our "Guinea Pig." And we've talked about erroneous non-errors - coding errors that don't cause the application to stop processing, but don't perform the way we want them to. We've talked briefly about how to identify these kind of errors, by using some of the debugging techniques described earlier, and commenting the code when it gets a bit too complex to follow. We've looked at "sabotaging" our application - attempting to make it break down, so that we can make it more robust in the production environment.

By this time you should have a grasp of all that invisible technology underlying your scripting, and be able to identify and deal with problems in the code, as well as to be able to write robust code that will stand up to a large, multi-user environment.

# Exercises

These exercises use `profile.mdb`, which is available from the Wrox website. The structure of the database is described in Appendix C.

**1.** The following ASP code contains the minimum code to create your own error testing page. Create a page called `errors.asp` with this code, and modify it to create the following errors:

[Microsoft][ODBC Driver Manager] Data source name not found and no default driver specified

ADODB.Field error '800a0bcd'

Either BOF or EOF is True, or the current record has been deleted; the operation requested by the application requires a current record.

[Microsoft][ODBC Microsoft Access Driver] Too few parameters. Expected 1.

```
<%
  cstring = "DSN=profile;"
  Set cn = Server.CreateObject("ADODB.Connection")
  cn.Open cstring
  cn.Execute("")
  cn.Close
  Set rs = Nothing
  Set cn = Nothing
%>
<HTML>

<HEAD>
<TITLE>Error Testing Page</TITLE>
</HEAD>

<BODY>
</BODY>
</HTML>
```

**2.** Using `searchprofiles.asp`, write code in the page that displays the values of various variables at several different points during the execution of the code. Write some code to display the `status` property of the `connection` object when it is opened and when it is closed.

# Quiz

**1.** How does an ASP page connect with a data source? What are the links in the ASP/ADO chain?

**2.** What does ODBC stand for? What is ODBC used for?

**3.** What kind of ODBC connection should you use for a file-based database? What kind should you use for a SQL Server database?

**4.** In order to view the SQL statement of an ADO operation, what must we do to ensure that we will see the variable value?

**5.** What are some of the best techniques for identifying the source of "Erroneous Non-errors?"

**6.** What is the very important and often-overlooked debugging technique?

# Quiz Answers

**1.** An ASP page connects to a data source by creating instances of ADO objects. ADO encapsulates OLE DB. OLE DB connects to ODBC, which in turn connects to the data source.

**2.** ODBC stands for "Open Database Connectivity." ODBC is used for connecting to a variety of data sources from outside the typical programming interface for that data source. For example, you can connect to any ODBC-compliant database using Active Server Pages and ADO.

**3.** A System DSN is recommended for connecting to file-based databases. A System DSN or a DSN-less connection can be used to connect to SQL Server databases. In most cases, a DSN-less connection is recommended for SQL Server databases.

**4.** If the execution of an SQL statement is causing processing to stop, we must comment out the line of code that executes the SQL statement, and any subsequent lines that work with any recordset generated by the command, prior to the point in the page where we wish to display the SQL statement.

**5.** Viewing the values of the SQL statement and various relevant variables in the page can help. When the code or application is complex, judicious use of commenting can be helpful as well.

**6.** "Sabotaging your code," testing the application by trying to make it blow up, is extremely important in the development process. It prevents the developer from having to do a lot of high-priority debugging after the application is already in production.

Welcome to the Microsoft

Setup cannot install system files or update shared files if the files are in use. Before o
any open applications.

Continue                                    Exit Setup

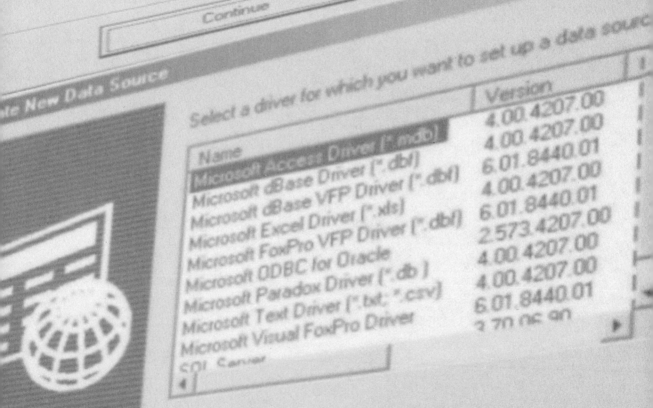

te New Data Source

Select a driver for which you want to set up a data sourc

| Name | Version |
|------|---------|
| Microsoft Access Driver (*.mdb) | 4.00.4207.00 |
| Microsoft dBase Driver (*.dbf) | 4.00.4207.00 |
| Microsoft dBase VFP Driver (*.dbf) | 6.01.8440.01 |
| Microsoft Excel Driver (*.xls) | 4.00.4207.00 |
| Microsoft FoxPro VFP Driver (*.dbf) | 6.01.8440.01 |
| Microsoft ODBC for Oracle | 2.573.4207.00 |
| Microsoft Paradox Driver (*.db ) | 4.00.4207.00 |
| Microsoft Text Driver (*.txt; *.csv) | 4.00.4207.00 |
| Microsoft Visual FoxPro Driver | 6.01.8440.01 |
| SQL Server | 2.70.06.90 |

Finish                                      Cancel

# Recordset Parameters

The previous chapters have mainly dealt with simple `Recordset` objects that used the `Open` method with just one or two parameters. This chapter takes the `Recordset` object to the next level by going into the details of the other parameters of the `Open` method of the `Recordset` object.

The `Recordset` object offers more flexibility in opening recordsets than just reading data and moving to the next record. These include such options as using cursors and locking, which control how a `Recordset` object will manipulate the data. We will also expand on the `Connection` parameter and show you various ways that it can be used.

Microsoft Access refers to compiled SQL statements as queries and Microsoft SQL Server refers to them as stored procedures. To keep our terminology consistent and to avoid confusion we are going to refer to queries as stored procedures.

In this chapter we will cover the following topics:

❑ The `Source` parameter
❑ The `Connection` parameter
❑ The `Cursor Type` parameter
❑ The `Lock Type` parameter
❑ The `Options` parameter

## Parameter Overview

When we are discussing parameters in this chapter, we are not referring to parameter data that we pass to a SQL string or a stored procedure. We are referring to the actual parameters of the `Open` method of the `Recordset` object. Let's take a quick look at the syntax of the `Open` method of the `Recordset` object:

```
object.Open Source, ActiveConnection, CursorType, LockType, Options
```

The `object` part of this statement evaluates to a valid `Recordset` object. Remember that we create a `Recordset` object in our ASP code using the `CreateObject` method as shown below.

```
Set objRS = Server.CreateObject("ADODB.Recordset")
```

The Open method opens the Recordset object and populates it with records from a table, SQL string or stored procedure. The Recordset object consists of records and fields, which respectively relate to rows of data and columns in the database.

The parameters of the Open method tell ADO how we want to open the Recordset object. We almost always use a Source parameter. This tells the Open method where the data is coming from and can be in one of the following forms:

❑ A database table name

❑ A SQL statement – we've used SQL statements already in this book so you should be familiar with them

❑ A stored procedure – these are just SQL statements that are stored in the database with a name assigned by you

❑ A Command object – this is another ADO object that can be used to specify a SQL string or stored procedure with or without parameters

❑ A URL – this can be used to specify the relative path to an existing recordset stored as a file

We have seen and used the ActiveConnection parameter previously; this parameter lets the Open method know how it should access the database. This parameter can be in the form of a Connection object or a Connection string.

There are some new parameters that have not been discussed before. The CursorType parameter specifies what type of cursor the database should use when opening the recordset. We will define what a cursor is in just a little bit.

LockType specifies what type of locking the database should use on the recordset.

The last parameter of the Open method is the Options parameter. This tells the database how it should interpret the Source parameter.

The Recordset.Open parameters must be specified in order. If you leave out a parameter to use the default that is provided by ADO then you must insert a comma in its place before specifying the next parameter as shown below.

```
objRS.Open objCmd,,adOpenForwardOnly
```

# Errors

One of the most common places to receive a database error is when opening a Recordset object. Misspelling a stored procedure name or having misspelled a column name or table name when using SQL statements could cause the error.

Another common mistake that causes errors when opening a recordset is to specify the wrong CursorType parameter with the wrong LockType parameter. You can also cause an error by specifying the wrong Options parameter for the Source parameter used.

In order to troubleshoot these errors, it is essential that you understand the different parameters and how they relate to one another.

Chapter 12 will go into error handling in detail and will list some of the most common mistakes encountered and how to correct them.

# Source Parameter

The Source parameter is a variant data type that specifies the source of the data to be populated in the Recordset object. As we described above, this can be in the form of a table name, a SQL string, a stored procedure, a Command object or a URL. Before the Recordset object is opened (executed using the Open method), this parameter can be read or written, meaning you can read what has been already set in this parameter or you can set it to a valid source.

To optimize the performance of the Open method when using a SQL string, a stored procedure or table name, you should specify the appropriate Options parameter. The Options parameter will be covered last in this section.

All of the examples in this chapter will be using the same column name from the Boats table in the Sailors database. This will allow you to concentrate on the various recordset parameters while getting the same results. To this end, most of the screen shots will look alike and will not be shown for every example. Also, most of the code is repetitive and will not be explained past the first example.

## Table Names

When you need all data from a specific table you can use the table name as the Source parameter. Using the table name will return all columns in all rows of the table into the Recordset object. This is in essence the same as specifying:

```
SELECT * FROM tablename
```

Where tablename is the name of the table you want to retrieve data from.

Before using a table name as the Source parameter ensure the table contains all of the data that you need to perform the task at hand. You also need to take into consideration the number of rows in the table. Using a very large table will diminish the performance of your application. In this case you might consider using a SQL statement or a stored procedure which specifies a criteria that will limit the number of rows returned.

## Try It Out – Using A Table Name Source

Create a Web page that uses the `Boats` table in the Sailors database as the `Source` parameter. After opening the recordset, display each boat name on the page. Your code should produce something similar to this:

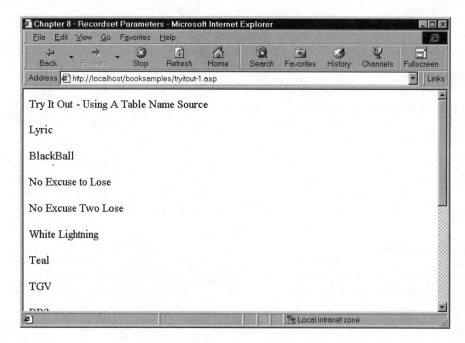

Here's our example code to list boat names. You can find this code in the file `TryItOut1.asp`, available for download with all the code from this book from the Wrox website.

```
<HTML>
<HEAD>
<META NAME="GENERATOR" Content="Microsoft Visual Studio 6.0">
<TITLE>Chapter 8 - Recordset Parameters</TITLE>
</HEAD>
<BODY>

<!--Display the page data-->
Try It Out - Using A Table Name Source<BR><BR>

<%
  'Create the recordset object
  Set objRS = Server.CreateObject("ADODB.Recordset")

  'Open the recordset
  objRS.Open "boats","DSN=Sailors"

  'Loop through the recordset displaying the boat name field
  Do While Not objRS.EOF

    Response.Write objRS("BoatName") & "<P>"
    objRS.MoveNext
```

```
   Loop

    'Close and dereference database objects
    objRS.Close
    Set objRS = Nothing
%>

</BODY>
</HTML>
```

### How It Works – Using A Table Name Source

We start our Web page by including the standard HTML headers that start every Web page. This example and those that follow were built using Microsoft Visual InterDev. You can use Microsoft FrontPage or any Web authoring tool of your choice.

```
<HTML>
<HEAD>
<META NAME="GENERATOR" Content="Microsoft Visual Studio 6.0">
<TITLE>Chapter 8 - Recordset Parameters</TITLE>
</HEAD>
<BODY>
```

To display a comment in HTML we use the standard tags for a comment, which begin with a less than sign followed by an exclamation sign and two dashes. To end the comment, use two dashes and a 'greater than' sign. Here we are using an HTML comment to help document our code and then display the first line of text in our Web page.

```
<!--Display the page data-->
Try It Out - Using A Table Name Source<BR><BR>
```

After switching to server-side script, we create our Recordset object.

```
<%
'Create the recordset object
Set objRS = Server.CreateObject("ADODB.Recordset")
```

Using the Open method of the Recordset object we open the recordset passing it the appropriate parameters. Here we are specifying that the Source parameter to be used is the table name of Boats and the ActiveConnection property is set to a connection string.

Using a connection string creates a database connection but it is applied only to this object. It is not available to other objects as a Connection object.

```
'Open the recordset
objRS.Open "boats","DSN=Sailors"
```

Next, we loop through the Recordset object displaying each boat name on the Web page.

```
'Loop through the recordset displaying the boat name field
Do While Not objRS.EOF

    Response.Write objRS("BoatName") & "<P>"
    objRS.MoveNext

Loop
```

> A common mistake, even for experienced developers, is forgetting to code the
> `MoveNext` method of the `Recordset` object. Doing so will cause your code to hang in
> an infinite loop.

After we have finished using the `Recordset` object, we must close it using the `Close` method and set the
`Recordset` object equal to nothing, which will release the object and all associated resources from
memory.

```
'Close and dereference database objects
objRS.Close
Set objRS = Nothing
%>
```

Switching back to HTML code, we end our Web page using standard HTML tags.

```
</BODY>
</HTML>
```

# SQL Statements

Writing SQL statements has been the main `Source` parameter used in prior chapters. This section should
come as no surprise to you, and you should feel confident writing simple `SELECT` SQL statements. If you
code a stored procedure in Access and take a look at the SQL code that was generated you will notice a
semicolon at the end of the statement. Using a semicolon at the end of your SQL statement is optional
when using your SQL statement in ADO.

There are two ways to pass a SQL statement as a `Source` parameter. You can use the actual SQL
statement as the parameter value or you can assign the SQL statement to a string variable and pass the
variable as the `Source` parameter. The following code fragments demonstrate the two different methods.

```
objRS.Open "SELECT * FROM boats", "DSN=Sailors"
```

```
strSQL = "SELECT * FROM boats"
objRS.Open strSQL, "DSN=Sailors"
```

## Try It Out – Using A SQL Statement Source

Create a Web page that uses a SQL statement to select the boat names from the `Boats` table in the Sailors
database. Loop through the recordset and display each boat name on the Web page.

The result will look much the same as before. You can find the example code in `TryitOut2.asp`:

```
<HTML>
<HEAD>
<META NAME="GENERATOR" Content="Microsoft Visual Studio 6.0">
<TITLE>Chapter 8 - Recordset Parameters</TITLE>
</HEAD>
<BODY>

<!--Display the page data-->
Try It Out - Using A SQL Statement Source<BR><BR>
```

```
<%
 'Create the recordset object
 Set objRS = Server.CreateObject("ADODB.Recordset")

 'Open the recordset
 objRS.Open "SELECT boatname FROM boats;","dsn=Sailors"

 'Loop through the recordset displaying the boat name field
 Do While Not objRS.EOF

   Response.Write objRS("BoatName") & "<P>"
   objRS.MoveNext

 Loop

 'Close and dereference database objects
 objRS.Close
 Set objRS = Nothing
%>

</BODY>
</HTML>
```

### How It Works – Using A SQL Statement Source

We'll only look at the code that is different from our first example.

We open the `Recordset` object using a `Source` parameter that contains a SQL statement and the same `ActiveConnection` parameter is used as was used in the last example. This SQL statement only selects the `BoatName` column from the `Boats` table in the Sailors database.

```
'Open the recordset
objRS.Open "SELECT boatname FROM boats;","DSN=Sailors"
```

Thus it is only the boat names that are transferred to the client and not the whole `Boats` table. Next, we loop through the recordset and display all boat names on our Web page, as in our previous example.

# Stored Procedures

Stored procedures are just SQL statements that reside in the database under a saved name. A stored procedure is considered compiled once saved in the database and therefore offers superior performance to SQL statements passed in the `Source` parameter.

This is because the database goes through a process when you save a stored procedure in which it figures out the fastest access path to the data and which indexes to use. When you pass SQL statements in the `Source` parameter, the database must first compile the SQL statement and then execute it.

Stored procedures can be simple `SELECT` statements, or complex statements using `JOIN`s to join one or more tables. Stored procedures can accept parameters that restrict the access of data. They can also be action-stored procedures in which they insert, update and delete data from one or more tables depending on the parameters passed to it.

*We'll be looking at stored procedures in detail in chapter 14.*

## Try It Out – Using A Stored Procedure Source

Create a Web page that uses a stored procedure called qAllBoatNames as the Source parameter. This stored procedure will select all boat names from the Boats table in the Sailors database. After opening the recordset display all boat names on the Web page.

> *You must create the stored procedure before running this example – if you're not sure how to do this, refer to the How It Works section below.*

As before, the result will look the same as our first example, so we won't show the screenshot again.

The example code for the stored procedure (to be found in the file qAllBoatNames) looks like this:

```
SELECT Boats.BoatName
FROM Boats;
```

Here is the example code (from TryItOut3.asp):

```
<HTML>
<HEAD>
<META NAME="GENERATOR" Content="Microsoft Visual Studio 6.0">
<TITLE>Chapter 8 - Recordset Parameters</TITLE>
</HEAD>
<BODY>

<!--Display the page data-->
Try It Out - Using A Stored Procedure Source<BR><BR>

<%
  'Create the recordset object
  Set objRS = Server.CreateObject("ADODB.Recordset")

  'Open the recordset
  objRS.Open "qAllBoatNames","DSN=Sailors"

  'Loop through the recordset displaying the boat name field
  Do While Not objRS.EOF

    Response.Write objRS("BoatName") & "<P>"
    objRS.MoveNext

  Loop

  'Close and dereference database objects
  objRS.Close
  Set objRS = Nothing
%>

</BODY>
</HTML>
```

### How It Works – Using A Stored Procedure Source

This time we start by creating the stored procedure needed for our example. As you can see, this stored procedure is really quite simple. We are selecting the `BoatName` column from the `Boats` table. Notice that Access has placed a semicolon at the end of our SQL statement and has also prefixed our column name with the table name that we are selecting the column from.

```
SELECT Boats.BoatName
FROM Boats;
```

To create this stored procedure, open the Sailors database in Access. Select the **Queries** tab and click on the **New** button.

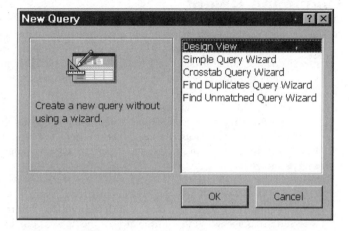

Select **Design View** in the **New Query** dialog and click on the **OK** button. Click on the **Close** button in the **Show Table** dialog. Next, click on the **SQL** button in the far left-hand side of the toolbar. Notice that **Select**; is displayed and is highlighted. Delete this SQL statement and enter the SQL statements for our stored procedure.

Click on the **Save** button on the toolbar and enter `qAllBoatNames` for the stored procedure name in the **Save As** dialog.

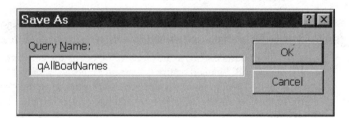

At this point you can close the stored procedure and test it by clicking on the **Open** button.

> **We will be using this same stored procedure in the rest of our examples in this chapter.**

Again we'll only look at the code that is different in this example from previously.

We open our `Recordset` object using the stored procedure that we created as the `Source` parameter:

```
'Open the recordset
objRS.Open "qAllBoatNames","DSN=Sailors"
```

Again we can use a connection string for the `ActiveConnection` parameter. Finally we loop through all of the records and display them on our web page.

# Command Object

Using the `Command` object as a `Source` parameter provides a lot of flexibility in the types of SQL statements and stored procedures we can use. We are going to use the `Command` object to execute our newly created stored procedure from the last example. This will demonstrate using a `Command` object as the `Source` parameter for the `Recordset` object's `Open` method.

When we use the `Command` object with a `Recordset` object we also need to use a `Connection` object. Using the `Recordset` object or the `Command` object separately allows us to use a connection string for the `ActiveConnection`. Both the `Recordset` object and the `Command` object require an `ActiveConnection` parameter, and when we use them together we must use a `Connection` object for this parameter.

However, since we will be using a `Command` object as the `Source` parameter, we can omit the `ActiveConnection` parameter in our `Open` method. You may be wondering why we can do this. The `Recordset` object will inherit the value of the `Command` object's `ActiveConnection` property. This is why we are forced to use a `Connection` object. Using a connection string only creates a connection for that object; it doesn't allow us to pass that connection to another object.

Likewise the `Source` parameter of the `Recordset` object actually inherits the `CommandText` property of the `Command` object to use as the source.

## Try It Out – Using A Command Object Source

Create a Web page that uses a `Command` object as the `Source` parameter. The stored procedure from the last example will be used as the `Command` object's `CommandText` property. You will need to also create a `Connection` object and check for errors after opening the `Connection` object and after executing the `Open` method of the `Recordset` object. Loop through the recordset and display all boat names on the Web page.

Here's the example code (found in `TryItOut4.asp`):

```
<HTML>
<HEAD>
<META NAME="GENERATOR" Content="Microsoft Visual Studio 6.0">
<TITLE>Chapter 8 - Recordset Parameters</TITLE>
</HEAD>
<BODY>

<!--Display the page data-->
Try It Out - Using A Command Object Source<BR><BR>
```

```
<%
'Instruct VBScript to ignore the error and continue
'with the next line of code
On Error Resume Next

'Create and open the database object
Set objConn = Server.CreateObject("ADODB.Connection")
objConn.Open "DSN=Sailors"

'Check for errors
If objConn.Errors.Count > 0 Then
  'Create an error object to access the ADO errors collection
  Set objErr = Server.CreateObject("ADODB.Error")
  'Declare Boolean flag for critical errors
  Dim blnCriticalError
  'Write all errors to the page
  For Each objErr In objConn.Errors
    If objErr.Number <> 0 Then
      Response.Write "Number: " & objErr.Number & "<P>"
      Response.Write "Description: " & objErr.Description & "<P>"
      Response.Write "Source: " & objErr.Source & "<P>"
      Response.Write "SQLState: " & objErr.SQLState & "<P>"
      Response.Write "NativeError: " & objErr.NativeError & "<P>"
      blnCriticalError = True
    End If
  Next
  'Dereference all objects
  Set objErr = Nothing
  If blnCriticalError Then
    Response.End
  End If
End If

'Declare ADO variables
Dim adCmdStoredProc
adCmdStoredProc = 4

'Create the command object
Set objCmd = Server.CreateObject("ADODB.Command")

'Set the command object properties
Set objCmd.ActiveConnection = objConn
objCmd.CommandText = "qAllBoatNames"
objCmd.CommandType = adCmdStoredProc

'Create the recordset object and open the recordset
Set objRS = Server.CreateObject("ADODB.Recordset")
objRS.Open objCmd

'Check for errors
If objConn.Errors.Count > 0 Then
  'Create an error object to access the ADO errors collection
  Set objErr = Server.CreateObject("ADODB.Error")
  'Write all errors to the page
  For Each objErr In objConn.Errors
    If objErr.Number <> 0 Then
      Response.Write "Number: " & objErr.Number & "<P>"
      Response.Write "Description: " & objErr.Description & "<P>"
      Response.Write "Source: " & objErr.Source & "<P>"
      Response.Write "SQLState: " & objErr.SQLState & "<P>"
      Response.Write "NativeError: " & objErr.NativeError & "<P>"
      blnCriticalError = True
    End If
```

```
      Next
      'Dereference all objects
      Set objErr = Nothing
      If blnCriticalError Then
         Response.End
      End If
   End If
End If

'Loop through the recordset displaying the boat name field
Do While Not objRS.EOF

   Response.Write objRS("BoatName") & "<P>"
   objRS.MoveNext

Loop

'Close and dereference database objects
Set objCmd = Nothing
objRS.Close
Set objRS = Nothing
objConn.Close
Set objConn = Nothing
%>

</BODY>
</HTML>
```

### How It Works - Using a Command Object Source

Don't let the size of this code fool you, it really is quite simple and we will step through it all. First, we create our Web page using standard HTML tags and display our first line of text on the page.

```
<HTML>
<HEAD>
<META NAME="GENERATOR" Content="Microsoft Visual Studio 6.0">
<TITLE>Chapter 8 - Recordset Parameters</TITLE>
</HEAD>
<BODY>

<!--Display the page data-->
Try It Out - Using A Command Object Source<BR><BR>
```

In order to trap ADO errors, we must instruct VB Script to ignore all errors so we can handle them ourselves. We do this by using the On Error Resume Next statement. Error handling will be discussed in detail in Chapter 12.

```
<%
'Instruct VBScript to ignore the error and continue
'with the next line of code
On Error Resume Next
```

We create a Connection object and open the connection passing it the name of the DSN for the Sailors database.

```
'Create and open the database object
Set objConn = Server.CreateObject("ADODB.Connection")
objConn.Open "DSN=Sailors"
```

This next section in our code checks for and handles errors. If you don't fully understand what we are doing in this section don't worry. Chapter 12 will cover error handling in detail.

### Error Handling

We should always check for errors, especially since we are using multiple ADO objects in which setting the properties of one object depends on the other object being created and opened. We start our error handling routine by checking to see if the `Errors Collection` contains any errors. The `Errors Collection` object is one of the objects in the ADO object model and belongs to the `Connection` object. We check the `Count` property of the `Errors Collection` object to see if the count is greater than zero, which indicates that one or more errors exist in the collection.

```
'Check for errors
If objConn.Errors.Count > 0 Then
```

In order to access an error in the `Errors Collection` we must create an `Error` object as shown below.

```
'Create an error object to access the ADO errors collection
Set objErr = Server.CreateObject("ADODB.Error")
```

We declare a variable that will be used to determine if the error we received was critical and indicates that we should stop processing our script.

```
'Declare Boolean flag for critical errors
Dim blnCriticalError
```

We access the errors in the `Errors Collection` in a `For Each` loop setting the `Error` object equal to an error in the `Errors Collection`.

```
'Write all errors to the page
For Each objErr In objConn.Errors
```

Some errors are just informational and have an error number of zero. We can ignore these errors as we are doing below and just display the errors that have an error number not equal to zero.

If a true error exists, we display the various error properties on the Web page. Notice that we also set the `blnCriticalError` variable to `True` to indicate we have a serious error.

```
   If objErr.Number <> 0 Then
      Response.Write "Number: " & objErr.Number & "<P>"
      Response.Write "Description: " & objErr.Description & "<P>"
      Response.Write "Source: " & objErr.Source & "<P>"
      Response.Write "SQLState: " & objErr.SQLState & "<P>"
      Response.Write "NativeError: " & objErr.NativeError & "<P>"
      blnCriticalError = True
   End If
Next
```

After we have processed all of the errors in the `Errors Collection`, we need to dereference our `Error` object to release it from memory and free its resources.

```
'Dereference all objects
Set objErr = Nothing
```

The last thing we need to do in our error handling routine is to check to see if we encountered a serious error. If the `blnCriticalError` variable is `True` we want to stop processing our script. We do this by using the `End` method of the `Response` object. This will stop our code dead in its tracks.

```
If blnCriticalError Then
   Response.End
End If
End If
```

## Using the Command Object

Unlike VB, ASP does not allow us to set a reference to the ADO object library so that all enumerations are available. So we must declare variables for the various values that we assign to the properties of the objects in the ADO object model. Here we are declaring a variable for the `Command` object property `CommandType` that indicates what type of command we are trying to execute. The value can be looked up in the ADO documentation or you can use VB and set a reference to the Microsoft ActiveX Data Objects 2.x Library. The .x value indicates the latest release of ADO that you have and should be 2.1 as at the time of writing. Once you have a reference set in VB you can use the object browser and look up the appropriate enumeration value. Using this method ensures you are using the correct value for the enumeration.

> You also have the option of including the `adovbs.inc` file, which provides a listing of constants and their values. This is discussed further in the case study.

```
'Declare ADO variables
Dim adCmdStoredProc
adCmdStoredProc = 4
```

Now we need to create the `Command` object and set its various properties. The first property we want to set is the `ActiveConnection` property. We set this property to the `Connection` object that we created above.

Next we set the `CommandText` property to the stored procedure name that we created in the last example, and then set the `CommandType` property to `adCmdStoredProc`. The `CommandType` property tells the `Command` object what type of command we are executing. Like the `Options` property in the `Recordset` object, specifying this property will help to optimize the performance of this object. This prevents ADO from having to go through the steps of trying to figure out what type of command we are trying to execute.

```
'Create the command object
Set objCmd = Server.CreateObject("ADODB.Command")

'Set the command object properties
Set objCmd.ActiveConnection = objConn
objCmd.CommandText = "qAllBoatNames"
objCmd.CommandType = adCmdStoredProc
```

Now we can create our `Recordset` object and open it. Notice that the only parameter we are specifying is the `Source` parameter. Remember we said earlier that the `ActiveConnection` parameter would be inherited from the `Command` object.

```
'Create the recordset object and open the recordset
Set objRS = Server.CreateObject("ADODB.Recordset")
objRS.Open objCmd
```

After performing a database operation we need to once again check for errors. This error handling code is a duplicate of the previous error handling code minus the declaration of our `blnCriticalError` variable. This is because ASP would give us an error about a duplicate variable being declared.

```
'Check for errors
If objConn.Errors.Count > 0 Then
   'Create an error object to access the ADO errors collection
   Set objErr = Server.CreateObject("ADODB.Error")
   'Write all errors to the page
   For Each objErr In objConn.Errors
      If objErr.Number <> 0 Then
        Response.Write "Number: " & objErr.Number & "<P>"
        Response.Write "Description: " & objErr.Description & "<P>"
        Response.Write "Source: " & objErr.Source & "<P>"
        Response.Write "SQLState: " & objErr.SQLState & "<P>"
        Response.Write "NativeError: " & objErr.NativeError & "<P>"
        blnCriticalError = True
      End If
   Next
   'Dereference all objects
   Set objErr = Nothing
   If blnCriticalError Then
      Response.End
   End If
End If
```

Now that our `Recordset` object contains data, we want to loop through the recordset and display all boat names on our Web page.

```
'Loop through the recordset displaying the boat name field
Do While Not objRS.EOF

   Response.Write objRS("BoatName") & "<P>"
   objRS.MoveNext

Loop
```

Once we have displayed all boat names, we must close and dereference all of our database objects. Notice there are more objects this time.

```
'Close and dereference database objects
Set objCmd = Nothing
objRS.Close
Set objRS = Nothing
objConn.Close
Set objConn = Nothing
%>
```

Last we use standard HTML tags to end our page.

```
</BODY>
</HTML>
```

# The ActiveConnection Parameter

Without a connection we could not perform any operations against the database. The ActiveConnection parameter provides a connection to the database thus allowing us to access the data. It can be in one of two forms:

First, we can pass a connection string that contains the DSN that will be used to open the database. Using this method will only create a database connection for the object we specify. The first three examples demonstrated this method when we opened the Recordset object.

The second method is to use an actual Connection object as we did in the last example. This allows us to use the same Connection object for all our ADO objects. Using this method keeps the database open and available for subsequent use by the other objects. The previous example demonstrated this method by setting the ActiveConnection property of the Command object to the actual Connection object. The Recordset object inherited this connection from the Command object.

# The CursorType Parameter

A cursor controls the navigation of records and how the records will be updated in a Recordset object. It also controls how you see changes in the data in your recordset. There are four types of cursors that ADO uses: adOpenForwardOnly, adOpenKeyset, adOpenDynamic, and adOpenStatic. We will be discussing the details of each of these cursors in the sections that follow.

A cursor can be updateable or non-updateable. This means that you can either update the fields in a record within the recordset or not. For obvious reasons, the non-updateable type of cursor is faster because the database does not have to keep track of the changes in your recordset. It simply passes you the recordset data and forgets about it.

Scrollable cursors can allow updates to the recordset but do not necessarily have to. This all depends on what type of locking options you use. The LockType parameter will be discussed later in this chapter.

## The adOpenForwardOnly Cursor

The default cursor if none is specified is adOpenForwardOnly. As its name implies, this cursor only allows you to navigate forward in the recordset. This cursor also does not allow updates to the recordset.

This is the ideal cursor for quick access to records if you only need to read and process the data in one pass. Because the database does not have to keep track of changes to data in this type of cursor, the overhead associated with using this type of cursor is low and it is very efficient.

Create a Web page that uses a forward only cursor on the recordset. The Source parameter should use the `qAllBoatNames` stored procedure and a connect string for the `ActiveConnection` parameter. Loop through the recordset displaying all boat names on the Web page.

Here's the example code (found in `TryItOut5.asp`):

```
<HTML>
<HEAD>
<META NAME="GENERATOR" Content="Microsoft Visual Studio 6.0">
<TITLE>Chapter 8 - Recordset Parameters</TITLE>
</HEAD>
<BODY>

<!--Display the page data-->
Try It Out - Using A Forward Only Cursor<BR><BR>

<%
  'Declare ADO variables
  Dim adOpenForwardOnly
  adOpenForwardOnly = 0

  'Create the recordset object
  Set objRS = Server.CreateObject("ADODB.Recordset")

  'Open the recordset
  objRS.Open "qAllBoatNames","DSN=Sailors",adOpenForwardOnly

  'Loop through the recordset displaying the boat name field
  Do While Not objRS.EOF

    Response.Write objRS("BoatName") & "<P>"
    objRS.MoveNext

  Loop

  'Close and de-reference database objects
  objRS.Close
  Set objRS = Nothing
%>

</BODY>
</HTML>
```

### How It Works – Using A Forward Only Cursor

We start with the code that is different in this example. We must declare the ADO variables that we will be using as our `Recordset` parameters. Here we are specifying a cursor type variable. We looked up the value using the VB object browser.

```
<%
'Declare ADO variables
Dim adOpenForwardOnly
adOpenForwardOnly = 0
```

Next, we create our `Recordset` object and open the recordset. Notice that we have specified the stored procedure name as the `Source` parameter and connection string for the `ActiveConnection` parameter. The `CursorType` parameter is specified as `adOpenForwardOnly`, which means we can only move forward in our recordset and cannot update any data.

```
'Create the recordset object
Set objRS = Server.CreateObject("ADODB.Recordset")

'Open the recordset
objRS.Open "qAllBoatNames","DSN=Sailors",adOpenForwardOnly
```

Finally we loop thorough the recordset and display each boat name on our Web page.

# The adOpenKeySet Cursor

A keyset driven cursor supports forward and backward navigation through the recordset. It also allows you to update the data in the recordset if the appropriate LockType parameter is specified.

> *We'll be covering the LockType parameter next in this chapter.*

You can see updates made by other users in your recordset but you will not be able to see records that other users add to the data source. Also, records deleted by other users will be inaccessible in your recordset.

This cursor also supports bookmarks in your recordset and allows you to resynchronize your recordset with the database; thus refreshing your recordset and picking up added records.

## Try It Out - Using A Keyset Cursor

Create a Web page that uses a Keyset cursor and the qAllBoatNames stored procedure. Loop through the recordset and display all boat names on your Web page.

Again, the basics of this example are very similar to our previous examples, so we won't show the whole code here – you can find it in TryItOut6.asp.

### How It Works - Using a Keyset Cursor

We'll just look at the new lines of code. We need to declare our ADO variable for the keyset cursor and again we used the VB object browser to determine the value.

```
<%
'Declare ADO variables
Dim adOpenKeyset
adOpenKeyset = 1
```

Once we have created our Recordset object, we can open the recordset passing the correct parameters. Here we are using the adOpenKeyset variable as the CursorType parameter.

```
'Create the recordset object
Set objRS = Server.CreateObject("ADODB.Recordset")

'Open the recordset
objRS.Open "qAllBoatNames","DSN=Sailors",adOpenKeyset
```

Once our Recordset object is opened, we loop through the recordset displaying all boat names on our Web page.

# adOpenDynamic Cursor

The dynamic cursor supports forward and backward navigation in your recordset but bookmarks are not supported in this cursor (although features may vary for providers other than Access – you will need to check if you are using a different provider).

So what's the upside to a dynamic cursor? All changes to the underlying data are visible. This means that any record that is added, updated or deleted is immediately visible in your recordset. There is no need to resynchronize your cursor with the database. Resynchronization is when the database updates your cursor to reflect any changes in the data, thus making your cursor in sync with the database.

As you can imagine, there is a price to pay for using this type of cursor. There is additional overhead associated with this type of cursor because the database must provide all changes to the data to your cursor while it is open. So you should only use this type of cursor when changes to the data in the database are absolutely critical to the task at hand.

## Try It Out - Using A Dynamic Cursor

Create a Web page that uses a dynamic cursor and the qAllBoatNames stored procedure. After opening the recordset, display all boat names on your Web page.

We won't show our complete example code again – it is available for download in TryItOut7.asp. Instead we'll just show the new lines of code.

### How It Works - Using a Dynamic Cursor

Starting with the code that is different, we declare our ADO variable for the dynamic cursor that we will be using.

```
<%
'Declare ADO variables
Dim adOpenDynamic
adOpenDynamic = 2
```

After creating the Recordset object, we open the recordset specifying a dynamic cursor as the CursorType parameter.

```
'Create the recordset object
Set objRS = Server.CreateObject("ADODB.Recordset")

'Open the recordset
objRS.Open "qAllBoatNames","DSN=Sailors",adOpenDynamic
```

We loop through the entire recordset displaying all boat names on our Web page.

# adOpenStatic Cursor

The static cursor uses a static copy of data from the database. This means that no changes to the data are visible in your recordset. Also this type of cursor is only supported if the `CursorLocation` property of the `Recordset` object is set to use a client cursor. This makes this type of cursor ideal for use in disconnected recordsets. This means that the recordset is opened and then the `ActiveConnection` property is set to nothing. This disconnects the recordset from the database connection and you can then close the database. Using this method in a web page is ideal as you can get the data you need and then free the database connection while you perform other processing.

Complete recordset navigation is supported in this type of cursor as well as bookmarks. You can use the `Resync` method to resynchronize your recordset with the database.

## Try It Out - Using A Static Cursor

Create a Web page that opens the `qAllBoatNames` stored procedure using a static cursor. Once the recordset is opened, display all boat names on your Web page.

You can find the example code in `TryItOut8.asp` – we won't show it all here, as again the framework is the same as in our previous examples.

### How It Works - Using a Static Cursor

We start where the code differs from the last example. This time we must declare two ADO variables. As we mentioned above the static cursor is only valid if we set the `CursorLocation` property of the recordset to a client side cursor, so we must declare a variable for it. A client side cursor uses the local cursor library services that often provide features not supported in the driver supplied cursor.

```
<%
'Declare ADO variables
Dim adOpenStatic
Dim adUseClient
adOpenStatic = 3
adUseClient = 3
```

We create our `Recordset` object and then set the cursor location before the recordset is opened. The `CursorLocation` property is read/write while the `Recordset` object is closed and read only after the object is opened.

Next, we open the `Recordset` object specifying the static cursor.

```
'Create the recordset object and set the cursor location
Set objRS = Server.CreateObject("ADODB.Recordset")
objRS.CursorLocation = adUseClient

'Open the recordset
objRS.Open "qAllBoatNames","DSN=Sailors",adOpenStatic
```

Once our recordset is opened, we loop through the recordset displaying all boat names on our Web page.

# The LockType Parameter

The LockType parameter specifies what type of locking should be used on our cursor when we are editing the data in our recordset. There are four basic types of locking methods available in ADO. They are adLockReadOnly, adLockPessimistic, adLockOptimistic, and adLockBatchOptimistic.

Most of the locking mechanisms can be used with all cursors. The correct combination of cursor type and lock type can provide flexibility and powerful use of ADO recordsets. We will be going into the details of each lock type in the following sections.

## adLockReadOnly Lock

This is the default lock type used when no LockType parameter has been specified. As its name implies, this lock type specifies that the fields in the recordset can be read only, no updates are allowed.

As you might imagine, the resources used with this type of lock are very low because the database does not have to keep track of when you are editing the fields in the recordset.

### Try It Out - Using A Read Only Lock

Create a Web page that uses a forward only cursor and a read only lock. Use the qAllBoatNames stored procedure to retrieve the data. Once the recordset has been opened, loop through the recordset and display all boat names on your Web page.

Using a forward only cursor and a read only lock allows us to only navigate in a forward motion using the MoveNext property of the recordset and to only read the fields in the recordset. You'll find the code for this example in TryItOut9.asp.

#### How It Works - Using A Read Only Lock

Again, we'll only look at the lines of code that are different from our basic example. Since we are using an extra ADO variable, we must look up the correct number for this variable using the VB object browser. Here we are specifying variables for the cursor type and the lock type to be used.

```
<%
'Declare ADO variables
Dim adOpenForwardOnly
Dim adLockReadOnly
adOpenForwardOnly = 0
adLockReadOnly = 1
```

We create the Recordset object first and then open the recordset specifying the Source, ActiveConnection, CursorType and the LockType parameters.

```
'Create the recordset object
Set objRS = Server.CreateObject("ADODB.Recordset")

'Open the recordset
objRS.Open "qAllBoatNames", "DSN=Sailors", adOpenForwardOnly, adLockReadOnly
```

After our recordset is opened, we loop through the recordset and display each boat name on our Web page.

# adLockPessimistic Lock

Pessimistic locking forces the database to lock the entire record when we first start editing a recordset. This means when the first field in the recordset has changed, the database will lock the entire record. This ensures we have complete control over the record and no other user can edit this record while we are.

The record is not actually updated until we call the `Update` method of the `Recordset` object. The database just locks the record so we have complete control over it while editing.

After we have completed editing all fields by assigning them new values in the current row of the recordset, we must call the `Update` method to have the database apply the changes in our recordset to the database thus releasing the lock on that record in the table.

## Try It Out – Using A Pessimistic Lock

Create a web page that uses a dynamic cursor and pessimistic locking to edit a record. After opening the recordset using the `qAllBoatNames` stored procedure, display the first record on the web page and then change the boat name. Update the recordset and the display the new boat name on the web page.

The result should look something like this:

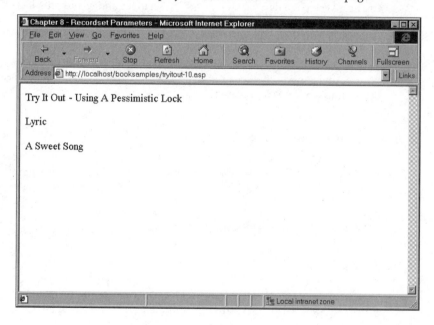

You can find the code in `TryItOut10.asp`:

```html
<HTML>
<HEAD>
<META NAME="GENERATOR" Content="Microsoft Visual Studio 6.0">
<TITLE>Chapter 8 - Recordset Parameters</TITLE>
</HEAD>
<BODY>

<!--Display the page data-->
Try It Out - Using A Pessimistic Lock<BR><BR>

<%
'Declare ADO variables
Dim adOpenDynamic
Dim adLockPessimistic
adOpenDynamic = 2
adLockPessimistic = 2

'Create the recordset object
Set objRS = Server.CreateObject("ADODB.Recordset")

'Open the recordset
objRS.Open "qAllBoatNames","DSN=Sailors",adOpenDynamic,adLockPessimistic

'Display the first record
Response.Write objRS("BoatName") & "<P>"

'Set the boat name in the recordset to a new name
objRS("BoatName") = "A Sweet Song"

'Update the recordset
objRS.Update

'Display the new name from the recordset
Response.Write objRS("BoatName") & "<P>"

'Close and dereference database objects
objRS.Close
Set objRS = Nothing
%>

</BODY>
</HTML>
```

### How It Works - Using A Pessimistic Lock

We'll only look at the new code in detail. We declare our two ADO variables that we will be using, one for the cursor type and the other for the lock type.

```
<%
'Declare ADO variables
Dim adOpenDynamic
Dim adLockPessimistic
adOpenDynamic = 2
adLockPessimistic = 2
```

Next we create our `Recordset` object and open our recordset specifying the appropriate parameters.

```
'Create the recordset object
Set objRS = Server.CreateObject("ADODB.Recordset")

'Open the recordset
objRS.Open "qAllBoatNames","DSN=Sailors",adOpenDynamic,adLockPessimistic
```

We display the first boat name in the recordset. Notice that we are not looping through the recordset in this example. We will only be working with the first record. If we needed to find a specific record we could loop through the recordset until we find the record we need to process and then make the changes to it.

```
'Display the first record
Response.Write objRS("BoatName") & "<P>"
```

Because we have specified a `LockType` parameter other than `adLockReadOnly`, we can edit fields in the current row of our recordset by setting the field to a new value as shown below.

Here we are assigning the `BoatName` field a new value of "**A Sweet Song**". Once we set the first value, the database will lock the row in the table of the database of the field we are editing so no other user can update that row. We can proceed to edit the other fields in our recordset if needed but in our case we only have one field.

```
'Set the boat name in the recordset to a new name
objRS("BoatName") = "A Sweet Song"
```

After we have finished editing the fields in the current row of the recordset, we must update the row of data in the database. Using the `Update` method of the `Recordset` object does this for us by having the database apply the changes from our recordset to the table in the database. Once the updates have been made, the database releases the lock on the current row in the table.

```
'Update the recordset
objRS.Update
```

Now that we have changed our boat name, we want to display the new boat name from the recordset on our Web page.

```
'Display the new name from the recordset
Response.Write objRS("BoatName") & "<P>"
```

Once all processing has been completed, we close and deference our database objects. Using standard HTML tags we end our Web page.

```
'Close and dereference database objects
objRS.Close
Set objRS = Nothing
%>

</BODY>
</HTML>
```

# adLockOptimistic Lock

The optimistic locking method locks records only after you call the `Update` method of the `Recordset` object. When using this method it is important to check for errors after each update to ensure no errors have occurred updating the record you were editing.

If you edit a row in your recordset and call the `MoveNext` method of the `Recordset` object without first calling the `Update` method, ADO will call the `Update` method for you and automatically lock the record so it can apply the updates. To cancel any changes you have made before moving to the next record, you must call the `CancelUpdate` method to discard the changes.

## Try It Out – Using An Optimistic Lock

Create a web page that uses a dynamic cursor and optimistic locking. Use the `qAllBoatNames` stored procedure to open and populate the recordset. Display the boat name in the first row of the recordset, change it, update it, and then display the new boat name.

The basic code is the same as in the previous example – you can find it in `TryItOut11.asp`.

### How It Works - Using An Optimistic Lock

We start where the code is different from before. We declare the ADO variables that we are going to be using in this page, getting the values from the VB object browser.

```
<%
'Declare ADO variables
Dim adOpenDynamic
Dim adLockOptimistic
adOpenDynamic = 2
adLockOptimistic = 3
```

After we create our `Recordset` object, we open the recordset using the `Source`, `ActiveConnection`, `CursorType` and `LockType` parameters.

```
'Create the recordset object
Set objRS = Server.CreateObject("ADODB.Recordset")

'Open the recordset
objRS.Open "qAllBoatNames","DSN=Sailors",adOpenDynamic,adLockOptimistic
```

Once the recordset has been opened, we display the boat name from the first row of our recordset. Next we change the boat name assigning it a new value.

```
'Display the first record
Response.Write objRS("BoatName") & "<P>"

'Set the boat name in the recordset to a new name
objRS("BoatName") = "Lyric"
```

At this point no locking has occurred in the database. Once we call the `Update` method, the database will lock the row and will apply the update.

After the updates have been applied, we display the new boat name on our web page from our recordset.

```
'Update the recordset
objRS.Update

'Display the new name from the recordset
Response.Write objRS("BoatName") & "<P>"
```

We end our web page by closing and de-referencing our database objects and using standard HTML tags.

# adLockBatchOptimistic Lock

The `adLockBatchOptimistic` lock allows us to apply our updates in a batch instead of updating each row of our recordset after a change is made. This allows for efficient processing if all we need to do is update one field in each row of our recordset. We can loop through our recordset and change the field in question and then apply all of the updates at once.

This type of lock is also great if you are using a disconnected recordset. You can open the recordset and then disconnect it from the database and close the database connection. You can perform your processing and update the recordset as needed. Once you have completed your updates, you can open another database connection, reconnect your recordset and apply your updates.

## Try It Out - Using A Batch Optimistic Lock

Create a web page that uses a static cursor and a batch optimistic lock. Display the first boat name in the recordset and then change it. Move to the next record and display that boat name and then change. Apply the updates to the database using the `UpdateBatch` method and then move to the first record. Display the first two records again using data from the recordset.

Here's what the example should produce:

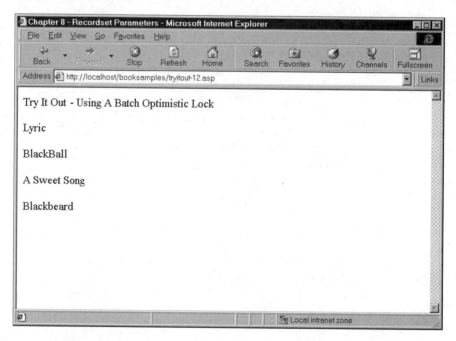

You can find the code for this example in `TryItOut12.asp`.

```
<HTML>
<HEAD>
<META NAME="GENERATOR" Content="Microsoft Visual Studio 6.0">
<TITLE>Chapter 8 - Recordset Parameters</TITLE>
</HEAD>
<BODY>

<!--Display the page data-->
Try It Out - Using A Batch Optimistic Lock<BR><BR>

<%
'Declare ADO variables
Dim adOpenStatic
Dim adLockBatchOptimistic
adOpenStatic = 3
adLockBatchOptimistic = 4

'Create the recordset object
Set objRS = Server.CreateObject("ADODB.Recordset")

'Open the recordset
objRS.Open "qAllBoatNames","DSN=Sailors",adOpenStatic,adLockBatchOptimistic

'Display the first record
Response.Write objRS("BoatName") & "<P>"

'Set the boat name in the recordset to a new name
objRS("BoatName") = "A Sweet Song"

'Move to the next record
objrs.MoveNext

'Display the next record
Response.Write objRS("BoatName") & "<P>"

'Set the boat name in the recordset to a new name
objRS("BoatName") = "Blackbeard"

'Update the recordset
objRS.UpdateBatch

'Move to the first record
objRS.MoveFirst

'Display the new name for the first record
Response.Write objRS("BoatName") & "<P>"

'Move to the next record
objrs.MoveNext

'Display the new name in the next record
Response.Write objRS("BoatName") & "<P>"

'Close and dereference database objects
objRS.Close
Set objRS = Nothing
%>

</BODY>
</HTML>
```

## How It Works - Using A Batch Optimistic Lock

Starting with the code that is different from the last example, we declare the ADO variables that we will be using as parameters and set their values.

```
<%
'Declare ADO variables
Dim adOpenStatic
Dim adLockBatchOptimistic
adOpenStatic = 3
adLockBatchOptimistic = 4
```

Next, we create our Recordset object and open the recordset specifying the Source, ActiveConnection, CursorType and LockType parameters.

```
'Create the recordset object
Set objRS = Server.CreateObject("ADODB.Recordset")

'Open the recordset
objRS.Open "qAllBoatNames","DSN=Sailors",adOpenStatic,adLockBatchOptimistic
```

Once our recordset is open, we display the first boat name in our recordset and set the BoatName field to a new name.

```
'Display the first record
Response.Write objRS("BoatName") & "<P>"

'Set the boat name in the recordset to a new name
objRS("BoatName") = "A Sweet Song"
```

Now we advance the recordset to the next record. If we were using the regular optimistic or pessimistic LockType parameter this could cause the Update method to be invoked for us, updating the database. But, since we are using a batch optimistic lock, no updates are applied until we specifically call the UpdateBatch method.

We now display the next boat name on our web page and then assign it a new name.

```
'Move to the next record
objrs.MoveNext

'Display the next record
Response.Write objRS("BoatName") & "<P>"

'Set the boat name in the recordset to a new name
objRS("BoatName") = "Blackbeard"
```

Now that we are done updating the boat names, it's time to apply the updates to the database by calling the UpdateBatch method. This will apply all changes in our recordset to the database.

```
'Update the recordset
objRS.UpdateBatch
```

After our updates have been applied to the database, we want to reposition our recordset to the first record by using the MoveFirst method of the Recordset object. Then we display the new name of the first boat in the recordset and then move to the next record and display that boat name.

```
'Move to the first record
objRS.MoveFirst

'Display the new name for the first record
Response.Write objRS("BoatName") & "<P>"

'Move to the next record
objrs.MoveNext

'Display the new name in the next record
Response.Write objRS("BoatName") & "<P>"
```

After we have finished our processing we close and deference our database objects. We end our page by using standard HTML tags.

# Options Parameter

The Options parameter specifies how the database should interpret the Source parameter *only* if the Source parameter does not contain a Command object. Remember when we used the Command object? Well, we set the type of command that we were executing in the Command object's CommandType property. That is why we would not need to set it in the Recordset object.

You can improve the performance of your code by specifying this option. The default parameter if one has not been specified is adCmdUnknown. This means that ADO must go through the process of trying to figure out which type of Source parameter you have specified and this adds extra overhead to your processing.

The following table lists the available values for this parameter from the CommandTypeEnum, and is pretty self-explanatory.

| Constant | Value | Description |
|---|---|---|
| adCmdUnknown | 8 | This is the default if no Options parameter is specified and it indicates the Source parameter is unknown. |
| adCmdText | 1 | Specifies a SQL statement is being used. |
| adCmdTable | 2 | Specifies that a table name was used by an internally generated SQL statement – note that in this chapter we have only covered the direct use of a table name, shown at the end of this table. |
| adCmdStoredProc | 4 | Specifies that a stored procedure is being used. |
| adCmdFile | 256 | Specifies a persisted recordset is being used. |
| adCmdTableDirect | 512 | Specifies that a table name is being used. |

# Summary

We have gone into the details of the various parameters of the `Recordset` object in this chapter. You should now be familiar with these parameters and know when you must use them and why you should use them. Even though all of these parameters are optional you should now understand why it is important for performance reasons to specify all of them.

Having gone into the details of the cursor types and lock types you should now understand how the combinations of these two parameters work together. You should know when to use the various cursors when you need to see the changes to the data made by other users. You should also be familiar with the locking options and know when to use each one for the given task at hand.

To summarize this chapter, you should know:

- ❑ What type of sources can be used with the `Source` parameter
- ❑ The two different types of connections that can be used
- ❑ The various types of cursors and when to use them
- ❑ The various types of locks and how to use them with the cursor specified

# Exercise 1

Using a keyset cursor and a pessimistic lock, create a web page that will update a boat name. Use a SQL statement that will select all boat names from the `Boats` table in the Sailors database. Once the recordset has been opened, loop through the recordset until you find the boat name "BB3" and update it to "BBC". Display a message on your web page that the boat name was updated.

Your code could produce a result similar to this:

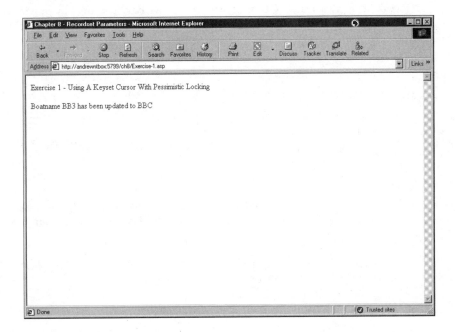

You can find the code for this exercise in the file `Exercise-1.asp`.

### How It Works

To start our web page we use standard HTML tags to define our page. Then we display the first line of text on the web page.

```
<HTML>
<HEAD>
<META NAME="GENERATOR" Content="Microsoft Visual Studio 6.0">
<TITLE>Chapter 8 - Recordset Parameters</TITLE>
</HEAD>
<BODY>

<!--Display the page data-->
Exercise 1 - Using A Keyset Cursor With Pessimistic Locking<BR><BR>
```

We must declare our ADO variables that we are going to be using. We got these values from the VB object browser.

```
<%
Dim adOpenKeyset
Dim adLockPessimistic
Dim adCmdText
adOpenKeyset = 1
adLockPessimistic = 2
adCmdText = 1
```

Next, we create our `Recordset` object and open the recordset passing it the `Source`, `ActiveConnection`, `CursorType`, `LockType` and `Options` parameters. Notice that our `Source` parameter is an actual SQL string and as such we have specified the `adCmdText` `Option` parameter.

```
'Create a recordset object
Set objRS = Server.CreateObject("ADODB.Recordset")

'Open the recordset
objRS.Open "SELECT boatname FROM boats;", "DSN=Sailors", _
  adOpenKeyset, adLockPessimistic, adCmdText
```

We want to loop through the recordset looking for the boat name of `'BB3'`.

```
'Loop through the recordset and update boat name 'BB3'
Do While not objRS.EOF

  If objRS("boatname") = "BB3" Then
```

Once we find a match, we update the `BoatName` field in the recordset and then apply these changes to the database using the `Update` method. Then we display a message on our Web page that the record has been changed.

At this point it does not make sense to continue looping through the recordset, as we know this is the only boat with this name, so we exit the loop using `Exit Do`.

```
    'A match was found, so update the boat name
    objRS("boatname") = "BBC"
    objRS.Update
    'Display a message that the boat name was updated
    Response.Write "Boatname BB3 has been updated to " & _
        objRS("boatname")
    Exit Do
  End If
```

If a match has not been found, we advance the recordset using the `MoveNext` method of the `Recordset` object and then start our loop over.

```
    'No match was found so move to the next record
    objRS.MoveNext

Loop
```

To finish things off, we close and de-reference our database objects and end our page using standard HTML tags.

```
'Close and dereference database objects
objRS.Close
Set objRS = Nothing
%>

</BODY>
</HTML>
```

# Exercise 2

Using a `Connection` object, a `Command` object and a `Recordset` object, create a web page that will perform the same type of update as the last example reversing the name of the boat back to the original name. This time however, you will use the stored procedure `qAllBoatNames` and use a dynamic cursor with optimistic locking.

The result will look similar to the previous example, and you can find the code in the file `Exercise-2.asp`.

### How It Works

This exercise looks like a lot of code, however just read on for a moment. It is the same code that we have used before and requires very little explanation.

We start our web page in the same manner as we have done before by using standard HTML tags and displaying our first line of text.

```
<HTML>
<HEAD>
<META NAME="GENERATOR" Content="Microsoft Visual Studio 6.0">
<TITLE>Chapter 8 - Recordset Parameters</TITLE>
</HEAD>
<BODY>

<!--Display the page data-->
Exercise 2 - Using A Dynamic Cursor With Optimistic Locking<BR><BR>
```

Next, we instruct VB script to ignore any errors it encounters because we are going to be handling them ourselves.

```
<%
'Instruct VBScript to ignore the error and continue
'with the next line of code
On Error Resume Next
```

We create our `Connection` object and open it using the `Sailors` DSN. Then we check for errors using the same error handling code that we saw earlier in the chapter.

```
'Create and open the database object
Set objConn = Server.CreateObject("ADODB.Connection")
objConn.Open "DSN=Sailors"

'Check for errors
If objConn.Errors.Count > 0 Then
  'Create an error object to access the ADO errors collection
  Set objErr = Server.CreateObject("ADODB.Error")
  'Declare Boolean flag for critical errors
  Dim blnCriticalError
  'Write all errors to the page
  For Each objErr In objConn.Errors
    If objErr.Number <> 0 Then
      Response.Write "Number: " & objErr.Number & "<P>"
      Response.Write "Description: " & objErr.Description & "<P>"
      Response.Write "Source: " & objErr.Source & "<P>"
      Response.Write "SQLState: " & objErr.SQLState & "<P>"
      Response.Write "NativeError: " & objErr.NativeError & "<P>"
      blnCriticalError = True
    End If
  Next
```

```
        'Dereference all objects
        Set objErr = Nothing
        If blnCriticalError Then
           Response.End
        End If
End If
```

Next, we declare our ADO variables getting the values from the VB object browser.

```
'Declare ADO variables
Dim adCmdStoredProc
Dim adOpenDynamic
Dim adLockOptimistic
adCmdStoredProc = 4
adOpenDynamic = 2
adLockOptimistic = 3
```

Now, we create our Command object and set its ActiveConnection property to the Connection object. We then set the CommandText property to the stored procedure to be executed and set the CommandType property to adCmdStoredProc, which tells the Command object how to interpret the CommandText property.

```
'Create the command object
Set objCmd = Server.CreateObject("ADODB.Command")

'Set the command object properties
Set objCmd.ActiveConnection = objConn
objCmd.CommandText = "qAllBoatNames"
objCmd.CommandType = adCmdStoredProc
```

We can now create our Recordset object and open it. Notice that we have not specified the ActiveConnection or the Options parameters. If you recall our discussion from earlier, we stated that the Recordset object would inherit the Connection object from the Command object. Well, the Recordset object also inherits the Options parameter from the Command object's CommandType property.

```
'Create the recordset object and open the recordset
Set objRS = Server.CreateObject("ADODB.Recordset")
objRS.Open objCmd,,adOpenDynamic,adLockOptimistic
```

After opening our recordset we need to check for errors using the same error handling code as above.

```
'Check for errors
If objConn.Errors.Count > 0 Then
   'Create an error object to access the ADO errors collection
   Set objErr = Server.CreateObject("ADODB.Error")
   'Write all errors to the page
   For Each objErr In objConn.Errors
     If objErr.Number <> 0 Then
        Response.Write "Number: " & objErr.Number & "<P>"
        Response.Write "Description: " & objErr.Description & "<P>"
        Response.Write "Source: " & objErr.Source & "<P>"
        Response.Write "SQLState: " & objErr.SQLState & "<P>"
        Response.Write "NativeError: " & objErr.NativeError & "<P>"
        blnCriticalError = True
     End If
   Next
   'Dereference all objects
   Set objErr = Nothing
   If blnCriticalError Then
      Response.End
   End If
End If
```

Now we are ready to loop through the recordset looking for the boat name of BBC. Once we find this record, we set the new value of the BoatName field and then we update the record by calling the Update method. After updating the database, we display a message on our Web page and exit the loop.

If no match was found we move to the next record and continue processing.

```
'Loop through the recordset and update boatname BBC
Do While not objRS.EOF

  If objRS("boatname") = "BBC" Then

    'A match was found, so update the boatname
    objRS("boatname") = "BB3"
    objRS.Update
    Response.Write "Boatname BBC has been updated to " & _
      objRS("boatname")
    Exit Do

  End If

  'No match was found so move to the next record
  objRS.MoveNext

Loop
```

To wrap things up, we close and dereference all of our database objects. Last we end the page by using the standard HTML tags.

```
'Close and dereference database objects
Set objCmd = Nothing
objRS.Close
Set objRS = Nothing
objConn.Close
Set objConn = Nothing
%>

</BODY>
</HTML>
```

# Quiz

**1.** What is the Source parameter used for?

**2.** What is the CursorType parameter used for?

**3.** What is the LockType parameter used for?

**4.** When would you want to use a forward only cursor?

**5.** Why is there extra overhead when using a dynamic cursor?

**6.** What type of lock parameter would you use to update all changed records in your recordset at one time?

# Quiz Answers

**1.** It specifies the source of command used to retrieve data to be placed into the recordset.

**2.** It controls the navigation of the records in the recordset and specifies how data is updated in the database. It also specifies how you will see updates in the recordset.

**3.** It specifies what type of locking should be placed on the cursor when we are editing data in the recordset.

**4.** When you need to read data in a forward motion only. You cannot navigate the recordset backwards.

**5.** Because all changes to the data in the database are immediately shown in a dynamic cursor. This includes records that have been added and deleted.

**6.** A batch optimistic lock.

Setup cannot install system files or update shared files if the files are in use. Before c...
any open applications.

WARNING: This program is protected by copyright law and international treaties.

You may install Microsoft Data Access 2.1 on a single computer. Some Microsoft products
with additional rights, which are stated in the End User License Agreement included with y...

Please take a moment to read the End User License Agreement now. It contains all of the te...
conditions that pertain to this software product. By choosing to continue, you indicate accept...
these terms.

Exit Setup

Continue

...e New Data Source

Select a driver for which you want to set up a data sourc...

| Name | Version |
|------|---------|
| Microsoft Access Driver (*.mdb) | 4.00.4207.00 |
| Microsoft dBase Driver (*.dbf) | 4.00.4207.00 |
| Microsoft dBase VFP Driver (*.dbf) | 6.01.8440.01 |
| Microsoft Excel Driver (*.xls) | 4.00.4207.00 |
| Microsoft FoxPro VFP Driver (*.dbf) | 6.01.8440.01 |
| Microsoft ODBC for Oracle | 2.573.4207.00 |
| Microsoft Paradox Driver (*.db ) | 4.00.4207.00 |
| Microsoft Text Driver (*.txt; *.csv) | 4.00.4207.00 |
| Microsoft Visual FoxPro Driver | 6.01.8440.01 |
| SQL Server | 3.70.06.90 |

Finish

Cancel

# RecordSet Methods and Properties

## Introduction

There are two ways to work with a database using ADO. One technique is to incorporate all of the selecting, sorting, editing, and deleting into SQL statements. (In Chapter 10 we will utilize action queries using the SQL keywords UPDATE, INSERT, and DELETE to makes changes in our data.) The second technique, covered in this chapter, is to perform these tasks using methods available to the recordset. SQL statements can handle far more complex objectives than methods. However, for some simple tasks, the various recordset methods work very well. In addition, methods can be applied after a SQL statement has performed an initial action. Furthermore, as a site designer you will come across legacy code which relies on these methods.

There are certain scenarios in which using recordset methods make sense. In cases where we must iterate through each record in a table or large recordset, these methods can be advantageous. Also, complex updates, which would normally require painful string manipulation, can be much simpler using these methods. It's good to be prepared for these situations, to understand the recordset method approach as opposed to encapsulating all changes in SQL statements.

Many students confuse the tactics of the two techniques. SQL statements are generally used over three blocks of code:

- ❏ open the recordset with a given SQL statement
- ❏ use the resulting recordset
- ❏ close the recordset

But when we use recordset methods we generally have more code:

- ❏ open the recordset without a SQL statement
- ❏ apply methods over several lines
- ❏ use the resulting recordset
- ❏ close the recordset

In this chapter we focus on recordset methods that allow the finding, sorting, inserting, editing, and deleting of data. We've previously discussed the recordset Open and Close methods, so they are not included in our discussion here.

# Supported Methods

Some methods only work on recordsets opened with certain combinations of cursor type and lock type. For an obvious example, a recordset opened as ReadOnly will not support a method that creates a new record.

ADO allows you to check a recordset's capabilities before performing an operation, by using the Supports method. There is one parameter, which is the constant value corresponding to the method that you want to check. For example, to do a quick check that a recordset named oRS supports the Delete method, you could use:

```
Response.Write oRS.Supports(adDelete)
```

If the Supports method returns a value of "true", then the specified method is supported by the recordset. A more enlightened technique is to give yourself a reminder of what it is that you are checking:

```
Response.Write "adDelete " & oRS.Supports(adDelete)
```

If you want to catch errors at run time, you can use the result of the Supports method as the truth expression for an IF statement as follows:

```
If oRS.Supports(adDelete) Then
  Response.Write "Run code that does the delete"
Else
  Response.Write "Notify user of inability to delete"
End If
```

You cannot check support for all methods; ADO 2.0 allows testing only for the following ten actions, which are listed in the CursorOptionEnum values section of ADOvbs.inc. ADO 2.1 adds a few more. Remember that, if you want to use the constants listed in the left column, you must include the ADOvbs.inc file in your page, located as follows:

```
<BODY>
<!--#include file="ADOvbs.inc"-->
<%
```

| Constant | Value |
|---|---|
| AdAddNew | &H01000400 |
| AdApproxPosition | &H00004000 |
| AdBookmark | &H00002000 |
| AdDelete | &H01000800 |

| Constant | Value |
|---|---|
| AdHoldRecords | &H00000100 |
| AdMovePrevious | &H00000200 |
| AdNotify | &H00040000 |
| AdResync | &H00020000 |
| AdUpdate | &H01008000 |
| AdUpdateBatch | &H00010000 |

There is some debate among programmers about checking your recordset with the Supports method. Some programmers believe that it is a useful test to prevent run–time errors as a result of attempting to execute an unallowable method. Other writers have proclaimed that it would be a lame programmer indeed who used a recordset without knowing how it was opened.

There are times when it is worth checking. Consider a page that is using a recordset that was opened and held in a session recordset, and thus may have been set up by another member of the programming team. I tell students that it is certainly useful to use Supports to confirm that they opened a recordset with the proper parameters, but as you get further along, it is generally unnecessary.

## Try It Out – Supports Method

Write a page that helps you test the availability of recordset methods for various types of recordsets. This page would be useful at design time when you are deciding how to work with a recordset, but would not have a use after deployment. Start by encapsulating the code for printing the availability of methods in a procedure, then open a recordsets and test it for the ability to perform various methods. One solution yields code and a screen shot as follows:

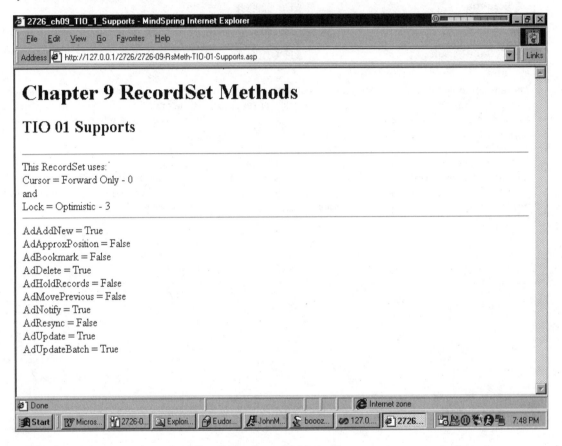

The above screen came from the following code, available in file `2726-09-RsMeth-TIO-01-Supports.asp`.

```
<HTML>
<HEAD>
<TITLE>2726_ch09_TIO_1_Supports</TITLE>
</HEAD>
<BODY>
<H1>Chapter 9 RecordSet Methods</H1>
<H2>TIO 01 Supports</H2>
<!--#include file="ADOvbs.inc"-->
<%
  Sub SupportOptionsWriter
```

```
     Select Case oRSs.CursorType
     Case 0
       vCursorType = "Forward Only - 0"
     Case 1
       vCursorType = "Keyset - 1"
     Case 2
       vCursorType = "Dynamic - 2"
     Case 3
       vCursorType = "Static - 3"
     End Select
     Select Case oRSs.LockType
     Case 1
       vLockType = "Read Only - 1"
     Case 2
       vLockType = "Pessimistic - 2"
     Case 3
       vLockType = "Optimistic - 3"
     Case 4
       vLockType = "Batch Optimistic - 4"
     End Select

     Response.Write "<HR> This RecordSet uses:<BR>"
     Response.Write "Cursor = " & vCursorType & "<BR>and<BR>"
     Response.Write "Lock = " & vLockType & "<HR>"

     Response.Write "AdAddNew = " & oRSs.Supports(AdAddNew) & "<BR>"
     Response.Write "AdApproxPosition = " &  oRSs.Supports(AdApproxPosition) & "<BR>"
     Response.Write "AdBookmark = " &  oRSs.Supports(AdBookmark) & "<BR>"
     Response.Write "AdDelete = " &  oRSs.Supports(AdDelete) & "<BR>"
     Response.Write "AdHoldRecords = " &  oRSs.Supports(AdHoldRecords) & "<BR>"
     Response.Write "AdMovePrevious = " &  oRSs.Supports(AdMovePrevious) & "<BR>"
     Response.Write "AdNotify = " &  oRSs.Supports(AdNotify) & "<BR>"
     Response.Write "AdResync = " &  oRSs.Supports(AdResync) & "<BR>"
     Response.Write "AdUpdate = " &  oRSs.Supports(AdUpdate) & "<BR>"
     Response.Write "AdUpdateBatch = " &  oRSs.Supports(AdUpdateBatch) & "<BR>"
   End Sub
%>

<%
  'Now let us use the subprocedure
  Set oRSs=Server.CreateObject("ADODB.Recordset")
  oRSs.Open "People", "DSN=Sailors",adOpenForwardOnly,adLockOptimistic
  Call SupportOptionsWriter
  oRSs.Close
  Set oRSs=nothing
%>
</BODY>
</HTML>
```

### How It Works – Supports Method

This code is in four parts. The first three are in the procedure named `SupportOptionsWriter`. The first puts an English description of the cursor type into a variable named `vCursorType`. The second does the same for the lock type. Those English words are written to the screen so we will remember what type of recordset we are using. The third section, still within the sub, writes out the Boolean value for each function that can be tested by the `Supports` method. The fourth section creates a recordset and calls it `SupportOptionWriter`.

We start with the usual set–up; we will be using the ADO constants, so don't forget the include.

```
<HTML>
<HEAD>
<TITLE>2726_ch09_TIO_1_Supports</TITLE>
</HEAD>
<BODY>
<H1>Chapter 9 RecordSet Methods</H1>
<H2>TIO 01 Supports</font></H2>
<!--#include file="ADOvbs.inc"-->
```

Now we create the sub procedure and within it assign an English name to the cursor type:

```
<%
  Sub SupportOptionsWriter

    Select Case oRSs.CursorType
    Case 0
      vCursorType = "Forward Only - 0"
    Case 1
      vCursorType = "Keyset - 1"
    Case 2
      vCursorType = "Dynamic - 2"
    Case 3
      vCursorType = "Static - 3"
    End Select
```

We do the same for the lock type:

```
    Select Case oRSs.LockType
    Case 1
      vLockType = "Read Only - 1"
    Case 2
      vLockType = "Pesimistic - 2"
    Case 3
      vLockType = "Optimistic - 3"
    Case 4
      vLockType = "Batch Optimistic - 4"
    End Select
```

Then we write out both of those to the screen. This helps us understand what recordset we are looking at in the browser.

```
    Response.Write "<HR> This RecordSet uses:<BR>"
    Response.Write "Cursor = " & vCursorType & "<BR>and<BR>"
    Response.Write "Lock = " & vLockType & "<HR>"

    Response.Write "AdAddNew = " & oRSs.Supports(AdAddNew) & "<BR>"
    Response.Write "AdApproxPosition = " & oRSs.Supports(AdApproxPosition) & "<BR>"
    Response.Write "AdBookmark = " & oRSs.Supports(AdBookmark) & "<BR>"
    Response.Write "AdDelete = " & oRSs.Supports(AdDelete) & "<BR>"
    Response.Write "AdHoldRecords = " & oRSs.Supports(AdHoldRecords) & "<BR>"
    Response.Write "AdMovePrevious = " & oRSs.Supports(AdMovePrevious) & "<BR>"
    Response.Write "AdNotify = " & oRSs.Supports(AdNotify) & "<BR>"
    Response.Write "AdResync = " & oRSs.Supports(AdResync) & "<BR>"
    Response.Write "AdUpdate = " & oRSs.Supports(AdUpdate) & "<BR>"
    Response.Write "AdUpdateBatch = " & oRSs.Supports(AdUpdateBatch) & "<BR>"
  End Sub
%>
```

That finishes our procedure, it is now pretty easy to use it as follows; open a recordset and call the sub.

```
<%
  'Now let us use the subprocedure
  Set oRSs=Server.CreateoObject("ADODB.Recordset")
  oRSs.Open "People", "DSN=Sailors",adOpenForwardOnly,adLockOptimistic
  Call SupportOptionsWriter
  oRSs.Close
  Set oRSs=nothing
%>
</BODY></HTML>
```

Note in screens resulting from the above code that not all cursor and lock types are available for all datastore, drivers and providers. For example, when you ask an Access database for a dynamic cursor you will get a keyset, since dynamic is not supported. But that is part of the purpose of the `Supports` method – you can test what features your recordset actually has.

# Find

When we need to read from or write to a specific record, the `Find` method is employed. `Find` is similar to the `WHERE` clause of a SQL statement. Unlike a `WHERE` clause, however, the `Find` method only supports a single field name and value pair. You cannot use multiple search criteria with the `Find` method.

After using the `Find` method, we know the pointer will be at a specific record, and any subsequent methods such as `Update` or `Delete` will change the "found" record under the pointer.

## Find Syntax

The `Find` method is generally used with a single parameter, a string containing the fieldname, operator, and value to compare. If the value to search is a character string, we should enclose the value in single quotes:

```
oRS.Find "FieldName = 'TextToFind'"
```

Usually, however, we get the data from a form. In that case, we can concatenate the value from the form into our search string. For instance, if the form had a field called `FieldOfWords`, then the syntax would be as follows:

```
oRS.Find "Field = '" & varFieldOfWords & "'"
```

Just as with SQL statements, proper use of quotation marks is essential. Say, for example, we left out the single quote marks around the value to search for in the above code, and the user entered `Fallingwater` in the form field. When our code executes the `Find` method, the database will attempt to find a record where `Field` equals the value of *another* field called `Fallingwater`. This is not the intended effect; we wanted to find the record where `Field` *contains* the value "Fallingwater".

Usually the data for a search comes from a form rather than being hard-coded, and so the syntax spans two pages. The first page would be an HTML form with the following code:

```
<FORM ACTION="Response.asp" METHOD=Post>
<INPUT TYPE=text NAME="FieldName">
```

This would be followed by a response page, which would contain:

```
<%
  Dim varFieldName
  varFieldName = Request("FieldName")

  Dim oRS
  Set oRS=Server.CreateObject("ADODB.Recordset")
  oRS.Open "People", "DSN=Sailors"
  oRS.find "PeopleNameLast = '" & varFieldName & "'"
  ' use the matching record
```

Searching for numeric data works in the same way, the only difference being that we do not place single quotes around numeric data.

## Try It Out – Find

Create a pair of pages that ask for a sailor's last name, then use the recordset `Find` method to get the sailor's first name, and report that back to the visitor. Remember, in this chapter we want to practice recordset methods, not SQL statements.

We start with a form page as follows, the code is available in file `2726-09-RSMeth-FindForm.asp`:

```
<HTML><HEAD>
<META NAME="GENERATOR" Content="Microsoft Visual Studio 6.0">
<TITLE>2726 09 Methods TIO-02 Find Form</TITLE>
</HEAD>
<BODY>
<H1>Chapter 9 Recordset Methods<BR>
Try It Out #02 Find Form</H1>
<H2>Find a sailor's first name</H2>
Please type the sailors last name,<BR>
then click on submit.
<FORM ACTION="2726-09-RSMeth-FindResponse.asp" METHOD=POST>
<INPUT TYPE=text NAME=PeopleNameLast
VALUE="Please type last name here" size = 40>
<BR>
<INPUT TYPE=submit>
</FORM></BODY></HTML>
```

The above form produces the following page:

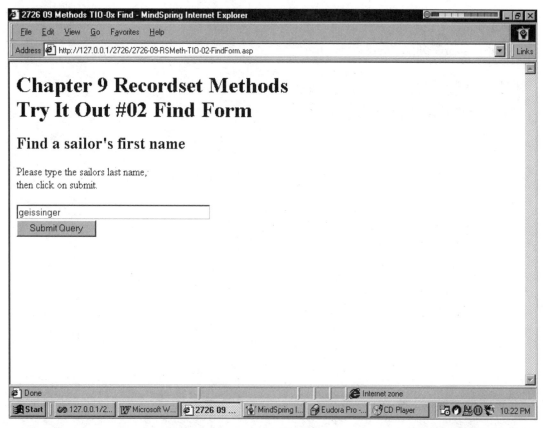

The response page code, file `2726-09-RSMeth-FindResponse.asp`, would be coded as follows:

```
<HTML>
<HEAD>
<META NAME="GENERATOR" Content="Microsoft Visual Studio 6.0">
<TITLE>2726 09 Methods TIO-0x Find</TITLE>
</HEAD>
<BODY>

<H1>Chapter 9 Recordset Methods
Try It Out #02 Find</H1>
<!--#include file="ADOvbs.inc"-->
<%
  Dim varPeopleNameLast
  varPeopleNameLast = Request("PeopleNameLast")
  Dim oRS
  Set oRS=Server.CreateObject("ADODB.Recordset")
  oRS.Open "People", "DSN=Sailors",adOpenKeyset,adLockReadOnly
  oRS.Find "PeopleNameLast = " & chr(39) & varPeopleNameLast & chr(39)

  Response.Write "The first name of " & oRS("PeopleNameLast")
  Response.Write " is <H3>" & oRS("PeopleNameFirst") & "</H2>"
  oRS.Close
  Set oRS=nothing
%>
</BODY>
</HTML>
```

The above response page code, combined with a user input of "geissinger", produces the following screen:

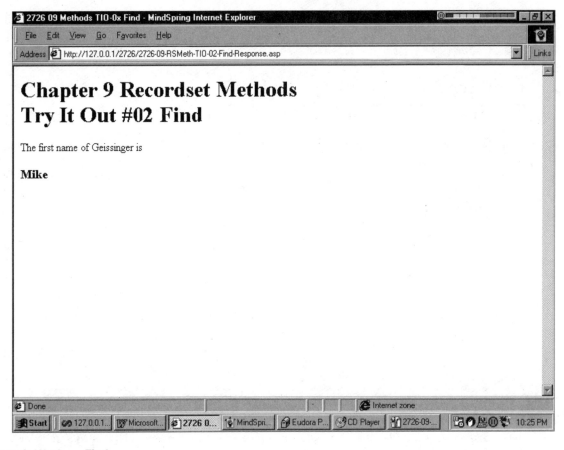

## How it Works – Find

The form page is nothing new, we just need to remember that we are using the post method and that the name of our field is PeopleNameLast.

```
<FORM ACTION="2726-09-RSMeth-Find-Response.asp" METHOD=post>
<INPUT TYPE=text NAME=PeopleNameLast VALUE="Please type last name here" size = 40>
```

Now, in the response we need to pick up the value of PeopleNameLast from the Request object and put that value into our variable varPeopleNameLast:

```
...
<TITLE>2726 09 Methods TIO-0x Find</TITLE>
...
<BODY>
<H1>Chapter 9 Recordset Methods
Try It Out #02 Find</H1>
<!--#include file="ADOvbs.inc"-->
<%
  Dim varPeopleNameLast
  varPeopleNameLast = Request("PeopleNameLast")
```

Then we open a recordset. Since we want to use the `Find` method, we cannot use the default parameter for the cursor type (`ForwardOnly`); rather, we specify an `OpenKeyset`.

```
Dim oRS
Set oRS=Server.CreateObject("ADODB.Recordset")
oRS.Open "People", "DSN=Sailors",adOpenKeyset,adLockReadOnly
```

Now that the recordset is open, we can apply the `Find` method. If the entered data was `Geissinger` then our objective is to get code that reads `PeopleNameLast = 'Geissinger'`.

```
oRS.Find "PeopleNameLast = '" & varPeopleNameLast & "'"
```

Finally we display the result from the found record:

```
Response.Write "The first name of " & oRS("PeopleNameLast")
Response.Write " is <H3>" & oRS("PeopleNameFirst") & "</H2>"
%></BODY></HTML>
```

# Find Traps

There are a few traps with `Find`. First is that there may not be a matching record. Assuming we are searching in the forward direction, the recordset will have a property of `EOF=True`, which can be tested, as below.

```
oRS.Find "FieldName = " & chr(39) & varTextToMatch & chr(39)
If oRS.EOF Then
  Response.Write "No match found for FieldName = " & varTextToMatch
Else
  'use the record
End If
```

Another trap is that if you use an `OpenForwardOnly` cursor type with `Find`, you will get a Microsoft OLE DB Provider for ODBC Drivers error '80040e29', indicating that the `rowset` cannot scroll backwards. Since the default cursor type is forward only, you cannot use either of the following `Rs.Open` statements if you intend to use `Find`:

```
oRS.Open "People", "DSN=Sailors"
oRS.Find "PeopleNameLast = '" & varPeopleNameLast & "'"
'fails since default cursor type is ForwardOnly
```

```
oRS.Open "People", "DSN=Sailors",adOpenKeyset,adLockReadOnly
oRS.Find "PeopleNameLast = '" & varPeopleNameLast & "'"
'fails since cursor type 0 is ForwardOnly
```

However, all of the `RecordSet.Open` lock types will work.

# Filter Property

The `Filter` property provides a means to select a subset of records from a recordset. However, its use is limited since it is not available for all datastore/provider/driver combinations. The non-supporting failure results in a VBScript runtime error '800a01b6', indicating that the object doesn't support this property or method. For example, neither the native OLEDB provider nor the ODBC driver for Access can utilize this property. However, for people using SQL data stores the most logical point for filtering is in the SQL statement itself. Once the recordset is created from a filter–enabled source it can then be subjected to a re-selection process using the filter property, as in the following examples:

```
RS.Filter "ItemPrice > 24.99"
Rs.Filter "ItemPrice
```

A filter can then be removed, to re-expose all the records of a recordset, by using one of the following lines of code, the second being an empty string.

```
RS.Filter adFilterNone
'or
RS.Filter ""
```

# AddNew

The recordset method `AddNew` will create a new, "virtual" record in the recordset. After calling this method, the pointer will be sitting on the emerging record and will thus be ready for changing its data. As you will learn later in the chapter, to effect those changes, you must run an `Update` or `UpdateBatch` method. `AddNew` also offers a syntax form where you can both create the new record and fill its fields with data in one statement. Although convenient, you must be very careful of the syntax.

## Syntax

The `AddNew` method can be used with or without arguments. When `AddNew` is used with an argument, that argument can contain one piece of information corresponding to one field in the target recordset, or it can contain an array of values corresponding to multiple fields in the recordset.

Typically, the `AddNew` method is used *without* arguments. Then, we set the values of the individual fields in the following statements, and after that we use the `Update` method to commit our changes to the database. For example, if we wished to allow users to create a new record in the `People` table, we could create an entry form for them as follows:

```
<FORM ACTION="addnewpeople.asp" METHOD="post">
Last Name: <INPUT TYPE="text" NAME="PeopleNameLast"><BR>
First Name: <INPUT TYPE="text" NAME="PeopleNameFirst"><BR>
<INPUT TYPE="submit">
</FORM>
```

The ASP to process this form could use the following syntax:

```
oRS.AddNew
oRS.Fields("PeopleNameLast") = Request.Form("PeopleNameLast")
oRS.Fields("PeopleNameFirst") = Request.Form("PeopleNameFirst")
oRS.Update
```

The code above is equivalent to the following:

```
strSQL = "INSERT INTO People (PeopleNameLast,PeopleNameFirst) " _
   & " VALUES ('" & Request.Form("PeopleNameLast") & "'," _
   & "'" & Request.Form("PeopleNameFirst") & "')"
oCN.Execute strSQL
```

This first technique makes code easier to read if you are doing some calculating to come up with the data or if the data is coming from a variable, for example as in the following code.

```
varNameFirst = Request.Form(NameFirst)
varNameLast = Request.Form(NameLast)

oRS.AddNew
oRS("PeopleNameLast") = Ucase(varNameLast)
oRS("PeopleNameFirst") = varNameFirst
oRS("PeopleDOB") = #07/15/1968#
oRS.Update
```

Carefully consider the use of quotes. There are three kinds of information that can be confused:

❑   The field name

❑   Data that is hard-wired

❑   Data that is in a variable (usually from a form)

Ensure that you use the proper syntax for denoting field names. For instance, above we have placed the field name in quotes within parentheses. For data that is hard-coded, be careful to use quotes where appropriate.

Data that comes from a variable is more difficult. Keep in mind that HTML forms do not have a date or number type, only a text input field. Therefore, validation and/or conversion may be needed. Most database systems take a date or number field as text and convert it, as long as the data is a recognizable date and the recipient field is of date/time type. But some databases can be particular. You can accommodate them by validating the date with the `IsDate` function, and then running date data through the `cDate` function to convert it to a date. Of course, prior to that, you should check that it is a recognizable date that can be converted, as in the following code.

```
varClassEntered = Request.Form("ClassEntered")

If Not(IsDate(varClassEntered)) Then
   Response.Write "This is not an understandable date<BR>"
   Response.Write "<A HREF='Form.asp'>Click here to correct</A>"
   Response.End
End If
… code to execute if the Date is OK
```

A second technique is to specify a single field and datum on the `AddNew` line. You cannot insert more then one piece of data with this technique. In the following sample, we add a new record with "Cooper" specified for the `PeopleNameLast` field:

```
oRS.AddNew "PeopleNameLast", "Cooper"
oRS.Update
```

Another way to use the AddNew method is to use arrays as the arguments for the method. The first parameter is an array containing the fields to be modified. The second parameter contains the actual values for these fields. Here is what the statement would look like:

```
Dim arrFields(1)
Dim arrValues(1)
arrFields(0) = "PeopleNameFirst"
arrValues(0) = "Bob"
arrFields(1) = "PeopleNameLast"
arrValues(1) = "Smith"
oRS.AddNew arrFields, arrValues
```

Don't forget to **dim**ension your arrays if you choose to use this syntax.

With all AddNew code you must be careful to catch empty and/or null data. For example, an empty FirstName field in the form will result in an empty varNameFirst in the response page, and an empty variable being used as the source of data in the AddNew. This will not cause an error, but the data will be missing from the database. This is different in SQL, where you must use NULL, since an empty string will cause an error.

### Common Errors with the RecordSet AddNew Method:

❑ Incorrectly bracketing characters, for example quotes around a number

❑ Mixing up the order of fields and data

❑ Missing data for a mandatory field

❑ Trying to insert a record without specifying values for all mandatory (non–NULL) fields

We'll look at a couple of Try It Out examples for the AddNew method – if you find the first straightforward you can always skip the second one and move on to the next section.

### Try It Out – Add New Sailor

Create a pair of pages to allow a user to create a new record in the People table. Again, we want to use the AddNew method of the Recordset object rather than writing a SQL action query.

First, we need to create an input form to allow the user to enter the sailor's name. This code is available as 2726-09-RSMeth-TIO-03A-AddNew-Sailor-Form.asp:

```
<%@ Language=VBScript %>
<HTML>
<HEAD>
<META NAME="GENERATOR" Content="Microsoft Visual Studio 6.0">
<TITLE>2726 09 Methods TIO-03A AddNew Sailor Form</TITLE>
</HEAD>
<BODY>
<H1>Chapter 9 Recordset Methods</H1>
<H2>Try It Out #3-A AddNew Sailor Form</H2>
<P>Enter the name for the new sailor to add:</P>
<P>
<FORM ACTION="2726-09-RSMeth-TIO-03A-AddNew-Sailor-Response.asp" METHOD="post">
First Name: <INPUT TYPE="text" NAME="PeopleNameFirst"><BR>
Last Name: <INPUT TYPE="text" NAME="PeopleNameLast"><BR>
<INPUT TYPE="submit">
</FORM>
</P>
</BODY>
</HTML>
```

The HTML above produces a page that looks like this:

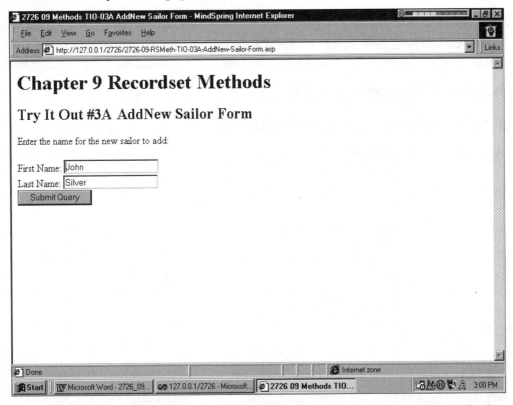

Next, we write a page that will process the user's input and return a message. The code for this page is in file `2726-09-RSMeth-TIO-03A-AddNew-Sailor-Response.asp`, as follows:

```
<HTML>
<HEAD>
<META NAME="GENERATOR" Content="Microsoft Visual Studio 6.0">
<TITLE>2726 09 Methods TIO-03A AddNew Sailor Response</TITLE>
</HEAD>
<BODY>
<H1>Chapter 9 Recordset Methods</H1>
<H2>Try It Out #3-A AddNew Sailor Response</H2>
<!--#include file="ADOvbs.inc"-->
<%
  Dim oRS
  Set oRS=Server.CreateObject("ADODB.Recordset")
  oRS.Open "people", "DSN=Sailors",adOpenKeyset,adLockOptimistic
  oRS.AddNew
  oRS.Fields("PeopleNameFirst")=Request.Form("PeopleNameFirst")
  oRS.Fields("PeopleNameLast")=Request.Form("PeopleNameLast")
  oRS.Update
  Response.Write "<P>A new sailor has been created " _
           & "using the following values:</P>" _
           & "<P>First Name: " & oRS.Fields("PeopleNameFirst") _
           & "<BR>Last Name: " & oRS.Fields("PeopleNameLast") & "</P>"
  oRS.Close
%>
</BODY>
</HTML>
```

The results of running the script will look similar to this:

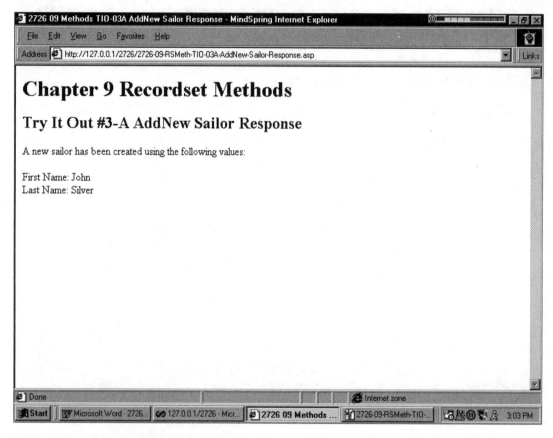

### How It Works – Add New Sailor

In the input page, we create a form containing the two required fields for this table.

```
<FORM ACTION="2726-09-RSMeth-TIO-03A-AddNew-Sailor-Response.asp" METHOD="post">
First Name: <INPUT TYPE="text" NAME="PeopleNameFirst"><BR>
Last Name: <INPUT TYPE="text" NAME="PeopleNameLast"><BR>
<INPUT TYPE="submit">
</FORM>
```

Note that in a production form we should probably add a client-side validation function to ensure that data is entered for both fields.

In the response page, we open a recordset for the table to which we are adding a record. Note that we are using an Optimistic lock type in conjunction with the AddNew method, as indicated by the fourth parameter in our method call.

```
oRS.Open "people", "DSN=Sailors",adOpenKeyset,adLockOptimistic
```

Next, we invoke the AddNew method on the Recordset object. This creates a temporary record, but does not yet actually affect the data in the table.

```
oRS.AddNew
```

Then, we set the values of the required fields in the record.

```
oRS.Fields("PeopleNameFirst")=Request.Form("PeopleNameFirst")
oRS.Fields("PeopleNameLast")=Request.Form("PeopleNameLast")
```

We must invoke the Update method on the Recordset object to perform the actual insertion of the record.

```
oRS.Update
```

Then, we can use the same Recordset object to retrieve the data and present it back to the user.

```
Response.Write "<P>A new sailor has been created " _
  & "using the following values:</P>" _
  & "<P>First Name: " & oRS.Fields("PeopleNameFirst") _
  & "<BR>Last Name: " & oRS.Fields("PeopleNameLast") & "</P>"
```

Finally, we close the Recordset object.

```
oRS.Close
```

## Try It Out – New Boat Class

We have worked with the People table quite a bit, so for our second example let's try turning to the BoatClass table. Create a form that allows the addition of a new boat class, and test it by adding the following two classes of boats:

| Name | Weight | Length | Date Entered |
|------|--------|--------|--------------|
| Star | 1800 pounds | 26 feet | 18 July, 1926 |
| Tornado | 1200 pounds | 22 feet | 20 March, 1969 |

One solution follows and it starts with a form, the code for which is available in file 2726-09-RSMeth-TIO-3B-AddNew-BoatClass-Form.asp.

```
<%@ Language=VBScript %>
<!--#include file = "ADOVBS.inc"-->
<HTML><HEAD>
<META NAME="GENERATOR" Content="Microsoft Visual Studio 6.0">
<TITLE>2726 09 Methods TIO-03B AddNew BoatClass Form</TITLE>
</HEAD>
<BODY>
<H1>Chapter 9 Recordset Methods</H1>
<H2>TIO #03B AddNew BoatCLass Form</H2>
<H3>Form to enter a New Class of Boats</H3>
<FORM ACTION="2726-09-RSMeth-TIO-03B-AddNew-BoatClass-Response.asp" METHOD=post>
Please provide the following information for the new class<BR>
Name <INPUT TYPE=text NAME=ClassName><BR>
Length <INPUT TYPE=text NAME=ClassLengTH> in feet<BR>
Weight <INPUT TYPE=text NAME=ClassWeight> in pounds<BR>
Date <INPUT TYPE=text NAME=ClassEntered>Please enter as mm/dd/yy<BR>
<INPUT TYPE=submit>
</FORM></BODY></HTML>
```

The above code creates the following screen:

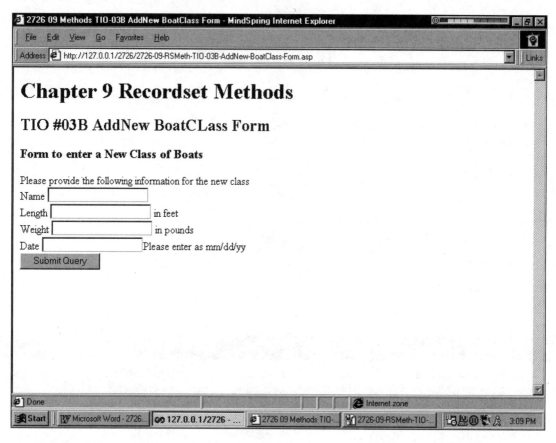

And then we write a second page, `2726-09-RSMeth-TIO-03B-AddNew-BoatClass-Response.asp`, to respond to the form, coded as follows.

```
<!-- #include file="ADOvbs.inc" -->
<HTML><HEAD>
<META NAME="GENERATOR" Content="Microsoft Visual Studio 6.0">
<TITLE>2726 09 Methods TIO-03 AddNew Response</TITLE>
</HEAD>
<BODY>
<H1>Chapter 9 Recordset Methods<BR>
TIO #03 AddNew Response</H1>
<%
  varClassName = Request.Form("ClassName")
  varClassLength = Request.Form("ClassLength")
  varClassWeight = Request.Form("ClassWeight")
  varClassEntered = Request.Form("ClassEntered")

  If NOT IsDate(varClassEntered) Then
    Response.Write "This is not an understandable date<BR>"
    Response.Write "<A HREF='2726-09-RSMeth-TIO-03B-AddNew-BoatClass-Form.asp'>" & _
                   "Click here to correct</A>"
    Response.End
  End If
```

```
Dim oRS
Set oRS=Server.CreateObject("ADODB.Recordset")
oRS.Open "BoatClass", "DSN=Sailors",adOpenDynamic,adLockPessimistic

oRS.AddNew
oRS("ClassName") = varClassName
oRS("ClassLength") = varClassLength
oRS("ClassWeight") = varClassWeight
oRS("ClassEntered") = varClassEntered
Response.Write "Your new class has been entered"

'Read list, with new record, back to user
Response.Write "List of all classes"
Response.Write "<TABLE BORDER=1><TR>"
Response.Write "<TH>ID</TH><TH>Name</TH><TH>Length</TH>"
Response.Write "<TH>Weight</TH><TH>Date Entered</TH>"
Response.Write "</TR><TD>"
Response.Write _
oRS.GetString(adClipString,,"</TD><TD>","</TD></TR><TR><TD>"," ")
Response.Write "<TABLE BORDER=1>"
Response.Write "</TABLE></TD></TR>"
%>
<A HREF="2726-09-RSMeth-TIO-03B-AddNew-BoatClass-Form.asp">
Click to enter another class</A>
</BODY></HTML>
```

The above response page code produces the page below.

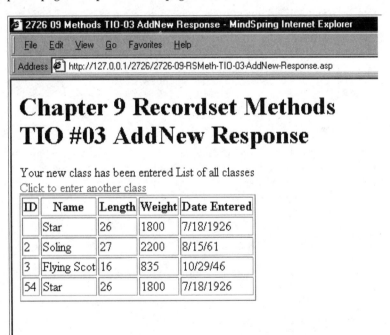

### How It Works – New Boat Class

The form page is straightforward. Just remember that the method of the form and the names of the fields form the following lines.

```
<TITLE>2726 09 Methods TIO-03B AddNew BoatClass Form</TITLE>

<FORM ACTION="2726-09-RSMeth-TIO-03B-AddNew-BoatClass-Response.asp" METHOD=post>
Please provide the following information for the new class<BR>
Name <INPUT TYPE=text NAME=ClassName><BR>
Length <INPUT TYPE=text NAME=ClassLengTH> in feet<BR>
Weight <INPUT TYPE=text NAME=ClassWeight> in pounds<BR>
Date <INPUT TYPE=text NAME=ClassEntered>Please enter as mm/dd/yy<BR>
```

In the response page we start by gathering the data from the `Request` object and storing it in variables.

```
<TITLE>2726 09 Methods TIO-03B AddNew BoatClass Response</TITLE>

<%
  varClassName = Request.Form("ClassName")
  varClassLength = Request.Form("ClassLength")
  varClassWeight = Request.Form("ClassWeight")
  varClassEntered = Request.Form("ClassEntered")
```

Then we check to be sure that the date entered can be interpreted as a date. The expression `IsDate(varClassEntered)` will be true if the data is readable, so we want that converted to a false using `NOT`, so that we can run abort code only in the case that the date is not readable.

```
If NOT IsDate(varClassEntered) Then
   Response.Write "This is not an understandable date<BR>"
   Response.Write "<A HREF='2726-09-RSMeth-TIO-03B-AddNew-BoatClass-Form.asp'>" & _
                  "Click here to correct</A>"
   Response.End
End If
```

Assuming the date is acceptable, we open up a recordset for the `BoatClass`. Since we will be adding a record, we must open with a movable cursor and with a lock type that allows writing. In this case we sacrifice speed to gain security with the `pessimistic` lock. We will discuss other lock options under the `Update/UpdateBatch` methods.

```
Dim oRS
Set oRS=Server.CreateObject("ADODB.Recordset")
oRS.Open "BoatClass", "DSN=Sailors",adOpenDynamic,adLockPessimistic
```

In the following code we create the new record and then fill its fields with data from the form.

```
oRS.AddNew
oRS("ClassName") = varClassName
oRS("ClassLength") = varClassLength
oRS("ClassWeight") = varClassWeight
oRS("ClassEntered") = varClassEntered
```

Now that the new record has been created and filled, we give the visitor some feedback by listing all of the classes, including the new one. One improvement to the table is the addition of a header row by lines four and five below. Also, when using the RecordSet GetString method you must add the first `<TR><TD>` and the final `</TD></TR>` outside the GetString method.

```
  Response.Write "Your new class has been entered"

  'Read list, with new record, back to user
  Response.Write "List of all classes"
  Response.Write "<TABLE BORDER=1><TR>"
  Response.Write "<TH>ID</TH><TH>Name</TH><TH>Length</TH>"
  Response.Write "<TH>Weight</TH><TH>Date Entered</TH>"
  Response.Write "</TR><TD>"
  Response.Write _
oRS.GetString(adClipString,,"</TD><TD>","</TD></TR><TR><TD>"," ")
  Response.Write "<TABLE BORDER=1>"
  Response.Write "</TABLE></TD></TR>"
%>
```

# Update and Batch Update

When opening a recordset we must set a lock type. One option, adLockBatchOptimistic, allows the batching of writes. As described in the previous chapter, no updates will be written to the database until the UpdateBatch method is called. All of the other lock options will perform the update when the Update method is called. We will discuss UpdateBatch further in the next section.

## Update Syntax

The Update method is similar to the AddNew method in that it can be used without parameters, or with an associated set of fieldnames and values. Like AddNew, the Update method is usually used without parameters, and the specifics of the fields and values to be added or updated are handled in the code preceding the Update, as shown below:

```
oRS.Open "People", "DSN=Sailors", adOpenDynamic, adLockOptimistic
oRS.AddNew
oRs("PeopleNameLast") = "Cooper"

oRS.Update
```

For example, if we wished to allow users to modify an existing record in the People table, we could create an entry form for them, consisting of input fields for the record to be found, as well as the updated values for this record.

```
<P>First Name of Person to Modify:
<INPUT TYPE="text" NAME="oldPeopleNameFirst"><BR>
Last Name of Person to Modify:
<INPUT TYPE="text" NAME="oldPeopleNameLast"></P>

<P>Updated First Name:
<INPUT TYPE="text" NAME="newPeopleNameFirst"><BR>
Updated Last Name:
<INPUT TYPE="text" NAME="newPeopleNameLast"></P>
```

The ASP to process this data would first need to find the record to be updated, and then it would apply the change. Note that this code is similar to the AddNew example above, but in order to modify a record, we simply start changing values in the record, rather than specifying an AddNew method first.

```
' (code to find record goes here)

oRS.Fields("PeopleNameFirst") = Request.Form("newPeopleNameFirst")
oRS.Fields("PeopleNameLast") = Request.Form("newPeopleNameFirst")
oRS.Update
```

The code above is similar to the following SQL update query:

```
...
strSQL = "UPDATE People SET " _
    & "PeopleNameFirst = '" &  Request.Form("newPeopleNameFirst") & "'," _
    & "PeopleNameLast = '" & Request.Form("newPeopleNameLast") & "' " _
    & "WHERE PeopleNameFirst = '" & Request.Form("oldPeopleNameFirst") & "' " _
    & "AND PeopleNameLast = '" & Request.Form("oldPeopleNameLast") & "'"
oCN.Execute strSQL
```

There is a major difference, however. The SQL action query above will update the first and last names for *all* records in the table matching our criteria. Unless we use a Do ... Loop construct to iterate through the records in the recordset, the Update example we looked at will only update the *first* record found to be matching our criteria.

Like the AddNew method, the Update method supports an alternative syntax, which allows us to put the field names and values for these fields in the same statement. The same caveats apply here as for the AddNew method. Here is what the statement would look like:

```
Dim arrFields(1)
Dim arrValues(1)
' code to find record goes here
arrFields(0) = "PeopleNameFirst"
arrValues(0) = "Bob"
arrFields(1) = "PeopleNameLast"
arrValues(1) = "Smith"
oRS.Update arrFields, arrValues
```

Again, don't forget to **dim**ension your arrays if you choose to use this syntax.

## Try It Out – Update Sailor Name

Create a system for sailors to change (update) their names. A form will ask for the sailor's ID and the new first and last names that they want to use. Then create a response page that will find the sailor, and update the names accordingly.

First, we will set up a form to allow the user to enter the existing and updated values. The code for this page is available as `2726-09-RsMeth-TIO-04-Update-Form.htm`:

```
<%@ Language=VBScript %>
<HTML>
<HEAD>
<META NAME="GENERATOR" Content="Microsoft Visual Studio 6.0">
</HEAD>
<BODY>
<H1>Chapter 9 Recordset Methods</H1>
```

```
<H2>Try It Out #4 Update Form</H2>
<P>Update a sailor's name:</P>
<P>
<FORM ACTION="2726-09-RSMeth-TIO-04-UpdateResponse.asp" METHOD="post">
<P>ID of Person to Modify:
<INPUT TYPE="text" NAME="PeopleID"><BR>
</P>

<P>Updated First Name:
<INPUT TYPE="text" NAME="newPeopleNameFirst"><BR>
Updated Last Name:
<INPUT TYPE="text" NAME="newPeopleNameLast"></P>
<INPUT TYPE="submit">
</FORM>
</P>
</BODY>
</HTML>
```

This HTML results in a page that looks like this:

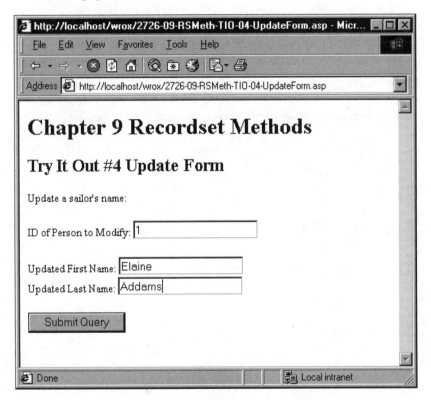

Next, we need to create a page that will accept the data and process the update. The code is in file 2726-09-RSMeth-TIO-04-UpdateResponse.asp.

```
<%@ Language=VBScript %>
<!--#INCLUDE FILE="ADOvbs.inc" -->
<HTML>
<HEAD>
<META NAME="GENERATOR" Content="Microsoft Visual Studio 6.0">
</HEAD>
```

```
<BODY>
<H1>Chapter 9 Recordset Methods</H1>
<H2>Try It Out #4 Update Response</H2>
<%
  Dim oRS
  Set oRS=Server.CreateObject("ADODB.Recordset")
  oRS.Open "People", "DSN=Sailors", adOpenKeyset, adLockOptimistic
  oRS.Find "PeopleID=" & Request.Form("PeopleID")
  If oRS.EOF Then
    Response.Write "<P>This sailor was not found.</P>"
  Else
    Response.Write "<P>This sailor is being updated as follows:</P>" _
                & "<P>Old First Name: " & oRS.Fields("PeopleNameFirst") _
                & "<BR>Old Last Name: " & oRS.Fields("PeopleNameLast") & "</P>"
    oRS.Fields("PeopleNameFirst")=Request.Form("newPeopleNameFirst")
    oRS.Fields("PeopleNameLast")=Request.Form("newPeopleNameLast")
    oRS.Update
    Response.Write "<P>The sailor has been updated as follows:</P>" _
                & "<P>New First Name: " & oRS.Fields("PeopleNameFirst") _
                & "<BR>New Last Name: " & oRS.Fields("PeopleNameLast") & "</P>"
  End If
  oRS.Close
%>
</BODY>
</HTML>
```

The output of the page looks something like this:

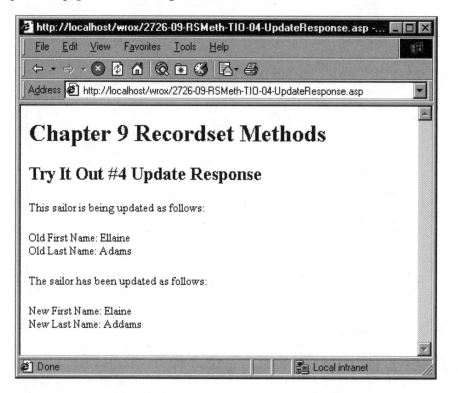

### *How It Works – Update Sailor Name*

The form page is similar to others we have worked with, be sure to note the values for the ACTION and METHOD attributes of the form.

```
<FORM ACTION="2726-09-RSMeth-TIO-04-UpdateResponse.asp" METHOD="post">
<P>ID of Person to Modify:
<INPUT TYPE="text" NAME="PeopleID"><BR>
</P>

<P>Updated First Name:
<INPUT TYPE="text" NAME="newPeopleNameFirst"><BR>
Updated Last Name:
<INPUT TYPE="text" NAME="newPeopleNameLast"></P>
<INPUT TYPE="submit">
</FORM>
```

In the response form, we first open a recordset. Note that we are using a lock type of Optimistic again. Then, we use the Find method along with the information from the form submitted by the user, to make the current record the one matching the sailor's ID.

```
Dim oRS
Set oRS=Server.CreateObject("ADODB.Recordset")
oRS.Open "People", "DSN=Sailors", adOpenKeyset, adLockOptimistic
oRS.Find "PeopleID=" & Request.Form("PeopleID")
```

Next, we check to ensure that a record has been found. If not, we tell the user.

```
If oRS.EOF Then
  Response.Write "<P>This sailor was not found.</P>"
```

If a record has been found, we show the user the old values then proceed to make updates to the field values.

```
Else
  Response.Write "<P>This sailor is being updated as follows:</P>" _
    & "<P>Old First Name: " & oRS.Fields("PeopleNameFirst") _
    & "<BR>Old Last Name: " & oRS.Fields("PeopleNameLast") & "</P>"
  oRS.Fields("PeopleNameFirst")=Request.Form("newPeopleNameFirst")
  oRS.Fields("PeopleNameLast")=Request.Form("newPeopleNameLast")
```

Then, we use the Update method to enact our changes on the database, and show the user our new value.

```
  oRS.Update
  Response.Write "<P>The sailor has been updated as follows:</P>" _
    & "<P>New First Name: " & oRS.Fields("PeopleNameFirst") _
    & "<BR>New Last Name: " & oRS.Fields("PeopleNameLast") & "</P>"
End If
```

Finally, we close the recordset.

```
oRS.Close
```

# UpdateBatch

ADO also supports batch updates to a recordset. When using a batch update, as you will remember from the previous chapter, all changes to a recordset, not just to a row, are written to the database when the UpdateBatch method is called. To use UpdateBatch, we must use a recordset with a lock type of BatchOptimistic and a cursor of Keyset or Static type.

## UpdateBatch Syntax

UpdateBatch is very similar to the Update method discussed previously, with two main differences. First, the UpdateBatch is not called until after all the rows in a recordset have been updated. Also, unlike the Update method, you cannot specify a field and value within the method call. All field updates must take place in the code preceding the UpdateBatch method call.

```
oRS.UpdateBatch
```

UpdateBatch has an optional parameter specifying which records to update; adAffectCurrent for only the record under the pointer, adAffectGroup to write for all records in the current filter, or adAffectAll for all the records in the recordset. Note that adAffectAll is the default behavior.

```
oRS.UpdateBatch adAffectCurrent
```

### Try It Out – UpdateBatch

Change the club code to "wsc" for all of the people in clubs "scow". Do not perform the update to the database until all of the records have been updated. The code is shown below and can be downloaded as file 2726-09-RSMeth-TIO-04B-BatchUpdate.asp.

```
<%@ Language=VBScript %>
<!-- #include file="ADOvbs.inc" -->
<HTML>
<HEAD>
<META NAME="GENERATOR" Content="Microsoft Visual Studio 6.0">
</HEAD>
<BODY>
<H1>Chapter 9 Recordset Methods</H1>
<H2>Try It Out #4B Batch Update</H2>
<P>
<%
  Dim oRS
  Set oRS=Server.CreateObject("ADODB.Recordset")
  oRS.Open "people", "DSN=Sailors", adOpenKeyset, adLockBatchOptimistic
  Do Until oRS.EOF
    If oRS.Fields("PeopleClubCode") = "scow" Then
      oRS.Fields("PeopleClubCode") = "wsc"
      Response.Write "Moved sailor:" & oRS.Fields("PeopleNameFirst") _
              & " " & oRS.Fields("PeopleNameLast") & "<BR>"
    End If
    oRS.Update
    oRS.MoveNext
  Loop
  oRS.UpdateBatch
  oRS.Close
%>
</P>
</BODY>
</HTML>
```

The resulting page will look something like this:

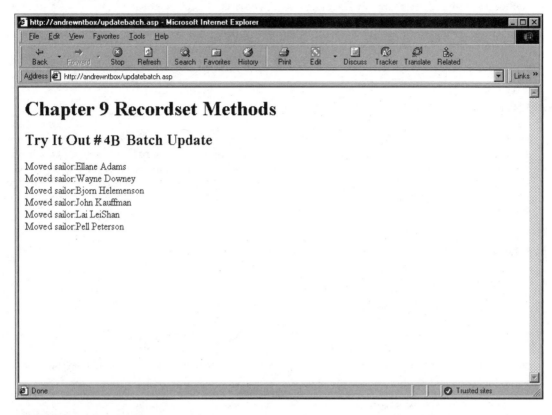

### How It Works – UpdateBatch

First, we open a recordset using a lock type of `BatchOptimistic`.

```
<%
  Dim oRS
  Set oRS=Server.CreateObject("ADODB.Recordset")
  oRS.Open "people", "DSN=Sailors", adOpenKeyset, adLockBatchOptimistic
```

Then, we iterate through the records in the recordset, checking that there are still records remaining. If the value of `PeopleClubCode` is "scow", then we update that field to contain "wsc". Don't forget the `MoveNext` in the loop!

```
Do Until oRS.EOF
   If oRS.Fields("PeopleClubCode") = "scow" Then
     oRS.Fields("PeopleClubCode") = "wsc"
     Response.Write "Moved sailor:" & oRS.Fields("PeopleNameFirst") _
             & " " & oRS.Fields("PeopleNameLast") & "<BR>"
   End If
   oRS.Update
   oRS.MoveNext
Loop
```

Now, at this point, no changes have taken place in the actual database. We must call the `UpdateBatch` method to commit these changes to the database. Then we close our recordset.

```
oRS.UpdateBatch
oRS.Close
%>
```

# Delete

The purpose of the `Delete` method is obvious, but it is important to clearly identify what is going to be deleted. This problem is solved at two levels. The first technique is to ensure that the current record is the correct record to be deleted. The second technique is to use the correct parameter regarding what to delete. The parameter has two values of interest to us: `adAffectCurrent`, which deletes one record only, and `adAffectGroup`, which deletes all records selected by the current filter. Note that `adAffectCurrent` is the default behavior.

## Syntax

The strict syntax is simple, as follows:

```
oRS.Delete adAffectCurrent
```

We normally want to delete a specific record, so the trick is to get that to be the current record. Your best approach is to use a `WHERE` clause in a SQL statement in the source parameter of the `RecordSet.Open` method. If you are trying to be completely independent of SQL however, and you only need to search on a single field, you can use the `Find` method as follows:

```
oRS.Find "MyFieldName='MyTextData'"
oRS.Delete adAffectCurrent
oRS.Update
```

There is the possibility of not finding a match, in which case the pointer would be at EOF. So we can test for that situation and only delete if a match is found.

```
oRS.Find "MyFieldName='MyTextData'"
If oRS.EOF Then
  Response.Write "Match not found"
Else
  oRS.Delete adAffectCurrent
  oRS.Update
End If
```

When discussing deletes, it is important to consider the consequences of a mistake. I like to create a form that asks for the information to match, then finds that information and displays it to the user for confirmation. Only after confirmation do we then actually do the delete. To summarize, the first page is the form, the second the confirmation, and the third the delete code.

Make pages to delete a class of boat. The first page will present the user with a list of classes and a form to enter one of the classes. Of course, this could be done with less visitor errors by creating a list box, but let's look at simpler code here, taken from file 2726-09-RSMeth-TIO-05-DeleteForm.asp.

```
<%@ Language=VBScript %>
<!-- #include file="ADOvbs.inc" -->
<HTML><HEAD>
<META NAME="GENERATOR" Content="Microsoft Visual Studio 6.0">
<TITLE>2726 09 Methods TIO-05 Delete Form</TITLE>
</HEAD>
<BODY>
<H1>Chapter 9 Recordset Methods<BR>
TIO #05 Delete Form</H1>

<FORM ACTION="2726-09-RSMeth-TIO-05-DeleteConfirm.asp" METHOD=post ID=form1
NAME=form1>
Class Name <INPUT TYPE=text NAME="ClassName">
<INPUT TYPE=submit>
</FORM>

<%
  'Read list to user (this could be done in a list box)
  Dim oRS
  Set oRS=Server.CreateObject("ADODB.Recordset")
  oRS.Open "BoatClass", "DSN=Sailors",adOpenDynamic,adLockBatchOptimistic
  Response.Write "List of all classes"
  Response.Write "<TABLE BORDER=1><TR>"
  Response.Write "<TH>ID</TH><TH>Name</TH><TH>Length</TH>"
  Response.Write "<TH>Weight</TH><TH>Date Entered</TH>"
  Response.Write "</TR><TD>"
  Response.Write _
oRS.GetString(adClipString,,"</TD><TD>","</TD></TR><TR><TD>"," ")
  Response.Write "<TABLE BORDER=1>"
  Response.Write "</TABLE></TD></TR>"
%>
</BODY></HTML>
```

The above deletion form page gives the following screen:

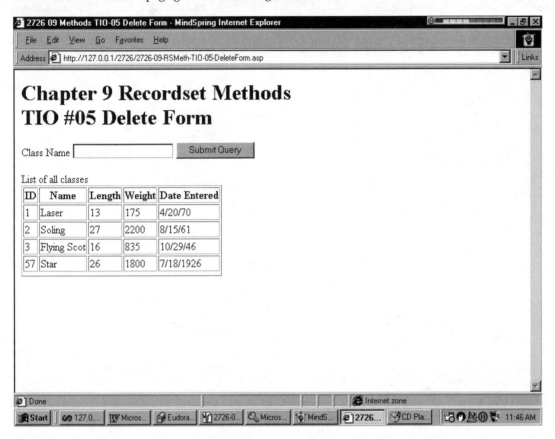

If we enter **Star** in the field above and submit, ASP will call up the following code for the confirmation page. This code is in file `2726-09-RSMeth-TIO-05-DeleteConfirm.asp`:

```
<%@ Language=VBScript %>
<!-- #include file="ADOvbs.inc" -->
<HTML>
<HEAD>
<META NAME="GENERATOR" Content="Microsoft Visual Studio 6.0">
<TITLE>2726 09 Methods TIO-05 Delete Confirm</TITLE>
</HEAD>
<BODY>
<H1>Chapter 9 Recordset Methods<BR>
TIO #05 Delete Confirm</H1>
<%
  Dim varClassName
  varClassName = Request.Form("ClassName")

  Dim oRS
  Set oRS=Server.CreateObject("ADODB.Recordset")
  oRS.Open "BoatClass", "DSN=Sailors",adOpenDynamic
```

```
   oRS.Find "ClassName='" & varClassName & "'"
   If oRS.EOF Then
     Response.Write "Match not found"
   Else
%>
   <FORM ACTION="2726-09-RSMeth-TIO-05-DeleteAction.asp" METHOD=post>
   Are you sure you want to delete the <%=varClassName%> class?
   <BR>Length <%=oRS("ClassLength")%>
   <BR>Weight <%=oRS("ClassWeight")%><BR>
   <INPUT TYPE=radio NAME=COnfirm VALUE="yes">Yes
   <INPUT TYPE=radio NAME=COnfirm VALUE="no" checked>No
   <INPUT TYPE=hidden NAME=ClassID VALUE=<%=oRS("ClassID")%>>
   <INPUT TYPE=submit VALUE="submit">
   </FORM>
<%
   End If
   oRS.Close
   Set oRS=nothing
%>
</BODY>
</HTML>
```

The above confirmation code gives the following result:

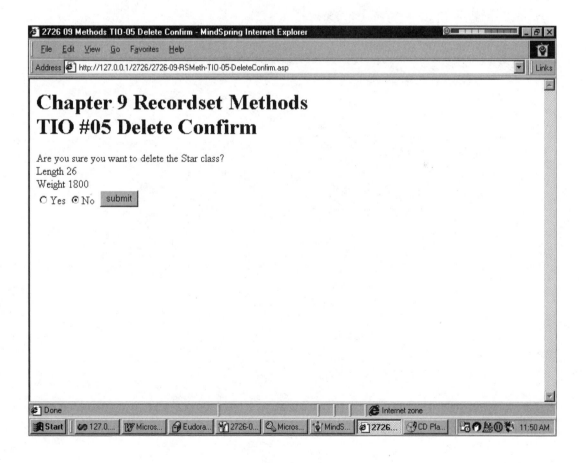

If the visitor selects No and clicks submit, she will return to the form page. But if she clicks on Yes then ASP evokes the following code, located in file 2726-09-RSMeth-TIO-05-DeleteAction.asp:

```
<%@ Language=VBScript %>
<HTML>
<!-- #include file="ADOvbs.inc" -->
<HEAD>
<META NAME="GENERATOR" Content="Microsoft Visual Studio 6.0">
<TITLE>2726 09 Methods TIO-05 Delete Action</TITLE>
</HEAD>
<BODY>
<H1>Chapter 9 Recordset Methods<BR>
TIO #05 Delete Action</H1>
<%
  Dim varConfirm
  varConfirm = Request.Form("Confirm")
  If varConfirm="no" Then
    Response.Redirect "2726-09-RSMeth-TIO-05-DeleteForm.asp"
  End If

  Dim varClassID
  varClassID = Request.Form("ClassID")

  Dim oRS
  Set oRS=Server.CreateObject("ADODB.Recordset")
  oRS.Open "BoatClass", "DSN=Sailors",adOpenDynamic,adLockOptimistic
  oRS.Find "ClassID=" & varClassID
  If oRS.EOF Then
    Response.Write "Matching ClassID not found"
  Else
    oRS.Delete adAffectCurrent
  End If

  oRS.MoveFirst
  Response.Write "List of all classes"
  Response.Write "<TABLE BORDER=1><TR>"
  Response.Write "<TH>ID</TH><TH>Name</TH><TH>Length</TH>"
  Response.Write "<TH>Weight</TH><TH>Date Entered</TH>"
  Response.Write "</TR><TD>"
  Response.Write _
oRS.GetString(adClipString,,"</TD><TD>","</TD></TR><TR><TD>"," ")
  Response.Write "<TABLE BORDER=1>"
  Response.Write "</TABLE></TD></TR>"
  oRS.Close
  Set oRS=nothing
%>
</BODY>
</HTML>
```

The above delete action code produces the following page:

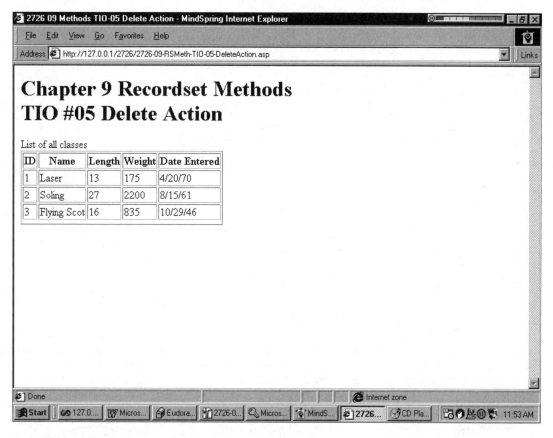

## How It Works – Delete a Record

To review, we have three pages. The first shows the list of boat classes and asks the user to select one to delete. The second page performs a check that the record exists, and poses a confirmation question to the user. The third page zaps the boat class and displays the new list, without the deleted boat class.

The first page, the form, presents no difficulty, but we do have to remember the METHOD, ACTION and NAME of the input field for use in future pages.

```
...
<TITLE>2726 09 Methods TIO-05 Delete Form</TITLE>
</HEAD>
<BODY>
<H1>Chapter 9 Recordset Methods<BR>
TIO #05 Delete Form</H1>

<FORM ACTION="2726-09-RSMeth-TIO-05-DeleteConfirm.asp" METHOD=post ID=form1
NAME=form1>
Class Name <INPUT TYPE=text NAME="ClassName">
<INPUT TYPE=submit>
</FORM>
```

To reduce errors on page one, we present the choices on screen as follows:

```
<%
  'Read list to user (this could be done in a list box)
  Dim oRS
  Set oRS=Server.CreateObject("ADODB.Recordset")
  oRS.Open "BoatClass", "DSN=Sailors",adOpenDynamic,adLockBatchOptimistic
  Response.Write "List of all classes"
  Response.Write "<TABLE BORDER=1><TR>"
  Response.Write "<TH>ID</TH><TH>Name</TH><TH>Length</TH>"
  Response.Write "<TH>Weight</TH><TH>Date Entered</TH>"
  Response.Write "</TR><TD>"
  Response.Write _
oRS.GetString(adClipString,,"</TD><TD>","</TD></TR><TR><TD>"," ")
  Response.Write "<TABLE BORDER=1>"
  Response.Write "</TABLE></TD></TR>"
%>
</BODY></HTML>
```

Now we examine page two, the response page, which starts by copying the data that the user typed, from the form collection of the Request object into a variable.

```
...
<!-- #include file="ADOvbs.inc" -->
...
<TITLE>2726 09 Methods TIO-05 Delete Confirm</TITLE>
...
<%
  Dim varClassName
  varClassName = Request.Form("ClassName")
```

Using that variable we open a recordset of all the records. Since we plan on performing a Find method, we open with a dynamic cursor. But on this second page we are confirming the user's wishes, not performing the deletion, so we can use the default read-only cursor:

```
  Dim oRS
  Set oRS=Server.CreateObject("ADODB.Recordset")
  oRS.Open "BoatClass", "DSN=Sailors",adOpenDynamic
```

Having opened the recordset, we check if we have a match for what the user typed:

```
  oRS.Find "ClassName='" & varClassName & "'"
  If oRS.EOF Then
    Response.write "Match not found"
  Else
%>
```

And if we have found a match, we can proceed to display the information about that match on a form. The form gives the visitor the opportunity to perform or halt the deletion.

```
    <FORM ACTION="2726-09-RSMeth-TIO-05-DeleteAction.asp" METHOD=post>
    Are you sure you want to delete the <%=varClassName%> class?
    <BR>Length <%=oRS("ClassLength")%>
    <BR>Weight <%=oRS("ClassWeight")%><BR>
    <INPUT TYPE=radio NAME=COnfirm VALUE="yes">Yes
    <INPUT TYPE=radio NAME=COnfirm VALUE="no" checked>No
    <INPUT TYPE=hidden NAME=ClassID VALUE=<%=oRS("ClassID")%>>
    <INPUT TYPE=submit VALUE="submit">
    </FORM>
<%
```

A little cleaning up, including closing off the If . . . Then statement, finishes this page.

```
      End If
      oRS.Close
      Set oRS=nothing
%>
</BODY>
</HTML>
```

Page three starts by looking at what the user selected in the confirmation page. If the visitor selects **No** and clicks **submit** she will return to the form page.

```
...
<!-- #include file="ADOvbs.inc" -->
...
<TITLE>2726 09 Methods TIO-06 Delete Action</TITLE>
...
Dim varConfirm
varConfirm = Request.Form("Confirm")
If varConfirm="no" Then
  Response.redirect "2726-09-RSMeth-TIO-05-DeleteForm.asp"
End If
```

If she clicks **Yes** to confirm the deletion, then we pick up the ClassID from the form collection and open a recordset of all the records. This time we intend to delete, so we must avoid the default read-only lock. Instead we choose optimistic, since we expect few people at a time to be deleting boat classes.

```
  Dim varClassID
  varClassID = Request.Form("ClassID")

  Dim oRS
  Set oRS=Server.CreateObject("ADODB.Recordset")
  oRS.Open "BoatClass", "DSN=Sailors",adOpenDynamic,adLockOptimistic
```

Using that ClassID we can do a Find for the record of interest. Although the verification on the previous page should have caught any problems, we nevertheless do another check. If the record is found, it is deleted. To summarize these next lines: *they came, they saw, they deleted*.

```
  oRS.Find "ClassID=" & varClassID
  If oRS.EOF Then
    Response.Write "Matching ClassID not found"
  Else
    oRS.Delete adAffectCurrent
  End If
```

It is important to give users some feedback indicating that what they think they did was in fact done. In this case we build a table showing the classes that remain after their deletion. The page ends with the usual clean up.

```
  oRS.MoveFirst
  Response.Write "List of all classes"
  Response.Write "<TABLE BORDER=1><TR>"
  Response.Write "<TH>ID</TH><TH>Name</TH><TH>Length</TH>"
  Response.Write "<TH>Weight</TH><TH>Date Entered</TH>"
  Response.Write "</TR><TD>"
  Response.Write _
oRS.GetString(adClipString,,"</TD><TD>","</TD></TR><TR><TD>"," ")
  Response.Write "<TABLE BORDER=1>"
  Response.Write "</TABLE></TD></TR>"
  oRS.Close
  Set oRS=nothing
%>
</BODY>
</HTML>
```

# Editing Data in Records

Although not strictly a method of recordsets, it is logical to include a note on editing the data of records. After all, we have looked at adding and deleting records, so changing an existing record is the third leg of the stool.

The technique is simple, consisting of four steps:

- ❑ Open the recordset
- ❑ Get the pointer to the record of interest
- ❑ Make changes by setting fields equal to a value
- ❑ Lock in those changes with an update

The first step is to open the recordset. The trick here is to get the correct parameters. We need a controllable cursor that is not the forward only cursor. Since we will be writing, we will also avoid the read–only lock type.

You then perform a `Find` to get the cursor to the record of interest. If possible, find data in a unique field to avoid having to sort out two records with the same data. Even in this case, you will have to check for the situation of a no-match.

Third, you make the changes with one of the following simple codes:

```
oRS("MyFieldName") = "MyNewTextData"
oRS("MyFieldName") = "MyNewNumericData"
oRS("MyFieldName") = "MyNewDateData"
```

If your data is in a variable you can use the following code for all three data types:

```
oRS("MyFieldName") = "MyVariableHoldingData"
```

# Navigation Through Records

I opened this chapter talking about two approaches to changing data, using SQL statements and using recordset methods. This chapter focused on the latter. However, the techniques to navigate through the records of a recordset are employed in both approaches. ADO offers us up to five methods, depending on the cursor type we have selected.

The most commonly used method is `MoveNext` because it is the basis for stepping through the records in a loop. In fact, judging from the number of times PWS hangs in my classes, `MoveNext` is not used enough in draft pages. What happens when you move to the end of the records? When the pointer gets to the last record it turns the `recordset`'s `EOF` property to "True". If you try to perform another `MoveNext` you will get a **VBScript runtime error '800a01a8'**, noting that an object is required for the line with the offending `MoveNext`. This method is available for all recordsets, as in the following common example:

```
Do Until oRSs.EOF
   Response.Write oRSs("PeopleNameLast") & "<BR>"
   oRSs.MoveNext
Loop
```

A second common navigation method is MoveFirst. The meaning is obvious, setting the current record to the first record. Be careful not to confuse that with BOF, which is only achieved by MoveFirst followed by MovePrevious. By strict definition the forward only cursor type goes through the recordset once only. However, some datastore/provider/driver combinations will accept a MoveFirst. The problem is that they may re-submit the opening of the recordset in order to do so and thus reduce performance. Other combinations will just refuse to implement MoveFirst on a forward only cursor; you must use a more flexible cursor. You can test your situation with code like the following:

```
Do Until oRSs.EOF
   Response.Write oRSs("PeopleNameFirst") & "<BR>"
   oRSs.MoveNext
Loop
oRSs.MoveFirst
Do Until oRSs.EOF
   Response.Write oRSs("PeopleNameLast") & "<BR>"
   oRSs.MoveNext
Loop
```

MoveLast and MovePrevious are used less frequently. MoveLast works with a forward only cursor, but MovePrevious does not. Again, moving to the last record does not set EOF to "True"; that must be done with an additional MoveNext. You can see this by running the following code:

```
'Create and open a recordset named oRSs
oRSs.MoveLast
Response.Write oRSs.EOF
oRSs.MoveNext
Response.Write oRSs.EOF
```

ADO supports one additional command, Move. This must be followed by a parameter indicating how many records to jump and in which direction. You can move four records back with the following example:

```
oRSs.Move -4
```

Move considers the current record to be number one (not zero) when counting. For example look at the results of the following code.

```
Set oRS=Server.CreateObject("ADODB.Recordset")
oRS.Open "People", "DSN=sailors",2,2
For i=1 to 6
   Response.Write oRS("PeopleNameFirst") & "<BR>"
   oRS.MoveNext
Next
oRS.Move -4
Response.Write "<HR>" & oRS("PeopleNameFirst")
```

# Summary

There are two techniques for working with recordsets using ASP-ADO. The first, which is covered in other chapters, uses a SQL statement to select, sort or change data. In this chapter we discussed several methods of the recordset which allow us to achieve the same goals. We must pay particular attention to open the recordset with cursor and lock types that support the methods we intend to use. Prior to use we can confirm those requirements by testing with the Supports method. The most common methods are those which find, add, and delete records. For each of these techniques attention must be paid to the nature of the updates. ADO offers a series of Move commands to assist navigation through the records of a recordset. Although the Move methods are used by both SQL–based and Method-based approaches, they are limited in both cases by the types of cursors set for the recordset.

# Exercises

These exercises use one or both of the two sample databases available from the Wrox website. The structures of the databases are described in Appendix A for Sailors.mdb and Appendix B for Clothier.mdb.

1. Use Clothier to create a series of eight pages (using RecordSet methods instead of SQL statements) for employees to maintain the catalog. An initial (home) page will list the items and provide hyperlinks to pages to add new items, edit existing items, and delete discontinued items. Each of these three options will need its own form page and response page. In our solution the edit response page is split into two, one to display existing details and one to carry out the changes. Before testing your delete page you may want to make a backup of the items table, so that you can restore all of its records after testing the delete and edit functions.

2. Create a page that includes the procedure you made in the first Try It Out, to display supported functions of a recordset. Now write code that will make a table of all 16 combinations of cursor and lock types, and their available functions, using looping.

# Exercise Answers

Note: answers presented are also available from the Wrox site.

**1.** The first page is the home page, `2726-09-RSMeth-Exercise-01-HomePage.asp`.

```
<%@ Language=VBScript %>
<HTML>
<HEAD>
<META NAME="GENERATOR" Content="Microsoft Visual Studio 6.0">
<TITLE>2726 09 Methods Exercise #01 Home Page</TITLE>
</HEAD>
<BODY>
<H1>Chapter 9 Recordset Methods Example Code for Exercise #1 - Intranet Home Page</H1>
<TABLE BORDER=1 WIDTH=70%>
<TBODY><TR>
<TD colSpan=3>
<DIV ALIGN=center>Click Below to:</DIV>
</TD>
</TR><TR>
<TD><A HREF="2726-09-RSMeth-Exercise-01-AddForm.asp">
Add a New Item</A></TD>
<TD><A HREF="2726-09-RSMeth-Exercise-01-EditForm.asp">
Edit an Item</A></TD>
<TD><A HREF="2726-09-RSMeth-Exercise-01-DeleteForm.asp">
Delete an Item</A></TD>
</TR></TABLE>
<H2>Our Items</H2>
<%
'List items
  Dim oRS
  Set oRS=Server.CreateObject("ADODB.Recordset")
  oRS.Open "Items", "DSN=clothier"
  Response.Write "<TABLE BORDER=1><TR>"
  Response.Write "<TH>Item<BR>Num</TH><TH>Item<BR>Name</TH>"
  Response.Write "<TH>Department</TH><TH>Type</TH><TH>Price</TH>"
  Response.Write "<TH>Vendor</TH><TH>Qty /<BR>Box</TH>"
  Response.Write "<TH>Date Release</TH>"
  Response.Write "</TR><TD>"
  Response.write oRS.GetString(,,"</TD><TD>","</TD></TR><TR><TD>"," ")
  Response.Write "<TABLE BORDER=1>"
  Response.Write "</TABLE></TD></TR>"
%>
</BODY>
</HTML>
```

The next page is the add form page, `2726-09-RSMeth-Exercise-01-AddForm.asp`:

```
<%@ Language=VBScript %>
<HTML>
<HEAD>
<META NAME="GENERATOR" Content="Microsoft Visual Studio 6.0">
<TITLE>2726 09 Methods Exercise #01 Add New Form</TITLE>
</HEAD>
<BODY>
<H1>Chapter 9 Recordset Methods Example Code for Exercise #1
- Intranet Add New Item Form</H1>Please provide the following information for
the New Item
```

```
<FORM ACTION="2726-09-RSMeth-Exercise-01-AddResponse.asp" METHOD=post>
<INPUT NAME="Name" SIZE=20 >
<EM>type as name</EM><BR>
<INPUT NAME="Department" SIZE=20>
<EM>type as dept</EM><BR>
<INPUT NAME="Type" SIZE=20 >
<EM>type as type</EM><BR>
<INPUT NAME="PriceBuy" SIZE=20 >
<EM>type as price</EM><BR>
<INPUT NAME="Vendor" SIZE=20 >
<EM>type as vendor</EM><BR>
<INPUT NAME="QtyPerBox" SIZE=20 >
<EM>type as qty per box</EM><BR>
<INPUT NAME="DateRelease" SIZE=20 >
<EM>type as date release</EM><BR>
<INPUT TYPE=submit><INPUT TYPE=reset>
</FORM>

</BODY>
</HTML>
```

This requires the add response page, `2726-09-RSMeth-Exercise-01-AddResponse.asp`:

```
<%@ Language=VBScript %>
<HTML>
<HEAD>
<META NAME="GENERATOR" Content="Microsoft Visual Studio 6.0">
<TITLE>2726 09 Methods Exercise #01 Add New Response</TITLE>
</HEAD>
<BODY>
<!-- #include file="ADOvbs.inc" -->
<H1>Chapter 9 Recordset Methods Example Code for Exercise #1
- Intranet Add New Items Response</H1>
<%
  Dim oRS
  Dim varName, varDepartment, varType
  Dim varPriceBuy, varVendor, varQtyPerBox
  Dim varDateRelease

  varName=Request.form("Name")
  varDepartment=Request.form("Department")
  varType=Request.form("Type")
  varPriceBuy=Request.form("PriceBuy")
  varVendor=Request.form("Vendor")
  varQtyPerBox=Request.form("QtyPerBox")
  varDateRelease=Request.form("DateRelease")

  Response.Write IsDate(varDateRelease)

  Set oRS=Server.CreateObject("ADODB.Recordset")
  oRS.Open "items", "DSN=clothier",adOpenDynamic,adLockOptimistic

  oRS.AddNew _
             Array("ItemName","ItemDepartment",_
             "ItemType", "ItemPriceBuy",        "ItemVendor",_
             "ItemQtyPerBox", "ItemDateRelease"_
             ), Array(_
             varName, varDepartment,_
             varType, varPriceBuy, varVendor,_
             varQtyPerBox, varDateRelease)
  oRS.Close
  Set oRS=nothing
%>
Your new item has been added<BR>
<A HREF="2726-09-RSMeth-Exercise-01-HomePage.asp">
HomePage</A>
</BODY>
</HTML>
```

We also have an option for editing items and therefore need an edit form page, `2726-09-RSMeth-EditForm.asp`:

```asp
<%@ Language=VBScript %>
<HTML>
<HEAD>
<META NAME="GENERATOR" Content="Microsoft Visual Studio 6.0">
<TITLE>2726 09 Methods Exercise #01 Edit Form</TITLE>
</HEAD>
<BODY>
<H1>Chapter 9 Recordset Methods Example Code for Exercise #1
- Intranet Edit Item Form</H1>
Please select an item to Edit by clicking on the name of the item

<TABLE border = 1>
<%
  Dim Orsi
  Set oRSi = Server.CreateObject("ADODB.Recordset")
  Orsi.Open "items", "DSN=CLothier"
  Do while NOT oRSi.EOF
    Response.Write "<TR><TD>" & oRSi("ItemID") & "</TD>"
    Response.Write "<TD><A HREF="
    Response.write "2726-09-RSMeth-Exercise-01-EditResponseDetails.asp"
    Response.Write "?ItemID=" & oRSi("ItemID") & ">"
    Response.Write oRSi("ItemName") & "</a></TD></TR>"
    Orsi.MoveNext
  Loop
  oRSi.Close
  Set oRSi=nothing
%>
</TR></TABLE>
</BODY></HTML>
```

We next want to have a response page for the edit form, `2726-09-RSMeth-EditResponseDetails.asp`. Note in the code below that for the ACTION we send back not only the URL of the response-write page, but appended to that URL is one name/value pair. The name/value pair is appended to the URL with the question mark.

```asp
<%@ Language=VBScript %>
<HTML>
<HEAD>
<META NAME="GENERATOR" Content="Microsoft Visual Studio 6.0">
<TITLE>2726 09 Methods Exercise #01 Edit Response Get Details</TITLE>
</HEAD>
<BODY>
<!--#include file="ADOvbs.inc"-->
<H1>Chapter 9 Recordset Methods Example Code for Exercise #1
- Intranet Edit Item - Get Details</H1>
<%
Dim oRS
Dim varName
varItemID=Request.QueryString("ItemID")
Response.Write "Item ID = " & varItemID
Set oRS=Server.CreateObject("ADODB.Recordset")
oRS.Open "items","DSN=clothier",adOpenKeyset
oRS.find "ItemID = " & varItemID

%>
<FORM ACTION="2726-09-RSMeth-Exercise-01-EditResponseWrite.asp?ItemID=<%=varItemID%>"
METHOD=get>
<TABLE BORDER=1>
<TR>
<TD>Information</TD>
<TD>Current</TD>
<TD>New</TD>
```

```
</TR>
<TR>
<TD> Item ID </TD>
<TD><%=oRS("ItemID")%></TD>
<TD><Input Type=hidden Name=ItemID VALUE=<%=varItemID%>>
<EM>no change allowed</EM></TD>
</TR>
<TR>
<TD> Item Name </TD>
<TD><%=oRS("ItemName")%></TD>
<TD><Input Type=Text Name=ItemName></TD>
</TR>
<TR>
<TD> Item Department </TD>
<TD><%=oRS("ItemDepartment")%></TD>
<TD><Input Type=Text Name=ItemDepartment></TD>
</TR>
<TR>
<TD> Type </TD>
<TD><%=oRS("ItemType")%></TD>
<TD><Input Type=Text Name=ItemType></TD>
</TR>
<TR>
<TD> Price Buy </TD>
<TD><%=oRS("ItemPriceBuy")%></TD>
<TD><Input Type=Text Name=ItemPriceBuy></TD>
</TR>
<TR>
<TD> Vendor Code </TD>
<TD><%=oRS("ItemVendor")%></TD>
<TD><Input Type=Text Name=ItemVendor></TD>
</TR>
<TR>
<TD> Quantity per box </TD>
<TD><%=oRS("ItemQtyPerBox")%></TD>
<TD><Input Type=Text Name=ItemQtyPerBox></TD>
</TR>
<TR>
<TD> Date of Release </TD>
<TD><%=oRS("ItemDateRelease")%></TD>
<TD><Input Type=Text Name=ItemDateRelease></TD>
</TR>
</TABLE>
<BR><INPUT TYPE=submit value="Save Changes">
</FORM>
<%
  oRS.Close
  Set oRS=nothing
%>
</BODY>
</HTML>
```

Once the user has input the new details, they need to be written to the database, using 2726-09-RSMeth-EditResponseWrite.asp.

```
<%@ Language=VBScript %>
<HTML>
<HEAD>
<META NAME="GENERATOR" Content="Microsoft Visual Studio 6.0">
<TITLE>2726 09 Methods Exercise #01 Edit Response Write</TITLE>
</HEAD>
<BODY>
<!--#include file="ADOvbs.inc"-->
<H1>Chapter 9 Recordset Methods Example Code for Exercise #1
- Intranet Edit Items Response Write</H1>
<%
```

```
Dim oRS
Dim varName
varItemID=Request.Querystring("ItemID")
varItemName = Request.Querystring("ItemName")
varItemDepartment = Request.Querystring("ItemDepartment")
varItemType = Request.Querystring("ItemType")
varItemPriceBuy = Request.Querystring("ItemPriceBuy")
varItemVendor = Request.Querystring("ItemVendor")
varItemQtyPerBox = Request.Querystring("ItemQtyPerBox")
varItemPriceBuy = Request.Querystring("ItemPriceBuy")

'following  lines for testing
'Response.Write varItemID & "<BR>"
'Response.Write "varItemName = " & varItemName & "<BR>"

Set oRS=Server.CreateObject("ADODB.Recordset")
oRS.Open "items", "DSN=clothier",adOpenKeyset,adLockOptimistic
oRS.find "ItemID = " & varItemID
If oRS.EOF Then
  Response.Write "There was an error in finding your item"
  Response.write "<A HREF='2726-09-RSMeth-"
  Response.write "Exercise-01-HomePage.asp'>HomePage</A>"
End If

'Perform updates
If varItemName<>"" Then oRS("ItemName") = varItemName
If varItemDepartment<>"" Then oRS("ItemDepartment") = varItemDepartment
If varItemTypePriceBuy<>"" Then oRS("ItemTypePriceBuy") = varItemTypePriceBuy
If varItemVendor<>"" Then oRS("ItemVendor") = varItemVendor
If varItemQtyPerBox<>"" Then oRS("ItemQtyPerBox") = varItemQtyPerBox
If varItemPriceBuy<>"" Then oRS("ItemPriceBuy") = varItemPriceBuy
oRS.Update
%>
<BR><H2>Changes saved</H2><BR>
<A HREF="2726-09-RSMeth-Exercise-01-HomePage.asp">
HomePage</A>
</BODY>
</HTML>
```

The final option is to select data for deletion, using `2726-09-RSMeth-DeleteForm.asp`:

```
<%@ Language=VBScript %>
<HTML>
<HEAD>
<META NAME="GENERATOR" Content="Microsoft Visual Studio 6.0">
<TITLE>2726 09 Methods Exercise #01 Add New Form</TITLE>
</HEAD>
<BODY>
<H1>Chapter 9 Recordset Methods Example Code for Exercise #1
- Intranet Delete Item Form</H1>Please select an item to delete

<FORM ACTION="2726-09-RSMeth-Exercise-01-DeleteResponse.asp" METHOD=post>
<SELECT NAME="ItemID">
<%
  Dim Orsi
  Set oRSi = Server.CreateObject("ADODB.Recordset")
  Orsi.Open "items", "DSN=CLothier"
  Do while NOT oRSi.EOF
    Response.Write "<OPTION NAME=" & oRSi("ItemID") & ">"
    Response.Write OrSI("ItemID") & " '"
    Response.Write oRSi("ItemName")
    Response.Write "' " & OrSI("ItemType")
    Response.Write " from " & OrSI("ItemDepartment")
    Orsi.MoveNext
  Loop
```

```
  oRSi.Close
  Set oRSi=nothing
%>
</SELECT><BR>
<INPUT TYPE=submit value="Begin to Delete Selected Item"><BR><INPUT TYPE="Reset">
</FORM></BODY></HTML>
```

We then come to the final page, `2726-09-RSMeth-DeleteResponse.asp`:

```
<%@ Language=VBScript %>
<HTML>
<HEAD>
<META NAME="GENERATOR" Content="Microsoft Visual Studio 6.0">
<TITLE>2726 09 Methods Exercise #01 Delete Response</TITLE>
</HEAD>
<BODY>
<!-- #include file="ADOvbs.inc" -->
<H1>Chapter 9 Recordset Methods Example Code for Exercise #1
- Intranet Delete Items Response</H1>
<%
  Dim oRS
  Dim varName
  varItemID=Request.Form("ItemID")
  varItemID = Left(varItemID, Instr(varItemID," ")-1)

  Set oRS=Server.CreateObject("ADODB.Recordset")
  oRS.Open "items", "DSN=clothier",adOpenDynamic,adLockPessimistic
  oRS.find "ItemID = " & varItemID
%>
<BR>
The following item has been deleted:
<BR>Item ID = <%=oRS("ItemID")%>
<BR>Item Name = <%=oRS("ItemName")%>
<BR>Item Department = <%=oRS("ItemDepartment")%>
<BR>Item Type = <%=oRS("ItemType")%>
<%
  oRS.Delete
  oRS.Close
  Set oRS=nothing
%>
<BR>
<A HREF="2726-09-RSMeth-Exercise-01-HomePage.asp">
HomePage</A>
</BODY>
</HTML>
```

**2.** The following code is in file `2726-09-RSMeth-Exercise-02-Supports.asp`.

```
'Put in here the Sub SupportsOptionsWriter from the first Try It Out of chapter 9

<TABLE BORDER=1><TR>
<%
  'Now let us use the subprocedure
  For CountLock=1 to 4
    Response.Write "<TR>"
    For CountCursor=0 to 3
      Set oRSs=Server.CreateObject("ADODB.Recordset")
      oRSs.Open "People", "DSN=Sailors",CountCursor,CountLock
      Response.Write "<TD>"
      Call SupportOptionsWriter
      Response.Write "</TD>"
      oRSs.Close
      Set oRSs=nothing
    Next   'CountCursor
```

```
    Response.Write "</TR>"
  Next 'CountLock
%>
</TR></TABLE>
</BODY>
</HTML>
```

Remember that not all datastore/driver/provider combinations support all cursor and lock types. Don't be surprised if your request for a type is changed by ADO.

# Chapter 9 Quiz

**1.** When planning to use the `Delete` recordset method, which cursor and lock types will work?

**2.** Why will the following code fail?

```
<TR>
<TD><%=oRS.ItemID%></TD><TD><INPUT TYPE=Text NAME=ItemID> Item ID</TD>
</TR>
```

**3.** Compare the advantages of changing data using SQL statements and using recordset methods.

**4.** Which lock type is best when there is likely to be only one person at a time changing a record, but when that person will be making changes to many records?

# Chapter 9 Quiz Answers

**1.** Cursors:

> AdOpenKeyset   1
> AdOpenDynamic 2
> AdOpenStatic 3
> (AdOpenForwardOnly 0 will not work)

Lock Types:
> AdLockPessimistic 2
> AdLockOptimistic 3
> AdLockBatchOptimistic 4
> (AdLockReadOnly 1 will not work)

**2.** The wrong syntax was used to refer to the `ItemID`. It should be as follows:

```
<TR>
<TD><%=oRS("ItemID")%></TD><TD><INPUT TYPE=Text NAME=ItemID> Item ID</TD>
</TR>
```

**3.** SQL statements use less commands against the recordset. SQL statements are generally faster. For simple changes `Recordset` methods can be easier to write and maintain.

**4.** Use `adLockBatchOptimistic`. Since there is only one user at a time we can use one of the "optimistics". Since there will be many changes we want to hit the database only once after all the changes, and thus use `BatchOptimistic`.

Setup cannot install system files or update shared files if the files are in use. Before c any open applications.

Exit Setup

Continue

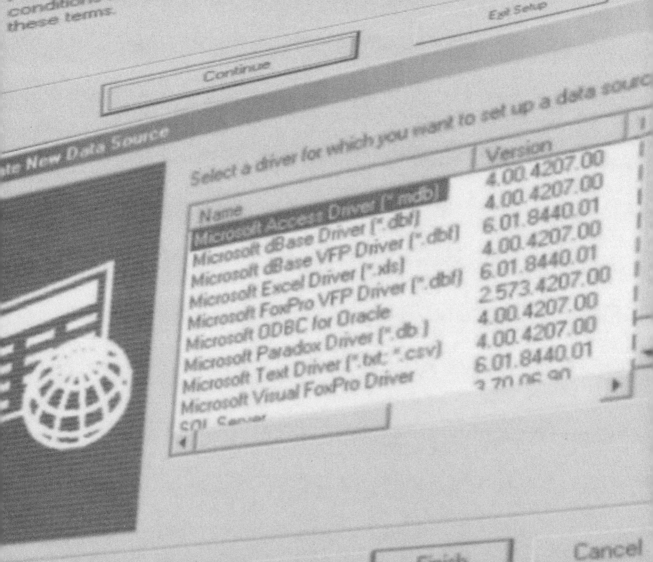

w Data Source

Select a driver for which you want to set up a data sourc

| Name | Version |
|---|---|
| Microsoft Access Driver (*.mdb) | 4.00.4207.00 |
| Microsoft dBase Driver (*.dbf) | 4.00.4207.00 |
| Microsoft dBase VFP Driver (*.dbf) | 6.01.8440.01 |
| Microsoft Excel Driver (*.xls) | 4.00.4207.00 |
| Microsoft FoxPro VFP Driver (*.dbf) | 6.01.8440.01 |
| Microsoft ODBC for Oracle | 2.573.4207.00 |
| Microsoft Paradox Driver (*.db ) | 4.00.4207.00 |
| Microsoft Text Driver (*.txt; *.csv) | 4.00.4207.00 |
| Microsoft Visual FoxPro Driver | 6.01.8440.01 |
| SQL Server | 3.70.06.90 |

Finish    Cancel

# SQL Statements To Modify Data

So far, in this book, the emphasis has been on retrieving data using the SELECT statement. We have used the SELECT statement to obtain data from the database, which we have then processed or used to populate forms. But the data has to get *into* the database somehow, and we also need a means of updating existing data. This chapter will show how we can do just that.

We will focus on the three SQL statements that *modify* data in the database. We will cover the syntax of these SQL statements, and use them to build forms that allow us to **input**, **update** and **delete** data.

This chapter takes a different approach from the previous ones. For each of our examples we will be building more than one web page. At the end of the chapter these will fit together to form a complete set, to allow all three types of modification to be carried out. This process will help you to get a full understanding of where the data comes from and how to modify it. You should also gain a solid foundation from which you can build your own web pages that modify data.

In this chapter we will cover:

- ❏ The distinction between adding and updating data
- ❏ Where the data comes from
- ❏ The INSERT statement
- ❏ The UPDATE statement
- ❏ The DELETE statement

## Distinction Between Adding and Updating

We can either *insert* a row or column of data into a table, or we can *update* an entire row or certain columns of data. The distinction between adding/inserting and updating data can sometimes be confusing.

When we add a row to a table we can do so independently of its data. That is, we can insert an *empty* row in our table, if the columns do not require data. (This can be specified when you define each column in a table.) Or we could insert a row with data in just one or two columns. Or we can even insert a whole row, putting data into every column all at the same time. Let's take a look for a moment at the following INSERT statement:

```
INSERT INTO People (PeopleNameLast) VALUES('Doe')
```

We know only the sailor's last name (Doe) and have no other information about her at the moment. However, we want to go ahead and insert this sailor into the `People` table in the `Sailors` database. We can do so using the `INSERT` statement above. We specify only the sailor's last name, and insert a new row of data into the `People` table.

Once we have inserted a record, we can update it, in much the same fashion. We now have the sailor's last name in the table – imagine that we just found out their first name. We can insert it using the following `UPDATE` statement:

```
UPDATE People SET PeopleNameFirst = 'John' WHERE PeopleNameLast = 'Doe'
```

> *If we knew all of the information about the sailor we could insert or update it all into the row in one go. We'll see how to do that later.*

So, there is a definite distinction between adding data and updating data. Likewise there is a definite distinction between the `INSERT` statement and the `UPDATE` statement, as shown above. We will be going into the details of these two statements shortly.

# Where Does The Data Come From?

Data can come from just about anywhere. However, the data that we are dealing with here comes primarily from our web pages, cookies, server functions, and server variables. Let's take a quick look at each of these in turn.

We create pages in our web applications for the distinct purpose of managing data. This data is entered by the user and displayed in tables, graphs, and reports. Sometimes the data becomes useless unless it is updated, so we create web pages that allow the user to update the existing data. At some point in time the data has no more meaningful value and the user will delete the data, again using web pages that we have designed.

Another source of data is from cookies. The next chapter will be discussing cookies and database information, so we won't go into all the details here. For now, we just need to know that the cookie can be used to retrieve data from the user's machine and look up their user information in the database. But how did the data get into the cookie in the first place? The user entered some data on a web page and we inserted the data into the database. We then used that data and wrote a cookie on the user's machine.

Server functions are another means of obtaining data. Any type of built–in function that is accessible from an Active Server Page can provide us with data that we could insert into our database. The `date` and `time` functions are the most commonly used, for adding date and timestamps.

Server variables come in two forms. First, ASP provides a built–in function that is part of the `Request` object and is called `ServerVariables`. The data provided by the `ServerVariables` function contains very useful information about the user's computer, such as what type of browser they are using and what their Internet Protocol (IP) address is. It also contains some very important HTTP header information. The second type of server variables is the actual variant variables that we define in our Active Server Pages. We use these variables for processing and passing data around in our ASP code. Both of these categories of variables can be used as a source of data.

Where you get the data that gets inserted into your database is entirely up to you, and the processing being performed. It also depends largely on the type of data that needs to be stored.

# Inserting A Record

To add records to our tables we must use the INSERT statement. Using this statement, we can also insert data into one or more columns of the table, as we demonstrated above. The INSERT statement is only used to insert new rows into our tables. Once a row of data exists, we can then only manipulate that data using the UPDATE statement or the DELETE statement.

Let's take a look at the format of the INSERT statement:

```
INSERT INTO tablename (column1, column2, column3) VALUES (value1, value2, value3)
```

The tablename parameter specifies the table that the data should be inserted into.

The column parameters specify the columns in the table into which we want to insert the data. Note that we don't have to specify and fill all of the columns in the table. In fact, if the table includes an AutoNumber field, we wouldn't want to insert a value, as the database does this automatically.

The value parameters specify the data values that we want to insert. The punctuation (or lack of) used with these values indicates the data type. The rules for data types were covered in Chapter 4.

> Although the columns can be specified in any order, it is very important to match the ordering of the columns with the values that you are inserting (e.g. value1 gets inserted into column1 and value2 gets inserted into column2, etc.). There should be no orphan values or columns in the INSERT statement.

You can only insert one row of data into a table at any given time. You can use the same INSERT statement and pass it different values from a loop, which will insert multiple rows, but only one at a time.

Also, any column in the row that is not specified in the INSERT statement gets the default value or NULL value inserted into it by the database. In Access, when you define a column in a table, you can specify a default value for that column which will be used if no data is passed for it when a record is inserted. If the column does not require data and no default value has been specified, then a NULL value is entered into that column when a row of data is inserted which is missing data for that column.

One final point before we try out the INSERT statement. Imagine we have a table that uses an AutoNumber field to uniquely identify each record. After inserting a new record, you might want to know what number has been automatically assigned to it, just in case you need to use this number later on.

Consider the following section of code:

```
Dim maxnum

' Create and open Connection Object
Set objConn = Server.CreateObject("ADODB.Connection")
objConn.Open "DSN=myDSN;"

' Execute INSERT INTO query
strSQL = "INSERT INTO mytable (strfield1, intfield2, datefield3) VALUES ('value1', _
value2, #value3#)
objConn.Execute(strSQL)

' Get AutoNumber field value of record just inserted
' Use the alias "maxnum" for your field
strSQL = "SELECT Max(autonumberfieldname) AS maxnum FROM mytable"
Set objRs = objConn.Execute(strSQL)
maxnum = objRs("maxnum").Value

' Tidy up
objRs.Close
Set objRs = Nothing
objConn.Close
Set objConn = Nothing
```

Note the **alias** used in getting the maxnum value. The Max() function is what is known as an **aggregate** function. It works not with the value of an individual record, but with a group of records, in this case all of them. The most commonly used aggregate functions include Max(), Min(), Avg(), and Sum(). When you use an aggregate function on a field, you are not actually returning the field, but a new one created by the query. The ODBC driver will usually assign an arbitrary name to this field, but since you want to be able to get hold of its value, and you don't know what name the ODBC driver will give to it, you assign it one yourself by using an alias, in this case maxnum. Then you refer to the value of that field by its alias.

> In Access, it is illegal to mix aggregate and non-aggregate functions in a single SQL statement. In some other databases, this is not the case. However, it is good practice to not mix aggregate and non-aggregate functions together in the same SQL statement.

Since your code has just inserted the new record, by immediately getting the maximum AutoNumber field value, you are getting the value from the record you've just inserted.

## Try It Out – Add a New Club

Build an HTML web page that contains a form, allowing a user to enter the required fields to populate the Clubs table in the Sailors database. We will be inserting data into all of the columns except ClubBurgeeFile and ClubBurgee.

The only fields *requiring* input should be the Club Code and the Club Name fields. A validation should be made before submitting the form, to check that these fields are present. Input into the other fields should be *optional*. The form will post the values to the TryItOut-2.asp page that we will be demonstrating next.

The form should appear as shown:

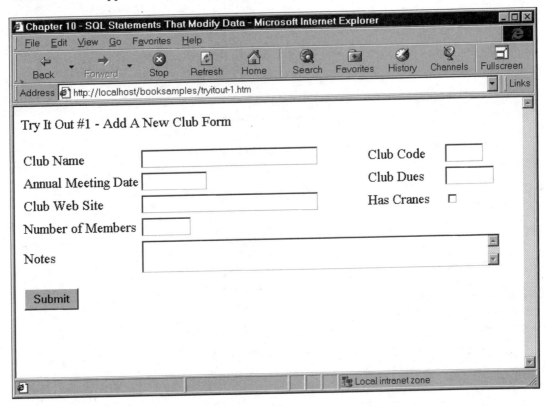

The code for this page is contained in `TryItOut-1.htm`, and is listed below:

```
<HTML>
<HEAD>
<META NAME="GENERATOR" Content="Microsoft Visual Studio 6.0">
<TITLE>Chapter 10 - SQL Statements That Modify Data</TITLE>
</HEAD>
<BODY>
<P>Try It Out #1 - Add A New Club Form</P>

<FORM ACTION=TryItOut-2.asp METHOD=post NAME=frmAdd>
 <INPUT TYPE=hidden NAME=Action VALUE=Add>
 <TABLE>
  <TR>
  <TD>Club Name</TD>
  <TD><INPUT TYPE=text NAME=txtClubName SIZE=30></TD>
  <TD WIDTH=10></TD>
  <TD>Club Code</TD>
  <TD><INPUT TYPE=text NAME=txtClubCode SIZE=5></TD>
  </TR>
  <TR>
  <TD NOWRAP>Annual Meeting Date</TD>
  <TD><INPUT TYPE=text NAME=txtMeetingDate SIZE=10></TD>
  <TD WIDTH=10></TD>
  <TD>Club Dues</TD>
  <TD><INPUT TYPE=text NAME=txtClubDues SIZE=7></TD>
  </TR>
  <TR>
```

```
<TD>Club Web Site</TD>
<TD><INPUT TYPE=text NAME=txtWebSite SIZE=30></TD>
<TD WIDTH=10></TD>
<TD NOWRAP>Has Cranes</TD>
<TD><INPUT TYPE=checkbox NAME=chkCrane VALUE=1></TD>
</TR>
<TR>
<TD>Number of Members</TD>
<TD><INPUT TYPE=text NAME=txtMembers SIZE=7></TD>
</TR>
<TR>
<TD>Notes</TD>
<TD COLSPAN=4><TEXTAREA ROWS=2 COLS=50 NAME=txtNotes></TEXTAREA></TD>
</TR>
<TR>
<TD HEIGHT=60><INPUT TYPE=button NAME=btnSubmit VALUE=Submit></TD>
</TR>
</TABLE>
</FORM>

<SCRIPT LANGUAGE=vbscript>
Sub btnSubmit_OnClick()
 'The only required fields at this point are
 'club name and club code
 If Len(frmAdd.txtClubName.value) = 0 Then
  Alert "You must enter a club name"
  frmAdd.txtClubName.focus
  Exit Sub
 ElseIf Len(frmAdd.txtClubCode.value) = 0 Then
  Alert "You must enter a club code"
  frmAdd.txtClubCode.focus
  Exit Sub
 End If

 'If we make it this far then submit the form
 Call frmAdd.submit()
End Sub
</SCRIPT>

</BODY>
</HTML>
```

### How It Works – Add a New Club

This is an HTML web page that displays a form for the user to enter data into. When the user clicks the submit button, all values are posted to the TryItOut-2.asp web page, which we'll be creating later.

We start our page using the standard HTML tags that define the beginning of any web page. Notice that this page was created using Microsoft Visual InterDev. You can use any web authoring tool of your choice. After our headers are written, we display our first line of text.

```
<HTML>
<HEAD>
<META NAME="GENERATOR" Content="Microsoft Visual Studio 6.0">
<TITLE>Chapter 10 - SQL Statements That Modify Data</TITLE>
</HEAD>
<BODY>
<P>Try It Out #1 - Add A New Club Form</P>
```

We now start our form that will provide the input fields for the user to enter data into. We specify that this form will post its data to the TryItOut-2.asp web page by specifying the METHOD and ACTION properties of the FORM tag. We have given the form a NAME of frmAdd. We add a hidden field in the form that will pass the value of Add. Later in the chapter we'll be including update and delete functions, and this field will be used by our TryItOut-2.asp page to decide which of the three actions to take.

```
<FORM ACTION=TryItOut-2.asp METHOD=post NAME=frmAdd>
<INPUT TYPE=hidden NAME=Action VALUE=Add>
```

Within the form we build a table. Using a table helps us to present our data and fields in a consistent manner, keeping all data elements aligned properly on the page, thus providing a more appealing visual interface for the user.

The first row of our table contains five columns. The first column contains the data that is displayed on our page, while the second column contains the input field for the club name. This is a text box field that has been assigned a NAME of txtClubName, and we specify the SIZE property to indicate how long it should be. Specifying a SIZE property of 30 indicates that our text box will be long enough to display 30 characters.

The third column in this row is used as a separator column. This keeps the data in the fourth column distinct from the text box in the second column. In order to have this column work the way we intend it to, we specify the WIDTH property of the TD tag. This will create a column that contains 10 pixels, which will keep the data in the two bordering columns spaced apart just right to create a pleasing appearance.

The fourth and fifth columns contain more data for display and another input field, this time for the club code:

```
<TABLE>
 <TR>
 <TD>Club Name</TD>
 <TD><INPUT TYPE=text NAME=txtClubName SIZE=30></TD>
 <TD WIDTH=10></TD>
 <TD>Club Code</TD>
 <TD><INPUT TYPE=text NAME=txtClubCode SIZE=5></TD>
 </TR>
```

The next row of the table contains two more text boxes for user input:

```
 <TR>
 <TD NOWRAP>Annual Meeting Date</TD>
 <TD><INPUT TYPE=text NAME=txtMeetingDate SIZE=10></TD>
 <TD WIDTH=10></TD>
 <TD>Club Dues</TD>
 <TD><INPUT TYPE=text NAME=txtClubDues SIZE=7></TD>
 </TR>
```

Again, the next row has text boxes for user input. The fifth column of this row deserves a little more explanation. Here we are using a checkbox to indicate whether or not a club has a crane (useful for putting boats in the water and taking them back out). Notice that we specify an INPUT TYPE of checkbox, and assign the checkbox a NAME. We give it a VALUE of 1 to help us determine if the checkbox is checked or not. We will go into the details of this value in the next example, when we read it from this page.

```
 <TR>
 <TD>Club Web Site</TD>
 <TD><INPUT TYPE=text NAME=txtWebSite SIZE=30></TD>
 <TD WIDTH=10></TD>
 <TD NOWRAP>Has Cranes</TD>
 <TD><INPUT TYPE=checkbox NAME=chkCrane VALUE=1></TD>
 </TR>
```

A further row contains only two columns, one for the data to be displayed and one for the input field:

```
<TR>
<TD>Number of Members</TD>
<TD><INPUT TYPE=text NAME=txtMembers SIZE=7></TD>
</TR>
```

The next row also contains only two columns, one for the data and one for a `textarea` field. This is like a text box except that it can contain multiple rows, and the width is specified as columns. Since the `Notes` column in the `Clubs` table is a memo field and can contain just over 1 gigabyte of data, it becomes clear why we use a `textarea` field instead of a text box. A `textarea` field has a beginning and an ending tag. We specify how wide the `textarea` field should be using the `COLS` property, and how high it should be using the `ROWS` property.

Since this field is so large, we must specify that it spans across four columns, by using the `COLSPAN` property in the `TD` tag. This helps to keep our data aligned properly on the page.

```
<TR>
<TD>Notes</TD>
<TD COLSPAN=4><TEXTAREA ROWS=2 COLS=50 NAME=txtNotes></TEXTAREA></TD>
</TR>
```

The last row of our table contains a button that will be used to submit the data. There are three possible button types that we can use. The first is an actual `submit` button, which would automatically submit the data in our form. The second type is a `reset` button, which would clear the data from all fields in the form. The last type is the `normal` button, which we are using here. The reason we use a `normal` button is that we want to control when the form values are submitted, and by using this type of button we can choose whether to submit the values or not. We'll explain the code behind this button in just a minute.

Notice that we have specified the `HEIGHT` property of the `TD` tag. This will give us the proper spacing between this row and the previous row, separating the button and the last row of data, again for an attractive appearance.

```
<TR>
<TD HEIGHT=60><INPUT TYPE=button NAME=btnSubmit VALUE=Submit></TD>
</TR>
</TABLE>
</FORM>
```

After ending our table and our form we need to write some client–side script. This script will be executed when the user clicks on the submit button. We are only validating that some data has been entered into the club name and club code fields. We are not validating that the data is correct.

```
<SCRIPT LANGUAGE=vbscript>
Sub btnSubmit_OnClick()
```

In order to validate the required fields, we check the length of the field using the `Len` function of VBScript. This returns the length of the string evaluated. If the length of the field is equal to zero, the user has not entered any data and we prompt them to enter some data using the `Alert` function. (This is similar to the `MsgBox` function except that we can only specify the text to be displayed, and we can only have one button, usually OK, which accepts the alert message.) After the user clicks on the OK button in the alert, we set the focus to the field that is blank and we exit the subroutine. We perform this same routine for both the club name and club code fields:

```
'The only required fields at this point are
'club name and club code
If Len(frmAdd.txtClubName.value) = 0 Then
  Alert "You must enter a club name"
  frmAdd.txtClubName.focus
  Exit Sub
ElseIf Len(frmAdd.txtClubCode.value) = 0 Then
  Alert "You must enter a club code"
  frmAdd.txtClubCode.focus
  Exit Sub
End If
```

If we pass both tests, we find ourselves at the last line of code in this subroutine. At this point everything has checked out OK and we call the submit method of the form. This will submit the values entered, and call the page that we specified in the ACTION property of this form.

```
'If we make this far then submit the form
Call frmAdd.submit()
End Sub
</SCRIPT>
```

The last two lines of code contain standard HTML code to end our page.

At this point we are ready for testing. Start this page and click on the submit button. You should receive a message that the club name is a required field. Notice that the focus goes to the club name field. Enter some data in this field and click Submit again. Once again you receive a message but this time it is for the club code field, and after clicking on OK in the message, the focus is set to the club code field.

This is all of the testing we can do at this point. We have to build the next web page before we can see the data being inserted into the database.

## Try It Out – Process the Add Using the Insert Into Statement

This example will process the data that was posted from TryItOut-1.htm and insert it into the database. We will be building a dynamic INSERT statement that will only insert fields that contain data. Once the data has been inserted into the database, we will write a message to confirm that fact, and also display the SQL string that was used to insert the data. This way, you can see how the SQL string has been built in the code.

The page we are about to create will give a result similar to the following:

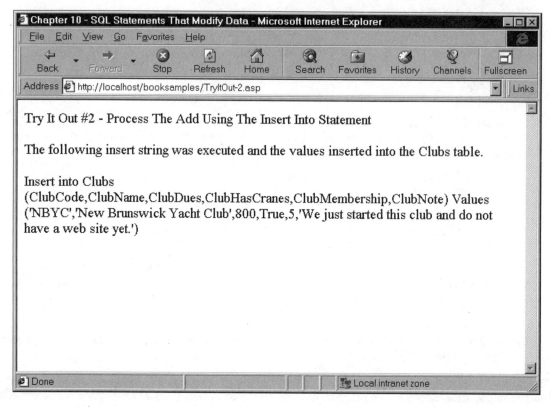

The code for `TryItOut-2.asp` appears below:

```
<HTML>
<HEAD>
<META NAME="GENERATOR" Content="Microsoft Visual Studio 6.0">
<TITLE>Chapter 10 - SQL Statements That Modify Data</TITLE>
</HEAD>
<BODY>
Try It Out #2 - Process The Add Using The Insert Into Statement<BR><BR>

<%
  'Declare variables needed
  Dim strInsert
  Dim strValues
  Dim adCmdText
  Dim blnCriticalError

  'Set required variables
  adCmdText = 1

'***************************************************************
'* If an Add was requested, add the new club to the database
'***************************************************************
  If Request.Form("Action") = "Add" Then
```

```
'Start building the SQL strings with the required fields
strInsert = "Insert into Clubs (ClubCode,ClubName"
strValues = "Values('" & CStr(Request.Form("txtClubCode")) & _
            "','" & CStr(Request.Form("txtClubName")) & "'"

'Add meeting date if present
If Len(Request.Form("txtMeetingDate")) > 0 Then
  'Add the column name to the insert string
  strInsert = strInsert & ",ClubAnnualMeeting"
  'Add the value to the value string
  strValues = strValues & ",'" & _
    Cstr(Request.Form("txtMeetingDate")) & "'"
End If

'Add club dues if present
If Len(Request.Form("txtClubDues")) > 0 Then
  'Add the column name to the insert string
  strInsert = strInsert & ",ClubDues"
  'Add the value to the value string
  strValues = strValues & "," & _
  CCur(Request.Form("txtClubDues"))
End If

'Add web site URL if present
If Len(Request.Form("txtWebSite")) > 0 Then
  'Add the column name to the insert string
  strInsert = strInsert & ",ClubWWWSite"
  'Add the value to the value string
  strValues = strValues & ",'" & _
  Cstr(Request.Form("txtWebSite")) & "'"
End If

'Add cranes if checked
If Request.Form("chkCrane") = 1 Then
  'Add the column name to the insert string
  strInsert = strInsert & ",ClubHasCranes"
  'Add True to the value string
  strValues = strValues & ",True"
End If

'Add club membership number if present
If Len(Request.Form("txtMembers")) > 0 Then
  'Add the column name to the insert string
  strInsert = strInsert & ",ClubMembership"
  'Add the value to the value string
  strValues = strValues & "," & _
    CLng(Request.Form("txtMembers"))
End If

'Add notes if present
If Len(Request.Form("txtNotes")) > 0 Then
  'Add the column name to the insert string
  strInsert = strInsert & ",ClubNote"
  'Add the value to the value string
  strValues = strValues & ",'" & _
  Cstr(Request.Form("txtNotes")) & "'"
End If

'Create and open the database object
Set objConn = Server.CreateObject("ADODB.Connection")
objConn.Open "DSN=Sailors"

'Create the command object
Set objCmd = Server.CreateObject("ADODB.Command")

'Set the command object properties
Set objCmd.ActiveConnection = objConn
objCmd.CommandText = strInsert & ") " & strValues & ")"
objCmd.CommandType = adCmdText
```

```
   'Execute the command
    objCmd.Execute

  'Display the insert string
  Response.Write "The following insert string was executed and " & _
                 "the values inserted into the Clubs table.<P>"
  Response.Write strInsert & " ) " & strValues & " ) "

  End If

  'Close and dereference database objects
  Set objCmd = Nothing
  objConn.Close
  Set objConn = Nothing
%>

</BODY>
</HTML>
```

### How It Works – Process the Add Using the Insert Into Statement

This looks like a lot of code but most of it is repetitive, dealing with the different fields from the request form. So let's begin to step through it line by line, but skip over the repeated bits.

After starting our web page, using standard HTML tags, and displaying our first line of text, we declare the variables that will be common to the entire page and set the required values:

```
<HTML>
<HEAD>
<META NAME="GENERATOR" Content="Microsoft Visual Studio 6.0">
<TITLE>Chapter 10 - SQL Statements That Modify Data</TITLE>
</HEAD>
<BODY>
Try It Out #2 - Process The Add Using The Insert Into Statement<BR><BR>
<%
  'Declare variables needed
  Dim strInsert
  Dim strValues
  Dim adCmdText
  Dim blnCriticalError

  'Set required variables
  adCmdText = 1
```

Keeping in mind that by the end of the chapter this page will also be used to update and delete the club data, we will set this page up to be able to process any given step, based on the Action field from the request form.

With that being said, we first check to see if the Action field from the request form contains the value of Add. If it does, we will start processing the insert section of code. (Since this is all we have coded at this point, this is the only section of code that will be added to this page for the time being.)

```
'*************************************************************
'* If an Add was requested, add the new club to the database
'*************************************************************
If Request.Form("Action") = "Add" Then
```

We begin by building two separate SQL strings. Once we have completed processing all of the fields from the request form, we will join them together to form the complete SQL statement to insert data.

The strInsert variable will contain the first part of our SQL statement. This consists of the INSERT INTO statement which will insert data into the table Clubs.

Remember the syntax for the INSERT INTO statement? Well, for each value that we want to insert, we must specify the column name that we want to insert it into. We do this in the strInsert variable, listing each column name in the Clubs table that we are inserting data into. Here we know that the club code and club name were required fields on the input form, so we go ahead and list these two columns in our strInsert variable.

The second variable, strValues, will contain the matching value to be inserted into the column. There must be a one for one match with the column names. We can go ahead and add the club code and club name from the request form.

Remember that all variables in ASP are variants. For this reason we specifically convert the fields from the request form to their appropriate data types. Here, since we are inserting two string values, we convert these two fields to string data types using the built-in CStr function. Also notice that all string values that are to be inserted must be enclosed by single quote marks.

```
'Start building the SQL strings with the required fields
strInsert = "Insert into Clubs (ClubCode,ClubName"

strValues = "Values('" & CStr(Request.Form("txtClubCode")) & _
 "','" & CStr(Request.Form("txtClubName")) & "'"
```

Now that we have our two partial SQL statements started, we just need to check each optional field from the request form to see if they contain any data, and append them to our two variables.

Here we are checking to see if the length of the value in the meeting date field is greater than zero, which would indicate that the field contains data. If it does, we append the column name of ClubAnnualMeeting to the strInsert variable, and append the txtMeetingDate field from the request form to the strValues variable.

We can convert date values to string data types to insert them into the database, as we are doing here. Alternatively, you can insert date values into the database if you enclose the date in pound signs (#). My personal preference is to treat the date as a string value, so we must also enclose the value in single quote marks.

```
'Add meeting date if present
If Len(Request.Form("txtMeetingDate")) > 0 Then
 'Add the column name to the insert string
 strInsert = strInsert & ",ClubAnnualMeeting"
 'Add the value to the value string
 strValues = strValues & ",'" & _
  Cstr(Request.Form("txtMeetingDate")) & "'"
End If
```

Here we are performing the same type of check as the last one. However, the ClubDues is a currency field in the database, and we must convert the field from the request form to currency using the CCur function. The currency data type is like a numeric data type and as such does not require single quote marks surrounding the value.

```
'Add club dues if present
If Len(Request.Form("txtClubDues")) > 0 Then
  'Add the column name to the insert string
  strInsert = strInsert & ",ClubDues"
  'Add the value to the value string
  strValues = strValues & "," & _
   CCur(Request.Form("txtClubDues"))
End If
```

We have another string value to check and insert if it is present. Even though the `ClubWWWSite` column in the database is a hyperlink data type, we can insert the value as a string data type:

```
'Add web site URL if present
If Len(Request.Form("txtWebSite")) > 0 Then
  'Add the column name to the insert string
  strInsert = strInsert & ",ClubWWWSite"
  'Add the value to the value string
  strValues = strValues & ",'" & _
   Cstr(Request.Form("txtWebSite")) & "'"
End If
```

The checkbox field presents a unique challenge to work with. Since the checkbox can be either checked or not checked, we have to determine a way to see if it is checked. Since we can only retrieve the *value* of the field from the request form, we set the value to 1 when we defined the checkbox. If the checkbox was checked, then the value will be 1. If it was not checked, the value will be nothing.

> *The default value for a checkbox when checked, if a value is not specified, is 'on'. Setting a value of 1 makes the field easier to process as a Boolean value if you choose to do so.*

If we have received a value of 1, we then set the value to be inserted as `True`, because the `ClubHasCranes` column in the database is a `Yes/No` data type which accepts only `Yes/No` and `True/False` values.

```
'Add cranes if checked
If Request.Form("chkCrane") = 1 Then
  'Add the column name to the insert string
  strInsert = strInsert & ",ClubHasCranes"
  'Add True to the value string
  strValues = strValues & ",True"
End If
```

The `txtMembers` field in the request form must be converted to a long data type, because the `ClubMembership` column in the database is a number data type. We do this using the `CLng` function, as it converts variant data types to long numeric data types.

```
'Add club membership number if present
If Len(Request.Form("txtMembers")) > 0 Then
  'Add the column name to the insert string
  strInsert = strInsert & ",ClubMembership"
  'Add the value to the value string
  strValues = strValues & "," & _
   CLng(Request.Form("txtMembers"))
End If
```

The `txtnotes` field in the request form is converted to a string data type when added to the database, as the `ClubNote` column is a memo data type, which is just a really long string.

```
'Add notes if present
If Len(Request.Form("txtNotes")) > 0 Then
 'Add the column name to the insert string
 strInsert = strInsert & ",ClubNote"
 'Add the value to the value string
 strValues = strValues & ",'" & _
   Cstr(Request.Form("txtNotes")) & "'"
End If
```

We have completed checking all of the fields from the request form and it is now time to move onto creating our database object. We create it and open our database connection using the `Sailors` DSN.

```
'Create and open the database object
Set objConn = Server.CreateObject("ADODB.Connection")
objConn.Open "DSN=Sailors"
```

Next, we create our `Command` object and set the `ActiveConnection` property to the `Connection` object. We set the `CommandText` property to our two SQL strings. Notice that we must terminate the first SQL string with a right parenthesis to terminate the column names, and do the same thing for the second SQL string to terminate the values. We specify that we are executing a SQL string by setting the `CommandType` property to `adCmdText`. A full explanation of the `Command` object will be given in Chapter 13. We then execute the `Command` object.

```
'Create the command object
Set objCmd = Server.CreateObject("ADODB.Command")

'Set the command object properties
Set objCmd.ActiveConnection = objConn
objCmd.CommandText = strInsert & ") " & strValues & ")"
objCmd.CommandType = adCmdText

'Execute the command
objCmd.Execute
```

If we make it this far in our code, the row was inserted into the database. We want to display a message indicating this fact. We will also display the actual SQL string that was used to insert the data. This is for demonstration purposes so that you can see what the completed SQL string is supposed to look like. After displaying our message and SQL string, we must terminate our step processing using the `End If` statement.

```
'Display the insert string
Response.Write "The following insert string was executed and " & _
  "the values inserted into the Clubs table.<P>"
Response.Write strInsert & ") " & strValues & ")"

End If ' End If for step processing
```

We must close and de–reference our database objects to release them from memory. To end our page we use the standard HTML tags that end a web page.

```
'Close and dereference database objects
Set objCmd = Nothing
objConn.Close
Set objConn = Nothing
%>

</BODY>
</HTML>
```

At this point, you should be able to enter values into the input form (`TryItOut-1.asp`), submit the form and have this web page confirm the insertion of those values into the database. You can open the `Sailors` database and look in the `Clubs` table to verify that the data was inserted.

# Updating A Record

When we refer to updating records, we are actually talking about updating the data in the various columns in a row. The UPDATE statement can update many rows at one time or just one row of data. It can be used to update single fields or multiple fields. We control which fields are updated by using the WHERE clause in the UPDATE statement. Let's take a look at the UPDATE statement format.

```
UPDATE tablename SET column1 = value1, column2 = value2, column3 = value3 WHERE
criteria
```

The `tablename` parameter specifies the table that contains the data we want to update.

The `column` parameters specify the columns which we want to update.

The `value` parameters specify the new data values that we want to update the columns with.

The `criteria` parameter specifies which rows are selected for update.

Notice that the UPDATE statement contains the SET keyword, which sets the contents of the named column equal to the value being passed. A comma separates each additional column/value pair.

The `criteria` parameter evaluates to a Boolean expression that the database uses to compare rows with. This could be as simple as:

```
WHERE ClubCode = 'SCOW'
```

or more complex, such as:

```
WHERE Dept = 'Sales' AND Age BETWEEN 18 AND 30
```

The WHERE clause will limit the number of rows that are updated, as only rows that meet the criteria will be updated. To control the update to a specific row of data, you must use a unique value in that row. This is usually a column that has been defined as a unique key. This key is not duplicated in any other row of data in that table. Note that if you omit the WHERE clause, all records will be updated. Refer back to Chapter 4 for details on the comparison operators which can be used with the WHERE clause.

## Try It Out – Update Club Form

Create a web page that will allow the user to update the existing information for a club. The first step in this process should allow the user to select the club that they want to update. The second step should display a form with the existing information for that club, and allow the user to make the appropriate updates. They can then submit the form and have the updates applied to the Clubs table in the Sailors database. The actual web page that will perform the updates will be built in the next example. The first page looks like this:

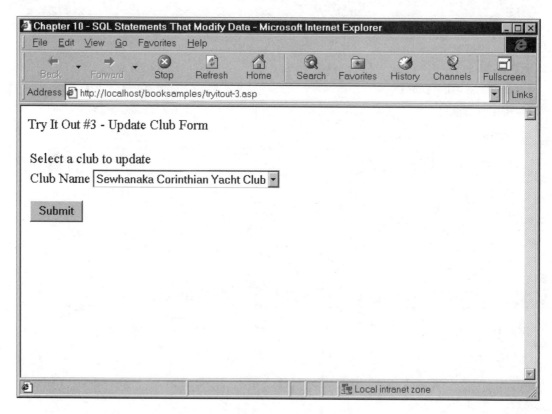

The user selects the name of the club that they want to update details for, and then clicks on the Submit button. This results in something similar to the following:

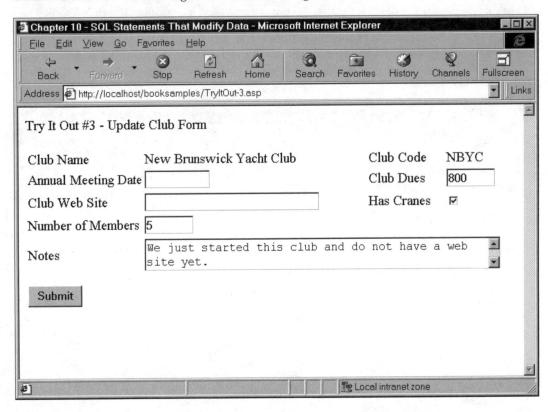

The code to produce these pages is contained in `TryItOut3.asp`, and is listed below.

```
<HTML>
<HEAD>
<META NAME="GENERATOR" Content="Microsoft Visual Studio 6.0">
<TITLE>Chapter 10 - SQL Statements That Modify Data</TITLE>
</HEAD>
<BODY>
Try It Out #3 - Update Club Form<BR><BR>

<%
'************************************************************
'* Step 1: Display a list of club names to select from
'************************************************************
  If Len(Request.Form("FormAction")) = 0 Then

  'Create the recordset object
  Set objRS = Server.CreateObject("ADODB.Recordset")

  'Open the recordset getting a list of all clubs
  objRS.Open "Select ClubCode, ClubName from Clubs","DSN=Sailors"
%>
<FORM ACTION=TryItOut-3.asp METHOD=post NAME=frmDisplay>
<INPUT TYPE=hidden NAME=FormAction VALUE=Step2>
<INPUT TYPE=hidden NAME=txtClubName>
<TABLE>
```

```
<TR>
<TD COLSPAN=2>Select a club to update</TD>
</TR>
<TR>
<TD>Club Name</TD>
<TD><SELECT NAME=cboClubs>
<%
  'Loop through the recordset adding each club to the combo box
  Do While Not objRS.EOF
%>
    <OPTION VALUE="<%=objRS("ClubCode")%>">
    <%=objRS("ClubName")%></OPTION>
<%
    objRS.MoveNext
  Loop

  'Close and dereference database objects
  objRS.Close
  Set objRS = Nothing
%>
</SELECT></TD>
<TR>
<TD HEIGHT=60><INPUT TYPE=submit NAME=btnSubmit VALUE=Submit></TD>
</TR>
</TABLE>
</FORM>

<SCRIPT LANGUAGE=vbscript>
Sub Window_OnLoad()
  'Save the club name currently displayed, just in case the
  'user wants to update this club
  frmDisplay.txtClubName.value = _
  frmDisplay.cboClubs(frmDisplay.cboClubs.selectedIndex).text
End Sub

Sub cboClubs_OnClick()
  'Save the club name the user selects by clicking on the combo box
  frmDisplay.txtClubName.value = _
  frmDisplay.cboClubs(frmDisplay.cboClubs.selectedIndex).text
End Sub

Sub cboClubs_OnChange()
  'Save the club name the user selects by scrolling the combo box
  'with the arrow keys
  frmDisplay.txtClubName.value = _
  frmDisplay.cboClubs(frmDisplay.cboClubs.selectedIndex).text
End Sub
</SCRIPT>

<%
'**************************************************************
'* Step 2: Display the form for editing a club
'**************************************************************
  ElseIf Request.Form("FormAction") = "Step2" Then

  'Create the recordset object
  Set objRS = Server.CreateObject("ADODB.Recordset")

  'Set the SQL string
  strSQL = "Select * from Clubs Where ClubCode = '" & _
  Request.Form("cboClubs") & "'"

  'Open the recordset getting the club details for this club
  objRS.Open strSQL,"DSN=Sailors"
%>
```

```
<FORM ACTION=TryItOut-4.asp METHOD=post NAME=frmUpdate>
<INPUT TYPE=hidden NAME=Action VALUE=Update>
<INPUT TYPE=hidden NAME=txtClubCode
VALUE=<%=Request.Form("cboClubs")%>>
<TABLE>
<TR>
<TD>Club Name</TD>
<TD><FONT COLOR=navy><%=Request.Form("txtClubName")%></font></TD>
<TD WIDTH=10></TD>
<TD>Club Code</TD>
<TD><FONT COLOR=navy><%=Request.Form("cboClubs")%></font></TD>
</TR>
<TR>
<TD NOWRAP>Annual Meeting Date</TD>
<TD><INPUT TYPE=text NAME=txtMeetingDate SIZE=10
VALUE=<%=objRS("ClubAnnualMeeting")%>></TD>
<TD WIDTH=10></TD>
<TD>Club Dues</TD>
<TD><INPUT TYPE=text NAME=txtClubDues SIZE=7
VALUE=<%=objRS("ClubDues")%>></TD>
</TR>
<TR>
<TD>Club Web Site</TD>
<TD><INPUT TYPE=text NAME=txtWebSite SIZE=30
<%
  strWebSite = objRS("ClubWWWSite")
  intPos = InStr(1,strWebSite,"#")
  If intPos > 0 Then
    strWebSite = Left(strWebSite,intPos-1)
  End If
  Response.Write "VALUE=" & strWebSite
%>></TD>
<TD WIDTH=10></TD>
<TD NOWRAP>Has Cranes</TD>
<TD><INPUT TYPE=checkbox NAME=chkCrane VALUE=1
<%
  If objRS("ClubHasCranes") Then Response.Write "Checked"%>></TD>
</TR>
<TR>
<TD>Number of Members</TD>
<TD><INPUT TYPE=text NAME=txtMembers SIZE=7
VALUE=<%=objRS("ClubMembership")%>></TD>
</TR>
<TR>
<TD>Notes</TD>
<TD COLSPAN=4>
<TEXTAREA ROWS=2 COLS=50 NAME=txtNotes><%=objRS("ClubNote")%>
</TEXTAREA></TD>
</TR>
<TR>
<TD HEIGHT=60><INPUT TYPE=submit NAME=btnSubmit VALUE=Submit></TD>
</TR>
</TABLE>
</FORM>

<%
  'Close and dereference database objects
  objRS.Close
  Set objRS = Nothing

End If 'End If for step processing
%>
```

```
</BODY>
</HTML>
```

### How It Works – Update Club Form

This web page contains two steps. The first step allows the user to select the name of the club for which they have new data, and the second step displays the existing data for that club so that the user can edit it.

We start our page by using the standard HTML tags that define our page and we display the first line of text.

```
<HTML>
<HEAD>
<META NAME="GENERATOR" Content="Microsoft Visual Studio 6.0">
<TITLE>Chapter 10 - SQL Statements That Modify Data</TITLE>
</HEAD>
<BODY>
Try It Out #3 - Update Club Form<BR><BR>
```

Since this is a multiple step web page, we are going to use a hidden field in the first form, called FormAction. The value in this field will indicate to us the next step of processing to take place.

The first time this page is run, the FormAction field will contain no data. We check to see if it has a length of zero, which indicates that this is indeed the first processing of this page. All of the server-side and client-side script, as well as the HTML, is processed in this step. No code in the second step is processed if this is the first time round.

```
<%
'*************************************************************
'* Step 1: Display a list of club names to select from
'*************************************************************
If Len(Request.Form("FormAction")) = 0 Then
```

We create a Recordset object and then open it to get a list of all club names and club codes from the Clubs table.

```
'Create the recordset object
Set objRS = Server.CreateObject("ADODB.Recordset")

'Open the recordset getting a list of all clubs
objRS.Open "Select ClubCode, ClubName from Clubs","DSN=Sailors"
%>
```

Now that we have our data in a recordset, we start building the form. Notice that the action the form will take is to post the data back to itself. This is how we are able to create a multiple step web page. Also notice the hidden field FormAction and that the VALUE specifies Step2. When the form is submitted, the FormAction field will contain a value of Step2 and we will know that we should process the second step of this web page. The second hidden field will be used to contain the club name that the user chooses. This field will be used in the next step for display purposes only.

```
<FORM ACTION=TryItOut-3.asp METHOD=post NAME=frmDisplay>
<INPUT TYPE=hidden NAME=FormAction VALUE=Step2>
<INPUT TYPE=hidden NAME=txtClubName>
```

As in the first example, we use a table to help us to keep our form fields aligned properly. The first row of our table specifies the instructions for the user. Notice that we are telling this column that it should span across two columns, by specifying the COLSPAN property in the TD tag.

The second row displays some data and a combo box. This combo box will contain a list of all club names for the user to select from. It has two parts, the SELECT element, which identifies this field as a combo box, and an OPTION element, which we will go into next. Both of these elements has a beginning and ending tag.

```
<TABLE>
<TR>
<TD COLSPAN=2>Select a club to update</TD>
</TR>
<TR>
<TD>Club Name</TD>
<TD><SELECT NAME=cboClubs>
```

Using our recordset data we populate the combo box by adding the OPTION elements to it. The OPTION element has two parts that we are going to use. The first is the VALUE, which is a number or text that the user does not see, but which will allow us to tell which option was selected. The second part is the actual text which appears in the combo box.

So, we loop through our recordset, adding an OPTION element, setting its VALUE and the display text. Notice that we are using the club code as the VALUE and the display text consists of the club name. When we are through, we close and de–reference our database objects, and end our combo box.

```
<%
  'Loop through the recordset adding each club to the combo box
  Do While Not objRS.EOF
%>
    <OPTION VALUE="<%=objRS("ClubCode")%>">
    <%=objRS("ClubName")%></OPTION>
<%
    objRS.MoveNext

  Loop

  'Close and dereference database objects
  objRS.Close
  Set objRS = Nothing
%>
</SELECT></TD>
</TR>
```

The last row in our table contains the Submit button. Since we have no validations to make, we can use a submit type instead of a normal type of button. Notice that we are once again using the HEIGHT property of the TD tag to separate the button from the rest of the form fields. This just helps to make a more pleasing visual interface for the user.

We end our form and our table, and then we're ready to write some client–side script.

```
<TR>
<TD HEIGHT=60><INPUT TYPE=submit NAME=btnSubmit VALUE=Submit></TD>
</TR>
</TABLE>
</FORM>
```

Later, we are going to be using the club code in our WHERE clause in the SELECT statement, to retrieve the data for the club name that the user chose. This club code will be accessible in the next step, as it is saved as the value of cboClubs when the user chooses a club from the combo box. However, we will not be able to retrieve the club name. This is where the client–side script comes in.

We will save the club name that the user selects, in the hidden field, `txtClubName`, that was defined at the beginning of our form. At this point the user has not clicked or scrolled the combo box and could simply click on the Submit button. If this were the case no club name would have been set. So, in the `Window_OnLoad` event, we set the club name in our hidden field to the first option that is displayed in our combo box, just in case.

We do this using the `text` property for the current `selected Index` of the combo box, to retrieve the club name and save it in the `txtClubName` hidden field:

```
<SCRIPT LANGUAGE=vbscript>
Sub Window_OnLoad()
   'Save the club name currently displayed, just in case the
   'user wants to update this club
   frmDisplay.txtClubName.value = _
   frmDisplay.cboClubs(frmDisplay.cboClubs.selectedIndex).text
End Sub
```

If the user clicks on an option in the combo box we will trap that event here using the `OnClick` event for the `cboClubs` field. Once again we set our hidden field to the text that is currently displayed in the combo box.

```
Sub cboClubs_OnClick()
   'Save the club name the user selects by clicking on the combo box
   frmDisplay.txtClubName.value = _
   frmDisplay.cboClubs(frmDisplay.cboClubs.selectedIndex).text
End Sub
```

If the user does not click the combo box to select an option but chooses to scroll through the list using the arrow keys, the `OnChange` event will fire and we can save the selection they have made using this code. The last line in this code fragment ends our client–side script:

```
Sub cboClubs_OnChange()
   'Save the club name the user selects by scrolling the combo box
   'with the arrow keys
   frmDisplay.txtClubName.value = _
   frmDisplay.cboClubs(frmDisplay.cboClubs.selectedIndex).text
End Sub
</SCRIPT>
```

Now we can begin the second step of our web page. The second time our web page is run the `FormAction` field will contain a value of `Step2` and we start our processing here.

```
<%
'************************************************************
'* Step 2: Display the form for editing a club
'************************************************************
ElseIf Request.Form("FormAction") = "Step2" Then
```

The first thing we want to do is create our `Recordset` object, set our SQL string to select the club data that the user wants to edit, and open our recordset.

Notice that we are getting the club code from the request form field `cboClubs`. The only information that is passed for the combo box is the VALUE of the item selected. The text data of the item that was selected is not available in the request form at this point – that is why we saved it in a hidden field, `txtClubName`.

```
'Create the recordset object
Set objRS = Server.CreateObject("ADODB.Recordset")

'Set the SQL string
strSQL = "Select * from Clubs Where ClubCode = '" & _
Request.Form("cboClubs") & "'"

'Open the recordset getting the club details for this club
objRS.Open strSQL,"DSN=Sailors"
%>
```

We start the form for the second part of our web page, and this time we specify an action of TryItOut-4.asp, which is the page we will be building next. Notice that there are two hidden fields in this form also. The first hidden field is to specify what action the TryItOut-4.asp page should process, and the second field contains the club code that will be needed to update the data. The value for the club code is being set using the value from the request form.

Again we use a table in our form to help us keep all fields aligned properly.

```
<FORM ACTION=TryItOut-4.asp METHOD=post NAME=frmUpdate>
<INPUT TYPE=hidden NAME=Action VALUE=Update>
<INPUT TYPE=hidden NAME=txtClubCode VALUE=<%=Request.Form("cboClubs")%>>
<TABLE>
```

We don't want the user to edit the club name or club code, so we display these fields as simple text, instead of placing them in a text box. We do change the font color of these fields to make them stand out somewhat.

Since we select every field in the Clubs table for the club code that was retrieved from the request form, we could use the recordset field for the club name instead of passing it from the request form. The reason we chose to do it this way was to demonstrate retrieving the selected text of the combo box for the option that the user chose. You will come across a situation one day where you will need to pass both the selected text and the value of the option that the user chose. It's just one of those things that's nice to know and remember for when you do need it.

```
<TR>
<TD>Club Name</TD>
<TD><FONT COLOR=navy><%=Request.Form("txtClubName")%></FONT></TD>
<TD WIDTH=10></TD>
<TD>Club Code</TD>
<TD><FONT COLOR=navy><%=Request.Form("cboClubs")%></FONT></TD>
</TR>
```

We start our next row in the table by building the text boxes that the user will enter and change data in. This is the same layout that was used on the form to add a new club. The only difference here is that we are setting the values using the data from the recordset. This way the user can see what data already exists before changing it.

```
<TR>
<TD NOWRAP>Annual Meeting Date</TD>
<TD><INPUT TYPE=text NAME=txtMeetingDate SIZE=10
VALUE=<%=objRS("ClubAnnualMeeting")%>></TD>
<TD WIDTH=10></TD>
<TD>Club Dues</TD>
<TD><INPUT TYPE=text NAME=txtClubDues SIZE=7 VALUE=<%=objRS("ClubDues")%>></TD>
</TR>
```

This next row of data deserves a little explanation. When you insert a web site URL in the database you insert it as `www.something.com`. If you were to open Access and take a look at it in the `Clubs` table, you would see that the database displays this URL in the same format that you entered it. However, when we retrieve this value in a field in our recordset it comes back as `WWW.Something.Com#http://WWW.Something.COM#`. This does not make a very pleasing display and could cause confusion to the user. Therefore we need to strip off the URL part and only display the show text of this address.

This is what this next bit of code does. First we set the hyperlink to a string variable, and then find the position of the first pound sign in the field, using the `InStr` function. (The `InStr` function finds a certain character or characters in a string and returns a value of the position of where it was found.) If the `intPos` variable is greater than zero then we have found the pound sign. We can set our string variable to include just the left portion of the string, using the `Left` function. Then, using the `Write` method of the `Response` object, we set the `VALUE` for this field to our string variable.

```
<TR>
<TD>Club Web Site</TD>
<TD><INPUT TYPE=text NAME=txtWebSite SIZE=30
<%
  strWebSite = objRS("ClubWWWSite")
  intPos = InStr(1,strWebSite,"#")
  If intPos > 0 Then
    strWebSite = Left(strWebSite,intPos-1)
  End If
  Response.Write "VALUE=" & strWebSite
%>></TD>
<TD WIDTH=10></TD>
```

Next we need to know whether to check the 'Has Cranes' checkbox. If the value from the database is set to `True`, we use the `Write` method of the `Response` object to make the checkbox checked, by writing the `checked` property:

```
<TD NOWRAP>Has Cranes</TD>
<TD><INPUT TYPE=checkbox NAME=chkCrane VALUE=1
<%
  If objRS("ClubHasCranes") Then Response.Write "Checked"
%>></TD>
</TR>
```

The last two fields in our form get set using data from the recordset:

```
<TR>
<TD>Number of Members</TD>
<TD><INPUT TYPE=text NAME=txtMembers SIZE=7 VALUE=<%=objRS("ClubMembership")%>></TD>
</TR>
<TR>
<TD>Notes</TD>
<TD COLSPAN=4>
<TEXTAREA ROWS=2 COLS=50 NAME=txtNotes><%=objRS("ClubNote")%>
</TEXTAREA></TD>
</TR>
```

Since we are not going to do any data validations, we will be using a `submit` button instead of a `normal` button to submit the values on this form. If you want to come back later and add data validation you should use a `normal` button, because you cannot cancel the `submit` button once it is clicked. Using a `normal` button allows you to perform any validations, and then call the `submit` method of the form, once all validations have been passed.

```
<TR>
<TD HEIGHT=60><INPUT TYPE=submit NAME=btnSubmit VALUE=Submit></TD>
</TR>
</TABLE>
</FORM>
```

To wrap up our web page we close and de-reference our database objects and end our page using standard HTML tags. Don't forget that we need our End If statement to terminate our step processing.

```
<%
  'Close and dereference database objects
  objRS.Close
  Set objRS = Nothing

End If
%>

</BODY>
</HTML>
```

You should now be able to run this page, select a club name to update and have the existing fields displayed in the update form. You won't be able to submit the data to be updated until we build the next page.

## Try It Out – Process the Update Using the Update Statement

Create a web page that will read the fields from the request form and then build an UPDATE statement, that will only update the fields that contain data.

Remember when we built the TryItOut-2.asp web page, our intention was to build one page that would handle all of our database maintenance for the Clubs table. In keeping with that thought, this page just expands on the existing one. The TryItOut-2.asp page inserted a new row of data into the Clubs table and this page will update existing data in that table.

The page will appear as shown:

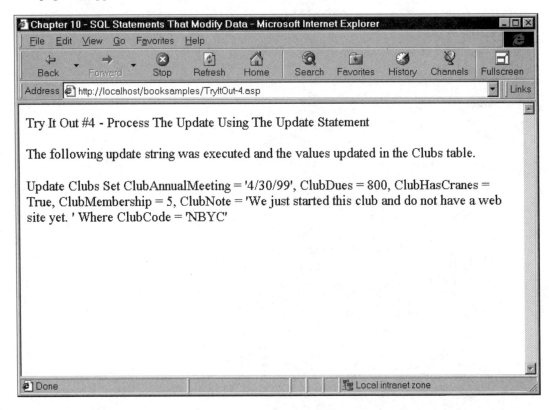

To start this page you need to make a copy of the `TryItOut-2.asp` page and name it `TryItOut-4.asp`. Modify it to give a file as follows.

```
<HTML>
<HEAD>
<META NAME="GENERATOR" Content="Microsoft Visual Studio 6.0">
<TITLE>Chapter 10 - SQL Statements That Modify Data</TITLE>
</HEAD>
<BODY>
Try It Out #4 - Process The Update Using The Update Statement<BR><BR>
<%

  'Declare variables needed
  Dim strInsert
  Dim strValues
  Dim strSQL
  Dim adCmdText
  Dim blnCriticalError
  Dim blnFirstParameter

'*********************************************************************************
'INSERT IN HERE THE CODE FROM TryItOut-02.asp, from and including the section
'"Set required variables" through to the end of the code to "Display the insert
string"
'*********************************************************************************
```

```
'****************************************************************
'* If an Update was requested, update the club in the database
'****************************************************************
  ElseIf Request.Form("Action") = "Update" Then

    'Start building the SQL string
    strSQL = "Update Clubs Set"

    'Set the first parameter flag to true
    blnFirstParameter = True

    'Update meeting date if present
    If Len(Request.Form("txtMeetingDate")) > 0 Then
      'Add the value to the SQL string
      strSQL = strSQL & " ClubAnnualMeeting = '" & _
      Cstr(Request.Form("txtMeetingDate")) & "'"
      'Set the first parameter flag to false
      blnFirstParameter = False
    End If

    'Update club dues if present
    If Len(Request.Form("txtClubDues")) > 0 Then
      'Add the value to the SQL string
      If blnFirstParameter Then
        strSQL = strSQL & " ClubDues = "
      Else
        strSQL = strSQL & ", ClubDues = "
      End If
      strSQL = strSQL & CCur(Request.Form("txtClubDues"))
      'Set the first parameter flag to false
      blnFirstParameter = False
    End If

    'Update web site URL if present
    If Len(Request.Form("txtWebSite")) > 0 Then
      'Add the value to the SQL string
      If blnFirstParameter Then
        strSQL = strSQL & " ClubWWWSite = '"
      Else
        strSQL = strSQL & ", ClubWWWSite = '"
      End If
      strSQL = strSQL & Cstr(Request.Form("txtWebSite")) & "'"
      'Set the first parameter flag to false
      blnFirstParameter = False
    End If

    'Update cranes if checked
    If Request.Form("chkCrane") = 1 Then
      'Add True to the SQL string
      If blnFirstParameter Then
        strSQL = strSQL & " ClubHasCranes = True"
      Else
        strSQL = strSQL & ", ClubHasCranes = True"
      End If
      'Set the first parameter flag to false
      blnFirstParameter = False
    End If

    'Update club membership number if present
    If Len(Request.Form("txtMembers")) > 0 Then
      'Add the value to the SQL string
      If blnFirstParameter Then
        strSQL = strSQL & " ClubMembership = "
      Else
        strSQL = strSQL & ", ClubMembership = "
      End If
```

```
        strSQL = strSQL & CLng(Request.Form("txtMembers"))
        'Set the first parameter flag to false
        blnFirstParameter = False
   End If

   'Update notes if present
   If Len(Request.Form("txtNotes")) > 0 Then
     'Add the value to the SQL string
     If blnFirstParameter Then
       strSQL = strSQL & " ClubNote = '"
     Else
       strSQL = strSQL & ", ClubNote = '"
     End If
     strSQL = strSQL & Cstr(Request.Form("txtNotes")) & "'"
     'Set the first parameter flag to false
     blnFirstParameter = False
   End If

   'Set the Where clause
   strSQL = strSQL & " Where ClubCode = '" & _
   Request.Form("txtClubCode") & "'"

   'Create and open the database object
   Set objConn = Server.CreateObject("ADODB.Connection")
   objConn.Open "DSN=Sailors"

   'Create the command object
   Set objCmd = Server.CreateObject("ADODB.Command")

   'Set the command object properties
   Set objCmd.ActiveConnection = objConn
   objCmd.CommandText = strSQL
   objCmd.CommandType = adCmdText

   'Execute the command
   objCmd.Execute

   'Display the update string
   Response.Write "The following update string was executed and " & _
           "the values updated in the Clubs table.<P>"
   Response.Write strSQL

 End If 'End If for step processing

 'Close and dereference database objects
 Set objCmd = Nothing
 objConn.Close
 Set objConn = Nothing
%>

</BODY>
</HTML>
```

### How It Works – Process the Update Using the Update Statement

Since the first part of this code has already been covered, we will only cover the areas that have changed, before going into the details of the second part of this web page.

If you copied the TryItOut-2.asp page and renamed it, you will need to change the text that is displayed from:

```
Try It Out #2 - Process The Add Using The Insert Into Statement<BR><BR>
```

to:

```
Try It Out #4 - Process The Update Using The Update Statement<BR><BR>
```

We have added a couple of extra variables that are needed for the second part of our web page. They are strSQL and blnFirstParameter.

```
<%
'Declare variables needed
Dim strInsert
Dim strValues
Dim strSQL
Dim adCmdText
Dim blnCriticalError
Dim blnFirstParameter

'Set required variables
adCmdText = 1
```

We will skip over the first section of code because it comes from the TryItOut-2.asp page.

We want to insert our new code after the messages from the end of the Add code. We start with an ElseIf statement to check if we should execute the second part of our code. If the Action field from the request form is equal to Update, then we will start executing code at this point in the page.

```
'Display the insert string
Response.Write "The following insert string was executed and " & _
  "the values inserted into the Clubs table.<P>"
Response.Write strInsert & ") " & strValues & ")"
'****************************************************************
'* If an Update was requested, update the club in the database
'****************************************************************
ElseIf Request.Form("Action") = "Update" Then
```

This time we will be building one SQL string and will only update the columns in the table for fields that contain data. We do this because we don't know which fields were changed on the form. We start by setting up our UPDATE statement, specifying that we want to update the Clubs table.

*If you only want to update fields that have changed, you could set a hidden field next to each of the regular fields in the update form. When the user changes the data in a field you could set a value in the hidden field. You would trap the changes to a field in the **OnChange** event for each of the normal fields. You could then check the value of the hidden fields to know which fields were changed.*

Because we don't know which field in the request form will contain data, we use a Boolean variable, set to True, to control the first column added. This ensures that this column does not contain a comma in front of it, but that the rest of the columns added do.

```
'Start building the SQL string
strSQL = "Update Clubs Set"

'Set the first parameter flag to true
blnFirstParameter = True
```

If the first field from the request form contains data, and we determine this by checking the length of the field, we append it to the SQL string. Since this is a string parameter we must convert it to a string using the `CStr` function and also enclose it in single quote marks. We then set our Boolean variable to `False`.

Notice that we are appending the parameter to the SQL string as `columnname = stringvalue`.

```
'Update meeting date if present
If Len(Request.Form("txtMeetingDate")) > 0 Then
 'Add the value to the SQL string
 strSQL = strSQL & " ClubAnnualMeeting = '" & _
  Cstr(Request.Form("txtMeetingDate")) & "'"
 'Set the first parameter flag to false
 blnFirstParameter = False
End If
```

If `club` does contain data in the request form, we append it to the SQL string, again checking to see if this is the first parameter added. We convert this field to a currency value using the `CCur` function and then set the Boolean variable to `False`.

```
'Update club dues if present
If Len(Request.Form("txtClubDues")) > 0 Then
 'Add the value to the SQL string
 If blnFirstParameter Then
  strSQL = strSQL & " ClubDues = "
 Else
  strSQL = strSQL & ", ClubDues = "
 End If
 strSQL = strSQL & CCur(Request.Form("txtClubDues"))
 'Set the first parameter flag to false
 blnFirstParameter = False
End If
```

We continue on with the rest of the fields, appending them to the SQL string if they are present. We use the same conversion functions as we did in `TryItOut-2.asp`, when we added these fields to the database.

After we have checked all of our fields from the request form, and appended the ones that contain data to the SQL string, it's time to add the `WHERE` clause. We are using the club code from the request form to control the updating of our data. We only want to update the row of data in the `Clubs` table that contains the club code we are specifying. We are getting the club code from our hidden field in the request form:

```
'Set the Where clause
strSQL = strSQL & " Where ClubCode = '" & _
 Request.Form("txtClubCode") & "'"
```

Next we open our `Connection` object:

```
'Create and open the database object
Set objConn = Server.CreateObject("ADODB.Connection")
objConn.Open "DSN=Sailors"
```

We create the `Command` object and set its parameters using our SQL string and our `Connection` object.

```
'Create the command object
Set objCmd = Server.CreateObject("ADODB.Command")

'Set the command object properties
Set objCmd.ActiveConnection = objConn
objCmd.CommandText = strSQL
objCmd.CommandType = adCmdText
```

We execute the `Command` object to update the row in the `Clubs` table that contains our club code:

```
'Execute the command
objCmd.Execute
```

If we make it this far, we have successfully updated the row of data in the `Clubs` table that contains our club code. We want to display a message, confirming this fact, for the user. For demonstration purposes we will also display the actual SQL string that was executed, so you can see the completed string that you have built.

```
'Display the update string
Response.Write "The following update string was executed and " & _
  "the values updated in the Clubs table.<P>"
Response.Write strSQL
```

The rest of this code is from the `TryItOut-2.asp` page and needs no further explanation.

```
End If 'End If for step processing

'Close and dereference database objects
Set objCmd = Nothing
objConn.Close
Set objConn = Nothing
%>

</BODY>
</HTML>
```

We are now ready to select a club name in the `TryItOut-3.asp` page, change some values on the update form, submit the changes, and have them updated in the database by this last page.

# Deleting A Record

At some point in time the data in our database will have outlived its usefulness and must be deleted. In the case of the `Clubs` table, a club could dissolve and we would want to clean up our tables by deleting any reference to that club. This would ensure that any queries against this table would not result in the presentation of outdated information.

We can delete data from the database in one of several ways. We can delete a single row of data, or multiple rows in one table, or we can delete multiple rows in multiple tables. We will be concentrating our efforts here on deleting one row of data in one table. So let's take a look at the format of the `DELETE` statement before continuing on:

```
DELETE column* FROM tablename WHERE criteria
```

The `column*` parameter specifies individual columns to be deleted or using a star character indicates that all columns should be deleted.

The `tablename` parameter specifies the table that contains the data we want to delete.

The `criteria` parameter specifies what rows should be selected for deleting.

Again, the `criteria` parameter evaluates to a Boolean expression that the database uses to compare rows to. Any rows that meet the criteria will be deleted. Be aware that omitting the `WHERE` clause will result in all columns being deleted.

> **Be careful when deleting data and ensure you have a backup beforehand. Once you issue the DELETE statement, the delete is irreversible.**

## Try It Out – Delete Club Form

Before we can delete a club from the `Clubs` table, we need to know which one the user wants to delete. Given this, we need to create another web page that gives the user a list of club names from the `Clubs` table and allows them to choose one. After they click on the submit button, we want to prompt the user with a message box verifying their decision.

Once we execute the `DELETE` statement, there is no turning back. The delete will be performed and it is irreversible. This is why it is important to confirm the user's choice of club name before executing the `DELETE` statement.

The values from this page will be posted to our next example's web page. The selection form is shown below:

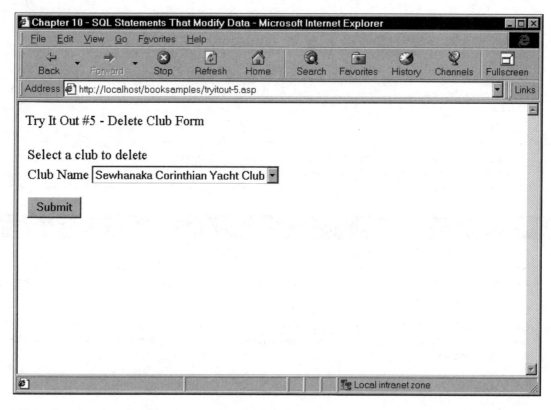

The code to produce this form, `TryItOut-5.asp`, is shown below:

```
<HTML>
<HEAD>
<META NAME="GENERATOR" Content="Microsoft Visual Studio 6.0">
<TITLE>Chapter 10 - SQL Statements That Modify Data</TITLE>
</HEAD>
<BODY>
Try It Out #5 - Delete Club Form<BR><BR>

<%
  'Create the recordset object
  Set objRS = Server.CreateObject("ADODB.Recordset")

  'Open the recordset getting a list of all clubs
  objRS.Open "Select ClubCode, ClubName from Clubs","DSN=Sailors"
%>

<FORM ACTION=TryItOut-6.asp METHOD=post NAME=frmDisplay>
<INPUT TYPE=hidden NAME=Action VALUE=Delete>
<TABLE>
<TR>
<TD COLSPAN=2>Select a club to delete</TD>
</TR>
<TR>
```

```
<TD>Club Name</TD>
<TD><SELECT NAME=cboClubs>
<%
   'Loop through the recordset populating the combo box
   Do While Not objRS.EOF
%>
     <option VALUE="<%=objRS("ClubCode")%>">
     <%=objRS("ClubName")%></option>
<%
     objRS.MoveNext

   Loop

   'Close and dereference database objects
   objRS.Close
   Set objRS = Nothing
%>
</SELECT></TD>
</TR>
<TR>
<TD HEIGHT=60><INPUT TYPE=button NAME=btnSubmit VALUE=Submit></TD>
</TR>
</TABLE>
</FORM>

<SCRIPT LANGUAGE=vbscript>
Sub btnSubmit_OnClick()
   'Prompt the user to ensure they want to delete the club
   lngRC = MsgBox("Deleting a Club is irreversible." & vbCRLF & _
   "Are you sure you want to delete " & _
   frmDisplay.cboClubs(frmDisplay.cboClubs.selectedIndex).text & _
   "?",vbOKCANCEL,"Try It Out #5 - Delete Club Form")

   'If the user chose OK then proceed
   If lngRC = vbOK Then
     Call frmDisplay.submit()
   End If
End Sub
</SCRIPT>

</BODY>
</HTML>
```

### How It Works – Delete Club Form

This page is very similar to the form page in Try It Out – Update Club Form, so our explanation can be brief. As before, we start our web page by using standard HTML tags to define our page and display our first line of text. Next, we move on to creating our Recordset object and getting a list of club codes and club names from the Clubs table.

When we start building our form, we specify that it should post the form fields to the TryItOut-6.asp web page that we will be building next. We insert a hidden field called Action and give it a value of DELETE, and then we insert a table into our form.

```
<FORM ACTION=TryItOut-6.asp METHOD=post NAME=frmDisplay>
 <INPUT TYPE=hidden NAME=Action VALUE=Delete>
 <TABLE>
```

The first row of our table contains instructions for the user on what to do. The second row starts to build our combo box that will contain a list of all club names from our recordset.

```
<TR>
<TD COLSPAN=2>Select a club to delete</TD>
</TR>
<TR>
<TD>Club Name</TD>
<TD><SELECT NAME=cboClubs>
```

As we demonstrated in the TryItOut-3.asp page, we loop through our recordset building the options for the combo box. We set each option value to the club code, and set the display text for each option to the club name. After we come to an end of file condition on our recordset, we close and de–reference our database objects.

The last row in our table contains the submit button. The TYPE property for this button is set to button because we want to control when the form gets submitted. If we had set the TYPE property to submit, we would have no way of canceling the submit process. We name our button btnSubmit.

We end our table and our form and are ready to move on to the client–side code.

```
<TR>
<TD HEIGHT=60><INPUT TYPE=button NAME=btnSubmit VALUE=Submit></TD>
</TR>
</TABLE>
</FORM>
```

When the user clicks on the button, we want to prompt them with a message box confirming their choice. We do this using the OnClick event in the button that we defined above.

We are using the standard MsgBox function that is built into the VBScript language. The MsgBox function accepts these parameters:

| Parameter | Description |
| --- | --- |
| Prompt | The message that is being displayed |
| Buttons | The buttons that should be displayed on the message box |
| Title | The title of the message box that should be displayed in the title bar |
| Helpfile | The help file containing the help topic specified in the context parameter |
| Context | The help topic context id |

We start by building the message that will be displayed to the user. Here we code the first line of the message and then append the vbCRLF character code to the string. This will provide a carriage return/line feed combination and force the second part of our message to the second line, providing a more visually pleasing appearance. Notice that we are expecting a return value from the message box, so we have specified the lngRC variable to accept the return value.

```
<SCRIPT LANGUAGE=vbscript>
Sub btnSubmit_OnClick()
 'Prompt the user to ensure they want to delete the club
 lngRC = MsgBox("Deleting a Club is irreversible." & vbCRLF & _
```

The second line of our message is built using a combination of text and the club name that has been selected by the user from the combo box.

```
"Are you sure you want to delete " & _
frmDisplay.cboClubs(frmDisplay.cboClubs.selectedIndex).text & _
```

We want to give the user a choice of continuing with or canceling the delete action, so we specify a combination of the OK and Cancel buttons. Next we include the title to be displayed in the title bar of the message box. We will not be using a help file or help topic so we omit these parameters.

```
"?",vbOKCANCEL,"Try It Out #5 - Delete Club Form")
```

Once the user clicks on the submit button they will see a message similar to the one shown below.

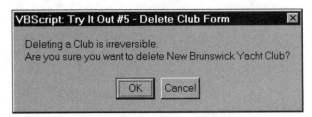

After the user has made their selection by clicking one of the two buttons, the next part of our code gets executed. If the user chooses the OK button, we call the submit method of the form and the form is submitted. If the user chooses Cancel, we simply carry on through the code and do nothing, giving them a chance to change their selection and try again. The last part of this code ends our web page using standard HTML tags.

```
    'If the user chose OK then proceed
    If lngRC = vbOK Then
        Call frmDisplay.submit()
    End If
  End Sub
</SCRIPT>

</BODY>
</HTML>
```

You can test your code at this point, but will not be able to perform a delete until we build the next example.

## Try It Out – Process the Delete Using the Delete Statement

This is the last part of code that will be added to our web page to handle all of our database maintenance for the Clubs table. After this code has been added will have a web page that will handle inserting, updating and deleting data in the Clubs table.

Using the TryItOut-4.asp page as a starting point, copy that page and name it TryItOut-6.asp. Add the code to delete a row of data from the Clubs table, based on the club code retrieved from the request form.

The result of running this page should be as follows:

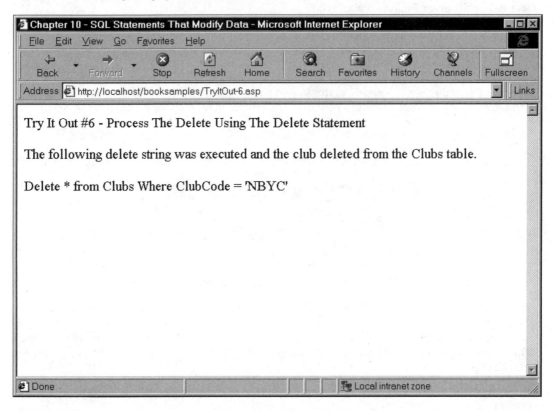

The code for `TryItOut-6.asp` is written below.

```
<HTML>
<HEAD>
<META NAME="GENERATOR" Content="Microsoft Visual Studio 6.0">
<TITLE>Chapter 10 - SQL Statements That Modify Data</TITLE>
</HEAD>
<BODY>
Try It Out #6 - Process The Delete Using The Delete Statement<BR><BR>

<%
  'Declare variables needed
  Dim strInsert
  Dim strValues
  Dim strSQL
  Dim adCmdText
  Dim blnCriticalError
  Dim blnFirstParameter


'****************************************************************************
''INSERT IN HERE THE CODE FROM TryItOut-02.asp, from and including the section
'"Set required variables" through to the end of the code to "Display the insert
string"
'****************************************************************************
*
```

```
'******************************************************************************
'* INSERT IN HERE THE CODE FROM TryItOut - 04.asp from and including the comment
'" If an Update was requested, update the club in the database" through to the end of
' the code to "Display the Update String"
'******************************************************************************


'****************************************************************
'* If a Delete was requested, delete the club from the database
'****************************************************************
  ElseIf Request.Form("Action") = "Delete" Then

    'Build the SQL string
    strSQL = "Delete * from Clubs Where ClubCode = '" & _
    Request.Form("cboClubs") & "'"

    'Create and open the database object
    Set objConn = Server.CreateObject("ADODB.Connection")
    objConn.Open "DSN=Sailors"

    'Create the command object
    Set objCmd = Server.CreateObject("ADODB.Command")

    'Set the command object properties
    Set objCmd.ActiveConnection = objConn
    objCmd.CommandText = strSQL
    objCmd.CommandType = adCmdText

    'Execute the command
    objCmd.Execute

    'Display the delete string
    Response.Write "The following delete string was executed and " & _
                "the club deleted from the Clubs table.<P>"
    Response.Write strSQL

  End If 'End If for step processing

  'Close and dereference database objects
  Set objCmd = Nothing
  objConn.Close
  Set objConn = Nothing
%>

</BODY>
</HTML>
```

### How It Works – Process The Delete Using The Delete Statement

The first part of this page has already been covered so we will forego any further explanation of it, other than to say the first section of code *inserted* a new row into the Clubs table and the second *updated* a row in the Clubs table.

You should change the first line of text that is displayed, to read:

```
Try It Out #6 - Process The Delete Using The Delete Statement<BR><BR>
```

The code we are now going to add will delete a row of data from the Clubs table, and we want to insert our delete code following the message from the update section as shown here. If the Action field passed from the form page has a value of Delete then we will execute this section of code in our page.

```
  'Display the update string
  Response.Write "The following update string was executed and " & _
    "the values updated in the Clubs table.<P>"
  Response.Write strSQL
```

```
'****************************************************************
'* If a Delete was requested, delete the club from the database
'****************************************************************
ElseIf Request.Form("Action") = "Delete" Then
```

Since we want to delete all columns in the row that matches the club code passed, our DELETE statement is straightforward.

We state that all columns should be deleted by using the star character (*), and specify the table from which the row should be deleted. The WHERE clause defines the condition of the delete, and we are setting it to delete the row of data that has a match between the ClubCode column and the club code value that was retrieved from the request form.

```
'Build the SQL string
strSQL = "Delete * from Clubs Where ClubCode = '" & _
  Request.Form("cboClubs") & "'"
```

In the same way as for our previous examples, we create and open our Connection object, and our Command object. We set the properties of the latter, using the Connection object and our SQL string that was just built. We then execute the Command object.

```
'Create and open the database object
Set objConn = Server.CreateObject("ADODB.Connection")
objConn.Open "DSN=Sailors"

'Create the command object
Set objCmd = Server.CreateObject("ADODB.Command")

'Set the command object properties
Set objCmd.ActiveConnection = objConn
objCmd.CommandText = strSQL
objCmd.CommandType = adCmdText

'Execute the command
objCmd.Execute
```

If we make it this far in the code all has gone well. We want to display a message to the user that the delete process has been successful. As before, we will also display the DELETE SQL string for demonstration purposes.

```
'Display the delete string
Response.Write "The following delete string was executed and " & _
  "the club deleted from the Clubs table.<P>"
Response.Write strSQL
```

The rest of the code is the same as before. (It provides the End If statement for our step processing. After that, we close and de–reference our database objects, and then end our web page using standard HTML tags.)

In order to use this all–inclusive web page, that performs all of our database maintenance for the Clubs table, you will need to make a modification to the TryItOut-1.htm and TryItOut-3.asp pages, as described below.

Change the ACTION property in this line of the TryItOut-1.htm page, to post the values to the TryItOut-6.asp page.

```
<FORM ACTION=TryItOut-2.asp METHOD=post NAME=frmAdd>
```

Change the ACTION property in this line of the TryItOut-3.asp page, to post the values to the TryItOut-6.asp page. Note that this is the second form listed in this page. The first form must post the values back to itself.

```
<FORM ACTION=TryItOut-4.asp METHOD=post NAME=frmUpdate>
```

After these changes have been made, the TryItOut-6.asp page will perform all database maintenance. If at this point you feel ambitious, you could create a simple web page that would allow the user to select an option to insert, update or delete clubs. This page could then call the appropriate Try It Out form page, either 1, 3, or 5, which in turn would call the TryItOut-6 action page.

# Summary

This chapter has shown you the basic syntax of the INSERT, UPDATE and DELETE statements. A practical demonstration has been given for each of these statements and you should now feel comfortable using each of them. The distinction between inserting and updating data has been covered and, as you saw from the syntax of the INSERT and UPDATE statements, they are very different from each other.

We have also explored where the data comes from that gets inserted into our database. Our examples used the data that the user entered in the forms on our web pages.

To summarize this chapter, you should now know:

- ❏ How to build and execute an INSERT statement using data from a form
- ❏ How to build and execute an UPDATE statement using data from a form
- ❏ How to build and execute a DELETE statement using data from a form
- ❏ The difference between inserting and updating data

# Exercise 1

Create a web page that will provide two functions. First it should provide a form that will allow the user to enter data, and second it should take that data and insert it into the database.

We will be using the BoatClass table in the Sailors database. The input form should validate that all data is present before submitting the form. The second step should build the INSERT statement, knowing that all data is present, and insert a new row of data into the BoatClass table. The results of running our code are shown in the following screenshots, first the form page:

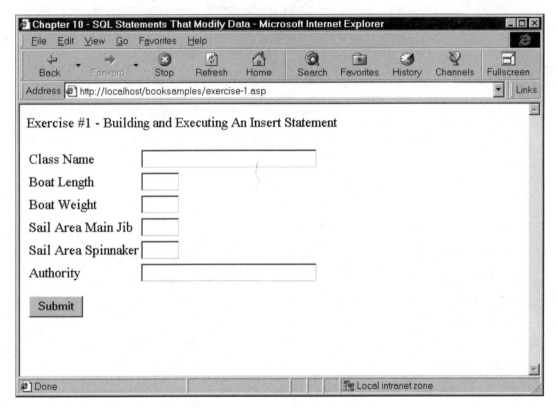

Then the response page:

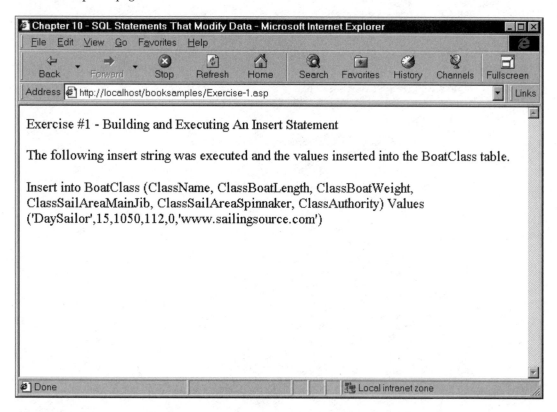

The code for this exercise is available in file `Exercise-1.asp`:

```
<HTML>
<HEAD>
<META NAME="GENERATOR" Content="Microsoft Visual Studio 6.0">
<TITLE>Chapter 10 - SQL Statements That Modify Data</TITLE>
</HEAD>
<BODY>
Exercise #1 - Building and Executing An Insert Statement<BR><BR>

<%
'************************************************************
'* Step 1: Display the entry form
'************************************************************
If Len(Request.Form("FormAction")) = 0 Then
%>

 <FORM ACTION=Exercise-1.asp METHOD=post NAME=frmAdd>
  <INPUT TYPE=hidden NAME=FormAction VALUE=Step2>
  <TABLE>
   <TR>
    <TD>Class Name</TD>
    <TD><INPUT TYPE=text NAME=txtClassName SIZE=30></TD>
   </TR>
   <TR>
    <TD NOWRAP>Boat Length</TD>
    <TD><INPUT TYPE=text NAME=txtBoatLength SIZE=5></TD>
   </TR>
```

```
  <TR>
   <TD NOWRAP>Boat Weight</TD>
   <TD><INPUT TYPE=text NAME=txtBoatWeight SIZE=5></TD>
   </TR>
   <TR>
   <TD NOWRAP>Sail Area Main Jib</TD>
   <TD><INPUT TYPE=text NAME=txtSailJib SIZE=5></TD>
   </TR>
   <TR>
   <TD NOWRAP>Sail Area Spinnaker</TD>
   <TD><INPUT TYPE=text NAME=txtSailSpinnaker SIZE=5></TD>
   </TR>
   <TR>
   <TD>Authority</TD>
   <TD><INPUT TYPE=text NAME=txtAuthority SIZE=30></TD>
   </TR>
   <TR>
   <TD HEIGHT=60>
     <INPUT TYPE=button NAME=btnSubmit VALUE=Submit></TD>
   </TR>
 </TABLE>
</FORM>

<SCRIPT LANGUAGE=vbscript>
Sub btnSubmit_OnClick()
 'Validate all fields contain data
 If Len(frmAdd.txtClassName.value) = 0 Then
  Alert "You must enter a class name"
  frmAdd.txtClassName.focus
  Exit Sub
 ElseIf Len(frmAdd.txtBoatLength.value) = 0 Then
  Alert "You must enter a boat length"
  frmAdd.txtBoatLength.focus
  Exit Sub
 ElseIf Len(frmAdd.txtBoatWeight.value) = 0 Then
  Alert "You must enter a boat weight"
  frmAdd.txtBoatWeight.focus
  Exit Sub
 ElseIf Len(frmAdd.txtSailJib.value) = 0 Then
  Alert "You must enter a sail jib"
  frmAdd.txtSailJib.focus
  Exit Sub
 ElseIf Len(frmAdd.txtSailSpinnaker.value) = 0 Then
  Alert "You must enter a sail spinnaker"
  frmAdd.txtSailSpinnaker.focus
  Exit Sub
 ElseIf Len(frmAdd.txtAuthority.value) = 0 Then
  Alert "You must enter a authority web site"
  frmAdd.txtAuthority.focus
  Exit Sub
 End If

 'If we make this far then submit the form
 Call frmAdd.submit()
End Sub
</SCRIPT>

<%
'**************************************************************
'* Step 2: Add the new boat class
'**************************************************************
ElseIf Request.Form("FormAction") = "Step2" Then

 'Declare variables needed
 Dim strSQL
 Dim adCmdText
```

```
'Set required variables here
adCmdText = 1

'Build the insert string
strSQL = "Insert into BoatClass (ClassName, ClassBoatLength, " & _
  "ClassBoatWeight, ClassSailAreaMainJib, " & _
  "ClassSailAreaSpinnaker, ClassAuthority) " & _
  "Values('" & CStr(Request.Form("txtClassName")) & "'," & _
  CLng(Request.Form("txtBoatLength")) & "," & _
  CLng(Request.Form("txtBoatWeight")) & "," & _
  CLng(Request.Form("txtSailJib")) & "," & _
  CLng(Request.Form("txtSailSpinnaker")) & ",'" & _
  CStr(Request.Form("txtAuthority")) & "')"

'Create and open the database object
Set objConn = Server.CreateObject("ADODB.Connection")
objConn.Open "DSN=Sailors"

'Create the command object
Set objCmd = Server.CreateObject("ADODB.Command")

'Set the command object properties
Set objCmd.ActiveConnection = objConn
objCmd.CommandText = strSQL
objCmd.CommandType = adCmdText

'Execute the command
objCmd.Execute

'Display the insert string
Response.Write "The following insert string was executed and " & _
  "the values inserted into the BoatClass table.<P>"
Response.Write strSQL

'Close and dereference database objects
Set objCmd = Nothing
objConn.Close
Set objConn = Nothing

End If 'End If for step processing
%>

</BODY>
</HTML>
```

### How It Works Exercise 1 – Building and Executing An Insert Statement

We start our page by using the standard HTML tags that define the beginning of our web page. We then display our first line of text.

```
<HTML>
<HEAD>
<META NAME="GENERATOR" Content="Microsoft Visual Studio 6.0">
<TITLE>Chapter 10 - SQL Statements That Modify Data</TITLE>
</HEAD>
<BODY>
Exercise #1 - Building and Executing An Insert Statement<BR><BR>
```

Since this web page contains multiple steps, we need to check which step to process. We are using a hidden field in the form called FormAction and the first time this web page is executed, this field contains no data. By checking the length of this field we can determine if this is the first time executing this page or not.

```
<%
'*****************************************************************
'* Step 1: Display the entry form
'*****************************************************************
If Len(Request.Form("FormAction")) = 0 Then
%>
```

We start this step by building a form that contains input fields for the user to enter data in. This form will post the results back to itself as indicated by the ACTION and METHOD properties of the FORM tag. Notice our hidden field called FormAction and notice that it has a value of Step2. When we post this form back to itself the next step to be executed will be step 2.

As we have done in the previous examples in this chapter, we include a table within our form to help keep our data fields aligned properly on our page.

```
<FORM ACTION=Exercise-1.asp METHOD=post NAME=frmAdd>
 <INPUT TYPE=hidden NAME=FormAction VALUE=Step2>
 <TABLE>
```

All of the input fields on this form are text boxes. We give each text box a NAME and set the SIZE property of each to indicate how many characters it should display.

```
<TR>
<TD>Class Name</TD>
<TD><INPUT TYPE=text NAME=txtClassName SIZE=30></TD>
</TR>
<TR>
<TD NOWRAP>Boat Length</TD>
<TD><INPUT TYPE=text NAME=txtBoatLength SIZE=5></TD>
</TR>
<TR>
<TD NOWRAP>Boat Weight</TD>
<TD><INPUT TYPE=text NAME=txtBoatWeight SIZE=5></TD>
</TR>
<TR>
<TD NOWRAP>Sail Area Main Jib</TD>
<TD><INPUT TYPE=text NAME=txtSailJib SIZE=5></TD>
</TR>
<TR>
<TD NOWRAP>Sail Area Spinnaker</TD>
<TD><INPUT TYPE=text NAME=txtSailSpinnaker SIZE=5></TD>
</TR>
<TR>
<TD>Authority</TD>
<TD><INPUT TYPE=text NAME=txtAuthority SIZE=30></TD>
</TR>
```

The last row in our table contains the submit button. Notice that we are using a standard button type because we will be including some client-side script to perform validations. If the user has not entered data in all fields we do not want to submit the form.

```
<TR>
<TD HEIGHT=60>
 <INPUT TYPE=button NAME=btnSubmit VALUE=Submit></TD>
</TR>
</TABLE>
</FORM>
```

Our client-side script is coded in the OnClick event of the Submit button. Here we are just validating that data has been entered. You are free to add validations to ensure the data is of the correct data types.

We are using the same validations that we used in our previous examples. We check to see if data has been entered by checking the length of the form field. If it has not, we display a message to the user prompting them to enter the data. We then set the focus to the field in question and exit the subroutine.

```vbscript
<SCRIPT LANGUAGE=vbscript>
Sub btnSubmit_OnClick()
 'Validate all fields contain data
 If Len(frmAdd.txtClassName.value) = 0 Then
  Alert "You must enter a class name"
  frmAdd.txtClassName.focus
  Exit Sub
 ElseIf Len(frmAdd.txtBoatLength.value) = 0 Then
  Alert "You must enter a boat length"
  frmAdd.txtBoatLength.focus
  Exit Sub
 ElseIf Len(frmAdd.txtBoatWeight.value) = 0 Then
  Alert "You must enter a boat weight"
  frmAdd.txtBoatWeight.focus
  Exit Sub
 ElseIf Len(frmAdd.txtSailJib.value) = 0 Then
  Alert "You must enter a sail jib"
  frmAdd.txtSailJib.focus
  Exit Sub
 ElseIf Len(frmAdd.txtSailSpinnaker.value) = 0 Then
  Alert "You must enter a sail spinnaker"
  frmAdd.txtSailSpinnaker.focus
  Exit Sub
 ElseIf Len(frmAdd.txtAuthority.value) = 0 Then
  Alert "You must enter a authority web site"
  frmAdd.txtAuthority.focus
  Exit Sub
 End If
```

If we make it this far in the validation code we know all fields contain data and we can submit the form by calling the Submit method of the form.

The end of the client-side script signifies the end of the first step in our web page.

```vbscript
 'If we make this far then submit the form
 Call frmAdd.submit()
End Sub
</SCRIPT>
```

We start the second part by declaring some variables that will be needed and setting their values where appropriate. We declare a variable to hold our SQL string, a variable to specify the type of command we will be executing.

```asp
<%
'***********************************************************
'* Step 2: Add the new boat class
'***********************************************************
ElseIf Request.Form("FormAction") = "Step2" Then

 'Declare variables needed
 Dim strSQL
 Dim adCmdText

 'Set required variables here
 adCmdText = 1
```

Since all fields were required in the request form, we can build our entire `Insert` statement at one time. We specify that we want to insert a row of data into the `BoatClass` table. Next we list all of the columns that we will be inserting data into. Lastly, we set all of the values using data from the request form and convert them to their appropriate data types. Keep in mind that string values must be enclosed by single quote marks.

```
'Build the insert string
strSQL = "Insert into BoatClass (ClassName, ClassBoatLength, " & _
 "ClassBoatWeight, ClassSailAreaMainJib, " & _
 "ClassSailAreaSpinnaker, ClassAuthority) " & _
 "Values('" & CStr(Request.Form("txtClassName")) & "'," & _
 CLng(Request.Form("txtBoatLength")) & "," & _
 CLng(Request.Form("txtBoatWeight")) & "," & _
 CLng(Request.Form("txtSailJib")) & "," & _
 CLng(Request.Form("txtSailSpinnaker")) & ",'" & _
 CStr(Request.Form("txtAuthority")) & "')"
```

We create and open our `Connection` object.

```
'Create and open the database object
 Set objConn = Server.CreateObject("ADODB.Connection")
 objConn.Open "DSN=Sailors"
```

We are now ready to create our `Command` object and set its properties using the `Connection` object, the SQL string and the variable that specifies what type of command we are going to be executing.

```
'Create the command object
 Set objCmd = Server.CreateObject("ADODB.Command")

 'Set the command object properties
 Set objCmd.ActiveConnection = objConn
 objCmd.CommandText = strSQL
 objCmd.CommandType = adCmdText
```

Next, we execute our command.

```
'Execute the command
 objCmd.Execute
```

Having made it this far in the code, we are now ready to display a message to the user indicating that the data has been inserted into the database. We also display the SQL string that was used to insert the data, for demonstration purposes.

```
'Display the insert string
 Response.Write "The following insert string was executed and " & _
 "the values inserted into the BoatClass table..<P>"
 Response.Write strSQL
```

After closing and de–referencing our database objects, we end our web page with an `End If` statement to terminate the step processing, and by inserting the standard HTML tags.

```
'Close and dereference database objects
 Set objCmd = Nothing
 objConn.Close
 Set objConn = Nothing

End If 'End If for step processing
%>

</BODY>
</HTML>
```

# Exercise 2

Having completed exercise one, it would only stand to reason that we should have a means that would allow us to update the BoatClass table. This is where this exercise comes in. The web page that you will create will contain three steps.

Step 1 should display a list of all boat class names in a combo box. The user will select the boat class that they want to update and submit the form.

Step 2 will build a form that displays the information for the boat class that was selected and allows the user to update the fields. Once again, all data will be required so there must be a client side validation routine. Once the user has completed their updates they will submit the form.

Step 3 will retrieve the fields from the request form and build an update statement. Once the update statement has been built, the SQL string will be executed and the results will be displayed.

The screen shot for Step 1 is shown below.

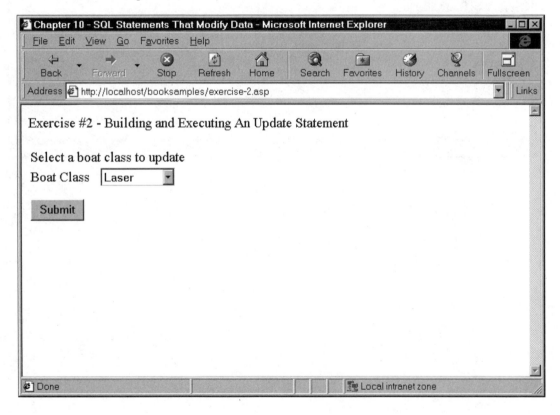

The screen shot for step 2 is shown next.

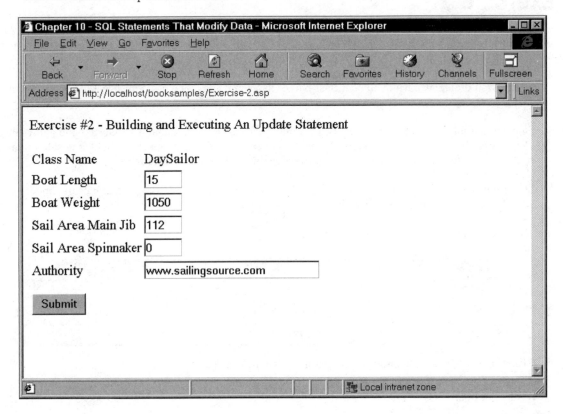

And last the screen shot for step 3 is shown next:

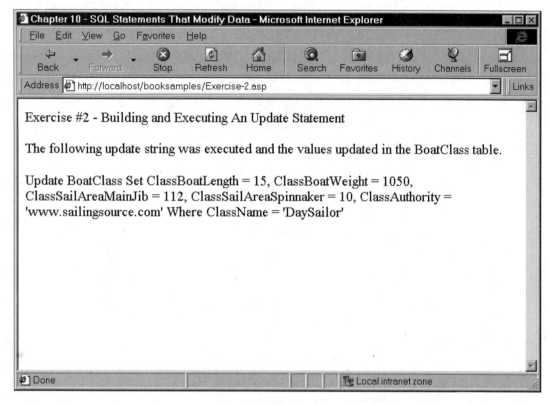

The code for this exercise is contained in file `Exercise-2.asp`.

```
<HTML>
<HEAD>
<META NAME="GENERATOR" Content="Microsoft Visual Studio 6.0">
<TITLE>Chapter 10 - SQL Statements That Modify Data</TITLE>
</HEAD>
<BODY>
Exercise #2 - Building and Executing An Update Statement<BR><BR>

<%
'Declare variables needed
Dim strSQL
Dim adCmdText

'Set required variables
adCmdText = 1

'***********************************************************
'* Step 1: Display a list of boat class names to select from
'***********************************************************
If Len(Request.Form("FormAction")) = 0 Then

 'Create the recordset object
 Set objRS = Server.CreateObject("ADODB.Recordset")
```

```
'Open the recordset getting a list of all boat classes
objRS.Open "Select ClassName from BoatClass","DSN=Sailors"
%>
<FORM ACTION=Exercise-2.asp METHOD=post NAME=frmDisplay>
 <INPUT TYPE=hidden NAME=FormAction VALUE=Step2>
 <TABLE>
  <TR>
  <TD COLSPAN=2>Select a boat class to update</TD>
  </TR>
  <TR>
  <TD>Boat Class</TD>
  <TD><SELECT NAME=cboBoatClass>
<%
  'Loop through the recordset adding class name to the combo box
  Do While Not objRS.EOF
%>
  <OPTION VALUE="<%=objRS("ClassName")%>">
   <%=objRS("ClassName")%></OPTION>
<%
  objRS.MoveNext

  Loop

  'Close and dereference database objects
  objRS.Close
  Set objRS = Nothing
%>
  </SELECT></TD>
  </TR>
  <TR>
  <TD HEIGHT=60><INPUT TYPE=submit NAME=btnSubmit VALUE=Submit></TD>
  </TR>
 </TABLE>
</FORM>

<%
'**********************************************************
'* Step 2: Display the update form
'**********************************************************
ElseIf Request.Form("FormAction") = "Step2" Then

'Build the SQL string
strSQL = "Select * from BoatClass where ClassName = '" & _
  CStr(Request.Form("cboBoatClass")) & "'"

'Create the recordset object
Set objRS = Server.CreateObject("ADODB.Recordset")

'Open the recordset getting the boat class details
objRS.Open strSQL,"DSN=Sailors"
%>
<FORM ACTION=Exercise-2.asp METHOD=post NAME=frmUpdate>
 <INPUT TYPE=hidden NAME=FormAction VALUE=Step3>
 <INPUT TYPE=hidden NAME=txtClassName
  VALUE="<%=objRS("ClassName")%>">
 <TABLE>
  <TR>
  <TD>Class Name</TD>
  <TD><FONT COLOR=navy><%=objRS("ClassName")%></FONT></TD>
  </TR>
  <TR>
  <TD NOWRAP>Boat Length</TD>
  <TD><INPUT TYPE=text NAME=txtBoatLength SIZE=5
    VALUE=<%=objRS("ClassBoatLength")%>></TD>
  </TR>
  <TR>
```

```html
      <TD NOWRAP>Boat Weight</TD>
      <TD><INPUT TYPE=text NAME=txtBoatWeight SIZE=5
        VALUE=<%=objRS("ClassBoatWeight")%>></TD>
      </TR>
      <TR>
      <TD NOWRAP>Sail Area Main Jib</TD>
      <TD><INPUT TYPE=text NAME=txtSailJib SIZE=5
        VALUE=<%=objRS("ClassSailAreaMainJib")%>></TD>
      </TR>
      <TR>
      <TD NOWRAP>Sail Area Spinnaker</TD>
      <TD><INPUT TYPE=text NAME=txtSailSpinnaker SIZE=5
        VALUE=<%=objRS("ClassSailAreaSpinnaker")%>></TD>
      </TR>
      <TR>
      <TD>Authority</TD>
      <TD><INPUT TYPE=text NAME=txtAuthority SIZE=30
        VALUE=<%=objRS("ClassAuthority")%>></TD>
      </TR>
      <TR>
      <TD HEIGHT=60>
        <INPUT TYPE=button NAME=btnSubmit VALUE=Submit></TD>
      </TR>
    </TABLE>
  </FORM>

<%
 'Close and dereference database objects
 objRS.Close
 Set objRS = Nothing
%>

<SCRIPT LANGUAGE=vbscript>
Sub btnSubmit_OnClick()
  'Validate all fields contain data
  If Len(frmUpdate.txtClassName.value) = 0 Then
    Alert "You must enter a class name"
    frmUpdate.txtClassName.focus
    Exit Sub
  ElseIf Len(frmUpdate.txtBoatLength.value) = 0 Then
    Alert "You must enter a boat length"
    frmUpdate.txtBoatLength.focus
    Exit Sub
  ElseIf Len(frmUpdate.txtBoatWeight.value) = 0 Then
    Alert "You must enter a boat weight"
    frmUpdate.txtBoatWeight.focus
    Exit Sub
  ElseIf Len(frmUpdate.txtSailJib.value) = 0 Then
    Alert "You must enter a sail jib"
    frmUpdate.txtSailJib.focus
    Exit Sub
  ElseIf Len(frmUpdate.txtSailSpinnaker.value) = 0 Then
    Alert "You must enter a sail spinnaker"
    frmUpdate.txtSailSpinnaker.focus
    Exit Sub
  ElseIf Len(frmUpdate.txtAuthority.value) = 0 Then
    Alert "You must enter a authority web site"
    frmUpdate.txtAuthority.focus
    Exit Sub
  End If

  'If we make this far then submit the form
  Call frmUpdate.submit()
End Sub
</SCRIPT>
```

```
<%
'*****************************************************************
'* Step 3: Update the boat class
'*****************************************************************
ElseIf Request.Form("FormAction") = "Step3" Then

 'Build the update string
 strSQL = "Update BoatClass Set " & _
  "ClassBoatLength = " & _
   CLng(Request.Form("txtBoatLength")) & ", " & _
  "ClassBoatWeight = " & _
   CLng(Request.Form("txtBoatWeight")) & ", " & _
  "ClassSailAreaMainJib = " & _
   CLng(Request.Form("txtSailJib")) & ", " & _
  "ClassSailAreaSpinnaker = " & _
   CLng(Request.Form("txtSailSpinnaker")) & ", " & _
  "ClassAuthority = '" & _
   CStr(Request.Form("txtAuthority")) & "' " & _
  "Where ClassName = '" & _
   CStr(Request.Form("txtClassName")) & "'"

'Create and open the database object
 Set objConn = Server.CreateObject("ADODB.Connection")
 objConn.Open "DSN=Sailors"

'Create the command object
 Set objCmd = Server.CreateObject("ADODB.Command")

 'Set the command object properties
 Set objCmd.ActiveConnection = objConn
 objCmd.CommandText = strSQL
 objCmd.CommandType = adCmdText

 'Execute the command
 objCmd.Execute

'Display the update string
 Response.Write "The following update string was executed and " & _
  "the values updated in the BoatClass table.<P>"
 Response.Write strSQL

 'Close and dereference database objects
 Set objCmd = Nothing
 objConn.Close
 Set objConn = Nothing

End If 'End If for step processing
%>

</BODY>
</HTML>
```

### How It Works Exercise 2 – Building and Executing An Update Statement

The first part of our page uses standard HTML tags to define the page and then we display our first line of text.

```
<HTML>
<HEAD>
<META NAME="GENERATOR" Content="Microsoft Visual Studio 6.0">
<TITLE>Chapter 10 - SQL Statements That Modify Data</TITLE>
</HEAD>
<BODY>
Exercise #2 - Building and Executing An Update Statement<BR><BR>
```

We define the variables that will be used throughout our page and set the appropriate values.

```
<%
'Declare variables needed
Dim strSQL
Dim adCmdText
Dim blnCriticalError

'Set required variables
adCmdText = 1
```

Step 1 of this page creates a `Recordset` object and gets all boat class names from the `BoatClass` table.

```
'****************************************************************
'* Step 1: Display a list of boat class names to select from
'****************************************************************
If Len(Request.Form("FormAction")) = 0 Then

 'Create the recordset object
 Set objRS = Server.CreateObject("ADODB.Recordset")

 'Open the recordset getting a list of all boat classes
 objRS.Open "Select ClassName from BoatClass","DSN=Sailors"
%>
```

We build a form that will post the fields back to itself. Notice that once again we have created a hidden field that will be used to control which step in the page is being processed.

```
<FORM ACTION=Exercise-2.asp METHOD=post NAME=frmDisplay>
 <INPUT TYPE=hidden NAME=FormAction VALUE=Step2>
```

Next, we build our table and display the instructions to the user, and insert a combo box that will contain the boat class names.

```
<TABLE>
 <TR>
 <TD COLSPAN=2>Select a boat class to update</TD>
 </TR>
 <TR>
 <TD>Boat Class</TD>
 <TD><SELECT NAME=cboBoatClass>
```

We loop through the recordset set populating the options for the combo box. Notice that this time we used the same field from our recordset for both the combo box `value` and `text`.

After we have added all of the boat class names, we close and de-reference our database objects.

```
<%
   'Loop through the recordset adding class name to the combo box
   Do While Not objRS.EOF
%>
   <option VALUE="<%=objRS("ClassName")%>">
    <%=objRS("ClassName")%></option>
<%
   objRS.MoveNext

   Loop

   'Close and dereference database objects
   objRS.Close
   Set objRS = Nothing
%>
   </SELECT></TD>
   </TR>
```

The last row in our table contains a submit button in which the TYPE property is set to submit, because we have no validations to make.

```
  <TR>
  <TD HEIGHT=60><INPUT TYPE=submit NAME=btnSubmit VALUE=Submit></TD>
  </TR>
  </TABLE>
</FORM>
```

Step 2 in our page builds a SELECT statement to select the data for the boat class name that was chosen by the user. After the SQL string has been built using data from the request form, we create and open our Recordset object.

```
<%
'*************************************************************
'* Step 2: Display the update form
'*************************************************************
ElseIf Request.Form("FormAction") = "Step2" Then

 'Instruct VBScript to ignore the error and continue
 'with the next line of code
On Error Resume Next

 'Build the SQL string
strSQL = "Select * from BoatClass where ClassName = '" & _
 CStr(Request.Form("cboBoatClass")) & "'"

 'Create the recordset object
Set objRS = Server.CreateObject("ADODB.Recordset")

 'Open the recordset getting the boat class details
objRS.Open strSQL,"DSN=Sailors"
%>
```

We build the form that allows the user to update the existing values. All edit fields are text boxes and their values have been set using the fields from the recordset.

```
<FORM ACTION=Exercise-2.asp METHOD=post NAME=frmUpdate>
 <INPUT TYPE=hidden NAME=FormAction VALUE=Step3>
 <INPUT TYPE=hidden NAME=txtClassName
  VALUE="<%=objRS("ClassName")%>">
 <TABLE>
  <TR>
  <TD>Class Name</TD>
  <TD><FONT COLOR=navy><%=objRS("ClassName")%></font></TD>
  </TR>
  <TR>
  <TD NOWRAP>Boat Length</TD>
  <TD><INPUT TYPE=text NAME=txtBoatLength SIZE=5
    VALUE=<%=objRS("ClassBoatLength")%>></TD>
  </TR>
  <TR>
  <TD NOWRAP>Boat Weight</TD>
  <TD><INPUT TYPE=text NAME=txtBoatWeight SIZE=5
    VALUE=<%=objRS("ClassBoatWeight")%>></TD>
  </TR>
  <TR>
  <TD NOWRAP>Sail Area Main Jib</TD>
  <TD><INPUT TYPE=text NAME=txtSailJib SIZE=5
    VALUE=<%=objRS("ClassSailAreaMainJib")%>></TD>
  </TR>
  <TR>
```

```
<TD NOWRAP>Sail Area Spinnaker</TD>
<TD><INPUT TYPE=text NAME=txtSailSpinnaker SIZE=5
  VALUE=<%=objRS("ClassSailAreaSpinnaker")%>></TD>
</TR>
<TR>
<TD>Authority</TD>
<TD><INPUT TYPE=text NAME=txtAuthority SIZE=30
  VALUE=<%=objRS("ClassAuthority")%>></TD>
</TR>
```

Because we need to perform client-side validations, we are using a normal button type for our Submit button.

```
<TR>
<TD HEIGHT=60>
  <INPUT TYPE=button NAME=btnSubmit VALUE=Submit></TD>
</TR>
</TABLE>
</FORM>
```

Next, we close and de-reference our database objects.

```
<%
'Close and dereference database objects
objRS.Close
Set objRS = Nothing
%>
```

Client-side validations are handled in our client-side script in the `OnClick` event for the `submit` button. As in the last exercise we are just validating that data exists, and not validating to ensure the data is of the correct data type.

```
<SCRIPT LANGUAGE=vbscript>
Sub btnSubmit_OnClick()
 'Validate all fields contain data
 If Len(frmUpdate.txtClassName.value) = 0 Then
  Alert "You must enter a class name"
  frmUpdate.txtClassName.focus
  Exit Sub
 ElseIf Len(frmUpdate.txtBoatLength.value) = 0 Then
  Alert "You must enter a boat length"
  frmUpdate.txtBoatLength.focus
  Exit Sub
 ElseIf Len(frmUpdate.txtBoatWeight.value) = 0 Then
  Alert "You must enter a boat weight"
  frmUpdate.txtBoatWeight.focus
  Exit Sub
 ElseIf Len(frmUpdate.txtSailJib.value) = 0 Then
  Alert "You must enter a sail jib"
  frmUpdate.txtSailJib.focus
  Exit Sub
 ElseIf Len(frmUpdate.txtSailSpinnaker.value) = 0 Then
  Alert "You must enter a sail spinnaker"
  frmUpdate.txtSailSpinnaker.focus
  Exit Sub
 ElseIf Len(frmUpdate.txtAuthority.value) = 0 Then
  Alert "You must enter a authority web site"
  frmUpdate.txtAuthority.focus
  Exit Sub
 End If
```

If all validations have passed, we find ourselves here ready to submit the form. We do this by calling the submit method of the form.

```
'If we make this far then submit the form
Call frmUpdate.submit()
End Sub
</SCRIPT>
```

The third step of this form starts by building the Update statement. The entire SQL string can be built at one time because all fields were required. We set each column name equal to the data values retrieved from the request form. Also notice that we are converting the data values to their appropriate data types. Once again don't forget to enclose the string values in single quote marks.

```
<%
'***********************************************************
'* Step 3: Update the boat class
'***********************************************************
ElseIf Request.Form("FormAction") = "Step3" Then

'Build the update string
strSQL = "UPDATE BoatClass SET " & _
  "ClassBoatLength = " & _
  CLng(Request.Form("txtBoatLength")) & ", " & _
  "ClassBoatWeight = " & _
  CLng(Request.Form("txtBoatWeight")) & ", " & _
  "ClassSailAreaMainJib = " & _
  CLng(Request.Form("txtSailJib")) & ", " & _
  "ClassSailAreaSpinnaker = " & _
  CLng(Request.Form("txtSailSpinnaker")) & ", " & _
  "ClassAuthority = '" & _
  CStr(Request.Form("txtAuthority")) & "' " & _
  "WHERE ClassName = '" & _
  CStr(Request.Form("txtClassName")) & "'"
```

We create and open our Connection object next:

```
'Create and open the database object
Set objConn = Server.CreateObject("ADODB.Connection")
objConn.Open "DSN=Sailors"
```

Next, we create our Command object and set its properties using the Connection object, SQL string and our adCmdText variable to tell the Command object what type of command we are executing.

```
'Create the command object
Set objCmd = Server.CreateObject("ADODB.Command")

'Set the command object properties
Set objCmd.ActiveConnection = objConn
objCmd.CommandText = strSQL
objCmd.CommandType = adCmdText
```

We execute the Command object:

```
'Execute the command
objCmd.Execute
```

Once again we need to display a message to the user indicating that the updates were applied. We also display the SQL string that was executed, for demonstration purposes.

```
'Display the update string
Response.Write "The following update string was executed and " & _
  "the values updated in the BoatClass table.<P>"
Response.Write strSQL
```

The last part of this step is to close and de-reference our database objects.

```
'Close and dereference database objects
Set objCmd = Nothing
objConn.Close
Set objConn = Nothing
```

We terminate our step processing with the End If statement and then end our page using standard HTML tags.

```
End If 'End If for step processing
%>

</BODY>
</HTML>
```

# Quiz

1. When do you want to use a `normal` type of button as a `submit` button?

2. Can we insert a blank row of data using the `INSERT` statement?

3. Does data that can be inserted into our database come from server variables or server functions?

4. Why is it important to check for errors after inserting or updating data in the database?

5. Can we delete more than one row of data at a time?

6. Does the criteria parameter in the `UPDATE` statement have to be a simple Boolean expression?

# Quiz Answers

1. When you need to control the submission of the form. This would normally be done after data validations have been performed

2. Yes, we can also insert data into just one or two columns of a table.

3. Actually, the data can come from both server variables and server functions.

4. Checking for errors after inserting or updating data will alert us to any problems that may arise, and we can halt our code after displaying the error message. This will also keep us from displaying a false message to the user that their data was inserted or updated when it was not.

5. We can delete as many rows of data that match the criteria that was passed in the DELETE statement.

6. No, we can use a complex expression, such as the one below, as long as it can be evaluated to a single Boolean value.

```
WHERE Dept = 'Sales' AND Age BETWEEN 18 AND 30
```

Setup cannot install system files or update shared files if the files are in use. Before c
any open applications.

Exit Setup

Continue

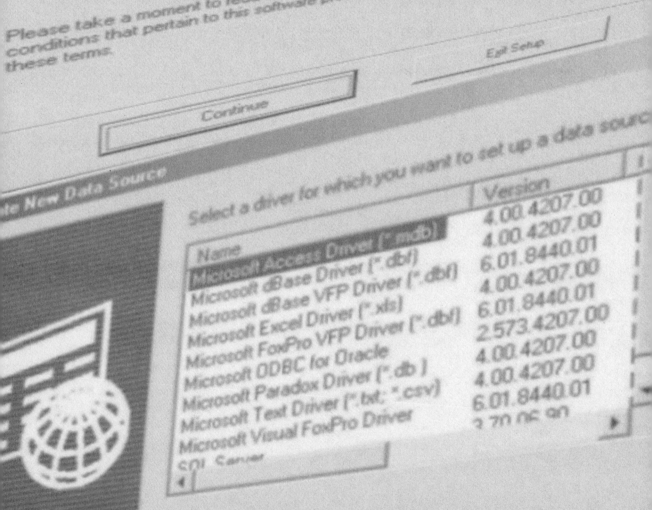

te New Data Source

Select a driver for which you want to set up a data sourc

| Name | Version |
|---|---|
| Microsoft Access Driver (*.mdb) | 4.00.4207.00 |
| Microsoft dBase Driver (*.dbf) | 4.00.4207.00 |
| Microsoft dBase VFP Driver (*.dbf) | 6.01.8440.01 |
| Microsoft Excel Driver (*.xls) | 4.00.4207.00 |
| Microsoft FoxPro VFP Driver (*.dbf) | 6.01.8440.01 |
| Microsoft ODBC for Oracle | 2.573.4207.00 |
| Microsoft Paradox Driver (*.db ) | 4.00.4207.00 |
| Microsoft Text Driver (*.txt; *.csv) | 4.00.4207.00 |
| Microsoft Visual FoxPro Driver | 6.01.8440.01 |
| SQL Server | 3.70.06.90 |

Cancel

# Databases and Cookies

From a programmer's standpoint, one great problem of the web is the lack of an intrinsic identification of visitors. Cookies provide a means of identifying visitors, with their approval, so that continuity can be established between visits. Cookies are limited in the amount of information they can hold but, by storing an identification number in a cookie, we can then use that ID with ASP-ADO to look up a returning visitor in our database, and thus have all of the visitor's data available.

## Review of Cookies

The following section provides a review of the purpose of cookies and a few key points to remember about cookies. If you have been working with ASP pages for very long you are probably already familiar with the basics and can skip to the section entitled "Using cookies with ADO and a Database." The topic of cookies is also covered in depth in Beginning and Professional Active Server Pages (ISBN 1-861001-34-7 and 1-861001-26-6) with additional information on cookies in the context of sessions and applications.

## Purpose of Cookies

Cookies were created to overcome the problem of identifying visitors to the site for the purpose of maintaining some continuity between requests. There is no mechanism built into the World Wide Web that states the name of the PC that is sending a request, or that provides the ability to sense that a series of requests are all coming from the same visitor. Recall that the WWW was originally designed to provide rapid and universal access to pages of information. There was no need for a system to track a series of requests as being from the same user. Implementation of that type of continuity would slow down the server.

However, modern sites provide a more interactive experience, which frequently requires that the server has an identification of the visitor. For example, visitors may proceed through many pages of forms to place an order; the server will have to know which was the last page completed by that user and be capable of holding information between submissions. Cookies were designed to hold information about a user, including an identifying number. When a visitor returns to a site after a few minutes or a few years the site can identify that user and serve appropriate pages.

# Key Points About Cookies

After teaching the concepts and techniques of cookies to several classes, I have found that the same concepts cause confusion for many people. This section provides explanations for those problems areas. Note that these explanations are in the context of a site designer working with ASP-ADO, and are generalities. Other site design tools offer their own techniques for working with cookies. In each case there are a few exceptions, but it helps my students to understand the core ideas first, then deal with exceptions later.

## Cookies are created by an ASP page

Many people wonder how the cookie gets set in the first place. It is not automatic. There is nothing built into the server or the browser that automatically sets cookies. The cookie-making process starts with several lines of code that you write in a page of your site. When the visitor opens that page, the lines of code instruct the browser to create the cookie. In summary, the script of the page instructs the browser to carry out the cookie baking.

## Cookies are located on the visitor's machine

Cookies are stored on the hard drive of the browser's machine. Each cookie has several pieces of data:

- ❏   Which domain (web site) set the cookie
- ❏   A date of expiration for this cookie
- ❏   One or more pieces of data
- ❏   Optional: keys that organize multiple data in folder-like groups

Note that the browser knows that a particular domain set a particular cookie.

## The mechanism of how cookies are stored and organized on the user's PC is browser-specific

As programmers, we can write an ASP page that tells the browser to create a cookie. We do not need to know any further specifics about how the browser creates the cookie since the browser performs the actual writing. Many students ask about the intricacies of how cookies are formatted and organized on the disk, but that topic is not part of ASP-ADO, it is part of a course in programming IE or Netscape. As programmers, we only need to know that all browsers have the ability to receive and carry out generic (not browser-specific) instructions regarding cookies. To summarize, to the programmer all browsers have the same interface regarding cookies. The details of carrying out the job vary between browsers, but that does not concern us in this book.

## Cookies do not persist unless instructed

Cookies, by default, only last as long as the browser is open. To make a cookie persist beyond the current session of the browser, you as the programmer must set an expiration date for some day in the future.

## Cookies have size limits

The WWW standards for browsers specify that they must support at least 300 cookies. That is a total from all websites, so the server that sets the 301$^{st}$ cookie erases the first cookie. In addition, each cookie size cannot exceed 4KB. There is also a limit of about 250 keys per cookie. In practical work, the limits on keys are not a problem. However, a very active web surfer could exceed the number of cookies supported by her browser. As covered below, it is important to have your site prepared for the non-existence of cookies.

## When a request is made to a domain, all of the cookies set by that domain are automatically sent along with the request

Prior to sending an URL request to the ISP, the browser checks to see if there are any cookies that have been set by that domain. If there are, then the browser copies the cookie's data into the header and sends it with the URL. Now consider this from the server side; this means that all of the cookies you set are available to you, as the programmer, in each and every page request sent from the browser. You can extract the cookie data and use it in the first response page. To repeat, when reading cookies you do not make a separate trip to the browser to get the cookies; all the cookies set by your domain are sitting right in the `Request` object, having been sent to the server by the browser with the original request.

## Looking at your cookies

Although it is not of direct concern to us to see the cookies (remember, the browser will set and serve cookies to ASP pages), they can be viewed easily. If you are using Microsoft Internet Explorer on Windows 98, you can look in `C:\Windows\Cookies` where you will see small text files holding each cookie; the name of the file is the user name and the domain name. In Netscape you can see them in `C:\program files\netscape\users\<profile name>\cookies.txt`. Note that, as a security measure, when a cookie file is opened the browser considers the cookie tampered with and thus non-existent.

## There are many ways that cookies are lost or ruined

Cookies suffer from a multitude of abuses, and thus can never be relied upon to be there when needed. Any of the following events can render a cookie unusable or inappropriate:

- Replacing or reformatting the hard drive
- Expiration of the cookie
- Movement of a visitor to a different PC
- Use of a PC by a different user
- Preference settings on a browser that prevent the setting of cookies
- Use of a firewall that prevents setting or reading cookies
- Switching between browser softwares
- Deletion or corruption of the cookie files

It is important to design your site to handle the possible absence of a cookie, not only from first-time visitors, but from returning browsers that have lost or rendered their cookies inappropriate.

## *Cookies are frequently used with a database*

Cookies can hold one datum or many. A minimalist approach is to store in the cookie only an identifier, which is then used to look up all other information in a database, using ASP-ADO. The large-cookie approach is to store all of the information that will be needed in the cookie itself. Generally, an intermediate tack is taken, with the most commonly and urgently needed information in the cookie; particularly the user's ID number, and less frequently used or secure information held in the database for look-up.

However, doing a look-up has time and server load costs, and so if there are one or two fundamental pieces of data we may want to include them in the cookie. For example, storing display preferences in a cookie would allow the building of pages with larger type for aging baby-boomers. Likewise, some basics on the visitor's area of interest would allow information of greatest appeal to the visitor to be immediately displayed. Another useful piece of data, if available, is the visitor's zip code, which allows geographic specialization.

Factors in favor of keeping data in cookies:

❑    The data is crucial to improving page loading speed

❑    The data is used frequently, for example building every page

❑    The information is not confidential

Factors in favor of keeping data in a database for look-up:

❑    Data is only used infrequently in the site

❑    You want to minimize the impact of the cookie on the user

❑    Cookies are likely to be unavailable, e.g. destroyed, unaccepted, or inapplicable

❑    The data needs to be kept secure

## *WebMaster strategies for visitors in a state of cookie-denial*

I mention several times in this chapter that if you use cookies you will have to address the possibility that a visitor does not accept cookies or has lost a cookie that you set. There are several ways to handle this problem. The first is to require that visitors sign in each time they visit the site. A second is to check if they have your cookie, and if not shunt them to a page which asks them to re-register and re-set their cookie.

A third option is to offer a set of pages that are cookie-less. This suite of pages would be weaker in features and more limited in scope than those for cookie-acceptors. At various points on these pages you could offer the chance for the visitor to change their mind about accepting a cookie.

Fourth, there is a product called Cookie Munger, which can emulate most aspects of cookies for cookie-deniers. More information is available by searching the Microsoft site for "Cookie Munger." A good paper resides, at the time of this publication, at
`http://msdn.microsoft.com/workshop/server/toolbox/cookie.asp`. The Munger searches both outgoing and incoming data streams, and if it sees cookie-like activity it excises the information and performs the same read or write task, but instead by adding extensions to the URL. Design drawbacks include performance hits that can become significant, cumbersome URLs that get book-marked, and other problems. Furthermore, in some cases it just doesn't work.

Lastly, in case you are thinking of avoiding cookies by using ASP sessions variables, remember that sessions require cookies.

## Cookies as an instrument of the Devil

Cookies have a bad reputation and thus you may encounter resistance from customers. The facts, though, are quite simple. First, it is impossible to set a cookie without the approval of the user. Second, cookies are generally only available to the domain that set them. Third, cookies do not have the ability to gather and report information about other activities of the user back to a web site.

Having said the above, there is also a level of responsibility required on the part of the programmer. Secure information such as a credit card number should not be stored in a cookie. Although it would be difficult for another web site to obtain the information, a hacker could find the cookie on the hard drive and derive the sensitive information.

# Examples of Using Cookies

Let's look at several levels of using cookies, the simplest requiring ASP only (no ADO). A simple case would be to store in a cookie a user's preference about how to display a page. The technique would work like this for a site called `www.MyCookieSite.com`:

❑ During the first visit to `www.MyCookieSite.com` the site uses a form page to ask the user if they prefer red or black color characters.

❑ That preference is set in a cookie by code contained in a second page that uses ASP.

❑ Subsequently when that user logs in to `www.MyCookieSite.com`, the browser sends along the cookie to the server. The ASP code checks the preference in the cookie and sets the character color to suit the preference. The visitor sees the page with the color he selected.

Now let's take a more sophisticated case where we use the cookie to store a membership number, and then use ADO to look that up in a database and derive additional information about the member.

❑ When the visitor joins `www.MyClub.org`, the site uses a form page to gather from the user their mailing address, including the zip code. The new member is added to the database and assigned a member number.

❑ That member number is set on the user's hard drive in a cookie, by code contained in a second page.

❑ The next time that the member logs in to `www.MyClub.org`, the browser sends along the member number in the cookie to the server. The ASP/ADO code uses that number in the WHERE clause of a SQL statement and gets the member's zip code. Based on that zip code, ASP builds the rest of the page to feature events in the area of the member.

# Syntax to Work with Cookies in Simple ASP (no ADO)

Prior to running through the techniques of using cookies with databases via ADO, let us briefly look at how to use cookies with just ASP. Again, if you are already using these types of commands, skip to the section titled "Using Cookies with ADO and a Database".

## Syntax to Set (Write) Cookies in Simple ASP (no ADO)

These techniques are explained in more depth in Beginning Active Server Pages (ISBN 1-861001-34-7) and Professional Active Server Pages (ISBN 1-861001-26-6), but I will run through them here. To set a persistent cookie you need three lines within ASP delimiters. The first line must go at the very beginning of the page, even before the `<HTML>` tag:

```
<%Response.Buffer=true%>
<HTML>

<BODY>
<%
  Response.Cookies("FirstCookie")="DataInCookie"
  Response.Cookies("FirstCookie").Expires = date + 365
%>
```

The first line is the trickiest. Normally ASP starts writing a header and then the HTML of the page as it is interpreting the ASP code. But the instructions to set a cookie must go into the header and if that header is already written then the cookie-setting commands will fail. So we must use `<%Response.Buffer=true%>` to tell ASP to wait on writing the page, because later in the page we want to write code into the header.

The first line of ASP code in the body sets the value of the data and the name of the cookie. However, cookies by default do not persist beyond the time the browser is open so we must specifically set an expiration date on the following line. In this case we pick up today's date, add a year's worth of days, and use that for the expiration date.

## Syntax to Read Cookies in Simple ASP (no ADO)

To read a cookie into a variable you need one line to get the cookie's data out of the `Request` object and into a variable. You can then use that variable as needed. There is no need to worry about buffering since you are not adding characters to the header.

```
<%
  Dim varCookie
  varCookie = Request.Cookies("FirstCookie")
  Response.Write varCookie
%>
```

In the above code we start by declaring the variable, then filling it. A following line writes the contents of the variable to the page. Reading a cookie does not require any buffering of the response, only setting a cookie requires page buffering.

Many students ask why the cookie data is first copied into a variable rather than used directly out of the `Request` object in a statement like the following:

```
Response.Write Request.Cookies("FirstCookie")
```

There is a rumor that Microsoft does not guarantee being able to extract cookie data from a request string more than once, however, if the data is extracted into a variable then the variable is, of course, available for the entire page. Although many programmers use the data directly without problems, I tend to take the more cautious approach. Don't be confused by this caveat. The cookie itself remains re-usable on the browser's hard disk. It is the copy of the cookie that was sent in the request that cannot be guaranteed for re-use. A subsequent request, with its new copy of the cookie, *will* be readable.

## Syntax for Cookies with Multiple Data with Simple ASP (no ADO)

There is one last topic before getting into cookies with ADO. Sometimes we want to hold more than one datum in a cookie. This is done by using **keys**, which are like subfolders within a cookie. Each key has a name and a value.

With multiple keys the code is as follows:

```
<%Response.Buffer=true%>
<HTML>

<BODY>
<%
  Response.Cookies("SecondCookie")("FirstDatum")="FirstDataInSecondCookie"
  Response.Cookies("SecondCookie")("SecondDatum")="SecondDataInSecondCookie"
  Response.Cookies("SecondCookie")("ThirdDatum")="ThirdDataInSecondCookie"
  Response.Cookies("SecondCookie").Expires = date + 365
%>
```

We can retrieve the data from multiple keys within a cookie with the following code:

```
<%
  Dim varSecondCookie1
  Dim varSecondCookie2
  Dim varSecondCookie3
  varSecondCookie1 = Request.Cookies("SecondCookie")("FirstDatum")
  varSecondCookie2 = Request.Cookies("SecondCookie")("SecondDatum")
  varSecondCookie3 = Request.Cookies("SecondCookie")("ThirdDatum")
  Response.Write varSecondCookie1 & "<BR>"
  Response.Write varSecondCookie2 & "<BR>"
  Response.Write varSecondCookie3 & "<BR>"
%>
```

Notice in the above code that we follow the name of the cookie with a key name. Also note that expiration is set for the entire cookie, you cannot set different expirations for each key within a cookie. If you need to have different expirations then you must use different cookies, not different keys within one cookie.

### Try It Out – Setting and Reading a Cookie with ASP Alone

Considering the dates of birth in our sailors list, it looks like we should accommodate folks that need glasses. Sailors trying to use laptops on yachts, where the bright sun makes reading a LCD screen difficult, exacerbate this problem. So we want to give sailors the ability to pick one of three types of displays: small, medium and large. Since this parameter will be utilized with every page, and is not sensitive, we can improve server speed by storing the setting in a cookie rather than in our `People` table for look–up.

You will have to create three pages. The first will be a "Set Preference" form to ask the sailor for her or his preference in type size. A second page will be a "Cookie Setter" that stores the preference in a cookie and offers a button to open the home page. The third is the "Home Page Using Preference" that will read the cookie and use that data to set its type style.

*If you haven't worked with HTML styles before, I suggest you study the following few ideas:*

❑   Style attributes are set for levels of text, for example `<P>`, `<H1>`, etc.

❑   Text for the remainder of the document will be formatted according to the style of its level

❑   Styles are set within the tags `<STYLE>` and `</STYLE>`

❑   Style tags are placed in the head section of the page

❑   Style attributes are set as Level {AttributeName: value} such as the following:
    `P {font-size: 14 pt}`

❑   Multiple attributes are separated by semi colons as follows:
    `P {font-size: 14 pt; color: black}`

*You can get a much better feel for all the features of styles from Chapters 1 and 2 of Frank Boumphrey's book: Professional Style Sheets (ISBN 1-861001-65-7). This book also carries you through XML, an improved formatting technique.*

The first page is a form that gets the font size preference from the user. The code for this page is available as `2726-11-Cook-TIO-01-SetPreferenceForm.htm`:

```
<HTML><HEAD>
<META NAME="GENERATOR" Content="Microsoft Visual Studio 6.0">
<TITLE>2726 chapt11 Cookies TIO 01 SetPreferences</TITLE>
</HEAD><BODY>

Please select the size font you prefer.
<FORM ACTION="2726-11-Cook-TIO-01-CookieSetter.asp" METHOD=get id=form1 NAME=form1>
<INPUT TYPE="radio" NAME="PrefFontSize" VALUE=small> Small
<INPUT TYPE="radio" NAME="PrefFontSize" VALUE=medium CHECKED> Medium
<INPUT TYPE="radio" NAME="PrefFontSize" VALUE=large> Large<BR><BR>
<INPUT TYPE=submit>
</FORM>

</BODY></HTML>
```

The above code produces the following form page:

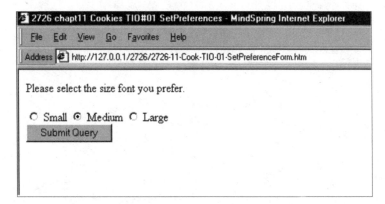

Then we need the response page that actually sets the cookie. `2726-11-Cook-TIO-01-CookieSetter.asp` contains the following code:

```
<%@ Language=VBScript%>
<%Response.Buffer=true%>
<HTML><HEAD>
<META NAME="GENERATOR" Content="Microsoft Visual Studio 6.0">
<TITLE>2726 chapt11 Cookies TIO 01 Create Cookie that holds the Preferences</TITLE>
</HEAD><BODY>
<%
 varPrefFontSize = Request.Querystring("PrefFontSize")
 Response.Write "Your cookie holds a font size preference of " & varPrefFontSize & _
 "<BR>"
  Response.Cookies("PrefFontSize")=varPrefFontSize
  Response.Cookies("PrefFontSize").Expires = date+365
%>
<A HREF="2726-11-Cook-TIO-01-HomePageUsingSizePreference.asp">
Now that the font size is set, click here to go to the home page.</A>
</BODY></HTML>
```

The preceding cookie-setting code produces the screen below, if the visitor selected medium.

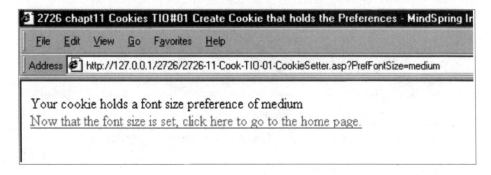

Now that the cookie is set we can use it in the following code for a home page, saved in file `2726-11-Cook-TIO-01-HomePageUsingPreference.asp`:

```
<%@ Language=VBScript %>
<HTML><HEAD>
<META NAME="GENERATOR" Content="Microsoft Visual Studio 6.0">
<TITLE>2726 chapt11 Cookies TIO 01 HomePage Using the Font Size Preferences</TITLE>
</HEAD><BODY>
<%
'--------------------
' the plan to set sailor preference in view
' get cookie
' use sailor preference in Select Case to set styles

'--------------------
' get cookie
'
  varPrefFontSize = Request.Cookies("PrefFontSize")
'next line for testing
'Response.Write "<HR>The cookie is " & varPrefFontSize & "<HR>"

'--------------------
' use sailor preference in Select Case to set styles
'
  Response.Write "<STYLE>"
  Select Case varPrefFontSize
    case "large"
      Response.Write "P {font-size: 26 pt}"
    case "medium"
      Response.Write "P {font-size: 16 pt}"
    case "small"
      Response.Write "P {font-size: 6 pt}"
  End Select
  Response.Write "</STYLE>"
%>
</HEAD>
<BODY>
<H2>Chapter 11 ASP-ADO and Cookies <BR><BR>
TIO #1 - Setting Page Styles According to Preferences</H2>
<P><P>Welcome to the Sailor Home Page.<BR><BR>
Your page is displayed as per your viewing preference</P>
</BODY></HTML>
```

The above home page code produces the screen below, again assuming that the medium size text was selected.

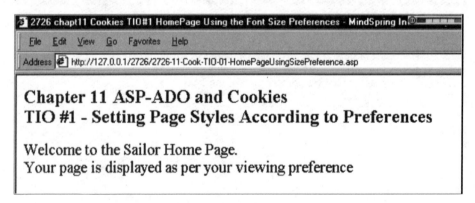

### How it Works – Setting and Reading a Cookie with ASP Alone

The first page is a simple HTML form. Remember that when using radio buttons on a form, one VALUE will be assigned to the NAME and then sent to the response page.

```
<FORM ACTION="2726-11-Cook-TIO-01-CookieSetter.asp" METHOD=get >
<INPUT TYPE="radio" NAME="PrefFontSize" VALUE=small> Small
<INPUT TYPE="radio" NAME="PrefFontSize" VALUE=medium CHECKED> Medium
<INPUT TYPE="radio" NAME="PrefFontSize" VALUE=large> Large<BR><BR>
<INPUT TYPE=submit>
</FORM>
</BODY></HTML>
```

The next page is the response page, as named in the ACTION attribute above. This page will be writing the cookie so we must be sure to buffer the page before starting the usual <HEAD> information:

```
<%@ Language=VBScript%>
<%Response.Buffer=true%>
<HTML><HEAD>
<META NAME="GENERATOR" Content="Microsoft Visual Studio 6.0">
<TITLE>2726 chapt11 Cookies TIO#01 Create Cookie that holds the Preferences</TITLE>
</HEAD><BODY>
```

Now we pick the data of the cookie out of the Request object and assign it to a variable. I like to report back to the user what she has selected.

```
<%
  varPrefFontSize = Request.Querystring("PrefFontSize")
  Response.Write "Your cookie holds a font size preference of " & varPrefFontSize & _
        "<BR>"
```

Once safely ensconced in a variable, we can use the data as the text for a cookie. Since cookies by default expire when the browser closes, we need to explicitly set an expiration:

```
  Response.Cookies("PrefFontSize")=varPrefFontSize
  Response.Cookies("PrefFontSize").Expires = date+365
%>
```

Now that the cookie is set we can give the user a hyperlink to the home page to try out the new convenience.

```
<A HREF="2726-11-Cook-TIO-01-HomePageUsingSizePreference.asp">
Now that the font size is set, click here to go to the home page.</A>
```

The home page that uses the cookie has two steps. After the housekeeping, here is the game plan laid out.

```
<%@ Language=VBScript %>
<HTML><HEAD>
<META NAME="GENERATOR" Content="Microsoft Visual Studio 6.0">
<TITLE>2726 chapt11 Cookies TIO#01 HomePage Using the Font Size Preferences</TITLE>
</HEAD><BODY>
<%
'--------------------
' the plan to use the font size cookie preference on this page
' get cookie
' use sailor preference in Select Case to set styles
```

To pick up the cookie we query the `Request` object and use that result to fill a variable. You can see the artifact of development where I checked the cookie on the browser screen. I looked at the results while building the page, then at the time of deployment added an apostrophe to the beginning of the line which turned the command into a comment and thus prevented execution of the `Response.Write`. I like to leave these in the code because later, when there is another round of problems and troubleshooting, these tools are available by just deleting the leading apostrophe.

```
'--------------------
' get cookie
'
varPrefFontSize = Request.Cookies("PrefFontSize")
' next line for testing
'Response.Write "<HR>The cookie is " & varPrefFontSize & "<HR>"
```

Now we run a `Select Case` against the variable that contains the cookie contents. Note that we must write the `<STYLE>` and `</STYLE>` tags regardless of the preference, so those are outside of the `Select Case`. Within the `Select Case` only one of the style definitions will be written.

```
'--------------------
' use sailor preference in Select Case to set styles
'
  Response.Write "<STYLE>"
  Select Case varPrefFontSize
    case "large"
      Response.Write "P {font-size: 26 pt}"
    case "medium"
      Response.Write "P {font-size: 16 pt}"
    case "small"
      Response.Write "P {font-size: 6 pt}"
  End Select
  Response.Write "</STYLE>"
%>
```

The remainder of the page contains simple HTML, which uses `<P><P>` styles that have been modified within the above code:

```
</HEAD>
<BODY>
<H2>Chapter 11 ASP-ADO and Cookies <BR><BR>
TIO #1 - Setting Page Styles According to Preferences</H2>
<P><P>Welcome to the Sailor Home Page.<BR><BR>
Your page is displayed as per your viewing preference<P><P>
</BODY></HTML>
```

# Using Cookies with ADO and a Database

Now that we have reviewed using cookies with ASP we can see how to enhance those techniques with ASP–ADO. The syntax is direct, but students can be confused by how to handle the information across multiple pages. Setting a cookie and making a new record in a database is generally done in three pages.

The first page gathers information in a form, this page requires neither ASP nor ADO, just simple HTML forms. That information is passed to an ASP/ADO response page, which performs two jobs. It sets the cookie on the user's PC, and writes the information to the database. Since the user sees neither of those processes, I usually include some text that repeats the data back to the user, and notes that a cookie has been set and they have been entered in the database, along with a hyperlink button to request the third page.

As a robust test we then write a third page to test our process, usually by reading the cookie and using it to look up the visitor's information. I usually add a button here that allows the user to catch a mistake. That button takes the visitor to an editing screen to correct the errors.

# Reading Cookies for Use in Database Look-Up

Once a cookie is set we can use it in subsequent visits to link the visitor to our database. For example, we can use the ID to find out the sailor's state and then feature on the web page regattas proximal to that sailor.

## Sample Syntax to Use a Cookie for Database Look-up

Cookies are used to obtain specific information from a database by including them in a SQL statement WHERE clause. This is usually performed over two blocks of code, the first is to get the cookie into a variable, and the second is to use the contents of that variable in the WHERE clause of a SQL statement that gets data from the specific record of the visitor:

```
<%
  Dim varCookieHolder
  varCookieHolder=Request.Cookies("MyCookie")

  Dim oRecordSet
  Set oRecordSet = Server.CreateObject("ADODB.Recordset")
  sqltext = "SELECT * FROM MyTable WHERE RecordID=" & varCookieHolder
  oRecordSet.Open sqltext, "DSN=MyDataSource"

  Response.Write "Data from Table is " & oRecordSet("MyField")
%>
```

The most common problem here is failure of the SQL statement when the cookie's data is different from expectations. For example, since MyCookie data could hold an ID for a record that has been deleted, you should check that the resulting recordset has a record prior to trying to use it. An additional problem could be when there is no cookie in the request. This condition must be tested and resolved prior to running a SQL statement with an empty WHERE clause.

## Try It Out – Setting a Cookie Using ASP–ADO

Our objective is to set a cookie with the user's ID number, then use that to look up the visitor's yacht club code in the database, and display that information on the home page. To make this example simpler, we will assume the visitors know their membership number from their membership card.

Firstly, let us look at the overall strategy that we will use. The four steps we will follow are:

- ❑ Get the visitor's membership number on a form.

- ❑ Second, we set a cookie that holds the visitor's ID number from the `People` table.

- ❑ Third we can use the ID from the cookie to find their record in the table.

- ❑ Lastly, from the correct record we can show the person's yacht club code.

This will require three pages. The first is a `CookieSetterForm` page that gathers the visitor's ID. The second page, `CookieSetter`, actually sets the cookie and confirms that act to the user. The third page, `CookieHome`, uses the emerging cookie and ADO to derive the name of the visitor's yacht club code.

The first page, in file `2726-11-Cook-TIO-02-CookiesWithADOCookieSetterForm.asp` follows:

```
<%@ Language=VBScript %>
<HTML>
<HEAD>
<META NAME="GENERATOR" Content="Microsoft Visual Studio 6.0">
<TITLE>2726-11-TI-02 Cookies With ADO CookieSetterForm</TITLE>
</HEAD>
<BODY>

<H1>Welcome to the Sailors Site, But First...</H1>
<P>Please provide your membership number so we can set your cookie.</P>
<FORM ACTION="2726-11-Cook-TIO-02-CookiesWithADOCookieSetter.asp" METHOD=post>
Please type your membership number here
<INPUT NAME='PeopleID'>
<INPUT TYPE=submit VALUE="Submit">
</FORM>
</BODY>
</HTML>
```

Which gives this result:

The second page, `2726-11-Cook-TIO-02-CookiesWithADOCookieSetter.asp`, takes the data and uses it to set a cookie, as follows:

```
<%@ Language=VBScript %>
<%Response.Buffer=true%>
<HTML>
<HEAD>
<META NAME="GENERATOR" Content="Microsoft Visual Studio 6.0">
<TITLE>2726-11-TI-O2 Cookies With ADO CookieSetter</TITLE>
</HEAD>
<BODY>

<%
  varPeopleID = Request.Form("PeopleID")
'next line for testing
'Response.Write varpeopleID

  Response.Cookies("PeopleIDNumber")=varPeopleID
  Response.Cookies("PeopleIDNumber").Expires = Date + 366
%>
A cookie has been set with your membership ID number of <%=varPeopleID%><BR>
<A HREF="2726-11-Cook-TIO-02-CookiesWithADOCookieHome.asp">
Click here to return to the home page</A>
</BODY>
</HTML>
```

The above code gives the following result:

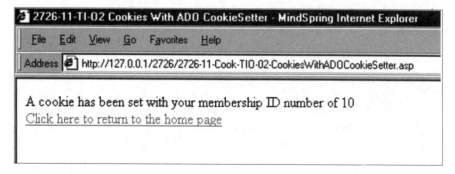

Then we finish by clicking back to the home page, whose code is in file `2726-11-Cook-TIO-02-CookiesWithADOCookieHome.asp` and below:

```
<%@ Language=VBScript %>
<HTML>
<HEAD>
<META NAME="GENERATOR" Content="Microsoft Visual Studio 6.0">
<TITLE>2726-11-TI-O2 Cookies With ADO Home</TITLE>
</HEAD>
<BODY>
<H1>Welcome to the Sailor's Home Site <BR><BR>
<%
  Dim oRS, varPeopleIDNumber
  varPeopleIDNumber = Request.Cookies("PeopleIDNumber")
  Set oRS=Server.CreateObject("ADODB.Recordset")
  sqltxt = "SELECT PeopleNameFirst, PeopleNameLast, PeopleClubCode"
  sqltxt = sqltxt & " FROM People "
  sqltxt = sqltxt & " WHERE PeopleID = " & varPeopleIDNumber & ";"
  oRS.Open sqltxt, "DSN=sailors"
```

```
  Response.Write oRS("PeopleNameFirst") & " "
  Response.Write oRS("PeopleNameLast")
%>
</H1>
Your yacht club code is <%=oRS("PeopleClubCode")%>
</BODY>
</HTML>
```

The above code produces the following screen:

### How it Works – Setting a Cookie Using ASP-ADO

The first page starts by informing the user that we need to set the cookie.

```
<%@ Language=VBScript %>
<HTML><HEAD>
<META NAME="GENERATOR" Content="Microsoft Visual Studio 6.0">
<TITLE>2726-11-TI-O2 Cookies With ADO CookieSetterForm</TITLE>
</HEAD><BODY>
<H1>Welcome to the Sailors Site, But First...</H1>
<P>Please provide your membership number so we can set your cookie.</P>
```

Continuing on the first page, we set up the form with a single text input field named PeopleID. The Submit button will direct the browser to pull up the CookieSetter page.

```
<FORM ACTION="2726-11-Cook-TIO-02-CookiesWithADOCookieSetter.asp" METHOD=post>
Please type your membership number here
<INPUT NAME='PeopleID'>
<INPUT TYPE=submit VALUE="Submit">
</FORM></BODY></HTML>
```

The second page takes the data and uses it to set a cookie. Of course, we want our cookie to persist beyond this session, so we set an expiry date.

```
<%@ Language=VBScript %>
<%Response.Buffer=true%>
...
<TITLE>2726-11-TI-O2 Cookies With ADO CookieSetter</TITLE>
</HEAD><BODY>

<%
  varPeopleID = Request.Form("PeopleID")
'Response.Write varpeopleID
```

```
    Response.Cookies("PeopleIDNumber")=varPeopleID
    Response.Cookies("PeopleIDNumber").Expires = Date + 366
%>
A cookie has been set with your membership ID number of <%=varPeopleID%><BR>
<A HREF="2726-11-Cook-TIO-02-CookiesWithADOCookieHome.asp">
Click here to return to the home page</A>
</BODY></HTML>
```

Now, in the home page, we can use ADO to use the cookie to look up a specific person's names and yacht club code. We start with the usual housekeeping, and then read the cookie from the Request object into a variable:

```
<TITLE>2726-11-TI-02 Cookies With ADO Home</TITLE>
</HEAD>
<BODY>
<H1>Welcome to the Sailor's Home Site <BR><BR>
<%
  Dim oRS, varPeopleIDNumber
  varPeopleIDNumber = Request.Cookies("PeopleIDNumber")
```

Then we create a SQL statement that has the cookie data in the WHERE clause, as in the lines below. Note that I have written a space both after People and before WHERE. That puts two spaces in the SQL statement when only one is needed. One of the most common student mistakes occurs when a space is left out of that position. I suggest that when students are building multi-line SQL statements they put a space both at the end of the FROM clause and the beginning of the WHERE clause. If, in the course of editing, one is removed, the statement will still have the other. SQL will never fail because of the extra space, so "better spaced than sorry".

```
    Set oRS=Server.CreateObject("ADODB.Recordset")
    sqltxt = "SELECT PeopleNameFirst, PeopleNameLast, PeopleClubCode"
    sqltxt = sqltxt & " FROM People "
    sqltxt = sqltxt & " WHERE PeopleID = " & varPeopleIDNumber & ";"
```

Finally, we use that SQL statement to open and read from a record set, as follows:

```
    oRS.Open sqltxt, "DSN=sailors"
    Response.Write oRS("PeopleNameFirst") & " "
    Response.Write oRS("PeopleNameLast")
%>
</H1>
Your yacht club code is <%=oRS("PeopleClubCode")%>
</BODY></HTML>
```

# Resetting a Cookie

There are two cases for setting a cookie. The first is that no cookie existed because the person was never registered, that is, they have no record in the database. But a frequent second type of case is that a person has a record in the People table but they have lost their cookie. This could be for many reasons, as discussed earlier in the chapter. In this case we want to reset a cookie.

In this second case, it is nice to give people a way to reset their cookie quickly and easily, without re-entering all of their information in the People table. In fact, we specifically want to avoid the latter since re-entering their data could easily lead to duplicate records for people.

In other words, we don't want to enter this person as a new record in the database like we would when first setting a cookie; rather we want to identify their existing record in the database and use that to set a cookie.

The solution to the second problem is to build a page that gives cookie-less visitors several options. Firstly, they could pick their name out of a drop-down list of names already in your `People` table. You can also give the visitor the option of visiting without a cookie. The third is that they can register, which will respond by both adding them as a record in the `People` table and setting a cookie on their hard drive. A fourth option is to ask the visitor to sign in at the beginning of each visit. The sign-in could be by name, member ID or a field like Email address. Although tedious, some visitors prefer signing in to setting a cookie.

You must also weigh up which options you want to offer in view of your security. In an Internet site, you would not want to reveal the names of all your visitors in a drop-down box. Likewise, with more than a few score members, you could not offer a drop-down list of names, and would have to gather the name by a text field and do a match with the database. But let us cover an example here for a departmental intranet with a few dozen users.

There are four pages or parts of pages that are needed for this process:

❑ First, our cookie-using home page must be modified to detect a missing cookie.

❑ Second, we must create a form for resetting a cookie, which offers a list of members.

❑ Third, we need a page that will set a cookie based on the selection in the above page.

❑ Last, when we reset a cookie, we will provide to the user a confirmation page.

## Try It Out – Resetting a Cookie

Our objective is to show on the home page the visitor's name and professional class, based on the person's ID stored as a cookie. We will do that by first reviewing the home page from the last Try It Out, which does not have a cookie check. Then we will modify that home page to check for cookies. If there is no cookie, then the visitor will be shunted to `ResetCookieForm.asp` and that leads to `ResetCookieResponse.asp`.

*One note on this exercise. In the course of this exercise you will probably want to delete a cookie for testing. After deleting the cookie it is best to re-start your browser.*

*You can delete a cookie by hand from IE by going to `C:\Windows\cookies`. It will probably be named `UserName@SiteName`. You can also sort by date and you will see your cookie as the most recently changed. In Netscape a cookie is located at:*
`c:\program files\netscape\users\<profile name>\cookies.txt`

The code for a typical home page that uses a cookie would look like:

```
<%@ Language=VBScript %>
<HTML><HEAD>
<META NAME="GENERATOR" Content="Microsoft Visual Studio 6.0">
<TITLE>2726-11-TI-O3 Reset Cookie Home Page No Check</TITLE>
</HEAD><BODY>
<H1>Welcome to the Sailor's Home Page</H1>
<P>(no cookie check)</P>
<%
  Dim varPeopleID
  Dim oRS
  varID=Request.Cookies("PeopleID")
  sqltxt = "SELECT PeopleNameLast, PeopleNameFirst, "
  sqltxt = sqltxt & "PeopleProfessionalClass FROM People "
  sqltxt = sqltxt & " WHERE PeopleID =" & varID & ";"
  Set oRS = Server.CreateObject("ADODB.Recordset")
  oRS.open sqltxt, "DSN=Sailors"

  Response.Write "Welcome " & oRS("PeopleNameFirst")
  Response.Write " " & oRS("PeopleNameLast") & "<BR>"
  Response.Write "<P>We have you registered as "
  Response.Write " of Professional Class "
  Response.Write oRS("PeopleProfessionalClass")
%>
</BODY></HTML>
```

And the above code (available as file `2726-11-Cook-TI-03-ResetCookieHomePageNoCheck.asp`) would produce the following page:

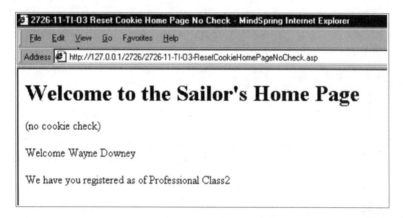

But when we consider that cookies may be unusable or unavailable we have to modify that home page to detect the absence of a cookie. If the cookie does not exist then the user is notified and asked to click to the Cookie Reset page, as follows. This code is available as file `2726-11-TI-03-ResetCookieHomePageWithCheck.asp`:

```
<HTML>
<HEAD>
<TITLE>2726-11-TI-O3 Reset Cookie Home Page With Check</TITLE>
</HEAD>

<BODY>
<%
  Dim varPeopleID, oRS
  varPeopleID=Request.Cookies("PeopleID")
  If varPeopleID = "" Then
```

```
   Response.Write "<H1>This is the Sailor's Home Page, but...</H1>"
   Response.Write  "<P>(failed cookie check)</P>"
   Response.Write "Sorry, we can not find your cookie<BR>"
   Response.Write "<A href='2726-11-TI-03-ResetCookieForm.asp'>"
   Response.Write "Please click here </A>to re-set your cookie"
  Else
   Response.Write "<H1>Welcome to the Sailor's Home Page</H1>"
   Response.Write  "<P>(passed cookie check)</P>"
   Set oRS = Server.CreateObject("ADODB.Recordset")
   sqltxt = "SELECT PeopleNameLast, PeopleNameFirst, "
   sqltxt = sqltxt & "PeopleProfessionalClass "
   sqltxt = sqltxt & " FROM People WHERE PeopleID=" & varPeopleID & ";"
   oRS.Open sqltxt, "DSN=Sailors"
   Response.Write "<P>We have you, " & oRS("PeopleNameFirst") & " "
   Response.Write oRS("PeopleNameLast") & ", "
   Response.Write "registered in Professional Class "
   Response.Write oRS("PeopleProfessionalClass") & "</P>"
  End If
%>
</BODY></HTML>
```

The above cookie-checking page gives the same result as the last page if a cookie is present, but if the cookie is missing, then we get the following:

The user would click to reset a new cookie, and would hit the following code, file `2726-11-TI-03-ResetCookieForm.asp`, to allow selection of the cookie to set:

```
<%@ Language=VBScript %>
<HTML><HEAD>
<META NAME="GENERATOR" Content="Microsoft Visual Studio 6.0">
<TITLE>2726-11-TI-03 Reset Cookie Form</TITLE>
</HEAD><BODY>
<H1>Reset Cookie</H1>
<P>Sorry, but we are having problems identifying you.</P>
<P>Please select your name from the list below</P>
<FORM ACTION="2726-11-TI-03-ResetCookieResponse.asp" METHOD=get>
<SELECT NAME="PeopleName">

<%
  Dim oRSPeople
  Set oRSPeople=Server.CreateObject("ADODB.Recordset")
  sqltxt = "Select PeopleNameLast, PeopleNameFirst from People"
  sqltxt = sqltxt & " ORDER BY PeopleNameLast;"
  oRSPeople.Open sqltxt, "DSN=Sailors"
  Do while not oRSPeople.EOF
    Response.Write "<OPTION NAME=>"
```

```
      Response.Write orsPeople("PeopleNameLast") & ", "
      Response.Write orsPeople("PeopleNameFirst") & "</OPTION>"
      oRSPeople.MoveNext
  Loop
%>
</SELECT>
<INPUT TYPE="Submit">
<INPUT TYPE="Reset">
</FORM></BODY></HTML>
```

Which produces the following page:

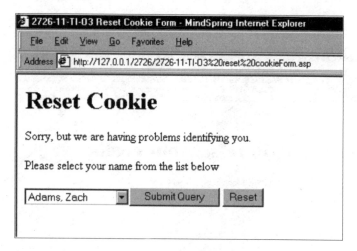

The form needs a response, which in this case actually sets the cookie, and we would confirm that by informing the user of setting a cookie and giving her a hyperlink back to the home page, where she can use the new cookie. The code for this page is taken from 2726-11-TI-03-ResetCookieResponse.asp and is listed below:

```
<%@ Language=VBScript%>
<%Response.Buffer = true%>
<HTML>
<HEAD>
<META NAME="GENERATOR" Content="Microsoft Visual Studio 6.0">
<TITLE>2726-11-TI-03 Reset Cookie Response</TITLE>
</HEAD>
<BODY>

<P> </P>
<H1>This page will re-set your cookie </H1>
<%
  varPeopleNameTotal = Request.Querystring("PeopleName")
  varPeopleNameLast = left(varPeopleNameTotal,instr(varPeopleNameTotal, ",")-1)
  varPeopleNameFirst = right(varPeopleNameTotal,len(varPeopleNameTotal)- _
                       instr(varPeopleNameTotal, ",")-1)

  Dim oRSPeopleIDLookUp
  Set oRSPeopleIDLookUp=Server.CreateObject("ADODB.Recordset")

  sqltxt = "Select PeopleID from People"
  sqltxt = sqltxt & " WHERE PeopleNameLast = '" & varpeoplenamelast & "'"
  sqltxt = sqltxt & " AND PeopleNameFirst = '" & varpeoplenamefirst & "';"
  oRSPeopleIDLookUp.Open sqltxt, "DSN=Sailors"
```

```
    Response.Cookies("PeopleID") = oRSPeopleIDLookUp("PeopleID")
    Response.Cookies("PeopleID").Expires = date + 365
%>
We have re-set your cookie, the identification is now for:<BR><BR>
<%=varPeopleNameFirst%> <%=varPeopleNameLast%>
with the ID number <%=oRSPeopleIDLookUp("PeopleID")%>
<BR><BR>Click here to re-try
<A HREF="2726-11-TI-03-ResetCookieHomePageWithCheck.asp">
homepage</A>
with your new cookie
</BODY>
</HTML>
```

Which gives the user the following page, reporting back to the user that the cookie has been set.

### How It Works – Resetting a Cookie

The home page in its original form could not handle visitors without a cookie. The following code would put a blank into varPeopleID. That causes a logical failure, but not an ASP error since VBScript accepts putting "nothing" into a variable.

```
<TITLE>2726-11-TI-03 Reset Cookie Home Page No Check</TITLE>
...
varID=Request.Cookies("PeopleID")
```

However, the following code would fail because SQL will not accept a null value for the expression of the WHERE clause.

```
sqltxt = "SELECT PeopleNameLast, PeopleNameFirst, "
sqltxt = sqltxt & "PeopleProfessionalClass FROM People "
sqltxt = sqltxt & " WHERE PeopleID =" & varID & ";"
set oRS = Server.CreateObject("ADODB.Recordset")
oRS.open sqltxt, "DSN=Sailors"
```

So we use the code of the improved page, which has an If to determine if the cookie is empty:

```
<TITLE>2726-11-TI-03 Reset Cookie Home Page With Check</TITLE>
...
Dim varPeopleID, oRS
varPeopleID=Request.Cookies("PeopleID")
If varPeopleID = "" Then
```

In the following code we determine if the cookie is empty, and if so give the "Sorry but … " message with a hyperlink to a form to reset the cookie (2726-11-TI-03-ResetCookieForm.asp). After getting this to work, you may consider changing the code to automatically redirect the user using Response.Buffer=true and Response.Redirect. However, I find that students understand the concepts better on their first try by clicking through the pages.

```
Response.Write "<H1>This is the Sailor's Home Page, but...</H1>"
Response.Write  "<P>(failed cookie check)</P>"
Response.Write "Sorry, we can not find your cookie<BR>"
Response.Write "<A HREF='2726-11-TI-03-ResetCookieForm.asp'>"
Response.Write "Please click here </A>to reset your cookie"
```

If the cookie exists we perform the following code to get the name and professional class of the visitor from the database. Note that we use the cookie as the expression of the WHERE clause in the SQL statement. Since the PersonID is a number, we do not concatenate quotes around the variable in the last line below:

```
Else
  Response.Write "<H1>Welcome to the Sailor's Home Page</H1>"
  Response.Write  "<P>(passed cookie check)</P>"
  Set oRS = Server.CreateObject("ADODB.Recordset")
  sqltxt = "SELECT PeopleNameLast, PeopleNameFirst, "
  sqltxt = sqltxt & "PeopleProfessionalClass "
  sqltxt = sqltxt & " FROM People WHERE PeopleID=" & varPeopleID & ";"
```

Then we can write the text of the home page using data from the recordset:

```
  oRS.open sqltxt, "DSN=Sailors"
  Response.Write "<P>We have you, " & oRS("PeopleNameFirst") & " "
  Response.Write oRS("PeopleNameLast") & ", "
  Response.Write "registered in Professional Class "
  Response.Write oRS("PeopleProfessionalClass") & "</P>"
End If
%>
```

But let us get back to the path of visitors without a cookie. They got the "Sorry but…" message on the home page and click to come to 2726-11-TI-03-ResetCookieForm.asp. Our objective is to set up a list of the available names from which to choose. The first part of that code, below, creates a form and a list box using the <SELECT> tag.

```
<TITLE>2726-11-TI-03 Reset Cookie Form</TITLE>

<FORM ACTION="2726-11-TI-03-ResetCookieResponse.asp" METHOD=get>
<SELECT NAME="PeopleName">
```

Then we create a recordset of the members so we can put them into a list box:

```
<%
  Dim oRSPeople
  Set oRSPeople=Server.CreateObject("ADODB.Recordset")
  sqltxt = "Select PeopleNameLast, PeopleNameFirst from People"
  sqltxt = sqltxt & " ORDER BY PeopleNameLast;"
  oRSPeople.Open sqltxt, "DSN=Sailors"
```

Then we actually populate the list box by looping through that recordset creating an `<OPTION>` tag for each member. As always, be sure to include the `RS.MoveNext` in the loop.

```
Do while not oRSPeople.EOF
  Response.Write "<OPTION NAME= >"
  Response.Write orsPeople("PeopleNameLast") & ", "
  Response.Write orsPeople("PeopleNameFirst") & "</OPTION>"
  oRSPeople.MoveNext
Loop
%>
</SELECT>
```

After the user has made a selection, the `Action` of the `FORM` tag rolls us to `2726-11-TI-03-ResetCookieResponse.asp`. Since we will be setting a cookie we must start by turning on the response buffer:

```
<%@ Language=VBScript%>
<%Response.Buffer = true%>
<HTML>
<HEAD>
<META NAME="GENERATOR" Content="Microsoft Visual Studio 6.0">
<TITLE>2726-11-TI-03 Reset Cookie Response</TITLE>
```

Our incoming data is the name of the member selected from the list box, in the form of last name, and comma, and the first name. We need to not only harvest that data from the querystring, but also parse apart the first and last names so we can compare the names with the database and extract the person ID. Our clue to separating the names is the comma. The third line below puts into the last name variable all of the text to the left of the comma:

```
<%
  varPeopleNameTotal = Request.Querystring("PeopleName")
  varPeopleNameLast = left(varPeopleNameTotal,instr(varPeopleNameTotal, ",")-1)
```

The line below puts the first name into a variable:

```
varPeopleNameFirst = right(varPeopleNameTotal,len(varPeopleNameTotal)- _
                          instr(varPeopleNameTotal, ",")-1)
```

Now we can create a recordset that selects out the one record matching the first and last names. Note that we are applying two tests in the `WHERE` clause; one for the last name and one for the first name.

```
Dim oRSPeopleIDLookUp
Set oRSPeopleIDLookUp=Server.CreateObject("ADODB.Recordset")

sqltxt = "Select PeopleID from People"
sqltxt = sqltxt & " WHERE PeopleNameLast = '" & varpeoplenamelast & "'"
sqltxt = sqltxt & " AND PeopleNameFirst = '" & varpeoplenamefirst & "';"
oRSPeopleIDLookUp.Open sqltxt, "DSN=Sailors"
```

We can now use the `PeopleID` data, from the one correct record sitting in the recordset, to write a cookie.

```
  Response.Cookies("PeopleID") = oRSPeopleIDLookUp("PeopleID")
  Response.Cookies("PeopleID").Expires = date + 365
%>
```

Lastly, we wrap up with some notices to the user about what we have done:

```
We have reset your cookie, the identification is now for:<BR><BR>
<%=varPeopleNameFirst%> <%=varPeopleNameLast%>
with the ID number <%=oRSPeopleIDLookUp("PeopleID")%>
<BR><BR>Click here to re-try
<A HREF="2726-11-TI-O3-ResetCookieHomePageWithCheck.asp">
homepage</A>
with your new cookie
</BODY></HTML>
```

# Summary

Cookies allow a site programmer to overcome one of the major problems of the Internet – the lack of identification of visitors. However, cookies are only usable with the approval of the visitor. Programmers must write code that will compensate for unusable or non-existent cookies.

Cookies are ideal for holding information about how a page should be presented. For example, data such as a zip code can be applied, with ADO, to a database, in order to build a page optimized for the visitor's neighborhood. In this technique, frequently used data is stored directly in the cookie.

An alternative approach is to hold only an ID number in the cookie. That datum is then used to select the visitor's record from all those in a database. From that record, information can be extracted about the visitor for use in the site. That data can be used to customize pages for the visitor.

# Exercises

These exercises use one or both of the two sample databases available from the Wrox website. The structures of the databases are described in Appendix A for Sailors.mdb and Appendix B for Clothier.mdb.

**1.** Some visitors to the Clothier site prefer to see the items listed alphabetically by type (hat, shirt, etc.), other visitors prefer ordering by department (Men's Sportswear, Women's Formals). Create a way for visitors to set a preference, and then create a products page that lists items in a table in the preferred order.

**2.** Build on the above exercise. Within the grouping of type or department, allow the visitor to set a preference of ordering by price, either increasing or decreasing.

# Exercise Answers (with Annotation)

**1.** There will be three pages. First we allow the user to specify his preferences in a form. Note that the NAME of the two radio buttons is the same, while the VALUE is different.

The code for this page is in file 2726-11-Cook-Exr01-SetPreferenceForm.htm:

```
<HTML>
<HEAD>
<META NAME="GENERATOR" Content="Microsoft Visual Studio 6.0">
<TITLE>Chapter 11 Exercise 01 Set Preference Form</TITLE>
</HEAD>
<BODY>

<H1> Set Preferences Page</H1>
<P><P>Please select your preference in ordering the clothing items.</P></P>

<FORM ACTION="2726-11-Cook-Exr01-SetPreferenceResponse.asp" METHOD=get>
<INPUT TYPE="radio" NAME="Group" VALUE="type" CHECKED> Group by Type of Item (hat,
jacket, pants)<BR><BR>
<INPUT TYPE="radio" NAME="Group" VALUE="dept"> Group by Department (Juniors, Men's
Formals)<BR><BR>
<INPUT TYPE="Submit">
<INPUT TYPE="Reset">
</FORM>
</BODY>
</HTML>
```

Then we pick up that preference and use it to set a cookie as below, in file 2726-11-Cook-Exr01-SetPreferenceResponse.asp.

```
<%@ Language=VBScript %>
<%Response.Buffer=true%>
<HTML>
<HEAD>
<META NAME="GENERATOR" Content="Microsoft Visual Studio 6.0">
<TITLE>Chapter 11 Exercise 01 Set Preference Response</TITLE>
</HEAD>
<BODY>
<%
  Dim varGroup
  varGroup = Request.Querystring("Group")
  Response.Write ' Next line for testing
' Response.Write varGroup
  Response.Cookies("Group") = varGroup
  Response.Cookies("Group").Expires = date + 365
%>
<P>A notation has been made for you that you prefer your items grouped by
<%
  Select Case varGroup
  Case "type"
    Response.Write " the <i>type</i> of the item."
  Case "dept"
    Response.Write " the <i>department</i> of the item."
  End Select
%>
</P>

<P><A HREF="2726-11-Cook-Exr01-SetPreferenceHome.asp">
Click Here to go to Home page and use your newly-set preference.</A></P>
</BODY>
</HTML>
```

And last we use that cookie to set the ORDER BY clause of the SQL statement that provides the recordset for the table. Whereas the last page received text from a form, which required stripping the quotes, this page receives information from a cookie which arrives without quotes. The code is in file 2726-11-Cook-Exr01-SetPreferenceHome.asp:

```
<%@ Language=VBScript %>
<HTML>
<HEAD>
<META NAME="GENERATOR" Content="Microsoft Visual Studio 6.0">
</HEAD>
<BODY>

<H1>Our Items</H1>
Arranged as per your preference in your cookie.

<%
  Dim oRS, sqltxt, varGroup
  varGroup = Request.Cookies("Group")

  sqltxt = "SELECT * FROM Items "
  Select Case varGroup
    Case "type"
      sqltxt = sqltxt & " ORDER BY ItemType;"
    Case "dept"
      sqltxt = sqltxt & " ORDER BY ItemDepartment;"
  End Select
'Response.Write "<BR>" & sqltxt & "<BR>"

%>
<TABLE BORDER=1>
<TH>ID Number</TH><TH>Name</TH>
<TH>Department</TH><TH>Type</TH>
<TH>Price  to Buy</TH><TH>Vendor Code</TH>
<TH>Qty per box</TH><TH>Date of Release</TH>
<TR><TD>
<%
  Set oRS=Server.CreateObject("ADODB.Recordset")
  oRS.Open sqltxt, "DSN=clothier"
  Response.Write oRS.GetString (,,"<TR><TD>","</TD></TR><TR><TD>"," ")
%>
</TD></TR></TABLE>
</BODY>
</HTML>
```

**2.**  Rather than modify (and lose) your answer to Exercise 1, I suggest you copy your pages with a new name. Don't forget to change:

❑  The names of your pages to include "Exercise 2"

❑  The ACTION of your form

❑  The reference of your hyperlinks

❑  Your cookie name, so there is no interference with Exercise 1

As with exercise one, we need three pages. However, this time we need to set two data items into the cookie, so we will be using keys within the cookie.

The first page, 2726-11-Cook-Exr02-SetPreferenceForm.htm, gets the preferences from the user. Note that the two sets of radio buttons have different NAMEs.

```
<HTML>
<HEAD>
<META NAME="GENERATOR" Content="Microsoft Visual Studio 6.0">
<TITLE>Chapter 11 Exercise 01 Set Preference Form</TITLE>
</HEAD>
<BODY>

<H1> Set Preferences Page</H1>
<P><P>Please select your preference in ordering the clothing items.</P></P>

<FORM ACTION="2726-11-Cook-Exr02-SetPreferenceResponse.asp" METHOD=get>
<INPUT TYPE="radio" NAME="Group" VALUE="type" CHECKED> Group by Type of Item<BR><BR>
<INPUT TYPE="radio" NAME="Group" VALUE="dept"> Group by Department<BR><BR>
<HR>
<INPUT TYPE="radio" NAME="PriceOrder" VALUE="Asc"> Within Groups, Order by ascending
price<BR><BR>
<INPUT TYPE="radio" NAME="PriceOrder" VALUE="Des" CHECKED> Within Groups, Order by
descending price<BR><BR>
<INPUT TYPE="Submit">
<INPUT TYPE="Reset">
</FORM>
</BODY>
</HTML>
```

Next we gather those preferences and use them to set the data into keys of a cookie. In order to avoid conflicts with exercise one, we will use a different cookie name. A hyperlink at the bottom of the page leads the visitor back to the home page. The code is available in file 2726-11-Cook-Exr02-SetPreferenceResponse.asp:

```
<%@ Language=VBScript %>
<%Response.Buffer=true%>
<HTML>
<HEAD>
<META NAME="GENERATOR" Content="Microsoft Visual Studio 6.0">
<TITLE>Chapter 11 Exercise 01 Set Preference Response</TITLE>
</HEAD>
<BODY>
<%
  Dim varGroup, varPriceOrder
  varGroup = Request.querystring("Group")
  varPriceOrder = Request.querystring("PriceOrder")

  Response.Cookies("Clothier")("Group") = varGroup
  Response.Cookies("Clothier")("PriceOrder") = varPriceOrder
  Response.Cookies("Clothier").Expires = date + 365
%>
<P>A notation has been made for you<BR><BR>
that you prefer your items grouped by<BR><BR>
<%
  Select Case varGroup
  Case "type"
    Response.Write " the <i>type</i> of the item, "
  Case "dept"
    Response.Write " the <i>department</i> of the item, "
  End Select

  Response.Write "<BR><BR>and within the group ordered by price from "
  Select Case varPriceOrder
  Case "Asc"
    Response.Write "<i>lowest to highest</i>."
  Case "Des"
    Response.Write "<i>highest to lowest</i>."
  End Select
```

```
%>
</P>

<P><A HREF="2726-11-Cook-Exr02-SetPreferenceHome.asp">
Click Here to go to Home page and use your newly-set preference.</A></P>
</BODY>
</HTML>
```

Now we can use both of the preferences in the home page, `2726-11-Cook-Exr02-SetPreferenceHome.asp`:

```
<%@ Language=VBScript %>
<HTML>
<HEAD>
<META NAME="GENERATOR" Content="Microsoft Visual Studio 6.0">
</HEAD>
<BODY>

<H1>Our Items</H1>
Arranged as per your preference in your cookie.

<%
  Dim oRS, sqltxt, varGroup, varPriceOrder
  varGroup = Request.Cookies("Clothier")("Group")
  varPriceOrder = Request.Cookies("Clothier")("PriceOrder")
'Response.Write "hello" & varGroup & " " & varPriceOrder

  sqltxt = "SELECT * FROM Items "
  Select Case varGroup
    Case "type"
      sqltxt = sqltxt & " ORDER BY ItemType"
    Case "dept"
      sqltxt = sqltxt & " ORDER BY ItemDepartment"
  End Select

  Select Case varPriceOrder
    Case "Asc"
      sqltxt = sqltxt & ",ItemPriceBuy;"
    Case "Des"
      sqltxt = sqltxt & ",ItemPriceBuy DESC;"
  End Select

'Response.Write "<BR>" & sqltxt & "<BR>"

%>
<TABLE BORDER=1>
<TH>ID Number</TH><TH>Name</TH>
<TH>Department</TH><TH>Type</TH>
<TH>Price  to Buy</TH><TH>Vendor Code</TH>
<TH>Qty per box</TH><TH>Date of Release</TH>
<TR><TD>
<%
  Set oRS=Server.CreateObject("ADODB.Recordset")
  oRS.Open sqltxt, "DSN=clothier"
  Response.Write oRS.GetString (,,"</TD><TD>","</TD></TR><TR><TD>"," ")
%>
</TD></TR></TABLE>
</BODY>
</HTML>
```

# Quiz

**1.** Which object is used to get the contents of a cookie?

**2.** Which object is used to create a cookie?

**3.** Cookies can contain multiple keys. Which of the following can be different and which must be the same: Key name, Key data, Key expiration date?

**4.** When using ASP solutions, which of the following pages must have an ASP extension and which can be HTML?
Page that uses a cookie
Form to get data for cookie
Response page to write the cookie
Confirmation page that reads the cookie

**5.** Name several ways in which a programming strategy that relies on cookies can fail.

**6.** Which of the following criteria favor holding data in cookies rather then in a server-side database?
Speed to load page
Security
Large amounts of data
Data which is used on every page

**7.** Consider the types of failures that can occur when using cookies and list solutions that should be coded by the programmer.

**8.** Programmers frequently use an ID number in a cookie and use it to look up a specific record by using the cookie in the WHERE clause of opening a recordset. Assuming the following first line works, why will the second line fail?

```
iPeopleID = Request.Form("PeopleID")
SELECT PeopleName, FROM People WHERE PeopleID = '" & iPeopleID & "';
```

# Quiz Answers

**1.** Request.

**2.** Response.

**3.** Each key has its own name and data, but all the keys of one cookie have the same expiration date.

**4.** A page that uses the cookie must use ASP to access the Request object.
A form page does not need ASP, only the HTML form tags.
A response page needs ASP to pick up the results of the form from the Request object and to write the cookie using the Response object.
A confirmation page would use ASP to read the cookie out of the Request object, and then to set up a recordset with the cookie data in the WHERE clause.

**5.** The visitor moves from machine to machine.
Hard drive is replaced.
Different users work from the same PC.
A firewall prevents the setting of cookies.

**6.** Pages load faster using data in cookies rather than a database look-up.
Data is more secure in a database than in a cookie.
Databases can hold vastly more data and in a better organization, than cookies.
Frequently used data, such as an identifier of a person's group or viewing preference, is more effectively stored in cookies.

**7.** *Cookie does not exist.*
Code must redirect the user to pages to register a cookie.
Or a cookie-less version of pages should be available.
*Record in database no longer exists which matches the cookie.*
Code must check for a returned recordset which is empty.
*Cookie data from an old database is unusable in a new database.*
Cookie must be reformatted or parsed to be usable in new schema.

**8.** In SQL statements numeric data should not be in quotes. The following will work.

```
iPeopleID = Request.Form("PeopleID")
sqltxt = "SELECT PeopleName FROM People WHERE PeopleID = " & iPeopleID & ";
```

Setup cannot install system files or update shared files if the files are in use. Before c
any open applications.

WARNING: This program is protected by copyright law and international treaties.

You may install Microsoft Data Access 2.1 on a single computer. Some Microsoft products
with additional rights, which are stated in the End User License Agreement included with yo

Please take a moment to read the End User License Agreement now. It contains all of the ter
conditions that pertain to this software product. By choosing to continue, you indicate accepta
these terms.

Exit Setup

Continue

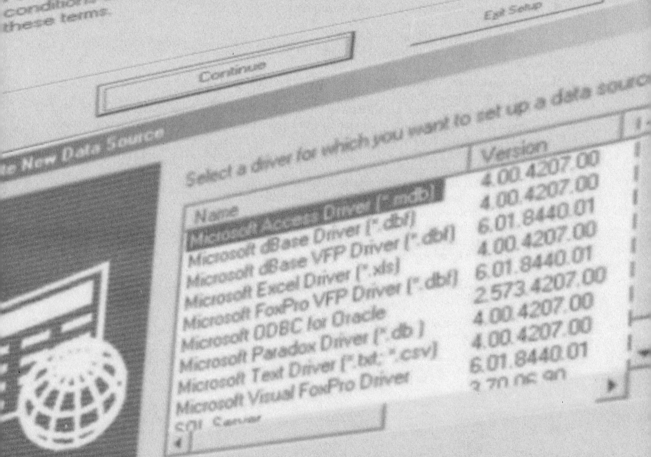

New Data Source

Select a driver for which you want to set up a data sourc

| Name | Version |
|---|---|
| Microsoft Access Driver (*.mdb) | 4.00.4207.00 |
| Microsoft dBase Driver (*.dbf) | 4.00.4207.00 |
| Microsoft dBase VFP Driver (*.dbf) | 6.01.8440.01 |
| Microsoft Excel Driver (*.xls) | 4.00.4207.00 |
| Microsoft FoxPro VFP Driver (*.dbf) | 6.01.8440.01 |
| Microsoft ODBC for Oracle | 2.573.4207.00 |
| Microsoft Paradox Driver (*.db ) | 4.00.4207.00 |
| Microsoft Text Driver (*.txt; *.csv) | 4.00.4207.00 |
| Microsoft Visual FoxPro Driver | 6.01.8440.01 |
| SQL Server | 3.70.06.90 |

Finish          Cancel

# The Errors Collection

Error handling is an important part of building applications. You need to be able to gracefully handle the *expected* errors, and have a mechanism for handling the *unexpected* ones. This allows you to control the flow of your code when an error occurs, providing the end user with more meaningful error messages and recommended actions to take.

If you have ever worked with the Visual Basic Error object, you know how robust it can be, and the benefits it provides when trapping and displaying errors. The current version of ASP has virtually no error handling and what error handling that is available is provided by the scripting language in use, which in our case is VBScript. VBScript error handling is very limited, providing only an 'On Error Resume Next' statement and limited methods and properties. Fortunately for us, the Visual Basic Scripting language is fairly simple compared to Visual Basic and Visual Basic for Applications. We'll be taking a look at the VBScript Error object shortly.

> *The limitation of ASP error handling has been removed in IIS 5.0, which includes a more complete error object built right into the ASP object, similar to Visual Basic. However, since IIS 5.0 is not widely used at this time, we will concentrate our efforts on dealing with IIS 4.0.*

We will also cover the ADO Errors collection and demonstrate how to trap and handle errors received from ADO. The errors received in this collection are not actually from ADO itself, but are passed to ADO from the specific database driver you are using. For example: If you are accessing a Microsoft Access database, you will probably be using a Microsoft Access driver, which will pass any errors back to ADO, which in turn will pass all errors received back to you. How this works will be explained later. ADO errors, which are related to such items as invalid use of ADO method or properties, do not show up in the Errors collection but instead show up in the VB Script Error object.

In this chapter we will cover the following topics:

- ❑ Why error handling is important
- ❑ How to get error information
- ❑ Using error information during development
- ❑ Using error information after development
- ❑ Common Errors
- ❑ ASP Help

# Introduction

This section introduces you to the ASP and ADO error objects. We will demonstrate some practical examples on error handling, and show you how to determine the difference between **real errors** and **validation errors**. We will also take a look at the difference between **development errors** versus **production errors**, otherwise known as syntax versus data errors. By the end of this section you should have a good understanding of the difference between ASP and ADO errors.

## Why Using Error Handling Is Important

Error handling is essential in that we want to shield our users from potentially confusing and/or meaningless error messages. For instance, if we were to pass all the errors generated by ADO directly to the web page, we might see the following error:

```
Number: 0
Description: [Microsoft][ODBC SQL Server Driver][SQL Server]Warning, null value
eliminated from aggregate.
Source: Microsoft OLE DB Provider for ODBC Drivers
```

This however is not really an error that you care about, or wish the client to see. This error is caused because some rows of the recordset contain nulls – however the recordset will be returned as normal and the rest of the page will be built.

Handling all errors and checking these errors in the development environment will help to ensure a successful implementation of your application in production. You as the developer must determine which errors are valid and which errors are not, during the development life cycle.

## The Errors Collection and the ASP Object Model

As we mentioned earlier, the ASP object model does not support error handling - this is handled by the built-in **error object** of the scripting language, in this case VB Script. This `Error` object is very limited in that it only supports the 'On Error Resume Next' statement. The table below lists the properties and methods of this `Error` object.

| Properties | Description |
| --- | --- |
| Number | Contains the error number. This is a read and write property. |
| Description | Contains the error message. This is a read and write property. |
| Source | Contains the source of the error. This is a read and write property. |
| HelpFile | Contains a fully qualified path and name of the help file. |
| HelpContext | Contains the context id of the help topic in the help file. |
| Clear | Clears the `Error` object of all information. |
| Raise | Raises a custom error. You supply the number, description and source properties. |

You can use the `Raise` method to raise your own custom errors and the `Clear` method to clear any pre-existing errors. Suppose you had a routine that performed edit checks on the fields on the form. You could set various error messages and error numbers within that routine and raise the appropriate error to display to the user. We'll see how to use the `Clear` method in later examples.

Suppose you had a calculation that is to be performed using variables in your code. Let's say that one of the variables contains a zero. With error handling in place you would receive the following error:

```
Number: 11
Description: Division by zero,
Source: Microsoft VBScript runtime error
```

## Try It Out – Trap an Error and Clear It

Create a page that traps and checks for errors and displays those errors on the web page. Once an error has been detected and reported on the web page, you should clear the error.

Create a web page with the following code – you can find this source in the file `TryItOut1.asp`.

```
<HTML>
<HEAD>
<META NAME="GENERATOR" Content="Microsoft Visual Studio 6.0">
<TITLE>Try It Out #1</TITLE>
</HEAD>
<BODY>

<!--Display the page data-->
Try It Out #1 - Trap an Error and Clear It<BR><BR>

<%
'Instruct VBScript to ignore the error and continue
'with the next line of code
On Error Resume Next

'Declare the variables
Dim intX
Dim intY
Dim intResult

'Set the variables
intX = 10
intY = 0

'Perform the calculation
intResult = intX / intY

'Check for errors
If err.Number <> 0 Then
  'Write the errors
  Response.Write "Number: " & err.Number & "<P>"
  Response.Write "Description: " & err.Description & "<P>"
  Response.Write "Source: " & err.Source & "<P>"
  'Clear the error
  err.Clear
End If
%>
</BODY>
</HTML>
```

The output of the page should look like this:

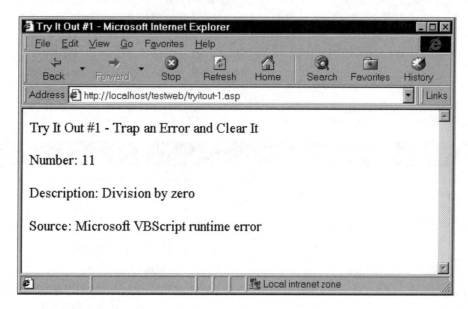

### How It Works – Trap an Error and Clear It

The first line of code contains an HTML comment and the second writes the data to be displayed on the page. After the text we use a couple of BR tags to give us a line break after the text and to insert a blank line.

```
<!--Display the page data-->
Try It Out #1 - Trap an Error and Clear It<BR><BR>
```

Next, we start our server side script with a comment about what the next line of code is going to do. Here we are telling VBScript to ignore any errors it encounters and execute the next line of code. Then we declare (with Dim statements) our variables that we are going to be using.

> *Remember, we do not have to declare our variables in VBScript as we have not used the Option Explicit statement. However, we declare them to make the code easier to follow, because we now know where the variables came from and when they entered the scope.*

```
'Instruct VBScript to ignore the error and continue
'with the next line of code
On Error Resume Next

'Declare the variables
Dim intX
Dim intY
Dim intResult
```

> Note: The On Error Resume Next is the only On Error statement available in VBScript.

We set the values of the variables that we just declared.

```
'Set the variables
intX = 10
intY = 0
```

We perform our calculation and then immediately check for an error. We do this by checking to see if the Error object contains an error number other than zero. If the error number of the Error object is not equal to zero then an error has occurred and we want to display the error information on the web page using Response.Write.

After we have written all of the error information we then want to clear the error object so we don't mistakenly check the same error condition later on in our code.

```
'Perform the calculation
intResult = intX / intY

'Check for errors
If err.Number <> 0 Then
  'Write the errors
  Response.Write "Number: " & err.Number & "<P>"
  Response.Write "Description: " & err.Description & "<P>"
  Response.Write "Source: " & err.Source & "<P>"
  'Clear the error
  err.Clear
End If
%>
```

Now it is up to you as the developer to determine whether or not to report this error to the user, as shown above, or to give the user a more polite response such as:

Calculation could not be performed due to an invalid value

We can change the message that is displayed by setting up a select case statement within the error handling code, as shown below.

```
If err.Number <> 0 Then
  'Determine what the error is
  Select Case err.Number
  Case 11
    Response.Write "Calculation could not be performed " & _
                   "due to an invalid value"
  Case Else
    Response.Write "An Unknown error has occurred " & _
                   "and the calculation could not be performed"
  End Select
  'Clear the error
  err.Clear
End If
```

We check for the error numbers that we expect, in this case only one error, number 11. (Remember from our earlier example that error 11 is for a division by zero.) We then display the appropriate messages. The Case Else statement handles the error numbers that we have not explicitly checked for and displays a generic message.

**439**

Ideally, you would protect your code from these types of errors by validating the data that is coming in. For instance, in the example above, we would check to be sure that value of intY is other than zero before attempting to divide by that number.

# VBScript vs ADO Errors

While the VBScript Error object provides a limited set of methods and properties, ADO provides a complete errors collection. When an error occurs during the execution of a command, one or more errors are placed in the **ADO errors collection**. The Errors collection properties and methods are listed in the table below.

| Properties | Description |
| --- | --- |
| Count | Contains the number of errors in the collection. |
| Item | Returns a specific error from the collection by name or ordinal number. |

| Methods | Description |
| --- | --- |
| Clear | Removes all error objects in the collection. |
| Refresh | Updates the error objects with information from the provider. |

The Error object itself contains the following properties:

| Properties | Description |
| --- | --- |
| Number | Contains the error number. |
| Description | Contains the error message. |
| Source | Contains the object name or application that generated the error. |
| SQLState | A five-character string containing the SQL state for a given error object. |
| NativeError | Contains the database specific error information. |
| HelpFile | A fully qualified help file name if available |
| HelpContext | A long value containing the help topic if available. |

The ADO errors collection is actually part of the ADO Connection object, which is shown in the diagram below:

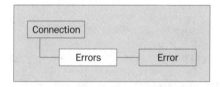

Notice that `Connection` and `Error` are actual objects while `Errors` is actually a collection of the `Error` objects. That is to say that the `Errors` collection contains one or more `Error` objects. When a database error occurs, the **Error** is placed in the `Errors` collection of the `Connection` object. So what do you do if you've been using a `Recordset` object without an explicit `Connection` object? As we mentioned in Chapter 6, when you open a connection to the database using a `Recordset` object, a `Connection` object is actually created behind the scenes. Therefore, you can access the `Errors` collection through the recordset's ActiveConnection property. To get the number of the first Error object in the Errors collection you could do the following:

```
oRS.ActiveConnection.Errors(0).Number
```

# Development Errors vs Production Errors

Development errors are usually keying errors that can be caught during testing, such as typing a query name or stored procedure name that does not exist, or a select statement with a field name that does not exist. Keying errors will probably account for 80% of your errors, so this is always the first place to check when an error occurs. The other 20% usually pertain to access permissions or invalid or missing parameters. Production errors usually involve corrupt or missing data.

## Try It Out – Cause an ADO Query Error

Create a page that runs the qDemoQueryGrid query in the Sailors database. Intentionally misspell the query name so an error occurs.

Create a new web page using the code below. You can find this example code in `TryItOut2.asp`.

```
<HTML>
<HEAD>
<META NAME="GENERATOR" Content="Microsoft Visual Studio 6.0">
<TITLE></TITLE>
</HEAD>
<BODY>

<!--Display the page data-->
Try It Out #2 -Cause an ADO Query Error<BR><BR>

<%
'Instruct VBScript to ignore the error and continue
'with the next line of code
On Error Resume Next

'Create and open the connection object
Set objConn = Server.CreateObject("ADODB.Connection")
objConn.Open "DSN=Sailors"

'Check for errors
If objConn.Errors.Count > 0 Then
  'Create an error object to access the ADO errors collection
  Set objErr = Server.CreateObject("ADODB.Error")
  'Declare boolean flag for critical errors
  Dim blnCriticalError
  'Write all errors to the page
  For Each objErr In objConn.Errors
```

```
      If objErr.Number <> 0 Then
        Response.Write "Number: " & objErr.Number & "<P>"
        Response.Write "Description: " & objErr.Description & "<P>"
        Response.Write "Source: " & objErr.Source & "<P>"
        Response.Write "SQLState: " & objErr.SQLState & "<P>"
        Response.Write "NativeError: " & objErr.NativeError & "<P>"
        blnCriticalError = True
      End If
    Next
    'Dereference all objects
    Set objErr = Nothing
    If blnCriticalError Then
      Response.End
    End If
End If

'Declare variables and set their values
Dim adOpenForwardOnly
Dim adCmdStoredProc
adOpenForwardOnly = 0
adCmdStoredProc = 4

  'Create the recordset object and open the recordset
Set objRS = Server.CreateObject("ADODB.Recordset")
strSQL = "DemoQueryGrid"
objRS.Open strSQL, objConn, adOpenForwardOnly, , adCmdStoredProc

'Check for errors
If objConn.Errors.Count > 0 Then
  'Create an error object to access the ADO errors collection
  Set objErr = Server.CreateObject("ADODB.Error")
  'Write all errors to the page
  For Each objErr In objConn.Errors
    If objErr.Number <> 0 Then
      Response.Write "Number: " & objErr.Number & "<P>"
      Response.Write "Description: " & objErr.Description & "<P>"
      Response.Write "Source: " & objErr.Source & "<P>"
      Response.Write "SQLState: " & objErr.SQLState & "<P>"
      Response.Write "NativeError: " & objErr.NativeError & "<P>"
      blnCriticalError = True
    End If
  Next
  'Dereference all objects
  Set objErr = Nothing
  If blnCriticalError Then
    Response.End
  End If
End If

'Loop through the recordset displaying the last name field
Do While Not objRS.EOF
  Response.Write objRS("PeopleNameLast") & "<P>"
  objRS.MoveNext
Loop

'Close and dereference database objects
objRS.Close
Set objRS = Nothing
objConn.Close
Set objConn = Nothing
%>
</BODY>
</HTML>
```

Run the page on
your browser:

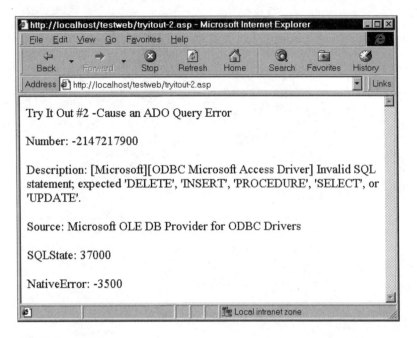

### How It Works – Cause an ADO Query Error

As in the previous example we have an HTML comment and then we display our page data.

```
<!--Display the page data-->
Try It Out #2 -Cause an ADO Query Error<BR><BR>
```

We start our server script by instructing VBScript to ignore any errors so we can trap them. Then we create our `Connection` object and open the Sailors database.

```
<%
'Instruct VBScript to ignore the error and continue
'with the next line of code
On Error Resume Next

'Create and open the connection object
Set objConn = Server.CreateObject("ADODB.Connection")
objConn.Open "dsn=Sailors"
```

Next, we set up an error handler to trap ADO errors. We first check to see if the `Connection` object's error count is greater than zero, indicating that we have an error.

Then we create an `Error` object to access the errors collection, and dimension a Boolean variable that we will set to True if we have any critical errors.

```
'Check for errors
If objConn.Errors.Count > 0 Then
  'Create an error object to access the ADO errors collection
  Set objErr = Server.CreateObject("ADODB.Error")
  'Declare boolean flag for critical errors
  Dim blnCriticalError
```

We need to loop through the `Errors` collection and retrieve each `Error` object using a `For Each` loop. Sometimes when you connect to a database you will get one or more informational messages that have a zero error number. We want to ignore these and only write errors that have a non-zero error number. If we have a real error we will set the Boolean variable to True, which we will check later.

```
'Write all errors to the page
For Each objErr In objConn.Errors
  If objErr.Number <> 0 Then
    Response.Write "Number: " & objErr.Number & "<P>"
    Response.Write "Description: " & objErr.Description & "<P>"
    Response.Write "Source: " & objErr.Source & "<P>"
    Response.Write "SQLState: " & objErr.SQLState & "<P>"
    Response.Write "NativeError: " & objErr.NativeError & "<P>"
    blnCriticalError = True
  End If
Next
```

Once we have retrieved all of the errors, we set our `Error` object to nothing and check our Boolean flag. If we had a serious error we will halt execution of our page by using the `Response` object's End method. This method will stop the code from executing any further and write out any data in the buffer.

```
'Dereference all objects
Set objErr = Nothing
If blnCriticalError Then
  Response.End
End If
End If
```

Next, we declare our ADO variables and set their values. Now we create our `Recordset` object, set our SQL string and open the recordset, returning any rows of data that the database finds.

```
'Declare variables and set their values
Dim adOpenForwardOnly
Dim adCmdStoredProc
adOpenForwardOnly = 0
adCmdStoredProc = 4

'Create the recordset object and open the recordset
Set objRS = Server.CreateObject("ADODB.Recordset")
strSQL = "DemoQueryGrid"
objRS.Open strSQL, objConn, adOpenForwardOnly, , adCmdStoredProc
```

Once again we check for errors and write any errors that have a non-zero error number to the page.

```
'Check for errors
If objConn.Errors.Count > 0 Then
  'Create an error object to access the ADO errors collection
  Set objErr = Server.CreateObject("ADODB.Error")
  'Write all errors to the page
  For Each objErr In objConn.Errors
    If objErr.Number <> 0 Then
      Response.Write "Number: " & objErr.Number & "<P>"
      Response.Write "Description: " & objErr.Description & "<P>"
      Response.Write "Source: " & objErr.Source & "<P>"
      Response.Write "SQLState: " & objErr.SQLState & "<P>"
      Response.Write "NativeError: " & objErr.NativeError & "<P>"
      blnCriticalError = True
    End If
  Next
  'Dereference all objects
  Set objErr = Nothing
  If blnCriticalError Then
    Response.End
  End If
End If
```

If we have no errors and make it this far in the code, then we loop through the recordset and write the PeopleLastName field on the page.

```
'Loop through the recordset displaying the last name field
Do While Not objRS.EOF
  Response.Write objRS("PeopleNameLast") & "<P>"
  objRS.MoveNext
Loop
```

The last thing we want to do is clean up our object references. First, we close the Recordset object and set it to nothing, which releases the object from memory. Next we close the Connection object and also release that object.

```
'Close and dereference database objects
objRS.Close
Set objRS = Nothing
objConn.Close
Set objConn = Nothing
%>
```

The error that is displayed on the web page is very misleading and does not really indicate that we have misspelled the query name. This is where you have to do tedious debugging to ensure that all of your statements are spelled correctly. Replace the misspelled query name with qDemoQueryGrid and see what results you now get.

When retrieving data from a SQL Server database we use this statement when executing a stored procedure.

```
strSQL = "up_select_author"
```

This stored procedure does not exist and would produce the following error in your web page:

```
Number: -2147217900
Description: [Microsoft][ODBC SQL Server Driver][SQL Server]Could not find stored
procedure 'up_select_author'.
Source: Microsoft OLE DB Provider for ODBC Drivers
SQLState: 37000
NativeError: 2812
```

These types of errors are easy to spot and can be easily corrected, unlike the error returned from Access. Keep in mind the difference in the error handling messages when you are coding and debugging data access code.

What do you do when your application is in production and the data does not exist? You need to be aware of these types of situations and include the proper error handling. In this case you would need to check whether the recordset is either at EOF or BOF, which indicates that no data has been returned. Your code could then take the appropriate actions.

# True Errors vs Data Validation Errors

True errors are usually easy to catch because you do not get the expected results returned in your recordset or in your web page. A true error is when you misspell a column or table name in your SQL statement or misspell a stored procedure name. Assume you are selecting data from Access and are using the following SQL statement:

```
strSQL = "select classname, classboatweight, classsailareaspinnakr " & _
  "from boatclass order by classname"
```

You mistyped the column name `classsailareaspinnaker` as `classsailareaspinnakr` and the resulting error would look like this:

```
Number: -2147217904
Description: [Microsoft][ODBC Microsoft Access Driver] Too few parameters. Expected 1.
Source: Microsoft OLE DB Provider for ODBC Drivers
SQLState: 07001
NativeError: -3010
```

This time you use the same select statement and try to select data from SQL Server. The error message that is returned now is much more representative of the actual error at hand.

```
Number: -2147217900
Description: [Microsoft][ODBC SQL Server Driver][SQL Server]Invalid column name
'classsailareaspinnakr'.
Source: Microsoft OLE DB Provider for ODBC Drivers
SQLState: S0022
NativeError: 207
```

> **Again we must stress the importance of checking your code for syntax errors first, when dealing with data access errors from Access.**

## Try It Out – Select Statement Error

Create a page that selects certain fields and displays them in a table. Intentionally misspell one of the column names so an error occurs.

Here's the example code (available in the file `TryItOut3.asp`).

```
<HTML>
<HEAD>
<META NAME="GENERATOR" Content="Microsoft Visual Studio 6.0">
<TITLE></TITLE>
</HEAD>
<BODY>

<!--Display the page data-->
Try It Out #3 - Select Statement Error<BR><BR>

<%
'Instruct VBScript to ignore the error and continue
'with the next line of code
On Error Resume Next
```

```
'Create and open the connection object
Set objConn = Server.CreateObject("ADODB.Connection")
objConn.Open "dsn=Sailors"

'Check for errors
If objConn.Errors.Count > 0 Then
  'Create an error object to access the ADO errors collection
  Set objErr = Server.CreateObject("ADODB.Error")
  'Declare boolean flag for critical errors
  Dim blnCriticalError
  'Write all errors to the page
  For Each objErr In objConn.Errors
    If objErr.Number <> 0 Then
      Response.Write "Number: " & objErr.Number & "<P>"
      Response.Write "Description: " & objErr.Description & "<P>"
      Response.Write "Source: " & objErr.Source & "<P>"
      Response.Write "SQLState: " & objErr.SQLState & "<P>"
      Response.Write "NativeError: " & objErr.NativeError & "<P>"
      blnCriticalError = True
    End If
  Next
  'Dereference all objects
  Set objErr = Nothing
  If blnCriticalError Then
    Response.End
  End If
End If

'Declare variables and set their values
Dim adOpenForwardOnly
Dim adCmdText
adOpenForwardOnly = 0
adCmdText = 1

 'Create the recordset object and open the recordset
Set objRS = Server.CreateObject("ADODB.Recordset")
strSQL = "SELECT classname, classboatweight, classsailareaspinnakr " & _
  "FROM boatclass ORDER BY classname"
objRS.Open strSQL, objConn, adOpenForwardOnly, , adCmdText

'Check for errors
If objConn.Errors.Count > 0 Then
  'Create an error object to access the ADO errors collection
  Set objErr = Server.CreateObject("ADODB.Error")
  'Write all errors to the page
  For Each objErr In objConn.Errors
    If objErr.Number <> 0 Then
      Response.Write "Number: " & objErr.Number & "<P>"
      Response.Write "Description: " & objErr.Description & "<P>"
      Response.Write "Source: " & objErr.Source & "<P>"
      Response.Write "SQLState: " & objErr.SQLState & "<P>"
      Response.Write "NativeError: " & objErr.NativeError & "<P>"
      blnCriticalError = True
    End If
  Next
  'Dereference all objects
  Set objErr = Nothing
  If blnCriticalError Then
    Response.End
  End If
End If
%>
```

```
<!--Build the header row of the table-->
<TABLE BORDER=1 CELLSPACING=1>
  <TR>
  <TH>Class Name</TH>
  <TH>Boat Weight</TH>
  <TH>Sail Area Spinnaker</TH>
  </TR>
<%
'Loop through the recordset displaying the
'data in a table
Do While Not objRS.EOF
%>
  <TR>
  <TD><%=objRS("classname")%></TD>
  <TD><%=objRS("classboatweight")%></TD>
  <TD><%=objRS("classsailareaspinnaker")%></TD>
  </TR>
<%
  objRS.MoveNext
Loop

'Close and dereference database objects
objRS.Close
Set objRS = Nothing
objConn.Close
Set objConn = Nothing
%>
</TABLE>
</BODY>
</HTML>
```

The result of running this page is shown below:

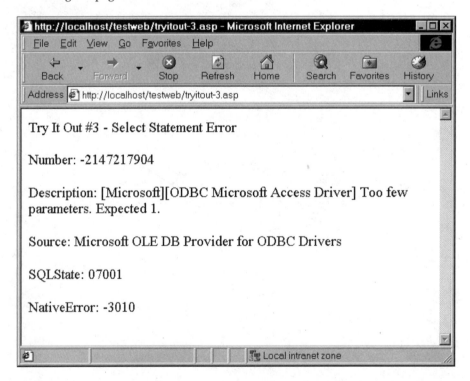

### How It Works – Select Statement Error

Let's take a look at the code that generates this error. The first part of the code is identical to the previous example except for the page data, so we won't go into it again.

As in the last example, we create the `Recordset` object. However, instead of setting our SQL string to execute a query, we code a select statement and intentionally misspell a column name. After we open the recordset we check for errors using the same error logic we used in the previous example.

```
'Create the recordset object and open the recordset
Set objRS = Server.CreateObject("ADODB.Recordset")
strSQL = "SELECT classname, classboatweight, classsailareaspinnakr " & _
   "FROM boatclass ORDER BY classname"
objRS.Open strSQL, objConn, adOpenForwardOnly, , adCmdText

'Check for errors
If objConn.Errors.Count > 0 Then
   'Create an error object to access the ADO errors collection
```

After the `End If` statement from the error handling code, we want to terminate the server side script and build a table containing data from the recordset, using HTML table tags. We build the header rows first.

```
End If
%>
<!--Build the header row of the table-->
<TABLE BORDER=1 CELLSPACING=1>
   <TR>
   <TH>Class Name</TH>
   <TH>Boat Weight</TH>
   <TH>Sail Area Spinnaker</TH>
   </TR>
```

Now we can loop through the recordset, building a row of data using the fields from the recordset. Notice the termination of the script before the HTML table row definitions.

```
<%
'Loop through the recordset displaying the
'data in a table
Do While Not objRS.EOF
%>
   <TR>
   <TD><%=objRS("classname")%></TD>
   <TD><%=objRS("classboatweight")%></TD>
   <TD><%=objRS("classsailareaspinnaker")%></TD>
   </TR>
<%
   objRS.MoveNext
Loop
```

After the loop we can close our recordset and dereference our objects.

```
'Close and dereference database objects
objRS.Close
Set objRS = Nothing
objConn.Close
Set objConn = Nothing
%>
```

When you run the active server page you can see that the error reported is not a true representation of the error at hand. This is why it is important to check for keying errors first when trying to debug these types of errors.

## Validation Errors

In a production environment the errors are of a different nature, such as fields containing null values or spaces. We call these **data validation errors**. Let's use the same SQL statement as above, but correct the column name of `classsailareaspinnaker` to `classsailareaspinnaker`. If we save the code and execute our active server page now, our web page will be built and display the following results:

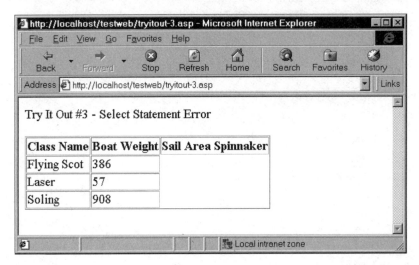

This is not the result we expected nor is it what we want our users to see. What we need to do is check the field `classsailareaspinnaker` for null values using the `IsNull` function, and correct it before it gets displayed.

Let's take a quick look at the code that checks for null values. We have to check the field name in the recordset in the server script. If the value of this field is null we set the variable to zero (0), otherwise we set the variable to the actual field data. This way we always display a number in our table, even though that number might be 0. If the value is null it prints a blank. In the HTML text we replaced the recordset field with the variable.

```
<%
'Loop through the recordset displaying the
'data in a table
Do While Not objRS.EOF
  'Check for null values and set the column
  'data to zero if null
  If IsNull(objRS("classsailareaspinnaker")) Then
    strSailArea = 0
  Else
    strSailArea = objRS("classsailareaspinnaker")
  End If
%>
  <TR>
  <TD><%=objRS("classname")%></TD>
  <TD><%=objRS("classboatweight")%></TD>
  <TD><%=strSailArea%></TD>
  </TR>
<%
  objRS.MoveNext
Loop
```

Save your code and execute the active server page again. This time we get satisfactory results as shown below.

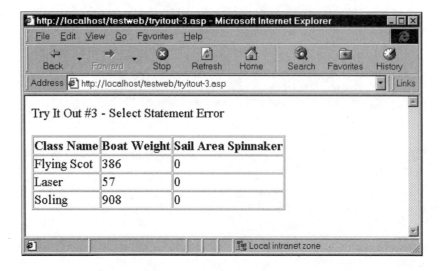

# How to Get Error Information

Using the various properties of the VBScript `Error` object and the ADO `Error` object, we can quickly determine what the errors are, in most cases. The error number provided can be used to search online help to get more detailed information about the errors that we received. This section covers the properties of the VBScript and ADO `Error` objects.

## Information About Errors

There are two types of scripting engine errors: compilation and run-time. The interaction between the scripting host (ASP) and the scripting engine (VBScript) happens in two phases. First, the scripting engine parses the script to perform a syntactical validation; if it finds an error, the execution is aborted and you receive a **compilation error**. When this phase is over, it begins the page construction with the execution of the script code. In this phase the script engine raises a **run-time error** which we can trap.

If you have compilation errors in your code, such as an unmatched `If` – `End If` pair, ASP will display a message similar to the following in your browser:

```
Microsoft VBScript compilation error '800a03f6'
Expected 'End'
/testweb/testsqlerror.asp, line 65
```

On the other hand, misspelling a method name leads to a run-time error, not to a compilation error.

Run-Time errors have to be retrieved from the VBScript `Error` object. This error object can only contain one error, and you need to check to see if the error `Number` property is greater than zero to determine if an error has occurred.

The ADO errors collection can contain more than one error, so you need to query the Errors collection to see if the Count property is greater than zero.

# Error Syntax

The error syntax varies slightly between the VBScript Error object and the ADO Error object. However, both error objects contain the same basic properties, which include the error number, description and the source. The ADO Error object provides additional properties related to the state of the database in use, and the actual SQL error number that occurred in the database.

## VBScript

To retrieve error information from the VBScript Error object you simply need to access the different properties that are listed below.

```
Response.Write err.Number
Response.Write err.Description
Response.Write err.Source
```

After you have successfully processed the error information and you want to continue executing your code, you should clear the previous error. This is performed using the Clear method as demonstrated below.

```
err.Clear
```

## ADO

As we saw above, the ADO Errors collection is different from the VBScript Error object because it is a collection of Error objects. The syntax to access the error properties is very similar to VBScript. First we create an Error object, which we will use to access all of the error properties contained in the Errors collection. By specifying Each objErr in objConn.Errors we are in essence setting the Error object to an error in the Errors collection of the Connection object. The syntax to display each error property is listed below.

```
Set objErr = Server.CreateObject("ADODB.Error")
For Each objErr In objConn.Errors
    Response.Write objErr.Number
    Response.Write objErr.Description
    Response.Write objErr.Source
    Response.Write objErr.SQLState
    Response.Write objErr.NativeError
    Response.Write objErr.HelpFile
    Response.Write objErr.HelpContext
Next
```

We do not need to worry about clearing the Errors collection because, on our next database operation, ADO will clear the Errors collection and then write any new errors, if any exist. If you do want to clear the Errors collection you can use the following syntax:

```
ObjConn.Errors.Clear
```

# Using Error Information in Development

Handling and displaying errors in development is a key part of developing Active Server Pages. You need a method of quickly identifying and displaying the errors that you receive, to resolve these errors and move on. This section will discuss just one method of handling errors. You as a developer must decide what method meets your shop standards and best practices.

## Try It Out – Development Error Page

Create an error page that displays all errors received in the development environment. This page will format the errors received in a table, making it easier to read than the methods we have been using up to this point.

First you will need to create the include file. You can find this code in `ErrorHandler.inc`.

```
<%
Function CheckForErrors(objConnection)

  'Declare variables
  Dim blnDisplayErrMsg

  If objConnection.Errors.Count > 0 Then

    'Create the FileSystemObject and open the error log
    Set objFile = Server.CreateObject("Scripting.FileSystemObject")
    Set objLog = objFile.OpenTextFile( _
                 Server.MapPath("ErrorLog.txt"),8,True)

    'Check for an open error from VBScript
    If Err.Number > 0 Then
      Response.Write "Error opening log file<P>"
      Response.Write "Error Number: " & Err.Number & _
                     ", Error Description: " & Err.Description
    End If

    'Create an error object to access the ADO errors collection
    Set objErr = Server.CreateObject("ADODB.Error")

    'Log all errors to the error log
    For Each objErr In objConnection.Errors
      If objErr.Number = 0 Then
        blnDisplayErrMsg = False
      Else
        objLog.WriteLine(objErr.Number & "|" & _
                  objErr.Description & "|" & objErr.Source & "|" & _
                  objErr.SQLState & "|" & objErr.NativeError)
        blnDisplayErrMsg = True
      End If
    Next

    'Close the log file and dereference all objects
    objLog.Close
    Set objLog = Nothing
    Set objFile = Nothing
    Set objErr = Nothing

    If blnDisplayErrMsg Then
%>
```

```
    <!--Display the error table window-->
    <Script Language=VBScript>
      window.open "http://Localhost/TestWeb/ErrorTable.asp", _
              "ErrorWindow","width=800,height=600,scrollbars=yes"
    </script>
  <%
      'Halt Execution
      Response.End
    End If
  End If
End Function
%>
```

Next you need to create the main page that contains the error, using the same basic code from the previous Try It Out with a few minor modifications. Ensure that the same error exists in the SELECT statement. You can find this code in the file TryItOut4.asp.

```
<!-- #include file="ErrorHandler.inc" -->
<HTML>
<HEAD>
<META NAME="GENERATOR" Content="Microsoft Visual Studio 6.0">
<TITLE></TITLE>
</HEAD>
<BODY>

<!--Display the page data-->
Try It Out #4 - Development Error Table<BR><BR>

<%
'Instruct VBScript to ignore the error and continue
'with the next line of code
On Error Resume Next

'Create and open the connection object
Set objConn = Server.CreateObject("ADODB.Connection")
objConn.Open "dsn=Sailors"

'Check for errors
Call CheckForErrors(objConn)

'Declare variables and set their values
Dim adOpenForwardOnly
Dim adCmdText
adOpenForwardOnly = 0
adCmdText = 1

 'Create the recordset object and open the recordset
Set objRS = Server.CreateObject("ADODB.Recordset")
strSQL = "SELECT classname, classboatweight, classsailareaspinnakr " & _
  "FROM boatclass ORDER BY classname"
objRS.Open strSQL, objConn, adOpenForwardOnly, , adCmdText

'Check for errors
Call CheckForErrors(objConn)
%>

<!--Build the header row of the table-->
<TABLE BORDER=1 CELLSPACING=1>
  <TR>
  <TH>Class Name</TH>
  <TH>Boat Weight</TH>
  <TH>Sail Area Spinnaker</TH>
  </TR>
<%
```

```
'Loop through the recordset displaying the
'data in a table
Do While Not objRS.EOF
  'Check for null values and set the column
  'data to zero if null
  If IsNull(objRS("classsailareaspinnaker")) Then
    strSailArea = 0
  Else
    strSailArea = objRS("classsailareaspinnaker")
  End If
%>
  <TR>
  <TD><%=objRS("classname")%></TD>
  <TD><%=objRS("classboatweight")%></TD>
  <TD><%=strSailArea%></TD>
  </TR>
<%
  objRS.MoveNext
Loop

'Close and dereference database objects
objRS.Close
Set objRS = Nothing
objConn.Close
Set objConn = Nothing
%>
</TABLE>
</BODY>
</HTML>
```

Then you need to create the error table page (found in ErrorTable.asp):

```
<HTML>
<HEAD>
<META NAME="GENERATOR" Content="Microsoft Visual Studio 6.0">
<TITLE>Error Table</TITLE>
</HEAD>
<BODY>
<!--Start the table and build the header-->
<TABLE BORDER=1>
<TR>
<TH BGCOLOR=navy><FONT COLOR=white>Number</FONT ></TH>
<TH BGCOLOR=navy><FONT COLOR=white>Description</FONT ></TH>
<TH BGCOLOR=navy><FONT COLOR=white>Source</FONT ></TH>
<TH BGCOLOR=navy><FONT COLOR=white>SQL State</FONT ></TH>
<TH BGCOLOR=navy><FONT COLOR=white>Native Error</FONT ></TH>
</TR>
<%
'Perform error handling
On Error Resume Next
Set objFile = Server.CreateObject("Scripting.FileSystemObject")
Set objLog = objFile.OpenTextFile(Server.MapPath("ErrorLog.txt"))

'If we could not open the file display the error message
If Err.Number > 0 Then
  Response.Write "Error opening log file<P>"
  Response.Write "Error Number: " & Err.Number & _
    ", Error Description: " & Err.Description
End If

'If the file is not empty then process it
If Not objLog.AtEndOfStream Then
```

```
  'Process the file until we reach EOF
  Do While Not objLog.AtEndOfStream
    'Read the data into a variable
    strText = objLog.ReadLine
    'Split the text into an array
    arrText = Split(strText,"|")
%>
    <!--Build a row of data-->
    <TR>
    <TD NOWRAP BGCOLOR=silver><%=arrText(0)%></TD>
    <TD NOWRAP BGCOLOR=silver><%=arrText(1)%></TD>
    <TD NOWRAP BGCOLOR=silver><%=arrText(2)%></TD>
    <TD NOWRAP BGCOLOR=silver><%=arrText(3)%></TD>
    <TD NOWRAP BGCOLOR=silver><%=arrText(4)%></TD>
    </TR>
<%
  Loop
End If
'Close the file
objLog.Close

'To clear the file
'Open the file with no parameters thus overwriting it
Set objLog = objFile.CreateTextFile(Server.MapPath("ErrorLog.txt"))
objLog.Close

'Dereference the objects
Set objLog = Nothing
Set objFile = Nothing
%>
</TABLE>
</BODY>
</HTML>
```

Finally, you can run the main page on your browser. This is what you should see:

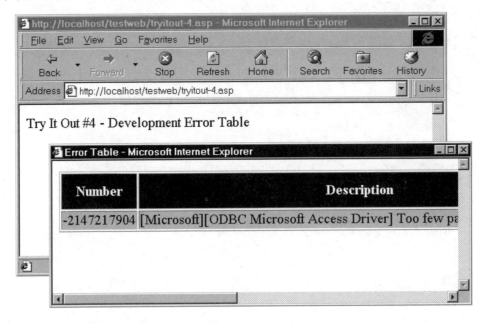

## How It Works – Development Error Page

The `ErrorTable.asp` page will provide a method of displaying errors in a standard format, and will be displayed in a separate window from the page that had the error. Before we can develop this page however, we must provide a common mechanism to trap and save the errors that have occurred. We will provide this functionality in an **include file** that will contain all of our ADO error handling code. An include file can contain common code that can be included in multiple active server pages, thus reducing the amount of code to be written, and allowing code to be maintained in one place. However, it is worth remembering that each include file represents a page request, so where possible you should avoid including the same page multiple times. We've called the include file once at the top of our main script. Let's start by examining the code that makes up the `ErrorHandler.inc` file.

Keeping in mind that the code in the include file is simply server-side script, we need to start by coding the begin script (`<%`) tag. Since the code in this include file will operate as a function that will accept any `Connection` object passed to it, we code the function statement first. Next, we check to see if the `Errors` collection of the `Connection` object has a `Count` property greater than zero, which indicates we have one or more errors.

If errors exist, we need to create a text file that will be used to log all of our errors. We do this by opening a file using the `FileSystemObject`. The `OpenTextFile` method accepts four parameters:

❑   filename - which is self-explanatory.

❑   I/O mode – which consists of `ForAppending`, `ForReading` and `ForWriting`. Instead of using the actual constant for I/O Mode we are using the corresponding value of 8 for the mode of `ForAppending`. This is because some versions of VBScript do not properly recognize the constant names.

❑   create file – this is a Boolean value that instructs VBScript to create the file if it does not exist.

❑   file format – this parameter has four constants:

   ❑   `TristateFalse`

   ❑   `TristateMixed`

   ❑   `TristateTrue`

   ❑   `TristateUseDefault`

   We are not specifying a file format parameter and will simply take the default value of `TriStateFalse`, which opens our file in ASCII format.

Place the file in a directory in which all users have write access – note that this may mean you cannot use a folder under the web root, as we have specified below. We use the `MapPath` function of the `Server` object to get the current path that this Web page is running in. This is where our `ErrorLog.txt` file will be created.

```
<%
If objConn.Errors.Count > 0 Then

  'Create the FileSystemObject and open the error log
  Set objFile = Server.CreateObject("Scripting.FileSystemObject")
  Set objLog = objFile.OpenTextFile( _
    Server.MapPath("ErrorLog.txt"),8,True)
```

After opening the file, we want to ensure the file has indeed been opened and we did not receive an error. Here we are checking the VBScript `Error` object to see if the error number is greater than zero. If it is, we are going to write the error information to the web page.

```
'Check for an open error from VBScript
If Err.Number > 0 Then
  Response.Write "Error opening log file<P>"
  Response.Write "Error Number: " & Err.Number & _
    ", Error Description: " & Err.Description
End If
```

Now we come to the heart of the matter at hand - logging the ADO errors from the `Errors` collection. We start by creating an `Error` object that will be used to access the ADO `Errors` collection.

Next we loop through the `Errors` collection and write a record containing all of the error properties. Notice that we are using the `WriteLine` command to write a record to the error log. We are separating each error property in the record with a pipe character. This will make it easier for us to read it back in the `ErrorTable.asp` page.

We are using a Boolean flag, as in our previous error handling examples, to determine if the error received was indeed a true error.

```
'Create an error object to access the ADO errors collection
Set objErr = Server.CreateObject("ADODB.Error")

'Log all errors to the error log
For Each objErr In objConn.Errors
  If objErr.Number = 0 Then
    blnDisplayErrMsg = False
  Else
    objLog.WriteLine(objErr.Number & "|" & _
      objErr.Description & "|" & objErr.Source & "|" & _
      objErr.SQLState & "|" & objErr.NativeError)
    blnDisplayErrMsg = True
  End If
Next
```

After we have written all of the errors, we need to close the log file and de-reference all of our objects as we no longer need them. Next, we check the Boolean variable to see if a true error has been recorded. Lastly, we close the script, using the end script (`%>`) tag, in preparation for our HTML code.

```
'Close the log file and dereference all objects
objLog.Close
Set objLog = Nothing
Set objFile = Nothing
Set objErr = Nothing

If blnDisplayErrMsg Then
%>
```

In order to automatically display the ErrorTable.asp page we need to open a separate window that will contain this page. We specify the URL for the page to be opened, along with the window name and window features. (Note that when you run this code on your own machine you'll probably want to change the URL path to where you've stored the file on your own machine). If no features are specified, the new window is created with all of the features of the browser intact. By specifying just a subset of features we are able to control how the window will be displayed. After our new window has been opened, we halt execution of our code.

```
  <!--Display the error table window-->
  <Script Language=VBScript>
    window.open "http://Localhost/TestWeb/ErrorTable.asp", _
      "ErrorWindow","width=800,height=600,scrollbars=yes"
  </script>
<%
    'Halt Execution
    Response.End
  End If
End If
%>
```

The ErrorHandler.inc include file can be saved in the same directory as your ASP files. One alternative would be to create a subdirectory called Includes.

To create the web page that has an error and uses the ErrorHandler.inc file, we used the same basic code from the previous Try It Out with a few minor modifications. The first part of the code is the same as the previous example except for the first line. Here we are including the error handling include file:

```
<!-- #include file="ErrorHandler.inc" -->
<HTML>
<HEAD>
<META NAME="GENERATOR" Content="Microsoft Visual Studio 6.0">
<TITLE></TITLE>
</HEAD>
<BODY>
```

The difference comes when we actually check for ADO errors. Here we have removed all of the error handling code and replaced it with a single line, which calls the error handling function, passing it the Connection object we are using.

```
'Create and open the connection object
Set objConn = Server.CreateObject("ADODB.Connection")
objConn.Open "dsn=Sailors"
```

```
' Check for errors
Call CheckForErrors(objConn)
```

```
'Create the recordset object and open the recordset
Set objRS = Server.CreateObject("ADODB.Recordset")
strSQL = "select classname, classboatweight, classsailareaspinnakr " & _
  "from boatclass order by classname"
objRS.Open strSQL, objConn, adOpenForwardOnly, , adCmdText
```

```
'Check for errors
Call CheckForErrors(objConn)
%>
```

```
<!--Build the header row of the table-->
```

Ensure the same error exists in the SELECT statement that existed in the previous Try It Out. This will facilitate our testing of the ErrorTable.asp file.

Now let's take a look at the ErrorTable.asp page. The idea of this page is really simple - we want to open the error log, read all of the records and place them into a table, then close the file. To ensure we don't get duplicate errors we will clear the log file after we have finished using it.

We start the page like any other page except we have no actual page data. We start by building a table and the header rows. We are setting the background color of the header rows to navy and the font color to white. Feel free to change the color of the header and the table rows.

```
<BODY>
<!--Start the table and build the header-->
<TABLE BORDER=1>
<TR>
<TH BGCOLOR=navy><FONT COLOR=white>Number</FONT ></TH>
<TH BGCOLOR=navy><FONT COLOR=white>Description</FONT ></TH>
<TH BGCOLOR=navy><FONT COLOR=white>Source</FONT ></TH>
<TH BGCOLOR=navy><FONT COLOR=white>SQL State</FONT ></TH>
<TH BGCOLOR=navy><FONT COLOR=white>Native Error</FONT ></TH>
</TR>
```

We start our server side script by turning on error handling. Then we create our `FileSystemObject` object and open our log file. We don't specify any parameters this time because we are only reading the file and the default parameters of the `OpenTextFile` method specify read only.

```
<%
'Perform error handling
On Error Resume Next
Set objFile = Server.CreateObject("Scripting.FileSystemObject")
Set objLog = objFile.OpenTextFile( _
                Server.MapPath("ErrorLog.txt"))
```

Of course we must check for errors that might have occurred opening the log file. We do this by checking the VBScript error number. If any errors did occur we will write them on the page.

```
'If we could not open the file display the error message
If Err.Number > 0 Then
  Response.Write "Error opening log file<P>"
  Response.Write "Error Number: " & Err.Number & _
    ", Error Description: " & Err.Description
End If
```

We want to check to make sure the error log file is not empty, and do so by checking to see if an EOF condition has occurred. If all is OK then we proceed into a loop until the EOF condition is set to true. The first thing we want to do in the loop is to read a record from the error log and assign it to a variable. Then we use the `Split` function to extract the different error information from the string. The `Split` function creates a one-dimensional array containing all of the data it found, using the separator that we specify.

```
'If the file is not empty then process it
If Not objLog.AtEndOfStream Then

  'Process the file until we reach EOF
  Do While Not objLog.AtEndOfStream
    'Read the data into a variable
    strText = objLog.ReadLine
    'Split the text into an array
    arrText = Split(strText,"|")
%>
```

*Testing has shown that using the optional `count` and `compare` parameters of the Split function renders the Split function inoperable.*

Now that our variables contain all of the error information we need, it's time to build a row in our table. We do this by beginning a row, and then writing each column and its data using the server-side text array that contains our error information. This is why the variables are enclosed in the server side scripting tags. We finish up by closing the table row.

```
<!--Build a row of data-->
<TR>
<TD NOWRAP BGCOLOR=silver><%=arrText(0)%></TD>
<TD NOWRAP BGCOLOR=silver><%=arrText(1)%></TD>
<TD NOWRAP BGCOLOR=silver><%=arrText(2)%></TD>
<TD NOWRAP BGCOLOR=silver><%=arrText(3)%></TD>
<TD NOWRAP BGCOLOR=silver><%=arrText(4)%></TD>
</TR>
```

We continue processing records by going back to the beginning of the loop. Once we have met an EOF condition on the file, we fall out of the loop and we will close the file.

```
<%
  Loop
End If
'Close the file
objLog.Close
```

In order to clear the log file we simply open it for creation, taking the default parameters, which will overwrite the file, and then we close it.

We de-reference all of our objects and then we are through.

```
'To clear the file
'Open the file with no parameters thus overwriting it
Set objLog = objFile.CreateTextFile(Server.MapPath("ErrorLog.txt"))

objLog.Close

'Dereference the objects
Set objLog = Nothing
Set objFile = Nothing
%>
</TABLE>
```

Now you have an include file that can be used in all of your pages that use ADO, and a standard means of displaying these errors.

Some things to try:

❑ Change the look of the ErrorTable.asp using different formatting options
❑ Add a pagename and timestamp to the error when writing it.

# Using Error Information in Production

Production error handling is going to be similar to that which you use in development. You still want to trap and record the errors – you just don't want to popup a separate window displaying the errors. The user does not usually care what the error is - they just want to know how to make it work. This section will demonstrate how to handle production errors and what course of action to take. Keep in mind that this is only one of many possible ways to handle errors, and you must find and choose the best method that meets your needs.

## The Correct Course of Action

The correct course of action to be taken when an error occurs depends on what your code is doing. If you are opening a recordset to be used to build a table and an error occurs, then you definitely do not want to continue processing. If you have an equation that is calculated and the results displayed and you receive an error, then you can continue to process as long as no code depends on this calculation. The correct course of action to take is entirely up to you and the business at hand.

### Try It Out – Production Error Handler

We can expand on our previous discussion and create a production error handler. This error handler will display a graceful message to the user and halt execution of all code once an error has been received and logged.

The code for the active server page is listed below (you can find it in `TryItOut5.asp`):.

```
<!-- #include file="ProductionErrorHandler.inc" -->
<HTML>
<HEAD>
<META NAME="GENERATOR" Content="Microsoft Visual Studio 6.0">
<TITLE></TITLE>
</HEAD>
<BODY>

<!--Display the page data-->
Try It Out #5 - Production Error Handler<BR><BR>

<%
'Instruct VBScript to ignore the error and continue
'with the next line of code
On Error Resume Next

'Create and open the connection object
Set objConn = Server.CreateObject("ADODB.Connection")
objConn.Open "DSN=Sailors"

'Check for errors
Call CheckForErrors(objConn)

'Declare variables and set their values
Dim adOpenForwardOnly
Dim adCmdText
adOpenForwardOnly = 0
adCmdText = 1
```

```
  'Create the recordset object and open the recordset
Set objRS = Server.CreateObject("ADODB.Recordset")
strSQL = "SELECT classname, classboatweight, classsailareaspinnakr " & _
  "FROM boatclass ORDER BY classname"
objRS.Open strSQL, objConn, adOpenForwardOnly, , adCmdText

'Check for errors
Call CheckForErrors(objConn)
%>

<!--Build the header row of the table-->
<TABLE BORDER=1 CELLSPACING=1>
  <TR>
  <TH>Class Name</TH>
  <TH>Boat Weight</TH>
  <TH>Sail Area Spinnaker</TH>
  </TR>
<%
'Loop through the recordset displaying the
'data in a table
Do While Not objRS.EOF
  'Check for null values and set the column
  'data to zero if null
  If IsNull(objRS("classsailareaspinnaker")) Then
    strSailArea = 0
  Else
    strSailArea = objRS("classsailareaspinnaker")
  End If
%>
  <TR>
  <TD><%=objRS("classname")%></TD>
  <TD><%=objRS("classboatweight")%></TD>
  <TD><%=strSailArea%></TD>
  </TR>
<%
  objRS.MoveNext
Loop

'Close and dereference database objects
objRS.Close
Set objRS = Nothing
objConn.Close
Set objConn = Nothing
%>
</TABLE>
</BODY>
</HTML>
```

Next, the code for the `ProductionErrorHandler.inc` file is listed below:

```
<%
Function CheckForErrors(objConnection)

  'Declare variables
  Dim blnDisplayErrMsg

  If objConnection.Errors.Count > 0 Then

    'Create the FileSystemObject and open the error log
    Set objFile = Server.CreateObject("Scripting.FileSystemObject")
    Set objLog = objFile.OpenTextFile( _
        Server.MapPath("ErrorLog.txt"),8,True)

'Check for an open error from VBScript
    If Err.Number > 0 Then
      Response.Write "Error opening log file<P>"
      Response.Write "Error Number: " & Err.Number & _
                  ", Error Description: " & Err.Description
    End If

    'Create an error object to access the ADO errors collection
    Set objErr = Server.CreateObject("ADODB.Error")

    'Log all errors to the error log
    For Each objErr In objConnection.Errors
      If objErr.Number = 0 Then
        blnDisplayErrMsg = False
      Else
        objLog.WriteLine(objErr.Number & "|" & _
            objErr.Description & "|" & objErr.Source & "|" & _
            objErr.SQLState & "|" & objErr.NativeError)
        blnDisplayErrMsg = True
      End If
    Next

    'Close the log file and dereference all objects
    objLog.Close
    Set objLog = Nothing
    Set objFile = Nothing
    Set objErr = Nothing

    If blnDisplayErrMsg Then
      'Display a graceful message to the user
      Response.Write "An unforseen error has occurred and processing " & _
      "must be stopped. You can try your request again later or " & _
      "you can call our Help Desk at 888-888-1234"
      'Halt Execution
      Response.End
    End If
  End If
End Function
%>
```

Finally, run the main page in your browser:

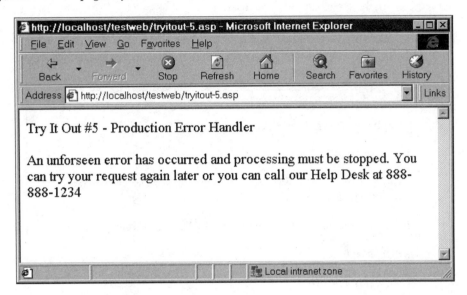

### How It Works – Production Error Handler

The Active Server Pages code is the same as in the last example except that we are replacing the
`ErrorHandler.inc` file with the new `ProductionErrorhandler.inc` file, so we don't need to go
into the details of the code again.

```
<!-- #include file="ProductionErrorHandler.inc" -->
<HTML>
<HEAD>
<META NAME="GENERATOR" Content="Microsoft Visual Studio 6.0">
<TITLE></TITLE>
</HEAD>
<BODY>
```

The `ProductionErrorHandler.inc` file is slightly different to the `ErrorHandler.inc` file that we
used to trap development errors. Instead of displaying a separate window containing all of the errors, we
will display a graceful message for the user, letting them know we had an error. Once the message is
displayed we will stop further execution of the code by using the `Response.End` command.

```
'Close the log file and dereference all objects
objLog.Close
Set objLog = Nothing
Set objFile = Nothing
Set objErr = Nothing

If blnDisplayErrMsg Then
  'Display a graceful message to the user
  Response.Write "An unforseen error has occurred and processing " & _
    "must be stopped. You can try your request again later or " & _
    "you can call our Help Desk at 888-888-1234"
  'Halt Execution
  Response.End
End If
End If
%>
```

**465**

This graceful error message is preferred to the standard error message from ADO, shown below, which does not indicate anything meaningful to the user:

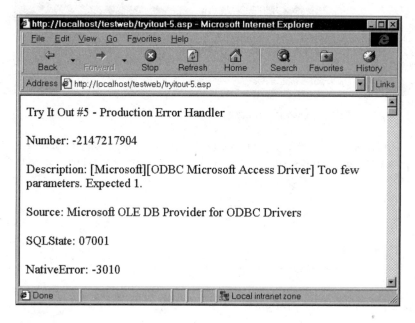

## Continuing Execution

Sometimes it is OK to continue execution. Let's assume that we display a form and the user inputs some values for a server side calculation. If we receive an error on the calculation we can continue execution of the code, as shown in the code fragment below.

```
<%
  Dim intTotal
  Dim intMonths
  Dim intResult
  Dim blnProceed

  'Assign the variables the values the user entered
  intTotal = Request.Form("txtTotal")
  intMonths = Request.Form("txtMonths")

  'Set up error handling
  On Error Resume Next

  'Perform the calculation
  intResult = intTotal / intMonths

  'Check for errors
  If err.Number > 0 Then
    blnProceed = False
  Else
    blnProceed = True
  End If
%>
```

Let's look at this code fragment in a little detail. First we dimension our variables, then we assign the variables values retrieved from the form that the user submitted. Then we set up our error handler and perform the calculation.

If we have an error after performing the calculation we can set a Boolean value that will tell our code which processing path to take. We could instruct our code to display an error message to the user letting them know they entered an invalid value, and send them back to the input form.

# Common Errors

While you are developing an Active Server Page, you will undoubtedly come across errors. Some are simple and very obvious while others are not so obvious. This section will examine some of the more common errors and show you why they occurred and how to fix them.

To be consistent, we are going to break this section into two parts. The first section will cover the common active server page scripting errors while the second section will cover errors returned from ADO.

## Common VBScript Errors

Experience has shown that the most common scripting error deals with the End If statement. This scripting error has multiple causes and solutions and can be one of the most frustrating errors to find, especially in large scripts containing several hundred lines of code.

When dealing with large scripts where there are multiple If, Else and End If statements it is very easy to overlook an End If statement. It is very hard to find where you missed it, and it will result in a compilation error as shown here:

```
Microsoft VBScript compilation error '800a03f6'
Expected 'End'
/testweb/testsqlerror.asp, line 60
```

The line number is very misleading and does not correspond to the actual line number in your code. Indenting your code between If Else End If statements is a good visual aid, or an easy way to find the missing statement is to actually print out your code and look at it on paper. This makes it easy to match the If, Else and End If pairs to determine which one is missing.

Another common mistake is typing the End If statement as one word instead of two separate words. If you are a VB developer, you know that VB will automatically handle this for you and separate the two statements. This error is easier to spot and correct, as the actual error is straightforward.

```
Microsoft VBScript compilation error '800a0400'
Expected statement
/testweb/testsqlerror.asp, line 59
EndIf
^
```

At first glance this next error might not be so obvious, especially if you have a large script with multiple If, Else, End If statements, but it is a common one. You might be thinking to yourself "I know I coded all of my End If statements". Actually this error is misleading because the End If statements are coded correctly and are all there.

```
Microsoft VBScript compilation error '800a0400'
Expected statement
/testweb/testsqlerror.asp, line 59
End If
^
```

The thing to check here is to ensure you terminated your server side script before starting to code the HTML. The code that is causing this problem is listed here.

```
   <TH>Last Name</TH>
   </TR>

   If Not objRS.EOF or objRS.BOF Then
```

The corrected code has the beginning server side script tag as shown here.

```
   <TH>Last Name</TH>
   </TR>
<%
   If Not objRS.EOF or objRS.BOF Then
```

This next error is on the flip side of the previous one and is much easier to spot. Here we forgot to end our server script before starting to code the HTML. Simply place the end server-side script tag before the line of code in question and you will be all set.

```
Microsoft VBScript compilation error '800a0400'
Expected statement
/testweb/testsqlerror.asp, line 36
<form action="messages.asp" method="POST" name="form1">
^
```

The following error is not as common as the previous ones but you will eventually run across it sooner or later. It is pretty much self-explanatory and easy to fix. Notice the underscore characters and the caret pointing to the error in the line of code. This can be helpful when you have a long line of code in error. This will point out the section of your code that has the error, and in this case we have forgotten to code the Then keyword.

```
Microsoft VBScript compilation error '800a03f9'
Expected 'Then'
/testweb/testsqlerror.asp, line 47
If Not objRS.EOF or objRS.BOF
----------------------------^
```

When dealing with SQL statements, especially if you are passing a lot of parameters from a request form, it is easy to forget to properly terminate the string. However, this scripting error is also self-explanatory in that it tells you that you forgot to terminate the string, and points out the string in question.

```
Microsoft VBScript compilation error '800a0409'
Unterminated string constant
/testweb/testsqlerror.asp, line 22
strSQL = "select stor_name, discounttype, lowqty, highqty from stores
---------------------------------------------------------------^
```

When using include files it is important to ensure you have spelled the name correctly and have specified the correct directory, otherwise you are going to see this error. Double check that the directory, if one is specified, is correct and contains the file in question. Also double-check the spelling of the include file name.

```
Active Server Pages error 'ASP 0126'
Include file not found
/testweb/testsqlerror.asp, line 26
The include file 'includes/ErrorHandler.inc' was not found.
```

When dealing with SQL data, a common error is not to get the results expected on your web page. If you know that you have data in the recordset, view the script in the browser by right clicking on the page in the browser and choosing **View** on the popup menu. The script will show you the results that are being displayed. Then go back and check your code. A common error is that you did not code the server side variable correctly, as shown below.

```
<TD><%objRS("au_id")%></TD>
```

The correct syntax is shown here with the equal sign in front of the `Recordset` object. This is sometimes a hard error to find.

```
<TD><%=objRS("au_id")%></TD>
```

You might also come across circumstances where you have used a recordset field in an expression on the server side or client side and it will cause an error. Sometimes an error will be generated and sometimes it is simply acceptable, depending on the statement being evaluated. This next example deals with a client side error that does not generate an error, but does not display the results expected either. When we examine our scripting code everything appears OK and looks like it should work:

```
<Script language=vbscript>
Sub Window_OnLoad()
  If "<%=objRS("au_id")%>" = "111-11-1111" Then
    form1.txtKey.value = "<%=objRS("au_id")%>"
  End IF
End Sub
</script>
```

Once the web page has loaded, we can view the source code in the browser and see where the problem is. The recordset field that is being used in the evaluation contains no data. There are a couple of things to check here. One, ensure the recordset is being opened. Next, make sure the recordset is not being closed before this code is generated - this is the problem in our case. Lastly, ensure the recordset field contains data, that is, it is not null or contains spaces.

```
<Script language=vbscript>
Sub Window_OnLoad()
  If "" = "111-11-1111" Then
    form1.txtKey.value = ""
  End IF
End Sub
</script>
```

The last scripting error that we are going to cover is a script timeout. This error has multiple causes but the most common is that the script has timed out waiting on a response from a database or server component. You should investigate the cause of the error before attempting to increase the script timeout value.

```
error 'ASP 0113'
Script timed out
/testweb/testsqlerror.asp
The maximum amount of time for a script to execute was exceeded. You can change this
limit by specifying a new value for the property Server.ScriptTimeOut or by changing
the value in the IIS administration tools.
```

# Common ADO Errors

The solutions to database errors are usually very easy to fix as ADO does a good job of reporting the errors returned by the ODBC driver in use. This section deals with the most common ADO errors encountered from Microsoft Access and Microsoft SQL Server.

The errors covered in this section are listed in the examples in the following order:

- ❑ Number
- ❑ Description
- ❑ Source
- ❑ SQL State
- ❑ Native Error

This first error is not really an error at all but just informational messages. When opening an Access database you will receive this message most of the time. According to the error message, IM006, during the SQLConnect function the driver's SQLSetConnectAttr function returned a SQL_SUCCESS_WITH_INFO message, hence the zero return code for the error number.

```
0
[Microsoft][ODBC Driver Manager] Driver's SQLSetConnectAttr failed
Microsoft OLE DB Provider for ODBC Drivers
IM006
0
```

SQL Server contains multiple databases with the default database being Master. When you set up a DSN you specify that the DSN should point to a database other than the default, if the logon id you are using has access to multiple databases on the same server. If your user id has access to multiple databases you will see the following messages when connecting to SQL Server.

```
0
[Microsoft][ODBC SQL Server Driver][SQL Server]Changed database context to 'pubs'.
Microsoft OLE DB Provider for ODBC Drivers
01000
5701
```

```
0
[Microsoft][ODBC SQL Server Driver][SQL Server]Changed language setting to us_english.
Microsoft OLE DB Provider for ODBC Drivers
01000
5703
```

You should check in both sets of messages that the error number is zero. If it is, you can code not to display these messages.

Another common error that you will run across is a DSN error. This is caused most of the time because you forgot to set up the DSN. In other circumstances it is possible that you misspelled the DSN in your code. Double check to ensure the DSN is set up, and double-check your code to ensure that you are spelling it correctly. The message displayed when trying to connect to Access and SQL Server is the same.

```
-2147467259
[Microsoft][ODBC Driver Manager] Data source name not found and no default driver
specified
Microsoft OLE DB Provider for ODBC Drivers
IM002
0
```

Another common mistake is not specifying the correct user id or password when trying to connect to a database. Ensure you have spelled the user id and password correctly. Since we have not been dealing with any secure Access databases, only the message from SQL Server is shown.

```
-2147217843
[Microsoft][ODBC SQL Server Driver][SQL Server]Login failed for user 'saa'.
Microsoft OLE DB Provider for ODBC Drivers
28000
18456
```

Given the very nature of SQL Server, it provides some great security features, one of which is permissions at the table level. Beyond that is what functions you can actually perform against that table. This next error indicates that you do not have select permissions for a specific table. In the same spectrum you will often see a similar message that you do not have insert rights to insert data into a table. The corrective action would be to check with your database administrator to get the appropriate permissions.

```
2147217911
[Microsoft][ODBC SQL Server Driver][SQL Server]SELECT permission denied on object
'authors', database 'pubs', owner 'dbo'.
Microsoft OLE DB Provider for ODBC Drivers
42000
229
```

Along with the previous example this next SQL Server error denies you access to a stored procedure. Again, check with your database administrator to get the appropriate permissions.

```
-2147217911
[Microsoft][ODBC SQL Server Driver][SQL Server]EXECUTE permission denied on object
'up_select_authors', database 'pubs', owner 'dbo'.
Microsoft OLE DB Provider for ODBC Drivers
42000
229
```

Sometimes I type so fast, I often misspell words, as shown in the next example. However, as we discussed before, the messages that are returned back from Access are not very descriptive. The actual problem exists because the query we are trying to execute was misspelled.

```
-2147217900
[Microsoft][ODBC Microsoft Access Driver] Invalid SQL statement; expected 'DELETE',
'INSERT', 'PROCEDURE', 'SELECT', or 'UPDATE'.
Microsoft OLE DB Provider for ODBC Drivers
37000
-3500
```

The SQL Server version of this message is much more descriptive. Double check to ensure you have spelled the stored procedure name correctly, and also check to ensure the stored procedure actually exists under the owner prefix that you specified.

*Owner prefixes will be covered in detail in the next chapter.*

```
-2147217900
[Microsoft][ODBC SQL Server Driver][SQL Server]Could not find stored procedure
'up_select_author'.
Microsoft OLE DB Provider for ODBC Drivers
37000
2812
```

> **dbo.up_select_authors is not the same as willist.up_select_authors**
>
> **Ensure you are specifying the correct owner of the stored procedure.**

Another common mistake is to specify the wrong option on the execute statement. This doesn't seem to be a problem when dealing with an Access database, but definitely is when dealing with SQL Server. When using inline SQL you must specify the option of adCmdText. When you use a stored procedure you should specify adCmdStoredProc.

```
-2147217900
[Microsoft][ODBC SQL Server Driver]Syntax error or access violation
Microsoft OLE DB Provider for ODBC Drivers
37000
0
```

Sometimes a stored procedure has so many parameters it is very easy to overlook one. As you can see, Access doesn't return a very descriptive message letting you know that you forgot to provide a parameter to a parameter query.

```
2147217900
[Microsoft][ODBC Microsoft Access Driver] Invalid SQL statement; expected 'DELETE',
'INSERT', 'PROCEDURE', 'SELECT', or 'UPDATE'.
Microsoft OLE DB Provider for ODBC Drivers
37000
-3500
```

The good thing about SQL Server is that it will tell you exactly which parameter you forgot. If your parameters are self describing then you can quickly tell what data you should pass, as shown in this message.

```
-2147217900
[Microsoft][ODBC SQL Server Driver][SQL Server]Procedure 'up_parmsel_checks_paid'
expects parameter '@date', which was not supplied.
Microsoft OLE DB Provider for ODBC Drivers
37000
201
```

The last error we'll discuss does not display an error message, but deals with recordset data and should be mentioned here. Even as an experienced developer I make this common mistake. For example: I will sometimes forget to code `objRS.MoveNext` before the `Loop` statement to advance the recordset and the code will get stuck in a loop. The symptoms of this type of error are:

- ❏ Web page does not display
- ❏ No error messages are displayed
- ❏ The mouse pointer in your browser displays an arrow and hourglass, or the web server will begin to become slow and unresponsive to requests. Also, the hard drives of the server will begin to chatter incessantly as it hits the swap file.

The solution is to hit **Stop** on your browser.

# ASP Help

Most of the time, the errors that you receive from Active Server Pages are pretty self-explanatory, as we have demonstrated in the previous examples. However, there will come a time when you receive an error that is not so simple and you cannot figure it out. Where do you turn for help?

## ASP-ADO Errors

The first place to go when you need help with ASP errors is the **MSDN Library**. There are MSDN Library CDs that come with either Visual Studio or Visual Basic, or you can access it online at `http://msdn.microsoft.com/library/`. Under the Tools and Technologies section is a section for Active Server Pages. This section provides invaluable information and can even step you through debugging an ASP script.

For ADO errors you should turn to the Platform SDK in the MSDN Library. Here you will find information on Microsoft Data Access 2.1 SDK under Data Access Services. You will find a whole section on ADO error codes along with other valuable information relating to ADO.

Sometimes you just can't seem to find the answer that you are looking for in the MSDN Library. There is a wealth of information available on the Internet – here are just a few.

For scripting answers and general information you should go to the Microsoft Windows Scripting Technologies web site at `http://msdn.microsoft.com/scripting/`.

Microsoft Technet is also a valuable source of information and provides a search function. You can find Technet at `http://www.microsoft.com/technet/`.

Peer support is available in the MS ASP newsgroups usually manned by ASP specialists.

ASPToday has a daily article on ASP development at `http://www.asptoday.com`

## ASP Roadmap

The **ASP Roadmap** gets installed with Microsoft FrontPage and should be your starting point when you first start developing Active Server Pages. Along with some valuable information you will also find some samples and step-by-step instructions for building an ASP page.

# Summary

In this chapter we have examined why error handling is important and have demonstrated some techniques that you can employ to trap and display errors in both a development and production environment. We have taken at look at both the VBScript `Error` object and the ADO `Errors` collection. To sum up, you should know how to:

❑ Implement error handling for both ASP and ADO
❑ Retrieve error information
❑ Use error information to react or not react to problems
❑ Avoid some of the common errors in ASP and ADO
❑ Get help with ASP and ADO errors and questions

# Exercise

Create a web page to display the production error log file. Add a button that will clear the log file upon request. All functionality should be contained in the same page. Your page should display something similar to this:

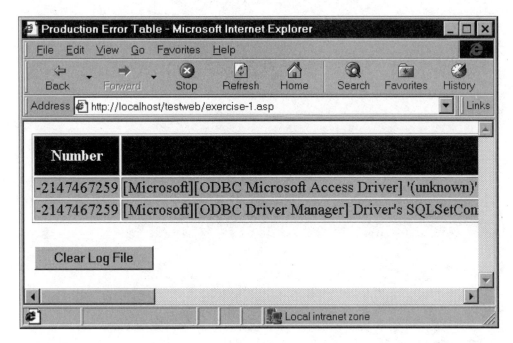

# Exercise Answer

The code for the web page is shown below (available in `Exercise-1.asp`):

```
<HTML>
<HEAD>
<META NAME="GENERATOR" Content="Microsoft Visual Studio 6.0">
<TITLE>Error Table</TITLE>
</HEAD>
<BODY>
<%
'****************************************************************************
'* Step 1 - Display the error log table
'****************************************************************************

If Len(Request.Form("FormAction")) = 0 Then
%>
  <!--Start the form-->
  <FORM ACTION="Exercise-1.asp" METHOD="post" NAME="form1">
  <INPUT TYPE=hidden NAME=FormAction VALUE=Step2>

  <!--Start the table and build the header-->
  <TABLE BORDER=1>
  <TR>
  <TH BGCOLOR=navy><FONT COLOR=white>Number</FONT ></TH>
  <TH BGCOLOR=navy><FONT COLOR=white>Description</FONT ></TH>
  <TH BGCOLOR=navy><FONT COLOR=white>Source</FONT ></TH>
  <TH BGCOLOR=navy><FONT COLOR=white>SQL State</FONT ></TH>
  <TH BGCOLOR=navy><FONT COLOR=white>Native Error</FONT ></TH>
  </TR>
<%
  'Perform error handling
  On Error Resume Next
  Set objFile = Server.CreateObject("Scripting.FileSystemObject")
  Set objLog = objFile.OpenTextFile(Server.MapPath("ProductionErrorLog.txt"))

  'If we could not open the file display the error message
  If Err.Number > 0 Then
    Response.Write "Error opening log file<P>"
    Response.Write "Error Number: " & Err.Number & _
      ", Error Description: " & Err.Description
  End If

  'If the file is not empty then process it
  If Not objLog.AtEndOfStream Then

    'Process the file until we reach EOF
    Do While Not objLog.AtEndOfStream
      'Read the data into a variable
      strText = objLog.ReadLine
      'Split the text into an array
      arrText = Split(strText,"|")
%>
      <!--Build a row of data-->
      <TR>
      <TD NOWRAP BGCOLOR=silver><%=arrText(0)%></TD>
      <TD NOWRAP BGCOLOR=silver><%=arrText(1)%></TD>
      <TD NOWRAP BGCOLOR=silver><%=arrText(2)%></TD>
      <TD NOWRAP BGCOLOR=silver><%=arrText(3)%></TD>
      <TD NOWRAP BGCOLOR=silver><%=arrText(4)%></TD>
      </TR>
<%
    Loop
  End If
```

```
   'Close the file
   objLog.Close

   'Dereference the objects
   Set objLog = Nothing
   Set objFile = Nothing
%>
   </TABLE>
   <TABLE>
   <TR><TD>  </TD></TR>
   <TR><TD>
     <INPUT TYPE=submit ID=btnClear NAME=btnClear VALUE="Clear Log File">
   </TD></TR>
   </TABLE>
   </FORM>

<%
'***************************************************************************
'* Step 2 - Clear the log file
'***************************************************************************

ElseIf Request.Form("FormAction") = "Step2" Then

   'Perform error handling
   On Error Resume Next

   'Create the file system object
   Set objFile = Server.CreateObject("Scripting.FileSystemObject")

   'Open the log file with parameters to clear it by overwriting any
   'existing data
   Set objLog = _
     objFile.CreateTextFile(Server.MapPath("ProductionErrorLog.txt")

   'If we could not open the file display the error message
   If Err.Number > 0 Then
     Response.Write "Error opening log file<P>"
     Response.Write "Error Number: " & Err.Number & _
       ", Error Description: " & Err.Description
   End If

   'Close the file
   objLog.Close

   'Dereference the objects
   Set objLog = Nothing
   Set objFile = Nothing

   'Write a message indicating the log file was cleared
   Response.Write "The log file has been cleared"
End If
%>
</TABLE>
</BODY>
</HTML>
```

Let's take a look at how this code works. First, this page performs multiple functions by breaking the server side script up into separate steps.

We have a form in the first step that will post all data back to the same page when the Submit button is clicked. The form also contains a hidden field, FormAction, which indicates which step in the script should be processed next. We start the page by checking the length of the field from the request form. If the length of this field is zero, it indicates that this is the first time executing this page and we want to process the first step of the script.

```
<HTML>
<HEAD>
<META NAME="GENERATOR" Content="Microsoft Visual Studio 6.0">
<TITLE>Error Table</TITLE>
</HEAD>
<BODY>
<%
'************************************************************************
'* Step 1 - Display the error log table
'************************************************************************

If Len(Request.Form("FormAction")) = 0 Then
%>
```

We start the first step by building a form, which contains the hidden field FormAction. Next, we build the table header rows for the error log table.

```
<!--Start the form-->
<FORM ACTION="Exercise-1.asp" METHOD="post" NAME="form1">
<INPUT TYPE=hidden NAME=FormAction VALUE=Step2>

<!--Start the table and build the header-->
<TABLE BORDER=1>
<TR>
<TH BGCOLOR=navy><FONT COLOR=white>Number</FONT ></TH>
<TH BGCOLOR=navy><FONT COLOR=white>Description</FONT ></TH>
<TH BGCOLOR=navy><FONT COLOR=white>Source</FONT ></TH>
<TH BGCOLOR=navy><FONT COLOR=white>SQL State</FONT ></TH>
<TH BGCOLOR=navy><FONT COLOR=white>Native Error</FONT ></TH>
</TR>
```

This section of code should be familiar, as it is the same as the previous examples and does not need further explanation.

```
<%
'Perform error handling
On Error Resume Next
Set objFile = Server.CreateObject("Scripting.FileSystemObject")
Set objLog = objFile.OpenTextFile(Server.MapPath("ProductionErrorLog.txt"))

'If we could not open the file display the error message
If Err.Number > 0 Then
  Response.Write "Error opening log file<P>"
  Response.Write "Error Number: " & Err.Number & _
    ", Error Description: " & Err.Description
End If

'If the file is not empty then process it
If Not objLog.AtEndOfStream Then

  'Process the file until we reach EOF
  Do While Not objLog.AtEndOfStream
    'Read the data into a variable
    strText = objLog.ReadLine
    'Split the text into an array
    arrText = Split(strText,"|")
%>
```

```
      <!--Build a row of data-->
      <TR>
      <TD NOWRAP BGCOLOR=silver><%=arrText(0)%></TD>
      <TD NOWRAP BGCOLOR=silver><%=arrText(1)%></TD>
      <TD NOWRAP BGCOLOR=silver><%=arrText(2)%></TD>
      <TD NOWRAP BGCOLOR=silver><%=arrText(3)%></TD>
      <TD NOWRAP BGCOLOR=silver><%=arrText(4)%></TD>
      </TR>
<%
    Loop
  End If

  'Close the file
  objLog.Close

  'Dereference the objects
  Set objLog = Nothing
  Set objFile = Nothing
%>
```

We close the error log table and start a new table to display the submit button. We include a blank row in the new table to provide the proper spacing of the submit button from the error log table. This ends the code for the first step of our page.

```
</TABLE>
<TABLE>
<TR><TD>  </TD></TR>
<TR><TD>
  <INPUT TYPE=submit ID=btnClear NAME=btnClear VALUE="Clear Log File">
</TD></TR>
</TABLE>
</FORM>
```

Once the page has been processed for the first time and the user clicks on the Submit button, the second step of our page will be processed. This is because the request form contains a field called FormAction and that field contains the value of Step2. We start the second stage of processing by creating the FileSystemObject and opening the file in create mode, which will clear the file.

```
<%
'****************************************************************************
'* Step 2 - Clear the log file
'****************************************************************************

ElseIf Request.Form("FormAction") = "Step2" Then

  'Perform error handling
  On Error Resume Next

  'Create the file system object
  Set objFile = Server.CreateObject("Scripting.FileSystemObject")

  'Open the log file with parameters to clear it by overwriting any
  'existing data
  Set objLog = _
    objFile.CreateTextFile(Server.MapPath("ProductionErrorLog.txt")
```

We perform the proper error handling as before and close the file, de-referencing all of our objects.

```
'If we could not open the file display the error message
If Err.Number > 0 Then
  Response.Write "Error opening log file<P>"
  Response.Write "Error Number: " & Err.Number & _
    ", Error Description: " & Err.Description
End If

'Close the file
objLog.Close

'Dereference the objects
Set objLog = Nothing
Set objFile = Nothing
```

We display a message to the user letting them know that the log file has been cleared, and then we end this section of code, which brings us to the end of the page.

```
'Write a message indicating the log file was cleared
  Response.Write "The log file has been cleared"
End If
%>
</TABLE>
</BODY>
</HTML>
```

# Quiz

**1.** Where does the `Error` object fit in to ASP?

**2.** What three common properties do the VBScript `Error` object and the ADO `Error` object share?

**3.** Why can we raise a custom error using the VBScript `Error` object but not the ADO `Error` object?

**4.** What is the one key statement that allows us to handle errors?

**5.** How can we determine how many errors are contained in the ADO `Errors` collection?

**6.** What is the single most common scripting error?

# Quiz Answers

**1.** The Error object is a built-in object of VBScript.

**2.** The three most common properties are number, description, and source.

**3.** Because the ADO Error object consists of a collection of errors returned by the ODBC driver in use. Either the underlying datastore or the actual ODBC driver generates the errors returned. The VBScript Error object is designed by its very nature to provide a means of returning errors and as a mechanism to allow you to raise your own custom errors.

**4.** On Error Resume Next tells ASP to ignore the error and resume with the next statement, which would be where we would have our error handling code placed.

**5.** By querying the Errors collection's Count property.

**6.** Forgetting an End If statement or forgetting to code a MoveNext for a Recordset object.

Setup cannot install system files or update shared files if the files are in use. Before c[...] any open applications.

Exit Setup

Continue

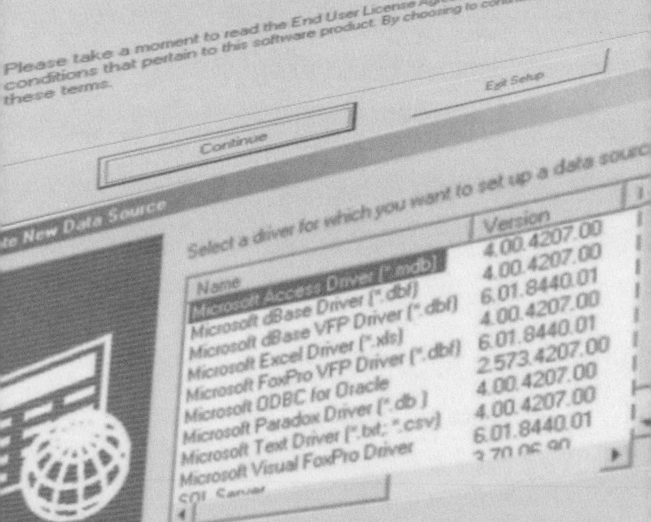

te New Data Source

Select a driver for which you want to set up a data sourc[...]

| Name | Version |
|------|---------|
| Microsoft Access Driver (*.mdb) | 4.00.4207.00 |
| Microsoft dBase Driver (*.dbf) | 4.00.4207.00 |
| Microsoft dBase VFP Driver (*.dbf) | 6.01.8440.01 |
| Microsoft Excel Driver (*.xls) | 4.00.4207.00 |
| Microsoft FoxPro VFP Driver (*.dbf) | 6.01.8440.01 |
| Microsoft ODBC for Oracle | 2.573.4207.00 |
| Microsoft Paradox Driver (*.db ) | 4.00.4207.00 |
| Microsoft Text Driver (*.txt; *.csv) | 4.00.4207.00 |
| Microsoft Visual FoxPro Driver | 6.01.8440.01 |
| SQL Server | 2.70.06.90 |

Finish

Cancel

# Command Object

In previous chapters we covered the Recordset object and the Connection object in detail. You have learned all the slick things that can be done with them. After having read those chapters, you may be wondering why you need the Command object.

Experience has shown that the Command object is probably the most misunderstood and least used object in the ADO object model. The reason for this might lie in the fact that the Command object can be difficult to use if you're new to ADO. Thus, new users might be put off using it except when absolutely necessary, and only learn as much about it as needed to get the job done. After reading this chapter you will have a better understanding of the Command object, and should feel comfortable using it in more situations.

This chapter focuses on nothing but the Command object - we will show you when you *need* to use the Command object and when it is *useful* to use it. We will also demonstrate some useful techniques when using the Command object. But before we dive into those areas we will explore the structure of the Command object and show you all of its associated objects. This will help you to better understand how the Command object works and where it fits into the ADO object model. It will also help you to better understand the examples demonstrated in this chapter.

In this chapter we will cover:

- ❏ The Command object structure
- ❏ When you must use the Command object
- ❏ When it is useful to use the Command object
- ❏ Command object parameters
- ❏ Stuffing techniques

# Command Object Overview

Before we continue, it would be prudent for us to take a look at what the Command object really is and what it does. The Command object represents a specific command that is to be executed. This command can be in the form of a SQL SELECT, INSERT, UPDATE, or DELETE statement, or can contain the name of a stored procedure to be executed.

> *Stored procedures will be covered in detail in chapter 14. Basically, a stored procedure is a set of SQL statements, stored and compiled within the database itself. In Access they are referred to as queries, but for simplicity we will use the standard term stored procedures.*

A command can also contain Data Definition Language. Data Definition Language comprises SQL statements that alter your database structure, such as ALTER TABLE or DROP INDEX.

The following code fragment shows a simple SELECT statement that could be executed with the Command object. This SELECT statement is selecting just one column, BoatName, from the table Boats.

```
SELECT BoatName FROM Boats
```

The Command object would be able to execute this SQL statement, but we would have to create and set the Recordset object equal to the Command object. This is because the Command object cannot be used to receive *records* from the database. However, the Command object can be used to receive *values* returned from a SQL statement or stored procedure. All of this will be explained and demonstrated later in this chapter.

The Command object can also be used to alter the structure of the database, using the Data Definition Language. This functionality depends on the rights of the user in the database being used. The structural changes can be in the form of altering tables, and adding or deleting columns or parameters. This next SQL code fragment shows a column named YearManufactured being added to the Boats table.

```
ALTER TABLE Boats ADD YearManufactured INT Null
```

So basically the Command object contains a command to be executed against the database. This command may or may not return a result or a recordset.

# Command Object Structure

Before we dive into the specifics of the Command object, it might be helpful to know exactly where the Command object fits into the ADO object model. The following diagram shows the entire ADO object model, and the highlighted boxes show the Command object and its related objects. This should help you to better understand where we are in the model, when working with the Command object.

As you can see, the Connection object is at the very top of the model and is required by all other objects in the ADO object model. This makes sense given the very nature of the Connection object. It establishes a connection to our database and without it we wouldn't be able to perform any work against the database. Looking at the Command object, we see that it contains a Parameters collection that is made up of one or more Parameter objects. The Command object requires the Connection object in order to execute any commands.

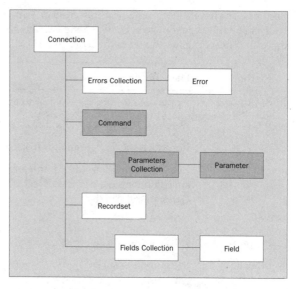

As with any other object in the ADO object model, the Command object contains various methods and properties. So let's take a look at the basic methods and properties of the Command object.

| Method | Description |
|---|---|
| Cancel | Cancels the current executing command |
| CreateParameter | Creates a new Parameter object with the specified properties |
| Execute | Executes the SQL statement or stored procedure specified in the CommandText property |

| Property | Description |
|---|---|
| ActiveConnection | Specifies a valid Connection object or connect string |
| CommandText | The text of the command you want to execute |
| CommandTimeout | Specifies how long to wait while executing before terminating and generating an error |
| CommandType | Indicates the type of command being executed as specified in the CommandText property |
| Name | Assigns/Retrieves a name to/of a Command object |
| Prepared | Indicates whether to save a compiled version of a command before execution |
| State | Read-Only property to describe the current state of an object, for example open, closed, or executing. |

The `Parameters` collection contains a collection of `Parameter` objects. To add or modify parameters in the `Parameters` collection we have to use the `Parameter` object. The `Parameters` collection has its own methods and properties as shown in the table below.

| Method | Description |
| --- | --- |
| Append | Appends a `Parameter` object to the collection. |
| Delete | Deletes a `Parameter` object from the collection. |
| Item | Returns a specific parameter from the collection by name or ordinal reference. |
| Refresh | Retrieves provider-side parameter information for the stored procedure specified by the `Command` object. The stored procedure's parameters and data types are returned. |

| Property | Description |
| --- | --- |
| Count | Read-Only property that returns the number of `Parameter` objects in the collection. |

The `Parameter` object itself contains its own methods and properties, which are shown next. These methods and properties apply to each `Parameter` object in the `Parameters` collection.

| Method | Description |
| --- | --- |
| AppendChunk | Appends large text or binary data to a `Parameter` object |

| Property | Description |
| --- | --- |
| Attributes | Indicates one or more characteristics of an object |
| Direction | Indicates the parameter direction - input, output or both |
| Name | Assigns/Retrieves a name to/from a `Parameter` object |
| NumericScale | Indicates the scale of a numeric value in a `Parameter` object |
| Precision | Indicates the degree of precision for numeric values in a `Parameter` object |
| Size | Indicates the maximum size for a `Parameter` object |
| Type | Indicates the data type for a `Parameter` object |
| Value | Indicates the actual value for a `Parameter` object |

We have taken a look at the basic objects that make up the `Command` object. Having looked at their methods and properties here should help you to better understand these objects and their relationship to each other. We will be getting into more detail when we actually use these objects. Use this section as a reference when we start to talk about and use the various methods and properties of these objects.

# When You Must Use a Command Object

This section will cover the details of when you *must* use a Command object. We will be covering several different scenarios and will be providing examples for you to try. By going through the examples, you will get a better understanding of how the Command object works. You will also become more familiar and comfortable with using the Command object.

There are several circumstances when you need to use a Command object. One such circumstance is when executing any Data Definition Language that modifies your database structure. Modifying your database structure includes actions such as altering a table or stored procedure. These types of database updates do not use the Recordset object, as they return no records, so you should use a Command object.

Another example would be when you need to update data in a table and pass parameters to the SQL string or stored procedure. This can be in the form of inserting, updating and deleting rows from a table. The Command object is ideal for this type of operation, especially if you need to persist the data in the Command object and execute it again. This would be handy if you were processing a loop that updated different rows in a table, and you were passing parameters to the Command object. If you use a SQL string, you can set the Prepared property of the Command object to True, and subsequent executions of the command would execute faster than the first one. This is because the database would compile the command on the first execution and use the compiled version for subsequent executions.

The data contained in the CommandText property of the Command object can be either actual SQL statements or the name of a stored procedure. The command being executed can either accept parameters or not. It all depends on the actions that are being performed.

Before we continue, let's touch briefly on the ActiveConnection property of the Command object. This property can contain either an active Connection object or a connect string. Which method you use depends on what type of command you are performing and whether or not you persist the data in the Command object. The thing to watch out for here is that if you use a connection string you will be unable to check for errors. This is because the Errors collection is part of the Connection object. Refer to our earlier diagram to see where the Errors collection fits into the ADO object model.

All of our examples will use an active Connection object so that we may check for errors. This is especially useful in debugging, as our error handler routine displays all the errors on your Web page. We will explain the error handling routine only briefly here, as it was covered in much more detail in Chapter 12.

## Try It out - Altering the database structure - Add a column

This example demonstrates adding a new column to the `Boats` table in the Access `Sailors` database, using the Data Definition Language. Remember we mentioned earlier that the Data Definition Language is actually just SQL statements that modify the structure of your database. We are using the `Command` object here to alter the database structure and insert a new column. You can see the result of our code in this screenshot:

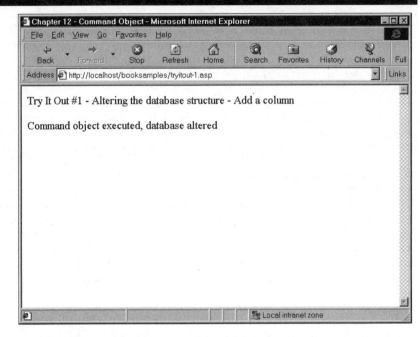

The code that will produce this for us is as follows. It can also be found in `TryItOut-1.asp`.

```
<HTML>
<HEAD>
<META NAME="GENERATOR" Content="Microsoft Visual Studio 6.0">
<TITLE>Chapter 12 - Command Object</TITLE>
</HEAD>
<BODY>

<!--Display the page data-->
Try It Out #1 - Altering the database structure - Add a column<BR><BR>

<%
'Instruct VBScript to ignore the error and continue
'with the next line of code
On Error Resume Next

'Create and open the database object
Set objConn = Server.CreateObject("ADODB.Connection")
objConn.Open "DSN=Sailors"

'Check for errors
If objConn.Errors.Count > 0 Then
  'Create an error object to access the ADO errors collection
  Set objErr = Server.CreateObject("ADODB.Error")
  'Declare Boolean(and other places) flag for critical errors
  Dim blnCriticalError
  'Write all errors to the page
  For Each objErr In objConn.Errors
```

```
  If objErr.Number <> 0 Then
    Response.Write "Number: " & objErr.Number & "<P>"
    Response.Write "Description: " & objErr.Description & "<P>"
    Response.Write "Source: " & objErr.Source & "<P>"
    Response.Write "SQLState: " & objErr.SQLState & "<P>"
    Response.Write "NativeError: " & objErr.NativeError & "<P>"
    blnCriticalError = True
  End If
 Next
 'Dereference all objects
 Set objErr = Nothing
 If blnCriticalError Then
   Response.End
 End If
End If

'Declare variables
Dim adCmdText
adCmdText = 1

'Create the command object and set the various properties
Set objCmd = Server.CreateObject("ADODB.Command")
Set objCmd.ActiveConnection = objConn
objCmd.CommandText = "ALTER TABLE Boats ADD YearManufactured INT Null"
objCmd.CommandType = adCmdText
objCmd.CommandTimeout = 30
objCmd.Prepared = False
objCmd.Execute

'Check for errors
If objConn.Errors.Count > 0 Then
 'Create an error object to access the ADO errors collection
 Set objErr = Server.CreateObject("ADODB.Error")
 'Write all errors to the page
 For Each objErr In objConn.Errors
  If objErr.Number <> 0 Then
    Response.Write "Number: " & objErr.Number & "<P>"
    Response.Write "Description: " & objErr.Description & "<P>"
    Response.Write "Source: " & objErr.Source & "<P>"
    Response.Write "SQLState: " & objErr.SQLState & "<P>"
    Response.Write "NativeError: " & objErr.NativeError & "<P>"
    blnCriticalError = True
  End If
 Next
 'Dereference all objects
 Set objErr = Nothing
 If blnCriticalError Then
   Response.End
 End If
End If

'Dereference objects
Set objCmd = Nothing
objConn.Close
Set objConn = Nothing
%>

<!--Display a message that the database was altered-->
Command object executed, database altered
</BODY>
</HTML>
```

### How It Works – Altering the database structure – Add a column

We start out by including the standard HTML tags used to define a page.

```
<HTML>
<HEAD>
<META NAME="GENERATOR" Content="Microsoft Visual Studio 6.0">
<TITLE>Chapter 12 - Command Object</TITLE>
</HEAD>
<BODY>
```

We write the page data using standard HTML tags, and start the server-side script by turning on error handling.

```
<!--Display the page data-->
Try It Out #1 - Altering the database structure - Add a column<BR><BR>

<%
'Instruct VBScript to ignore the error and continue
'with the next line of code
On Error Resume Next
```

We create the `Connection` object and open the `Sailors` database using the DSN that was set up in Chapter 2. Because of the type of operation that we are performing, an active `Connection` object is required.

```
'Create and open the database object
Set objConn = Server.CreateObject("ADODB.Connection")
objConn.Open "DSN=Sailors"
```

After we open the database we need to check the ADO `Errors` collection for any errors, by seeing if the `Count` property is greater than zero. If an error has occurred, we then create an `Error` object that will allow us to access the `Errors` collection. Next, we loop through the `Errors` collection checking each error. If the error number is not equal to zero then a serious error has occurred, and we write the errors on the web page, and set a flag to let us know what action to take after we have checked all errors.

One thing to note here is that if a serious error did occur, we stop all processing of our script by using the `End` method of the `Response` object.

> *Remember that error handling, the ADO `Errors` collection, and this particular error handling routine are all explained in detail in Chapter 12.*

```
'Check for errors
If objConn.Errors.Count > 0 Then
  'Create an error object to access the ADO errors collection
  Set objErr = Server.CreateObject("ADODB.Error")
  'Declare Boolean flag for critical errors
  Dim blnCriticalError
  'Write all errors to the page
  For Each objErr In objConn.Errors
    If objErr.Number <> 0 Then
      Response.Write "Number: " & objErr.Number & "<P>"
      Response.Write "Description: " & objErr.Description & "<P>"
      Response.Write "Source: " & objErr.Source & "<P>"
      Response.Write "SQLState: " & objErr.SQLState & "<P>"
      Response.Write "NativeError: " & objErr.NativeError & "<P>"
      blnCriticalError = True
    End If
```

```
Next
 'Dereference all objects
 Set objErr = Nothing
 If blnCriticalError Then
  Response.End
 End If
End If
```

Next we need to define our ADO verbs. These are enumerations (of constant value) that are used by the various properties to tell ADO what the property indicates. Not all ADO verbs are recognized by ASP, so we define what we need here and set their values. For example, adCmdText is represented by a value of 1.

These values can be found in the MSDN Library. This is available at http://msdn.microsoft.com/default.asp. If you look in the index of the library and key in ADOEnums, you will see a listing of all ADO enumerations.

> As Microsoft documentation is not always the most up to date, perhaps an even better method would be to open a Visual Basic project and set a reference to Microsoft ActiveX Data Objects 2.x Library. Substitute the x in the version number with the latest version you have installed. Then you can use the object browser in VB to look at the enumerations and get their values. You can also use the adovbs.inc include file.

```
'Declare variables
Dim adCmdText
adCmdText = 1
```

The next thing we need to do is create a Command object in our code. Then we set the ActiveConnection property to a valid Connection object that we defined and opened above.

```
'Create the command object and set the various properties
Set objCmd = Server.CreateObject("ADODB.Command")
Set objCmd.ActiveConnection = objConn
```

The CommandText property contains a string value containing our SQL command that we want executed. This property does not have to contain SQL statements, it can also contain the name of a stored procedure. The SQL statement we will be executing adds a column named YearManufactured to the Boats table. We specify that this column is an integer data type and can contain null values.

```
objCmd.CommandText = "ALTER TABLE Boats ADD YearManufactured INT Null"
```

At this point, the properties listed above are the only properties *required*. The properties that follow are optional and are included here to *optimize* the execution of our command. The CommandType property specifies what type of command you are executing. By setting this property to adCmdText, we are telling ADO that we are executing a command that contains a SQL string. This prevents ADO from having to make calls to our database provider to figure out what type of command we are trying to execute. The following table lists the available options for the CommandType property that we are using in this chapter. The complete list can be found in the ADO documentation.

| | |
|---|---|
| adCmdText | Specifies a textual command such as a SQL string. |
| adCmdTable | Specifies a table name. |
| adCmdStoredProc | Specifies that a stored procedure is being used. |
| adCmdUnknown | Specifies that the CommandText property is unknown. This is the default value, and instructs the database provider to identify the type of call. |

```
objCmd.CommandType = adCmdText
```

The `CommandTimeout` property specifies how long the `Command` object should wait while executing a command, before terminating the command and generating an error. The default value is 30 seconds and this property is listed here to demonstrate its use. This property accepts a long value in seconds.

```
objCmd.CommandTimeout = 30
```

The `Prepared` property is a Boolean value specifying whether or not the database provider should compile a version of the command before execution. It will slow down the first call of this command, but if you are executing this command in a loop, it will significantly increase the performance for the following calls. Once the database provider has compiled the command, subsequent calls will use the compiled version. This property is not available by all database providers. As with any Boolean value, the default value for this property is False.

```
objCmd.Prepared = False
```

Finally, we execute our command and check for errors using the same error handling routine as above.

```
objCmd.Execute

'Check for errors
If objConn.Errors.Count > 0 Then
 'Create an error object to access the ADO errors collection
 Set objErr = Server.CreateObject("ADODB.Error")
 'Write all errors to the page
 For Each objErr In objConn.Errors
  If objErr.Number <> 0 Then
   Response.Write "Number: " & objErr.Number & "<P>"
   Response.Write "Description: " & objErr.Description & "<P>"
   Response.Write "Source: " & objErr.Source & "<P>"
   Response.Write "SQLState: " & objErr.SQLState & "<P>"
   Response.Write "NativeError: " & objErr.NativeError & "<P>"
   blnCriticalError = True
  End If
 Next
 'Dereference all objects
 Set objErr = Nothing
 If blnCriticalError Then
  Response.End
 End If
End If
```

We need to close the database connection and de-reference our objects to release them from memory.

```
'Dereference objects
Set objCmd = Nothing
objConn.Close
Set objConn = Nothing
%>
```

If we made it this far in our code, we have successfully executed our command and there were no errors returned. That being said, we need to display a message indicating our command has successfully executed. After we display our message, we end the page by writing the standard HTML tags.

```
<!--Display a message that the database was altered-->
Command object executed, database altered
</BODY>
</HTML>
```

If you run this Web page and get the message above, you can then open Access, look at the Boats table and see the added column.

## Try It Out - Altering the database structure - Drop a column

Since we have a method of altering the database by *adding* a column, it follows that we would come across a circumstance where we would need to *drop* a column. This is where this next example fits in. This example drops the column we have added to the Boats table. As with the previous example, this example also uses the Data Definition Language, because we are altering the structure of the database.

> **Be aware that dropping a column that contains data is irreversible. Ensure the SQL statement you are using will drop the correct column in the correct table. Also, having a current backup of your database cannot hurt.**

The following screenshot shows the result of running our code:

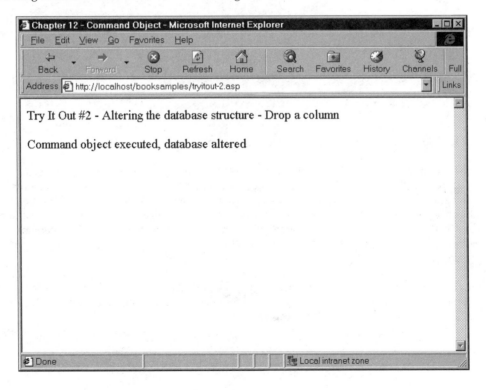

**495**

The code for this example can be found in `TryItOut-2.asp` and is almost the same as for the previous example, with the following changes.

In the heading section our page title is different:

```
<!--Display the page data-->
Try It Out #2 - Altering the database structure - Drop a column<BR><BR>
```

There are also differences in the section where we set the Command object.

```
'Create the Command object and set the various properties
Set objCmd = Server.CreateObject("ADODB.Command")
Set objCmd.ActiveConnection = objConn
objCmd.CommandText = "ALTER TABLE Boats DROP COLUMN YearManufactured"
objCmd.CommandType = adCmdText
objCmd.Execute
```

### How It Works – Altering the database structure – Drop a column

Most of the code is the same as in the previous example so we won't explain it again.

As before, we create our Command object and set its active connection to our Connection object. Next, we set the CommandText property to our SQL string, and set the CommandType property to specify that we are including text for execution. Finally, we execute the command. In this case the SQL string causes a column to be dropped.

Notice that we have not used the CommandTimeout or the Prepared properties, as we are taking the default values for those properties.

```
'Create the Command object and set the various properties
Set objCmd = Server.CreateObject("ADODB.Command")
Set objCmd.ActiveConnection = objConn
objCmd.CommandText = "ALTER TABLE Boats DROP COLUMN YearManufactured"
objCmd.CommandType = adCmdText
objCmd.Execute
```

The rest of the code works the same as in the previous example.

Another case you might run into, more likely than not, is that you will need to receive a value back from a stored procedure or SQL statement. The return value could be a return code, a row count of records, or a count of rows affected by the last command. This type of processing is ideal for, and requires, the Command object. This is because you can set the parameters for the Parameter object, pass parameters to the stored procedure or SQL statement, and receive a parameter from the stored procedure or SQL statement once it finishes executing. (A stored procedure that returns a value does not always have to accept parameters - it depends on the processing being performed.)

Since Access does not support return values from a stored procedure, we will use SQL Server for this next example. You can follow along and try this example but you will need to set up the Sailors database in SQL Server. This is covered in detail in Appendix D.

## Try It Out – Receiving a Return Value From SQL Server

This example calls a SQL Server stored procedure that returns the number of boats listed on the Boats table as a return value. The Command object receives this return value from the procedure as a return parameter and then displays the returned value on the Web page. This example will introduce you to the Parameter object and the Parameter collections.

The following screenshot shows the result of running our code:

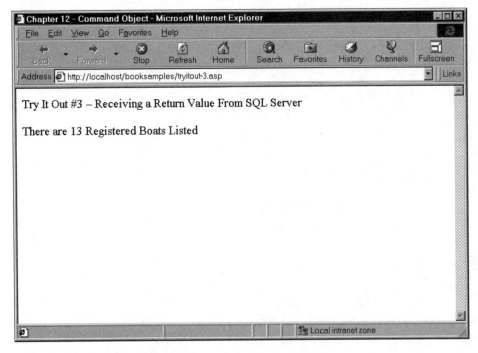

The code for the stored procedure is available as up_select_count_of_boats.

```
CREATE procedure up_select_count_of_boats AS
DECLARE @count INT
SELECT @count=count(boatsid) FROM boats
RETURN @count
```

The code for the web page is in TryItOut-3.asp.

```
<HTML>
<HEAD>
<META NAME="GENERATOR" Content="Microsoft Visual Studio 6.0">
<TITLE>Chapter 12 - Command Object</TITLE>
</HEAD>
<BODY>

<!--Display the page data-->
Try It Out #3 - Receiving a Return Value From SQL Server<BR><BR>
```

```
<%
'Instruct VBScript to ignore the error and continue
'with the next line of code
On Error Resume Next

'Create and open the database object
Set objConn = Server.CreateObject("ADODB.Connection")
objConn.Open "DSN=SQLSailor;uid=sa;pwd"""

'Check for errors
If objConn.Errors.Count > 0 Then
 'Create an error object to access the ADO errors collection
 Set objErr = Server.CreateObject("ADODB.Error")
 'Declare Boolean flag for critical errors
 Dim blnCriticalError
 'Write all errors to the page
 For Each objErr In objConn.Errors
  If objErr.Number <> 0 Then
    Response.Write "Number: " & objErr.Number & "<P>"
    Response.Write "Description: " & objErr.Description & "<P>"
    Response.Write "Source: " & objErr.Source & "<P>"
    Response.Write "SQLState: " & objErr.SQLState & "<P>"
    Response.Write "NativeError: " & objErr.NativeError & "<P>"
    blnCriticalError = True
  End If
 Next
 'Dereference all objects
 Set objErr = Nothing
 If blnCriticalError Then
   Response.End
 End If
End If

'Declare variables
Dim adCmdStoredProc
Dim adInteger
Dim adParamReturnValue
adCmdStoredProc = 4
adInteger = 3
adParamReturnValue = 4

'Create the command and parameter objects
Set objCmd = Server.CreateObject("ADODB.Command")
Set objParm = Server.CreateObject("ADODB.Parameter")

'Set the command object properties
Set objCmd.ActiveConnection = objConn
objCmd.CommandText = "call dbo.up_select_count_of_boats"
objCmd.CommandType = adCmdStoredProc

'Set the parameter and append it to the parameters collection
Set objParm = objCmd.CreateParameter("Return",adInteger,adParamReturnValue,,0)
objCmd.Parameters.Append objParm

objCmd.Execute

'Check for errors
If objConn.Errors.Count > 0 Then
 'Create an error object to access the ADO errors collection
 Set objErr = Server.CreateObject("ADODB.Error")
 'Write all errors to the page
 For Each objErr In objConn.Errors
```

```
  If objErr.Number <> 0 Then
    Response.Write "Number: " & objErr.Number & "<P>"
    Response.Write "Description: " & objErr.Description & "<P>"
    Response.Write "Source: " & objErr.Source & "<P>"
    Response.Write "SQLState: " & objErr.SQLState & "<P>"
    Response.Write "NativeError: " & objErr.NativeError & "<P>"
    blnCriticalError = True
  End If
Next
'Dereference all objects
Set objErr = Nothing
If blnCriticalError Then
  Response.End
End If
End If

Response.Write "There are " & objCmd.Parameters.Item("Return").Value & _
  " Registered Boats Listed"

'Close and dereference database objects
Set objParm = Nothing
Set objCmd = Nothing
objConn.Close
Set objConn = Nothing
%>
</BODY>
</HTML>
```

### How It Works: Creating the stored procedure

We want to create our stored procedure first, so start SQL Server Enterprise Manager and expand the server group where your Sailors database is located. Expand the Databases group and then expand the Sailors database. Right click on the Stored Procedures group and select New Stored Procedure from the popup menu.

If you notice, the first line of our stored procedure is already there, minus the actual stored procedure name. Highlight the [PROCEDURE NAME] name and replace it with up_select_count_of_boats. Case sensitivity does not matter for SQL Server.

```
CREATE PROCEDURE up_select_count_of_boats AS
```

We need to declare a variable to hold the count of boats in the Boats table. The variable we are going to use is @count and we specify that it is an integer data type.

```
DECLARE @count INT
```

Next, we select the count of the column BoatsID and assign the count to the variable @count. In other words we are selecting the count of the number of rows.

```
SELECT @count=count(boatsid) FROM boats
```

To have SQL Server return a value, we specify the RETURN function and pass it the value that we want to return. The return value that we pass to the RETURN function must be an integer, no other data types are allowed when using return values. Also, you cannot return a Null value. If you attempt to do so, a warning message is generated and a value of 0 through –14 will be returned.

```
RETURN @count
```

### Creating the ASP page

Now for the Active Server Page code, we start our page as we have done in the previous examples. We use the standard HTML headers and display our first line of text.

```
<!--Display the page data-->
Try It Out #3 - Receiving a Return Value From SQL Server<BR><BR>
```

Next, we turn on error handling, and create and open our database object.

Notice that this example is using a different DSN that points to the SQL Server version of our Sailors database. (Appendix D describes how to set up both the database and the DSN.) Also notice that we must include the user id (uid) that is authorized to access the database and we also include the password (pwd), which in this case is blank. If you did not set up this database yourself, ensure that you use the user id and password supplied by your database administrator.

```
<%
'Instruct VBScript to ignore the error and continue
'with the next line of code
On Error Resume Next

'Create and open the database object
Set objConn = Server.CreateObject("ADODB.Connection")
objConn.Open "DSN=SQLSailor;uid=sa;pwd"
```

Once again we check for errors after opening our database connection.

Again we declare the variables that we are using, with their enumeration value that we have looked up in either the ADO documentation or the VB object browser.

```
'Declare variables
Dim adCmdStoredProc
Dim adInteger
Dim adParamReturnValue
adCmdStoredProc = 4
adInteger = 3
adParamReturnValue = 4
```

Next we create our Command object and a Parameter object. We will be appending this Parameter object to the Parameters collection in just a little while.

```
'Create the command and parameter objects
Set objCmd = Server.CreateObject("ADODB.Command")
Set objParm = Server.CreateObject("ADODB.Parameter")
```

Now we set our ActiveConnection property to our Connection object. Then we set our CommandText property to the SQL statement that we want executed.

Notice that we are executing a stored procedure and we must specify this as such in the CommandType property.

```
'Set the command object properties
Set objCmd.ActiveConnection = objConn
objCmd.CommandText = "call dbo.up_select_count_of_boats"
objCmd.CommandType = adCmdStoredProc
```

To set the `Parameter` object we must execute the `CreateParameter` method of the `Command` object. The `CreateParameter` method accepts five arguments, which are listed in the table below.

| | |
|---|---|
| Name | A string value that identifies the parameter name. |
| Type | A long value from the `DataTypeEnum` that specifies what data type the parameter is. |
| Direction | A long value from the `ParameterDirectionEnum` that indicates the direction of the parameter. A parameter can be an input parameter, an output parameter, or both input and output parameter. A parameter can also be a return value. |
| Size | A long value that indicates the maximum length of the parameter value in bytes. |
| Value | The actual value of the parameter data. |

As you can see from our example, we are using `Return` as the parameter name, specifying that the parameter is an integer data type and the direction is a return value. We have not specified a size because we are using an integer data type, which is always four bytes long. The last argument is set as a default value.

Once we have set our `Parameter` properties, we need to append the `Parameter` object to the `Parameters` collection. We do this by using the `Append` method of the `Parameters` collection. All parameters must be specified in the `Parameters` collection in the order that the SQL statement or stored procedure expects them.

```
'Set the parameter and append it to the parameters collection
Set objParm = objCmd.CreateParameter("Return",adInteger,adParamReturnValue,,0)
objCmd.Parameters.Append objParm
```

Next, we execute our `Command` object and check for errors.

```
objCmd.Execute

'Check for errors
If objConn.Errors.Count > 0 Then
 'Create an error object to access the ADO errors collection
 Set objErr = Server.CreateObject("ADODB.Error")
 'Write all errors to the page
 For Each objErr In objConn.Errors
  If objErr.Number <> 0 Then
    Response.Write "Number: " & objErr.Number & "<P>"
    Response.Write "Description: " & objErr.Description & "<P>"
    Response.Write "Source: " & objErr.Source & "<P>"
    Response.Write "SQLState: " & objErr.SQLState & "<P>"
    Response.Write "NativeError: " & objErr.NativeError & "<P>"
    blnCriticalError = True
  End If
 Next
 'Dereference all objects
 Set objErr = Nothing
 If blnCriticalError Then
  Response.End
 End If
End If
```

We display a line of text on our Web page using the return value in the `Parameters` collection. Notice that we are referencing the parameter by the name that we gave it above in the `Name` property.

```
Response.Write "There are " & objCmd.Parameters.Item("Return").Value & _
  " Registered Boats Listed"
```

Lastly, we close and de-reference our database objects, and end the page using the standard HTML tags.

```
'Close and dereference database objects
Set objParm = Nothing
Set objCmd = Nothing
objConn.Close
Set objConn = Nothing
%>
</BODY>
</HTML>
```

# When it is Useful to Use a Command Object

Sometimes we use a `Command` object just because it is more useful to do so. Suppose you need to create a dynamic SQL statement that performs an update on a table. You need to perform this SQL statement several times within a loop.

This is an ideal situation for the `Command` object because we are able to have the `CommandText` property of the `Command` object prepared (compiled) by the database, which slows down the first execution only. Subsequent executions use the compiled version, which is just like executing a stored procedure. The compiled version uses the placeholders that we specify, and we only need to pass the parameters when calling subsequent executions.

Another useful reason to use the `Command` object and the `Parameters` collection is that it simplifies adding string values that contain single quotes. If we were to pass these string values ourselves, we would have to replace all single quotes with two consecutive single quotes, to prevent an un-terminated string error. By using the `Parameter` object, all of this is taken care of for us.

And then sometimes we want to dynamically create a SQL statement and just execute it once, passing it the parameters we need. This next example demonstrates this technique.

## Try It Out – Passing parameters to a SQL string

This example demonstrates passing two parameters in a SQL statement. We are using the `Boats` table and will update the `BoatNote` column for a boat that matches the `BoatName` parameter. So, this example passes two input parameters and does not return a value. We will be using our Access `Sailors` database, and the DSN set up in Chapter 2, for this example and the others that follow. The following screenshot shows what we see if we run the code.

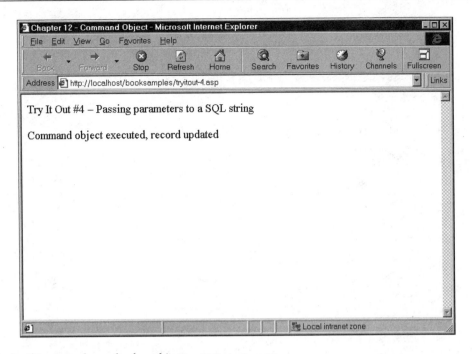

The code for this example can be found in `TryItOut-4.asp`.

```
<HTML>
<HEAD>
<META NAME="GENERATOR" Content="Microsoft Visual Studio 6.0">
<TITLE>Chapter 12 - Command Object</TITLE>
</HEAD>
<BODY>

<!--Display the page data-->
Try It Out #4 - Passing parameters to a SQL string<BR><BR>

<%
'Instruct VBScript to ignore the error and continue
'with the next line of code
On Error Resume Next

'Create and open the database object
Set objConn = Server.CreateObject("ADODB.Connection")
objConn.Open "DSN=Sailors"

'Check for errors
If objConn.Errors.Count > 0 Then
 'Create an error object to access the ADO errors collection
 Set objErr = Server.CreateObject("ADODB.Error")
 'Declare Boolean flag for critical errors
 Dim blnCriticalError
 'Write all errors to the page
```

```
For Each objErr In objConn.Errors
  If objErr.Number <> 0 Then
    Response.Write "Number: " & objErr.Number & "<P>"
    Response.Write "Description: " & objErr.Description & "<P>"
    Response.Write "Source: " & objErr.Source & "<P>"
    Response.Write "SQLState: " & objErr.SQLState & "<P>"
    Response.Write "NativeError: " & objErr.NativeError & "<P>"
    blnCriticalError = True
  End If
Next
'Dereference all objects
Set objErr = Nothing
If blnCriticalError Then
  Response.End
End If
End If

'Declare variables
Dim adCmdText
Dim adVarChar
Dim adParamInput
adCmdText = 1
adVarChar = 200
adParamInput = 1

'Create the command and parameter objects
Set objCmd = Server.CreateObject("ADODB.Command")
Set objParm = Server.CreateObject("ADODB.Parameter")

'Set the command object properties
Set objCmd.ActiveConnection = objConn
objCmd.CommandText = "UPDATE boats SET boatnote=? WHERE boatname=?"
objCmd.CommandType = adCmdText

'Set the parameters and append them to the parameters collection
Set objParm = objCmd.CreateParameter("boatnote",adVarChar,adParamInput,50, _
  "Now we have an excuse")
objCmd.Parameters.Append objParm
Set objParm = objCmd.CreateParameter("boatname",adVarChar,adParamInput,50, _
  "No Excuse to Lose")
objCmd.Parameters.Append objParm

objCmd.Execute

'Check for errors
If objConn.Errors.Count > 0 Then
  'Create an error object to access the ADO errors collection
  Set objErr = Server.CreateObject("ADODB.Error")
  'Write all errors to the page
  For Each objErr In objConn.Errors
    If objErr.Number <> 0 Then
      Response.Write "Number: " & objErr.Number & "<P>"
      Response.Write "Description: " & objErr.Description & "<P>"
      Response.Write "Source: " & objErr.Source & "<P>"
      Response.Write "SQLState: " & objErr.SQLState & "<P>"
      Response.Write "NativeError: " & objErr.NativeError & "<P>"
      blnCriticalError = True
    End If
  Next
  'Dereference all objects
  Set objErr = Nothing
  If blnCriticalError Then
```

```
  Response.End
 End If
End If

'Close and dereference database objects
Set objParm = Nothing
Set objCmd = Nothing
objConn.Close
Set objConn = Nothing
%>

<!--Display a message that the update was successful-->
Command object executed, record updated

</BODY>
</HTML>
```

### How It Works – Passing parameters to a SQL string

As always, we start our page in the same manner as in the previous examples, using standard HTML headers and displaying our first line of text:

```
<!--Display the page data-->
Try It Out #4 - Passing parameters to a SQL string<BR><BR>
```

Next, we turn on error handling, and create and open our database connection. We then check for errors to ensure nothing has gone wrong.

Again, we declare our variables and set their values, which we found in the MSDN library or the object browser in VB. Notice that this time we are using a `varchar` data type and the parameter direction being used is input:

```
'Declare variables
Dim adCmdText
Dim adVarChar
Dim adParamInput
adCmdText = 1
adVarChar = 200
adParamInput = 1
```

We create our `Command` and `Parameter` objects and then set the properties of the `Command` object. Notice that we are using a `CommandType` of adCmdText, which specifies we are using in-line SQL statements.

The placeholders that we specify this time will hold the data that we are passing, and will be input placeholders.

```
'Create the command and parameter objects
Set objCmd = Server.CreateObject("ADODB.Command")
Set objParm = Server.CreateObject("ADODB.Parameter")

'Set the command object properties
Set objCmd.ActiveConnection = objConn
objCmd.CommandText = "UPDATE boats SET boatnote=? WHERE boatname=?"
objCmd.CommandType = adCmdText
```

Remember, the parameters need to be passed in the corresponding order of the occurrence of the placeholders. So the first parameter we want to create contains the boat notes that we want to add. Notice that this time we are specifying the `size` argument, to limit the size of the character data that can be added. If you try to append more data to the parameter than is specified in the `size` argument, you will receive an error. We are also specifying that this is an input parameter.

To create the parameter, we set our `Parameter` object using the `CreateParameter` method of the `Command` object, as we did in the last example. We then append the `Parameter` object to the `Parameter` collection using the `Append` method of the `Parameters` collection.

After we create and append the first parameter to the `Parameters` collection, we create and append the second parameter to the `Parameters` collection:

```
'Set the parameters and append them to the parameters collection
Set objParm = objCmd.CreateParameter("boatnote",adVarChar,adParamInput,50,"Now we have
an excuse")
objCmd.Parameters.Append objParm
Set objParm = objCmd.CreateParameter("boatname",adVarChar,adParamInput,50,"No Excuse
to Lose")
objCmd.Parameters.Append objParm
```

Now we execute the command and check for errors, as in previous examples. If all goes well, we find ourselves at the section of the code where we close and de-reference our database objects. Last, we display a message that the record was updated, and we end our page.

At this point you should be able to open Access, open the `Boats` table and see the updated boat notes. Also, you should now be familiar with creating a parameter and appending it to the `Parameters` collection.

# Parameters

So far we have explored just one way to pass parameters to the `Command` object. However, there are several ways to pass parameters and with each method comes implications. This section will explore each of these methods and their implications.

## Creating multiple parameters with one Parameter object

Let's review the first way that we demonstrated passing parameters to the `Command` object, using the code fragment listed below. First we create a `Parameter` object, set the `CommandText` to a SQL string, and specify placeholders for our parameters. Then we use the `CreateParameter` method, passing it the various parameter details, to set our `Parameter` object. The `CreateParameter` method creates a parameter with all of the properties specified in the arguments of the method. Lastly, we append the `Parameter` object to the `Parameters` collection.

```
Set objParm = Server.CreateObject("ADODB.Parameter")

objCmd.CommandText = "UPDATE boats SET boatnote=? WHERE boatname=?"

Set objParm = objCmd.CreateParameter("boatnote",adVarChar,adParamInput,50, _
   "Now we have an excuse")
objCmd.Parameters.Append objParm
Set objParm = objCmd.CreateParameter("boatname",adVarChar,adParamInput,50, _
   "No Excuse to Lose")
objCmd.Parameters.Append objParm
```

This method is ideal if we have multiple simple parameters that we want to pass. We only have to create one `Parameter` object and we can reuse this object for each parameter we have to create.

## Creating a parameter without a Parameter object

Now let's take a look at a different twist using this example. If we know the parameters and their data types that we want to pass, we don't even have to explicitly use the `Parameter` object. We can create a parameter and append it to the `Parameters` collection all in one statement, as shown below.

```
objCmd.Parameters.Append
objCmd.CreateParameter("boatnote",adVarChar,adParamInput,50,"Now we have an excuse")
objCmd.Parameters.Append
objCmd.CreateParameter("boatname",adVarChar,adParamInput,50,"No Excuse to Lose")
```

You may be wondering why we can do this. This reason is that the `CreateParameter` method does some work behind the scenes. The `CreateParameter` method creates a `Parameter` object with the specified values that we pass, and assigns the parameter to the `Parameter` object that we specify. The `CreateParameter` method thus creates and returns a parameter with the required properties. Previously, we needed an object to hold the parameter that was created, before setting its properties and appending it to the `Parameters` collection. By using the statement above, we create and append the parameter all in one statement.

## Using a separate Parameter object for each parameter

What if we have parameters that are not as simple as the character or integer data that have been demonstrated so far? Then we need to revert to a third method of adding parameters to the `Parameters` collection. This method requires a different `Parameter` object for each parameter we intend to create. You may be wondering why we would have to do this. This is because we must set all or most of the individual properties of the `Parameter` object, and these properties are not covered in the `CreateParameter` method. The following code fragment demonstrates this, and we will go into the details of this method later in the chapter.

```
Set objParm1 = Server.CreateObject("ADODB.Parameter")
Set objParm2 = Server.CreateObject("ADODB.Parameter")

objParm1.Name = "TotalHours"
objParm1.Type = adDecimal
objParm1.Direction = adParamInput
objParm1.Precision = 8
objParm1.NumericScale = 2
objParm1.Value = 180.25
objCmd.Parameters.Append objParm1

objParm2.Name = "BillRate"
objParm2.Type = adCurrency
objParm2.Direction = adParamInput
objParm2.Value = 200.00
objCmd.Parameters.Append objParm2
```

Notice that we have created two separate `Parameter` objects, one for each of the parameters we are going to define. Before, when we used the `CreateParameter` method of the `Command` object, we were able to reuse the same `Parameter` object over and over.

## Referring to a parameter by ordinal reference

Let's revisit example three for a minute. Recall that we were receiving a return value from SQL Server, so we created a parameter and specified that it was a return value parameter. To refresh your memory, the code fragment below highlights the parameter being created and appended to the `Parameters` collection.

```
objCmd.CommandText = "{? = CALL dbo.up_select_count_of_boats}"
objCmd.CommandType = adCmdStoredProc

'Set the parameter and append it to the command object
Set objParm = objCmd.CreateParameter("Return",adInteger,adParamReturnValue,,0)
objCmd.Parameters.Append objParm
```

But since this is a just a return value and we don't particularly need to access the parameter by name, we can omit all of the properties of this parameter and define it as follows.

```
objCmd.CommandText = "{? = CALL dbo.up_select_count_of_boats}"
objCmd.CommandType = adCmdStoredProc

'Set the direction of the parameter
objCmd(0).Direction = adParamReturnValue
```

Here we are accessing the parameter by ordinal reference and just setting the default return value. How can we do this without first creating a `Parameter` object? We can do this because we have set the `ActiveConnection` property to a valid `Connection` object, and our first access of the `Parameters` collection, without first appending a parameter, will cause ADO to invoke the `Refresh` method. This will get the parameter information from the database provider.

So, that being said, let's take a look at the way the original example accessed the parameter to get the value that was returned. Here we specified that we wanted to access the `Parameters` collection, specify an `item` in the collection by `name`, and retrieve its `value` property.

```
Response.Write "There are " & objCmd.Parameters.Item("Return").Value & _
 " Registered Boats Listed"
```

Now let's take a look at another way to access the value, returned by the parameter that we set above. Since the `Parameters` collection is the default collection for the `Command` object, we can access the parameter in the same manner as we set its property above, by ordinal reference. Here the value is being returned and displayed on the page.

```
Response.Write "There are " & objCmd(0) & " Registered Boats Listed"
```

Of course, when working with just one or two parameters this is simple. But when you start working with a lot of parameters it can be hard to keep up with, plus you will probably start to notice a degradation in the performance of your code, due to the `Refresh` method being automatically invoked.

## Passing parameters directly

What if you know the parameters and their data types? Do you need to create placeholders for the parameters and also create the individual parameters? No! You can pass the parameters directly in your SQL code or pass them to the stored procedure. This next code fragment demonstrates this.

```
'Set the command object properties
Set objCmd.ActiveConnection = objConn
objCmd.CommandText = "UPDATE boats SET boatnote='Now we have an excuse' WHERE
boatname='No Excuse to Lose'"
objCmd.CommandType = adCmdText
objCmd.Execute
```

Using this method assumes you are only going to execute this SQL statement once, because the parameters are now static and cannot be changed. We will demonstrate and go into the details of this method later on in the chapter.

## Try It Out – Passing parameters to a stored procedure

This Web page creates two separate `Parameter` objects and sets their individual properties. After all of the properties have been set, the parameters are appended to the `Parameters` collection. This example uses a stored procedure in the Access `Sailors` database, that accepts two simple parameters. The results of the stored procedure are returned in a recordset and displayed in the Web page in a table, as shown:

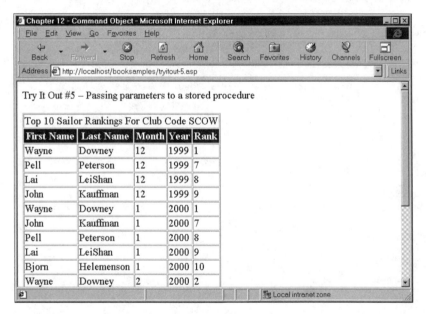

The stored procedure is in the file `qparmSailorRanking`.

```
PARAMETERS ClubCode Text, Ranking Long;
SELECT People.PeopleID, People.PeopleNameLast, People.PeopleNameFirst,
People.PeopleProfessionalClass, People.PeopleClubCode, Rank.Year, Rank.Month,
Rank.Rank
FROM People INNER JOIN Rank ON People.PeopleID = Rank.SailorID
WHERE (((People.PeopleClubCode)=[ClubCode]) AND ((Rank.Rank)<=[Ranking]))
ORDER BY Rank.Year, Rank.Month, Rank.Rank;
```

The web page code is available in TryItOut-5.asp.

```
<HTML>
<HEAD>
<META NAME="GENERATOR" Content="Microsoft Visual Studio 6.0">
<TITLE>Chapter 12 - Command Object</TITLE>
</HEAD>
<BODY>

<!--Display the page data-->
Try It Out #5 - Passing parameters to a stored procedure<BR><BR>

<%
'Instruct VBScript to ignore the error and continue
'with the next line of code
On Error Resume Next

'Create and open the database object
Set objConn = Server.CreateObject("ADODB.Connection")
objConn.Open "DSN=Sailors"

'Check for errors
If objConn.Errors.Count > 0 Then
 'Create an error object to access the ADO errors collection
 Set objErr = Server.CreateObject("ADODB.Error")
 'Declare Boolean flag for critical errors
 Dim blnCriticalError
 'Write all errors to the page
 For Each objErr In objConn.Errors
  If objErr.Number <> 0 Then
    Response.Write "Number: " & objErr.Number & "<P>"
    Response.Write "Description: " & objErr.Description & "<P>"
    Response.Write "Source: " & objErr.Source & "<P>"
    Response.Write "SQLState: " & objErr.SQLState & "<P>"
    Response.Write "NativeError: " & objErr.NativeError & "<P>"
    blnCriticalError = True
  End If
 Next
 'Dereference all objects
 Set objErr = Nothing
 If blnCriticalError Then
  Response.End
 End If
End If

'Declare variables
Dim adCmdStoredProc
Dim adInteger
Dim adVarChar
Dim adParamInput
adCmdStoredProc = 4
adInteger = 3
adVarChar = 200
adParamInput = 1

'Create the command and parameter objects
Set objCmd = Server.CreateObject("ADODB.Command")
Set objParm1 = Server.CreateObject("ADODB.Parameter")
Set objParm2 = Server.CreateObject("ADODB.Parameter")
Set objRS = Server.CreateObject("ADODB.Recordset")

'Set the command object properties
Set objCmd.ActiveConnection = objConn
objCmd.CommandText = "qparmSailorRanking"
objCmd.CommandType = adCmdStoredProc
```

```
'Set the parameters and append them to the parameters collection
objParm1.Name = "Club"
objParm1.Type = adVarChar
objParm1.Direction = adParamInput
objParm1.Size = 50
objParm1.Value = "SCOW"
objCmd.Parameters.Append objParm1

objParm2.Name = "Ranked"
objParm2.Type = adInteger
objParm2.Direction = adParamInput
objParm2.Value = 10
objCmd.Parameters.Append objParm2

Set objRS = objCmd.Execute

'Check for errors
If objConn.Errors.Count > 0 Then
 'Create an error object to access the ADO errors collection
 Set objErr = Server.CreateObject("ADODB.Error")
 'Write all errors to the page
 For Each objErr In objConn.Errors
  If objErr.Number <> 0 Then
   Response.Write "Number: " & objErr.Number & "<P>"
   Response.Write "Description: " & objErr.Description & "<P>"
   Response.Write "Source: " & objErr.Source & "<P>"
   Response.Write "SQLState: " & objErr.SQLState & "<P>"
   Response.Write "NativeError: " & objErr.NativeError & "<P>"
   blnCriticalError = True
  End If
 Next
 'Dereference all objects
 Set objErr = Nothing
 If blnCriticalError Then
  Response.End
 End If
End If
%>

<!--Build the table header rows-->
<TABLE BORDER=1 CELLSPACING=1>
 <TR>
 <TD COLSPAN=5 ALIGN=center>Top
  <%=objCmd.Parameters.Item("Ranked").Value%> Sailor Rankings
  For Club Code
  <%=objCmd.Parameters.Item("Club").Value%></TD>
 </TR>
 <TR>
 <TH BGCOLOR=navy><FONT COLOR=white>First Name</FONT></TH>
 <TH BGCOLOR=navy><FONT COLOR=white>Last Name</FONT></TH>
 <TH BGCOLOR=navy><FONT COLOR=white>Month</FONT></TH>
 <TH BGCOLOR=navy><FONT COLOR=white>Year</FONT></TH>
 <TH BGCOLOR=navy><FONT COLOR=white>Rank</FONT></TH>
 </TR>

<%
Do While Not objRS.EOF
%>

 <!--Build a row of data in the table-->
 <TR>
 <TD><%=objRS("PeopleNameFirst")%></TD>
 <TD><%=objRS("PeopleNameLast")%></TD>
 <TD><%=objRS("Month")%></TD>
 <TD><%=objRS("Year")%></TD>
 <TD><%=objRS("Rank")%></TD>
 </TR>
```

```
<%
 objRS.MoveNext
Loop

'Close and dereference database objects
objRS.Close
Set objRS = Nothing
Set objParm1 = Nothing
Set objParm2 = Nothing
Set objCmd = Nothing
objConn.Close
Set objConn = Nothing
%>

</BODY>
</HTML>
```

### How It Works: The stored procedure

This might look like a lot of complicated code for a stored procedure but it really is not, and we will step through it line by line. The first line contains the parameters and their data types that the stored procedure expects. When using Access to create a stored procedure, Access will terminate all SQL statements with a semi colon.

```
PARAMETERS ClubCode Text, Ranking Long;
```

The SELECT statement is selecting columns from two different tables, People and Rank. So the SELECT statement selects the columns using the table name as a prefix, just in case there are duplicate column names in the other table. Access automatically places the table names in our SQL statement. This helps to ensure we are getting the correct data from the correct table.

```
SELECT People.PeopleID, People.PeopleNameLast, People.PeopleNameFirst,
People.PeopleProfessionalClass, People.PeopleClubCode, Rank.Year, Rank.Month,
Rank.Rank
```

Since we have two separate tables we have to join these tables on a common column. That is, a column in both tables must contain the same data and relate to the other table. In this case the column happens to be PeopleID in the People table and SailorID in the Rank table. Both of these columns contain the same data - they are just named differently. The FROM statement selects data from the main table, which is People in this case, and inner joins the Rank table, specifying the columns that relate the two tables.

> *An inner join is when records from two tables are combined in the results, only if the value in the join fields match.*

```
FROM People INNER JOIN Rank ON People.PeopleID = Rank.SailorID
```

The WHERE clause specifies that only columns matching the parameters being passed should be selected.

```
WHERE (((People.PeopleClubCode)=[ClubCode]) AND ((Rank.Rank)<=[Ranking]))
```

Finally, the ORDER BY clause specifies how the results are sorted. In this case, we are specifying that the results should be sorted by year, then month, and then rank.

```
ORDER BY Rank.Year, Rank.Month, Rank.Rank;
```

### The Web page

As in previous examples, the first part of our Web page contains the standard HTML headers and our first line of text that we are displaying on the page.

```
<!--Display the page data-->
Try It Out #5 - Passing values to a stored procedure<BR><BR>
```

Next, we turn on error handling, create and open our database `Connection` object and check for errors, as before.

We define our variables and set their values. Notice that we have added the integer variables (we looked up the numbers that should be set in each variable, as discussed earlier).

```
'Declare variables
Dim adCmdStoredProc
Dim adInteger
Dim adVarChar
Dim adParamInput
adCmdStoredProc = 4
adInteger = 3
adVarChar = 200
adParamInput = 1
```

Now we create our objects. Notice that we are creating two `Parameter` objects and also a `Recordset` object. That is because this stored procedure returns records and the `Command` object cannot contain records.

```
'Create the command and parameter objects
Set objCmd = Server.CreateObject("ADODB.Command")
Set objParm1 = Server.CreateObject("ADODB.Parameter")
Set objParm2 = Server.CreateObject("ADODB.Parameter")
Set objRS = Server.CreateObject("ADODB.Recordset")
```

We set the `ActiveConnection` property of the `Command` object and then set the `CommandText` to a stored procedure name. Notice that we have not specified any placeholders for the parameters. This is because they are already contained in the stored procedure, and were defined in the first line of our stored procedure.

When executing a stored procedure we must specify the `adCmdStoredProc` value in the `CommandType` property. Setting this property lets the database know to look for the stored procedure, thus optimizing performance. If the database had to figure out what type of command we were executing, we would definitely notice a performance hit.

```
'Set the command object properties
Set objCmd.ActiveConnection = objConn
objCmd.CommandText = "qparmSailorRanking"
objCmd.CommandType = adCmdStoredProc
```

Now we set the various properties of the `Parameter` objects individually and append them to the `Parameters` collection.

```
'Set the parameters and append them to the parameters collection
objParm1.Name = "Club"
objParm1.Type = adVarChar
objParm1.Direction = adParamInput
objParm1.Size = 50
objParm1.Value = "SCOW"
objCmd.Parameters.Append objParm1
```

```
objParm2.Name = "Ranked"
objParm2.Type = adInteger
objParm2.Direction = adParamInput
objParm2.Value = 10
objCmd.Parameters.Append objParm2
```

We are doing things a little differently this time. We are setting the results of the execution of our Command object to the Recordset object. This has the same effect as specifying a objRS.Open command.

```
Set objRS = objCmd.Execute
```

Next we need to check for errors, in the same way as for previous examples.

After switching back to HTML code we build our header rows for our table. Notice that the first column in our table spans all five columns and contains the two fields from the parameters. We use the COLSPAN property of the TD tag to specify that the data should span multiple columns, and the ALIGN property to specify that the text in this column should be centered. This column makes up the description for our table.

The rest of the columns are header columns, specified by the TH tags. Notice that we are setting the background color of the column to navy, using the BGCOLOR property. We specify that the font color of the text should be white in the FONT tag.

```
<!--Build the table header rows-->
<TABLE border=1 cellspacing=1>
 <TR>
 <TD COLSPAN=5 ALIGN=center>Top
  <%=objCmd.Parameters.Item("Ranked").Value%> Sailor Rankings
  For Club Code
  <%=objCmd.Parameters.Item("Club").Value%></TD>
 </TR>
 <TR>
 <TH BGCOLOR=navy><FONT COLOR=white>First Name</FONT></TH>
 <TH BGCOLOR=navy><FONT COLOR=white>Last Name</FONT></TH>
 <TH BGCOLOR=navy><FONT COLOR=white>Month</FONT></TH>
 <TH BGCOLOR=navy><FONT COLOR=white>Year</FONT></TH>
 <TH BGCOLOR=navy><FONT COLOR=white>Rank</FONT></TH>
 </TR>
```

Switching back to server-side script, we build each row of our table in a Do While Not loop. Inside the loop we are using HTML to build the row of data, and specify that the data to be written should come from our recordset fields. Notice server-side script tags enclose the recordset fields, which signifies that the data is coming from the server. After a row of data has been built in the table, we advance the recordset by using the MoveNext method.

```
<%
Do While Not objRS.EOF
%>

 <!--Build a row of data in the table-->
 <TR>
 <TD><%=objRS("PeopleNameFirst")%></TD>
 <TD><%=objRS("PeopleNameLast")%></TD>
 <TD><%=objRS("Month")%></TD>
 <TD><%=objRS("Year")%></TD>
 <TD><%=objRS("Rank")%></TD>
 </TR>

<%
 objRS.MoveNext
Loop
```

After all the rows have been built and we have reached an end of file condition on our recordset, we close and de-reference all of our database objects. After that we end our page by using standard HTML tags.

```
'Close and dereference database objects
objRS.Close
Set objRS = Nothing
Set objParm1 = Nothing
Set objParm2 = Nothing
Set objCmd = Nothing
objConn.Close
Set objConn = Nothing
%>

</TABLE>
</BODY>
</HTML>
```

This next example uses the same stored procedure as the example we just discussed and the page is built the same way. However, the twist in this example is how we pass the parameters. We will not use the `Parameter` object or the `Parameters` collection. Instead we will pass the parameters directly to the stored procedure, since we know what the parameters and their data types are.

## Try It Out – Passing parameters to a stored procedure

As we just mentioned, this Web page (shown below) looks just like the last example and uses the same stored procedure. Given that, we do not have to recreate the stored procedure, which is saved as `qparmSailorRanking`.

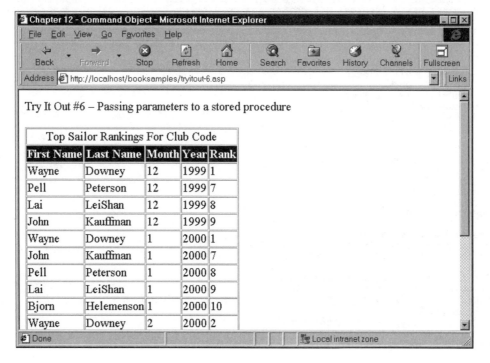

**Try It Out #6 – Passing parameters to a stored procedure**

| Top Sailor Rankings For Club Code | | | | |
|---|---|---|---|---|
| **First Name** | **Last Name** | **Month** | **Year** | **Rank** |
| Wayne | Downey | 12 | 1999 | 1 |
| Pell | Peterson | 12 | 1999 | 7 |
| Lai | LeiShan | 12 | 1999 | 8 |
| John | Kauffman | 12 | 1999 | 9 |
| Wayne | Downey | 1 | 2000 | 1 |
| John | Kauffman | 1 | 2000 | 7 |
| Pell | Peterson | 1 | 2000 | 8 |
| Lai | LeiShan | 1 | 2000 | 9 |
| Bjorn | Helemenson | 1 | 2000 | 10 |
| Wayne | Downey | 2 | 2000 | 2 |

### How It Works – Passing parameters to a stored procedure

We start this Web page the same way we started our last one by using the standard HTML headers and displaying our first line of text. Only code which is different from the last example is shown below.

```
<!--Display the page data-->
Try It Out #6 - Passing parameters to a stored procedure<BR><BR>
```

As before, we turn on error handling and create and open our `Connection` object. Then we check for errors.

The only variables that we are going to declare and set this time are the two variables that we are going to use for our parameter data. These two variables are going to be passed as part of the `CommandText` string data.

```
'Declare parameter variables
Dim adCmdStoredProc
Dim strClub
Dim lngRanking
adCmdStoredProc = 4
strClub = "SCOW"
lngRanking = 10
```

Now we create our `Command` object and `Recordset` object. Notice the absence of the `Parameter` objects, as we are not going to use them this time.

```
'Create the command and parameter objects
Set objCmd = Server.CreateObject("ADODB.Command")
Set objRS = Server.CreateObject("ADODB.Recordset")
```

We set our `ActiveConnection` property to a valid `Connection` object and then we set our `CommandText` property.

Since we are not using placeholders and will be passing the parameters as part of the `CommandText` string, we do not have to create the `Parameter` objects. The only thing that we need be concerned with here is that we specify our parameters correctly in the string. String and date parameters need to be enclosed in single quote marks and numeric parameters do not. Remember that if your string parameter contains any single quotes, you will have to insert another single quote immediately following the first one, or you will get an error about an un-terminated string. This is where using a `Parameter` object came in handy; we didn't have to worry about single quotes in our text strings.

The format of our `CommandText` string is `storedprocedure parameter1, parameter2`.

Notice again that we have specified that the `CommandType` is a stored procedure.

We execute our `Command` object, setting the records returned to the `Recordset` object.

```
'Set the command object properties and parameters
Set objCmd.ActiveConnection = objConn
objCmd.CommandText = "qparmSailorRanking '" & CStr(strClub) & "'," & _
  CLng(lngRanking)
objCmd.CommandType = adCmdStoredProc

Set objRS = objCmd.Execute
```

We again check for errors using our error handling code.

Next we build our table header in the exact same method as we did our last example. We also build the table rows in the same manner as the last example.

To wrap things up, we close and de-reference our database objects and end the page using HTML tags.

Once again, it is worth mentioning that you need to ensure you pass the parameters in the correct order that the stored procedure expects them, and you delimit all string and date parameters in single quotes. A comma separates each parameter.

# Stuffing Techniques

When we refer to **stuffing**, we are referring to appending large amounts of data into a parameter, which gets inserted into a large text field in the database. In Access this type of field is known as a `Memo` field and can contain up to 1.2 GB of text data (in other words 1.2 billion 8-bit characters). In SQL Server this type of field is known as a `Text` field and can contain just over 2 billion characters of data. This section will cover the details of stuffing data into a parameter using the `AppendChunk` method of the `Parameter` object.

There are just a few things that you should be aware of that are required in order to use the `AppendChunk` method. First, the data you are appending must be of a variant data type. This is not a problem when using this method from an active server page, but if you use VB you will need to declare your variable (that contains the data you want to append to the parameter) as a variant. Second, the `Attributes` property of the `Parameter` object must be set to `adFldLong`, which indicates a long field is being set.

OK, with that being said, what exactly does the `AppendChunk` method do? Well it does exactly what the method name implies; it appends chunks of data to the `Parameter` object. The first call to the `AppendChunk` method for a specific parameter writes data to the parameter, clearing any data that was there. Subsequent calls append data to the data already there.

Why use the `AppendChunk` method? Well, given the size of `Memo` and `Text` fields in the databases it is going to be a lot easier to manage smaller chunks of data than trying to manage 1.2 GB of data all in one string.

The example that we are going to work through uses a relatively small text string that is only 359 characters. But this example will demonstrate how to use the `AppendChunk` method in a loop, to append data to the `Parameter` object.

## Try It Out - Stuff a field using AppendChunk

This example uses the `AppendChunk` method of the `Parameter` object to append a large variant variable containing 359 bytes of character data. The data will be appended in chunks of 100 bytes each within a loop, until all data has been appended.

After the `Parameter` object contains all the data, we will add the `Parameter` object to the `Parameters` collection, and execute a SQL string that will update the `BoatNote` column in the `Boats` table for a specific boat.

Upon successful completion we will display a line of text indicating that the update was successful. This screenshot shows the result of running the code:

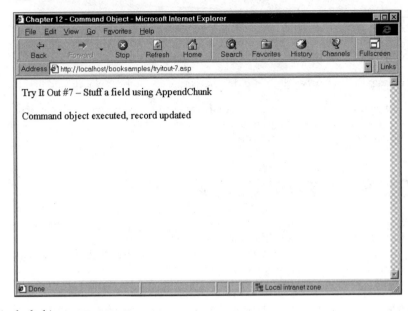

The code for this example is included in TryItOut_7.asp.

```
<HTML>
<HEAD>
<META NAME="GENERATOR" Content="Microsoft Visual Studio 6.0">
<TITLE>Chapter 12 - Command Object</TITLE>
</HEAD>
<BODY>

<!--Display the page data-->
Try It Out #7 - Stuff a field using AppendChunk<BR><BR>

<%
'Instruct VBScript to ignore the error and continue
'with the next line of code
On Error Resume Next

'Create and open the database object
Set objConn = Server.CreateObject("ADODB.Connection")
objConn.Open "DSN=Sailors"

'Check for errors
If objConn.Errors.Count > 0 Then
  'Create an error object to access the ADO errors collection
  Set objErr = Server.CreateObject("ADODB.Error")
  'Declare Boolean flag for critical errors
  Dim blnCriticalError
  'Write all errors to the page
  For Each objErr In objConn.Errors
    If objErr.Number <> 0 Then
      Response.Write "Number: " & objErr.Number & "<P>"
      Response.Write "Description: " & objErr.Description & "<P>"
      Response.Write "Source: " & objErr.Source & "<P>"
      Response.Write "SQLState: " & objErr.SQLState & "<P>"
      Response.Write "NativeError: " & objErr.NativeError & "<P>"
      blnCriticalError = True
    End If
  Next
```

```
 'Dereference all objects
 Set objErr = Nothing
 If blnCriticalError Then
  Response.End
 End If
End If

'Declare variables
Dim adCmdText
Dim adVarChar
Dim adLongVarChar
Dim adParamInput
Dim adFldLong
adCmdText = 1
adVarChar = 200
adLongVarChar = 201
adParamInput = 1
adFldLong = 128

'Declare text variable and set the text
Dim varText
varText = "For Sale, Laser class boat. This boat is in " & _
   "generally good shape. It was in a minor mishap a couple " & _
   "of months ago during a racing event. Damage was minor " & _
   "but a small gash was made in the side for the entire " & _
   "length of the boat. The damage has been repaired but " & _
   "the boat doesn't seem to be fit for racing anymore. " & _
   "A great deal can be made on this boat so hurry!"

'Create the command and parameter objects
Set objCmd = Server.CreateObject("ADODB.Command")
Set objParm1 = Server.CreateObject("ADODB.Parameter")
Set objParm2 = Server.CreateObject("ADODB.Parameter")

'Set the command object properties
Set objCmd.ActiveConnection = objConn
objCmd.CommandText = "update boats set boatnote=? where boatname=?"
objCmd.CommandType = adCmdText

'Set the parameters and append them to the parameters collection
objParm1.Attributes = adFldLong
objParm1.Name = "boatnote"
objParm1.Type = adLongVarChar
objParm1.Direction = adParamInput
objParm1.Size = 500

'Loop through the variant string appending chunks of data in
'100 byte increments to the parameter object
intStart = 1
intLength = 100
Do
   If (intStart + intLength) > Len(varText) Then
      intLength = Len(varText) - intStart + 1
   End If
   objparm1.AppendChunk Mid(varText, intStart, intLength)
   intStart = intStart + intLength
Loop While intLength = 100

objCmd.Parameters.Append objParm1
```

```
objParm2.Name = "boatname"
objparm2.Type = adVarChar
objParm2.Direction = adParamInput
objParm2.Size = 50
objparm2.Value = "No Excuse to Lose"
objCmd.Parameters.Append objParm2

objCmd.Execute

'Check for errors
If objConn.Errors.Count > 0 Then
 'Create an error object to access the ADO errors collection
 Set objErr = Server.CreateObject("ADODB.Error")
 'Write all errors to the page
 For Each objErr In objConn.Errors
  If objErr.Number <> 0 Then
   Response.Write "Number: " & objErr.Number & "<P>"
   Response.Write "Description: " & objErr.Description & "<P>"
   Response.Write "Source: " & objErr.Source & "<P>"
   Response.Write "SQLState: " & objErr.SQLState & "<P>"
   Response.Write "NativeError: " & objErr.NativeError & "<P>"
   blnCriticalError = True
  End If
 Next
 'Dereference all objects
 Set objErr = Nothing
 If blnCriticalError Then
  Response.End
 End If
End If

'Close and dereference database objects
Set objParm1 = Nothing
Set objParm2 = Nothing
Set objCmd = Nothing
objConn.Close
Set objConn = Nothing
%>

<!--Display a message that the update was successful-->
Command object executed, record updated

</BODY>
</HTML>
```

### How It Works – Stuff a Field using AppendChunk

As before, we start by building the first part of our Web page using the standard HTML headers and we display our first line of text.

```
<!--Display the page data-->
Try It Out #7 - Stuff a field using AppendChunk<BR><BR>
```

Next, we turn on error handling and create and open our database connection. We then check for errors using our error handling code.

We must declare the variables for the various `Parameter` object properties. Again, we found these values that are assigned to our variables either in the MSDN library, or in the VB object browser after having set a reference to the ADO object library. The new variables here are the `adFldLong` and `adLongVarChar` variables.

```
'Declare variables
Dim adCmdText
Dim adVarChar
Dim adLongVarChar
Dim adParamInput
Dim adFldLong
adCmdText = 1
adVarChar = 200
adLongVarChar = 201
adParamInput = 1
adFldLong = 128
```

Next we need to declare our variable to hold our character string. Remember that this variable must be a variant, which is already the case since we are using VBScript. You can key anything you want in this string, just ensure it contains over 100 characters because we are going to be appending data in 100 byte chunks. This string is 359 characters long.

```
'Declare text variable and set the text
Dim varText
varText = "For Sale, Laser class boat. This boat is in " & _
    "generally good shape. It was in a minor mishap a couple " & _
    "of months ago during a racing event. Damage was minor " & _
    "but a small gash was made in the side for the entire " & _
    "length of the boat. The damage has been repaired but " & _
    "the boat doesn't seem to be fit for racing anymore. " & _
    "A great deal can be made on this boat so hurry!"
```

Once again we are using two separate `Parameter` objects. Notice the lack of the `Recordset` object in this example. We don't need it this time as we are inserting data and are not retrieving any.

We set our `ActiveConnection` property to the `Connection` object and set the `CommandText` property to our SQL string. Notice the placeholders for the two parameters. Last we set the `CommandType` property to `adCmdText`, which indicates we are executing a text string as the command.

```
'Create the command and parameter objects
Set objCmd = Server.CreateObject("ADODB.Command")
Set objParm1 = Server.CreateObject("ADODB.Parameter")
Set objParm2 = Server.CreateObject("ADODB.Parameter")

'Set the command object properties
Set objCmd.ActiveConnection = objConn
objCmd.CommandText = "UPDATE boats SET boatnote=? WHERE boatname=?"
objCmd.CommandType = adCmdText
```

The first parameter we want to set is the parameter that will update the boat notes, and this is the column in our table that is a `Memo` data type. We must set the `Attributes` property to `adFldLong` in order to use the `AppendChunk` method. Also notice the `Type` property is set to `adLongVarChar` to indicate a large text parameter. We set the maximum `size` that we are going to be appending, which in this case is 500 characters. This should be set as close as possible to the maximum amount of data that you will be appending to the parameter. Notice the absence of the `value` property. This is because we are not setting the value directly but instead are using the `AppendChunk` method to do this indirectly.

```
'Set the parameters and append them to the parameters collection
objParm1.Attributes = adFldLong
objParm1.Name = "boatnote"
objParm1.Type = adLongVarChar
objParm1.Direction = adParamInput
objParm1.Size = 500
```

We set up a loop to process the data in 100 character chunks. We set a variable to hold our starting position in the variant string that we are going to be reading data from. We also set a variable to hold the length of the amount of data we want to read.

```
'Loop through the variant string appending chunks of data in
'100 byte increments to the parameter object
intStart = 1
intLength = 100
Do
```

If the starting position variable plus the length variable is greater than the length of the string we are reading, we know that we have reached the end of the length increments and must get the remaining amount of text.

```
If (intStart + intLength) > Len(varText) Then
```

We then set the length variable to the length of the string, minus the current starting position variable, plus one.

```
intLength = Len(varText) - intStart + 1
   End If
```

Next we append the string chunk to the parameter using the Mid function to extract a portion of text from the variant text string. The Mid function selects text from a string using three parameters. The first parameter is the string containing the text, the second parameter is a value specifying the starting position, and the third parameter is a value that specifies the ending position.

```
objparm1.AppendChunk Mid(varText, intStart, intLength)
```

The first call to the AppendChunk method will overwrite any existing data in our parameter. Subsequent calls append data to the parameter.

After we have appended the data to the parameter, we increment our starting position by the number of characters in our length variable. We then continue to process the loop until our length variable is no longer equal to 100.

```
   intStart = intStart + intLength
Loop While intLength = 100
```

After having appended all of the data to our parameter, we must append our parameter to the Parameters collection.

```
objCmd.Parameters.Append objParm1
```

The next parameter is straightforward and we covered it in a previous example, so we won't go over the details again. Basically we are adding a simple parameter for the boat name and are setting the value here. Then we append it to the Parameters collection.

```
objParm2.Name = "boatname"
objparm2.Type = adVarChar
objParm2.Direction = adParamInput
objParm2.Size = 50
objparm2.Value = "No Excuse to Lose"
objCmd.Parameters.Append objParm2
```

After we execute our Command object we need to check for errors, as in previous examples.

We close and de-reference all of our database objects including the two Parameter objects.

```
'Close and dereference database objects
Set objParm1 = Nothing
Set objParm2 = Nothing
Set objCmd = Nothing
objConn.Close
Set objConn = Nothing
%>
```

Lastly, we display a message that the record was updated and we end our page with HTML tags.

```
<!--Display a message that the update was successful-->
Command object executed, record updated

</BODY>
</HTML>
```

# Summary

This chapter has demonstrated various ways that parameters can be used with the Command object. We have taken a detailed look at the Command object, the Parameters collection and the Parameter object. Having gone through the examples in this chapter you should now feel comfortable using parameters with the Command object. We have also looked at the various ways you can create parameters using the Parameter object and the Parameters collection.

You should now know when you need to use the Command object and when it's useful to use. We have taken a look at how to append large amounts of data to a Parameter object and you should feel comfortable using this technique. By now you should be familiar with the various properties and methods of the Command object, Parameters collection and the Parameter object.

To summarize this chapter, you should be able to:

- ❑ alter the database structure using the Command object
- ❑ pass parameters to a SQL string
- ❑ pass parameters to a stored procedure
- ❑ receive a return value from a stored procedure using a parameter
- ❑ identify several ways to create a Parameter object and set its properties
- ❑ access a parameter by ordinal reference

# Exercises

The exercises in this section are designed to help reinforce the knowledge you have gained throughout this chapter. To keep things simple we are only going to be dealing with the Access Sailors database. There are two exercises in this section. Without looking at the supplied code, try to code the examples using only the screen shot provided, the exercise description given and the knowledge you have gained in this chapter.

# Exercise 1

This Web page passes two parameters to the `qparmSailRanking` stored procedure - the club code and the ranking. We do not have to build this stored procedure because we used it in some previous examples in this chapter. Display the data in any format you want on the Web page.

Using only one `Parameter` object, set the individual properties of this parameter for the club code. The club code is a `Text` field with a maximum number of 50 characters in the field, and is an input parameter. *Hint: the properties should be set individually.* After setting all of the properties, append the parameter to the `Parameters` collection. Use any club code listed in the `Sailors` database.

The second parameter should be created using the previously defined `Parameter` object. This parameter specifies the sailor ranking that should be retrieved and is an integer value. Create this parameter using a method that lets you specify the properties without having to set each one separately. *Hint: method is the keyword in the last sentence.* Use any value you want for the rankings and append this parameter to the `Parameters` collection.

The following screenshot shows what our code should produce:

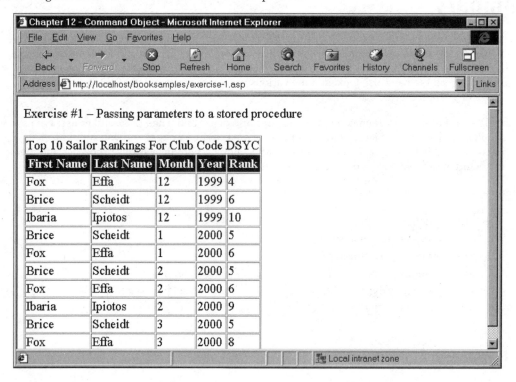

Here's the code, which is also in `Exercise-1.asp`.

```
<HTML>
<HEAD>
<META NAME="GENERATOR" Content="Microsoft Visual Studio 6.0">
<TITLE>Chapter 12 - Command Object</TITLE>
</HEAD>
<BODY>

<!--Display the page data-->
Exercise #1 - Passing parameters to a stored procedure<BR><BR>

<%
'Instruct VBScript to ignore the error and continue
'with the next line of code
On Error Resume Next

'Create and open the database object
Set objConn = Server.CreateObject("ADODB.Connection")
objConn.Open "DSN=Sailors"

'Check for errors
If objConn.Errors.Count > 0 Then
 'Create an error object to access the ADO errors collection
 Set objErr = Server.CreateObject("ADODB.Error")
 'Declare Boolean flag for critical errors
 Dim blnCriticalError
 'Write all errors to the page
 For Each objErr In objConn.Errors
  If objErr.Number <> 0 Then
    Response.Write "Number: " & objErr.Number & "<P>"
    Response.Write "Description: " & objErr.Description & "<P>"
    Response.Write "Source: " & objErr.Source & "<P>"
    Response.Write "SQLState: " & objErr.SQLState & "<P>"
    Response.Write "NativeError: " & objErr.NativeError & "<P>"
    blnCriticalError = True
  End If
 Next
 'Dereference all objects
 Set objErr = Nothing
 If blnCriticalError Then
  Response.End
 End If
End If

'Declare variables
Dim adCmdStoredProc
Dim adInteger
Dim adVarChar
Dim adParamInput
adCmdStoredProc = 4
adInteger = 3
adVarChar = 200
adParamInput = 1

'Create the command, parameter and recordset objects
Set objCmd = Server.CreateObject("ADODB.Command")
Set objParm = Server.CreateObject("ADODB.Parameter")
Set objRS = Server.CreateObject("ADODB.Recordset")
```

```
'Set the command object properties
Set objCmd.ActiveConnection = objConn
objCmd.CommandText = "qparmSailorRanking"
objCmd.CommandType = adCmdStoredProc

'Set the parameters and append them to the parameters collection
objParm.Name = "Club"
objParm.Type = adVarChar
objParm.Direction = adParamInput
objParm.Size = 50
objParm.Value = "DSYC"
objCmd.Parameters.Append objParm

Set objParm = objCmd.CreateParameter("Ranked",adInteger,adParamInput,,10)
objCmd.Parameters.Append objParm

Set objRS = objCmd.Execute

'Check for errors
If objConn.Errors.Count > 0 Then
 'Create an error object to access the ADO errors collection
 Set objErr = Server.CreateObject("ADODB.Error")
 'Write all errors to the page
 For Each objErr In objConn.Errors
  If objErr.Number <> 0 Then
   Response.Write "Number: " & objErr.Number & "<P>"
   Response.Write "Description: " & objErr.Description & "<P>"
   Response.Write "Source: " & objErr.Source & "<P>"
   Response.Write "SQLState: " & objErr.SQLState & "<P>"
   Response.Write "NativeError: " & objErr.NativeError & "<P>"
   blnCriticalError = True
  End If
 Next
 'Dereference all objects
 Set objErr = Nothing
 If blnCriticalError Then
  Response.End
 End If
End If
%>

<!--Build the table header rows-->
<TABLE border=1 cellspacing=1>
 <TR>
 <TD COLSPAN=5 ALIGN=center>Top
  <%=objCmd.Parameters.Item("Ranked").Value%> Sailor Rankings
  For Club Code
  <%=objCmd.Parameters.Item("Club").Value%></TD>
 </TR>
 <TR>
 <TH BGCOLOR=navy><FONT COLOR=white>First Name</FONT></TH>
 <TH BGCOLOR=navy><FONT COLOR=white>Last Name</FONT></TH>
 <TH BGCOLOR=navy><FONT COLOR=white>Month</FONT></TH>
 <TH BGCOLOR=navy><FONT COLOR=white>Year</FONT></TH>
 <TH BGCOLOR=navy><FONT COLOR=white>Rank</FONT></TH>
 </TR>

<%
Do While Not objRS.EOF
%>
```

```
<!--Build a row of data in the table-->
<TR>
<TD><%=objRS("PeopleNameFirst")%></TD>
<TD><%=objRS("PeopleNameLast")%></TD>
<TD><%=objRS("Month")%></TD>
<TD><%=objRS("Year")%></TD>
<TD><%=objRS("Rank")%></TD>
</TR>

<%
 objRS.MoveNext
Loop

'Close and dereference database objects
objRS.Close
Set objRS = Nothing
Set objParm = Nothing
Set objCmd = Nothing
objConn.Close
Set objConn = Nothing
%>

</TABLE>
</BODY>
</HTML>
```

### How It Works – Exercise 1

We start our page by using standard HTML header tags and we display our first line of text on the page.

```
<HTML>
<HEAD>
<META NAME="GENERATOR" Content="Microsoft Visual Studio 6.0">
<TITLE>Chapter 12 - Command Object</TITLE>
</HEAD>
<BODY>

<!--Display the page data-->
Exercise #1 - Passing parameters to a stored procedure<BR><BR>
```

We instruct VBScript to ignore all errors, then create our database `Connection` object and open the database. We then have to check for errors using the error code from chapter 14.

```
<%
'Instruct VBScript to ignore the error and continue
'with the next line of code
On Error Resume Next

'Create and open the database object
Set objConn = Server.CreateObject("ADODB.Connection")
objConn.Open "DSN=Sailors"

'Check for errors
If objConn.Errors.Count > 0 Then
 'Create an error object to access the ADO errors collection
 Set objErr = Server.CreateObject("ADODB.Error")
 'Declare Boolean flag for critical errors
 Dim blnCriticalError
 'Write all errors to the page
 For Each objErr In objConn.Errors
```

```
 If objErr.Number <> 0 Then
   Response.Write "Number: " & objErr.Number & "<P>"
   Response.Write "Description: " & objErr.Description & "<P>"
   Response.Write "Source: " & objErr.Source & "<P>"
   Response.Write "SQLState: " & objErr.SQLState & "<P>"
   Response.Write "NativeError: " & objErr.NativeError & "<P>"
   blnCriticalError = True
 End If
Next
'Dereference all objects
Set objErr = Nothing
If blnCriticalError Then
 Response.End
End If
End If
```

We declare our ADO variables and set their values. We used the VB object browser to find these values, after having set a reference to the ADO object library. We could also have looked them up in the MSDN library.

```
'Declare variables
Dim adCmdStoredProc
Dim adInteger
Dim adVarChar
Dim adParamInput
adCmdStoredProc = 4
adInteger = 3
adVarChar = 200
adParamInput = 1
```

We create our `Command` object and `Recordset` object and only one `Parameter` object.

```
'Create the command, parameter and recordset objects
Set objCmd = Server.CreateObject("ADODB.Command")
Set objParm = Server.CreateObject("ADODB.Parameter")
Set objRS = Server.CreateObject("ADODB.Recordset")
```

Next, we want to set our `ActiveConnection` property to our database `Connection` object, and set the `CommandText` to our stored procedure that we will be executing. Notice that we specified the `adCmdStoredProc` value for the `CommandType` property.

```
'Set the command object properties
Set objCmd.ActiveConnection = objConn
objCmd.CommandText = "qparmSailorRanking"
objCmd.CommandType = adCmdStoredProc
```

The first parameter we are supposed to create contains all the individual properties listed separately, as shown below. After we have assigned their values, we append the parameter to the `Parameters` collection.

```
'Set the parameters and append them to the parameters collection
objParm.Name = "Club"
objParm.Type = adVarChar
objParm.Direction = adParamInput
objParm.Size = 50
objParm.Value = "DSYC"
objCmd.Parameters.Append objParm
```

The second parameter is to use the same `Parameter` object as the first parameter. We need to set the properties of this parameter using the `CreateParameter` method of the `Command` object, which will clear all values in the `Parameter` object before it writes the new ones. This happens because the `CreateParameter` method creates a `Parameter` object behind the scenes and assigns it to the `Parameter` object we have defined. This allows us to reuse the same `Parameter` object over and over. Last we append this parameter to the `Parameters` collection.

```
Set objParm = objCmd.CreateParameter("Ranked",adInteger,adParamInput,,10)
objCmd.Parameters.Append objParm
```

We execute our `Command` object and set the recordset returned in the `Recordset` object. We then check for errors.

```
Set objRS = objCmd.Execute

'Check for errors
If objConn.Errors.Count > 0 Then
 'Create an error object to access the ADO errors collection
 Set objErr = Server.CreateObject("ADODB.Error")
 'Write all errors to the page
 For Each objErr In objConn.Errors
  If objErr.Number <> 0 Then
   Response.Write "Number: " & objErr.Number & "<P>"
   Response.Write "Description: " & objErr.Description & "<P>"
   Response.Write "Source: " & objErr.Source & "<P>"
   Response.Write "SQLState: " & objErr.SQLState & "<P>"
   Response.Write "NativeError: " & objErr.NativeError & "<P>"
   blnCriticalError = True
  End If
 Next
 'Dereference all objects
 Set objErr = Nothing
 If blnCriticalError Then
  Response.End
 End If
End If
%>
```

We build the header rows of the table and loop through the recordset building each data row in the table.

```
<!--Build the table header rows-->
<TABLE border=1 cellspacing=1>
 <TR>
 <TD COLSPAN=5 ALIGN=center>Top
  <%=objCmd.Parameters.Item("Ranked").Value%> Sailor Rankings
  For Club Code
  <%=objCmd.Parameters.Item("Club").Value%></TD>
 </TR>
 <TR>
 <TH BGCOLOR=navy><FONT COLOR=white>First Name</FONT></TH>
 <TH BGCOLOR=navy><FONT COLOR=white>Last Name</FONT></TH>
 <TH BGCOLOR=navy><FONT COLOR=white>Month</FONT></TH>
 <TH BGCOLOR=navy><FONT COLOR=white>Year</FONT></TH>
 <TH BGCOLOR=navy><FONT COLOR=white>Rank</FONT></TH>
 </TR>

<%
Do While Not objRS.EOF
%>
```

```
<!--Build a row of data in the table-->
<TR>
<TD><%=objRS("PeopleNameFirst")%></TD>
<TD><%=objRS("PeopleNameLast")%></TD>
<TD><%=objRS("Month")%></TD>
<TD><%=objRS("Year")%></TD>
<TD><%=objRS("Rank")%></TD>
</TR>

<%
objRS.MoveNext
Loop
```

To wrap things up, we close and de-reference our database objects to release them from memory. We end the page using standard HTML tags.

```
'Close and dereference database objects
objRS.Close
Set objRS = Nothing
Set objParm = Nothing
Set objCmd = Nothing
objConn.Close
Set objConn = Nothing
%>

</TABLE>
</BODY>
</HTML>
```

# Exercise 2

This exercise uses a SQL string that accepts one string parameter. We are selecting the first name and last name of all the people from the `People` table in the `Sailors` database that belong to a certain club. We are using the club code as the parameter. The results should be sorted by last name. You are free to display the data in any format you wish in the Web page.

Without explicitly using a `Parameter` object, create and append the one and only parameter to the `Parameters` collection. Don't forget to include the parameter placeholder in the SQL string.

The result should look something like the screenshot shown here:

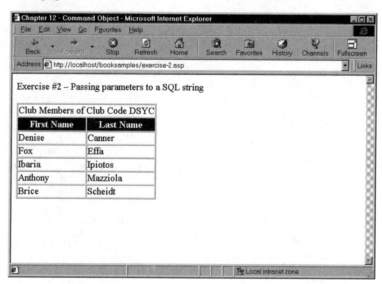

If you need the code, shown below, it is available as `Exercise-2.asp`.

```
<HTML>
<HEAD>
<META NAME="GENERATOR" Content="Microsoft Visual Studio 6.0">
<TITLE>Chapter 12 - Command Object</TITLE>
</HEAD>
<BODY>

<!--Display the page data-->
Exercise #2 - Passing parameters to a SQL string<BR><BR>

<%
'Instruct VBScript to ignore the error and continue
'with the next line of code
On Error Resume Next

'Create and open the database object
Set objConn = Server.CreateObject("ADODB.Connection")
objConn.Open "DSN=Sailors"

'Check for errors
If objConn.Errors.Count > 0 Then
 'Create an error object to access the ADO errors collection
 Set objErr = Server.CreateObject("ADODB.Error")
 'Declare Boolean flag for critical errors
 Dim blnCriticalError
 'Write all errors to the page
 For Each objErr In objConn.Errors
  If objErr.Number <> 0 Then
   Response.Write "Number: " & objErr.Number & "<P>"
   Response.Write "Description: " & objErr.Description & "<P>"
   Response.Write "Source: " & objErr.Source & "<P>"
   Response.Write "SQLState: " & objErr.SQLState & "<P>"
   Response.Write "NativeError: " & objErr.NativeError & "<P>"
   blnCriticalError = True
  End If
 Next
 'Dereference all objects
 Set objErr = Nothing
 If blnCriticalError Then
  Response.End
 End If
End If

'Declare variables
Dim adCmdText
Dim adVarChar
Dim adParamInput
adCmdText = 1
adVarChar = 200
adParamInput = 1

'Create the command and parameter objects
Set objCmd = Server.CreateObject("ADODB.Command")
Set objRS = Server.CreateObject("ADODB.Recordset")

'Set the command object properties
Set objCmd.ActiveConnection = objConn
objCmd.CommandText = "SELECT PeopleNameFirst, PeopleNameLast FROM People WHERE" & _
  "PeopleClubCode =  ? ORDER BY PeopleNameLast"
objCmd.CommandType = adCmdText
```

```
'Create and append a parameter to the parameters collection
objCmd.Parameters.Append objCmd.CreateParameter("ClubCode",adVarChar,adParamInput, _
 50,"DSYC")
Set objRS = objCmd.Execute

'Check for errors
If objConn.Errors.Count > 0 Then
 'Create an error object to access the ADO errors collection
 Set objErr = Server.CreateObject("ADODB.Error")
 'Write all errors to the page
 For Each objErr In objConn.Errors
  If objErr.Number <> 0 Then
   Response.Write "Number: " & objErr.Number & "<P>"
   Response.Write "Description: " & objErr.Description & "<P>"
   Response.Write "Source: " & objErr.Source & "<P>"
   Response.Write "SQLState: " & objErr.SQLState & "<P>"
   Response.Write "NativeError: " & objErr.NativeError & "<P>"
   blnCriticalError = True
  End If
 Next
 'Dereference all objects
 Set objErr = Nothing
 If blnCriticalError Then
  Response.End
 End If
End If
%>

<!--Build the table header rows-->
<TABLE border=1 cellspacing=1>
 <TR>
 <TD COLSPAN=5 ALIGN=center>Club Members of Club Code
  <%=objCmd.Parameters.Item("ClubCode").Value%></TD>
 </TR>
 <TR>
 <TH BGCOLOR=navy><FONT COLOR=white>First Name</FONT></TH>
 <TH BGCOLOR=navy><FONT COLOR=white>Last Name</FONT></TH>
 </TR>

<%
Do While Not objRS.EOF
%>

 <!--Build a row of data in the table-->
 <TR>
 <TD><%=objRS("PeopleNameFirst")%></TD>
 <TD><%=objRS("PeopleNameLast")%></TD>
 </TR>

<%
 objRS.MoveNext
Loop

'Close and dereference database objects
objRS.Close
Set objRS = Nothing
Set objCmd = Nothing
objConn.Close
Set objConn = Nothing
%>

</TABLE>
</BODY>
</HTML>
```

### How It Works – Exercise 2

We start our Web page by using standard HTML headers and display the first line of text.

```
<HTML>
<HEAD>
<META NAME="GENERATOR" Content="Microsoft Visual Studio 6.0">
<TITLE>Chapter 12 - Command Object</TITLE>
</HEAD>
<BODY>

<!--Display the page data-->
Exercise #2 - Passing parameters to a SQL string<BR><BR>
```

Next, we turn on error handling, create and open our database `Connection` object, and then check for errors.

```
<%
'Instruct VBScript to ignore the error and continue
'with the next line of code
On Error Resume Next

'Create and open the database object
Set objConn = Server.CreateObject("ADODB.Connection")
objConn.Open "DSN=Sailors"

'Check for errors
If objConn.Errors.Count > 0 Then
 'Create an error object to access the ADO errors collection
 Set objErr = Server.CreateObject("ADODB.Error")
 'Declare Boolean flag for critical errors
 Dim blnCriticalError
 'Write all errors to the page
 For Each objErr In objConn.Errors
  If objErr.Number <> 0 Then
   Response.Write "Number: " & objErr.Number & "<P>"
   Response.Write "Description: " & objErr.Description & "<P>"
   Response.Write "Source: " & objErr.Source & "<P>"
   Response.Write "SQLState: " & objErr.SQLState & "<P>"
   Response.Write "NativeError: " & objErr.NativeError & "<P>"
   blnCriticalError = True
  End If
 Next
 'Dereference all objects
 Set objErr = Nothing
 If blnCriticalError Then
  Response.End
 End If
End If
```

We declare our ADO variables and set their values.

```
'Declare variables
Dim adCmdText
Dim adVarChar
Dim adParamInput
adCmdText = 1
adVarChar = 200
adParamInput = 1
```

We create our `Command` and `Recordset` objects next. Notice that we have not declared a `Parameter` object.

```
'Create the command and parameter objects
Set objCmd = Server.CreateObject("ADODB.Command")
Set objRS = Server.CreateObject("ADODB.Recordset")
```

We set our `Command` objects `ActiveConnection`, `CommandText` and `CommandType` properties next.

Let's take a quick look at the SQL string that we are going to execute. We select the first and last names from the `People` table. We are only selecting people that have a matching club code of the parameter that was passed. We also sort the result set by last names.

Notice that we are using the `adCmdText` attribute in the `CommandType` property.

```
'Set the command object properties
Set objCmd.ActiveConnection = objConn
objCmd.CommandText = "Select PeopleNameFirst, PeopleNameLast From People Where
PeopleClubCode = ? Order by PeopleNameLast"
objCmd.CommandType = adCmdText
```

Without explicitly using a `Parameter` object we are able to create and append a parameter to the `Parameters` collection, using the `Append` method of the `Parameters` collection and the `CreateParameter` method of the `Command` object. This will work for simple parameters that are string and integer data types.

```
'Create and append a parameter to the parameters collection
objCmd.Parameters.Append objCmd.CreateParameter("ClubCode",adVarChar,adParamInput, _
    50,"DSYC")
```

Next we execute our `Command` object and set the `Recordset` object to the result set returned by the `Command` object. Then we check for errors.

```
Set objRS = objCmd.Execute

'Check for errors
If objConn.Errors.Count > 0 Then
  'Create an error object to access the ADO errors collection
  Set objErr = Server.CreateObject("ADODB.Error")
  'Write all errors to the page
  For Each objErr In objConn.Errors
   If objErr.Number <> 0 Then
     Response.Write "Number: " & objErr.Number & "<P>"
     Response.Write "Description: " & objErr.Description & "<P>"
     Response.Write "Source: " & objErr.Source & "<P>"
     Response.Write "SQLState: " & objErr.SQLState & "<P>"
     Response.Write "NativeError: " & objErr.NativeError & "<P>"
     blnCriticalError = True
   End If
  Next
  'Dereference all objects
  Set objErr = Nothing
  If blnCriticalError Then
    Response.End
  End If
End If
%>
```

We build the table header rows and then loop through the recordset, building the data rows.

```
<!--Build the table header rows-->
<TABLE border=1 cellspacing=1>
 <TR>
 <TD COLSPAN=5 ALIGN=center>Club Members of Club Code
  <%=objCmd.Parameters.Item("ClubCode").Value%></TD>
 </TR>
 <TR>
 <TH BGCOLOR=navy><FONT COLOR=white>First Name</FONT></TH>
 <TH BGCOLOR=navy><FONT COLOR=white>Last Name</FONT></TH>
 </TR>

<%
Do While Not objRS.EOF
%>

 <!--Build a row of data in the table-->
 <TR>
 <TD><%=objRS("PeopleNameFirst")%></TD>
 <TD><%=objRS("PeopleNameLast")%></TD>
 </TR>

<%
 objRS.MoveNext
Loop
```

Finally, we close and de-reference our database objects and end our page using HTML tags.

```
'Close and dereference database objects
objRS.Close
Set objRS = Nothing
Set objCmd = Nothing
objConn.Close
Set objConn = Nothing
%>

</TABLE>
</BODY>
</HTML>
```

# Quiz

1. What is the method of the `Parameter` object that allows us to place large amounts of data in a parameter?
2. Should we use the `Command` object to alter the database structure?
3. Is the `Parameters` collection required when passing parameters to a stored procedure?
4. Can we access a parameter by ordinal reference?
5. When we set our SQL string in the `CommandText` property, how do we indicate that the SQL string is expecting parameters?
6. Do we have to create a `Parameter` object in order to append the parameter to the `Parameters` collection?

# Quiz Answers

**1.** The AppendChunk method allows us to append large chunks of data to the Parameter object.

**2.** Yes, we alter the database structure using the Data Definition Language and should use the Command object to do this.

**3.** No, we can pass the parameters to the stored procedure directly in the CommandText property without creating and using the Parameters collection.

**4.** Yes we can but it is not advisable if you have a lot of parameters, as it is easy to get confused as to which parameter is which.

**5.** We use placeholders, which consists of a question mark where the parameter data will be placed when the Command object is executed.

**6.** Not if we are using simple parameters that contain string data or integer values. We can simply create the parameter and append it to the Parameters collection in one statement as shown below.

```
objCmd.Parameters.Append
objCmd.CreateParameter("boatname",adVarChar,adParamInput,50,"No Excuse to Lose")
```

Setup cannot install system files or update shared files if the files are in use. Before continuing close any open applications.

WARNING: This program is protected by copyright law and international treaties.

You may install Microsoft Data Access 2.1 on a single computer. Some Microsoft products are provided with additional rights, which are stated in the End User License Agreement included with your software.

Please take a moment to read the End User License Agreement now. It contains all of the terms and conditions that pertain to this software product. By choosing to continue, you indicate acceptance of these terms.

Continue

Exit Setup

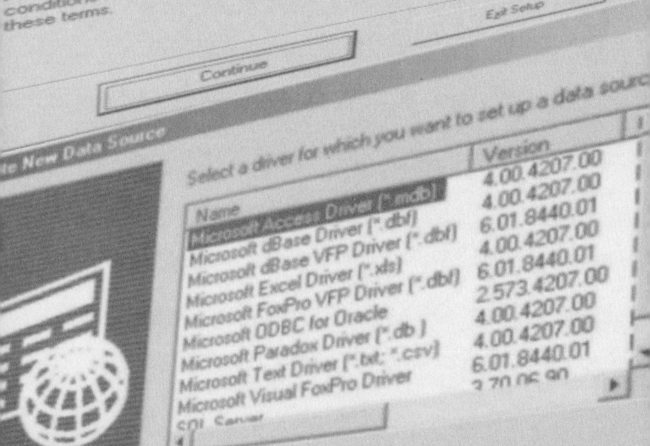

te New Data Source

Select a driver for which you want to set up a data source

| Name | Version |
|---|---|
| Microsoft Access Driver (*.mdb) | 4.00.4207.00 |
| Microsoft dBase Driver (*.dbf) | 4.00.4207.00 |
| Microsoft dBase VFP Driver (*.dbf) | 6.01.8440.01 |
| Microsoft Excel Driver (*.xls) | 4.00.4207.00 |
| Microsoft FoxPro VFP Driver (*.dbf) | 6.01.8440.01 |
| Microsoft ODBC for Oracle | 2.573.4207.00 |
| Microsoft Paradox Driver (*.db ) | 4.00.4207.00 |
| Microsoft Text Driver (*.txt; *.csv) | 4.00.4207.00 |
| Microsoft Visual FoxPro Driver | 6.01.8440.01 |
| SQL Server | 3.70.06.90 |

Finish

Cancel

# Stored Procedures and Passing Parameters

When we refer to **stored procedures** in terms of Microsoft Access we are really referring to queries. The large scale, enterprise relational databases refer to queries as stored procedures. So, what is a stored procedure? It depends on whom you ask. Basically, a stored procedure is a set of logical SQL code that selects columns and rows of data from one or more tables in your database. Stored procedures also allow you to write SQL statements that insert, update and delete data.

*The reason we use the term 'logical code' is because a stored procedure can logically execute its code, based on SQL statements and values contained in variables.*

In this chapter we will be referring to stored procedures and queries as one and the same and henceforth will use the term stored procedure. This chapter will introduce you to stored procedures and the benefits gained from using them. We will also cover some useful techniques for passing and retrieving values from stored procedures. By the end of the chapter you should have a firm grasp on stored procedures and what you can do with them.

We will cover the following topics in detail:

- ❑ Benefits of using stored procedures
- ❑ Applications of stored procedures
- ❑ Traps to avoid
- ❑ Passing values to a stored procedure
- ❑ Retrieving values from a stored procedure

## Benefits

There are many benefits of using stored procedures versus using actual SQL statements in your code (otherwise known as in-line). Probably the most beneficial is the fact that stored procedures are maintained outside of your code. Thus they can be used by other programs and applications. Stored procedures also execute faster because they are considered compiled when they are created in the database. That is, the database goes through a process in which it figures out the fastest access path to the data.

If you are using an enterprise database such as SQL Server, security is another added benefit. You can specify who has access rights to the stored procedure.

This section will cover just some of the major benefits of using stored procedures, and explain why they can be beneficial to you. It is up to you as the developer to determine when to use them.

# Maintainability

Since code for stored procedures resides in the database and not in your compiled program, maintaining stored procedures is a simple task. You simply need to change the code in the database, and the changes are immediately effective for all programs that use it.

## Simple Select Stored Procedures

With **simple select stored procedures** you can pretty much make any change you want as long as you do not drop column names from the SELECT list. For example, you can enhance the functionality of a stored procedure by adding column names to the SELECT list, and even join in one or more tables. This enhanced functionality is exposed to existing programs (although it's probably not needed), and all new programs can take advantage of the additional functionality.

## Parameterized Stored Procedures

Care must be taken when changing stored procedures that accept parameters in order to function. These **parameterized stored procedures** can include such types as SELECT, UPDATE, and DELETE. You cannot change the parameter list of the stored procedure in any way without affecting the existing programs that use the stored procedure, unless you add new parameters that specify default values. You can, however, increase the functionality by adding columns to the SELECT list in a select stored procedure, and even join in one or more tables. Again, this functionality is exposed to existing programs, but won't be taken advantage of. New programs can take advantage of these features, and will most likely be the reason for changing an existing stored procedure.

# Reusability

As we mentioned above, multiple programs can use the same stored procedure and this is often the case. This promotes continuity among your applications because they all use the same stored procedures. Along the same lines are **business rules** (which will be explained shortly). When a stored procedure contains business rules, you ensure all of your applications are implementing the same business rules when dealing with data from your database.

# Performance

Performance improvements of using a stored procedure versus using in-line SQL statements can be easily seen and measured. Stored procedures are considered compiled once they are created in the database. That is, the database goes through several steps when a stored procedure is created to ensure optimal performance when it is executed.

Performance improvements of a stored procedure can also be realized in the reduction of network traffic. You are typically sending less data across the network when calling a stored procedure versus using in-line SQL statements.

## Flexibility

Flexibility can be found in several areas. First is the fact that one stored procedure can call another. Second, since one stored procedure can call another, you can set up a stored procedure to return multiple recordsets, thus optimizing the performance of the stored procedure and reducing network traffic.

Since business rules are often implemented in stored procedures, you can shield the client from the complicated business rules, and change the stored procedures when the business rules change. This flexibility helps you to keep your business rules up to date and minimizes the impact on the client side.

You can also implement transactions in your stored procedures to help ensure data integrity, thus eliminating the need to code client transactions. This provides great flexibility in a multiple-tier system.

# Application

Applying stored procedures to your projects will make your life as a developer simpler. Suppose you used in-line SQL statements in your project. Imagine that your project consists of a couple of Active Server Pages, some ActiveX DLL server components, and of course the database. You use the same SQL code in a couple of your Active Server Pages and also one of your server components. It has become evident that you need to change the SQL code to perform the SELECT a little differently, and change the order the records are returned. You must update the SQL code in your Active Server Pages and the server component. Worst of all is that you now have to recompile your server component to reflect the change.

By using stored procedures, you could have simply made the change to the one stored procedure in question, and it would immediately have become effective in all Active Server Pages and the server component. Best of all is that the maintenance nightmare described above has become simple, and you've reduced the outage required to perform the maintenance on all of your code.

This section will describe three applications of stored procedures and why using stored procedures is important. Given some thought, you will be able to find more applications of stored procedures in your own environment.

## Active Server Pages

Typically, your web application will contain dozens of web pages. You will undoubtedly come across a situation where you need to use the same SQL code in more than one page. This is where a stored procedure will come in handy - you write the code once and share it among your web pages. If you need to update the SQL code, you update the stored procedure and the change is reflected immediately, and is available to all pages.

Another good use of stored procedures in your web pages is in situations where you can relieve the burden of processing off the web page and onto the database. Why would we want to do that? If you recall, Active Server Pages are interpreted and are thus slower than compiled programs, or even stored procedures. By moving some of the processing logic into stored procedures where appropriate, you increase the performance of your web pages, and therefore increase the performance of your application as a whole. Also, if you recall in our previous discussions, stored procedures are considered compiled and thus will run faster than actual SQL statements in your code.

Sometimes other web applications will access data from your database. By using stored procedures you ensure that they are accessing the data in a consistent manner and according to your standards. This is especially useful when dealing with SQL Server, as this enterprise database has a lot of built-in security features that prevent unauthorized access to data.

As you can see, using stored procedures in your Active Server Pages not only increases the performance of your web pages, but also helps to ensure the stability and integrity of your data.

# Business Rules

A lot of talk is floating around the industry about business rules, and applying your business rules on the backend (in other words, the database). But what are business rules? Business rules are the steps taken to perform a logical unit of work. A business rule is application-specific code whose primary purpose is to support the way that an organization does its business. Business rules are the core functionality of the application and represent the reason the application was written in the first place.

Let's assume that you are in the car insurance business. You calculate insurance rates for a driver based on the vehicle that they drive and their driving record. There is a standard formula that is used to perform these calculations. Using a specific formula and performing the calculation make up the business rules for determining an insurance rate.

As you can see, these rules can easily be applied and used in stored procedures. By using stored procedures you ensure the business rules are in a common place, and that any application that accesses the data to perform the rate calculation, performs the calculation according to the same business rules. This enforcement of the business rules provides consistent handling and ensures the integrity of your data.

By incorporating the business rules into the backend, the front-end programs do not need to worry about what formulae to use to perform the calculation. The maintenance associated with the front-end programs is also reduced because we have one central place for the business rules.

# Compiled Programs

Compiled programs include executable programs, ActiveX DLLs, and any other types of compiled code that access the database to retrieve and update data. This is probably the most important application of using stored procedures. Consider for a moment that you have an ActiveX server component running on your web site. This server component is heavily used by your web application and your web site is used 24 hours a day. If you are using in-line SQL statements and need to make a change to the SQL, you have a problem. However, if your server component were using stored procedures, you would simply need to make the appropriate changes to your stored procedure and you are done. The server component would then pick the new version of your stored procedure and you wouldn't have down time due to code maintenance.

Again, we can't stress enough the importance of using stored procedures versus in-line SQL statements. Maintenance of your compiled programs becomes much easier when you use stored procedures. I have often run across a situation where we have a stored procedure used both in our web pages and our server components, and we need to join another table and add some columns in the SELECT statement of a stored procedure. Doing so causes no change to any of the existing web pages or server components because of the use of stored procedures.

Even if you make no other use of stored procedures in your environment, at least consider using them in your compiled components.

# Traps

There are some common errors that even an experienced developer will run across when using stored procedures and passing parameters. A complete list of the most common errors can be found in Chapter 12, which covers error handling in depth. We will recap just a few of them here to help to prepare you for the examples that follow.

> *When you are trying the examples, you may need to refer back to this section for help in debugging your code.*

When dealing with SQL Server stored procedures, SQL Server may deny you access to a stored procedure, as the following error message indicates. Check with your database administrator to get the appropriate permissions to execute the stored procedure in question.

```
-2147217911
[Microsoft][ODBC SQL Server Driver][SQL Server]EXECUTE permission denied on object
'up_select_authors', database 'pubs', owner 'dbo'.
Microsoft OLE DB Provider for ODBC Drivers
42000
229
```

When dealing with Access you need to be aware of your spelling. Keying errors are commonplace and I often misspell words, as shown in the next example. However, as we can see, the messages that are returned back from Access are not very descriptive. The actual problem exists because the stored procedure we were trying to execute was misspelled.

```
-2147217900
[Microsoft][ODBC Microsoft Access Driver] Invalid SQL statement; expected 'DELETE',
'INSERT', 'PROCEDURE', 'SELECT', or 'UPDATE'.
Microsoft OLE DB Provider for ODBC Drivers
37000
-3500
```

The SQL Server version of this message is much more descriptive. Double check to ensure you have spelled the stored procedure name correctly, and also check to ensure the stored procedure actually exists under the owner prefix that you specified. The owner prefix will be discussed in detail later in this chapter.

```
-2147217900
[Microsoft][ODBC SQL Server Driver][SQL Server]Could not find stored procedure
'up_select_author'.
Microsoft OLE DB Provider for ODBC Drivers
37000
2812
```

Sometimes a stored procedure has so many parameters it is very easy to overlook one. As you can see, Access doesn't return a very descriptive message letting you know that you forgot to provide a parameter.

```
2147217900
[Microsoft][ODBC Microsoft Access Driver] Invalid SQL statement; expected 'DELETE',
'INSERT', 'PROCEDURE', 'SELECT', or 'UPDATE'.
Microsoft OLE DB Provider for ODBC Drivers
37000
-3500
```

The good thing about SQL Server is that it will tell you exactly which parameter you forgot. If your parameters are self-describing then you can quickly tell what data you should pass, as shown in this message.

```
-2147217900
[Microsoft][ODBC SQL Server Driver][SQL Server]Procedure 'up_parmsel_checks_paid'
expects parameter '@date', which was not supplied.
Microsoft OLE DB Provider for ODBC Drivers
37000
201
```

# Passing Values to a Stored Procedure

Passing parameters to stored procedures is a common everyday occurrence with database programming. Using parameters lets you limit the amount of data returned by the database so that you only have to deal with the data that you need. Likewise, using parameters with stored procedures that update data lets you only update the data in question, and not all rows in a table.

There are several methods of passing parameters to a stored procedure. The method used will depend on what actions the stored procedure is performing. This section will explore the various methods that are most commonly used. You must decide which method meets your shop's standards and best practices.

These examples illustrate the various techniques required to pass parameters to an Access stored procedure and to a SQL Server stored procedure. For the Access examples we'll be using the Sailors database which you should already have set up from Chapter 2. In order to try and use the SQL Server examples, you will need to have set up the Sailors database in SQL Server and created a DSN named SQLSailor. The specific instructions for doing this are included in Appendix D.

# Select Stored Procedures

**Select stored procedures** that accept parameters are very useful. They select only a subset of data that meets the criteria passed in the parameters. This makes this type of stored procedure very useful in terms of reuse and scalability. The two basic methods of passing parameters to a select stored procedure involve using either the ADO `Command` object or the `Recordset` object. The `Command` object uses the `CommandText` property to set the SQL statement or stored procedure to be executed, and sets the results set to a `Recordset` object. This was covered in detail in Chapter 13. The `Recordset` object uses a `Source` parameter to specify the SQL string or stored procedure to be executed, as was demonstrated in Chapter 8.

## Command Object

To recap what we covered in Chapter 13, the `Command` object defines a specific command that you will execute. Depending on the functionality of the providing database, the command object can contain one or more collections, properties and methods. The command object is very useful for executing SQL commands that select, insert, update and delete rows of data. It is also useful for modifying table structures and performing general maintenance on your database objects.

*Refer back to Chapter 13 and the ADO help documentation for a complete list and further information on the* `Command` *object.*

## Try It Out – Passing values to an Access select stored procedure using the command object

Using Microsoft Access as the database provider, create a web page to execute a select stored procedure that accepts parameters, using the `Command` object. We will be selecting data from the `Boats` table in the `Sailors` database. When we run our code we should get the following result:

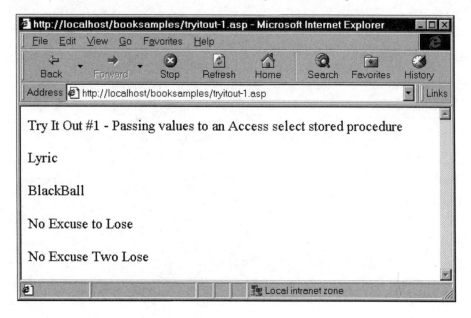

The first thing we want to do is create the stored procedure in the Access Sailors database. We can do this by opening the Sailors database and clicking on the **Queries** tab. Next, click on the **New** button and then select **Design View** in the **New Query** dialog, and then click on **OK**. The **Show Table** dialog is shown next but we do not want to select any tables. Simply click on the **Close** button to dismiss this dialog. Select **SQL View** from the **View** menu and enter the SQL statements below. Save the query as qparmBoats (This file is also available for download).

```
PARAMETERS Class Text;
SELECT Boats.BoatsID, Boats.BoatName
FROM Boats
WHERE (((Boats.BoatClass)=[Class]));
```

Next we need to create the web page using the following code, available as TryItOut-1.asp.

```
<HTML>
<HEAD>
<META NAME="GENERATOR" Content="Microsoft Visual Studio 6.0">
<TITLE></TITLE>
</HEAD>
<BODY>

<!--Display the page data-->
Try It Out #1 - Passing values to an Access select stored procedure<BR><BR>

<%
'Instruct VBScript to ignore the error and continue
'with the next line of code
On Error Resume Next

'Create and open the database object
Set objConn = Server.CreateObject("ADODB.Connection")

objConn.Open "DSN=Sailors"

'Check for errors
If objConn.Errors.Count > 0 Then
  'Create an error object to access the ADO errors collection
  Set objErr = Server.CreateObject("Error")
  'Declare Boolean flag for critical errors
  Dim blnCriticalError
  'Write all errors to the page
  For Each objErr In objConn.Errors
    If objErr.Number <> 0 Then
      Response.Write "Number: " & objErr.Number & "<P>"
      Response.Write "Description: " & objErr.Description & "<P>"
      Response.Write "Source: " & objErr.Source & "<P>"
      Response.Write "SQLState: " & objErr.SQLState & "<P>"
      Response.Write "NativeError: " & objErr.NativeError & "<P>"
      blnCriticalError = True
    End If
  Next
  'Dereference all objects
  Set objErr = Nothing
  If blnCriticalError Then
    Response.End
  End If
End If

'Declare variables and set their values
Dim strBoat
strBoat = "Laser"
```

```
'Create the command object and set the query to be executed
Set objCmd = Server.CreateObject("ADODB.Command")
Set objCmd.ActiveConnection = objConn
objCmd.CommandText = "{CALL qparmBoats ('" & CStr(strBoat) & "')}"
Set objRS = Server.CreateObject("ADODB.Recordset")
Set objRS = objCmd.Execute

'Check for errors
If objConn.Errors.Count > 0 Then
  'Create an error object to access the ADO errors collection
  Set objErr = Server.CreateObject("Error")
  'Write all errors to the page
  For Each objErr In objConn.Errors
    If objErr.Number <> 0 Then
      Response.Write "Number: " & objErr.Number & "<P>"
      Response.Write "Description: " & objErr.Description & "<P>"
      Response.Write "Source: " & objErr.Source & "<P>"
      Response.Write "SQLState: " & objErr.SQLState & "<P>"
      Response.Write "NativeError: " & objErr.NativeError & "<P>"
      blnCriticalError = True
    End If
  Next
  'Dereference all objects
  Set objErr = Nothing
  If blnCriticalError Then
    Response.End
  End If
End If

'Loop through the recordset displaying the last name field
Do While Not objRS.EOF
  Response.Write objRS("BoatName") & "<P>"
  objRS.MoveNext
Loop

'Close and dereference database objects
objRS.Close
Set objRS = Nothing
objConn.Close
Set objConn = Nothing
%>
</BODY>
</HTML>
```

### How It Works: The stored procedure

Let's take a quick look at the stored procedure itself. We are defining a parameter that will be used in the stored procedure to restrict the selection of records. Next we select the two columns from the Boats table, using the WHERE clause to select only records from the boatclass column that match the parameter passed.

```
PARAMETERS Class Text;
SELECT Boats.BoatsID, Boats.BoatName
FROM Boats
WHERE (((Boats.BoatClass)=[Class]));
```

### The Web Page

Now let's look at the code that makes up the active server page. We start the page out by including the standard HTML tags used to define a page.

```
<HTML>
<HEAD>
<META NAME="GENERATOR" Content="Microsoft Visual Studio 6.0">
<TITLE></TITLE>
</HEAD>
<BODY>
```

We write the page data using standard HTML tags, and start the server-side script by turning on error handling.

```
<!--Display the page data-->
Try It Out #1 - Passing values to an Access select stored procedure<BR><BR>

<%
'Instruct VBScript to ignore the error and continue
'with the next line of code
On Error Resume Next
```

We create the Connection object and open the Sailors database, using the DSN that we already set up in Chapter 2.

```
'Create and open the database object
Set objConn = Server.CreateObject("ADODB.Connection")
objConn.Open "DSN=Sailors"
```

After we open the database we should check the ADO Errors collection for any errors, by seeing if the Count property is greater than zero. If an error has occurred, we then create an Error object that will allow us to access the Errors collection. Next, we loop through the Errors collection checking each error. If the error number is not equal to zero then a serious error has occurred, and we write the errors on the web page, setting a flag to let us know what action to take after we have checked all errors. Error handling and the ADO Errors collection were explained in detail in Chapter 12.

```
'Check for errors
If objConn.Errors.Count > 0 Then
  'Create an error object to access the ADO errors collection
  Set objErr = Server.CreateObject("Error")
  'Declare Boolean flag for critical errors
  Dim blnCriticalError
  'Write all errors to the page
  For Each objErr In objConn.Errors
    If objErr.Number <> 0 Then
      Response.Write "Number: " & objErr.Number & "<P>"
      Response.Write "Description: " & objErr.Description & "<P>"
      Response.Write "Source: " & objErr.Source & "<P>"
      Response.Write "SQLState: " & objErr.SQLState & "<P>"
      Response.Write "NativeError: " & objErr.NativeError & "<P>"
      blnCriticalError = True
    End If
  Next
```

We de-reference our Error object to release it from memory and then check our flag. If the flag is True, then a serious error occurred and we want to stop processing. We do this by using the Response object's End method, which halts execution of our code immediately.

```
   'Dereference all objects
   Set objErr = Nothing
   If blnCriticalError Then
     Response.End
   End If
End If
```

We declare the variables that we are going to be using to pass parameters to the stored procedure, and set their values. These variables could be fields from the request form, or querystring values passed to our page. Using a little imagination here, you can see a multitude of possibilities for getting values to be passed to our stored procedure.

```
'Declare variables and set their values
Dim strBoat
strBoat = "Laser"
```

We will break down this next section of code into one-liners and discuss each line separately. In this next line of code we are creating the ADO `Command` object, similar to how we did with the `Connection` object:

```
'Create the command object and set the query to be executed
Set objCmd = Server.CreateObject("ADODB.Command")
```

Before we can use the `Command` object that we created, we have to set it to an active connection. Here we set the `Command` object's `ActiveConnection` property to the `Connection` object that we have created:

```
Set objCmd.ActiveConnection = objConn
```

Using the stored procedure we created earlier, we set the `CommandText` property of the `Command` object to call the stored procedure we created, and pass all of the parameters that the stored procedure expects. Notice that we are converting the variable to a specific variable type. This is because all variables in Active Server Pages are variants, and we want to convert them to their proper types.

> *Testing has shown that this is not necessary when dealing with Access, but it is a good habit to get into. When passing parameters to ActiveX DLLs, you will have to specify the correct data types that the DLL expects, or you will receive an error.*

Notice that we use single quote marks before and after the variable. This is because we must delimit our string parameters.

```
objCmd.CommandText = "{CALL qparmBoats ('" & CStr(strBoat) & "')}"
```

Next, we create a `Recordset` object to hold the records that will be returned when we execute the `Command` object. We execute the `Command` object, returning all records into the `Recordset` object:

```
Set objRS = Server.CreateObject("ADODB.Recordset")
Set objRS = objCmd.Execute
```

Again we perform our error checking in the same way as was described above:

```
'Check for errors
If objConn.Errors.Count > 0 Then
   'Create an error object to access the ADO errors collection
   Set objErr = Server.CreateObject("Error")
   'Write all errors to the page
   For Each objErr In objConn.Errors
     If objErr.Number <> 0 Then
        Response.Write "Number: " & objErr.Number & "<P>"
        Response.Write "Description: " & objErr.Description & "<P>"
        Response.Write "Source: " & objErr.Source & "<P>"
        Response.Write "SQLState: " & objErr.SQLState & "<P>"
        Response.Write "NativeError: " & objErr.NativeError & "<P>"
        blnCriticalError = True
     End If
   Next
   'Dereference all objects
   Set objErr = Nothing
   If blnCriticalError Then
     Response.End
   End If
End If
```

Next we loop through our recordset, writing the boat name on the web page, until we reach an end of file condition (EOF) on the recordset:

```
'Loop through the recordset displaying the last name field
Do While Not objRS.EOF
   Response.Write objRS("BoatName") & "<P>"
   objRS.MoveNext
Loop
```

We perform our cleanup by closing our Recordset and Connection objects and setting them equal to Nothing, which releases them from memory:

```
'Close and dereference database objects
objRS.Close
Set objRS = Nothing
objConn.Close
Set objConn = Nothing
%>
</BODY>
</HTML>
```

## Try It Out – Passing values to a SQL Server select stored procedure using the command object

Using Microsoft SQL Server as the database provider, create a web page to execute a select stored procedure that accepts parameters, using the Command object. The changes we want to make are the same as for the previous example. Our web page should give the result shown in the screenshot:

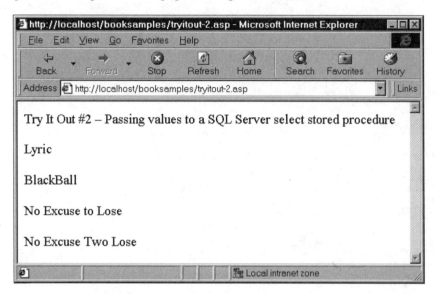

To create the stored procedure in SQL Server versions 6.5 and 7, open SQL Server Enterprise Manager and expand the Sailors database. Expand **Objects** and then **Stored Procedures**. Right click on **Stored Procedures**, select **New Stored Procedure** in the popup menu, and key in the following stored procedure. Click on the **Save Object** button to create the stored procedure, with the name up_parmsel_boats. We use the 'up' prefix to specify that this is a user created procedure. This file is available for download, with the name up_parmsel_boats.

```
CREATE PROCEDURE up_parmsel_boats (@class varchar(50)) AS

SELECT boatsid, boatname
  FROM boats
  WHERE boatclass = @class
```

If you are not using the administrator ID in the DSN to access the Sailors database, you will need to grant execute permission on this stored procedure to the public group. Right click on the stored procedure just created and select **Permissions** in the popup menu. Click on the **Execute** box for public users and then click on **Set**. Click **Close** to close the dialog.

The code for the web page is shown below and is also contained in TryItOut-2.asp.

```
<HTML>
<HEAD>
<META NAME="GENERATOR" Content="Microsoft Visual Studio 6.0">
<TITLE></TITLE>
</HEAD>
<BODY>
```

```
<!--Display the page data-->
Try It Out #2 - Passing values to a SQL Server select stored procedure<BR><BR>

<%
'Instruct VBScript to ignore the error and continue
'with the next line of code
On Error Resume Next

'Create and open the database object
Set objConn = Server.CreateObject("ADODB.Connection")
objConn.Open "DSN=SQLSailor;uid=sa;pwd="

'Check for errors
If objConn.Errors.Count > 0 Then
  'Create an error object to access the ADO errors collection
  Set objErr = Server.CreateObject("Error")
  'Declare Boolean flag for critical errors
  Dim blnCriticalError
  'Write all errors to the page
  For Each objErr In objConn.Errors
    If objErr.Number <> 0 Then
      Response.Write "Number: " & objErr.Number & "<P>"
      Response.Write "Description: " & objErr.Description & "<P>"
      Response.Write "Source: " & objErr.Source & "<P>"
      Response.Write "SQLState: " & objErr.SQLState & "<P>"
      Response.Write "NativeError: " & objErr.NativeError & "<P>"
      blnCriticalError = True
    End If
  Next
  'Dereference all objects
  Set objErr = Nothing
  If blnCriticalError Then
    Response.End
  End If
End If

'Declare variables and set their values
Dim adCmdText
Dim strBoat
adCmdText = 1
strBoat = "Laser"

'Create the command object and set the query to be executed
Set objCmd = Server.CreateObject("ADODB.Command")
Set objCmd.ActiveConnection = objConn
objCmd.CommandText = "{CALL dbo.up_parmsel_boats ('" & CStr(strBoat) & "')}"
objCmd.CommandType = adCmdText
Set objRS = Server.CreateObject("ADODB.Recordset")
Set objRS = objCmd.Execute

'Check for errors
If objConn.Errors.Count > 0 Then
  'Create an error object to access the ADO errors collection
  Set objErr = Server.CreateObject("Error")
  'Write all errors to the page
  For Each objErr In objConn.Errors
    If objErr.Number <> 0 Then
      Response.Write "Number: " & objErr.Number & "<P>"
      Response.Write "Description: " & objErr.Description & "<P>"
      Response.Write "Source: " & objErr.Source & "<P>"
      Response.Write "SQLState: " & objErr.SQLState & "<P>"
      Response.Write "NativeError: " & objErr.NativeError & "<P>"
      blnCriticalError = True
    End If
```

```
    Next
    'Dereference all objects
    Set objErr = Nothing
    If blnCriticalError Then
      Response.End
    End If
End If

'Loop through the recordset displaying the last name field
Do While Not objRS.EOF
    Response.Write objRS("BoatName") & "<P>"
    objRS.MoveNext
Loop

'Close and dereference database objects
objRS.Close
Set objRS = Nothing
objConn.Close
Set objConn = Nothing
%>
</BODY>
</HTML>
```

### How It Works: The stored procedure

This stored procedure performs the same function as its Access equivalent. We are specifying that `@class` is the parameter that this stored procedure expects, and we define what data type it is. SQL Server requires that all local variables specify the at (@) sign as a prefix. Next, we select the two columns from the `boats` table where the `boat` class equals the parameter passed.

```
CREATE PROCEDURE up_parmsel_boats (@class varchar(50)) AS

SELECT boatsid, boatname
  FROM boats
  WHERE boatclass = @class
```

### The Web Page

The first part of this web page is the same as in the last example so we won't go into the details again. One minor difference to be noted here is that when we open the `Connection` object, we must specify the user ID and password for a DSN that accesses a SQL Server database.

```
'Create and open the database object
Set objConn = Server.CreateObject("ADODB.Connection")
objConn.Open "DSN=SQLSailor;uid=sa;pwd"
```

The next section is also very similar to the last example, except that we are specifying the owner prefix of the stored procedure, along with the stored procedure name. The owner prefix is the SQL Server user ID of the person who created the stored procedure. In this case we use the prefix dbo (**data**base **o**wner), which is reserved for the database administrator user ID. The owner prefix is not required if the stored procedure was created by the database owner. It is required for any other user id, unless you are the owner that created the stored procedure.

> Note that, although the owner prefix is not required if executing a stored procedure that belongs to you or the dbo, always specifying the owner prefix makes converting your code for test or production easier, as you simply need to change the prefix. It also helps to let you know at a quick glance if the stored procedure is one you created or if someone else created it.

```
'Create the command object and set the query to be executed
Set objCmd = Server.CreateObject("ADODB.Command")
Set objCmd.ActiveConnection = objConn
objCmd.CommandText = "{CALL dbo.up_parmsel_boats ('" & CStr(strBoat) & "')}"
objCmd.CommandType = adCmdText
Set objRS = Server.CreateObject("ADODB.Recordset")
Set objRS = objCmd.Execute
```

The rest of the code is the same as in the previous example and does not need further explanation.

## Recordset Object

As we saw in Chapter 8, the Recordset object contains a group of records returned as a result of executing a command to select records, or executing a stored procedure. The Recordset object can only refer to a single record in the group at any one time, and can be used to change the records in the recordset. You can then apply these changes contained in the recordset back to the database. The recordsets that we will be dealing with here are used only for selecting records, we will not be performing any updates to the recordset.

As with other ADO objects, the Recordset object supports multiple collections, properties and methods. See the ADO online help in the MSDN site for further information.

**Try It Out – Passing values to an Access select stored procedure using the recordset object**

Using Microsoft Access as the database provider, create a web page to execute a select stored procedure that accepts parameters, using the Recordset object. The same changes will be made to the database as in the previous examples. Our code will produce the following result:

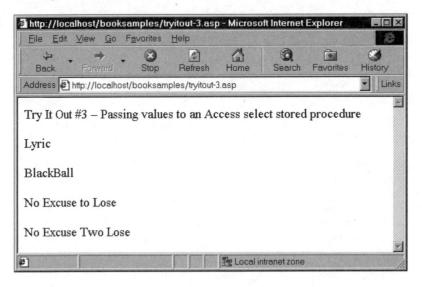

The stored procedure is the same as in the first example, (code as shown – qparmBoats).

```
PARAMETERS Class Text;
SELECT Boats.BoatsID, Boats.BoatName
FROM Boats
WHERE (((Boats.BoatClass)=[Class]));
```

The code for the new web page, from TryItOut-3.asp, is shown below.

```
<HTML>
<HEAD>
<META NAME="GENERATOR" Content="Microsoft Visual Studio 6.0">
<TITLE></TITLE>
</HEAD>
<BODY>

<!--Display the page data-->
Try It Out #3 - Passing values to an Access select stored procedure<BR><BR>

<%
'Instruct VBScript to ignore the error and continue
'with the next line of code
On Error Resume Next

'Create and open the database object
Set objConn = Server.CreateObject("ADODB.Connection")
objConn.Open "DSN=Sailors"

'Check for errors
If objConn.Errors.Count > 0 Then
  'Create an error object to access the ADO errors collection
  Set objErr = Server.CreateObject("Error")
  'Declare Boolean flag for critical errors
  Dim blnCriticalError
  'Write all errors to the page
  For Each objErr In objConn.Errors
    If objErr.Number <> 0 Then
      Response.Write "Number: " & objErr.Number & "<P>"
      Response.Write "Description: " & objErr.Description & "<P>"
      Response.Write "Source: " & objErr.Source & "<P>"
      Response.Write "SQLState: " & objErr.SQLState & "<P>"
      Response.Write "NativeError: " & objErr.NativeError & "<P>"
      blnCriticalError = True
    End If
  Next
  'Dereference all objects
  Set objErr = Nothing
  If blnCriticalError Then
    Response.End
  End If
End If

'Declare variables and set their values
Dim adOpenForwardOnly
Dim adCmdStoredProc
Dim strBoat
adOpenForwardOnly = 0
adCmdStoredProc = 4
strBoat = "Laser"

'Create the recordset object and open the recordset
Set objRS = Server.CreateObject("ADODB.Recordset")
strSQL = "qparmBoats '" & CStr(strBoat) & "'"
objRS.Open strSQL, objConn, adOpenForwardOnly, , adCmdStoredProc
```

**557**

```
'Check for errors
If objConn.Errors.Count > 0 Then
  'Create an error object to access the ADO errors collection
  Set objErr = Server.CreateObject("Error")
  'Write all errors to the page
  For Each objErr In objConn.Errors
    If objErr.Number <> 0 Then
      Response.Write "Number: " & objErr.Number & "<P>"
      Response.Write "Description: " & objErr.Description & "<P>"
      Response.Write "Source: " & objErr.Source & "<P>"
      Response.Write "SQLState: " & objErr.SQLState & "<P>"
      Response.Write "NativeError: " & objErr.NativeError & "<P>"
      blnCriticalError = True
    End If
  Next
  'Dereference all objects
  Set objErr = Nothing
  If blnCriticalError Then
    Response.End
  End If
End If

'Loop through the recordset displaying the last name field
Do While Not objRS.EOF
  Response.Write objRS("BoatName") & "<P>"
  objRS.MoveNext
Loop

'Close and dereference database objects
objRS.Close
Set objRS = Nothing
objConn.Close
Set objConn = Nothing
%>
</BODY>
</HTML>
```

### How It Works – Passing Values to an Access Select Stored Procedure Using the Recordset Object

This stored procedure is the same one as used in the last Access example and does not need to be explained here. The first part of the web page code is also the same as the previous examples, so we won't go into the details again.

The difference in this example comes after we have declared our variables and set their values. We create a `Recordset` object that will contain the records returned from the stored procedure that we are going to execute.

```
'Declare variables and set their values
Dim strBoat
strBoat = "Laser"

'Create the recordset object and open the recordset
Set objRS = Server.CreateObject("ADODB.Recordset")
```

Next, we set a string that contains the SQL statement that we want to execute. Here we are setting the string to the stored procedure name and the parameters it expects. Again we are specifying what specific data type the variable should be.

```
strSQL = "qparmBoats '" & CStr(strBoat) & "'"
```

Lastly, we open the recordset using the open method, passing it the required parameters. Let's take a look at the parameters.

The first parameter is the source parameter, which is a variant that accepts a string – the string contains the SQL statements or stored procedure to be executed. This parameter can also accept a valid Command object as demonstrated in the last two examples. Here, we are using a string that contains the stored procedure to be executed, along with its required parameters.

```
objRS.Open strSQL, objConn, adOpenForwardOnly, , adCmdStoredProc
```

The second parameter is a variant that accepts a valid Connection object, which we are using in our example, or a string containing the connect string parameters.

CursorType is the third parameter and determines what type of cursor should be used when opening the recordset. We are using a forward only cursor, which means we can only read forward in the recordset using the MoveNext method.

The LockType parameter is next and determines what type of locking should be performed on the recordset when it is opened. By not specifying this parameter, we are using the default parameter of adLockReadOnly, which means we can only read records from the recordset, we cannot perform any type of updates to the recordset.

The last parameter is the Options parameter, which is a long data type. This parameter determines how the source parameter should be evaluated. By using the adCmdStoredProc parameter, we are specifying that the source we passed is a stored procedure on the database.

*For more information on the Open method's parameters, see Chapter 8 or the ADO online help.*

The rest of the code is the same as used in the previous examples.

**Try It Out – Passing values to a SQL Server select stored procedure using the recordset object**

This time we will use Microsoft SQL Server as the database provider, and again create a web page to execute a select stored procedure that accepts parameters, using the `Recordset` object. The result of running our code is shown below:

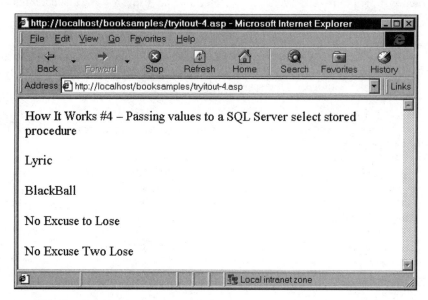

The stored procedure is the same one used in the last SQL Server example, and does not have to be recreated. It is saved in `up_parmsel_boats`.

```
CREATE PROCEDURE up_parmsel_boats (@class varchar(50)) as

SELECT boatsid, boatname
  FROM boats
  WHERE boatclass = @class
```

The code for the web page is given here and in `TryItOut-4.asp`.

```
<HTML>
<HEAD>
<META NAME="GENERATOR" Content="Microsoft Visual Studio 6.0">
<TITLE></TITLE>
</HEAD>
<BODY>

<!--Display the page data-->
How it works #4 - Passing values to a SQL Server select stored procedure<BR><BR>

<%
'Instruct VBScript to ignore the error and continue
'with the next line of code
On Error Resume Next

'Create and open the database object
Set objConn = Server.CreateObject("ADODB.Connection")
objConn.Open "DSN=SQLSailor;uid=sa;pwd"
```

```
'Check for errors
If objConn.Errors.Count > 0 Then
  'Create an error object to access the ADO errors collection
  Set objErr = Server.CreateObject("Error")
  'Declare Boolean flag for critical errors
  Dim blnCriticalError
  'Write all errors to the page
  For Each objErr In objConn.Errors
    If objErr.Number <> 0 Then
      Response.Write "Number: " & objErr.Number & "<P>"
      Response.Write "Description: " & objErr.Description & "<P>"
      Response.Write "Source: " & objErr.Source & "<P>"
      Response.Write "SQLState: " & objErr.SQLState & "<P>"
      Response.Write "NativeError: " & objErr.NativeError & "<P>"
      blnCriticalError = True
    End If
  Next
  'Dereference all objects
  Set objErr = Nothing
  If blnCriticalError Then
    Response.End
  End If
End If

'Declare variables and set their values
Dim adOpenForwardOnly
Dim adCmdStoredProc
Dim strBoat
adOpenForwardOnly = 0
adCmdStoredProc = 4
strBoat = "Laser"

'Create the recordset object and open the recordset
Set objRS = Server.CreateObject("ADODB.Recordset")
strSQL = "dbo.up_parmsel_boats ('" & CStr(strBoat) & "')"
objRS.Open strSQL, objConn, adOpenForwardOnly, , adCmdStoredProc

'Check for errors
If objConn.Errors.Count > 0 Then
  'Create an error object to access the ADO errors collection
  Set objErr = Server.CreateObject("Error")
  'Write all errors to the page
  For Each objErr In objConn.Errors
    If objErr.Number <> 0 Then
      Response.Write "Number: " & objErr.Number & "<P>"
      Response.Write "Description: " & objErr.Description & "<P>"
      Response.Write "Source: " & objErr.Source & "<P>"
      Response.Write "SQLState: " & objErr.SQLState & "<P>"
      Response.Write "NativeError: " & objErr.NativeError & "<P>"
      blnCriticalError = True
    End If
  Next
  'Dereference all objects
  Set objErr = Nothing
  If blnCriticalError Then
    Response.End
  End If
End If

'Loop through the recordset displaying the last name field
Do While Not objRS.EOF
  Response.Write objRS("BoatName") & "<P>"
  objRS.MoveNext
Loop
```

```
'Close and dereference database objects
objRS.Close
Set objRS = Nothing
objConn.Close
Set objConn = Nothing
%>
</BODY>
</HTML>
```

### How It Works – Passing Values to a SQL Server Select Stored Procedure Using the Recordset Object

The stored procedure is the same one used in the last SQL Server example and does not have to be explained here. Also, the majority of code for this example is the same as the code used in the last SQL Server example, and won't be covered again.

The difference in this example is that we are using a `Recordset` object only, as opposed to the `Command` object - `Recordset` object combination that we used in the last SQL Server example.

The only difference between this code and the previous (Access) example is that we are using SQL Server as the database and therefore the syntax is slightly different. Notice that we specify the owner prefix before the stored procedure name. See the previous SQL Server example's How It Works section for a detailed discussion on the owner prefix.

```
'Declare variables and set their values
Dim strBoat
strBoat = "Laser"
```

```
'Create the recordset object and open the recordset
Set objRS = Server.CreateObject("ADODB.Recordset")
strSQL = "dbo.up_parmsel_boats '" & CStr(strBoat) & "'"
objRS.Open strSQL, objConn, adOpenForwardOnly, , adCmdStoredProc
```

The remainder of the code is the same as in the previous examples.

# Action Stored Procedures

When we use the term **action stored procedure** we are referring to a stored procedure that performs some type of action on the database. This could be inserting a new row, updating an existing row, or deleting a row. Depending on the actions they are performing, action stored procedures don't always accept parameters and don't usually return records. For the purpose of our discussions though, our stored procedure will accept multiple parameters and insert a row into the database.

Again we will use two basic methods to perform these actions. This time we use the `Command` object and the `Connection` object. The `Recordset` object is not used because we are not retrieving any data, we simply want to perform some action on the database.

## Command Object

In order not to repeat the previous discussion on the `Command` object, we will just recap that the `Command` object defines a specific command that you will execute. This command can be in the form of SQL statements or a stored procedure. Again, refer back to Chapter 13 for a full explanation of the `Command` object. This section focuses on using action stored procedures that accept parameters.

**Try It Out – Passing values to an Access action stored procedure using the command object**

Using Microsoft Access as the database provider, create a web page to execute an action stored procedure that accepts parameters, using the Command object. We want to insert a record into the database. Our code will produce the following result:

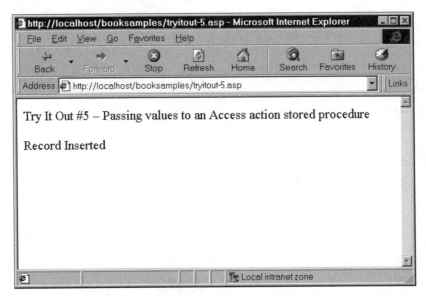

Let's start by creating the stored procedure needed in Access. Using the same instructions described in the first example, key in the SQL statements below. Save the stored procedure as qparmInsertBoatClass, or use the download file of the same name.

```
INSERT INTO BoatClass ( ClassName, ClassBoatLength, ClassBoatWeight,
ClassSailAreaMainJib, ClassSailAreaSpinnaker, ClassAuthority )
SELECT [Name] AS Expr1, [Length] AS Expr2, [Weight] AS Expr3, [MainJib] AS Expr4,
[Spinnaker] AS Expr5, [Authority] AS Expr6;
```

Next create a web page using the code below, which is also included in TryItOut-5.asp.

```
<HTML>
<HEAD>
<META NAME="GENERATOR" Content="Microsoft Visual Studio 6.0">
<TITLE></TITLE>
</HEAD>
<BODY>

<!--Display the page data-->
Try It Out #5 - Passing values to an Access action stored procedure<BR><BR>

<%
'Instruct VBScript to ignore the error and continue
'with the next line of code
On Error Resume Next
```

```
'Create and open the database object
Set objConn = Server.CreateObject("ADODB.Connection")
objConn.Open "DSN=Sailors"

'Check for errors
If objConn.Errors.Count > 0 Then
  'Create an error object to access the ADO errors collection
  Set objErr = Server.CreateObject("Error")
  'Declare Boolean flag for critical errors
  Dim blnCriticalError
  'Write all errors to the page
  For Each objErr In objConn.Errors
    If objErr.Number <> 0 Then
      Response.Write "Number: " & objErr.Number & "<P>"
      Response.Write "Description: " & objErr.Description & "<P>"
      Response.Write "Source: " & objErr.Source & "<P>"
      Response.Write "SQLState: " & objErr.SQLState & "<P>"
      Response.Write "NativeError: " & objErr.NativeError & "<P>"
      blnCriticalError = True
    End If
  Next
  'Dereference all objects
  Set objErr = Nothing
  If blnCriticalError Then
    Response.End
  End If
End If

'Declare variables and set their values
Dim adCmdText
Dim strClass
Dim lngLength
Dim lngWeight
Dim lngMainJib
Dim lngSpinnaker
Dim strAuthority
adCmdText = 1
strClass = "Mini Laser"
lngLength = 3
lngWeight = 45
lngMainJib = 6
lngSpinnaker = 0
strAuthority = "www.laser.com"

'Create the command object and set the query to be executed
Set objCmd = Server.CreateObject("ADODB.Command")
Set objCmd.ActiveConnection = objConn
objCmd.CommandText = "{call qparmInsertBoatClass ('" & CStr(strClass) & _
  "'," & CLng(lngLength) & "," & CLng(lngWeight) & _
  "," & CLng(lngMainJib) & "," & CLng(lngSpinnaker) & _
  ",'" & CStr(strAuthority) & "')}"
objCmd.CommandType = adCmdText
objCmd.Execute

'Check for errors
If objConn.Errors.Count > 0 Then
  'Create an error object to access the ADO errors collection
  Set objErr = Server.CreateObject("Error")
  'Write all errors to the page
  For Each objErr In objConn.Errors
    If objErr.Number <> 0 Then
      Response.Write "Number: " & objErr.Number & "<P>"
      Response.Write "Description: " & objErr.Description & "<P>"
      Response.Write "Source: " & objErr.Source & "<P>"
      Response.Write "SQLState: " & objErr.SQLState & "<P>"
      Response.Write "NativeError: " & objErr.NativeError & "<P>"
      blnCriticalError = True
```

```
      End If
   Next
   'Dereference all objects
   Set objErr = Nothing
   If blnCriticalError Then
      Response.End
   End If
End If

Response.Write "Record Inserted"

'Close and dereference database objects
objConn.Close
Set objConn = Nothing
%>
</BODY>
</HTML>
```

### How It Works: The stored procedure

Let's take a look at the SQL statements that make up this stored procedure. Since this is an append query in Access terms, we do not have to define the parameters. Instead, the parameters are implied by the fact that we are specifying them in the SELECT statement.

The first line of SQL specifies that we want to insert data into the BoatClass table, and the order of the data that will be inserted matches the order of the column names that are defined in the first line.

```
INSERT INTO BoatClass ( ClassName, ClassBoatLength, ClassBoatWeight,
ClassSailAreaMainJib, ClassSailAreaSpinnaker, ClassAuthority )
```

The second line of SQL selects the data to be inserted using the parameters that we pass. The parameters must be passed in the same order that is specified in this line of SQL.

```
SELECT [Name] AS Expr1, [Length] AS Expr2, [Weight] AS Expr3, [MainJib] AS Expr4,
[Spinnaker] AS Expr5, [Authority] AS Expr6;
```

### The Web Page

The first part of the web page code is the same as the previous Access examples. The difference comes when we declare our variables and assign them values. As you can see, there are a lot more variables than we used in the previous examples.

```
'Declare variables and set their values
Dim adCmdText
Dim strClass
Dim lngLength
Dim lngWeight
Dim lngMainJib
Dim lngSpinnaker
Dim strAuthority
adCmdText = 1
strClass = "Mini Laser"
lngLength = 3
lngWeight = 45
lngMainJib = 6
lngSpinnaker = 0
strAuthority = "www.laser.com"
```

This next section of code should be pretty routine to you by now, as we simply create our Command object and set it to an active Connection object.

```
'Create the command object and set the query to be executed
Set objCmd = Server.CreateObject("ADODB.Command")
Set objCmd.ActiveConnection = objConn
```

Setting the command text should look somewhat familiar, as the syntax hasn't changed. We are simply adding more parameters to the stored procedure that we are calling. Let's take a close look at the parameters again. The first and last variables that we defined are string data types, and the rest are long data types. We have to enclose our string parameters with a single quote mark on each side of the parameter. Again we convert the variables to specific data types.

After adding all of the parameters to the CommandText property, we execute the command.

```
objCmd.CommandText = "{CALL qparmInsertBoatClass ('" & CStr(strClass) & _
   "'," & CLng(lngLength) & "," & CLng(lngWeight) & _
   "," & CLng(lngMainJib) & "," & CLng(lngSpinnaker) & _
   ",'" & CStr(strAuthority) & "')}"
objCmd.CommandType = adCmdText
objCmd.Execute
```

The rest of the code is the same as the previous examples.

## Try It Out – Passing values to a SQL Server action stored procedure using the command object

This time we will use Microsoft SQL Server as the database provider, and create a web page to execute an action stored procedure that accepts parameters, using the Command object. Again, we will insert a record. The resulting web page should look like the following screenshot.

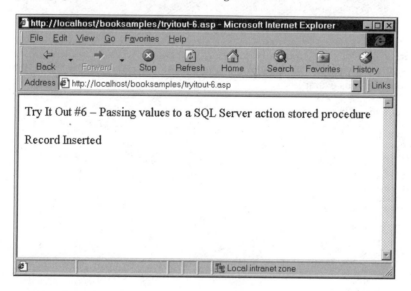

Using the procedures detailed in the second example, create a SQL Server stored procedure using the code below. Save it as up_parmins_boatclass. Alternatively, use the downloaded file of the same name.

```
CREATE PROCEDURE up_parmins_boatclass (@name varchar(50), @length int, @weight int,
  @mainjib int, @spinnaker int, @authority varchar(16)) AS

INSERT INTO boatclass
  (ClassName, ClassBoatLength, ClassBoatWeight, ClassSailAreaMainJib,
ClassSailAreaSpinnaker, ClassAuthority)
  VALUES(@name, @length, @weight, @mainjib, @spinnaker, @authority)
```

Create a new web page as below, using the code from TryItOut-6.asp.

```
<HTML>
<HEAD>
<META NAME="GENERATOR" Content="Microsoft Visual Studio 6.0">
<TITLE></TITLE>
</HEAD>
<BODY>

<!--Display the page data-->
Try It Out #6 - Passing values to a SQL Server action stored procedure<BR><BR>

<%
'Instruct VBScript to ignore the error and continue
'with the next line of code
On Error Resume Next

'Create and open the database object
Set objConn = Server.CreateObject("ADODB.Connection")
objConn.Open "DSN=SQLSailor;uid=sa;pwd"

'Check for errors
If objConn.Errors.Count > 0 Then
  'Create an error object to access the ADO errors collection
  Set objErr = Server.CreateObject("Error")
  'Declare Boolean flag for critical errors
  Dim blnCriticalError
  'Write all errors to the page
  For Each objErr In objConn.Errors
    If objErr.Number <> 0 Then
      Response.Write "Number: " & objErr.Number & "<P>"
      Response.Write "Description: " & objErr.Description & "<P>"
      Response.Write "Source: " & objErr.Source & "<P>"
      Response.Write "SQLState: " & objErr.SQLState & "<P>"
      Response.Write "NativeError: " & objErr.NativeError & "<P>"
      blnCriticalError = True
    End If
  Next
  'Dereference all objects
  Set objErr = Nothing
  If blnCriticalError Then
    Response.End
  End If
End If

'Declare variables and set their values
Dim adCmdText
Dim strClass
Dim lngLength
Dim lngWeight
Dim lngMainJib
Dim lngSpinnaker
Dim strAuthority
```

```
adCmdText = 1
strClass = "Mini Laser"
lngLength = 3
lngWeight = 45
lngMainJib = 6
lngSpinnaker = 0
strAuthority = "www.laser.com"

'Create the command object and set the query to be executed
Set objCmd = Server.CreateObject("ADODB.Command")
Set objCmd.ActiveConnection = objConn
objCmd.CommandText = "{CALL dbo.up_parmins_boatclass ('" & CStr(strClass) & _
  "'," & CLng(lngLength) & "," & CLng(lngWeight) & _
  "," & CLng(lngMainJib) & "," & CLng(lngSpinnaker) & _
  ",'" & CStr(strAuthority) & "')}"
objCmd.CommandType = adCmdText
objCmd.Execute

'Check for errors
If objConn.Errors.Count > 0 Then
  'Create an error object to access the ADO errors collection
  Set objErr = Server.CreateObject("Error")
  'Write all errors to the page
  For Each objErr In objConn.Errors
    If objErr.Number <> 0 Then
      Response.Write "Number: " & objErr.Number & "<P>"
      Response.Write "Description: " & objErr.Description & "<P>"
      Response.Write "Source: " & objErr.Source & "<P>"
      Response.Write "SQLState: " & objErr.SQLState & "<P>"
      Response.Write "NativeError: " & objErr.NativeError & "<P>"
      blnCriticalError = True
    End If
  Next
  'Dereference all objects
  Set objErr = Nothing
  If blnCriticalError Then
    Response.End
  End If
End If

Response.Write "Record Inserted"

'Close and dereference database objects
objConn.Close
Set objConn = Nothing
%>
</BODY>
</HTML>
```

### How It Works: The stored procedure

In SQL Server, we always specify the parameters that the stored procedure expects, and we do so in the first line of code. Notice also that we are specifying the data types of each parameter:

```
CREATE PROCEDURE up_parmins_boatclass (@name varchar(50), @length int, @weight int,
  @mainjib int, @spinnaker int, @authority varchar(16)) AS
```

This next line of SQL specifies that we are going to insert a row of data into the BoatClass table, and we are going to insert the parameters in the order listed by the column names. In other words, there is a one for one match between the column name and the parameter name. We can insert data into the row in any order we want, as long as it is listed in the stored procedure.

```
INSERT INTO boatclass
    (ClassName, ClassBoatLength, ClassBoatWeight, ClassSailAreaMainJib,
ClassSailAreaSpinnaker,
    ClassAuthority)
```

The last line of SQL specifies the parameters that contain the data to be inserted:

```
VALUES (@name, @length, @weight, @mainjib, @spinnaker, @authority)
```

### The Web Page

Examining the code for the web page, we don't find a lot of difference from the previous (Access) example. We still have to declare our variables and set their values.

```
'Declare variables and set their values
Dim adCmdText
Dim strClass
Dim lngLength
Dim lngWeight
Dim lngMainJib
Dim lngSpinnaker
Dim strAuthority
adCmdText = 1
strClass = "Mini Laser"
lngLength = 3
lngWeight = 45
lngMainJib = 6
lngSpinnaker = 0
strAuthority = "www.laser.com"
```

The only difference is in the stored procedure being used, and the fact that we must specify the owner if the stored procedure does not belong to either us or the administrator.

```
'Create the command object and set the query to be executed
Set objCmd = Server.CreateObject("ADODB.Command")
Set objCmd.ActiveConnection = objConn
objCmd.CommandText = "{call dbo.up_parmins_boatclass ('" & CStr(strClass) & _
    "'," & CLng(lngLength) & "," & CLng(lngWeight) & _
    "," & CLng(lngMainJib) & "," & CLng(lngSpinnaker) & _
    ",'" & CStr(strAuthority) & "')}"
objCmd.CommandType = adCmdText
objCmd.Execute
```

The rest of the code is the same as the previous examples.

## Connection Object

As discussed in Chapter 6, the Connection object is at the heart of the ADO object model. No actions can be performed and no data retrieved without an active connection to the database. This is where the Connection object comes into play. We can open and close connections to the database with this object, as well as start and end transactions.

The discussion here involves the Execute method of the Connection object. The Execute method allows us to pass, as one of the parameters to this method, a string containing the SQL statements or stored procedure to be executed. The only drawback is that the SQL code that we execute cannot return any rows of data. This makes the Connection object an ideal method for executing action stored procedures that accept parameters, but which do not require any data to be returned.

**Try It Out – Passing values to an Access action stored procedure using the connection object**

Using Microsoft Access as the database provider, create a web page to execute an action stored procedure that accepts parameters, using the `Connection` object. We wish to insert a record into the database. When we run our code, we see the following:

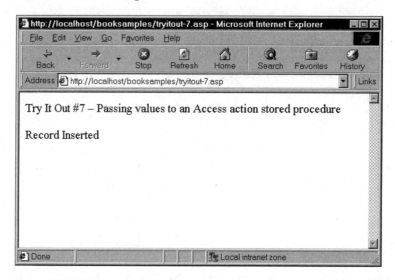

The stored procedure is the same as in the previous Access example (`qparmInsertBoatClass`):

```
INSERT INTO BoatClass ( ClassName, ClassBoatLength, ClassBoatWeight,
ClassSailAreaMainJib, ClassSailAreaSpinnaker, ClassAuthority )
SELECT [Name] AS Expr1, [Length] AS Expr2, [Weight] AS Expr3, [MainJib] AS Expr4,
[Spinnaker] AS Expr5, [Authority] AS Expr6;
```

The code for the web page, taken from `TryItOut-7.asp`, is as follows.

```
<HTML>
<HEAD>
<META NAME="GENERATOR" Content="Microsoft Visual Studio 6.0">
<TITLE></TITLE>
</HEAD>
<BODY>

<!--Display the page data-->
Try It Out #7 - Passing values to an Access action stored procedure<BR><BR>

<%
'Instruct VBScript to ignore the error and continue
'with the next line of code
On Error Resume Next

'Create and open the database object
Set objConn = Server.CreateObject("ADODB.Connection")
objConn.Open "DSN=Sailors"
```

```
'Check for errors
If objConn.Errors.Count > 0 Then
  'Create an error object to access the ADO errors collection
  Set objErr = Server.CreateObject("Error")
  'Declare Boolean flag for critical errors
  Dim blnCriticalError
  'Write all errors to the page
  For Each objErr In objConn.Errors
    If objErr.Number <> 0 Then
      Response.Write "Number: " & objErr.Number & "<P>"
      Response.Write "Description: " & objErr.Description & "<P>"
      Response.Write "Source: " & objErr.Source & "<P>"
      Response.Write "SQLState: " & objErr.SQLState & "<P>"
      Response.Write "NativeError: " & objErr.NativeError & "<P>"
      blnCriticalError = True
    End If
  Next
  'Dereference all objects
  Set objErr = Nothing
  If blnCriticalError Then
    Response.End
  End If
End If

'Declare variables and set their values
Dim strClass
Dim lngLength
Dim lngWeight
Dim lngMainJib
Dim lngSpinnaker
dim strAuthority
strClass = "Mini Laser"
lngLength = 3
lngWeight = 45
lngMainJib = 6
lngSpinnaker = 0
strAuthority = "www.laser.com"

'Create the command object and set the query to be executed
strSQL = "qparmInsertBoatClass ('" & CStr(strClass) & _
  "'," & CLng(lngLength) & "," & CLng(lngWeight) & _
  "," & CLng(lngMainJib) & "," & CLng(lngSpinnaker) & _
  ",'" & CStr(strAuthority) & "')"
objConn.Execute strSQL

'Check for errors
If objConn.Errors.Count > 0 Then
  'Create an error object to access the ADO errors collection
  Set objErr = Server.CreateObject("Error")
  'Write all errors to the page
  For Each objErr In objConn.Errors
    If objErr.Number <> 0 Then
      Response.Write "Number: " & objErr.Number & "<P>"
      Response.Write "Description: " & objErr.Description & "<P>"
      Response.Write "Source: " & objErr.Source & "<P>"
      Response.Write "SQLState: " & objErr.SQLState & "<P>"
      Response.Write "NativeError: " & objErr.NativeError & "<P>"
      blnCriticalError = True
    End If
  Next
  'Dereference all objects
  Set objErr = Nothing
  If blnCriticalError Then
    Response.End
  End If
End If
```

```
Response.Write "Record Inserted"

'Close and dereference database objects
objConn.Close
Set objConn = Nothing
%>
</BODY>
</HTML>
```

### How It Works – Passing Values to an Access Action Stored Procedure Using the Connection Object

This example uses the same stored procedure that we created earlier. Also the beginning of the web page is the same as the previous examples, so we won't cover them again here.

We still need to declare our variables as before and assign them values:

```
'Declare variables and set their values
Dim strClass
Dim lngLength
Dim lngWeight
Dim lngMainJib
Dim lngSpinnaker
dim strAuthority
strClass = "Mini Laser"
lngLength = 3
lngWeight = 45
lngMainJib = 6
lngSpinnaker = 0
strAuthority = "www.laser.com"
```

The SQL string should look exactly like the previous Access example. The difference comes when we actually need to execute the SQL string. We are using the Connection object's Execute method and only pass it one parameter.

> The Execute method actually accepts three parameters but only requires the first,
> CommandText. The other two (optional) parameters are described below.

The second parameter is RecordsAffected. This parameter is a variable supplied by you that is a long data type. The Connection object will update this variable with the number of records affected by the operation.

The third parameter is the Options parameter (also a long data type) that specifies how the database should evaluate the CommandText parameter. This parameter operates in a very similar fashion to the recordset's Open method.

```
'Create the command object and set the query to be executed
strSQL = "qparmInsertBoatClass ('" & CStr(strClass) & _
  "'," & CLng(lngLength) & "," & CLng(lngWeight) & _
  "," & CLng(lngMainJib) & "," & CLng(lngSpinnaker) & _
  ",'" & CStr(strAuthority) & "')"
objConn.Execute strSQL
```

Again, the rest of the code is the same as previous examples.

**Try It Out – Passing values to a SQL Server action stored procedure using the connection object**

This time we will use Microsoft SQL Server as the database provider, and create a web page to execute an action stored procedure that accepts parameters, using the Connection object. This screenshot shows what our web page should look like:

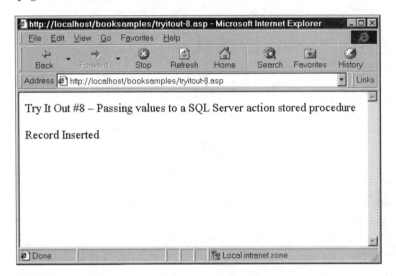

The stored procedure, up_parmins_boatclass, was created in the last SQL example.

```
CREATE PROCEDURE up_parmins_boatclass (@name varchar(50), @length int, @weight int,
  @mainjib int, @spinnaker int, @authority varchar(16)) as

INSERT INTO boatclass
  (ClassName, ClassBoatLength, ClassBoatWeight, ClassSailAreaMainJib,
ClassSailAreaSpinnaker, ClassAuthority)
  VALUES(@name, @length, @weight, @mainjib, @spinnaker, @authority)
```

The code for the web page is below, and in TryItOut-8.asp.

```
<HTML>
<HEAD>
<META NAME="GENERATOR" Content="Microsoft Visual Studio 6.0">
<TITLE></TITLE>
</HEAD>
<BODY>

<!--Display the page data-->
Try It Out #8 - Passing values to a SQL Server action stored procedure<BR><BR>

<%
'Instruct VBScript to ignore the error and continue
'with the next line of code
On Error Resume Next

'Create and open the database object
Set objConn = Server.CreateObject("ADODB.Connection")
objConn.Open "DSN=SQLSailor;uid=sa;pwd"
```

```
'Check for errors
If objConn.Errors.Count > 0 Then
  'Create an error object to access the ADO errors collection
  Set objErr = Server.CreateObject("Error")
  'Declare Boolean flag for critical errors
  Dim blnCriticalError
  'Write all errors to the page
  For Each objErr In objConn.Errors
    If objErr.Number <> 0 Then
      Response.Write "Number: " & objErr.Number & "<P>"
      Response.Write "Description: " & objErr.Description & "<P>"
      Response.Write "Source: " & objErr.Source & "<P>"
      Response.Write "SQLState: " & objErr.SQLState & "<P>"
      Response.Write "NativeError: " & objErr.NativeError & "<P>"
      blnCriticalError = True
    End If
  Next
  'Dereference all objects
  Set objErr = Nothing
  If blnCriticalError Then
    Response.End
  End If
End If

'Declare variables and set their values
Dim strClass
Dim lngLength
Dim lngWeight
Dim lngMainJib
Dim lngSpinnaker
dim strAuthority
strClass = "Mini Laser"
lngLength = 3
lngWeight = 45
lngMainJib = 6
lngSpinnaker = 0
strAuthority = "www.laser.com"

'Create the command object and set the query to be executed
strSQL = "dbo.up_parmins_boatclass ('" & CStr(strClass) & _
  "'," & CLng(lngLength) & "," & CLng(lngWeight) & _
  "," & CLng(lngMainJib) & "," & CLng(lngSpinnaker) & _
  ",'" & CStr(strAuthority) & "')"
objConn.Execute strSQL

'Check for errors
If objConn.Errors.Count > 0 Then
  'Create an error object to access the ADO errors collection
  Set objErr = Server.CreateObject("Error")
  'Write all errors to the page
  For Each objErr In objConn.Errors
    If objErr.Number <> 0 Then
      Response.Write "Number: " & objErr.Number & "<P>"
      Response.Write "Description: " & objErr.Description & "<P>"
      Response.Write "Source: " & objErr.Source & "<P>"
      Response.Write "SQLState: " & objErr.SQLState & "<P>"
      Response.Write "NativeError: " & objErr.NativeError & "<P>"
      blnCriticalError = True
    End If
  Next
  'Dereference all objects
  Set objErr = Nothing
  If blnCriticalError Then
    Response.End
  End If
End If
```

```
Response.Write "Record Inserted"

'Close and dereference database objects
objConn.Close
Set objConn = Nothing
%>
</BODY>
</HTML>
```

### How It Works – Passing Values to a SQL Server Action Stored Procedure Using the Connection Object

We explained the stored procedure that we are using in the last SQL Server example.

Looking at the web page code, the declare statements are the same as in the previous (Access) example:

```
'Declare variables and set their values
Dim strClass
Dim lngLength
Dim lngWeight
Dim lngMainJib
Dim lngSpinnaker
dim strAuthority
strClass = "Mini Laser"
lngLength = 3
lngWeight = 45
lngMainJib = 6
lngSpinnaker = 0
strAuthority = "www.laser.com"
```

The only difference here is that we are using a SQL Server stored procedure and all of the previous comments apply, regarding the use of the owner prefix:

```
'Create the command object and set the query to be executed
strSQL = "dbo.up_parmins_boatclass ('" & CStr(strClass) & _
  "'," & CLng(lngLength) & "," & CLng(lngWeight) & _
  "," & CLng(lngMainJib) & "," & CLng(lngSpinnaker) & _
  ",'" & CStr(strAuthority) & "')"
objConn.Execute strSQL
```

The rest of the code is the same as previous examples.

# Retrieving Values From a Stored Procedure

Sometimes it is desirable to execute some type of action stored procedure and have the stored procedure return a value indicating success or failure. Other times you might need to have the stored procedure return a single value, and you will opt to go this route instead of incurring the extra overhead of creating and using a recordset.

This section will demonstrate examples using SQL Server stored procedures and the Command object to retrieve the values returned by the stored procedure. SQL Server stored procedures are limited to returning only one value and the value must be an integer data type. This equates to a long data type in VB, VBA, and VBScript.

You can have the stored procedure return a value indicating the number of records it inserted, updated or deleted. You could also use a return value to return the number of records in a table. Another possible use is to use the return value to return a next key number, to be used as a numeric key for some operation, or perhaps a numeric key for a table. Last but not least you can use the return value to return a return code from the stored procedure to indicate success or failure.

By the time you reach the end of this section you should have a pretty good idea of the possibilities of using a return value in your own stored procedures.

# Retrieving a Return Code

Probably the single most used return value from a stored procedure is a return code. This will indicate the success or failure of the stored procedure. The savvy developer will develop a stored procedure that can return any number of different return codes based on the processing at hand.

### Try It Out – Retrieving a return code from SQL Server

Using Microsoft SQL Server as the database provider, create a web page to execute an action stored procedure that accepts parameters and returns a value, using the Command object. The return value will indicate whether the stored procedure worked successfully. The result should appear as follows:

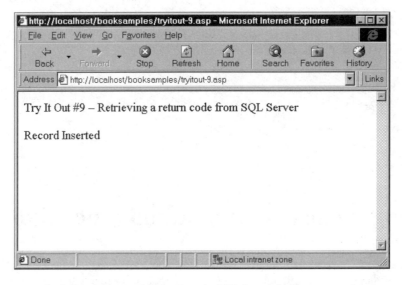

We need to create the following stored procedure in SQL Server before we can begin our web page. Using the methods we have already covered, create this stored procedure, and save it as up_parmins_boatclass_rc. It is also already available for a download as a file with the same name.

```
CREATE PROCEDURE up_parmins_boatclass_rc (@name varchar(50), @length int, @weight int,
  @mainjib int, @spinnaker int, @authority varchar(16)) as

INSERT INTO boatclass
  (ClassName, ClassBoatLength, ClassBoatWeight, ClassSailAreaMainJib,
    ClassSailAreaSpinnaker, ClassAuthority)
  VALUES(@name, @length, @weight, @mainjib, @spinnaker, @authority)

if @@error <> 0
  return @@error
else
  return 0
```

Next we need to create a web page. The code for this is shown below and is contained in TryItOut-9.asp.

```
<HTML>
<HEAD>
<META NAME="GENERATOR" Content="Microsoft Visual Studio 6.0">
<TITLE></TITLE>
</HEAD>
<BODY>

<!--Display the page data-->
Try It Out #9 - Retrieving a return code from SQL Server<BR><BR>

<%
'Instruct VBScript to ignore the error and continue
'with the next line of code
On Error Resume Next

'Create and open the database object
Set objConn = Server.CreateObject("ADODB.Connection")
objConn.Open "DSN=SQLSailor;uid=sa;pwd"

'Check for errors
If objConn.Errors.Count > 0 Then
  'Create an error object to access the ADO errors collection
  Set objErr = Server.CreateObject("Error")
  'Declare Boolean flag for critical errors
  Dim blnCriticalError
  'Write all errors to the page
  For Each objErr In objConn.Errors
    If objErr.Number <> 0 Then
      Response.Write "Number: " & objErr.Number & "<P>"
      Response.Write "Description: " & objErr.Description & "<P>"
      Response.Write "Source: " & objErr.Source & "<P>"
      Response.Write "SQLState: " & objErr.SQLState & "<P>"
      Response.Write "NativeError: " & objErr.NativeError & "<P>"
      blnCriticalError = True
    End If
  Next
  'Dereference all objects
  Set objErr = Nothing
  If blnCriticalError Then
    Response.End
  End If
End If
```

```
'Declare variables and set their values
Dim adCmdText
Dim adParamReturnValue
Dim strClass
Dim lngLength
Dim lngWeight
Dim lngMainJib
Dim lngSpinnaker
Dim strAuthority
adCmdText = 1
adParamReturnValue = 4
strClass = "Mini Laser"
lngLength = 3
lngWeight = 45
lngMainJib = 6
lngSpinnaker = 0
strAuthority = "www.laser.com"

'Create the command object and set the query to be executed
Set objCmd = Server.CreateObject("ADODB.Command")
Set objCmd.ActiveConnection = objConn
objCmd.CommandText = "{? = CALL dbo.up_parmins_boatclass_rc ('" & _
  CStr(strClass) & "'," & CLng(lngLength) & "," & _
  CLng(lngWeight) & "," & CLng(lngMainJib) & "," & _
  CLng(lngSpinnaker) & ",'" & CStr(strAuthority) & "')}"
objCmd.CommandType = adCmdText
objCmd(0).Direction = adParamReturnValue
objCmd.Execute

'Check for errors
If objConn.Errors.Count > 0 Then
  'Create an error object to access the ADO errors collection
  Set objErr = Server.CreateObject("Error")
  'Write all errors to the page
  For Each objErr In objConn.Errors
    If objErr.Number <> 0 Then
      Response.Write "Number: " & objErr.Number & "<P>"
      Response.Write "Description: " & objErr.Description & "<P>"
      Response.Write "Source: " & objErr.Source & "<P>"
      Response.Write "SQLState: " & objErr.SQLState & "<P>"
      Response.Write "NativeError: " & objErr.NativeError & "<P>"
      blnCriticalError = True
    End If
  Next
  'Dereference all objects
  Set objErr = Nothing
  If blnCriticalError Then
    Response.End
  End If
End If

If objCmd(0) = 0 Then
  Response.Write "Record Inserted"
Else
  Response.Write "Insert Failed, RC = " & objCmd(0)
End If

'Close and dereference database objects
objConn.Close
Set objConn = Nothing
%>
</BODY>
</HTML>
```

### How It Works: The stored procedure

This stored procedure is very similar to the `up_parmins_boatclass` stored procedure with one exception. This exception is listed in the last four lines of code in this stored procedure.

We are using the built-in error object of SQL Server to determine if the last SQL statement that we executed had an error. If the error code is not equal to zero we will return the error code, otherwise we return a zero to indicate success.

```
CREATE PROCEDURE up_parmins_boatclass_rc (@name varchar(50), @length int, @weight int,
   @mainjib int, @spinnaker int, @authority varchar(16)) as

INSERT INTO boatclass
   (ClassName, ClassBoatLength, ClassBoatWeight, ClassSailAreaMainJib,
ClassSailAreaSpinnaker, ClassAuthority)
   VALUES(@name, @length, @weight, @mainjib, @spinnaker, @authority)

if @@error <> 0
   return @@error
else
   return 0
```

### The Web Page

Taking a look at the web page code, we jump right into the middle of it. (The first part of the code is the same as for previous examples.)

```
'Create the command object and set the query to be executed
Set objCmd = Server.CreateObject("ADODB.Command")
Set objCmd.ActiveConnection = objConn
```

We are using the `Command` object again but with a simple twist. We are expecting a return value from the stored procedure and specify this as such by using the question mark at the beginning of our stored procedure call:

```
objCmd.CommandText = "{? = CALL dbo.up_parmins_boatclass_rc ('" & _
   CStr(strClass) & "'," & CLng(lngLength) & "," & _
   CLng(lngWeight) & "," & CLng(lngMainJib) & "," & _
   CLng(lngSpinnaker) & ",'" & CStr(strAuthority) & "')}"
objCmd.CommandType = adCmdText
```

Next we indicate that the first parameter in the `Command` collection needs to return a value. We specify the ordinal position of the parameter by addressing it by number, in this case `objCmd(0)`, which is actually a shorter version of `objCmd.Parameters(0)`. Next, we indicate the direction of the parameter, which is a return value. The use of the ordinal position number was covered in our discussion of the `Command` object in Chapter 13.

*A note here to those that may be wondering - the default for this parameter is input, hence we did not specify it on our previous examples, to keep them simple.*

Then we execute the `Command` object.

```
objCmd(0).Direction = adParamReturnValue
objCmd.Execute
```

We have one more little piece of code to examine in this page. After the error checking has been performed, we need to check the returned value in the Command object. Again, specifying the ordinal position of the parameter, we check to see if it is equal to zero. If it is, we write a message that the record was inserted, otherwise we write a message indicating failure, and write the return code returned by the stored procedure.

```
  If blnCriticalError Then
    Response.End
  End If
End If

If objCmd(0) = 0 Then
  Response.Write "Record Inserted"
Else
  Response.Write "Insert Failed, RC = " & objCmd(0)
End If

'Close and dereference database objects
objConn.Close
```

# Retrieving a Value

A value retrieved from a stored procedure can be any of the values that we mentioned at the beginning of this section, or more. However, we are going to concentrate on two simple examples that return a value that indicates how many records are in a table, and how many records we updated. If you give this some thought you can probably think of dozens of practical uses for this.

### Try It Out – Retrieving a return value from SQL Server

Using Microsoft SQL Server as the database provider, create a web page to execute an action stored procedure that accepts parameters and returns a value (the number of records in the table), using the Command object. Our code should produce the following result:

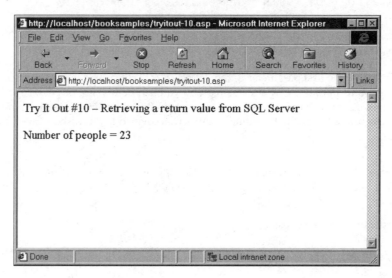

Again we start by creating a new stored procedure. Use the following code to create a stored procedure named up_select_count_of_people in SQL Server, or use the downloaded file.

```
CREATE PROCEDURE up_select_count_of_people AS

DECLARE @rc int

SELECT @rc=count(peopleid) FROM people

RETURN @rc
```

Next we need to create the web page, using the following code, taken from TryItOut-10.asp.

```
<HTML>
<HEAD>
<META NAME="GENERATOR" Content="Microsoft Visual Studio 6.0">
<TITLE></TITLE>
</HEAD>
<BODY>

<!--Display the page data-->
Try It Out #10 - Retrieving a return value from SQL Server<BR><BR>

<%
'Instruct VBScript to ignore the error and continue
'with the next line of code
On Error Resume Next

'Create and open the database object
Set objConn = Server.CreateObject("ADODB.Connection")
objConn.Open "DSN=SQLSailor;uid=sa;pwd"

'Check for errors
If objConn.Errors.Count > 0 Then
  'Create an error object to access the ADO errors collection
  Set objErr = Server.CreateObject("Error")
  'Declare Boolean flag for critical errors
  Dim blnCriticalError
  'Write all errors to the page
  For Each objErr In objConn.Errors
    If objErr.Number <> 0 Then
      Response.Write "Number: " & objErr.Number & "<P>"
      Response.Write "Description: " & objErr.Description & "<P>"
      Response.Write "Source: " & objErr.Source & "<P>"
      Response.Write "SQLState: " & objErr.SQLState & "<P>"
      Response.Write "NativeError: " & objErr.NativeError & "<P>"
      blnCriticalError = True
    End If
  Next
  'Dereference all objects
  Set objErr = Nothing
  If blnCriticalError Then
    Response.End
  End If
End If

'Declare variables and set their values
Dim adCmdText
Dim adParamReturnValue
adCmdText = 1
adParamReturnValue = 4
```

```
'Create the command object and set the query to be executed
Set objCmd = Server.CreateObject("ADODB.Command")
Set objCmd.ActiveConnection = objConn
objCmd.CommandText = "{? = CALL dbo.up_select_count_of_people}"
objCmd.CommandType = adCmdText
objCmd(0).Direction = adParamReturnValue
objCmd.Execute

'Check for errors
If objConn.Errors.Count > 0 Then
  'Create an error object to access the ADO errors collection
  Set objErr = Server.CreateObject("Error")
  'Write all errors to the page
  For Each objErr In objConn.Errors
    If objErr.Number <> 0 Then
      Response.Write "Number: " & objErr.Number & "<P>"
      Response.Write "Description: " & objErr.Description & "<P>"
      Response.Write "Source: " & objErr.Source & "<P>"
      Response.Write "SQLState: " & objErr.SQLState & "<P>"
      Response.Write "NativeError: " & objErr.NativeError & "<P>"
      blnCriticalError = True
    End If
  Next
  'Dereference all objects
  Set objErr = Nothing
  If blnCriticalError Then
    Response.End
  End If
End If

Response.Write "Number of people = " & objCmd(0)

'Close and dereference database objects
objConn.Close
Set objConn = Nothing
%>
</BODY>
</HTML>
```

### How It Works: The stored procedure

Let's take a quick look at this stored procedure. First, this stored procedure accepts no parameters and returns a value indicating how many rows of data it found. We declare a variable in our stored procedure to hold the number of rows found.

Next, we select the count of a column from the People table assigning it to the @rc variable we declared. Last, we return the count using the RETURN statement in SQL Server.

```
CREATE PROCEDURE up_select_count_of_people AS

DECLARE @rc int

SELECT @rc=count(peopleid) FROM people

RETURN @rc
```

### The Web Page

Taking a look at the web page, in the only code that is different from the previous examples, we will notice that we still have to set the CommandText to accept a return value, by placing the question mark before our call to the stored procedure. Again we set the direction of the parameter in the Parameters collection and then execute the Command object.

```
objCmd.CommandText = "{? = CALL dbo.up_select_count_of_people}"
objCmd.CommandType = adCmdText
objCmd(0).Direction = adParamReturnValue
objCmd.Execute
```

In the last part of the code, before we close and de-reference our database objects, we write a line of text to the web page along with the number of records in the table:

```
Response.Write "Number of people = " & objCmd(0)

'Close and dereference database objects
objConn.Close
```

## Try It Out – Retrieving a return value from SQL Server

Using Microsoft SQL Server as the database provider, create a web page to execute an action stored procedure that accepts parameters and returns a value (how many records were updated), using the Command object. The web page should look like this:

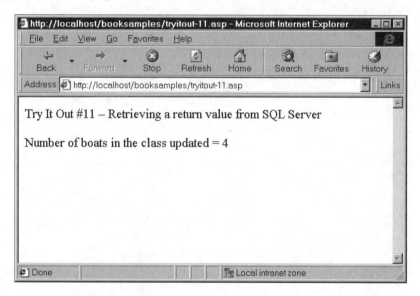

We start this example by creating (or downloading) another stored procedure in SQL Server, and saving it as up_parmupd_boat_certification.

```
CREATE PROCEDURE up_parmupd_boat_certification (@class varchar(50)) AS

UPDATE boats
  SET boatcertified = 1
  WHERE boatclass = @class

RETURN @@rowcount
```

Then we create a web page, using the code from TryItOut-11.asp.

```
<HTML>
<HEAD>
<META NAME="GENERATOR" Content="Microsoft Visual Studio 6.0">
<TITLE></TITLE>
</HEAD>
<BODY>

<!--Display the page data-->
Try It Out #11 - Retrieving a return value from SQL Server<BR><BR>

<%
'Instruct VBScript to ignore the error and continue
'with the next line of code
On Error Resume Next

'Create and open the database object
Set objConn = Server.CreateObject("ADODB.Connection")
objConn.Open "DSN=SQLSailor;uid=sa;pwd"

'Check for errors
If objConn.Errors.Count > 0 Then
  'Create an error object to access the ADO errors collection
  Set objErr = Server.CreateObject("Error")
  'Declare Boolean flag for critical errors
  Dim blnCriticalError
  'Write all errors to the page
  For Each objErr In objConn.Errors
    If objErr.Number <> 0 Then
      Response.Write "Number: " & objErr.Number & "<P>"
      Response.Write "Description: " & objErr.Description & "<P>"
      Response.Write "Source: " & objErr.Source & "<P>"
      Response.Write "SQLState: " & objErr.SQLState & "<P>"
      Response.Write "NativeError: " & objErr.NativeError & "<P>"
      blnCriticalError = True
    End If
  Next
  'Dereference all objects
  Set objErr = Nothing
  If blnCriticalError Then
    Response.End
  End If
End If

'Declare variables and set their values
Dim adCmdText
Dim adParamReturnValue
Dim strClass
adCmdText = 1
adParamReturnValue = 4
strClass = "laser"

'Create the command object and set the query to be executed
Set objCmd = Server.CreateObject("ADODB.Command")
Set objCmd.ActiveConnection = objConn
objCmd.CommandText = "{? = CALL dbo.up_parmupd_boat_certification ('" & _
  CStr(strClass) & "')}"
objCmd.CommandType = adCmdText
objCmd(0).Direction = adParamReturnValue
objCmd.Execute
```

```
'Check for errors
If objConn.Errors.Count > 0 Then
  'Create an error object to access the ADO errors collection
  Set objErr = Server.CreateObject("Error")
  'Write all errors to the page
  For Each objErr In objConn.Errors
    If objErr.Number <> 0 Then
      Response.Write "Number: " & objErr.Number & "<P>"
      Response.Write "Description: " & objErr.Description & "<P>"
      Response.Write "Source: " & objErr.Source & "<P>"
      Response.Write "SQLState: " & objErr.SQLState & "<P>"
      Response.Write "NativeError: " & objErr.NativeError & "<P>"
      blnCriticalError = True
    End If
  Next
  'Dereference all objects
  Set objErr = Nothing
  If blnCriticalError Then
    Response.End
  End If
End If

Response.Write "Number of boats in the class updated = " & objCmd(0)

'Close and dereference database objects
objConn.Close
Set objConn = Nothing
%>
</BODY>
</HTML>
```

### How It Works: The stored procedure

This stored procedure accepts one parameter, and will update all rows that match the criteria of the parameter passed. Immediately following the update statement, we use the built-in variable @@rowcount to determine the number of rows affected by our last SQL statement, and return that value to the caller of the stored procedure.

```
CREATE PROCEDURE up_parmupd_boat_certification (@class varchar(50)) AS

UPDATE boats
  SET boatcertified = 1
  WHERE boatclass = @class

RETURN @@rowcount
```

### The Web Page

Now, let's look at the web page code that is different from the previous examples. This stored procedure accepts one input parameter and returns one output value. After setting the direction of the return value we execute the Command object.

```
objCmd.CommandText = "{? = CALL dbo.up_parmupd_boat_certification ('" & _
  CStr(strClass) & "')}"
objCmd.CommandType = adCmdText
objCmd(0).Direction = adParamReturnValue
objCmd.Execute
```

Immediately before the code to close and de-reference our database objects, we write a statement to the web page indicating how many rows were updated using the return value from our stored procedure:

```
Response.Write "Number of boats in the class updated = " & objCmd(0)

'Close and dereference database objects
objConn.Close
```

## What About Access?

Access is not an enterprise database and as such does not have all of the capabilities that are provided by SQL Server, and cannot return values from a stored procedure. If you find that you need to use Access and you need a return value, you will have to code your stored procedure to return a single column in a single row in a recordset to simulate this feature. Unfortunately you will have to incur the extra overhead of using a recordset just to retrieve this single value.

# Summary

This chapter has covered the benefits of using stored procedures, and has demonstrated various techniques of calling stored procedures that accept parameters and return values. You should now understand the importance of using stored procedures in your code versus using in-line SQL statements.

You should also understand the concepts of, and when you should use, the Connection, Command and Recordset objects, and feel comfortable passing parameters to stored procedures.

In summary, you should understand

- ❑ The benefits of using stored procedures
- ❑ How to apply the use of stored procedures in your applications
- ❑ When to use the Command object to execute a stored procedures
- ❑ When to use the Connection object to execute a stored procedure
- ❑ When to use the Recordset object to open a stored procedure
- ❑ The difference between calling an Access and SQL Server stored procedure

## Exercise 1

Create a stored procedure in Access, called qparmSailorRanking, which will list the sailor ranking for a given club and specific rank. The parameters that are to be passed to the stored procedure are to limit the data to be returned, and should include the club code and the rank. List all ranks that are equal to or less than the rank parameter passed, and only data for the club code passed.

The following columns should be returned in the recordset: PeopleNameLast, PeopleNameFirst, PeopleClubCode, Year, Month and Rank.

Select data from the People table and join the Rank table. The relationship between the two tables is PeopleID in the People table and SailorID in the Rank table.

To keep the page simple you can assign the parameter values to variables, like we have done in the previous examples. Display the data on the web page any way you want. Our code produces a web page as shown in the following screenshot:

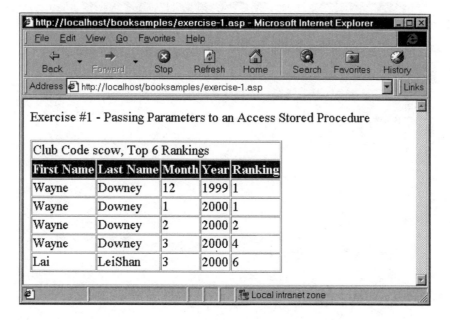

## Exercise 2

Create a stored procedure in SQL Server, called up_select_boatclass_count, that will select the number of distinct boat classes in the Boats table. The number of boat classes should be returned in a return value by the stored procedure. This stored procedure does not accept any input parameters.

Keeping the web page simple, display the data in any format you desire. The screenshot below shows the result of using our code:

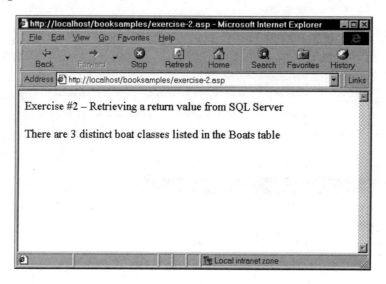

# Exercise Answers

## Exercise 1

The code for the stored procedure is contained in `qparmSailorRanking`, and is shown below.

```
PARAMETERS ClubCode Text, Ranking Long;
SELECT People.PeopleNameLast, People.PeopleNameFirst, People.PeopleClubCode,
Rank.Year, Rank.Rank, Rank.Month
FROM People INNER JOIN Rank ON People.PeopleID = Rank.SailorID
WHERE (((People.PeopleClubCode)=[ClubCode]) AND ((Rank.Rank)<=[Ranking]))
ORDER BY Rank.Year, Rank.Rank, Rank.Month;
```

The web page can be created using the following code, included in `Exercise-1.asp`.

```
<HTML>
<HEAD>
<META NAME="GENERATOR" Content="Microsoft Visual Studio 6.0">
<TITLE></TITLE>
</HEAD>
<BODY>

<!--Display the page data-->
Exercise #1 - Passing Parameters to an Access Stored Procedure <BR><BR>

<%
'Instruct VBScript to ignore the error and continue
'with the next line of code
On Error Resume Next
```

```
'Create and open the database object
Set objConn = Server.CreateObject("ADODB.Connection")
objConn.Open "DSN=Sailors"

'Check for errors
If objConn.Errors.Count > 0 Then
  'Create an error object to access the ADO errors collection
  Set objErr = Server.CreateObject("Error")
  'Declare Boolean flag for critical errors
  Dim blnCriticalError
  'Write all errors to the page
  For Each objErr In objConn.Errors
    If objErr.Number <> 0 Then
      Response.Write "Number: " & objErr.Number & "<P>"
      Response.Write "Description: " & objErr.Description & "<P>"
      Response.Write "Source: " & objErr.Source & "<P>"
      Response.Write "SQLState: " & objErr.SQLState & "<P>"
      Response.Write "NativeError: " & objErr.NativeError & "<P>"
      blnCriticalError = True
    End If
  Next
  'Dereference all objects
  Set objErr = Nothing
  If blnCriticalError Then
    Response.End
  End If
End If

'Declare variables and set their values
Dim adOpenForwardOnly
Dim adCmdStoredProc
Dim strClubCode
Dim lngRank
adOpenForwardOnly = 0
adCmdStoredProc = 4
strClubCode = "scow"
lngRank = 6

'Create the recordset object and open the recordset
Set objRS = Server.CreateObject("ADODB.Recordset")
strSQL = "qparmSailorRanking '" & CStr(strClubCode) & "'," & CLng(lngRank)
objRS.Open strSQL, objConn, adOpenForwardOnly, , adCmdStoredProc

'Check for errors
If objConn.Errors.Count > 0 Then
  'Create an error object to access the ADO errors collection
  Set objErr = Server.CreateObject("Error")
  'Write all errors to the page
  For Each objErr In objConn.Errors
    If objErr.Number <> 0 Then
      Response.Write "Number: " & objErr.Number & "<P>"
      Response.Write "Description: " & objErr.Description & "<P>"
      Response.Write "Source: " & objErr.Source & "<P>"
      Response.Write "SQLState: " & objErr.SQLState & "<P>"
      Response.Write "NativeError: " & objErr.NativeError & "<P>"
      blnCriticalError = True
    End If
  Next
  'Dereference all objects
  Set objErr = Nothing
  If blnCriticalError Then
    Response.End
  End If
End If
```

```
%>
<!--Build the table header rows-->
<TABLE BORDER=1 CELLSPACING=1>
   <TR>
   <TD colspan=5>Club Code <%=objRS("PeopleClubCode")%>, Top <%=lngRank%> Rankings</TD>
   </TR>
   <TR>
   <TH BGCOLOR=navy><FONT COLOUR=white>First Name</FONT></TH>
   <TH BGCOLOR=navy><FONT COLOUR=white>Last Name</FONT></TH>
   <TH BGCOLOR=navy><FONT COLOUR=white>Month</FONT></TH>
   <TH BGCOLOR=navy><FONT COLOUR=white>Year</FONT></TH>
   <TH BGCOLOR=navy><FONT COLOUR=white>Ranking</FONT></TH>
   </TR>
<%
'Loop through the recordset displaying the last name field
Do While Not objRS.EOF
%>
   <TR>
   <TD><%=objRS("PeopleNameFirst")%></TD>
   <TD><%=objRS("PeopleNameLast")%></TD>
   <TD><%=objRS("Month")%></TD>
   <TD><%=objRS("Year")%></TD>
   <TD><%=objRS("Rank")%></TD>
   </TR>
<%
   objRS.MoveNext
Loop

'Close and dereference database objects
objRS.Close
Set objRS = Nothing
objConn.Close
Set objConn = Nothing
%>
</BODY>
</HTML>
```

### How It Works: The stored procedure

Let's take a quick look at the stored procedure before we jump into the code. As before, we define our input parameters first, which in this case consist of a text value for the club code and a long value for the ranking.

```
PARAMETERS ClubCode Text, Ranking Long;
```

Next, we code our SELECT statement using fields from two separate tables:

```
SELECT People.PeopleNameLast, People.PeopleNameFirst, People.PeopleClubCode,
Rank.Year, Rank.Rank, Rank.Month
```

The FROM statement lists the primary table we are selecting data from, and the second table is joined to the first table using the key fields that we specify:

```
FROM People INNER JOIN Rank ON People.PeopleID = Rank.SailorID
```

The WHERE statement contains the criteria by which data will be selected, and uses the parameters that we specified:

```
WHERE (((People.PeopleClubCode)=[ClubCode]) AND ((Rank.Rank)<=[Ranking]))
```

Lastly, we order certain fields in ascending order to return the rows in a more logical order:

```
ORDER BY Rank.Year, Rank.Rank, Rank.Month;
```

### The Web Page

Now let's take a look at the web page code. The first part of the code needs no explanation and we will not go into it. We start by declaring our variables and setting their values.

```
'Declare variables and set their values
Dim adOpenForwardOnly
Dim adCmdStoredProc
Dim strClubCode
Dim lngRank
adOpenForwardOnly = 0
adCmdStoredProc = 4
strClubCode = "scow"
lngRank = 6
```

We then create our `Recordset` object and our SQL string, passing the parameters we defined to the stored procedure. Then we open the `Recordset` object.

```
'Create the recordset object and open the recordset
Set objRS = Server.CreateObject("ADODB.Recordset")
strSQL = "qparmSailorRanking '" & CStr(strClubCode) & "'," & CLng(lngRank)
objRS.Open strSQL, objConn, adOpenForwardOnly, , adCmdStoredProc
```

After the error checking code we switch back to HTML and build the header rows of our table. Notice that we create one standard row of data before the header rows. This row contains the club code, which we get from the recordset. We could have used the parameter that we passed to the stored procedure, but I wanted to demonstrate using the recordset field. The second part of the line uses a parameter that we passed to the stored procedure, to write the ranking number.

```
   If blnCriticalError Then
     Response.End
   End If
End If
%>
<!--Build the table header rows-->
<TABLE BORDER=1 CELLSPACING=1>
   <TR>
   <TD colspan=5>Club Code <%=objRS("PeopleClubCode")%>, Top <%=lngRank%> Rankings</TD>
   </TR>
   <TR>
   <TH BGCOLOR=navy><FONT COLOUR=white>First Name</FONT></TH>
   <TH BGCOLOR=navy><FONT COLOUR=white>Last Name</FONT></TH>
   <TH BGCOLOR=navy><FONT COLOUR=white>Month</FONT></TH>
   <TH BGCOLOR=navy><FONT COLOUR=white>Year</FONT></TH>
   <TH BGCOLOR=navy><FONT COLOUR=white>Ranking</FONT></TH>
   </TR>
```

The last part of the code we want to pay attention to is looping through the recordset. Here we create a row of data in the table using the various fields from the recordset. The rest of the code that follows is the standard code that we have already covered in this chapter.

```
<%
'Loop through the recordset displaying the last name field
Do While Not objRS.EOF
%>
  <TR>
  <TD><%=objRS("PeopleNameFirst")%></TD>
  <TD><%=objRS("PeopleNameLast")%></TD>
  <TD><%=objRS("Month")%></TD>
  <TD><%=objRS("Year")%></TD>
  <TD><%=objRS("Rank")%></TD>
  </TR>
<%
  objRS.MoveNext
Loop
```

# Exercise 2

The code for the stored procedure, up_select_boatclass_count, is shown below.

```
CREATE PROCEDURE up_select_boatclass_count AS

SELECT distinct boatclass FROM boats

RETURN @@rowcount
```

The code for the web page is given in Exercise-2.asp, and is shown below.

```
<HTML>
<HEAD>
<META NAME="GENERATOR" Content="Microsoft Visual Studio 6.0">
<TITLE></TITLE>
</HEAD>
<BODY>

<!--Display the page data-->
Exercise #2 - Retrieving a return value from SQL Server<BR><BR>

<%
'Instruct VBScript to ignore the error and continue
'with the next line of code
On Error Resume Next

'Create and open the database object
Set objConn = Server.CreateObject("ADODB.Connection")
objConn.Open "DSN=SQLSailor;uid=sa;pwd"

'Check for errors
If objConn.Errors.Count > 0 Then
  'Create an error object to access the ADO errors collection
  Set objErr = Server.CreateObject("Error")
  'Declare Boolean flag for critical errors
  Dim blnCriticalError
  'Write all errors to the page
  For Each objErr In objConn.Errors
    If objErr.Number <> 0 Then
      Response.Write "Number: " & objErr.Number & "<P>"
      Response.Write "Description: " & objErr.Description & "<P>"
      Response.Write "Source: " & objErr.Source & "<P>"
      Response.Write "SQLState: " & objErr.SQLState & "<P>"
      Response.Write "NativeError: " & objErr.NativeError & "<P>"
      blnCriticalError = True
    End If
```

```
      Next
       'Dereference all objects
       Set objErr = Nothing
       If blnCriticalError Then
         Response.End
       End If
    End If

    'Declare variables and set their values
    Dim adCmdText
    Dim adParamReturnValue
    adCmdText = 1
    adParamReturnValue = 4

    'Create the command object and set the query to be executed
    Set objCmd = Server.CreateObject("ADODB.Command")
    Set objCmd.ActiveConnection = objConn
    objCmd.CommandText = "{? = CALL dbo.up_select_boatclass_count}"
    objCmd.CommandType = adCmdText
    objCmd(0).Direction = adParamReturnValue
    objCmd.Execute

    'Check for errors
    If objConn.Errors.Count > 0 Then
       'Create an error object to access the ADO errors collection
       Set objErr = Server.CreateObject("Error")
       'Write all errors to the page
       For Each objErr In objConn.Errors
         If objErr.Number <> 0 Then
           Response.Write "Number: " & objErr.Number & "<P>"
           Response.Write "Description: " & objErr.Description & "<P>"
           Response.Write "Source: " & objErr.Source & "<P>"
           Response.Write "SQLState: " & objErr.SQLState & "<P>"
           Response.Write "NativeError: " & objErr.NativeError & "<P>"
           blnCriticalError = True
         End If
       Next
       'Dereference all objects
       Set objErr = Nothing
       If blnCriticalError Then
         Response.End
       End If
    End If

    Response.Write "There are " & objCmd(0) & " distinct boat classes " & _
       "listed in the Boats table"

    'Close and dereference database objects
    objConn.Close
    Set objConn = Nothing
    %>
    </BODY>
    </HTML>
```

### How It Works: The stored procedure

Taking a look at this stored procedure, we see that it will return data in a recordset as well as returning a value. In our case we are only interested in the return value and not the data. The stored procedure is pretty basic. We select all of the distinct boat classes from the Boats table. After that, we return the number of rows returned by the SELECT statement.

```
CREATE PROCEDURE up_select_boatclass_count AS

SELECT DISTINCT boatclass FROM boats

RETURN @@rowcount
```

### The Web Page

Looking at the details of this code that are different from the previous examples, we notice that we are creating the Command object and setting its active connection. Next we specify what stored procedure to execute, and specify that we are expecting a return value. We set the direction of the parameter, and then execute the Command object.

```
'Create the command object and set the query to be executed
Set objCmd = Server.CreateObject("ADODB.Command")
Set objCmd.ActiveConnection = objConn
objCmd.CommandText = "{? = CALL dbo.up_select_boatclass_count}"
objCmd.CommandType = adCmdText
objCmd(0).Direction = adParamReturnValue
objCmd.Execute
```

After checking for errors, we simply write a line to the web page using the Response object and specify the value that was returned from the stored procedure:

```
Response.Write "There are " & objCmd(0) & " distinct boat classes " & _
    "listed in the Boats table"
```

# Quiz

**1.** Why should we use stored procedures in our compiled program?

**2.** What is an owner prefix in SQL Server?

**3.** What are the two different kinds of stored procedures that we discussed in this chapter?

**4.** What is an action stored procedure?

**5.** When would you use the Connection object with a stored procedure?

**6.** What are the three types of return values that are returned from a stored procedure?

# Quiz Answers

**1.** Because we can change the SQL statements in the stored procedure and the changes become effective immediately. Also, we do not have to recompile our programs, and pre-compiled queries run faster.

**2.** The owner prefix is your SQL Server user ID and is used to specify the owner of a stored procedure. If you are the owner of a stored procedure or if the database administrator (dbo) is the owner of a stored procedure, you do not have to specify the prefix when executing a stored procedure.

**3.** Select stored procedures and action stored procedures. Both kinds of stored procedures may or may not accept parameters and may or may not return values.

**4.** An action stored procedure is a stored procedure that performs some type of action on the data in the database. This can be inserting a row of data, updating a row of data, or deleting a row of data.

**5.** You use the `Connection` object to execute an action stored procedure. If you recall, this type of stored procedure does not return any data in a recordset and does not return any values.

**6.** We used three types of return values in our examples. They are: return codes, row counts and records affected.

Setup cannot install system files or update shared files if the files are in use. Before c̲
any open applications.

WARNING: This program is protected by copyright law and international treaties.

You may install Microsoft Data Access 2.1 on a single computer. Some Microsoft products
with additional rights, which are stated in the End User License Agreement included with j̲

Please take a moment to read the End User License Agreement now. It contains all of the te̲
conditions that pertain to this software product. By choosing to continue, you indicate accepta̲
these terms.

Exit Setup

Continue

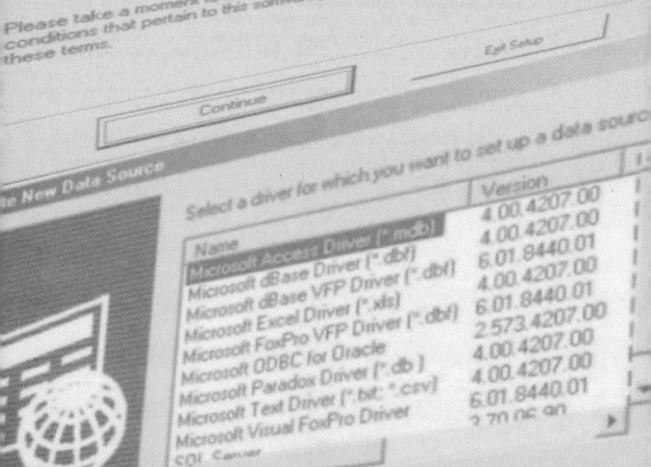

New Data Source

Select a driver for which you want to set up a data sourc̲

| Name | Version |
|------|---------|
| Microsoft Access Driver (*.mdb) | 4.00.4207.00 |
| Microsoft dBase Driver (*.dbf) | 4.00.4207.00 |
| Microsoft dBase VFP Driver (*.dbf) | 6.01.8440.01 |
| Microsoft Excel Driver (*.xls) | 4.00.4207.00 |
| Microsoft FoxPro VFP Driver (*.dbf) | 6.01.8440.01 |
| Microsoft ODBC for Oracle | 2.573.4207.00 |
| Microsoft Paradox Driver (*.db ) | 4.00.4207.00 |
| Microsoft Text Driver (*.txt; *.csv) | 4.00.4207.00 |
| Microsoft Visual FoxPro Driver | 6.01.8440.01 |
| SQL Server | 2.70.06.90 |

Finish      Cancel

# Irregular Data

## Introduction

Most of the time, you deal with text, numeric, and date data types, and they are not terribly difficult to handle. These fields are all variants of either text or numeric data. However, from time to time you have to deal with special kinds of data, such as stored images, sound files, and other *binary* objects (sequences of un-interpreted bytes). These are generally referred to in the database as **BLOB** fields ("**B**inary **L**arge **OB**ject").

> *In Access, they are referred to as "OLE (Object Linking and Embedding) Object" fields, but you will also see them referred to in the documentation as BLOB fields. In SQL Server, they are referred to as "image", "varbinary" and "binary" fields. Oracle refers to them as RAW, LONG RAW, or LONG TEXT fields.*

In any case, they are dealt with in an entirely different way than text, numeric, or date fields. For one thing, each of these has to be "displayed", that is interpreted by the browser, using some sort of device, such as a media player. And an image has to be interpreted before it can be displayed with the pixels arranged correctly. In this chapter, we will discuss how these data types are stored in the database, and how to work with them. For the purpose of keeping the language as universal as possible, I will generally refer to them as BLOB fields.

There are two basic approaches to using these kinds of data with a database, when using ASP/ADO. One is to store the actual images, sound files, movies, etc., in a folder on a web site, and store only the file names in the database. The second approach is to store the binary objects in a database, and retrieve them directly. I refer to these as the *Easy Way* and the *Hard Way*. Of course, it's always best to go the Easy Way, but there are times when you are constrained from doing what you'd like to, and then you have to take the Hard Way. For example, you may have a client with an existing database, who doesn't want to make any changes to its structure. Or it may be integrated with a front end that would have to be modified in order to modify the structure of the database. Murphy's law being what it is, chances are you will eventually come up against this type of situation. So you'd better be prepared!

In the process of discussing these BLOB fields, we will build some web pages that display several kinds of BLOB fields, using Access and SQL Server. We will also build an ActiveX COM object (DLL) that can be used to display Access BLOB data. If you don't have Microsoft Visual Basic 6, the DLL is available for free download from the Wrox web site. We'll build our web pages both the Easy Way and the Hard Way, to display the following:

- ❑  A Bitmap stored in an Access database.
- ❑  A Wave file stored in an Access database.
- ❑  A Bitmap stored in a SQL Server database.

We will also discuss some methods for inputting and updating BLOB data in Access and SQL Server, and some of the tools used for doing so, such as SAFileUp and ASPUpload.

We are also going to talk briefly about one other type of "irregular" data - the Memo field (in SQL Server, this is called a Text field). The Memo (Text) field is a special kind of text data field that can be of any size. There is virtually no limit to its size (SQL Server – 2 GB, Access - 1.2 GB). There are a few issues regarding working with these fields that make them an exception as well. At the end of the chapter, we'll discuss those issues.

# How Binary Data is Stored

Access stores BLOB data as OLE objects. Object Linking and Embedding is a technology that Microsoft invented some time ago, as a way of unifying the way that different types of files and data are dealt with. You'd be surprised how often it comes into play in the Windows environment. In fact, ADO uses OLE to "talk with" databases! Object Linking means exactly what its name implies: a link to a file is maintained. The contents of the file are not stored in the database, but a link to it is. Embedding means to make a copy of a file and store the contents in the database. Each method has its strong and weak points. When you link an object, you can update the contents of the database by editing the file. However, if the file is moved or deleted, the link becomes bad. When you embed the object in the database, it is safe from the wiles of the "outside world," but it can be difficult to edit. Access has some rudimentary tools for editing binary objects, but nothing worthy of mention.

When Access stores a BLOB object, it stores it with a **header** included, which identifies what kind of object it is storing (bitmap, sound file, metafile, etc.), and what kind of device will be used to "display" or "play" (interpret) the object. The advantage of this is that the type of object is always known. The disadvantage is that you must strip the header from the data before attempting to display it.

Access has some tools for converting (*filtering* is the term that Access uses) unsupported object types to supported ones. The obvious drawback to this is that you must have the correct filter for the object you need to store. If you don't, you're out of luck. It also has a "Package" object that can be used to store almost any kind of file. When you can, use a Package. You will not always have a choice about how the data is stored, however. For instance, if you are working on a project with an existing database that a client created, you will be stuck with the format used by the client. In this case, you will just have to work with the data "as is".

SQL Server stores the raw data, without any header information. The data in the field is exactly what was in the file that is stored. The advantages and disadvantages of this are exactly the opposite of Access. Yes, you can store any kind of binary data in a SQL Server database. That's a big plus. *However*, there is nothing in the database itself which identifies what *kind* of binary data is stored. This can make retrieving the data a difficult task, especially if you're working with a database you didn't create. On the other hand, you don't have to strip out the header to display the data when working outside of SQL Server. In addition, stripping out the header information in an Access OLE field is one big headache, as we will discover.

# Working With Binary Data

## The Easy Way

The easiest, but if you have lots of files not necessarily the most efficient, way to work with binary data is to store the files in a folder and to store the file names in your database. In fact, there are circumstances in which you don't even have to store the file names in the database. If, for example, your table has a uniquely identified field, such as an AutoNumber (or, in SQL Server, *Identity* field), you can simply name your files with the value of the record to which they belong, with the correct extension for that file type. For example, if you had a table with an AutoNumber field, and you wanted to store and fetch a photograph associated with record number "1", you could name the image "1photo.jpg". Then, you can build your image source tag using the value of the AutoNumber Field:

```
<img src="images/<%=rs("id")%>photo.jpg">
```

The example web site we'll be talking about in this chapter, my Personal Profile Web site, does just that. The `profile` table in the Access database has an *image* field, with a *text* data type, in which the names of image files are stored. The default value of the field is "none." When someone sends me an image, I change the name of the file to the file name of that person's picture. You can get a copy of the database and other related files from the Wrox website.

In the Personal Profile display page, an image source tag is dynamically built, using ASP and ADO. When the recordset is opened, the value of the image field is stored in a variable called `image`. It is checked for a value of `none`, and if this is the case, it sets the value to `none.jpg` and a default image is displayed.

I don't have a picture!

Take a look at the following blocks of code:

```
<%

image = rs("image").value
if image = "none" then image = "none.jpg"

%>
```

The image tag is then dynamically built, by inserting ASP scripting tags into an HTML `<IMG>` tag:

```
<img src="_private/images/<%=image%>" align="left" border="0">
```

## Try It Out – Building a Dynamic Image Tag from a Stored File Name

For all exercises in this chapter, we are going to use files from an example website available for download from the Wrox website. You can copy the whole area on to your website or you can just copy the essential files as you need them, such as the profile database. You will need to have a copy of `profile.mdb`, and a System DSN named `profile` pointing to the location of the `profile.mdb` file on your machine. (Refer to chapter 2 if you need a reminder of how to set up the DSN.)

Copy the following ASP/ADO/HTML source code and save it in your web site as "`easyblobs.asp`:"

```
<%

' ** Note: This ASP code appears above the HTML for the page. It opens the recordset,
' ** gets the data, and closes it, before any HTML is sent to the browser.
' ** This speeds up the execution, and maximizes processor and memory on the server.
' ** The more the server has to switch back and forth between processing server-side
' ** scripting and HTML, the more resources are used.
' ** I find it good practice to execute as much server-side scripting as possible before
' ** any HTML, and to not mix up ASP scripting and HTML as much as is
' ** practically possible under the circumstances.

Dim image, fname, lname, rs, cn
Set cn = Server.CreateObject("ADODB.Connection")
cn.Open "DSN=profile;"
Set rs = cn.Execute ("SELECT fname, lname, image FROM profile WHERE email " & _
    "LIKE 'takempis@bellsouth.net'")
image = rs("image").value
fname = rs("fname").value
lname = rs("lname").value
rs.Close
Set rs = Nothing
cn.Close
Set cn = Nothing
%>

<HTML>
<HEAD>
<TITLE>Blob Fields in Access and SQL Server - The Easy Way</TITLE>
</HEAD>

<BODY>

<H1 ALIGN="center"><FONT COLOR="#0000FF">BLOB Fields - The Easy Way</FONT></H1>

<HR>
```

```
<!-- Label to appear above the picture is created below, by stringing the first and
last names together with a space between them, and adding (in the HTML) a dash, and
the word "Photo" -->
<P ALIGN="center"><FONT COLOR="#008040"><STRONG><%=fname & " " & lname%> -
Photo</STRONG></FONT><BR>

<!-- The <IMG> tag is created dynamically, by inserting an ASP script with the file
name from the recordset, where the file name of the image in the path should be. -->
<IMG SRC="/_private/images/<%=image%>"></P>

<HR>
</BODY>
</HTML>
```

### How it works - Building a Dynamic Image Tag from a Stored File Name

As you can see, it's pretty straightforward. In this case, we have used an email address (a uniquely valued field in the profile table) to search for a particular person's record. The fname (first name), lname (last name), and image fields are pulled from the record, and the values are placed in ASP variables. Then they are used to dynamically build both the label for the picture (in other words the name of the person whose picture it is), and the image source tag itself. When you run the page in a browser, it should look something like this:

This technique has an additional advantage. It works the same way with Access and SQL Server. Since you're just storing the name of the file, you are simply building an image source tag with text data. Try to use this method whenever you can. It costs the client less money, because it takes less time.

# The Hard Way

Okay, you're stuck. You can't change the database, and you have to use BLOB data stored in a database. *Now* what are you going to do? Well, the easy part is, if you're building a web interface, you're going to use almost the same code as the above example in your page. In other words, if you have an image, you're going to create an image source tag. If you have a sound file, or some other form of media, you're most likely going to use an <EMBED> tag. Alternatively, you might even create a hyperlink to the file you want to retrieve from the database, as in the case of a sound file that plays "on demand."

**601**

## *The Display Page*

The first thing you're going to have to do is to create an ASP page that will function much like the file you're retrieving. Why is that? Well, you're going to be creating an image source tag, for example, and the image source is going to be data from a database. The file is referenced in the <IMG> tag, but it doesn't have a recognizable extension. The browser isn't going to know the **MIME** (Multipurpose Internet Mail Extensions) type for the item you are going to retrieve. MIME types are used to tell the browser (and other Internet application software, such as Mail and News readers) what kind of data is being sent, so that they can interpret it correctly. The browser attempts to determine what kind of data it is by one of several methods:

- ❏ The server can supply the MIME type to the browser, by sending an HTML header.
- ❏ Registry settings on the local computer can identify a MIME Type by several means.
- ❏ The extension of the file being downloaded can identify the MIME type.
- ❏ The browser can examine the contents and make an educated "guess."

If the browser doesn't know the MIME type, it will assume that the type is text/HTML. In the case of binary data, this would be a big mistake. After all, binary data is not text, and cannot be interpreted as such. Therefore, what we want to do is to create an ASP page that sends a header to the browser. This, after all, is a "failsafe" way to make sure that the browser knows the MIME type. Since the client computer may or may not have registry settings for all of the MIME types, and since the file has a different extension (.asp) than the type of data contained in it, and since relying on the browser to make an educated "guess" isn't always going to work, sending a header is the only way to make sure that the browser knows.

We use a separate ASP page because you can't send headers in an existing page after HTML has already been sent to the browser.  Even though a page may contain tags for other types of data than HTML text, the browser actually makes separate requests for each of the files referenced in the page. Therefore, each file is sent with its own set of headers, or can be interpreted by the file extension, as long as the browser recognizes it.

Luckily, the Response object of ASP has a property for doing just that. It's called the ContentType property. Consider the following code:

```
<%Response.ContentType = "image/bmp"%>
```

This tells the browser that the file being retrieved is an image file with a .bmp extension, in other words a bitmap. The following are a list of common MIME types that browsers recognize:

| | | |
|---|---|---|
| text/richtext | image/x-png | application/base64 |
| text/html | image/x-xbitmap | application/macbinhex40 |
| audio/x-aiff | image/bmp | application/pdf |
| audio/basic | image/x-jg | application/x-compressed |
| audio/wav | image/x-emf | application/x-zip-compressed |
| | image/x-wmf | application/x-gzip-compressed |
| image/gif | image/pjpeg | application/java |
| image/jpeg | video/avi | application/x-msdownload |
| image/tiff | video/mpeg | application/postscript |

You must determine the ContentType property based upon what kind of BLOB data you're fetching, and create the appropriate HTML in your page to insert that "file" (the file containing the BLOB data) into the page. For example:

```
<IMG SRC="sqlbitmap.asp">
<EMBED WIDTH="128" HEIGHT="128"
SRC="accesswave.asp" ALIGN="baseline" HIDDEN AUTOSTART="true" AUTOPLAY="true">
```

Now all you have to do is create the file that sends the BLOB data to the browser, using the Response.BinaryWrite method. This is used for sending binary data to the browser, rather than text data. The syntax for it is just the same as the syntax for the Response.Write method:

```
<%Response.BinaryWrite <data>%>
```

But now comes the really tricky part. Remember that Access includes a header with the data stored in the field, while SQL Server does not. It's not difficult to write a script for a SQL Server BLOB field. The following is the code for sqlbitmap.asp, which is an ASP file that retrieves a gif image from a SQL Server database named pubs and displays a logo:

```
<%
Response.Expires = 0     ' ** Make sure to get a fresh copy each time
                         ' ** It might not be the same image!
Response.Buffer = TRUE ' ** Send the whole thing at once
Response.Clear           ' ** Clear out the Response object

Set cn = Server.CreateObject("ADODB.Connection")
cn.Open "DSN=pubs;UID=wrox;PWD=;"
Set rs = cn.Execute("SELECT logo FROM pub_info WHERE pub_id='0736'")
Response.ContentType = "image/gif"   ' ** Set the MIME Type for a gif image
Response.BinaryWrite rs("logo")        ' ** Send the data to the browser
rs.Close
Set rs = Nothing
cn.Close
Set cn = Nothing
Response.End  ' ** Clear out the Response Object
%>
```

Note that there is no HTML in this page. All it does is fetch data and stream the data to the browser.

That wasn't too hard, was it? Thank goodness we knew what kind of image was stored in the database! If we had sent the wrong MIME type, it would have surely failed to display the image.

## Stripping the Access Header

What about Access? If we send the entire contents of the file, it *will* mess up the image. How are we going to strip out the image header? Well, if we knew the header length, we could strip it out by getting the length of the data, and using the VBScript Right() function to get everything but the leftmost (header) data. Unfortunately, the header is of indeterminate length; it varies from one record to another. Oh, what will we do?

We will build an ActiveX COM object (Actually, "ActiveX" and "COM" are synonymous, and used interchangeably) to strip out the header for us. If you do not have Microsoft Visual Basic 6, you can download "AccessBLOB.dll" from the Wrox web site. If you've never built a COM object before, don't worry. The following contains step-by-step instructions for building the DLL yourself.

### Try It Out – Building an ActiveX COM Object

(Note: The following information and code are adapted from Microsoft Knowledge Base article Q175261. I have modified the code to increase its functionality.)

**Step 1:** Create a New Project in Visual Basic: ActiveX DLL.

**Step 2:** Click the **Project** menu and select **References**. Select "Microsoft OLE DB ActiveX Data Objects 1.0 Library.

**Step 3:** Add a new Module to the Project. Click **Add Module**, Select the Module and Click **Open**.

**Step 4:** The following code goes in the (general) (declarations) section of the Module:

```
' Be sure not to be running VB in debug mode when using this API!
' The following 2 lines should all be on a single line
Public Declare Sub CopyMemory Lib "kernel32" Alias "RtlMoveMemory" (lpvDest As Any,
lpvSource As Any, ByVal cbCopy As Long)

Type PT
    Width As Integer
    Height As Integer
End Type

Type OBJECTHEADER
    Signature As Integer
    HeaderSize As Integer
    ObjectType As Long
    NameLen As Integer
    ClassLen As Integer
    NameOffset As Integer
    ClassOffset As Integer
    ObjectSize As PT
    OleInfo As String * 256
End Type
```

**Step 5:** The following code goes in the (general) (declarations) section of CLASS1.CLS:

```
Function DisplayBLOB(ByVal OleField As Variant)
        Dim Arr() As Byte
        Dim ObjHeader As OBJECTHEADER
        Dim Buffer As String
        Dim ObjectOffset As Long
        Dim BitmapOffset As Long
        Dim BitmapHeaderOffset As Integer
        Dim ArrBmp() As Byte
        Dim i As Long

        ' Resize the array, then fill it with
        ' the entire contents of the field
        ReDim Arr(OleField.ActualSize)
        Arr() = OleField.GetChunk(OleField.ActualSize)

        ' Copy the first 19 bytes into a variable
        ' of the OBJECTHEADER user defined type
        CopyMemory ObjHeader, Arr(0), 19

        ' Determine where the Access Header ends
        ObjectOffset = ObjHeader.HeaderSize + 1

        ' Grab enough bytes after the OLE header to get
        ' the bitmap header
        Buffer = ""
        For i = ObjectOffset To ObjectOffset + 512
            Buffer = Buffer & Chr(Arr(i))
        Next

        ' Find out if the Object is Paintbrush or Sound Recorder
        If InStr(Buffer, "PBrush") > 0 Then
            BitmapHeaderOffset = InStr(Buffer, "BM")
        ElseIf InStr(Buffer, "SoundRec") > 0 Then
            BitmapHeaderOffset = InStr(Buffer, "RIFF")
        End If
        If BitmapHeaderOffset > 0 Then

            ' Calculate the beginning of the bitmap
            BitmapOffset = ObjectOffset + BitmapHeaderOffset - 1

            ' Move the bitmap into its own array
            ReDim ArrBmp(UBound(Arr) - BitmapOffset)
            CopyMemory ArrBmp(0), Arr(BitmapOffset), UBound(Arr) - BitmapOffset + 1

            ' Return the bitmap
            DisplayBLOB = ArrBmp
        Else
            DisplayBLOB = "Error"
        End If
End Function
```

**Step 6:** Rename the project. On the **Project** menu, click on **Project1 Properties**. Type AccessBLOB in the **Project Name** field.

**Step 7:** Check the **Unattended Execution** check box. Click **OK** to close the **Project Properties** window.

**Step 8:** In the **Project** pane, select the CLASS1.CLS class. In the **Properties** pane, change the name of the class to GetBLOB.

**Step 9:** Compile the project to create AccessBLOB.dll. Click the **File** menu and select **Make AccessBLOB.dll**.

Congratulations. You've just built yourself a COM object!

Once you've built your COM object, you're going to have to register it on the web server. This is done by making a copy of AccessBLOB.dll in your \Windows\System32 folder (in NT, this would probably be your \WINNT\System32 folder).

Now it needs to be registered with your server. This is done using a system tool called RegSvr32 which you access through your **Start | Run** menu. To register the AccessBLOB.dll on your server, click **Start**, then **Run**, and then type in "**regsvr32 AccessBLOB.dll**" Once you've done this, your web server will be able to access the COM object any time a script calls for it. If you have VB 6 installed, you should have all the necessary run-time files to run this COM object.

Note: This COM object can strip headers from bitmaps and wave files. You can modify the code to strip headers from any OLE object that Access supports. When Access doesn't support a particular type of OLE object (such as an avi file), it will attempt to convert the file to another supported type. Be aware that your file may not end up as the type that it started out. An avi file, for example, can be converted to a metafile, depending on whether avi files are supported by your Access database. When this occurs, you are basically in the dark concerning what kind of file you are dealing with. If you want to add objects to the code supplied, you will have to do a good deal of research. You can use getblobinfo.asp, described a little later, to give you some clues. The Access help documentation may be helpful.

What objects are supported by your Access database are determined by a number of factors, such as what version of Access you are using, what filters you've installed, and what other applications you have installed (some applications add filters of their own).

## Getting the Header Info

Now we are going to want to use the COM object to get BLOB data from an Access database. My profile.mdb database has a table in it called blobs. There are two fields in the blobs table that we will deal with. One is called image and it refers to bitmaps. The other is sound and is specifically for .wav files. The email field is for identifying to which record in the profile table the image and sound belong.

I have created a page called hardblobs.htm. We will build it in sections. The first and easiest section is the actual page itself. The code for this page follows:

```
<HTML>

<HEAD>
  <TITLE>Blob Fields in Access and SQL Server - The Hard Way</TITLE>
</HEAD>

<BODY>

  <H1 ALIGN="center"><FONT COLOR="#0000FF"><EMBED WIDTH="128" HEIGHT="128"
    SRC="accesswave.asp" ALIGN="baseline" HIDDEN AUTOSTART="true" AUTOPLAY="true">
    BLOB Fields - The Hard Way</FONT></H1>

  <HR>

  <P ALIGN="center"><STRONG>Access - Photo</STRONG><BR>
  <IMG SRC="accessbitmap.asp"></P>

</BODY>
</HTML>
```

Note that there is no actual ASP code in this page. That is because it has image source, embed, and hyperlink tags pointing to the pages which actually do the work.

There are two files that actually do the work here – they pull data from an Access database and display the results in the `hardblobs.htm` page.

❑  accessbitmap.asp

❑  accesswave.asp

What we want to do here is to create the `hardblobs.htm` page, then create the three pages that it refers to, and see the results.

Now, don't think that I've left you "out in the cold" as far as figuring out the way to get the MIME type and file type stored in an Access OLE field. In fact, I've developed a page for doing just that. It's called `getblobinfo.asp`. Here is a snapshot of its output:

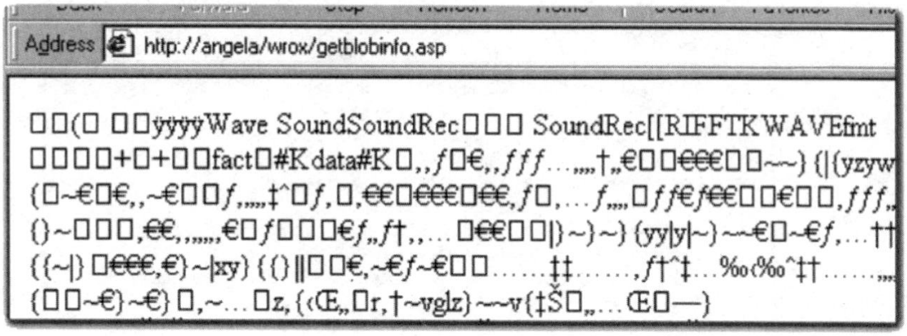

The code for this page follows:

```
<HTML>

<HEAD>
<TITLE>getblobinfo.asp</TITLE>
</HEAD>

<BODY>
<%
Set cn = Server.CreateObject("ADODB.Connection")
cn.Open "DSN=profile;"
Set rs = cn.Execute("SELECT sound FROM blobs WHERE email LIKE" & _
        "'takempis@bellsouth.net'")
Response.BinaryWrite rs.Fields("sound").GetChunk(1024)
rs.Close
Set rs = Nothing
cn.Close
Set cn = Nothing
Set sound = Nothing
%>
</BODY>
</HTML>
```

This page is used purely for diagnostics; that is, it is used to determine (1) what the device for this file is, and (2) where the actual code for the file begins (end of header). Note that in the screenshot above, the string SoundRec appears, which is the name of the device used to display the file. Also note, in the code for AccessBLOB.dll, that SoundRec is specifically mentioned as the identifier for a .wav file. Therefore, we know that we are looking at a .wav file, and therefore, we will use an image/wav value for the ContentType property of the Response object.

To determine where the header ends, we will need to know where the actual file begins. All of these types of files begin in the same way. There is a character code that signifies the start of the file. To find out what that character code is, you can open the file in WordPad (yes, you can open a binary file in WordPad or NotePad – it just isn't pretty). I use WordPad because some of these files are quite large. Make sure that when you use the Open File dialog box, you set the file type to "(*.*)." This indicates that you want to open files of any type. Here's a snapshot of a .wav file in WordPad:

You may have to open several files to make the identification. As you can see, both the output of getblobinfo.asp and the .wav file in WordPad begin with the string "RIFF." They are very similar in other ways, but by opening several other .wav files, you can see that the only common beginning letters are "RIFF." So, obviously, that is the common string.

Now, in the COM object, the InStr() function is used to determine where the buffer for storing the binary data begins. The InStr() function returns a numeric value indicating the number of bytes or characters (a character is 1 byte in length) from the beginning of a string of bytes or characters, that a sub string starts at. The AccessBLOB.GetBLOB's displayBLOB function handles the math for all of this, and returns the contents of the file stored. All you have to do to modify the DLL's ability to retrieve various types of files is to add an If...Else statement to the following section of code:

```
If InStr(Buffer, "PBrush") > 0 Then
    BitmapHeaderOffset = InStr(Buffer, "BM")
ElseIf InStr(Buffer, "SoundRec") > 0 Then
    BitmapHeaderOffset = InStr(Buffer, "RIFF")
End If
```

The first part looks for the device used to "play" the object. The second part identifies the beginning of the file for that type of object. In the above code, Pbrush identifies the object as a bitmap. SoundRec identifies the object as a .wav file. The COM object doesn't have to know what kind of object is stored; it gets that information from the data in the field.

You should be able to see how you could add different object types to the DLL to enhance its functionality.

## The "Display" File (Access)

Let's look first at accessbitmap.asp:

```
<%
Response.Expires = 0
Response.Buffer = TRUE
Response.Clear
Set cn = Server.CreateObject("ADODB.Connection")
cn.Open "DSN=profile;"
Set rs = cn.Execute("SELECT picture FROM blobs WHERE email LIKE" & _
        "'takempis@bellsouth.net'")
Response.ContentType = "image/bmp"
Set bitmap = Server.CreateObject("AccessBLOB.GetBLOB")
Response.BinaryWrite bitmap.DisplayBLOB(rs("picture"))
rs.Close
Set rs = Nothing
cn.Close
Set cn = Nothing
Set bitmap = Nothing
Response.End
%>
```

Again, note that this file contains no HTML, because it is simply going to stream out the contents of the file to the browser. We know that the picture is a bitmap, so we've set the ContentType to image/bmp. In almost every other way, this file resembles the one for getting a bitmap from a SQL Server BLOB field. However, let's look at the two lines that are crucially different:

```
Set bitmap = Server.CreateObject("AccessBLOB.GetBLOB")
Response.BinaryWrite bitmap.DisplayBLOB(rs("picture"))
```

Here is where the AccessBLOB COM object comes into play. As you can see, working with it is very similar to working with ADO COM objects. First, you create an instance of the object and store it in a variable (called bitmap). Then you invoke the DisplayBLOB() function of that object, passing to it the field from the database. This strips out the header, and then writes the value to the browser, using the Response.BinaryWrite method.

Now, let's look at `accesswave.asp`:

```
<%
Response.Expires = 0
Response.Buffer = TRUE
Response.Clear
Set cn = Server.CreateObject("ADODB.Connection")
cn.Open "DSN=profile;"
Set rs = cn.Execute("SELECT sound FROM blobs WHERE email LIKE" & _
"'takempis@bellsouth.net'")
Response.ContentType = "audio/wav"
Set sound = Server.CreateObject("AccessBLOB.GetBLOB")
Response.BinaryWrite sound.DisplayBLOB(rs("sound"))
rs.Close
Set rs = Nothing
cn.Close
Set cn = Nothing
Set sound = Nothing
Response.End
%>
```

This file pulls the contents of the `sound` field in the blobs table, which we know is a `.wav` file. It sets the `ContentType` property to `audio/wav` and does everything else in the same fashion as the `accessbitmap.asp` page.

## Try It Out – Putting It All Together

Make copies of the pages we've discussed: `hardblobs.htm`, `accesswave.asp`, `accessbitmap.asp`

Now all you have to do is open `hardblobs.htm` in your browser and you should see something like this:

I've visually depicted the embedded sound file. It's embedded, so it simply plays when the page is opened. An interesting aspect of this is that the browser has downloaded the data as the file types that they are. In your Temporary Internet Files folder, you should find copies of these files, and they can actually be opened in whatever the default device for that type of file.

Check this out: In Internet Explorer, click Tools | Internet Options. In the Temporary Internet Files section, click Settings and then click View Files. You should see the files accessbitmap.asp, and accesswave.asp displayed there; each with the .asp extension, but with an icon for that file type. If you open either of them, they will appear in the default device for that type of file.

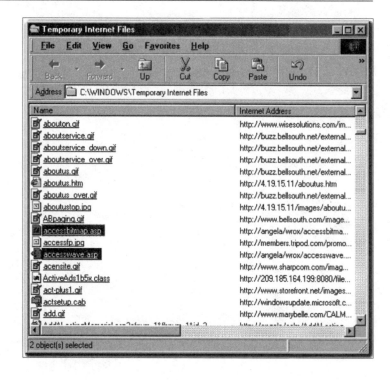

# Uploading BLOB Data

Uploading BLOB data to a database is particularly difficult, because in order to transmit binary data, the form that transmits the data must have a different *encoding type* than usual. The standard encoding type of an HTML form translates the data in the form into URL encoding, which has a whole host of illegal characters. When you use the POST method of the form, the translating is done for you, but the result with a binary object may be incredibly long, because the URL encoding for the illegal characters consists of the "%" symbol plus a two-character code.

Instead, you can change the encoding type of the form to multipart/form-data, which transmits the raw data from the form without any translation. Unfortunately, once you've done this, you can't use the Request object of ASP to read the data from the form.

So, how do we get around this predicament? Fortunately, there are a number of commercially distributed ASP components available for doing this. The most popular ones are SAFileUp from Software Artisans (http://www.softartisans.com) and ASPUpLoad from Persits Software (http://www.aspupload.com). You'll find that most hosting services support at least one of these components. Each one of them has numerous properties and methods for handling uploaded files and form fields that have been submitted using the multipart/form-data encoding method. For the purposes of this chapter, we will use SAFileUp, which is probably the most popular.

# The Easy Way and The Hard Way

We will be using the same form code for discussing both the Easy Way and the Hard Way of uploading binary data to your ASP/ADO application. Because of the fact that you may or may not have access to SAFileUp, we will not have any "Try-it-Outs" for this section, but if you do have access to SAFileUp, you may be able to use some of the code provided, and it should in any case give you an idea of what needs to be done.

The following is the form code for uploading a file to a web site. It can reside in an HTML page, or an ASP page. It is simply a form, with no other special qualities than the fact that the encoding type is different, and it has a "FILE" type form field:

```
<HTML>

<HEAD>
<TITLE>Update My Image</TITLE>
</HEAD>

<BODY>

<P ALIGN="center"><FONT size="4"><STRONG>Profile - Update My Image</STRONG></FONT></P>

<form method="POST" action="upload.asp" enctype="multipart/form-data">
  <P>Email Address: <input type="text" name="email" size="50" maxlength="100"><BR>
  Image: <input type="FILE" name="myfile"></P>
  <P><input type="submit" value="Upload" name="B1"></P>
</form>
</BODY>
</HTML>
```

Note the FILE form field. This is a special type of form field that is specifically used for uploading files of any type. This is one of the things that makes uploading files difficult, as this form field type is not supported by some older browsers. For example, MS Internet Explorer 3 and below do not support this type of form field. If the browser supports the form field, there will be a Browse button next to it. This button enables the user to browse their system for the file to upload. Also, note the <FORM> tag and the encoding type used. When this file is displayed in a browser, it should look something like this:

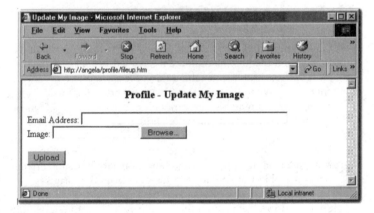

We will use this form to update a profile in the Personal Profile web site in both the Easy Way and the Hard Way.

## The Easy Way

The Easy way, again, is to upload the file to a location on the server, and to upload the file name to the database. Why is this? First, working with BLOB fields in ADO consumes processor and memory, and is less efficient in terms of performance. Secondly, if you upload to the database, you're going to have to fetch data from the database, which adds to the performance hit. Third, as mentioned earlier, the FILE form field is not supported by some browsers. Finally, in order to INSERT or UPDATE a BLOB field in a database, you will not be able to use a SQL statement. You will have to open an updateable recordset, and update it with the recordset's Update method. This is more of a performance hit as well, and may not be supported on the system that the application resides. However, if the hosting service has kept up with the latest updates, and has the most recent version of MDAC installed on their server, both Access and SQL Server's ODBC providers will support the updateable recordset, and the Update method.

So, how do we make a form handler that will upload the file to the server, and the file name to the database? Consider the following ASP/ADO code:

```
<%
Dim status, email, image, rs, cn, strSQL, fl, newpath, cstring

cstring = "DSN=profile;"

' ** The "status" variable is used to determine whether
' ** everything was successful or not
status = ""

' ** Create the File upload object
Set upl = Server.CreateObject("SoftArtisans.FileUp")

' ** Check to make sure that it is a JPEG file. This application requires
' ** a JPEG file with a ".jpg" extension. This may or may not be necessary.
' ** However, it is important in almost any case to know the file type, which
' ** can be derived from the file extension.
if TRIM(upl.UserFileName) <> "" then
  if InStr(LCase(upl.UserFileName), ".jpg") = 0 then
    status = "Photo file is incorrect format. It must be .JPG format."
  end if
end if

' ** check to make sure that a file was uploaded
if upl.Form("myfile").IsEmpty then
  status = "Photo was not uploaded"
end if

' ** check to make sure that an email address was supplied
if upl.Form("email") = "" then
  status = "No email address was supplied"
end if

' ** if everything is in order, save the image and record the file name in the
database
if status = "" then

' ** get the path to the image location of the profile database profile images
  fl = Server.MapPath("_private/images/")

' ** add the file name to the path
  newpath = fl & upl.UserFileName
```

```
' ** update the record containing the new image with the file name
  Set cn = Server.CreateObject("ADODB.Connection")
  cn.Open cstring
  strSQL = "UPDATE profile SET image = '" & upl.UserFileName & "' WHERE email" & _
           "LIKE '" & email & "'"
  cn.Execute(strSQL)
  cn.Close
  Set cn = Nothing

' ** save the file to the correct location
  upl.SaveAs newpath
  status = "Your photo has been uploaded."
else

' ** Clear the file from memory on the server
  upl.Flush
  Session("message") = status
end if
Set upl = Nothing
%>
<HTML>

<HEAD>
<TITLE>Profile Image Update</TITLE>
</HEAD>

<BODY>

<P ALIGN="center"><FONT size="4"><STRONG>Profile Image Update</STRONG></FONT></P>

<! - Display status message -- >
<P ALIGN="center"><%=status%></P>
</BODY>
</HTML>
```

Okay, the first thing to do is to create an instance of the FileUp object:

```
Set upl = Server.CreateObject("SoftArtisans.FileUp")
```

This is the object that we will be working with to upload the image, and to work with the additional form field(s). We're using a variable named status to determine whether or not the upload is successful. There are several reasons why it might not be. We initially set the value of this string to "", which indicates that all is well.

We test for several problem areas:

❑ **Is the file a ".jpg" file?** The reason for this is that in this case, the application is using a dynamically-drawn image source tag. The image must be an acceptable format (such as .jpg, .gif, or .bmp). This code could be amended to allow the other two image file formats, but it must at least check to see whether it is an acceptable format for the browser. I left it at .jpg for simplicity's sake in the demo. We check by using the FileUp object's UserFileName property, which is the name of the file uploaded:

```
if InStr(LCase(upl.UserFileName), ".jpg") = 0 then …
```

We're not sure whether the file extension will have the same case, so we use the Lcase() function to make it all lower case, and test it against .jpg.

- ❑ **Is there a file at all?** The `FileUp` object also has a property called `IsEmpty`, which can be used to determine this. It returns `True` or `False`.

- ❑ **Was an email address supplied?** In order to access values from form fields, we use the `FileUp` object's `Form` collection. It works exactly the same way that the `Request` object's `Form` collection works. In this case, we simply test for an empty string.

Next, we update the `image` field in the table, to reflect the new image name. Again, we use the `FileUp` object's `UserFileName` property in the `SQL UPDATE` statement that updates the table, and we use the email address supplied to indicate which record should be updated.

Finally, we use the `FileUp` object's `SaveAs` method to save the file to the drive. This method takes the full path to the folder and the file name as an argument. We have determined the path by using the `Server.MapPath()` method, which takes a virtual path (a relative path, in this case), and returns the actual path to the folder. We concatenated the file name to the path to get the full path that we want to save the file to. The `SaveAs` method can be used to change the name of the file as well, since the file name is supplied as well as the path. The name of the file can be anything you want to name it. This comes in handy when you want to make sure that the file has a unique name, and doesn't overwrite any existing files. By using a uniquely valued field from the database, you can give the file a unique name, if you wish. For the purposes of this demonstration, you can leave the file name the same.

One last word of caution in regards to saving the file to the hard drive. The permissions must be set on the folder to be uploaded to, to allow the `IUSER<Machine_Name>` IIS anonymous user account to upload files. Otherwise, you may get an error message from `SAFileUp`: "Error occurred when moving cached file to final destination". You will have to get the Network Administrator for the hosting service to set this permission.

After everything is complete, the status message is displayed in the browser window.

## The Hard Way

Now, if you want to save the BLOB data directly to the database, you can use `SAFileUp` to do so (as well as `ASPUpLoad`). As mentioned previously, this is done by opening a recordset containing the record we want to update, setting the recordset as Updateable, and then updating the record with the BLOB data. It is done the same way using both Access and SQL Server. The difference is that when updating the Access database, no header information is included with the BLOB data. This is fine, as long as all of the database fields store the data the same way. However, you won't be able to access the BLOB data in the Access database using the Access front end any more, as it does require the header information. Still, you can access it via ASP/ADO, and in the same way that you would access BLOB data stored in a SQL Server database.

This demonstration uses the same form that the Easy Way uses. The form handler page is different, in some respects. Let's take a look at the code (this demonstration uses the blobs table in the profile.mdb database):

```
<%
Dim cstring, rs, email
cstring = "DSN=profile;"

' ** The "status" variable is used to determine whether
' ** everything was successful or not
status = ""

' ** Create the File upload Object
Set upl = Server.CreateObject("SoftArtisans.FileUp")

' ** Check to make sure that it is a JPEG file. This application requires
' ** a JPEG file with a ".jpg" extension. This may or may not be necessary.
' ** However, it is important in almost any case to know the file type, which
' ** can be derived from the file extension.
if TRIM(upl.UserFileName) <> "" then
  if InStr(LCase(upl.UserFileName), ".jpg") = 0 then
    status = "Photo file is incorrect format. It must be .JPG format."
  end if
end if

' ** check to make sure that a file was uploaded
if upl.Form("myfile").IsEmpty then
  status = "Photo was not uploaded"
end if

' ** check to make sure that an email address was supplied
if upl.Form("email") = "" then
  status = "No email address was supplied"
end if

' ** if everything is in order, save the image to the database
if status = "" then

' ** update the record containing the new image with the file name
  set rs = Server.CreateObject("ADODB.RecordSet")
  strSQL = "SELECT * FROM blobs WHERE email LIKE '" & email & "'"
  rs.Open strSQL, cstring, 2, 3
  upl.SaveAsBlob rs.Fields("picture")
  rs.Update
  rs.Close
  Set rs = Nothing
else

' ** Clear the file from memory on the server
  upl.Flush
  Session("message") = status
end if
Set upl = Nothing
%>
<HTML>

<HEAD>
<TITLE>Profile - Upload BLOB to the Database</TITLE>
<META NAME="GENERATOR" content="Microsoft FrontPage 3.0">
</HEAD>

<BODY>

<P ALIGN="center"><FONT size="4"><STRONG>Profile - Upload BLOB to the
Database</STRONG></FONT></P>

<P><%=status%></P>
</BODY>
</HTML>
```

As you can see, the steps are very much the same, up to a point. The form input information is checked, and the `status` variable is used to verify that everything is okay.

The difference is what is actually done with the data. The file name isn't stored anywhere, as we are not storing the file name, but the actual contents of the file. The first thing that is done is to open an updateable recordset, and then select the record to update. Then the `FileUp` object's `SaveAsBlob` method is used to save the blob to the recordset. It takes the field to update as its argument. Finally, the recordset's `Update` method is called to commit the change to the database, and the status message is printed to the page, just as before.

This method does have one advantage over the Easy Way: you don't need any special permissions settings for the folder containing your files.

# Working With Access Memo and SQL Server Text Fields

In MS Access, it is called a Memo field. In SQL Server, it is called a Text field. What is it? In a sense, it is a field that can be virtually any length at all (up to about 2 GB). In actuality, it's a pointer to a location where the data is stored, almost like the File Allocation Table of your operating system. A database table typically has fields of fixed length, so in order to store data of indeterminate length, or data which may grow in length, the Memo (Text) field was created. It is actually a fixed length field containing a pointer (address) to the beginning of the data that belongs to it.

Because of this, and because of certain "features" of the software, this kind of data has to be given special treatment in your ADO operations.

## SQL Server Table Structure

SQL Server has this quirk: if you perform a `SELECT` SQL statement which includes data from a Text field, the Text field must be the last field referred to in the statement, or you will have problems. There are two solutions to this:

> Structure your table so that Text fields are at the end. This allows you to use `SELECT *`... without any problems. When you use `SELECT *`... all the fields in the table are returned in the physical order in which they appear in the table.

> If you can't restructure the table, don't use `SELECT *`.... Instead, use a fields list in your `SELECT` SQL statements, and place the Text fields at the end of the fields list:

```
SELECT field1, field2, field3, field4, field7, field8, field5, field6 FROM mytable
```

# In Search of the Lost Data

ADO has a quirk, too. I would call it a "bug" but maybe it's just a "feature." After you've performed a SELECT statement that returns a recordset, the data in Memo (Text) fields has a funny way of *disappearing* on you! I have yet to see the documentation for this, but I know it from bitter experience. You populate a recordset from a query, and start working with it, and when you get to the data in the Memo field, it is suddenly NULL. Apparently, it has been lost, scrambled, or leaked into Memory somewhere.

> *With SQL Server, you can overcome this problem by using the GetChunk() method of the Fields collection of the RecordSet. For example:*
>
> *mytest = rs.Fields("mytextfield").GetChunk(12345)*
>
> *The GetChunk() method of the Fields collection of a Recordset object takes the number of bytes to get as its argument. However, I've seen no documentation about this in regard to Access.*

The solution to this in Access (and it works with SQL Server too, if you use it without the GetChunk() method), is to grab the value of the Memo field immediately after opening your recordset. If you are looping through records, grab the value as soon as you move the cursor to the next record in your loop. Example (from viewprofile.asp):

```
<%
cstring = "DSN=profile;"

Dim job
Dim hobbies
Dim bio

' ** This function replaces CRLFs with HTML encoding for CRLFs
Function newstr(str)
  newstr = Replace(str, VbCrLf, "<BR>")
End Function

Set cn = Server.CreateObject("ADODB.Connection")
cn.Open cstring
q = "SELECT * FROM profile WHERE email = '" & email & "'"
Set rs = cn.Execute(q)

' ** These are all Memo fields
job = newstr(rs("job").value)
hobbies = newstr(rs("hobbies").value)
bio = newstr(rs("bio").value)

%>
```

# Summary

In this chapter, we've dealt with two different kinds of "irregular" data: BLOB fields and Memo (Text) fields. We've discussed the "Easy Way" to deal with this type of data: store the files on the web server and store the filenames in the database. Then use dynamically built HTML/ASP to display the file. We've talked at length about the "Hard Way" of retrieving raw data stored in BLOB fields in Access and SQL Server.

We've discussed how BLOB data is stored in Access and SQL Server:

- **Access**: BLOB data is stored as OLE (Object Linking and Embedding) objects, with a header included identifying the type of object, and the device for viewing it.
- **SQL Server**: BLOB data is stored in raw form, with no header.

We've discussed how to retrieve BLOB data from both kinds of databases:

- **Access**: The header must be stripped. A custom-built COM object strips the header and identifies the type of object being retrieved.
- **SQL Server**: The type of object must be known. The data can be retrieved in raw fashion.

We've built a custom ActiveX COM object, to strip out header information from an Access OLE object field, and learned how to register it on the web server, as well as customize it further to deal with additional object types.

We've discussed using ASP combined with ADO to display the data in a web page. We built four web pages, one HTML page for displaying the data retrieved, and three ASP pages to stream the data to the browser. In the process, we learned about MIME types for different kinds of data, and how to use the Response.ContentType property to inform the browser of the type of data being streamed.

We have successfully displayed a bitmap and a .wav file from an Access database, and a .gif file from a SQL Server database, all in the same page.

We've looked at the downloaded files in the Temporary Internet Files folder, to see how the downloaded data is stored with a .asp extension, but with an icon for the type of object that it contains.

We've looked at uploading BLOB data to both a folder on the server, and directly to the database, using third-party COM objects that make it comparatively easy. We used SAFileUp for our example component, because it is probably the most widely used and accepted by most hosting services.

We've discussed several issues dealing with Memo (Text) fields in Access and SQL Server. We've discussed structuring SQL Server tables with Text fields at the end, or alternatively, using a fields list in SELECT statements, to make sure that Text fields appear at the end of the SELECT statement.

Finally, we've learned how to avoid losing the data in Memo and Text fields after opening a recordset, by immediately placing their values in ASP variables.

# Exercises

These exercises use `profile.mdb` available from the Wrox website. The structure of the database is also described in Appendix C.

**1.** Modify `AccessBLOB.dll` to accommodate two additional types of files, .gif and .mid files. The blobs table has a record for `shiningdi@aol.com` that has a gif file in the image field and a midi file in the sound field. Use WordPad and `getblobinfo.asp` to determine the new parameters to plug into the `DisplayBLOB()` function.

*Note: You will have to unregister AccessBLOB.dll, and copy the new version over it to use it again. This may require re-booting your system before you can overwrite the dll. If you're running NT, stopping and starting the web server will probably suffice, to unregister a COM object, use the same utility (regsvr32) that you use to register it. The syntax is:*

```
regsvr32 AccessBLOB.dll /u
```

**2.** Create two new asp pages, `accessgif.asp` and `accessmidi.asp`, that will use AccessBLOB to display a gif image and a midi file in a web page.

**3.** Create a new web page, or modify `hardblobs.htm` to display the gif and play the midi file. You can use the embed tag to play the midi file.

**4.** Create a hyperlink on the gif image that will display the image by itself. Create a hyperlink to the midi file that will play the midi file.

# Quiz

**1.** What is the advantage of the Access OLE Object field?

**2.** What is the disadvantage of the Access OLE Object field?

**3.** What is the "Easy Way" to display binary files?

**4.** What is the disadvantage of the SQL Server BLOB fields?

**5.** How do you register an ActiveX dll with the server?

**6.** How do you tell the browser what kind of data you are sending to it?

**7.** Where should you put Access Memo Fields when designing an Access database for the Web?

**8.** How do you prevent Memo and Text field data from disappearing in your ASP/ADO pages?

# Quiz Answers

**1.** It stores the type of object being stored in the field

**2.** You must strip the header before streaming the data

**3.** Store the files in a folder on the web and store the filenames in the database. Use ASP/HTML to insert the files into the page

**4.** The type of object being stored is not stored with the object. If you didn't create the database, you may have a hard time figuring out what's in there

**5.** Start|Run (Command Line) – `regsvr32 dllname.dll`

**6.** Use the `Response.ContentType` property

**7.** Trick question! You can put them anywhere. *SQL Server Text fields* should be placed at the end of the table

**8.** When using SQL Server, use the `GetChunk()` method of the `Recordset` object's `Fields` collection to get the value in the field. With Access (or SQL Server, if you wish), grab the value of the field as soon as the recordset is opened, and place it in an ASP variable

Setup cannot install system files or update shared files if the files are in use. Before c
any open applications.

WARNING: This program is protected by copyright law and international treaties.

You may install Microsoft Data Access 2.1 on a single computer. Some Microsoft product
with additional rights, which are stated in the End User License Agreement included with y

Please take a moment to read the End User License Agreement now. It contains all of the te
conditions that pertain to this software product. By choosing to continue, you indicate accep
these terms.

Exit Setup

Continue

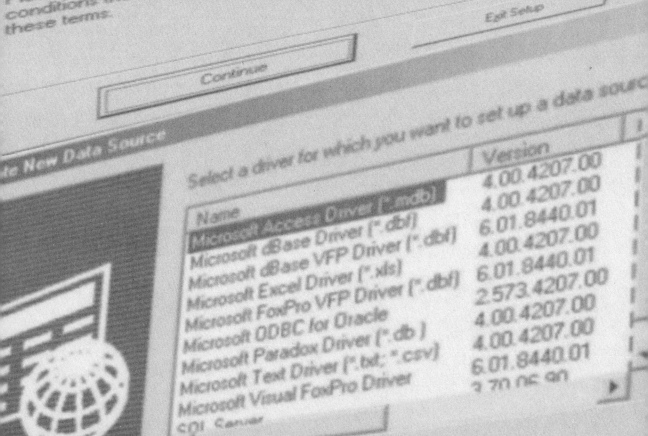

te New Data Source

Select a driver for which you want to set up a data sourc

| Name | Version |
|------|---------|
| Microsoft Access Driver (*.mdb) | 4.00.4207.00 |
| Microsoft dBase Driver (*.dbf) | 4.00.4207.00 |
| Microsoft dBase VFP Driver (*.dbf) | 6.01.8440.01 |
| Microsoft Excel Driver (*.xls) | 4.00.4207.00 |
| Microsoft FoxPro VFP Driver (*.dbf) | 6.01.8440.01 |
| Microsoft ODBC for Oracle | 2.573.4207.00 |
| Microsoft Paradox Driver (*.db ) | 4.00.4207.00 |
| Microsoft Text Driver (*.txt; *.csv) | 4.00.4207.00 |
| Microsoft Visual FoxPro Driver | 6.01.8440.01 |
| SQL Server | 3.70.06.90 |

Cancel

# ADO Tips and Tricks

As ASP pages and database access get more complex, more issues and bugs start to arise. This chapter is designed to help tackle some of the most common issues that developers are faced with when developing applications. In general, most of the issues that arise when developing an application in ASP and ADO are data related. The issue usually stems from a lack of data, invalid SQL statements, or invalid data from the end user.

The topics we'll cover in this chapter are as follows:

- ❏ Null values in recordsets
- ❏ Cleaning SQL statements
- ❏ Validating Dates
- ❏ Retrieving the number of records in a recordset
- ❏ Printing empty cells in HTML tables
- ❏ Handling multiple recordsets
- ❏ Refreshing the Command object

We've encountered some of these in earlier chapters, however this chapter provides a round up of the key things to look out for.

We'll be using a SQL Server database for some of the examples in this chapter – the pubs database. This is an example database supplied with SQL Server, which contains tables of authors and books for a fictitious publishing company. To see how to set up a DSN for this database refer back to chapter 2.

## SQL Data Shortcomings

Most of the time when you're debugging issues that are hard to reproduce, the best place to start is to check the data you're using. Often the issues that arise stem from the improper use of Null values, or invalid SQL statements that are partially generated from user input.

When these unexpected data-related issues arise, they can be very time-consuming to solve. Most of the time the issue won't arise where the problem actually resided, especially when using a language that has no data types like VBScript or when variables are dimensioned as variants. Let's look at how to deal with some of these common problems.

# Null Values in Recordsets

One of the most common unexpected issues that arises when programming with recordsets is a Null value where a string or number of some type was expected. When a Null value is read from a recordset and placed into a variable in ASP, the variable type is actually Null, and not the data type of the field.

There are several ways to deal with this issue, depending on whether we want to make allowances for Null variables, or test for them and then take action when they arise.

For the first approach, the easiest solution to get around the Null issue is to simply concatenate an empty string to the value as it is read from the recordset:

```
objRS.Fields.Item("Name").Value & ""
```

This will work for most of the issues that arise, but won't always solve the issue when dealing with numeric values.

Alternatively, we can test for Null variables in a number of ways. The best way to determine the variable type is to utilize the TypeName function. The TypeName function expects a variable of any data type (variant) to be passed to it, and returns a string holding the name of the data type that the variable contains:

```
Response.Write TypeName(objRS.Fields.Item("Name").Value)
```

This allows a developer to easily see what type of data the variable contains, which can be very useful when debugging.

VBScript also comes with another built in function that can determine if a variable is holding a Null variable - IsNull. This function takes any variable and returns a True if it is Null and False otherwise:

```
If IsNull(objRS.Fields.Item("Name").Value Then …
```

Another method is to build a function that accepts a variant and returns a string. The logic of the function can determine whether the value is Null and if so, return an empty string. This same type of function can be used to convert other data types such as Integer, Long, and Boolean.

```
Function CleanNull(strValue)
  If IsNull(strValue) Then
    CleanNull = ""
  Else
    CleanNull = strValue
  End If
End Function
```

The above function is very similar to the CInt, CStr, CBool, CLng, and CDate functions which are a part of VBScript. CInt and its related functions provide a mechanism to convert variables from one type to another (type casting).  However, if any of these functions are passed a Null value they will raise the error 94, Invalid use of Null. Building your custom functions also allows the flexibility to handle any special cases that arise.

## Try It Out — Dealing with Null Values

Start by creating a connection to a data source and open a recordset that contains a Null value. Next, loop through the recordset and `Response.Write` the data that contains the null value, wrapping it in the `CStr` function.

Here is our example code which can be found in `NullTEST.asp`:

```
<%@ Language=VBScript %>
<HTML>
<BODY>

<%
  Dim objRS
  Set objRS = Server.CreateObject("ADODB.Recordset")
  objRS.Open "SELECT * FROM Publishers", Application ("Pubs_ConnectionString")

  Do until objRS.EOF
    Response.Write  CStr(objRS("City"))  & "<BR>" & vbCrLf
    objRS.MoveNext
  Loop
%>

</BODY>
</HTML>
```

This code uses a connection to the SQL Server pubs database that has been stored in an ASP `Application` object:

```
  objRS.Open "SELECT * FROM Publishers", Application ("Pubs_ConnectionString")
```

You can modify this line to suit your own setup. As the recordset is read its contents are displayed until a Null value is encountered. At this point the code will stop executing the script and display the following error message:

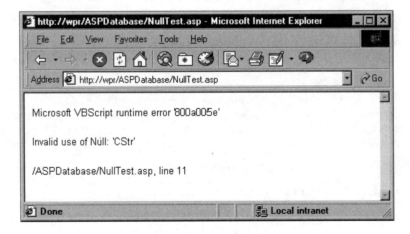

**627**

To counteract this simply concatenate an empty string to the data that is read from the recordset:

```
<%@ Language=VBScript %>
<HTML>
<BODY>

<%
  Dim objRS
  Set objRS = Server.CreateObject("ADODB.Recordset")
  objRS.Open "SELECT * FROM Publishers", Application("Pubs_ConnectionString")

  Do until objRS.EOF
    Response.Write  CStr(objRS("City") & "") & "<BR>" & vbCrLf
    objRS.MoveNext
  Loop
%>

</BODY>
</HTML>
```

# Cleaning SQL Statements

When working with ASP pages that update data sources it is very common to forget about certain characters that will cause a SQL statement to fail. The most common character is the apostrophe (single quote). The apostrophe is commonly used in a SQL statement to encapsulate a string (or varchar in SQL Server).

A likely place where the apostrophe issue can arise is on an ASP page that adds or updates a record, where a description field is filled from a text box that the user keys in. If the user enters a string like Bob's Bait and Tackle, the SQL statement will produce an error because the database engine will expect the SQL statement to end after the second b, causing the SQL string to be invalid. The SQL statement below is an example of what the database engine will actually try to process:

```
INSERT INTO MyTable (MyField) VALUES ('Bob's Bait and Tackle')
```

You can see that the ASP code is just pulling the values from the Form or QueryString:

```
sql = "INSERT INTO MyTable (MyField) VALUES ('" & Request.Form("UserInput") & "')"
```

A way to cope with the apostrophe issue is to surround all strings that are values for fields in double quotes. The only problem with this is that it creates another issue; double quotes in the string will cause the SQL statement to fail.

The best and safest way to solve this issue is to build a custom function that expects a string and cleans out the string of any unwanted characters that will cause the SQL statement to fail. This can be done fairly easily by using the Instr function within a Do While loop. The Instr function is part of VBScript and provides a way to determine where one string is in another. Below, we call InStr and pass it three parameters:

```
InStr(1,"Active Server Pages","rv")
```

- ❑ 1 is the starting point for the function
- ❑ Active Server Pages is the string to search
- ❑ rv is the string we are looking for

In this example `InStr` would return a result of 10.

Now let's build a custom function using the `Instr` function. The only drawback to this solution is that the data is not always identical to what the user keyed in.

```
Function CleanForSQL(strValue)

    'create another copy
    Dim strTemp
    strTemp = strValue

    'clean out single quotes
    Do Until InStr(1, strTemp, "'") = 0
        strTemp = Left(strTemp, InStr(1, strTemp, "'") - 1) & _
            Right(strTemp, Len(strTemp) - InStr(1, strTemp, "'"))
    Loop

    'clean out double quotes
    Do Until InStr(1, strTemp, Chr(34)) = 0
        strTemp = Left(strTemp, InStr(1, strTemp, Chr(34)) - 1) & _
            Right(strTemp, Len(strTemp) - InStr(1, strTemp, Chr(34)))
    Loop

    'return the clean string
    CleanForSQL = strTemp
End Function
```

In the code above the `Instr` function is used to search for single and double quotes. If one is found the string is altered and the quote is removed. The loop then continues until the string doesn't contain any quotes.

## Try It Out — Removing Invalid SQL Characters

Start by developing two ASP pages: one to retrieve the data from the user and one to insert the record into the table. This example inserts a record into SQL Server, but it can be tested with almost any data source.

The following code is a normal ASP page that is designed to capture the information from the user. It can be found in file `InvalidSQL.asp`.

```
<%@ Language=VBScript %>

<HTML>
<HEAD>
<META NAME="GENERATOR" Content="Microsoft Visual Studio 6.0">
</HEAD>
<BODY>
<FORM ID="frmExample" NAME="frmExample" ACTION="InvalidSQLInsert.asp" METHOD="POST">

  String:<BR>
  <INPUT TYPE="text" ID="txtString" NAME="txtString">
  <P>
  <INPUT TYPE="submit" VALUE="Submit" ID=submit1 NAME="Insert">

</FORM>
</BODY>
</HTML>
```

Our form should look like this:

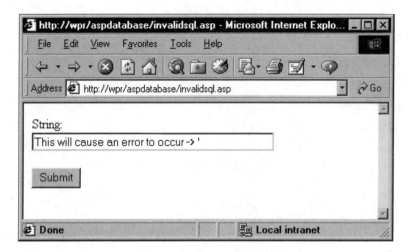

The second page retrieves the information from the form on the first page and inserts a record into the table within the database. This code uses a DSN called MyDSN, which points to the pubs database. You'll need to create an extra table in this database called test.

```
<%@ Language=VBScript %>

<%
  Dim txtString
  txtString = Request.Form("txtString")

  If Not IsEmpty(txtString) Then
    Dim objConn
    Set objConn = Server.CreateObject("ADODB.Connection")
    objConn.Open "DSN=MyDSN"
    objConn.Execute "INSERT INTO Test (Test) VALUES ( '" & txtString & "')"
    Set objConn = Nothing
  End If
%>

<HTML>
<HEAD>
</HEAD>
<BODY>
  Record inserted.
</BODY>
</HTML>
```

The second page will work successfully as long as the data entered by the user is valid. If the user enters a value that is invalid it will result in an error.

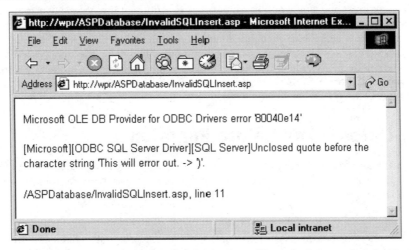

To solve this issue add a function to the second page to clean (filter) the information that is retrieved from the user. This code is available in InvalidSQLInsert.asp.

```
<%@ Language=VBScript %>

<%

  Function CleanForSQL(strValue)
    'create another copy
    Dim strTemp
    strTemp = strValue

    'clean out single quotes
    Do Until InStr(1, strTemp, "'") = 0
      strTemp = Left(strTemp, InStr(1, strTemp, "'") - 1) & _
         Right(strTemp, Len(strTemp) - InStr(1, strTemp, "'"))
    Loop

    'return the clean string
    CleanForSQL = strTemp
  End Function

  Dim txtString
  txtString = Request.Form("txtString")

  If Not IsEmpty(txtString) Then
    Dim objConn
    Set objConn = Server.CreateObject("ADODB.Connection")
    objConn.Open "DSN=MyDSN"
    objConn.Execute "INSERT INTO Test (Test) VALUES ( '" & CleanForSQL(txtString) & _
       "')"
    Set objConn = Nothing
  End If
%>

<HTML>
<HEAD>
</HEAD>
<BODY>
  Record inserted.
</BODY>
</HTML>
```

The code sample above is an example of combining our custom function to clean a string, with an INSERT statement that is executed by a Connection object. The code starts by defining the custom function that accepts a string and removes any single quotes from it. The execution of the ASP page actually starts on the line that dimensions the variable txtString. Next, the variable is filled with a value from the form collection which has been entered by a user. Once the value is captured from the user the code creates a connection to the database and executes an INSERT statement against the test table. However, the string entered by the user could be invalid so the code first validates the string by calling the CleanForSQL function to remove any single quotes. When the CleanForSQL function finishes it returns back a cleaned version of the string and the Execute method is called.

# Validating Dates – The IsDate Function

Because there are various ways for users to enter dates, validating them can be challenging at times. This is because most ASP applications don't use date controls in the same way as many form-based applications do (such as Visual Basic applications). Most of the input from the user in an ASP application is entered into a plain text box.

The issue with an invalid date becomes very noticeable when trying to update a database. The best way to ensure that a valid date has been read from the users is to utilize the IsDate function. This function is very useful because it accepts a variable of any type and returns a Boolean indicating whether or not the variable is a valid date. However, you should be aware that IsDate may sometimes accept a format that your database setup will reject – additional checking for your particular database is a good idea.

The IsDate function is most often used in client-side script. This enables the date to be validated before it is sent back to the server. (Note that this client-side VBScript can only be relied upon to work with Internet Explorer and not Netscape). Your code could look like this:

```
<%@ Language=VBScript %>
<HTML>
<HEAD>
<META NAME="GENERATOR" Content="Microsoft Visual Studio 6.0">
</HEAD>
<BODY>
<SCRIPT Language=VBScript>

Sub Validate
  If Not IsDate(document.all.txtDate.Value) Then
    Msgbox "Invalid date"
    document.all.txtDate.Focus
  Else
    Msgbox CDate(document.all.txtDate.Value) & " is a valid date."
  End If
End Sub

</SCRIPT>

<INPUT TYPE="TEXT" ID="txtDate" NAME="txtDate">
<INPUT TYPE="BUTTON" ONCLICK="Validate" VALUE="Validate" ID="btnValidate"
NAME="btnValidate">

</BODY>
</HTML>
```

# Retrieving the Number of Records

There are many times when the record count of a recordset is needed in an application to either perform some type of business logic or to simply display the count to the user. Whatever the need may be, it is important to open the recordset with the proper lock type and cursor location to avoid having to loop through all of the records counting them manually in code. There are two possible locations for a cursor: client and server. When a client-side cursor is used all of the data is brought down to the client (caller). When a server-side cursor is used the data is brought down to the client in pieces (a few records at a time).

If a record count is unavailable, ADO will return a –1 (long) when the RecordCount property is called. This will not only look strange to the user, it also has the potential to cause an error in the application if it is expecting a non negative number.

The best way to prevent the RecordCount property from returning a –1 is to specify the CursorLocation as adUseClient. This ensures that all of the data resides on the caller, which will enable the RecordsetCount function to return the proper record count.

If a server-side cursor must be used there are still ways to retrieve the right record count. If the cursor type is set to either adOpenKeyset or adOpenStatic, the recordset count will be accurate. This is because these cursors are blind to changes made by other users. Basically, it's a snapshot in time. If the cursor type is set to adOpenForwardOnly or adOpenDynamic the recordset will not have referenced all of the records and therefore will return a –1 for the RecordCount. This is because the adOpenForwardOnly cursor is used to scroll forward through a recordset, and does not know the size of the recordset until it reaches the end. The adOpenDynamic cursor provides the ability to see any other changes to the recordset made by other users, and must therefore constantly check for additions, edits, and deletes. Because of this, the adOpenDynamic cursor cannot provide a record count because it could be constantly changing.

The RecordCount property may also return –1 if the provider specified does not support the proper functionality; however most providers, such as Microsoft Jet 4.0 OLEDB and SQL OLEDB, do support this. For more information on what each specific provider supports reference their text file located in the C:\Program Files\Common Files\System\ole db directory (note that your drive letter may be different).

## Try It Out — Getting a Valid Record Count

First start out by creating a simple recordset and select all of the records from a table. Before opening the recordset make sure the CursorLocation is set to 2 (adUseServer).

```
<%@ Language=VBScript %>
<HTML>
<HEAD>
<META NAME="GENERATOR" Content="Microsoft Visual Studio 6.0">
</HEAD>
<BODY>

<%
   Dim objRec
   Set objRec = Server.CreateObject("ADODB.Recordset")
   objRec.CursorLocation = 2 'adUseServer
   objRec.Open "SELECT * FROM authors", "DSN=MyDSN "
   Response.Write "RecordCount: " & objRec.RecordCount
%>

</BODY>
</HTML>
```

The code example above will return a record count of –1 because the location of the cursor is set to use the server.

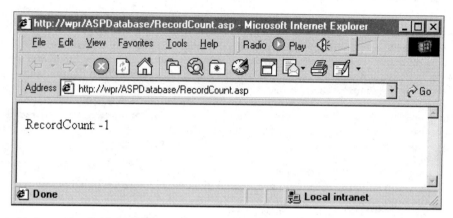

To solve this issue simply change the cursor location to use the client, as noted above. The code for this is in RecordCount.asp.

```
<%@ Language=VBScript %>
<HTML>
<HEAD>
<META NAME="GENERATOR" Content="Microsoft Visual Studio 6.0">
</HEAD>
<BODY>

<%
  Dim objRec
  Set objRec = Server.CreateObject("ADODB.Recordset")
  objRec.CursorLocation = 3 'adUseClient
  objRec.Open "SELECT * FROM authors", "DSN=MyDSN "
  Response.Write "RecordCount: " & objRec.RecordCount
%>

</BODY>
</HTML>
```

This results in the following:

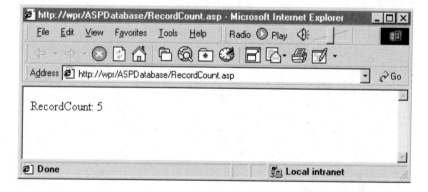

# Empty HTML Table Cells

Generating HTML tables is a very common feature of many ASP pages. HTML tables allow the data to be displayed in a very user-friendly manner. However, there is one small detail that will make an HTML table appear very strange, and that is a cell with no text. When a cell is built with no text between the <TD> and </TD> tags, the indented field disappears, as you can see below:

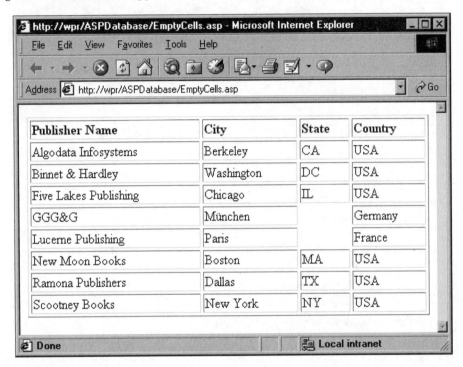

To solve this issue and make the cells appear the same, place an " " character in the empty cells. The " " character tells the browser on the client to insert a space into the cell as it is processing the HTML. The browser is basically trimming the context of the cell before displaying it to the user. One might think that simply adding a regular space character in front of the </TD> might solve the issue, but it doesn't. To make the cell appear you need to insert an HTML special character such as   or some visible text.

The following screenshot shows a table where   has been added before the </TD> tag, so that every cell ends in a space:

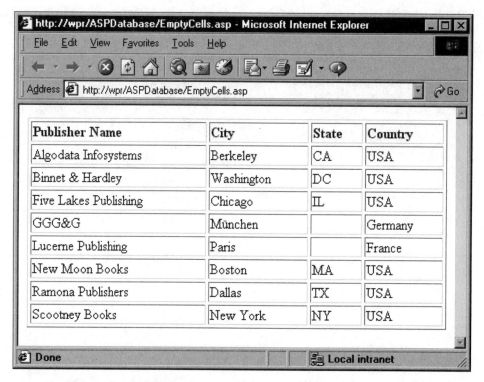

Here is our code which can be found in EmptyCells.asp.

```
<%@ Language=VBScript %>
<HTML>
<HEAD>
<META NAME="GENERATOR" Content="Microsoft Visual Studio 6.0">
</HEAD>
<BODY>

<%
  Dim objConn
  Dim objRec

  Set objConn = Server.CreateObject("ADODB.Connection")
  objConn.ConnectionString = "DSN=Pubs"
  objConn.Open

  Set objRec = Server.CreateObject("ADODB.Recordset")
  Set objRec.ActiveConnection = objConn
  objRec.Source = "SELECT pub_name, city, state, country FROM " & _
          "Publishers ORDER BY pub_name"
  objRec.Open
%>

<TABLE BORDER="1" CELLPADDING="1" CELLSPACING="3" WIDTH="100%">
<THEAD>
  <TR>
```

```
      <TD><STRONG>Publisher Name</STRONG></TD>
      <TD><STRONG>City</STRONG></TD>
      <TD><STRONG>State</STRONG></TD>
      <TD><STRONG>Country</STRONG></TD>
   </TR>
</THEAD>

<%
  Do Until objRec.EOF
    Response.Write "<TR>" & vbCrLf
    Response.Write "<TD>" & objRec("pub_name") & " </TD>" & vbCrLf
    Response.Write "<TD>" & objRec("city") & " </TD>" & vbCrLf
    Response.Write "<TD>" & objRec("state") & " </TD>" & vbCrLf
    Response.Write "<TD>" & objRec("country") & " </TD>" & vbCrLf
    Response.Write "</TR>" & vbCrLf
    objRec.MoveNext
  Loop
%>

</TABLE>
</BODY>
</HTML>
```

Another possible way to solve this issue is to build a function on the ASP page that expects a variable holding a string. If the string is Null or has a length of zero it returns a string with a value of " ", otherwise it returns back the string that was sent in.

```
'server-side function to check for empty/null strings
Function CheckString(strValue)
  If Len(strValue & "") = 0 Then
    CheckString = " "
  Else
    CheckString = strValue
  End If
End Function
```

The code sample above is a function used to analyze the data that is read from the recordset and determines whether or not a   character is necessary. This way of solving the issue is better because it only adds a   character if needed, however it uses an extra method call that can slow down performance.

# Multiple Recordsets

ADO has the ability to return multiple recordsets from a single SQL statement. For example, the statement "SELECT * FROM TableA; SELECT * FROM TableB", will return two recordsets. All that is needed to return two or more recordsets is a semicolon between the individual statements. Another way to return multiple recordsets is from complex stored procedures.

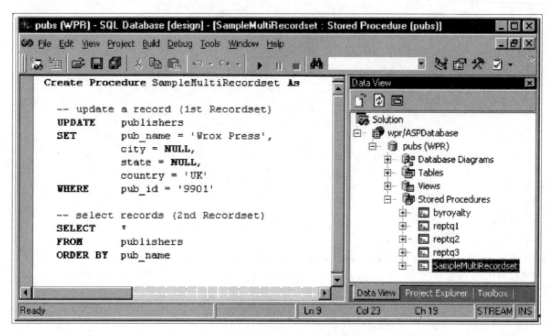

The above screen shot is an example of a stored procedure that returns multiple recordsets. The first recordset is actually an UPDATE statement and the second is a normal SELECT statement. This type of stored procedure is not uncommon, and as projects grow they can get much more complex.

When a stored procedure that returns multiple recordsets is called, it may not be obvious how to access all of the data. Even more so, the ASP developer might not be aware of the internal code of the stored procedure, especially if the roles of the ASP developer and the database administrator of the project have been separated among two or more people.

If the sample stored procedure (SampleMultiRecordset) is called, and the data is displayed the normal way, the recordset will be closed. When code is expecting an open recordset it can either result in no data or even an error.

To prevent this error from happening, simply check the state of the recordset by looking at the value of the State property. Here are the possible values for this property:

| Value | Description | Constant Name |
|-------|-------------|---------------|
| 0 | The object is closed. This is the default. | adStateClosed |
| 1 | The object is open. | adStateOpen |
| 2 | The object is connecting | adStateConnecting |
| 4 | The object is executing a command | adStateExecuting |
| 8 | Rows of the recordset are being fetched. | adStateFetching |

You can find the constants defined in the file `adovbs.inc`. In this case we would want to check the recordset is open:

```
If objRS.State = 1 Then 'adStateOpen ...
```

This will now prevent any errors, but it still doesn't display all of the data that the stored procedure returns. To get to the next recordset the `NextRecordset` routine must be called:

```
Set objRS = objRS.NextRecordset
```

If this returns `Nothing` then there are no more recordsets, otherwise it returns a reference to the next recordset.

## Try It Out — Dealing with Multiple Recordsets

Start by creating a stored procedure similar to the one in the beginning of this section. The stored procedure should update or insert a record, and then return a recordset by selecting the data from the data source.

Then develop a simple ASP page to access the stored procedure and display the data in the recordset without calling the `NextRecordset` method. The code is in `MultiRecError.asp`:

```
<%@ Language=VBScript %>
<HTML>
<HEAD>
<META NAME="GENERATOR" Content="Microsoft Visual Studio 6.0">
</HEAD>
<BODY>

<%
  Dim objConn
  Dim objComm
  Dim objRS
  Dim objField
  Dim strTextToWrite
  Dim lngRSCount

  'connect to the database
  Set objConn = Server.CreateObject("ADODB.Connection")
  objConn.ConnectionString = "Provider=sqloledb;Data Source=wpr;" & _
    "Initial Catalog=pubs;User Id=sa;Password=;"
  objConn.Open

  'call the stored proc that returns multiple recordsets
  Set objComm = Server.CreateObject("ADODB.Command")
  Set objComm.ActiveConnection = objConn

  'Call the stored proc
  objComm.CommandText = "SampleMultiRecordset"
  objComm.CommandType = 4 'adCmdStoredProc
  Set objRS = objComm.Execute

  lngRSCount = 0

  'Display the recordset
  Response.Write "<TABLE BORDER=1 CELLPADDING=1 CELLSPACING=3>" & vbCrLf
  Response.Write "<TR><TD COLSPAN=" & objRS.Fields.Count & _
    "><STRONG>" & objRS.Source & "</STRONG></TD></TR>" & vbCrLf
```

```
  Response.Write "<TR><TD>"
  strTextToWrite = objRS.GetString(,,"</TD><TD>","</TD></TR>" & _
    vbCrLf & "<TR><TD>"," ")
  'Trim off the last 8 characters
  Response.Write Left(strTextToWrite,Len(strTextToWrite) - 8)

  Response.Write "</TABLE>" & vbCrLf
  Response.Write "<P>" & vbCrLf
  lngRSCount = lngRSCount + 1

  'Clean up
  Set objField = Nothing
  If Not objRS Is Nothing Then If objRS.State = 1 Then objRS.Close
  Set objRS = Nothing
  Set objComm = Nothing
  If Not objConn Is Nothing Then If objConn.State = 1 Then objConn.Close
  Set objConn = Nothing
%>

</BODY>
</HTML>
```

The ASP page should look like the code above and generate an error like the following:

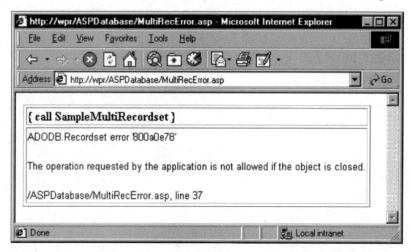

The following code is a full example of how to call the `SampleMultiRecordset` stored procedure and display the data in all of the recordsets no matter how many recordsets are returned, and no matter what they are holding. The code is in the file `MultiRecordsets.asp`:

```
<%@ Language=VBScript %>
<HTML>
<HEAD>
<META NAME="GENERATOR" Content="Microsoft Visual Studio 6.0">
</HEAD>
<BODY>

<%
  Dim objConn
  Dim objComm
  Dim objRS
  Dim objField
  Dim strTextToWrite
  Dim lngRSCount
```

```
'connect to the database
Set objConn = Server.CreateObject("ADODB.Connection")
objConn.ConnectionString = "Provider=sqloledb;Data Source=wpr;" & _
  "Initial Catalog=pubs;User Id=sa;Password=;"
objConn.Open

'call the stored proc that returns multiple recordsets
Set objComm = Server.CreateObject("ADODB.Command")
Set objComm.ActiveConnection = objConn

'Call the stored proc
objComm.CommandText = "SampleMultiRecordset"
objComm.CommandType = 4 'adCmdStoredProc
Set objRS = objComm.Execute

lngRSCount = 0

'Display all of the different recordset in the recordset object
Do Until objRS Is Nothing
  Response.Write "<TABLE BORDER=1 CELLPADDING=1 CELLSPACING=3>" & vbCrLf
  Response.Write "<TR><TD COLSPAN=" & objRS.Fields.Count & _
    "><STRONG>" & objRS.Source & "</STRONG></TD></TR>" & vbCrLf
  If objRS.State = 1 Then 'adStateOpen
    Response.Write "<TR><TD>"
    strTextToWrite = objRS.GetString(,,"</TD><TD>","</TD></TR>" & _
      vbCrLf & "<TR><TD>"," ")
    'Trim off the last 8 characters
    Response.Write Left(strTextToWrite,Len(strTextToWrite) - 8)
  End If
  Response.Write "</TABLE>" & vbCrLf
  Response.Write "<P>" & vbCrLf
  lngRSCount = lngRSCount + 1
  Set objRS = objRS.NextRecordset
Loop

Response.Write "There were " & lngRSCount & " recordsets." & vbCrLf

'Clean up
Set objField = Nothing
If Not objRS Is Nothing Then If objRS.State = 1 Then objRS.Close
Set objRS = Nothing
Set objComm = Nothing
If Not objConn Is Nothing Then If objConn.State = 1 Then objConn.Close
Set objConn = Nothing
%>

</BODY>
</HTML>
```

The code above starts by opening a connection to the pubs database and calls the stored procedure. Next the code enters a Do Until...Loop until the recordset is nothing. Within the loop, the code builds an HTML table displaying all of the data within the current recordset. Once the table is built, the code moves to the next recordset by calling the NextRecordset routine. If the NextRecordset routine returns a recordset, the code stays in the loop and displays the new recordset, else it drops out of the loop and cleans up the ADO variables used.

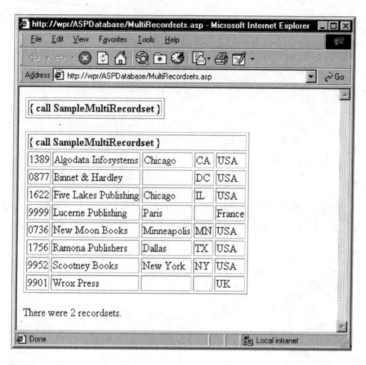

This screen shot is what the code example above generates for the user. Note that two recordsets are displayed. The first one is from the update statement and contains no records, while the second is a result from the select statement, which does contain data.

Not all data source providers support multiple recordsets. Reference any provider documentation to see if it supports multiple recordset, or try a quick sample. If the provider doesn't support multiple recordsets an error will be displayed stating so.

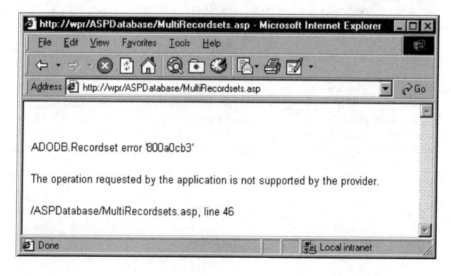

# Refreshing Command Objects

Utilizing an instance of the Command object to access data is generally faster and more efficient than simply concatenating a SQL statement into a single string and using the Recordset object. However, calling stored procedures that have a lot of parameters can be challenging to program, especially if they have uncommon data types.

The following screen shot displays a stored procedure (AddAuthor) that inserts a record into the author table in the pubs database. The stored procedure expects nine parameters, one of which is of type bit.

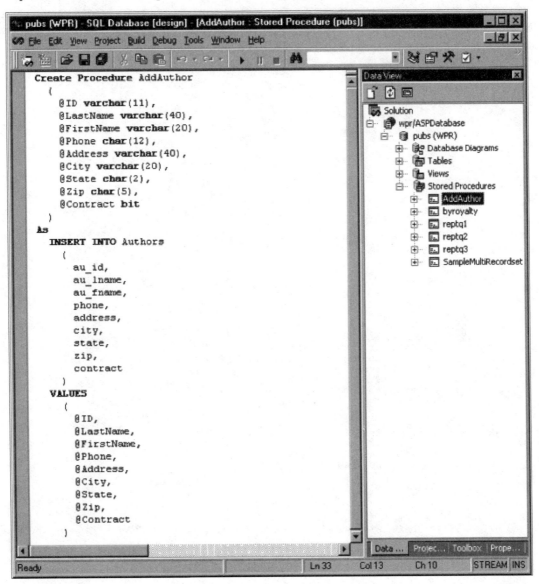

Accessing this stored procedure can be hard to code because of its number of parameters and various data types. One way to make the programming a little easier is to use the `Refresh` method belonging to the `Parameters` collection of the `Command` object. The `Refresh` method looks at the `ConnectionString` and `CommandText` properties, and the `Parameters` collection, and then queries the data source to fill in any missing or inaccurate information in the `Parameters` collection.

Even though the `Refresh` method can be used in production code, it is strongly advised to only use it when developing or debugging. By calling this method an unnecessary round trip is made from the web server service to the database service (across processes and usually across machines).

## Try It Out — Refreshing the Command Objects

Start out by creating a stored procedure similar to the one in the beginning of the section which contains multiple parameters. Next create an ASP page to call upon this stored procedure. The code for this file is in file `RefreshCommand.asp`.

```asp
<%@ Language=VBScript %>
<HTML>
<HEAD>
<META NAME="GENERATOR" Content="Microsoft Visual Studio 6.0">
</HEAD>
<BODY>

<%
  Dim objConn
  Dim objComm
  Dim objPara

  'connect to the database
  Set objConn = Server.CreateObject("ADODB.Connection")
  objConn.ConnectionString = "DSN=Pubs"
  objConn.Open

  'get the information about the stored proc
  Set objComm = Server.CreateObject("ADODB.Command")
  Set objComm.ActiveConnection = objConn
  objComm.CommandText ="AddAuthor"
  objComm.CommandType = 4 'adCmdStoredProc
  objComm.Parameters.Append objComm.CreateParameter("@ID",adVariant)
  objComm.Parameters.Append objComm.CreateParameter("@LastName",adVariant)
  objComm.Parameters.Append objComm.CreateParameter("@FirstName",adVariant)
  objComm.Parameters.Append objComm.CreateParameter("@Phone",adVariant)
  objComm.Parameters.Append objComm.CreateParameter("@Address",adVariant)
  objComm.Parameters.Append objComm.CreateParameter("@City",adVariant)
  objComm.Parameters.Append objComm.CreateParameter("@State",adVariant)
  objComm.Parameters.Append objComm.CreateParameter("@Zip",adVariant)
  objComm.Parameters.Append objComm.CreateParameter("@Contract",adVariant)
  objComm.Parameters.Refresh
%>

  <TABLE BORDER=1 CELLPADDING=1 CELLSPACING=3 WIDTH=100%>
    <TR>
      <TD COLSPAN=3><%=objComm.CommandText%></TD>
    </TR>
    <TR>
      <TD><STRONG>Name</STRONG></TD>
      <TD><STRONG>Type</STRONG></TD>
      <TD><STRONG>Size</STRONG></TD>
    </TR>
```

```
<%
  For Each objPara in objComm.Parameters
    Response.Write "<TR><TD>" & objPara.Name & "</TD>" & vbCrLf
    Response.Write "<TD>" & objPara.Type & "</TD>" & vbCrLf
    Response.Write "<TD>" & objPara.Size & "</TD>" & vbCrLf
  Next
%>

</TABLE>
</BODY>
</HTML>
```

The code above starts by connecting to the data source. Next the basic information about the stored procedure is filled into the instance of the command class. Even though none of the parameters are of data type variant, initially setting them to this type provides ADO with enough information to look up the real data types and other settings.

The following screen shot is what the code above generated. Notice that the command text changed to signify the parameters, and each `Parameter` object now holds the proper data types and size. Also notice that ADO added a parameter called RETURN_VALUE with a data type of 3 (adInteger) and a size of zero. This parameter is always the first parameter in every `Command` object and is where a recordset is placed.

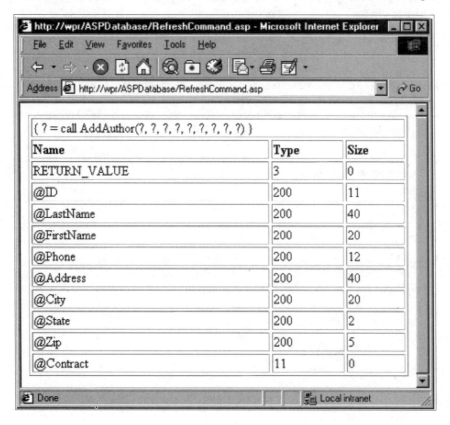

| Name | Type | Size |
|------|------|------|
| RETURN_VALUE | 3 | 0 |
| @ID | 200 | 11 |
| @LastName | 200 | 40 |
| @FirstName | 200 | 20 |
| @Phone | 200 | 12 |
| @Address | 200 | 40 |
| @City | 200 | 20 |
| @State | 200 | 2 |
| @Zip | 200 | 5 |
| @Contract | 11 | 0 |

`{ ? = call AddAuthor(?, ?, ?, ?, ?, ?, ?, ?, ?) }`

# Additional Books

For further information, and more advanced topics, you may want to refer to additional books. Using ADO in ASP pages brings together several important techniques: HTML, ASP, ADO and a database management system. Most ASP/ADO programmers have a half dozen coffee-stained books on their desk. Here are the ones which I keep within an arm's length and which I recommend to my students.

You are probably one of the tens of thousands of programmers that have read *Beginning Active Server Pages 2.0* (ISBN 1-861001-34-7). That is the best introduction to this study in that it covers the exact ASP topics that are considered the prerequisites for this book.

If you forget the HTML tags as frequently as I do you will want a copy of the *Instant HTML Programmers Reference* (ISBN 1-861001-56-8). This nugget packs all the tags along with an example for each and browser compatibility charts into a size which fits right into that space under the monitor.

You may also have studied *Professional Active Server Pages 2.0* (ISBN 1-861001-26-6) which spends time on more advanced topics than this book, including scaling to enterprise-wide data and Microsoft Index Server. Pro ASP also gives you more ASP tools against which you can apply your ADO techniques. If you have already crushed a few mice under toppling stacks of books consider the more succinct *ASP 2.0 Programmers Reference* (ISBN 1-861002-45-9) which gives you just the methods, properties, parameters and useful constants in a compact format. For under $20, you can't beat it.

An important feature of this book is that it covers only those topics that are most useful for beginners. If you want exhaustive coverage of the ADO methods and properties I suggest the ADO Programmer's References. David Sussman and Alex Homer's *ADO 2.0 Programmer's Reference* (ISBN 1-861001-83-5) is a handy volume, which lists the methods, properties, events and parameters in every corner of ADO for under $20. The ADO 2.1 version is 200 pages longer to cover the new features (ISBN 1-861002-68-8).

Finally *ADO RDS Programming with ASP* (ISBN 1-861001-64-9) provides a further step up in coding with ADO, including topics such as data shaping.

# Summary

This chapter touched on issues from null values in recordsets to tricks for developing, to complex stored procedures. No single chapter, or single book for that matter, could talk about all of the issues and problems ASP developers are faced with when using ADO, but hopefully this will help solve some of the most common ones that arise.

# Quiz

**1.** What is used to insert a space into an empty cell in an HTML table?

**2.** How does one determine if there are any more recordsets in a recordset object?

**3.** What cursor location must be used in order for the `RecordCount` property to return a valid record count?

**4.** What are the two cursor types that will allow the `RecordCount` property to return a valid record count?

# Quiz answers

1.   

2.  If the `NextRecordset` method of the `Recordset` object returns nothing, there are no more recordsets

3.  Client-side (`adUseClient`)

4.  `adOpenKeyset` or `adOpenStatic`

Setup cannot install system files or update shared files if the files are in use. Before c
any open applications.

WARNING: This program is protected by copyright law and international treaties.

You may install Microsoft Data Access 2.1 on a single computer. Some Microsoft products
with additional rights, which are stated in the End User License Agreement included with y

Please take a moment to read the End User License Agreement now. It contains all of the te
conditions that pertain to this software product. By choosing to continue, you indicate accept
these terms.

Exit Setup

Continue

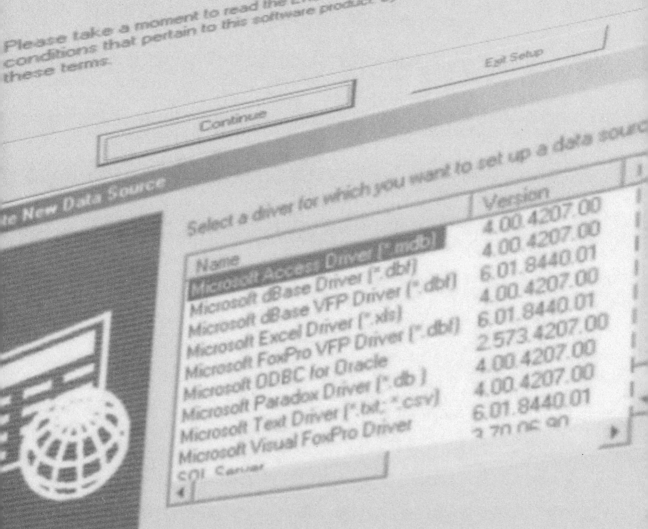

te New Data Source

Select a driver for which you want to set up a data sourc

| Name | Version |
| --- | --- |
| Microsoft Access Driver (*.mdb) | 4.00.4207.00 |
| Microsoft dBase Driver (*.dbf) | 4.00.4207.00 |
| Microsoft dBase VFP Driver (*.dbf) | 6.01.8440.01 |
| Microsoft Excel Driver (*.xls) | 4.00.4207.00 |
| Microsoft FoxPro VFP Driver (*.dbf) | 6.01.8440.01 |
| Microsoft ODBC for Oracle | 2.573.4207.00 |
| Microsoft Paradox Driver (*.db ) | 4.00.4207.00 |
| Microsoft Text Driver (*.txt; *.csv) | 4.00.4207.00 |
| Microsoft Visual FoxPro Driver | 6.01.8440.01 |
| SQL Server | 3.70.06.90 |

Cancel

# Performance Testing and Performance Improvements

*What is the essence of great power? Speed, Silence and Space.*

## Introduction

Big things are made up of lots of little things.

In any application, performance is an important issue, especially in a network application, and *most* especially in an Internet (the Mother of all networks!) application. The more simultaneous users you have, the more those little chunks of time, processor, and memory add up. Consider the Microsoft web site, which has three million visitors a day. Imagine what a tiny one per cent improvement in performance would mean on a site like that.

This chapter will discuss performance issues related to ADO, particularly in regards to Internet ASP applications. We will talk about some testing software that is readily available, and will also create some of our own, using ASP and ADO. By the time you've finished this chapter, you will be able to develop your own performance-testing web pages, and be able to use some of the software that comes with your own operating system.

We will discuss the various techniques for working with databases, and which techniques are more and less efficient in various situations. And we will discuss the advantages and disadvantages of using Access and SQL Server databases, in terms of performance.

## Server Issues

We are only briefly going to touch on server issues. Most of the time, these are out of control of the developer. If you are fortunate enough to have your own web server, some of this information may come in handy. You will find more details about tuning performance on the server in the IIS help files.

# Processor Bottlenecks

When the CPU usage of your system is very high, and the network card usage is well below capacity, you have what is known as a **processor bottleneck**. Solutions to processor bottlenecking include:

❑ upgrading the CPU

❑ adding another CPU to the system

❑ replicating web sites

❑ running web sites from more than one computer

❑ moving processor-intensive web applications (such as database applications) to a different computer

ADO is a processor-intensive technology! In general, dual processors are recommended for servers running ADO web applications.

# Processor Throttling (IIS 5 only)

When running multiple web sites on a single computer (as is the case with most hosting services), you can use **processor throttling** to prevent a site from "hogging" the processor, and slowing or preventing access to other web sites in the process. Out-of-process applications such as CGI (Common Gateway Interface), ISAPI (Internet Server Application Program Interfaces), and WAM (Web Application Manager – an Internal IIS COM component that controls loading and interfacing with ISAPI DLLs – this can be run in-process or out-of-process), can cause the processor to spend an inordinate amount of time serving one request, thereby holding up the line for other requests on the network.

When processor throttling is enabled for a web site, the processor usage is monitored by the system. The Server Administrator sets the maximum amount of allowable processor time for out-of-process applications to use during a specific time interval. If the amount of time is exceeded, an event log is written. If the amount of time is exceeded by 150 per cent, the out-of-process applications for that web site have their CPU priority set to idle. This is the lowest priority setting that an application can have without being totally halted. If it is exceeded by 200 per cent, all out-of-process applications for that web site are halted for the time interval specified in the processor throttling settings.

# Connection Pooling

**Connection pooling** enables a middle-tier application to share and maintain database connections. Through IIS, you can enable connection pooling for a web site, and set the duration for the timeout of the connection.

*Note: IIS 4 and 5 processes always use connection pooling. With IIS 3, you must set this explicitly.*

Since your application will almost always be logging into the system with the same user name and password (set by the connection string you specify in your scripting), the connection can be shared.

Explicitly destroying the connection in your code is also excellent practice. This saves resources by destroying the connection immediately, rather than waiting for the connection to time out. An ADO connection will destroy itself based upon several different conditions, such as idle time, and being "out of scope" (which it is once the ASP page has been processed and delivered). While explicitly closing and destroying the connection consumes resources as well, I believe that this process improves performance overall on the server, by freeing up resources quickly.

# Tools – Packaged Operating System

NT Server comes packaged with a number of tools that can help you to monitor (for diagnostic purposes) performance on your system. Some of these tools are also available for NT Workstation, as well as Windows 98. Let's take a look at some of these.

## System Monitor (Windows 9x)

This is a tool for monitoring the activity and performance of any number of objects on your system. It monitors **counters** on your system, at intervals which you specify. You can select the objects and the counters that are monitored, and there are many to select from. Some of the most useful objects that you can choose will include your Processor, Memory, Internet Information Services, and Web Services. You can select from a variety of counters in any of these and many more services. A few are shown below:

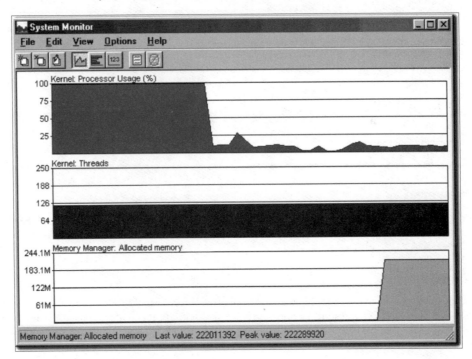

## Performance Monitor

Performance Monitor is similar to System Monitor, but has additional capacities, such as the ability to generate **logs** and **alerts**. A log is similar to what you see in the monitor itself, but is saved to a file that you can refer to later. An alert can react to the counter value in a wide variety of ways. With Performance Monitor, you can view any number of counters in a single pane, such as in the illustration below:

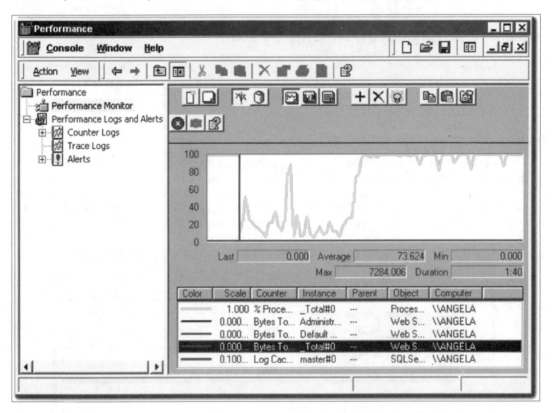

## Event Viewer

Windows NT includes an event-monitoring service that logs events of numerous types, generated by the various applications and services on the system and network. You can use the Event Viewer to examine these logs.

## Task Manager

Task Manager is used to view ongoing tasks and threads. It can be used to temporarily set the priority of processes (it does not save the settings once the process is ended). It can also be used to view memory and processor usage in real time, but does not log or track this information as the System Monitor or Performance Monitor does.

### Network Monitor

Network Monitor can be used to monitor information on traffic to and from a computer. You can also use it to view header information included in HTTP and FTP requests to your server. Network Monitor captures **frames** (individual packets of data transmitted over the network), and you can filter the protocols captured, as well as view the data transmitted via those protocols.

## Tools – Wcat

Wcat (**W**eb **c**apacity **a**nalysis **t**ool), a free download located at `http://msdn.microsoft.com/workshop/server/toolbox/wcat.asp`, and available in the IIS 4 Resource kit, runs simulated workloads on client-server configurations. You can use it to test the response of your server to HTTP requests, requests for Active Server Pages, SSL (Secure Sockets Layer, used to encrypt data transmissions), and a lot more.

By using this tool repeatedly, and tweaking your hardware and software configuration, you can fine-tune the performance of your system, optimizing for the particular needs of your web application(s). It comes with a number of prepared simulations, but you can create your own as well.

Wcat can be used on Windows 95/98 and NT platforms, and can be used with most Internet web servers, at least those that run on Microsoft Windows platforms. Another tool available is the Microsoft Web Application Stress Tool (aka Homer), which can be found at `http://homer.rte.microsoft.com`. It is designed for stress testing ASP applications.

# Database Issues

## Access vs. SQL Server

SQL Server was developed with the Internet in mind, although it can certainly shine in any kind of network situation. It is a database *server*, rather than a stand-alone database. It can be accessed through virtually any kind of network connection, including TCP/IP. The maximum size of a SQL Server database is 1, 048,516 *terabytes* (a terabyte is 1,000 gigabytes), meaning that it has virtually no size limitation. The maximum number of concurrent client connections per server is 32,767. However, by using replication, you can link several SQL Servers together to increase the number of concurrent client connections to any amount you wish.

SQL Server can be used to create stored procedures that can accept parameters, and perform a multitude of tasks. The stored procedures are cached, which increases performance. In general, SQL Server yields much faster results than Access, and it can be configured to perform a great number of maintenance activities automatically. It even includes its own e-mail server.

SQL Server can be *administered remotely* (from a computer over the Internet, for example) using SQL Enterprise Manager, and can be *accessed remotely* by other database applications via ODBC. In other words, an ODBC System DSN to access a SQL Server database doesn't have to reside on the same LAN as the database itself. It can reside anywhere that has access to the SQL Server via TCP/IP (in other words, anywhere in the world that has a connection to the Internet). That is because SQL Server is a client-server Database Management System, designed as a literal "database server", just as Internet Information Server is a "web server". It can be accessed via TCP/IP, as the SQL Server can have its own permanent IP address on the Internet.

Microsoft Access was originally developed as a straightforward desktop database application. It was not designed with the Internet in mind and is not *scaleable*. As such, it has a number of liabilities, which you should consider when designing an Internet database application. The maximum size of an Access database is 2 gigabytes, which isn't bad. However, the maximum number of concurrent users is 255, and in many cases you'd be lucky to manage 20 users. That means trouble when your web site is popular. An Access database can't accept parameters with stored procedures via ODBC (you can pass parameters to stored *queries* in Access, but not to stored *procedures*). And the System DSN to access an Access database must reside on the same LAN as the database itself, as Access is a file-based DBMS (not a client-server application).

It does have several advantages over SQL Server, though. Access is much less expensive to purchase than SQL Server. It is part of Microsoft Office, which means that most people in business already have it. It uses much less RAM than SQL Server. You also need to own a copy of SQL Server and its Enterprise Manager, to administer a SQL Server database remotely. An Access database is a file, which can be uploaded and downloaded to the web server. A SQL Server database, while being a file, must remain in the SQL Server's database folder, and cannot be uploaded and downloaded.

You can work with a SQL Server database using Access, but your ability to administer the database is severely limited. You can do this by downloading the MS Access Upsizing tools, a free download from the Microsoft web site. With the SQL Server browser (one of the Upsizing tools), you can execute scripts to modify the SQL Server database. However, you must either have the scripts, or be able to write them using SQL Server Transact-SQL, the extended version of ANSI SQL that SQL Server supports. The Upsizing tool is shown below:

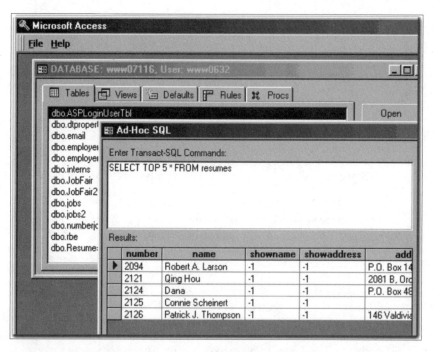

You can also create a System DSN that points to the remote SQL Server, create a database with Access, and create linked tables that allow you to manipulate the data contained in the SQL Server database through Access. But you can't use these linked tables to make changes in the database structure. However, Access 2000 does have some capacity to work with the structure of a SQL Server database.

Finally, you must host the web site on a WSP (Web-hosting Service Provider, also referred to as a hosting service) that supports SQL Server. This is also more expensive than hosting without it, due to the expense of SQL Server, and the level of training needed by the support personnel to administer it.

To conclude, if you *can* work with SQL Server, by all means do so. However, if you do not expect a lot of traffic on your web site, and do not expect it to grow significantly in the near future, you can certainly use Access.

# Indexing

Indexing is one *sure* way to speed up performance. An index is used by the database in much the same way that it is used in a book (like this one, for instance). It is a record of where information is kept. If you want to find something quickly, you look in the index.

When fields in the database are indexed, the database looks up the location of the data it wants in the index. Consider the following SQL statement:

```
SELECT * FROM profile WHERE email LIKE 'takempis@bellsouth.net'
```

If you were reading a book, and wanted to find all the references to "takempis@bellsouth.net", you would look in the index. The index stores the locations of all references. Similarly, when this field is indexed in a database, the database stores the locations of all fields with this value, in the index. Rather than having to go through the table record-by-record, reading every one, it simply pulls the information from the index.

When designing the database, be sure to index the fields that will be used in any WHERE clauses of your SQL statements. Only index the necessary fields, in order to preserve space and performance on the server, and to save time when the index may need to be updated.

# Coding Issues

Your coding is probably the most important aspect of optimizing performance, especially if you do not have the ability to administer the web server, or choose the database product that you are using. There are many ways to optimize your code, and we will discuss them in detail.

## Stored Procedures

If you are using SQL Server, you have the ability to create stored procedures that can perform a great variety of tasks. Because these stored procedures reside on the database, they can reduce the amount of bandwidth used in sending requests to the server. By creating stored procedures that execute multiple operations, you can execute multiple operations with a single request to the server.

With SQL Server, you have the ability to send parameters to the stored procedures as well, which enhances the ability to use them. Stored procedures are cached on the server, which makes multiple requests for them increasingly efficient. However, there are times when using a stored procedure is actually less efficient than sending a query to the server. When we look at our custom-built testing applications, we will get a closer look at this.

If you are using Access, you can use stored procedures that perform various operations as well. However, you can't send parameters to an Access stored procedure via ODBC. This is a definite drawback to Access. As stated earlier, you can send parameters to a stored query in Access, but the Access SQL language is severely limited compared to the SQL Server Transact-SQL language.

In ADO, you call stored procedures using the Command object. Consider the following code:

This is a SQL Server stored procedure:

```
CREATE PROCEDURE inserttest  AS

DECLARE @x AS int
DECLARE @mystr AS varchar(11)
DECLARE @newstr AS varchar(75)

SET @mystr = 'Newcategory'
SET @x = 0
WHILE @x < 500
BEGIN
   SET @newstr = @mystr + convert(varchar(4), @x)
   EXEC('INSERT INTO subcategories (Category, Subcategory) VALUES(''Facilities'', ''' +
@newstr  + ''' )')
SET @x = @x + 1
END
```

The ASP code to execute the stored procedure:

```
<%
   cstring = "DSN=psych;UID=takempis;PWD=knoxville;"
   Set cn = Server.CreateObject("ADODB.Connection")
   cn.Open cstring
   Set cmd = Server.CreateObject("ADODB.Command")
   ' Command Object code below
   cmd.ActiveConnection = cn
   cmd.CommandType = adCmdStoredProc
   cmd.CommandText = "inserttest"
   cmd.Execute
%>
```

The SQL Server stored procedure above is a test procedure that inserts 500 records into a database table. We will be using this stored procedure, and several others, later on in the testing section.

To execute a stored procedure, you first create an instance of the Command object, set the ActiveConnection property to an open Connection object, and then set the CommandType property of the Command object ("cmd") to adCmdStoredProc. After setting the CommandText property of the Command object to the name of the stored procedure, we use the execute method to execute the stored procedure. If the stored procedure returns a recordset, you can use the following to capture the recordset:

```
Set rs = cmd.Execute
```

Sending parameters to a stored procedure is done using the parameters collection of the Command object. Consider the following code:

The stored SQL Server procedure:

```
CREATE PROCEDURE paraminserttest

@mystr varchar(11)

AS

DECLARE @x AS int
DECLARE @newstr AS varchar(75)

SET @x = 0
WHILE @x < 500
BEGIN
  SET @newstr = @mystr + convert(varchar(4), @x)
  EXEC('INSERT INTO subcategories (Category, Subcategory) VALUES (''Facilities'', '''
+ @newstr + ''' )')
  SET @x = @x + 1
END
```

This is the ASP code to execute the procedure:

```
<%
  cstring = "DSN=psych;UID=takempis;PWD=knoxville;"

  Set cn = Server.CreateObject("ADODB.Connection")
  cn.Open cstring
  Set cmd = Server.CreateObject("ADODB.Command")
  cmd.ActiveConnection = cn
  cmd.CommandType = adCmdStoredProc
  cmd.CommandText = "paraminserttest"
  cmd.Parameters.Append cmd.CreateParameter("mystr", adVarChar, adParamInput, 11, _
    "MyParam")
  cmd.Execute
%>
```

*Note: You can use the* `Refresh` *method of the* `Command` *object's parameters collection to get the parameter information from the database. However, this adds a performance hit to the application, as a query must be sent to the database in order to get the parameter names and data types. For example, "*`cmd.Parameters.Refresh`*". Explicitly create your parameters whenever you can!*

The way to send parameters to a stored procedure is to *append* them to the parameters collection of the Command object. In this instance, I have optimized the code for this by creating the parameter and appending it at the same time. The Command object's CreateParameter() function takes five arguments (all optional):

1.  Name – the parameter name (mystr in the code above)

2.  Type – the data type of the parameter (default is adEmpty – no value specified)

3.  Direction – the direction (input/output) of the parameter. Defaults to adParamInput

4.  Size – the amount of storage to allocate for the parameter. Zero is the default

5.  Value – the value of the parameter

The parameter has to be created first, and then appended. The Append() method takes a parameter object as its argument. By using the CreateParameter() method as its argument (it returns a parameter object), I combined the two operations into one.

# BLOBS, MEMO, and Bit Fields

As we saw in Chapter 15, BLOB (**Binary Large Ob**ject) fields, such as Image fields in SQL Server, and OLE Object fields in Access, can consume a lot of resources when we get data from them. First, the data is not stored in the field itself, since the data can be of any length. Instead a pointer is stored in the field, which points to the location where the data is stored. Second, the data from a BLOB field must be read in chunks, rather than all at once, which adds to the performance hit. Finally, in an ASP page, the HTTP headers must be cleared and changed when streaming this data to the browser, which means that a separate page must be created for displaying the data.

The best way to store and fetch this type of data is to store the data in files on the server, and store the filenames in the database. See "The Easy Way" section of Chapter 15 for more details.

Memo fields ("Text" in SQL Server) are stored similarly. Since they can be of any length, a pointer is stored in the table and the data is stored elsewhere. Memo fields come in handy when you need to store a lot of text data, but they consume a lot of resources when you need to fetch data from them. In addition, the LIKE operator must be used in your WHERE clauses of SELECT statements to fetch the data, which is slower than the = operator.

BLOBS, Memo, and Bit ("Yes/No" in Access) fields are all non-indexable. Since these fields can't be indexed, using them in a WHERE clause of a SQL statement means that the entire table must be searched in order to retrieve the records desired. There are times when you must use these kinds of fields in a database, and there are times when you must use them as search criteria. Try to avoid it when you can.

# Storing ADO Objects in Sessions

Generally, this is *not* a good idea. From time to time, you may want to preserve a RecordSet or Connection object across pages, and it's tempting to store it in the Session object. Why is this a bad idea?

❑ You lose connection pooling. If connection pooling is set up on the server, the connection to the database used in this case cannot be shared.

❑ They consume session resources while they are in the session. By default, a session times out after 20 minutes. This means that the object can consume these resources for up to 20 minutes before being released. Programmatically reducing the session TimeOut property increases the chances of losing the object during user idle time (see next point).

❑ The object can be lost during the user idle time. Since the session times out after 20 minutes, if a user goes away from his browser for 20 minutes, the object is lost.

It is far better to open and close your connections between pages. While it might seem that it consumes more resources, in fact it consumes less.

# Optimizing Queries

Different types of SQL queries consume different amounts of resources. Queries that return very large recordsets, for example, should be avoided. If you are creating a search engine, you might want to consider limiting the number of records returned to a certain number, and use a "Next 10 Records" type of approach.

Using SELECT * is fine when you want to return all the fields in a table. But using it just to avoid typing in all the fields you want is plain lazy. If you only need some of the fields in the table, use a fields list in your SELECT statement, instead of *.

Certain operators also consume more resources than others. For example, LIKE consumes more than =. IN, NOT IN, and OR queries are heavy resource consumers. The != (Not Equal to) operator in SQL Server takes a particularly high load. Certain types of aggregate functions, such as SUM, should be avoided unless absolutely necessary.

## Query Analyzer (SQL Server)

If you have SQL Server, it comes with a great tool for optimizing your queries. It is called Query Analyzer, and not only can you *perform* queries with it, but as the name suggests, you can also *analyze* them.

Query Analyzer has a range of tools for analyzing the queries and scripts that you want to write or execute. "Show Execution Plan" can give you a graphic analysis of the execution plan required to execute your script. In the "Current Connection Options" menu item, you can select to display I/O statistics for running the query. This will display the amount of CPU usage required, and the time used to execute the query. An example is shown:

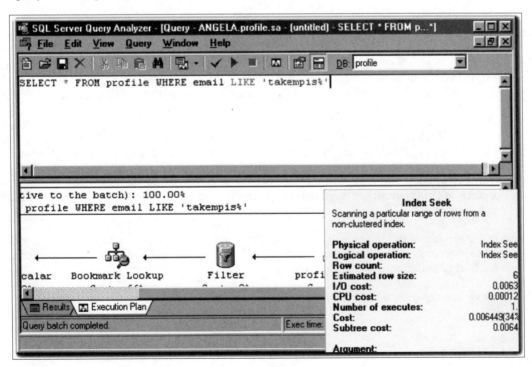

You can also have Query Analyzer perform an Index Analysis, which will recommend the best indexing structure for the table you are using, based upon the query or script that you are working with. If the analysis recommends a certain kind of indexing, it can build the indices for you on demand. (To do this you must be logged in as a user who has dbo permission for the database.)

## Cursor Types

ADO provides four types of cursors to work with:

❑ adOpenForwardOnly – movement through the recordset is forward only (of course!), and the recordset is read only.

❑ adOpenKeySet – returns a Keyset cursor. Data is up-to-date with the underlying source, but the number of records may not be. Movement forwards and backwards is supported.

❑ adOpenDynamic - data and records are both up-to-date, and movement both forwards and backwards is supported.

❑ adOpenStatic – the data is fixed at the time the cursor is created, with both forwards and backwards movement.

The forward only/read only cursor is the fastest by far, and is also the default cursor. Use it whenever possible. However, if you need to use the RecordCount property of the recordset, you need a cursor that supports movement backwards and forwards. Also, if you need to use bookmarks, the forward only cursor is not the right one to use.

# Testing ADO Performance With ASP - PerfTest

So far, we've discussed methods of analyzing your hardware, operating system, web server, and query performance. We've discussed analyzing your database needs, and how to optimize your database performance. We've discussed ways of fine-tuning your ADO code. But how do we *test* the ADO code?

We build ASP pages to test the code. How is this done? Well, the operative word here is "speed". The best way to test the optimization of a procedure is to see how long it takes to execute. And for that, we will use the VBScript Timer() function. This function returns a floating point number representing the number of seconds elapsed since midnight. By executing the Timer() function before beginning an operation, placing that value into a variable, performing the operation, and executing the Timer function again after the operation, we can subtract the beginning time from the ending time, and get the time it took for the operation to complete.

Note that the results of this testing will vary depending upon certain conditions on the machine, such as what other programs are running, network traffic, etc. These tests should be done numerous times, and under different conditions, to get the best results.

Once we've completed the testing, we will display the data in a bar chart, with the numbers shown under the bars.

We will be using the following ASP page to explain how to do this. The file is called
perftestAccess.asp:

```asp
<!--#INCLUDE FILE="ADOvbs.inc" -->
<! - adovbs is an include file containing all of the ADO enumerated constants. Since
there are quite a few of them, it is easier to refer to the various values of these
constants by their names, rather than by their numeric values -- >
<%
  Server.ScriptTimeout = 200
  cstring = "DSN=profile;"

  Dim nstart, nstop, spinsert, aspinsert, spselect, aspselect, spupdate
  Dim aspupdate, spparamselect, x, spdelete, aspdelete

  Set cn = Server.CreateObject("ADODB.Connection")
  cn.Open cstring
  Set cmd = Server.CreateObject("ADODB.Command")
  cmd.ActiveConnection = cn
  cmd.CommandType = adCmdStoredProc
  cmd.CommandText = "inserttest"
  nstart = Timer()
  For x = 0 to 500
    cmd.Execute
  Next
  nstop = Timer()
  spinsert = nstop - nstart

  cn.Close
  cn.Open cstring
  cmd.ActiveConnection = cn
  cmd.CommandText = "updatetest"
  nstart = Timer()
  For x = 0 to 500
    cmd.Execute
  Next
  nstop = Timer()
  spupdate = nstop - nstart

  cn.Close
  cn.Open cstring
  cmd.ActiveConnection = cn
  cmd.CommandText = "deletetest"
  nstart = Timer()
  For x = 0 to 500
    cmd.Execute
  Next
  nstop = Timer()
  spdelete = nstop - nstart

  cn.Close
  Set cmd = Nothing
  cn.Open cstring
  strSQL = "INSERT INTO profile ( fname, mname, lname, handle, " &_
           "usehandle, phone, email, password, address, city, " &_
           "state, zip, country, website, newsletter, job, hobbies, " &_
           "bio, other, [image], template, fontstyle, fontsize, " &_
           "fontcolor, bgimage, bgcolor, linkcolor, vlinkcolor, " &_
           "alinkcolor, tblbgimage, tblbgcolor, textcolor, tblborder ) " &_
       "VALUES ('Kevin', 'C', 'Spencer', 'Kevin', FALSE, " &_
           "'111-222-3333', 'takempis@aol.com', 'hello', 'address', " &_
           "'city', 'state', '11111', 'USA', 'http://www.takempis.com', " &_
           "TRUE, 'Internet Database Programming', 'programming', " &_
           "'I was born. I lived. I will die', 'whatever', 'none', " &_
           "1, 'Arial', 2, 29, 'rosesbg.jpg', 30, 29, 30, 28, " &_
           "'rosesbg.jpg', 18, 30, 0)"
```

```
    nstart = Timer()
    For x = 0 to 500
      cn.Execute(strSQL)
    Next

    nstop = Timer()
    aspinsert = nstop - nstart

    cn.Close
    cn.Open cstring
    strSQL = "UPDATE profile SET email = 'takempis@whatever.net' WHERE email LIKE _
                'takempis@aol.com'"
    nstart = Timer()
    For x = 0 to 500
      cn.Execute(strSQL)
    Next
    nstop = Timer()
    aspupdate = nstop - nstart

    cn.Close
    cn.Open cstring
    Set cmd = Server.CreateObject("ADODB.Command")
    cmd.ActiveConnection = cn
    cmd.CommandType = adCmdStoredProc
    cmd.CommandText = "paramselecttest"
    cmd.Parameters.Append cmd.CreateParameter("mystr", adVarChar, adParamInput, 75, _
                "takempis@whatever.net")
    nstart = Timer()
    Set rs = cmd.Execute
    While NOT rs.EOF
      rs.MoveNext
    Wend
    nstop = Timer()
    rs.Close
    cmd.Parameters.Delete("mystr")
    spparamselect = nstop - nstart

    cn.Close
    cn.Open cstring
    nstart = Timer()
    cn.Execute "DELETE FROM profile WHERE email LIKE 'takempis@whatever.net'"
    nstop = Timer()
    aspdelete = nstop - nstart

    cn.Close
    Set rs = Nothing
    Set cn = Nothing
    Set cmd = Nothing
%>
<HTML>

<HEAD>
<TITLE>Stored Procedures Performance Testing - Access</TITLE>
</HEAD>

<BODY>

<P ALIGN="center"><FONT SIZE="6" COLOR="#0000FF"><<PPerfTest - Stored Procedures vs.
ASP Scripting</STRONG></FONT></P>

<HR>
<DIV ALIGN="center"><CENTER>
```

```
<TABLE BORDER="0" CELLPADDING="0" BGCOLOR="#C0C0C0">
<TR>
<TD VALIGN="bottom" ALIGN="center"><IMG SRC="images/bluebar.gif"
WIDTH="60" HEIGHT="<%=FormatNumber((spinsert * 10), 0)%>" ALT="<%=spinsert%>"></TD>
<TD VALIGN="bottom" ALIGN="center"><IMG SRC="images/purplebar.gif"
WIDTH="60" HEIGHT="<%=FormatNumber((aspinsert * 10), 0)%>" ALT="<%=aspinsert%>"></TD>
<TD VALIGN="bottom" ALIGN="center"><IMG SRC="images/redbar.gif"
WIDTH="60" HEIGHT="<%=FormatNumber((spupdate * 10), 0)%>" ALT="<%=spupdate%>"></TD>
<TD VALIGN="bottom" ALIGN="center"><IMG SRC="images/pinkbar.gif"
WIDTH="60" HEIGHT="<%=FormatNumber((aspupdate * 10), 0)%>" ALT="<%=aspupdate%>"></TD>
<TD VALIGN="bottom" ALIGN="center"><IMG SRC="images/olivebar.gif"
WIDTH="60" HEIGHT="<%=FormatNumber((spdelete * 10), 0)%>" ALT="<%=spdelete%>"></TD>
<TD VALIGN="bottom" ALIGN="center"><IMG SRC="images/greenbar.gif"
WIDTH="60" HEIGHT="<%=FormatNumber((aspdelete * 10), 0)%>" ALT="<%=aspdelete%>"></TD>
<TD VALIGN="bottom" ALIGN="center"><IMG SRC="images/orangebar.gif"
WIDTH="60" HEIGHT="<%=FormatNumber((spparamselect * 10), 0)%>"
ALT="<%=spparamselect%>"></TD>
</TR>
<TR>
<TD VALIGN="top" ALIGN="center"><FONT FACE="Arial" SIZE="1"><%=spinsert%></FONT></TD>
<TD VALIGN="top" ALIGN="center"><FONT FACE="Arial" SIZE="1"><%=aspinsert%></FONT></TD>
<TD VALIGN="top" ALIGN="center"><FONT FACE="Arial" SIZE="1"><%=spupdate%></FONT></TD>
<TD VALIGN="top" ALIGN="center"><FONT FACE="Arial" SIZE="1"><%=aspupdate%></FONT></TD>
<TD VALIGN="top" ALIGN="center"><FONT FACE="Arial" SIZE="1"><%=spdelete%></FONT></TD>
<TD VALIGN="top" ALIGN="center"><FONT FACE="Arial" SIZE="1"><%=aspdelete%></FONT></TD>
<TD VALIGN="top" ALIGN="center"><FONT FACE="Arial"
SIZE="1"><%=spparamselect%></FONT></TD>
</TR>
</TABLE>
</CENTER></DIV>

<P ALIGN="center"><IMG SRC="images/bluebar.gif" ALT="Stored Procedure - Insert"
WIDTH="25" HEIGHT="5"> <FONT FACE="Arial" SIZE="2">Stored Procedure -
Insert</FONT><BR>
<IMG SRC="images/purplebar.gif" ALT="ASP Script - Insert" WIDTH="25" HEIGHT="5">
  <FONT FACE="Arial" SIZE="2">ASP Script - Insert</FONT><BR>
<IMG SRC="images/redbar.gif" ALT=" Stored Procedure - Update "WIDTH="25" HEIGHT="5">
  <FONT FACE="Arial" SIZE="2">Stored Procedure - Update</FONT><BR>
<IMG SRC="images/pinkbar.gif" ALT=" ASP Script - Update" WIDTH="25" HEIGHT="5">
  <FONT FACE="Arial" SIZE="2">ASP Script - Update</FONT><BR>
<IMG SRC="images/olivebar.gif" ALT=" Stored Procedure - Delete " WIDTH="25"
HEIGHT="5"> <FONT FACE="Arial" SIZE="2">Stored Procedure - Delete</FONT><BR>
<IMG SRC="images/greenbar.gif" ALT=" ASP Script - Delete " WIDTH="25" HEIGHT="5">
  <FONT FACE="Arial" SIZE="2">ASP Script - Delete<BR>
<IMG SRC="images/orangebar.gif" WIDTH="25" HEIGHT="5" ALT="Parameterized Query -
Select"> Parameterized Query - Select</FONT></P>
</BODY>
</HTML>
```

Now, let's have a look at the component parts of the page. What this page does is perform seven different tests, each comparing the results of using an Access stored query against sending the query to the database via hard-coded SQL in the ASP page. When it's run, the results look something like this:

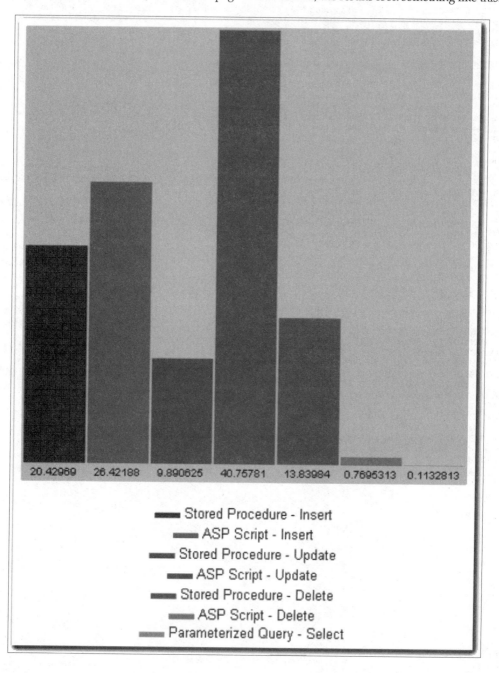

# How the Tests are Run

Let's start with the top of the page and work our way down, shall we?

```
<!--#INCLUDE FILE="ADOvbs.inc" -->
```

We include the ADOvbs.inc file, which has all of the ADO constant enumeration definitions. This is used for setting the CommandType property of the Command object, and the properties of the parameter we're going to create.

Next, we define the connection string and variables we're going to use.

```
<%
  Server.ScriptTimeout = 200
  cstring = "DSN=profile;"

  Dim nstart, nstop, spinsert, aspinsert, spselect, aspselect, spupdate
  Dim aspupdate, spparamselect, x, spdelete, aspdelete
```

Note that I've set the server's ScriptTimeout property to 200 (seconds). This is because each of these tests is designed to consume a good chunk of time. The default ScriptTimeout is 60. This script will take a couple of minutes to execute.

Why have we designed these operations to take a long time to execute? There are several reasons. We are creating loops that will execute 500 times, in order to get a good statistical result, and because we want the number of seconds elapsed to be measurable.

Now, if this next section of code looks familiar to you, it should. The code I gave for executing a stored procedure in a SQL Server database earlier is taken from another similar PerfTest page I created for testing SQL Server. We are going to start by performing a stored procedure (a stored query) in an Access database. Here's the query, which is stored in the Access profile.mdb database with the name inserttest:

```
INSERT INTO profile ( fname, mname, lname, handle, usehandle, phone, email,
              password, address, city, state, zip, country, website, newsletter,
              job, hobbies, bio, other, [image], template, fontstyle, fontsize,
              fontcolor, bgimage, bgcolor, linkcolor, vlinkcolor, alinkcolor,
              tblbgimage, tblbgcolor, textcolor, tblborder )
VALUES ('Kevin', 'C', 'Spencer', 'Kevin', FALSE, '111-222-3333', 'takempis@aol.com',
              'hello', 'address', 'city', 'state', '11111', 'USA',
              'http://www.takempis.com', TRUE, 'Internet Database
              Programming', 'programming', 'I was born. I lived. I will die',
              'whatever', 'none', 1, 'Arial', 2, 29, 'rosesbg.jpg', 30, 29, 30,
              28, 'rosesbg.jpg', 18, 30, 0);
```

And here's the part of the script that executes it:

```
Set cn = Server.CreateObject("ADODB.Connection")
cn.Open cstring
Set cmd = Server.CreateObject("ADODB.Command")
cmd.ActiveConnection = cn
cmd.CommandType = adCmdStoredProc
cmd.CommandText = "inserttest"
nstart = Timer()
For x = 0 to 500
  cmd.Execute
Next
nstop = Timer()
spinsert = nstop - nstart
```

The only difference between this code and the example code I gave you for the SQL Server stored procedure is the addition of the code that runs the timer. Note that I have put the code to run the stored query in a loop that executes 500 times. For SQL Server, you can put the code for the loop directly in the query. Here's an example from a similar stored procedure in a SQL Server database:

```
CREATE PROCEDURE inserttest  AS

DECLARE @x AS int
DECLARE @mystr AS varchar(11)
DECLARE @newstr AS varchar(75)

SET @mystr = 'Newcategory'
SET @x = 0
WHILE @x < 500
BEGIN
  SET @newstr = @mystr + convert(varchar(4), @x)
  EXEC('INSERT INTO subcategories (Category, Subcategory) VALUES (''Facilities'', '''
+ @newstr + ''' )')
  SET @x = @x + 1
END
```

Transact-SQL, the SQL language of SQL Server, is capable of doing a whole lot more than ANSI or Access SQL. You can, as you can see, store variables, perform loops, and dynamically create SQL statements by concatenating strings. We're using Access for this demonstration because SQL Server isn't widely used.

Each of the succeeding blocks of code performs similarly to the first. Here's the second, with my explanation of the code:

Access Stored Query:

```
UPDATE profile SET email = 'takempis@whatever.net'
WHERE email = 'takempis@aol.com';
```

ASP/ADO in page:

```
cn.Close
cn.Open cstring
cmd.ActiveConnection = cn
cmd.CommandText = "updatetest"
nstart = Timer()
For x = 0 to 500
  cmd.Execute
Next
nstop = Timer()
spupdate = nstop - nstart
```

Note that we close the connection, and then re-open it. This clears out the Command object and prevents any "leakage" from the data transmitted through the first connection. Occasionally, when you use the same connection to run more than one SQL statement without closing it in between, unexpected things can happen. Certain kinds of data may not be updated until the connection is closed. This behavior is erratic, but if the connection is closed and re-opened, all of the data will be up-to-date.

The code is almost exactly the same in every other aspect. The third block of code executes a stored query that deletes all of the records we've created and updated. It doesn't have a loop, since you wouldn't be deleting the same records 500 times.

Next, we create code that does the exact same thing, but using a query in the page:

```
cn.Close
Set cmd = Nothing
cn.Open cstring
strSQL = "INSERT INTO profile ( fname, mname, lname, handle, " &_
  "usehandle, phone, email, password, address, city, " &_
  "state, zip, country, website, newsletter, job, hobbies, " &_
  "bio, other, [image], template, fontstyle, fontsize, " &_
  "fontcolor, bgimage, bgcolor, linkcolor, vlinkcolor, " &_
  "alinkcolor, tblbgimage, tblbgcolor, textcolor, tblborder ) " &_
  "VALUES ('Kevin', 'C', 'Spencer', 'Kevin', FALSE, " &_
  "'111-222-3333', 'takempis@aol.com', 'hello', 'address', " &_
  "'city', 'state', '11111', 'USA',"'http://www.takempis.com', " &_
  "TRUE, 'Internet Database Programming', 'programming', " &_
  "'I was born. I lived. I will die', 'whatever', 'none', " &_
  "1, 'Arial', 2, 29, 'rosesbg.jpg', 30, 29, 30, 28, " &_
  "'rosesbg.jpg', 18, 30, 0)"
nstart = Timer()
For x = 0 to 500
  cn.Execute(strSQL)
Next
nstop = Timer()
aspinsert = nstop - nstart
```

Note that we destroy the Command object first. This is just good programming practice. Since we've executed all the stored procedures that we are going to on this page, we no longer need the Command object. We will be using the Connection object from here on in.

I created the query string before the loop, because the query string is created already in the stored query, and I want this to run in as close to the same fashion as the stored query, in order for the test to be accurate. All of the values inserted, updated, and deleted will be the same in all instances.

Next we update the table in the same fashion. After this, I added a parameterized query for demonstration purposes only, that selects the records we've created and updated, and moves through the recordset, one record at a time:

```
cn.Close
cn.Open cstring
Set cmd = Server.CreateObject("ADODB.Command")
cmd.ActiveConnection = cn
cmd.CommandType = adCmdStoredProc
cmd.CommandText = "paramselecttest"
cmd.Parameters.Append cmd.CreateParameter("mystr", adVarChar, adParamInput, 75, _
"takempis@whatever.net")
nstart = Timer()
Set rs = cmd.Execute
While NOT rs.EOF
  rs.MoveNext
Wend
 nstop = Timer()
rs.Close
cmd.Parameters.Delete("mystr")
spparamselect = nstop - nstart
```

I put this in simply to demonstrate a parameterized Access stored query. It doesn't really affect the testing properties of the page, since the page is for comparing stored procedures to hard-coded queries. However, I did display the results in the page.

Finally, I used a hard-coded DELETE SQL statement to delete the records we've created, cleaning up the database. The last block of code is cleanup code. It simply closes and destroys all objects left in the page:

```
  cn.Close
  Set rs = Nothing
  Set cn = Nothing
  Set cmd = Nothing
%>
```

Now we've stored all the values in variables, and we're ready to display the data in the page.

# Displaying the Results

"A picture is worth a thousand words." Therefore I wanted to be able to display the results graphically, so I created a bar chart. How did I do this? I used a series of graphics which I created. Each is a 5 X 25 pixel gif file of a single color.

In HTML, you can specify the width and height properties of an image in the image source tag. So, I created a table of two rows, set the horizontal alignment of both rows to center, and the vertical alignment of the top row to bottom. This way, when the table cells stretch to accommodate the height of the tallest image, all of the bars will sit on the bottom of the row, and stretch up. Here's the code for the table:

```
<DIV ALIGN="center"><CENTER>

<TABLE BORDER="0" CELLPADDING="0" BGCOLOR="#C0C0C0">
<TR>
<TD VALIGN="bottom" ALIGN="center"><IMG SRC="images/bluebar.gif"
WIDTH="60" HEIGHT="<%=FormatNumber((spinsert * 10), 0)%>" ALT="<%=spinsert%>"></TD>
<TD VALIGN="bottom" ALIGN="center"><IMG SRC="images/purplebar.gif"
WIDTH="60" HEIGHT="<%=FormatNumber((aspinsert * 10), 0)%>" ALT="<%=aspinsert%>"></TD>
<TD VALIGN="bottom" ALIGN="center"><IMG SRC="images/redbar.gif"
WIDTH="60" HEIGHT="<%=FormatNumber((spupdate * 10), 0)%>" ALT="<%=spupdate%>"></TD>
<TD VALIGN="bottom" ALIGN="center"><IMG SRC="images/pinkbar.gif"
WIDTH="60" HEIGHT="<%=FormatNumber((aspupdate * 10), 0)%>" ALT="<%=aspupdate%>"></TD>
<TD VALIGN="bottom" ALIGN="center"><IMG SRC="images/olivebar.gif"
WIDTH="60" HEIGHT="<%=FormatNumber((spdelete * 10), 0)%>" ALT="<%=spdelete%>"></TD>
<TD VALIGN="bottom" ALIGN="center"><IMG SRC="images/greenbar.gif"
WIDTH="60" HEIGHT="<%=FormatNumber((aspdelete * 10), 0)%>" ALT="<%=aspdelete%>"></TD>
<TD VALIGN="bottom" ALIGN="center"><IMG SRC="images/orangebar.gif"
WIDTH="60" HEIGHT="<%=FormatNumber((spparamselect * 10), 0)%>"
ALT="<%=spparamselect%>"></TD>
</TR>
<TR>
<TD VALIGN="top" ALIGN="center"><FONT FACE="Arial" SIZE="1"><%=spinsert%></FONT></TD>
<TD VALIGN="top" ALIGN="center"><FONT FACE="Arial" SIZE="1"><%=aspinsert%></FONT></TD>
<TD VALIGN="top" ALIGN="center"><FONT FACE="Arial" SIZE="1"><%=spupdate%></FONT></TD>
<TD VALIGN="top" ALIGN="center"><FONT FACE="Arial" SIZE="1"><%=aspupdate%></FONT></TD>
<TD VALIGN="top" ALIGN="center"><FONT FACE="Arial" SIZE="1"><%=spdelete%></FONT></TD>
<TD VALIGN="top" ALIGN="center"><FONT FACE="Arial" SIZE="1"><%=aspdelete%></FONT></TD>
<TD VALIGN="top" ALIGN="center"><FONT FACE="Arial"
SIZE="1"><%=spparamselect%></FONT></TD>
</TR>
</TABLE>
</CENTER></DIV>
```

See how the values of the variables create the height property of each graphic? I multiplied the values by 10, and used the FormatNumber() function to get rid of any decimal places. You don't want decimal places in the height property of an image! HTML doesn't support that. The second argument of the FormatNumber() function is the number of decimal places. The overall result is that the number of pixels is a manageable one for displaying the results.

# Analyzing the Results

The screenshot of the results above is from a test done on a Windows 98 machine with a Pentium 200 processor and 96 MB of RAM. The results are interesting. It seems to bear out the theory that stored procedures are more efficient for performing queries, with one exception: for some reason, the DELETE query in the stored procedure took much longer than the DELETE query that was hard-coded on the page.

Obviously, testing in different conditions would affect the results of the test. I have run some of these tests multiple times in order to compare results, and would recommend this to anyone that wants to test ADO. Here are some comparative results from other test pages I've created:

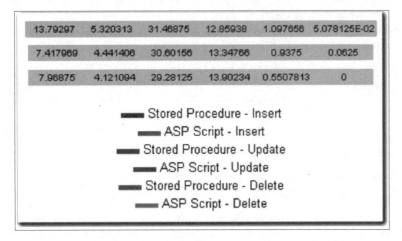

| 13.79297 | 5.320313 | 31.46875 | 12.85938 | 1.097656 | 5.078125E-02 |
| 7.417969 | 4.441406 | 30.60156 | 13.34766 | 0.9375 | 0.0625 |
| 7.96875 | 4.121094 | 29.28125 | 13.90234 | 0.5507813 | 0 |

▬▬ Stored Procedure - Insert
▬▬ ASP Script - Insert
▬▬ Stored Procedure - Update
▬▬ ASP Script - Update
▬▬ Stored Procedure - Delete
▬▬ ASP Script - Delete

I ran this test three times, with varying, but roughly proportionate results. This one yielded different results than expected. The stored procedures ran slower than the hard-coded ASP. I believe that this was due to the Transact-SQL that I used in the code, which assigned values to a number of variables, and had a loop in it (see the code for the inserttest stored procedure in the section above on stored procedures). In the results below, you can see that the stored procedures ran much faster. These used SELECT statements instead of INSERTs, UPDATEs, and DELETEs.

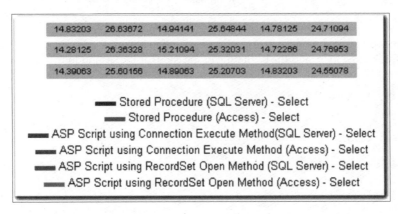

| 14.83203 | 26.63672 | 14.94141 | 25.64844 | 14.78125 | 24.71094 |
| 14.28125 | 26.36328 | 15.21094 | 25.32031 | 14.72266 | 24.76953 |
| 14.39063 | 25.60156 | 14.89063 | 25.20703 | 14.83203 | 24.55078 |

▬▬ Stored Procedure (SQL Server) - Select
▬▬ Stored Procedure (Access) - Select
▬▬ ASP Script using Connection Execute Method(SQL Server) - Select
▬▬ ASP Script using Connection Execute Method (Access) - Select
▬▬ ASP Script using RecordSet Open Method (SQL Server) - Select
▬▬ ASP Script using RecordSet Open Method (Access) - Select

The SELECT statements were simply SQL statements, without loops or variables:

```
CREATE PROCEDURE selecttest AS
SELECT * FROM Subcategories
```

One final note: you will notice that there are no demonstrations available for you to run tests on the SQL Server databases at Wrox. That is because these tests necessarily consume a *lot* of resources! All of the demonstrations and examples here use the Access profile.mdb database.

## Try it Out – Creating Your Own PerfTest Page

Now you're going to create your own PerfTest Active Server Page. This one will measure the difference in performance between the four different cursor types. It will use the profile.mdb file, and you will need to have set up an Access System DSN named profile that points to the database. If you don't have the database, it can be downloaded from the Wrox web site.

We are going to be creating recordsets with four different cursor types. If you remember, we are going to have to create the recordset first, set the CursorType property for it, and use the RecordSet.Open method to open the recordset. This is instead of using the Connection object's Execute method, which always returns a Forward Only cursor.

Since we are going to be setting the RecordSet object's CursorType property, we will need to include the ADOvbs.inc file. The complete code for this is available as file perftestcursor.asp.

Copy the following to the very first line at the top of your page:

```
<!--#INCLUDE FILE="ADOvbs.inc" -->
```

Next, we're going to set up the variables to store the information in, and then write 4 blocks of ASP/ADO code to get the values of those variables. Following that, we will create our Connection object, open it, and create our RecordSet object:

```
<%
  Server.ScriptTimeout = 200
  cstring = "DSN=profile;"

  Dim nstart, nstop,  x, openforwardonly, openkeyset, opendynamic, openstatic

  Set cn = Server.CreateObject("ADODB.Connection")
  cn.Open cstring
  Set rs = Server.CreateObject("ADODB.RecordSet")
```

Now for the loops. Each one is the same, with one exception: the CursorType of the recordset. I have put in the code for the first loop, and the beginning of the code for the second loop because, if you remember, you must close and re-open the connection before each new loop:

```
  rs.CursorType = adOpenForwardOnly
  nstart = Timer()
  For x = 0 to 150
    rs.Open "SELECT * FROM profile", cn
    While NOT rs.EOF
      rs.MoveNext
    Wend
    rs.Close
  Next
  nstop = Timer()
  openforwardonly = nstop - nstart

  cn.Close
  cn.Open cstring
  rs.CursorType = adOpenKeySet
  nstart = Timer()
```

*Note the looping through the recordset each time. This is because the difference in performance is related to the use of the recordset, not just to opening it. Looping through the recordset takes some time. That's why we've lessened the number of iterations of the test from 500 to 150.*

The rest of the second loop is identical to the rest of the first (before the empty line). Now you're going to want to add two more loops, creating `CursorTypes` of adOpenDynamic and adOpenStatic. Go ahead and write the code for these.

Next comes the cleanup code:

```
  cn.Close
  Set cn = Nothing
  Set rs = Nothing
%>
```

Okay, now to display the data. Copy the following HTML and ASP code to your page:

```
<HTML>

<HEAD>
<TITLE>Cursor Type Performance Testing</TITLE>
</HEAD>

<BODY>

<P ALIGN="center"><FONT SIZE="6" COLOR="#0000FF"><STRONG>PerfTest - Cursor
Types</STRONG></FONT></P>

<HR>
<DIV ALIGN="center"><CENTER>

<TABLE BORDER="0" CELLPADDING="0" bgCOLOR="#C0C0C0">
<TR>
<TD VALIGN="bottom" ALIGN="center"><IMG SRC="images/bluebar.gif" WIDTH="60"
HEIGHT="<%=FormatNumber((openforwardonly * 10), 0)%>" ALT="<%=openforwardonly%>"></TD>
<TD VALIGN="bottom" ALIGN="center"><IMG SRC="images/purplebar.gif" WIDTH="60"
HEIGHT="<%=FormatNumber((openkeyset * 10), 0)%>" ALT="<%=openkeyset%>"></TD>
<TD VALIGN="bottom" ALIGN="center"><IMG SRC="images/redbar.gif" WIDTH="60"
HEIGHT="<%=FormatNumber((opendynamic * 10), 0)%>" ALT="<%=opendynamic%>"></TD>
<TD VALIGN="bottom" ALIGN="center"><IMG SRC="images/pinkbar.gif" WIDTH="60"
HEIGHT="<%=FormatNumber((openstatic * 10), 0)%>" ALT="<%=openstatic%>"></TD>
</TR>
<TR>
<TD VALIGN="top" ALIGN="center"><FONT FACE="Arial"
SIZE="1"><%=openforwardonly%></FONT></TD>
<TD VALIGN="top" ALIGN="center"><FONT FACE="Arial"
SIZE="1"><%=openkeyset%></FONT></TD>
<TD VALIGN="top" ALIGN="center"><FONT FACE="Arial"
SIZE="1"><%=opendynamic%></FONT></TD>
<TD VALIGN="top" ALIGN="center"><FONT FACE="Arial"
SIZE="1"><%=openstatic%></FONT></TD>
</TR>
</TABLE>
</CENTER></div>

<P ALIGN="center"><IMG SRC="images/bluebar.gif" ALT="adOpenForwardOnly " WIDTH="25"
HEIGHT="5">
<FONT FACE="Arial" SIZE="2">adOpenForwardOnly</FONT><br>
<IMG SRC="images/purplebar.gif" ALT="adOpenKeyset " WIDTH="25" HEIGHT="5">
<FONT FACE="Arial" SIZE="2">adOpenKeyset</FONT><br>
<IMG SRC="images/redbar.gif" ALT=" adOpenDynamic " WIDTH="25" HEIGHT="5">
<FONT FACE="Arial" SIZE="2">adOpenDynamic</FONT><br>
<IMG SRC="images/pinkbar.gif" ALT=" adOpenStatic " WIDTH="25" HEIGHT="5">
<FONT FACE="Arial" SIZE="2">adOpenStatic</FONT><BR>
</P>
</BODY>
</HTML>
```

**673**

Save the page to your web server with the name `perftestcursor.asp`, and view it in a browser. Your results should look something like this:

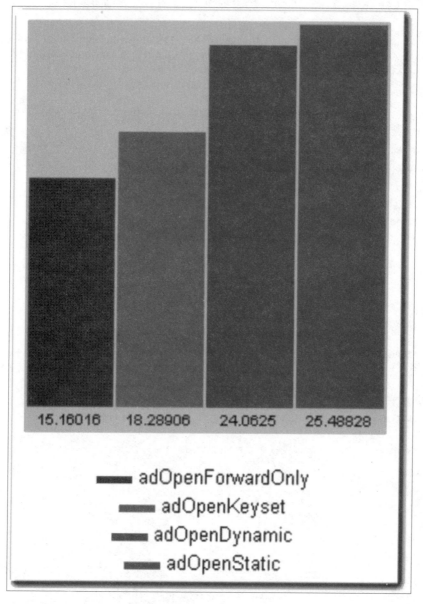

It certainly seems to bear out the theory that the `adForwardOnly` cursor type is the fastest!

# Summary

In this chapter, we've discussed various performance issues related to using ADO, with an emphasis on developing for the Internet. We've talked about the importance of speed, and discussed the various components that make up an Internet ADO application:

❑ The Hosting Platform – Operating System and Web Server

❑ The Database used

❑ The Code used

We've talked about ways of measuring and tweaking performance on the operating system and the web server, and discussed various readily available tools, such as System Monitor, Performance Monitor, Event Viewer, Task Manager, Network Monitor, and the freely downloadable Wcat utility.

We've talked about areas of the system and server that need to be addressed. We've discussed processor bottlenecks, processor throttling, and connection pooling.

We've discussed the relative strengths and weaknesses of using Access versus SQL Server. We have recommended SQL Server to be used wherever possible, as it has virtually unlimited capacity, in terms of speed, number of concurrent connections, and storage.

We've discussed coding issues:

❑ Stored procedures – why they are generally better to use for queries

❑ BLOBS, Memo, and Bit fields – their drawbacks to performance

❑ Storing ADO in sessions – why it's not a good idea

❑ Optimizing queries – using the SQL Server Query Analyzer

❑ Cursor types – which ones to use, and when

Finally, we have created a tool for testing ADO in ASP pages – `PerfTest`. This performs various operations and displays the results graphically in a bar chart. We can use variations of this tool to test all kinds of ADO operations on the web.

# Exercises

Some of these exercises use profile.mdb, which is available from the Wrox website. The structure of the database is described in Appendix C.

**1.** If you have NT, use the tools described in the Tools section of this chapter to analyze the performance of your system and web server. Do you have any processor bottlenecks? Should you use processor throttling? Connection pooling? Analyze your system and maximize it for the performance needs of your web site(s).

**2.** Download and install Wcat, and use it to test your web server for various types of loads. In particular, run some ASP tests with it.

**3.** Analyze the profile.mdb database, and determine whether it needs any particular indexing. What fields should be indexed?

**4.** If you have SQL Server, try out the Query Analyzer. Using a local database, test out some queries in it, and use the Index Analysis tool to decide whether and what kinds of indices you need to add to your database.

**5.** Create a new PerfTest ASP page. Use this page to combine the four ADO cursor types (adOpenForwardOnly, adOpenKeyset, adOpenDynamic, adOpenStatic) with the four lock types available (adLockReadOnly, adLockPessimistic, adLockOptimistic, adLockBatchOptimistic), to analyze the performances of combinations of these cursor and lock types. You should have 16 tests on the page. Each cursor type should be combined with each of the four lock types.

# Quiz

**1.** Why is performance an important issue in Internet ADO application development?

**2.** Define "Processor Bottlenecks, "Processor Throttling", and "Connection Pooling".

**3.** What is the greatest performance issue concerning ADO? In other words, what does it use the most?

**4.** What are some ways to remedy or prevent processor bottlenecking?

**5.** Why is SQL Server a much better database solution for Internet database applications?

**6.** What is the difference between System Monitor and Performance Monitor?

**7.** How are BLOB fields and Memo fields stored in a table?

**8.** Why shouldn't you store ADO objects in sessions?

**9.** What is the fastest cursor type?

# Quiz Answers

**1.** An Internet ADO application may be used by hundreds, thousands, or even millions of people. A small performance improvement therefore translates to a big performance improvement.

**2.** **Processor Bottleneck:** When the processor is maxing out while the Network card is still way under capacity.
**Processor Throttling:** A way of monitoring and reacting to processor overuse by a web application's out-of-process WAMs, CGIs, and ISAPIs.
**Connection Pooling:** A way of sharing connections between concurrent database users having the same user name and password.

**3.** ADO is processor-intensive.

**4.** Add another processor to the server.
Use replication to share a web site between more than one server.
Move processor-intensive web applications to a different server.

**5.** SQL Server has virtually unlimited capacity, and was designed with the Internet in mind.

**6.** Performance Monitor includes the ability to create logs and alerts.

**7.** They are not stored in the table. A pointer to the data's location is stored in the table.

**8.** Sessions can time out, and the ADO object can be lost. Connection pooling is not available to connections stored in sessions. They can also consume system resources while in a session, which can take a long time to time-out. It is better to explicitly destroy them and recreate them in the next page.

**9.** adOpenForwardOnly. This is the default CursorType.

Setup cannot install system files or update shared files if the files are in use. Before c any open applications.

WARNING: This program is protected by copyright law and international treaties.

You may install Microsoft Data Access 2.1 on a single computer. Some Microsoft products with additional rights, which are stated in the End User License Agreement included with y

Please take a moment to read the End User License Agreement now. It contains all of the te conditions that pertain to this software product. By choosing to continue, you indicate accept these terms.

Continue                    Exit Setup

e New Data Source

Select a driver for which you want to set up a data sourc

| Name | Version |
|------|---------|
| Microsoft Access Driver (*.mdb) | 4.00.4207.00 |
| Microsoft dBase Driver (*.dbf) | 4.00.4207.00 |
| Microsoft dBase VFP Driver (*.dbf) | 6.01.8440.01 |
| Microsoft Excel Driver (*.xls) | 4.00.4207.00 |
| Microsoft FoxPro VFP Driver (*.dbf) | 6.01.8440.01 |
| Microsoft ODBC for Oracle | 2.573.4207.00 |
| Microsoft Paradox Driver (*.db ) | 4.00.4207.00 |
| Microsoft Text Driver (*.txt; *.csv) | 4.00.4207.00 |
| Microsoft Visual FoxPro Driver | 6.01.8440.01 |
| SQL Server | 3.70.06.90 |

Finish                    Cancel

# The Sailors Case Study

You have made it through all of the chapters and find yourself here, ready to implement a complete application, using everything that you have learned throughout this book. By now you have covered all the essentials of ADO and recordset manipulation using Microsoft Access and SQL Server. You have seen how ASP and ADO can be used together to create web applications incorporating information from within a database. This case study will help you to reinforce what you have learned by implementing as much of the material covered as possible into a single application. We will be creating a Sailors web site, and integrating data from the Sailors database.

What will you need to implement this case study? First and foremost you will need the Sailors Access database. If you don't already have a copy of it, you should download the database from the Wrox web site at http://www.wrox.com. You will also need an editor to create Active Server Pages, Visual InterDev or FrontPage 98 are recommended, however Notepad is perfectly adequate for the task. The latest service pack for the software you are using should also be installed but certainly is not essential. Last but not least, you will need a web server. This can be a Personal Web Server or a web Server on your network. Chapter 2 covered setting up a Personal Web Server and the DSN that is needed to access the Sailors database. All code in this case study works with Internet Explorer versions 4 and 5.

This case study will implement the following features:

- Simple select stored procedures
- Parameterized stored procedures
- Action stored procedures
- Cookies
- Error handling

As you go through the text in this case study, you are encouraged to try the examples. After you get a page working, don't be afraid to experiment a little. If you wonder why something works the way it does and wonder "what if...?", then by all means try the "what if...?". This case study tries to bring as much of the book together as possible into one application.

Do you remember how to enter stored procedures in Access? You can read chapter 14 to jog your memory but I will give you a quick summary. Select Queries | New and then select Design View. Then hit Close and right click the empty Select Query Box. Now you just select SQL View.

# The Sailors Web Site

There are four main functions performed on this web site. The first function is to have the user login. Next, the user has the option of registering their boat, listing all registered boats and listing the sailor rankings. This is a simple web site with minimal security. There are no formal user tables with associated profiles that are used for security.

Because we are trying to demonstrate, in the case study, as much as possible of the material covered throughout this book, there is a definite lack of consistency in the code. For example, one web page may select a recordset one way, while another may select it a different way. Also, you may find that many of the pages will not work when first created. This is because they may refer to a page that will be created later on, and so you may have to be patient to test out your application.

We've divided this case study into three main sections, or groups of web pages, so that we can discuss related areas together. These three sections are the include files, logging on and registration, and web site user options. We can break these down a bit further, so we can see how the case study fits together.

## The Include Files

In the first section of the case study we'll look at all the include files we'll be using. These contain common functionality which is used in a number of places, as follows:

- Error handling
- Authentication checking
- Connecting to the database
- Disconnecting from the database
- Common functions
- Menu options
- ADO constants

We'll also discuss `global.asa`.

## Logging On and Registration

In this section we'll discuss the web pages that make up our login and registration pages, which verify that users are registered and ask them to register if not. We'll look at each of the following pages in turn:

- Default.asp
- Register.asp
- RegistrationConfirmation.asp
- WelcomeBack.asp
- LoginVerification.asp

### Web Site User Options

Finally we'll look at the pages that make up the options available to the user, starting from the menu page and then discussing each of the following:

- ❏ The 'Display Boats' page
- ❏ The 'Boat Registration' page
- ❏ The 'Display Ranking' page

All the code is shown here, however the entire case study is also available to download with the rest of the source code for this book, as described in the Introduction. With that said, let's dive into the details of the Sailors Web site.

# The Include Files

In order to keep the code in our web pages to a minimum, we will make extensive use of include files. If you recall, in Chapter 12, the code to check for errors after performing a SQL operation was contained in an include file called ProductionErrorHandler.inc. This helped to ensure that all error handling was performed in a consistent manner. If you also recall, it was a fair amount of code, and using an include file helped to keep our web pages manageable.

## Error Handling

We are going to use the same production error handling include file that we used in Chapter 12 with a few minor modifications. This include file will be included at the top of every web page that uses the database. This file contains a function called CheckForErrors, and we will call this function after every call to the database. It will be used after connecting to the database, and after executing action stored procedures and simple selects that are used in recordsets. The rest of the code is the same as you saw in Chapter 12. We are using the Server.MapPath function to place the ProductionErrorLog.txt file in the same directory as the web pages. This function maps a path to the current directory or a virtual directory when you specify part of a path name. The code for the ProductionErrorHandler.inc file is listed below.

```
<SCRIPT LANGUAGE=vbscript runat=server>
Function CheckForErrors(objConnection)
  'Declare variables
  Dim blnDisplayErrMsg

  If objConnection.Errors.Count > 0 Then

    'Create the FileSystemObject and open the error log
    Set objFile = Server.CreateObject("Scripting.FileSystemObject")
    Set objLog = objFile.OpenTextFile( _
      Server.MapPath("ProductionErrorLog.txt"),8,True)

    'Check for an open error from VBScript
    If Err.Number > 0 Then
      Response.Write "Error opening log file<P>"
      Response.Write "Error Number: " & Err.Number & _
        ", Error Description: " & Err.Description
    End If
```

```
        'Create an error object to access the ADO errors collection
        Set objErr = Server.CreateObject("ADODB.Error")

        'Log all errors to the error log
        For Each objErr In objConnection.Errors
          If objErr.Number = 0 Then
            blnDisplayErrMsg = False
          Else
            objLog.WriteLine(objErr.Number & "|" & _
              objErr.Description & "|" & objErr.Source & "|" & _
              objErr.SQLState & "|" & objErr.NativeError)
            blnDisplayErrMsg = True
          End If
        Next

        'Close the log file and dereference all objects
        objLog.Close
        Set objLog = Nothing
        Set objFile = Nothing
        Set objErr = Nothing

        If blnDisplayErrMsg Then
          'Display a graceful message to the user
          Response.Write "An unforseen error has occurred and processing " & _
            "must be stopped. You can try your request again later or " & _
            "you can call our Help Desk at 888-888-1234"
          'Halt Execution
          Response.End
        End If
      End If
  End Function
</SCRIPT>
```

## *Authentication Check*

One of the security features used to prevent unauthorized access to our web pages is to check to see whether the user has logged in and has been authorized. Since this code is used in multiple web pages it makes sense to also put this code in an include file. The code for the `AuthenticationCheck.inc` file is really fairly simple, and is shown below.

We check to see if a `Session` variable called `Authenticated` has been set to a value of `True`. If the variable has not been set to `True`, we redirect the browser to the `Default.asp` web page. If the client is viewing this page via a proxy server, the server may disallow a redirection like this. You could also insert a message with a hyperlink to direct the reader to `default.asp` if their proxy server won't allow you to redirect them automatically.

```
<%
'Authentication check
If Session("Authenticated") <> True Then
  Session("ErrorMessage") = "You Have not properly logged in."
  Response.Redirect "Default.asp"
End If
%>
```

> In order to redirect the browser to another URL, no HTTP headers can have been written. Therefore it is crucial that this code is contained as the first lines of code in your Web page. As has been shown in previous chapters, we could use Response.Buffer = True to execute the entire page before sending it to the browser. However, this method is not being used in this case study.

## Connecting to the Database

We are going to connect to the database in the same manner most of the time. Again it makes sense to place this common code in an include file. The `Connect.inc` file, shown below, sets up our error handling with the `On Error Resume Next` statement, and then an ADO `Connection` object is created and the database opened. We are using an application level variable to hold our connection string. This variable is defined in the `Global.asa` file, which will be discussed later. If problems arise with the connect string, it could be the case that your security settings on your web server are set too high. Try changing permissions to give execute properties to the browser. There are also a number of knowledge base articles available discussing this problem.

```
<%
'Instruct VBScript to ignore the error and continue
'with the next line of code
On Error Resume Next

'Create and open the database object
Set objConn = Server.CreateObject("ADODB.Connection")
objConn.Open Application("ConnectString")
%>
```

## Disconnecting From the Database

Along the same lines as *connecting* to the database we need a method to *disconnect* from the database. This is where the `DisConnect.inc` file comes into play. This include file, while simple, is important. Let's take a look at what the code does.

Not every web page will have a recordset so we must first check to see if a `Recordset` object exists. We do this by checking to see if the `objRS` object is actually an object, using the `IsObject` function. This function will return a Boolean value of `True` if the object exists. If it does exist, we close it and de-reference it, by setting it to `Nothing`. This will release it from memory. Next, we close the `Connection` object and also set it to `Nothing`.

```
<%
'Close and dereference database objects
If IsObject(objRS) Then
  objRS.Close
  Set objRS = Nothing
End If
objConn.Close
Set objConn = Nothing
%>
```

## Common Functions

Sometimes we develop a routine to solve a particular problem and realize that this routine could be useful in other web pages. It makes sense to put these routines into an include file also, so that they can be shared. This is where the `CommonFunctions.inc` file comes into play. This file contains specialized routines that can be shared in multiple web pages. Right now we only have one routine in this file, but with a little thought I'm sure you can come up with more.

Because we want to share these routines, and possibly in more than one place in our web page, we include these routines as server-side script. We do this by specifying that this is script to be run on the server, as indicated by the first line of code in the file. Whenever we want to use these routines we simply call them as if they were built-in functions of the VBScript language. We will demonstrate a call to this routine later in this case study.

The routine we have in our `CommonFunctions.inc` file is very simple – it converts single quote marks in a string to two consecutive single quote marks in the string. Why do we do this? If you recall our discussions in chapter 12 about passing string parameters, we need to delimit all string parameters with a single quote. If our string parameter has a single quote mark in it, then we are going to run into problems because the string would be terminated by the single quote mark within the string. The database would then give us an error about an un-terminated string. This routine accepts an input string, converts all single quote marks and then returns the new string to us. The code for `CommonFunctions.inc` is shown below.

```vbscript
<SCRIPT LANGUAGE=vbscript RUNAT=server>
Function ConvertString(strInput)
  Dim intPos
   intPos = 1
   Do
      intPos = InStr(intPos, strInput, "'", vbTextCompare)
      If intPos > 0 Then
        strInput = Left(strInput, intPos) + Right(strInput, Len(strInput) - _
          (intPos - 1))
         intPos = intPos + 2
      End If
   Loop While intPos > 0
   ConvertString = strInput
End Function
</SCRIPT>
```

## Menu Options

Since we display the menu options, which the user can choose to execute, on more than one page, we should place them in an include file. If we ever want to make a change to a menu option or add a new one, we make the change in one place and it immediately becomes effective in all pages. So let's take a look at the `MenuOptions.inc` file.

A quick look at this include file and you can see it is different from the other include files. This one contains straight HTML and no server–side script. We just build a table and display each option in a separate row. By putting our menu options in a table we have more control over the presentation of the data. Notice that the first column in the table uses the HEIGHT parameter to increase the height of the cell. This provides just a little extra spacing between the line 'Select an option' and the surrounding lines. Also, using a table groups our menu options a little closer together, more so than using HTML tags.

Notice that each of the hyperlinks contains an ONMOUSEOVER and an ONMOUSEOUT event. These are Dynamic HTML tag properties that specify what actions should be taken when the user moves the mouse over the hyperlink, and what action should be taken when they move the mouse away from the hyperlink. In the case of this example, these events set the text of the window status bar. The code opposite is the `MenuOptions.inc` file:

```
<TABLE>
  <TR>
  <TD HEIGHT=50>Select an option</TD>
  </TR>
  <TR>
  <TD><A HREF="DisplayBoats.asp"
    ONMOUSEOVER="window.status='Display Registered Boats'; return true"
    ONMOUSEOUT="window.status=''">
    Display a listing of all registered boats</FONT></TD>
  </TR>
  <TR>
  <TD><A HREF="RegisterNewBoat.asp"
    ONMOUSEOVER="window.status='Register a New Boat'; return true"
    ONMOUSEOUT="window.status=''">
    Register a new boat</FONT></TD>
  </TR>
  <TR>
  <TD><A HREF="DisplayRankings.asp"
    ONMOUSEOVER="window.status='Display Sailor Rankings'; return true"
    ONMOUSEOUT="window.status=''">
    Display sailor rankings</FONT></TD>
  </TR>
</TABLE>
```

Note: The ONMOUSEOVER code lines in this snippet and throughout this chapter have been specifically tailored for MS Internet Explorer 5. If your application is for IE4 only, then remove the code after and including the semi-colon; leaving the ending quotation marks only. For example the line:

```
ONMOUSEOVER="window.status='Display Registered Boats'; return true"
```

would become:

```
ONMOUSEOVER="window.status='Display Registered Boats'"
```

If the page was intended to be viewed by any browser, you could remove the ONMOUSE. . . events. There will be more about the ONMOUSEOVER and ONMOUSEOUT events when we discuss the default.asp page later.

## ADO Constants

Throughout the text in this book we have made use of ADO constants such as adCmdText and adOpenReadOnly. We declared the variables for these constants and set their values. When you install ADO on your computer, an include file is installed that includes all of the constants we have used and a whole lot more. This file is called ADOVBS.inc and can usually be found in the C:\Program Files\Common Files\System\ado\ directory.

We will be using this include file in the web pages that access the database. Copy this file to the same directory with the other include files used in this case study.

# Global.asa

Global.asa is an optional file in which you can declare objects and variables that have application and session level scope. There can be only one Global.asa file within your web application, it must be named Global.asa and it must reside in the root directory of your web application.

This file contains two procedures that get executed before anything else. The first of these is the Application_OnStart procedure. The code in this procedure gets executed when the application is accessed for the first time and the variables that are set stay active the entire time. The Session_OnStart procedure gets executed when an individual session is started and the variables that are set in this procedure stay active for that session only. An individual session is started when a user browses a page on the web site and the session ends when the user's session times out or they shut down their browser.

The OnEnd events, and any code we have placed in them, get executed when an application or session ends.

For the purposes of our case study, we are only using the Application_Onstart procedure to set the ConnectString variable, which will be used by all web pages needing to connect to the database. The code for Global.asa is shown below:

```
<SCRIPT LANGUAGE="VBScript" RUNAT="Server">
Sub Session_OnStart
End Sub

Sub Session_OnEnd
End Sub

Sub Application_OnStart
  Application("ConnectString") = "DSN=sailors"
End Sub

Sub Application_OnEnd
  Application("ConnectString") = ""
End Sub
</SCRIPT>
```

It is advisable to stop and start your web server once you have copied this file into the root directory of your application. This will ensure that the file is read and that the application variable is set.

# Logging On and Registration

We know that we want this web site to have minimum security. That being said, we want our users to be automatically logged in if we find a cookie on their machine. (We covered cookies in Chapter 11). If we don't find a cookie then we will prompt the user for their login values, which include First Name, Last Name and Password. If the user has not registered with us before, we will provide a hyperlink on the login page to a registration page. The following illustration provides the flow of the login process.

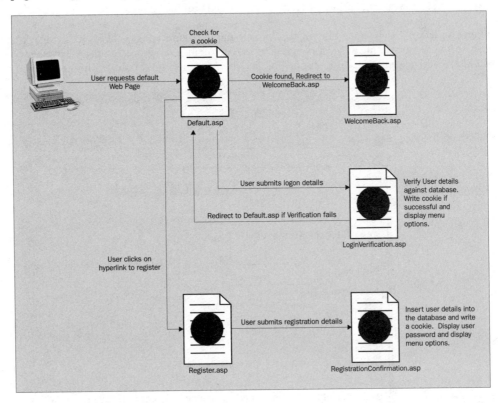

As you can see, our login process is quite extensive. Could we have done this in just one or two web pages? Absolutely! You may be wondering why we went to all of this trouble of using so many pages? There are actually several reasons.

First, we wanted to demonstrate how you could redirect the browser to another URL. Remember that we mentioned earlier, that if we want to redirect the browser to another web page, we should do so before any HTTP headers are written. The LoginVerification.asp page demonstrates significant script processing and redirection before the HTTP headers are written.

Next, we wanted to demonstrate the use of cookies. The Default.asp page checks for the existence of a cookie and if it finds one, will redirect the browser to the WelcomeBack.asp page. The LoginVerification.asp page writes a new cookie using information retrieved from the database, if the login details have been verified. Also, the RegistrationConfirmation.asp page writes a cookie after a user has been registered.

Last, we wanted to demonstrate how to use forms in one web page to submit information to another web page, and to have the receiving web page read and process those values.

## Try It Out – Default.asp Page

The `Default.asp` web page has three functions. First it checks to see if a cookie exists on the user's machine. If it does then it will redirect the browser to the `WelcomeBack.asp` page. The second function is to display a login form if no cookie has been found. The last function is to provide a hyperlink to the `Registration.asp` page if the user has not registered with us before.

When you set up a web site in IIS you can define what the default page will be. It can be any name you wish as long as you define it. Most people find it easier to just name the first page that is seen as either `Default.htm` or `Default.asp`, depending on whether or not server-side script needs to be executed.

The result of running the `Default.asp` page is shown here:

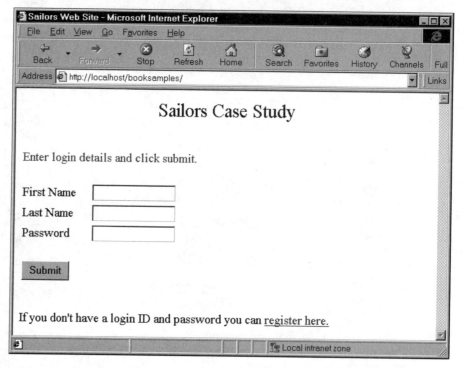

Below is the code for `Default.asp`:

```
<%
'Check to see if a cookie exists for this user
If Len(Request.Cookies("Sailor")("FirstName")) > 0 Then
   'Cookie exists

   'Authenticate the user for other Web pages
   Session("Authenticated") = True

   'Redirect the browser to the welcome back page
   Response.Redirect "WelcomeBack.asp"
End If
%>
```

```
<HTML>
<HEAD>
<META NAME="GENERATOR" Content="Microsoft Visual Studio 6.0">
<TITLE>Sailors Web Site</TITLE>
</HEAD>
<BODY>

<!--Display the page data-->
<DIV ALIGN=center>
  <BIG><BIG><FONT COLOR=navy>Sailors Case Study</FONT></BIG></BIG>
</DIV>
<BR><BR>

<%
'Check for an error message which indicates the previous
'login attempt failed
If Len(Session("ErrorMessage")) > 0 Then
  Response.Write "<FONT COLOR=red>" & _
    Session("ErrorMessage") & "</FONT><BR>"
End If
%>

<!--Display login form-->
<FORM ACTION=loginverification.asp METHOD=post NAME=frmDefault>
<TABLE>
  <TR>
  <TD COLSPAN=2><FONT COLOR=teal>Enter login details and click submit.</TD>
  </TR>
  <TR>
  <TD>  </TD>
  </TR>
  <TR>
  <TD>First Name</TD>
  <TD><INPUT TYPE=text NAME=txtFirstName SIZE=15></TD>
  </TR>
  <TR>
  <TD>Last Name</TD>
  <TD><INPUT TYPE=text NAME=txtLastName SIZE=15></TD>
  </TR>
  <TR>
  <TD>Password</TD>
  <TD><INPUT TYPE=text NAME=txtPassword SIZE=15></TD>
  </TR>
  <TR>
  <TD>  </TD>
  </TR>
  <TR>
  <TD><INPUT TYPE=submit NAME=btnSubmit VALUE=Submit></TD>
  </TR>
</TABLE>
</FORM>

<BR>
If you don't have a login ID and password you can
<A HREF="register.asp"
  ONMOUSEOVER="window.status='Register on the Sailors Web Site'; return true"
  ONMOUSEOUT="window.status=''">register here.</A>
</BODY>
</HTML>
```

### How It Works – Default.asp Page

We'll start by taking a look at the script at the top of the page. This server-side script checks for the existence of a cookie on the user's machine by using the `Request.Cookie` method. If you recall the discussions on cookies in Chapter 11, we use the `Request` object to check for cookies. The type of cookie we are using has multiple values for `Sailor` and is considered an index cookie. We access the different keys (`FirstName`, `LastName`, `Password`) within the index by specifying their key name. If a cookie is found that contains the `Sailor` index with the `FirstName` key, then we authenticate the user by setting the `Session` variable to True, redirecting the browser to the `WelcomeBack.asp` page. Notice that all of this processing happens before the first HTML header tag is written.

```
<%
'Check to see if a cookie exists for this user
If Len(Request.Cookies("Sailor")("FirstName")) > 0 Then
  'Cookie exists

  'Authenticate the user for other Web pages
  Session("Authenticated") = True

  'Redirect the browser to the welcome back page
  Response.Redirect "WelcomeBack.asp"
End If
%>
```

If we made it this far then no cookie was found or the cookie has expired. We then start the process of building the web page to be displayed. The beginning of this page contains the standard HTML header details and we will not go into the details of this.

```
<HTML>
<HEAD>
<META NAME="GENERATOR" Content="Microsoft Visual Studio 6.0">
<TITLE>Sailors Web Site</TITLE>
</HEAD>
<BODY>
```

The next section of code writes the first line of text in our page using standard HTML. Here we are using the `DIV` tag to set up a division of text and specify that the text should be centered using the `ALIGN` property. We also specify that the font should be larger than normal by using the `BIG` tag. Next we use the `FONT` tag to change the color of the font. The last line of code uses the `BR` tags to create two line breaks for spacing purposes. Instead of using the `BIG` tags to increase the size of the font you could use the `FONT` tag and specify the font size using the `SIZE` property.

```
<!--Display the page data-->
<DIV ALIGN=center>
  <BIG><BIG><FONT COLOR=navy>Sailors Case Study</FONT></BIG></BIG>
</DIV>
<BR><BR>
```

If you recall in the diagram earlier, the `LoginVerification.asp` page redirects the user back to the `Default.asp` page if the login values cannot be verified against the database. That page, which we'll take a look at later, set a message in a `Session` variable. We must check to see if any messages exist, (by checking the length of the `Session` variable `ErrorMessage`, and display the messages if there are any. Using the `Response.Write` method we write the message to the page. Also notice that we are using the `FONT` tag again to change the color of the text.

```
<%
'Check for an error message which indicates the previous
'login attempt failed
If Len(Session("ErrorMessage")) > 0 Then
  Response.Write "<FONT COLOR=red>" & _
    Session("ErrorMessage") & "</FONT><BR>"
End If
%>
```

We build the login form using the standard HTML FORM tag. The first line of code specifies that we want a form called frmDefault, and specifies that it should post values to the LoginVerification.asp page.

Next, we use a table in the form to help ensure that all of the fields have the appropriate alignment and spacing on the web page. Notice that we tell the first column of the table that the text in this column should span two columns, using the COLSPAN property of the TD tag. We also change the font color of the text.

We use the second row as a spacer row and indicate that a blank space should be written in the first column, using  . This separates the text in the first row from the text in the third row to give us a more appealing look.

```
<!--Display login form-->
<FORM ACTION=loginverification.asp METHOD=post NAME=frmDefault>
<TABLE>
  <TR>
  <TD COLSPAN=2><FONT COLOR=teal>Enter login details and click submit.</TD>
  </TR>
  <TR>
  <TD>  </TD>
  </TR>
```

We build the actual form fields using the INPUT element in the form. We specify the type of input element that the form should render, which in this case is a text field, and also specify the NAME of the field and the SIZE. The SIZE property specifies how many characters wide the input box should be. If we needed to restrict the amount of text that could be entered in the text box, we could use the MAXLENGTH property instead of (or as well as) the SIZE property. The difference is, the SIZE property controls the size of the text box but does not limit the amount of text that can be keyed in. The MAXLENGTH property also controls the size of the text box, but limits the amount of text that can be keyed in.

After having built all of our text fields in the form we need to specify another input type, which is Submit. This renders a Submit button on the form and we give it a NAME and a VALUE. The VALUE property specifies what text should be displayed on the button.

We finish the form by closing the table and the form using the /TABLE and /FORM tags.

```
<TR>
<TD>First Name</TD>
<TD><INPUT TYPE=text NAME=txtFirstName SIZE=15></TD>
</TR>
<TR>
<TD>Last Name</TD>
<TD><INPUT TYPE=text NAME=txtLastName SIZE=15></TD>
</TR>
<TR>
<TD>Password</TD>
<TD><INPUT TYPE=text NAME=txtPassword SIZE=15></TD>
</TR>
<TR>
<TD>  </TD>
</TR>
<TR>
<TD><INPUT TYPE=submit NAME=btnSubmit VALUE=Submit></TD>
</TR>
</TABLE>
</FORM>
```

The last part of our web page contains a hyperlink to let an unregistered user jump to the registration page. This is a standard hyperlink but contains two events that have not been mentioned in detail yet. The ONMOUSEOVER and ONMOUSEOUT events specify what actions should be taken when the user moves the mouse over the hyperlink, and what action should be taken when they move the mouse away from the hyperlink.

In the ONMOUSEOVER event we specify what text should be displayed in the window status area. This is the StatusBar text in the lower left–hand corner of your browser. By default, the hyperlink URL would be displayed but we want to give the user a little more info. We specify what the page does that is contained in the hyperlink. The ONMOUSEOUT event simply sets the text in the window status area to nothing.

```
<BR>
If you don't have a login ID and password you can
<A HREF="register.asp"
  ONMOUSEOVER="window.status='Register on the Sailors Web Site'; return true"
  ONMOUSEOUT="window.status=''">register here.</A>
```

The last part of the code ends the web page.

```
</BODY>
</HTML>
```

At this point you can test this web page to make sure it displays properly. Since you do not have a cookie you will not be redirected to another page. Also, you cannot click on the hyperlink to register until we build the next page.

## Try It Out – Register.asp Page

Since we don't yet have a user id and password in the Sailors database, the next logical step would be to build the Register.asp page. This page allows us to enter all of the required user information, and click on a submit button which will submit all of our details to be recorded in the database by the RegistrationConfirmation.asp page. The register.asp page should look like the following:

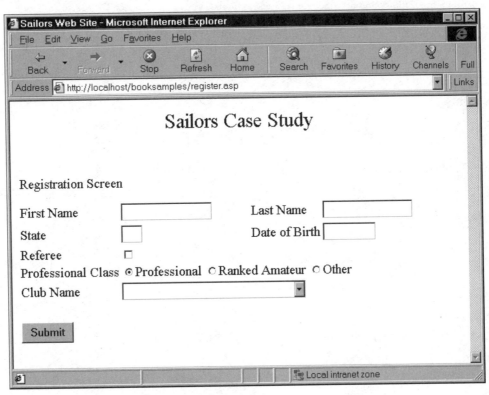

The qAllClubs stored procedure code is shown below:

```
SELECT Clubs.ClubName, Clubs.ClubCode
FROM Clubs
ORDER BY Clubs.ClubName;
```

The code for the register.asp web page is as follows:

```
<!-- #include file="adovbs.inc" -->
<!-- #include file="ProductionErrorHandler.inc" -->
<HTML>
<HEAD>
<META NAME="GENERATOR" Content="Microsoft Visual Studio 6.0">
<TITLE>Sailors Web Site</TITLE>
</HEAD>
<BODY>
```

```
<!--Display the page data-->
<DIV ALIGN=CENTER>
  <BIG><BIG><FONT COLOR=navy>Sailors Case Study</FONT></BIG></BIG>
</DIV>
<BR><BR>

<FORM ACTION=registrationconfirmation.asp method=post NAME=frmRegister>
<TABLE>
  <TR>
  <TD HEIGHT=50 COLSPAN=2><FONT COLOR=navy>Registration Screen
    </FONT></TD>
  </TR>
  <TR>
  <TD>First Name</TD>
  <TD><INPUT TYPE=text NAME=txtFirstName SIZE=15></TD>
  <TD WIDTH=50></TD>
  <TD>Last Name</TD>
  <TD><INPUT TYPE=text NAME=txtLastName SIZE=15></TD>
  </TR>
  <TR>
  <TD>State</TD>
  <TD><INPUT TYPE=text NAME=txtState SIZE=2></TD>
  <TD WIDTH=50></TD>
  <TD>Date of Birth</TD>
  <TD><INPUT TYPE=text NAME=txtDateofBirth SIZE=8></TD>
  </TR>
  <TR>
  <TD>Referee</TD>
  <TD><INPUT TYPE=checkbox NAME=chkReferee VALUE=1></TD>
  </TR>
  <TR>
  <TD>Professional Class</TD>
  <TD COLSPAN=4>
    <INPUT TYPE=radio NAME=optClass VALUE=1 checked>Professional
    <INPUT TYPE=radio NAME=optClass VALUE=2>Ranked Amateur
    <INPUT TYPE=radio NAME=optClass VALUE=3>Other
  </TD>
  </TR>
  <TR>
  <TD>Club Name</TD>
  <TD COLSPAN=3><SELECT NAME=cboClubs></SELECT></TD>
  </TR>
  <TR>
  <TD>  </TD>
  </TR>
  <TR>
  <TD><INPUT TYPE=button NAME=btnSubmit VALUE=Submit></TD>
  </TR>
</FORM>

  <!-- #include file="Connect.inc" -->

<%
'Check for database errors
Call CheckForErrors(objConn)

'Create the recordset object, set the SQL string and open the recordset
Set objRS = Server.CreateObject("ADODB.Recordset")
strSQL = "qAllClubs"
objRS.Open strSQL, objConn, adOpenForwardOnly, , adCmdStoredProc

'Check for database errors
Call CheckForErrors(objConn)
%>
```

```
<SCRIPT LANGUAGE=vbscript>
Sub Window_OnLoad()
<%
  Do While Not objRS.EOF
%>
    Set objOption = document.createElement("OPTION")
    objOption.text = "<%=objRS("ClubName")%>"
    objOption.value = "<%=objRS("ClubCode")%>"
    document.all.cboClubs.add objOption
<%
    objRS.MoveNext
  Loop
%>

  <!-- #include file="DisConnect.inc" -->

  Set objOption = Nothing
End Sub

Sub btnSubmit_OnClick()
  'Verify all fields have been entered
  If Len(frmRegister.txtFirstName.value) = 0 Then
    Alert "You must enter a first name"
    frmRegister.txtFirstName.focus
    Exit Sub
  ElseIf Len(frmRegister.txtLastName.value) = 0 Then
    Alert "You must enter a last name"
    frmRegister.txtLastName.focus
    Exit Sub
  ElseIf Len(frmRegister.txtState.value) = 0 Then
    Alert "You must enter a state abbreviation"
    frmRegister.txtState.focus
    Exit Sub
  ElseIf Len(frmRegister.txtDateofBirth.value) = 0 Then
    Alert "You must enter your date of birth"
    frmRegister.txtDateofBirth.focus
    Exit Sub
  ElseIf frmRegister.cboClubs.selectedindex = -1 Then
    Alert "You must select the club to which you belong"
    frmRegister.cboClubs.focus
    Exit Sub
  End If

  'If we get to this point all is OK, submit the form
  Call frmRegister.submit()
End Sub
</SCRIPT>

</BODY>
</HTML>
```

### How It Works – Register.asp Page

We want to start by building our `qAllClubs` stored procedure in the Sailors Access database. The procedure for creating an Access stored procedure is explained in the second example of Chapter 14. The SQL code for this stored procedure is really quite simple. We are selecting two columns from the `Clubs` table, and ordering the set of results by the `ClubName` column.

```
SELECT Clubs.ClubName, Clubs.ClubCode
FROM Clubs
ORDER BY Clubs.ClubName;
```

As you can see by the code listing, this page contains a lot more detail than the `Default.asp` page. So let's jump right in and take it step by step.

The first two lines of code are for our include files. The adovbs.inc file contains all of our ADO constants and the ProductionErrorHandler.inc file contains the function to check for errors.

The first part of the page contains the standard HTML tags that build the page header. Again we use the same HTML tags as our last example to write and center our first line of text in the page.

```
<!-- #include file="adovbs.inc" -->
<!-- #include file="ProductionErrorHandler.inc" -->
<HTML>
<HEAD>
<META NAME="GENERATOR" Content="Microsoft Visual Studio 6.0">
<TITLE>Sailors Web Site</TITLE>
</HEAD>
<BODY>

<!--Display the page data-->
<DIV ALIGN=center>
  <BIG><BIG><FONT COLOR=navy>Sailors Case Study</FONT></BIG></BIG>
</DIV>
<BR><BR>
```

We need to build a form to display the fields that require input from the user. Our form, named frmRegister, will display text fields, a check box, option buttons (also referred to as radio buttons), a combo box and of course a Submit button so the user can submit the form data. This will post details to the registrationconfirmation.asp page. The first part of our form contains the standard input boxes used in our last example.

```
<FORM ACTION=registrationconfirmation.asp METHOD=post NAME=frmRegister>
<TABLE>
  <TR>
  <TD HEIGHT=50 COLSPAN=2><FONT COLOR=navy>Registration Screen
    </FONT></TD>
  </TR>
  <TR>
  <TD>First Name</TD>
  <TD><INPUT TYPE=text NAME=txtFirstName SIZE=15></TD>
  <TD WIDTH=50></TD>
  <TD>Last Name</TD>
  <TD><INPUT TYPE=text NAME=txtLastName SIZE=15></TD>
  </TR>
  <TR>
  <TD>State</TD>
  <TD><INPUT TYPE=text NAME=txtState SIZE=2></TD>
  <TD WIDTH=50></TD>
  <TD>Date of Birth</TD>
  <TD><INPUT TYPE=text NAME=txtDateofBirth SIZE=8></TD>
  </TR>
```

This next section of code contains the checkbox that will indicate if the person registering is a referee. The value property is used in our server-side script to test if the check box has been checked. If it has it will contain a value of '1' and if it has not it will contain no value at all. We will cover this in detail in the next example when we check the fields from this form.

```
  <TR>
  <TD>Referee</TD>
  <TD><INPUT TYPE=checkbox NAME=chkReferee VALUE=1></TD>
  </TR>
```

The option buttons that we build next are also referred to as radio buttons. Notice that all three buttons have the same name but different values. This allows us to place these option buttons in a collection, in which only one button can be turned on (checked) at any given time. We will also explain this in detail in the next example.

One more thing to point out here is that all three option buttons exist in the same column in the table. Therefore we have to specify the COLSPAN property of the TD tag which we are doing here. We specify that this column in the table should span across four other columns in the table. This helps us to keep everything aligned properly.

```
<TR>
<TD>Professional Class</TD>
<TD COLSPAN=4>
   <INPUT TYPE=radio NAME=optClass VALUE=1 checked>Professional
   <INPUT TYPE=radio NAME=optClass VALUE=2>Ranked Amateur
   <INPUT TYPE=radio NAME=optClass VALUE=3>Other
</TD>
</TR>
```

Next, we build a combo box using the HTML SELECT element. This element requires an ending tag, which we have specified here. We have already seen how to code static options in the combo box, and how to load the combo box using a recordset while the form was being built. We are going to show you a different way to load this combo box, using the Window_OnLoad event. That comes just a little further on.

```
<TR>
<TD>Club Name</TD>
<TD COLSPAN=3><SELECT NAME=cboClubs></SELECT></TD>
</TR>
```

The last part of our form contains one table row that contains a blank space, which is specified as  . This will help to separate our Submit button from the rest of the fields in the form. This Submit button is built differently to how we did in the last example. Here we are using a standard button element and giving it a name of btnSubmit and a value of Submit. The value property is what will actually display on your web page.

```
<TR>
<TD>  </TD>
</TR>
<TR>
<TD><INPUT TYPE=button NAME=btnSubmit VALUE=Submit></TD>
</TR>
</FORM>
```

We include our include file that contains the code to connect to the database, and then call the function to check for errors. Notice that we are passing the Connection object as a parameter to the CheckForErrors function. This will allow us to open multiple Connection objects and use the same error handling function to check for errors.

```
<!-- #include file="Connect.inc" -->

<%
'Check for database errors
Call CheckForErrors(objConn)
```

Next, we create our `Recordset` object, and open our recordset using the stored procedure, `qAllClubs`, on the database. After opening our recordset we again call the function to check for errors.

```
<%
'Create the recordset object, set the SQL string and open the recordset
Set objRS = Server.CreateObject("ADODB.Recordset")
strSQL = "qAllClubs"
objRS.Open strSQL, objConn, adOpenForwardOnly, , adCmdStoredProc

'Check for database errors
Call CheckForErrors(objConn)
%>
```

We now switch to client-side script and process some code in the `Window_OnLoad` event. This is the first event to run when the web page loads in the browser. Remember we mentioned earlier that we would demonstrate a different way to load the combo box. Well here it is. We start by using some server-side script, which is used to loop through the `Recordset` object.

Next, we create an `Option` element for the combo box and set it to a variable, in this case `objOption`. Next we assign the `text` to the option variable using the recordset field `ClubName`. This is the text that you will see on your screen. Notice that we include server-side tags around the `Recordset` object, which indicates that this data will be coming from the server-side script. Next we assign the `value` to the option variable using the recordset field `ClubCode`. This is the value that will be read from the next page. We will explain more about that in the next example. Last, we add the option to the combo box, advance the recordset and start the loop over again. We now have a combo box with a dropdown list of all the available boat club names.

After we come out of the loop, we switch back to HTML and include our `Disconnect` include file which will close our recordset and database connection, and de-reference those objects. Last we de-reference our `objOption` object and end the `Window_OnLoad` event.

```
<SCRIPT LANGUAGE=vbscript>
Sub Window_OnLoad()
<%
  Do While Not objRS.EOF
%>
    Set objOption = document.createElement("OPTION")
    objOption.text = "<%=objRS("ClubName")%>"
    objOption.value = "<%=objRS("ClubCode")%>"
    document.all.cboClubs.add objOption
<%
    objRS.MoveNext
  Loop
%>

  <!-- #include file="DisConnect.inc" -->

  Set objOption = Nothing
End Sub
```

Before the user submits the form for processing, we want to validate that all data has been entered. We are not validating the data to see if it is correct, we'll leave that up to you to try later if you so desire. We are validating the code in the **Submit** button's `onclick` event, which indicates to us that the user wants to submit the form. We simply do an `If`, `ElseIf` pair until we get to the end of the validations.

We check the length of the field on the form to see if it is equal to zero, which indicates the user has not entered any data. If the length is zero we send a message to the user using the `Alert` function. This is very similar to the `MsgBox` function except we can only specify a message to be displayed. We cannot set the buttons that will be displayed, as the only button in the `Alert` function is the `OK` button.

After displaying the alert, we set focus to the field in question so the user can start entering data, they don't have to try and figure out which field was in error. Next we exit the procedure without doing any further validations.

```
Sub btnSubmit_OnClick()
   'Verify all fields have been entered
   If Len(frmRegister.txtFirstName.value) = 0 Then
      Alert "You must enter a first name"
      frmRegister.txtFirstName.focus
      Exit Sub
   ElseIf Len(frmRegister.txtLastName.value) = 0 Then
      Alert "You must enter a last name"
      frmRegister.txtLastName.focus
      Exit Sub
   ElseIf Len(frmRegister.txtState.value) = 0 Then
      Alert "You must enter a state abbreviation"
      frmRegister.txtState.focus
      Exit Sub
   ElseIf Len(frmRegister.txtDateofBirth.value) = 0 Then
      Alert "You must enter your date of birth"
      frmRegister.txtDateofBirth.focus
      Exit Sub
```

The validation of the combo box is a little different, as the user cannot enter text, they can only select it. Here we need to check the `selectedindex` property of the combo box. Just like the standard combo box in VB, this combo box also uses a base 0 index, so if an item is not selected then the `selectedindex` is – 1. If the first item is selected then the `selectedindex` is 0 and so on.

If all validation tests have been passed we come to the end of our code in this procedure and we will call the `submit` method of the form. This method will submit all of the values on the form and call the web page listed in the `action` property of our form, in other words the `registrationconfirmation` page.

```
   ElseIf frmRegister.cboClubs.selectedindex = -1 Then
      Alert "You must select the club to which you belong"
      frmRegister.cboClubs.focus
      Exit Sub
   End If

   'If we get to this point all is OK, submit the form
   Call frmRegister.submit()
End Sub
</SCRIPT>
```

We then end our page with the standard HTML tags (not shown).

## Try It Out – RegistrationConfirmation.asp Page

The `RegistrationConfirmation.asp` page reads all of the form fields from the request form, which in this case is the `Registration.asp` page. It builds the parameters to a stored procedure and executes that stored procedure, writing all of the information to the database. Upon successful completion of this it will write a cookie to the user's machine, display the user's password and give them a list of options for them to execute. The page looks like the following screenshot:

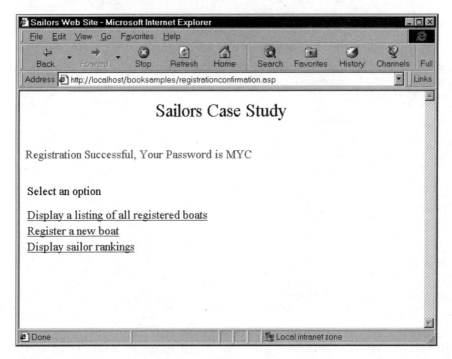

The stored procedure `qparmInsertPerson` is coded as below:

```
PARAMETERS FirstName Text, LastName Text, DOB DateTime, ProfessionalClass Long,
ClubCode Text, Referee Bit, State Text;
INSERT INTO People ( PeopleNameFirst, PeopleNameLast, PeopleDOB,
PeopleProfessionalClass, PeopleClubCode, PeopleReferee, PeopleState )
SELECT [FirstName] AS Expr1, [LastName] AS Expr2, [DOB] AS Expr3, [ProfessionalClass]
AS Expr4, [ClubCode] AS Expr5, [Referee] AS Expr6, [State] AS Expr7;
```

The code for this web page is shown below, and is in the file `RegistrationConfirmation.asp`.

```asp
<!-- #include file="adovbs.inc" -->
<!-- #include file="ProductionErrorHandler.inc" -->
<!-- #include file="Connect.inc" -->

<%
'Check for database errors
Call CheckForErrors(objConn)

'Set the referee variable
If Request.Form("chkReferee") = 1 Then
  bytReferee = 1
Else
  bytReferee = 0
End If

'Set the parameters for the insert stored procedure
strSQL = "qparmInsertPerson ('" & CStr(Request.Form("txtFirstName")) & _
  "','" & CStr(Request.Form("txtLastName")) & _
  "','" & CStr(Request.Form("txtDateofBirth")) & _
  "'," & CLng(Request.Form("optClass")) & _
  ",'" & CStr(Request.Form("cboClubs")) & _
  "'," & CByte(bytReferee) & _
  ",'" & CStr(Request.Form("txtState")) & "')"
'Execute the stored procedure to insert the person
objConn.Execute strSQL,,adCmdStoredProc

'Check for database errors
Call CheckForErrors(objConn)
%>

<!-- #include file="DisConnect.inc" -->

<%
'Save the user information to a cookie
Response.Cookies("Sailor")("FirstName") = Request.Form("txtFirstName")
Response.Cookies("Sailor")("LastName") = Request.Form("txtLastName")
Response.Cookies("Sailor")("Password") = Request.Form("txtPassword")

'Set the expiration date of the cookie to the last day of the
'current year
Response.Cookies("Sailor").Expires = "December 31, " & Year(Now)

'Authenticate the user for other Web pages
Session("Authenticated") = True
%>

<HTML>
<HEAD>
<META NAME="GENERATOR" Content="Microsoft Visual Studio 6.0">
<TITLE>Sailors Web Site</TITLE>
</HEAD>
<BODY>

<!--Display the page data-->
<DIV ALIGN=CENTER>
  <BIG><BIG><FONT COLOR=navy>Sailors Case Study</FONT></BIG></BIG>
</DIV>
<BR><BR>
  <FONT COLOR=teal>Registration Successful,
  Your Password is <%=Request.Form("cboClubs")%></FONT>
<BR><BR>

<!-- #include file="MenuOptions.inc" -->

</BODY>
</HTML>
```

### How It Works – RegistrationConfirmation.asp page – The Stored Procedure

Let's start with our stored procedure. It actually looks more complicated than it really is. First we define all of our parameters specifying the parameter name and the data type.

```
PARAMETERS FirstName Text, LastName Text, DOB DateTime, ProfessionalClass Long,
ClubCode Text, Referee Bit, State Text;
```

Next, we build the INSERT statement, specifying the table and the columns into which we are inserting data.

```
INSERT INTO People ( PeopleNameFirst, PeopleNameLast, PeopleDOB,
PeopleProfessionalClass, PeopleClubCode, PeopleReferee, PeopleState )
```

Last we SELECT the parameters as expressions, in the same order as the columns listed in the INSERT statement.

```
SELECT [FirstName] AS Expr1, [LastName] AS Expr2, [DOB] AS Expr3, [ProfessionalClass]
AS Expr4, [ClubCode] AS Expr5, [Referee] AS Expr6, [State] AS Expr7;
```

### The Web Page

This web page does not contain a lot of code but it does a lot of work. We start our page by including the include files that contain our ADO constants, check for errors and connect to the database. Notice that we haven't coded any HTML headers yet.

```
<!-- #include file="adovbs.inc" -->
<!-- #include file="ProductionErrorHandler.inc" -->
<!-- #include file="Connect.inc" -->

<%
'Check for database errors
Call CheckForErrors(objConn)
```

Remember in the last example we said we would go into the details of the check box. Well, here we go. The value of the check box is what actually gets read from the request form. If the field chkReferee has a value of 1 then we know that the checkbox was checked. If the value is nothing then we know that the checkbox was not checked.

So, in our code we check to see if the value is 1 and if so set a variable to 1, else we set the variable to 0. We have to do this validation here before we code our parameters for the stored procedure. The database is expecting a 0 or 1 value to the PeopleReferee field in the People table. If we passed the chkReferee field directly as a parameter to the stored procedure, we would receive an error if the checkbox were not checked.

Notice that we use the Request object to retrieve the form field and we have also started our server–side script.

```
<%
'Set the referee variable
If Request.Form("chkReferee") = 1 Then
  bytReferee = 1
Else
  bytReferee = 0
End If
```

We pass the rest of the fields from the request form directly, without having to set them to a variable first. We do convert the fields to their appropriate values first though.

The option buttons that were used in the last example all had a value set, and they also all had the same name, which allows us to access the buttons in a collection in the form in which they are built. When the form was submitted from the last page, it looked at the collection of option buttons and only passed the one that was checked. So if the first button were checked, we would receive a 1 for optClass because the value was set to 1. If the second option button were checked, we would receive a 2 because the value of the second option button was 2, and so on.

In the last example we mentioned that the combo box used the VALUE property to pass the value of the item selected. Since we required the user to select an entry in the combo box, we do not have to validate the option selected here. Here, we simply pass the value that is associated with cboClubs.

After all parameters have been built in the SQL string, we execute the SQL string using the Connection object, as demonstrated in Chapter 14. Next we check for errors using the CheckForErrors function. We then switch to HTML code and include our include file to close the Connection object.

The ConvertString function could be included to check the last name, since a last name that contains a single quote would cause an error.

```
'Set the parameters for the insert stored procedure
strSQL = "qparmInsertPerson ('" & CStr(Request.Form("txtFirstName")) & _
   "','" & CStr(Request.Form("txtLastName")) & _
   "','" & CStr(Request.Form("txtDateofBirth")) & _
   "'," & CLng(Request.Form("optClass")) & _
   ",'" & CStr(Request.Form("cboClubs")) & _
   "'," & CByte(bytReferee) & _
   ",'" & CStr(Request.Form("txtState")) & "')"
'Execute the stored procedure to insert the person
objConn.Execute strSQL,,adCmdStoredProc

'Check for database errors
Call CheckForErrors(objConn)
%>

<!-- #include file="DisConnect.inc" -->
```

Next we write a cookie on the user's machine with their login information, as was demonstrated in Chapter 11. Then we set the cookie to expire on December 31 of the current year.

```
<%
'Save the user information to a cookie
Response.Cookies("Sailor")("FirstName") = Request.Form("txtFirstName")
Response.Cookies("Sailor")("LastName") = Request.Form("txtLastName")
Response.Cookies("Sailor")("Password") = Request.Form("txtPassword")

'Set the expiration date of the cookie to the last day of the
'current year
Response.Cookies("Sailor").Expires = "December 31, " & Year(Now)
```

After we have written the cookie we want to authenticate the user so they can access the other web pages. We do this by creating a `Session` variable called `Authenticated`, and setting its value to `True`.

```
'Authenticate the user for other Web pages
Session("Authenticated") = True
%>
```

After we have gone through all of the previous processing, where we connected to the database, set the stored procedure parameters, inserted the user record into the database, disconnected from the database, wrote a cookie to the user's machine and authenticated the user, we *now* write the HTML headers for the beginning of our web page.

The first part of the code contains just the standard HTML headers and the beginning of the page text, as in the previous two examples.

```
<HTML>
<HEAD>
<META NAME="GENERATOR" Content="Microsoft Visual Studio 6.0">
<TITLE>Sailors Web Site</TITLE>
</HEAD>
<BODY>

<!--Display the page data-->
<DIV ALIGN=center>
   <BIG><BIG><FONT COLOR=navy>Sailors Case Study</FONT></BIG></BIG>
</DIV>
<BR><BR>
```

We want to inform the user of their password which, to keep this case study simple, is the club code of the club they chose on the Registration form. We use a different font color so that this information stands out from the rest of the text on the page.

```
   <FONT COLOR=teal>Registration Successful,
   Your Password is <%=Request.Form("cboClubs")%></FONT>
<BR><BR>
```

The last part of the code includes a file containing the menu options, and the last two lines of code end the page.

```
<!-- #include file="MenuOptions.inc" -->

</BODY>
</HTML>
```

At this point, we have a default page for our web site, a page to enter registration information, and a page to write the registration information to the database and write our cookie.

---

**If you have not done so at this point, register yourself in the Sailors database.**

---

## Try It Out – WelcomeBack.asp Page

The WelcomeBack.asp page welcomes the user back to our web site. The user would receive this page if the Default.asp page found a cookie and redirected their browser here. The page looks like this:

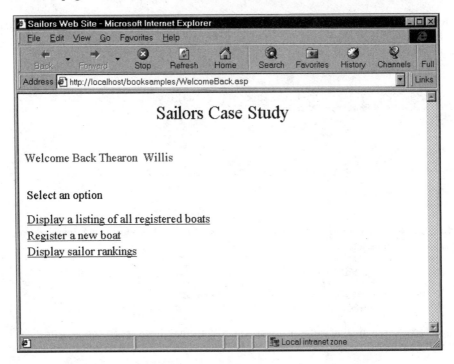

The code for this page is in Welcomeback.asp, shown below.

```
<!-- #include file="AuthenticationCheck.inc" -->
<HTML>
<HEAD>
<META NAME="GENERATOR" Content="Microsoft Visual Studio 6.0">
<TITLE>Sailors Web Site</TITLE>
</HEAD>
<BODY>

<!--Display the page data-->
<DIV ALIGN=center>
  <BIG><BIG><FONT COLOR=navy>Sailors Case Study</FONT></BIG></BIG>
</DIV>

<BR><BR>
  <FONT COLOR=teal>Welcome Back
  <%=Request.Cookies("Sailor")("FirstName")%> 
  <%=Request.Cookies("Sailor")("LastName")%></FONT>
<BR><BR>

<!-- #include file="MenuOptions.inc" -->

</BODY>
</HTML>
```

### How It Works – WelcomeBack.asp Page

This page is really simple and straight to the point. First we include the include file to see if the user has been authenticated. This include file checks that the `Session` variable `Authenticated` is set to `True`. If it is not, the browser will be redirected back to the `default.asp` page.

The rest of this section of code is the standard HTML code for the beginning of a page and also the first line of text on our web page.

```
<!-- #include file="AuthenticationCheck.inc" -->
<HTML>
<HEAD>
<META NAME="GENERATOR" Content="Microsoft Visual Studio 6.0">
<TITLE>Sailors Web Site</TITLE>
</HEAD>
<BODY>

<!--Display the page data-->
<DIV ALIGN=center>
  <BIG><BIG><FONT COLOR=navy>Sailors Case Study</FONT></BIG></BIG>
</DIV>

<BR><BR>
```

Reading the first name and last name from the cookie that we have found on the user's machine, we write a little welcome message.

```
  <FONT COLOR=teal>Welcome Back
  <%=Request.Cookies("Sailor")("FirstName")%> 
  <%=Request.Cookies("Sailor")("LastName")%></FONT>
<BR><BR>
```

Last, we include the file that contains the menu options that the user can choose from. The last two lines of code end the page with standard HTML.

```
<!-- #include file="MenuOptions.inc" -->

</BODY>
</HTML>
```

At this point, you should be able to shut down your browser, start it back up again, navigate to this web site, and automatically be sent to this page.

To test the next example that will be demonstrated, it will be necessary for you to delete your cookie. Using Windows Explorer, navigate to the **Cookies** folder and delete the cookie.

If you don't know where your temporary Internet files are stored, especially if you are on a Windows NT workstation, click on the View menu in Internet Explorer and select Internet Options. The following dialog appears:

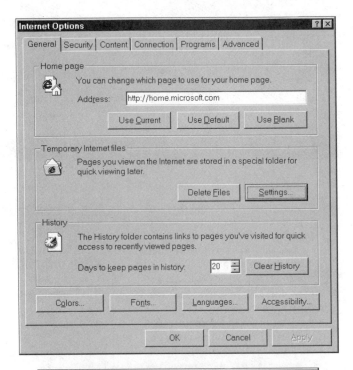

Click on the Settings button in the Temporary Internet Files section to see this dialog and to find out where your Temporary Internet Files folder is located.

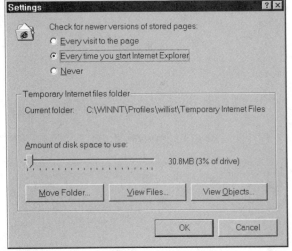

Your Cookies folder should be in the same directory as your Temporary Internet Files folder. Now that you know where it is, you need to know the name of the cookie. It will have the same name as your web site. In my case my web site name is BookSamples so my cookie name is also BookSamples.

Click on the cookie in Windows Explorer and press the Delete key, or right click the mouse on it and choose Delete from the menu. You will get a confirmation message warning you this is a cookie and asking if you are sure you want to delete it – click Yes.

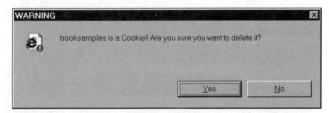

## Try It Out – LoginVerification.asp Page

The LoginVerification.asp page reads the login information that the user has entered into the default.asp page and verifies it against the database. If no match is found, the page sets an error message and redirects the browser back to the default.asp page. If a match was found it will write a new cookie on the user's machine and then display the menu options. The display should be as shown:

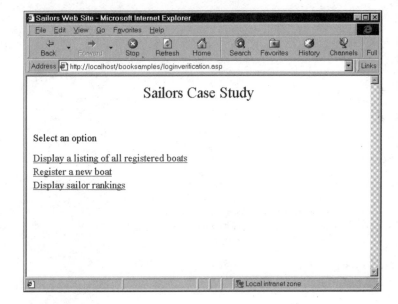

The stored procedure required is qparmVerifyLogin.

```
PARAMETERS FirstName Text, LastName Text, ClubCode Text;
SELECT People.PeopleNameFirst, People.PeopleNameLast, People.PeopleClubCode
FROM People
WHERE (((People.PeopleNameFirst)=[FirstName]) AND ((People.PeopleNameLast)=[LastName])
AND ((People.PeopleClubCode)=[ClubCode]));
```

The `LoginVerification.asp` web page code looks like this:

```
<!-- #include file="adovbs.inc" -->
<!-- #include file="ProductionErrorHandler.inc" -->
<!-- #include file="Connect.inc" -->

<%
'Check for database errors
Call CheckForErrors(objConn)

'Verify user information in the database
'Create the recordset object, set the SQL string and parameters
'and open the recordset
Set objRS = Server.CreateObject("ADODB.Recordset")
strSQL = "qparmVerifyLogin '" & CStr(Request.Form("txtFirstName")) & _
  "','" & CStr(Request.Form("txtLastName")) & _
  "','" & CStr(Request.Form("txtPassword")) & "'"
objRS.Open strSQL, objConn, adOpenForwardOnly, , adCmdStoredProc

'Check for database errors
Call CheckForErrors(objConn)

'Check for empty recordset which indicates user information
'was not found
If objRS.EOF or objRS.BOF Then
  Session("ErrorMessage") = "No record found - Please ensure all information was" & _
    "entered correctly"
  Response.Redirect "default.asp"
Else
  Session("ErrorMessage") = Empty
End If
%>

<!-- #include file="DisConnect.inc" -->

<%
'Save the user information to a cookie
Response.Cookies("Sailor")("FirstName") = Request.Form("txtFirstName")
Response.Cookies("Sailor")("LastName") = Request.Form("txtLastName")
Response.Cookies("Sailor")("Password") = Request.Form("txtPassword")

'Set the expiration date of the cookie to the last day of the
'current year
Response.Cookies("Sailor").Expires = "December 31, " & Year(Now)

'Authenticate the user for other Web pages
Session("Authenticated") = True
%>

<HTML>
<HEAD>
<META NAME="GENERATOR" Content="Microsoft Visual Studio 6.0">
<TITLE>Sailors Web Site</TITLE>
</HEAD>
<BODY>

<!--Display the page data-->
<DIV ALIGN=CENTER>
  <BIG><BIG><FONT COLOR=navy>Sailors Case Study</FONT></BIG></BIG>
</DIV>
<BR><BR>

<!-- #include file="MenuOptions.inc" -->

</BODY>
</HTML>
```

## How It Works – LoginVerification.asp Page – The Stored Procedure

We need to code our stored procedure first, which is a simple select with parameters. This stored procedure will return a recordset with the same fields that we passed as parameters, which are FirstName, LastName, and ClubCode. We will explain why we do this when we get into the code.

First we define the parameters that are going to be passed to this stored procedure.

```
PARAMETERS FirstName Text, LastName Text, ClubCode Text;
```

Next we code the SELECT statement selecting the only three columns that we need and that match the parameters being passed.

```
SELECT People.PeopleNameFirst, People.PeopleNameLast, People.PeopleClubCode
FROM People
```

Finally, we code the WHERE clause, selecting only the record that matches the parameters passed. All columns in the SELECT clause are listed here and must match exactly the parameters being passed.

```
WHERE (((People.PeopleNameFirst)=[FirstName]) AND ((People.PeopleNameLast)=[LastName])
AND ((People.PeopleClubCode)=[ClubCode]));
```

Now we start our web page by including the include files that contain our ADO constants and that will check for errors and connect to the database.

```
<!-- #include file="adovbs.inc" -->
<!-- #include file="ProductionErrorHandler.inc" -->
<!-- #include file="Connect.inc" -->

<%
'Check for database errors
Call CheckForErrors(objConn)
```

After we have an active connection to the database, we can set up the SQL string, passing it the appropriate parameters. Notice that we are going to open a recordset and thus create a Recordset object. This recordset will contain the same fields that match the parameters. Last, we open the recordset and check for errors.

```
<%
'Verify user information in the database

'Create the recordset object, set the SQL string and parameters
'and open the recordset
Set objRS = Server.CreateObject("ADODB.Recordset")
strSQL = "qparmVerifyLogin '" & CStr(Request.Form("txtFirstName")) & _
  "','" & CStr(Request.Form("txtLastName")) & _
  "','" & CStr(Request.Form("txtPassword")) & "'"
objRS.Open strSQL, objConn, adOpenForwardOnly, , adCmdStoredProc

'Check for database errors
Call CheckForErrors(objConn)
```

The reason that we selected the same fields that matched the parameters being passed was because Access cannot return a value in a stored procedure, as SQL Server can. We covered this in chapter 14. So, by returning a recordset we can check for an EOF (end of file) and BOF (beginning of file) condition on the recordset. If this evaluation is True, this indicates to us that the parameters that were passed did not find a match, and that the user does not exist in the database.

If no record was returned in the recordset, we set a `Session` variable called `ErrorMessage` with the appropriate error message, and redirect the browser back to the `default.asp` page. Otherwise we clear any previous existing messages, just in case there are any, and continue on.

```
'Check for empty recordset which indicates user information
'was not found
If objRS.EOF or objRS.BOF Then
   Session("ErrorMessage") = "No record found - Please ensure all information was" & _
   "entered correctly"
   Response.Redirect "default.asp"
Else
   Session("ErrorMessage") = Empty
End If
%>
```

We disconnect the recordset and database connection using the appropriate include file, and then write a new cookie to the user's machine, setting the expiration date on the cookie. We then authenticate the user so that they have access to the other web pages.

```
<!-- #include file="DisConnect.inc" -->

<%
'Save the user information to a cookie
Response.Cookies("Sailor")("FirstName") = Request.Form("txtFirstName")
Response.Cookies("Sailor")("LastName") = Request.Form("txtLastName")
Response.Cookies("Sailor")("Password") = Request.Form("txtPassword")

'Set the expiration date of the cookie to the last day of the
'current year
Response.Cookies("Sailor").Expires = "December 31, " & Year(Now)

'Authenticate the user for other Web pages
Session("Authenticated") = True
%>
```

Finally we start the headers for this web page. Again, these are the standard HTML headers as we have seen before. We also write the first line of text on the page as we have done in the previous examples.

```
<HTML>
<HEAD>
<META NAME="GENERATOR" Content="Microsoft Visual Studio 6.0">
<TITLE>Sailors Web Site</TITLE>
</HEAD>
<BODY>

<!--Display the page data-->
<DIV ALIGN=center>
   <BIG><BIG><FONT COLOR=navy>Sailors Case Study</FONT></BIG></BIG>
</DIV>
<BR><BR>
```

To wrap up this page, we include the file that contains the menu options and write the closing HTML tags for this page.

```
<!-- #include file="MenuOptions.inc" -->

</BODY>
</HTML>
```

# Login Process Summary

At this point, you should be able to login using the information you previously supplied in the registration page and the password that was returned, and see the page shown in the previous figure. After you have logged back in, try shutting down your browser and then start it back up. When you come back into your web site you should be redirected to the WelcomeBack.asp page.

To summarize the login process, we have created a series of web pages that will:

- ❑ Check for the existence of a cookie
- ❑ Redirect your browser
- ❑ Provide a login screen
- ❑ Validate the user's login details
- ❑ Provide a registration screen
- ❑ Register a new user
- ❑ Welcome back an existing user

We are now ready to create the other web pages that make up the rest of the functionality of our web site.

# Web Site User Options

We included an include file called MenuOptions.inc in some of our login pages. This was done so that we could validate the user and provide the appropriate messages, and also display the menu options that they could access. The Options.asp page contains mostly HTML code with very little script processing. It is displayed after the user has logged in, has navigated to another page, and chosen to return to the menu options.

## Try It Out – Options.asp

The Options.asp page contains the options that are available for the user. They can click on any of the hyperlinks to jump to another page in the web site. There are currently only three options, but with some thought you are sure to be able to come up with more. This is how our page looks:

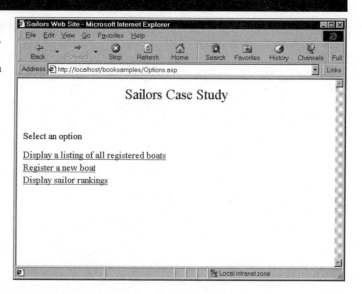

The code for the `Options.asp` page is given here:

```
<!-- #include file="AuthenticationCheck.inc" -->
<HTML>
<HEAD>
<META NAME="GENERATOR" Content="Microsoft Visual Studio 6.0">
<TITLE>Sailors Web Site</TITLE>
</HEAD>
<BODY>

<!--Display the page data-->
<DIV ALIGN=center>
  <BIG><BIG><FONT COLOR=navy>Sailors Case Study</FONT></BIG></BIG>
</DIV>
<BR><BR>

<!-- #include file="MenuOptions.inc" -->

</BODY>
</HTML>
```

### How It Works – Options.asp

The only script processing in this page is contained in the include file which we have coded first. If the user has not been authenticated they will be redirected to the `Default.asp` page.

The rest of the code in this first section contains the standard HTML headers and the first line of text on our page.

```
<!-- #include file="AuthenticationCheck.inc" -->
<HTML>
<HEAD>
<META NAME="GENERATOR" Content="Microsoft Visual Studio 6.0">
<TITLE>Sailors Web Site</TITLE>
</HEAD>
<BODY>

<!--Display the page data-->
<DIV ALIGN=center>
  <BIG><BIG><FONT COLOR=navy>Sailors Case Study</FONT></BIG></BIG>
</DIV>

<BR><BR>
```

The rest of the code in our web page contains an include file that includes the menu options to be displayed and the standard HTML tags that end our page.

```
<!-- #include file="MenuOptions.inc" -->

</BODY>
</HTML>
```

# The Display Boats Page

The next page we want to look at is a page to display all boats that are listed in our Boats table. This page will display Boat Name and Boat Class in a table. The end of the page will provide a hyperlink back to the Options.asp page.

**Try It Out – DisplayBoats.asp**

This page opens a recordset containing all of the boats listed in the Boats table, which are returned in the recordset sorted by boat class and then by boat name. A formatted table is built, using table headers and standard table rows, to display the data. The page is shown in the next screenshot:

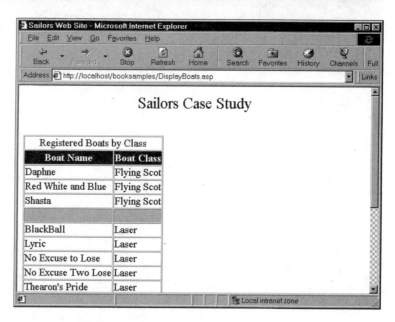

The stored procedure, qAllBoats, is coded as follows:

```
SELECT Boats.BoatClass, Boats.BoatName
FROM Boats
ORDER BY Boats.BoatClass, Boats.BoatName;
```

The web page file, DisplayBoats.asp, looks like this:

```
<!-- #include file="adovbs.inc" -->
<!-- #include file="AuthenticationCheck.inc" -->
<!-- #include file="ProductionErrorHandler.inc" -->

<HTML>
<HEAD>
<META NAME="GENERATOR" Content="Microsoft Visual Studio 6.0">
<TITLE>Sailors Web Site</TITLE>
</HEAD>
<BODY>

<!--Display the page data-->
<DIV ALIGN=CENTER>
  <BIG><BIG><FONT COLOR=navy>Sailors Case Study</FONT></BIG></BIG>
</DIV>
<BR><BR>
```

```
<!-- #include file="Connect.inc" -->

<%
'Check for database errors
Call CheckForErrors(objConn)

'Create the recordset object, set the SQL string and open the recordset
Set objRS = Server.CreateObject("ADODB.Recordset")
strSQL = "qAllBoats"
objRS.Open strSQL, objConn, adOpenForwardOnly, , adCmdStoredProc

'Check for database errors
Call CheckForErrors(objConn)
%>

<!--Build the table header rows-->
<TABLE border=1 cellspacing=1>
  <TR>
  <TD COLSPAN=2 ALIGN=CENTER>Registered Boats by Class</TD>
  </TR>
  <TR>
  <TH BGCOLOR=navy><FONT COLOR=white>Boat Name</FONT></TH>
  <TH BGCOLOR=navy><FONT COLOR=white>Boat Class</FONT></TH>
  </TR>

<%
'Set a variable to hold the last boatclass
Dim strLastClass
strLastClass = objRS("BoatClass")

'Loop through the recordset displaying the last name field
Do While Not objRS.EOF
  'If the current boat class is not equal to the last
  'boat class then build a seperator row in the table
  If objRS("BoatClass") <> strLastClass Then
%>
    <TR>
    <TD BGCOLOR=silver>  </TD>
    <TD BGCOLOR=silver>  </TD>
    </TR>
<%
    strLastClass = objRS("BoatClass")
  End If
%>
  <!--Build a row of data in the table-->
  <TR>
  <TD><%=objRS("BoatName")%></TD>
  <TD><%=objRS("BoatClass")%></TD>
  </TR>
<%
  objRS.MoveNext
Loop
%>
  <!--Build a seperator row in the table-->
  <TR>
  <TD BGCOLOR=silver>  </TD>
  <TD BGCOLOR=silver>  </TD>
  <TR>
  <!--Build the last row of data with a hyper link to the options page-->
  <TR>
  <TD COLSPAN=2><A HREF="Options.asp"
    ONMOUSEOVER="window.status='Return to Options Page';return true"
    ONMOUSEOUT="window.status=''">Return to Options Page</A></TD>
  </TR>
  </TABLE>

<!-- #include file="DisConnect.inc" -->

</BODY>
</HTML>
```

### How It Works – DisplayBoats.asp – The Stored Procedure

The stored procedure to select all of our boat names and boat classes is simple. We select the two columns from the Boats table and order them by boatclass and then by boatname. This ensures that all records returned are sorted by class, and within each class the boat names are sorted.

```
SELECT Boats.BoatClass, Boats.BoatName
FROM Boats
ORDER BY Boats.BoatClass, Boats.BoatName;
```

### The Web Page

Once again, the first part of our web page contains the include files that contain our ADO constants, the authentication routine, and our error handling function, the standard HTML headers, and the first line of text in our page.

```
<!-- #include file="adovbs.inc" -->
<!-- #include file="AuthenticationCheck.inc" -->
<!-- #include file="ProductionErrorHandler.inc" -->

<HTML>
<HEAD>
<META NAME="GENERATOR" Content="Microsoft Visual Studio 6.0">
<TITLE>Sailors Web Site</TITLE>
</HEAD>
<BODY>

<!--Display the page data-->
<DIV ALIGN=center>
  <BIG><BIG><FONT COLOR=navy>Sailors Case Study</FONT></BIG></BIG>
</DIV>
<BR><BR>
```

Since we are going to be opening a recordset, we need to include the include files to establish the database connection and then check for errors.

```
<!-- #include file="Connect.inc" -->

<%
'Check for database errors
Call CheckForErrors(objConn)
```

This stored procedure contains no parameters, as we want all rows in the Boats table returned. We create our Recordset object and set the SQL string. Next we open our recordset and check for errors.

```
<%
'Create the recordset object, set the SQL string and open the recordset
Set objRS = Server.CreateObject("ADODB.Recordset")
strSQL = "qAllBoats"
objRS.Open strSQL, objConn, adOpenForwardOnly, , adCmdStoredProc

'Check for database errors
Call CheckForErrors(objConn)
%>
```

We start building the table by writing the first column in our table. Notice that we specify the COLSPAN property of the TD tag so that this column will span across two normal columns. The second row of the table actually contains column headers, which are signified by the use of the TH tags. We set the background color of the column by specifying the BGCOLOR property of the TH tags. We then use the FONT tag to specify the color of the text in the header column.

```
<!--Build the table header rows-->
<TABLE BORDER=1 CELLSPACING=1>
  <TR>
  <TD COLSPAN=2 ALIGN=center>Registered Boats by Class</TD>
  </TR>
  <TR>
  <TH BGCOLOR=navy><FONT COLOR=white>Boat Name</FONT></TH>
  <TH BGCOLOR=navy><FONT COLOR=white>Boat Class</FONT></TH>
  </TR>
```

Now that the table headers have been written, we are almost ready to start writing our table rows. Before we do that we are going to use a variable to keep track of the last boat class. This way we can create a separator row in our table to separate the different boat classes.

We start by declaring a variable called strLastClass. Remember that all variables are variants so we cannot specify a data type. Next we set the variable to the boat class contained in the first row of our recordset.

```
<%
'Set a variable to hold the last boatclass
Dim strLastClass
strLastClass = objRS("BoatClass")
```

We set up a Do While loop to loop through the recordset. The first thing we do in the loop is to check to see if the current boat class in the recordset is not equal to the last boat class in our variable. If they are not equal, we write two blank columns setting the BGCOLOR property of the TD tag to silver. In order to have the color span the entire length of the column, we have to create a non-breaking space by using   The last thing we need to do here is update our variable with the current boat class.

Now we insert the recordset fields into our columns through the use of server-side script tags. Then we advance the recordset to the next record using the MoveNext property of the Recordset object, and we go back to the top of the loop.

```
'Loop through the recordset displaying the last name field
Do While Not objRS.EOF
  'If the current boat class is not equal to the last
  'boat class then build a seperator row in the table
  If objRS("BoatClass") <> strLastClass Then
%>
    <TR>
    <TD BGCOLOR=silver>  </TD>
    <TD BGCOLOR=silver>  </TD>
    </TR>
<%
    strLastClass = objRS("BoatClass")
  End If
%>
<!--Build a row of data in the table-->
  <TR>
  <TD><%=objRS("BoatName")%></TD>
  <TD><%=objRS("BoatClass")%></TD>
  </TR>
<%
  objRS.MoveNext
Loop
%>
```

We need a way for the user to get back to the `Options` page, so we create another separator row in the table and then place a hyperlink to the `Options.asp` page in the next row. We then end the table.

```
<!--Build a seperator row in the table-->
<TR>
<TD BGCOLOR=silver>  </TD>
<TD BGCOLOR=silver>  </TD>
<TR>
<!--Build the last row of data with a hyper link to the options page-->
<TR>
<TD COLSPAN=2><A HREF="Options.asp"
   ONMOUSEOVER="window.status='Return to Options Page'; return true"
   ONMOUSEOUT="window.status=''">Return to Options Page</A></TD>
</TR>
</TABLE>
```

The last part of our code disconnects the recordset by using the `disconnect` include file, and then we end our page using the standard ending HTML tags.

```
<!-- #include file="DisConnect.inc" -->

</BODY>
</HTML>
```

# The Boat Registration Page

Our new user might look at the boats listed in the last page and decide that they want to register their own boat. Therefore we need to provide a page to allow a user to register their boat on our web site. The registration process is very simple for the user as they only have to enter their boat details and click on the Submit button. Once the registration details have been inserted into the database, the web page will display a confirmation message to the user.

## Try It Out – RegisterNewBoat.asp

This web page will take on a new twist to the way we have been doing things. This case study would not be complete if we did not demonstrate how you could process multiple steps in a single Active Server Page. The `RegisterNewBoat.asp` page contains a form that the user can fill in with their boat information. When they click on the submit button, the form will post the data back to the `RegisterNewBoat.asp` page. This is shown in the following two screenshots:

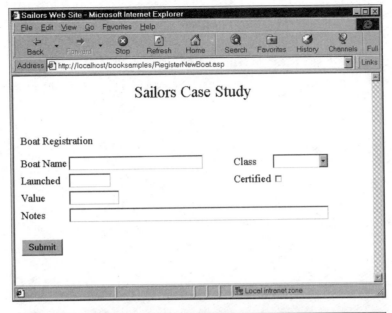

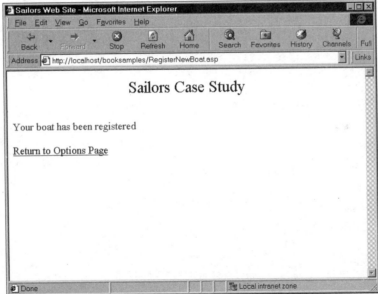

The first stored procedure we need is qAllBoatClasses, shown below.

```
SELECT BoatClass.ClassName
FROM BoatClass
ORDER BY BoatClass.ClassName;
```

We also need the stored procedure `qparmInsertBoat`.

```
PARAMETERS Name Text, Class Text, Launched DateTime, Certified Bit, Notes LongText,
[Value] Currency;
INSERT INTO Boats ( BoatName, BoatClass, BoatLaunched, BoatCertified, BoatNote,
BoatValue )
SELECT [Name] AS Expr1, [Class] AS Expr2, [Launched] AS Expr3, [Certified] AS Expr4,
[Notes] AS Expr5, [Value] AS Expr6;
```

The `RegisterNewBoat.asp` web page is coded as below.

```
<!-- #include file="adovbs.inc" -->
<!-- #include file="AuthenticationCheck.inc" -->
<!-- #include file="CommonFunctions.inc" -->
<!-- #include file="ProductionErrorHandler.inc" -->

<HTML>
<HEAD>
<META NAME="GENERATOR" Content="Microsoft Visual Studio 6.0">
<TITLE>Sailors Web Site</TITLE>
</HEAD>
<BODY>

<!--Display the page data-->
<DIV ALIGN=CENTER>
  <BIG><BIG><FONT COLOR=navy>Sailors Case Study</FONT></BIG></BIG>
</DIV>
<BR><BR>

<%
'********************************************************************
'* Step 1: Display the New Boat form for user input
'********************************************************************
If Len(Request.Form("FormAction")) = 0 Then
%>

  <FORM ACTION=RegisterNewBoat.asp method=post NAME=frmNewBoat>
  <INPUT TYPE=hidden NAME=FormAction VALUE=Step2>
  <TABLE>
    <TR>
    <TD HEIGHT=50 COLSPAN=2><FONT COLOR=navy>Boat Registration
      </FONT></TD>
    </TR>
    <TR>
    <TD>Boat Name</TD>
    <TD><INPUT TYPE=text NAME=txtBoatName SIZE=30></TD>
    <TD WIDTH=50></TD>
    <TD>Class</TD>
    <TD><SELECT NAME=cboClass></SELECT></TD>
    </TR>
    <TR>
    <TD>Launched</TD>
    <TD><INPUT TYPE=text NAME=txtLaunched SIZE=8></TD>
    <TD WIDTH=50></TD>
    <TD>Certified</TD>
    <TD><INPUT TYPE=checkbox NAME=chkCertified VALUE=1></TD>
    </TR>
    <TR>
    <TD>Value</TD>
    <TD><INPUT TYPE=text NAME=txtValue SIZE=10></TD>
    </TR>
    <TR>
    <TD>Notes</TD>
    <TD COLSPAN=4><INPUT TYPE=text NAME=txtNotes SIZE=60></TD>
    </TR>
```

```
  <TR>
  <TD>  </TD>
  </TR>
  <TR>
  <TD><INPUT TYPE=button NAME=btnSubmit VALUE=Submit></TD>
  </TR>
  </TABLE>
  </FORM>

<!-- #include file="Connect.inc" -->

<%
'Check for database errors
Call CheckForErrors(objConn)

'Create the recordset object and open the recordset
Set objRS = Server.CreateObject("ADODB.Recordset")
strSQL = "qAllBoatClasses"
objRS.Open strSQL, objConn, adOpenForwardOnly, , adCmdStoredProc

'Check for database errors
Call CheckForErrors(objConn)
%>

<SCRIPT LANGUAGE=vbscript>
Sub Window_OnLoad()
<%
  Do While Not objRS.EOF
%>
    Set objOption = document.createElement("OPTION")
    objOption.text = "<%=objRS("ClassName")%>"
    objOption.value = "<%=objRS("ClassName")%>"
    document.all.cboClass.add objOption
<%
    objRS.MoveNext
  Loop
%>
  <!-- #include file="DisConnect.inc" -->

  Set objOption = Nothing
End Sub

Sub btnSubmit_OnClick()
  'Verify required fields are complete
  If Len(frmNewBoat.txtBoatName.value) = 0 Then
    Alert "You must enter a boat name"
    frmNewBoat.txtBoatName.focus
    Exit Sub
  ElseIf frmNewBoat.cboClass.selectedIndex = -1 Then
    Alert "You must select your boat class"
    frmNewBoat.cboClass.focus
    Exit Sub
  ElseIf Len(frmNewBoat.txtLaunched.value) = 0 Then
    Alert "You must enter when your boat was launched"
    frmNewBoat.txtLaunched.focus
    Exit Sub
  ElseIf Len(frmNewBoat.txtValue.value) = 0 Then
    Alert "You must enter the value of your boat"
    frmNewBoat.txtValue.focus
    Exit Sub
  ElseIf Len(frmNewBoat.txtNotes.value) = 0 Then
    frmNewBoat.txtNotes.value = " "
  End If
```

```
      'If we get to this point all is OK, submit the form
      Call frmNewBoat.submit()
End Sub
</SCRIPT>

<%
'******************************************************************
'* Step 2: Process the new boat form the user has submitted
'******************************************************************
ElseIf Request.Form("FormAction") = "Step2" Then
%>

  <!-- #include file="Connect.inc" -->

<%
  'Check for database errors
  Call CheckForErrors(objConn)

  'Set the certified variable
  If Request.Form("chkCertified") = 1 Then
    bytCertified = 1
  Else
    bytCertified = 0
  End If

  'Run the boat name through the string conversion routine
  'just in case there are any single quotes
  strBoatName = ConvertString(Request.Form("txtBoatName"))

  'Set the parameters for the insert stored procedure
  strSQL = "qparmInsertBoat ('" & CStr(strBoatName) & _
    "','" & CStr(Request.Form("cboClass")) & _
    "','" & CStr(Request.Form("txtLaunched")) & _
    "'," & CByte(bytCertified) & _
    ",'" & CStr(Request.Form("txtNotes")) & _
    "'," & CCur(Request.Form("txtValue")) & ")"
  'Insert the new boat
  objConn.Execute strSQL,,adCmdStoredProc

  'Check for database errors
  Call CheckForErrors(objConn)
%>

  <!-- #include file="DisConnect.inc" -->

  <!--Display registration message-->
  <FONT COLOR=teal>Your boat has been registered</FONT>
  <BR><BR>
  <A HREF="Options.asp"
    ONMOUSEOVER="window.status='Return to Options Page'; return true"
    ONMOUSEOUT="window.status=''">Return to Options Page</A>
<%
End If
%>
</BODY>
</HTML>
```

### How It Works – RegisterNewBoat.asp – The Stored Procedures

This example needs two stored procedures. The first stored procedure selects all of the different boat classes from the BoatClass table and orders the results by the class name. This stored procedure will be used to populate a combo box for the user to select the type of boat they have.

```
SELECT BoatClass.ClassName
FROM BoatClass
ORDER BY BoatClass.ClassName;
```

This next stored procedure is used to insert the new boat details into the Boats table, so let's take a look at it line by line. First we declare all of the parameters that we will be passing to this stored procedure, as shown in the first line of code. Notice the last parameter in this list is called Value. Because Value is a property in Access, the parameter name has been automatically enclosed in brackets to distinguish it as a parameter name and not a property.

```
PARAMETERS Name Text, Class Text, Launched DateTime, Certified Bit, Notes LongText,
[Value] Currency;
```

The second line of code contains the INSERT statement for the columns that we will be inserting data into.

```
INSERT INTO Boats ( BoatName, BoatClass, BoatLaunched, BoatCertified, BoatNote,
BoatValue )
```

The last line of our stored procedure selects the parameters as expressions to be inserted.

```
SELECT [Name] AS Expr1, [Class] AS Expr2, [Launched] AS Expr3, [Certified] AS Expr4,
[Notes] AS Expr5, [Value] AS Expr6;
```

Since this page processes two separate steps and displays two separate results, we are going to divide this page into Step One, Step Two and Common Code. First we want to look at the first part of the common code.

## Common Code

The common code for this page includes the four include files at the top of the page. The first include file adds our ADO constants and the second file checks to see if the user has been authenticated and redirects their browser to the Default.asp page if they have not. The third include file contains some common functions that can be shared with other pages. And the last include file contains our error handling function.

The rest of the code in the common code section contains the standard HTML headers and the first line of text in our page.

It is worth noting that the common code will *always* execute, regardless of the specific step in the code that we are going to execute. Given this, be sure you do not duplicate variable names.

```
<!-- #include file="adovbs.inc" -->
<!-- #include file="AuthenticationCheck.inc" -->
<!-- #include file="CommonFunctions.inc" -->
<!-- #include file="ProductionErrorHandler.inc" -->

<HTML>
<HEAD>
<META NAME="GENERATOR" Content="Microsoft Visual Studio 6.0">
<TITLE>Sailors Web Site</TITLE>
</HEAD>
<BODY>

<!--Display the page data-->
<DIV ALIGN=center>
  <BIG><BIG><FONT COLOR=navy>Sailors Case Study</FONT></BIG></BIG>
</DIV>
<BR><BR>
```

### Step One

We have set up a hidden field on our form called `FormAction`. This field will contain the value of the next step to process in the page. The first time we access this page, this field does not exist so checking the length of this field will always return 0 for the first step.

```
<%
'***************************************************************
'* Step 1: Display the New Boat form for user input
'***************************************************************
If Len(Request.Form("FormAction")) = 0 Then
%>
```

We start building our form by specifying that the form will `post` the results to the `RegisterNewBoat.asp` page, which is the current page. We have named our form `frmNewBoat` and this name will be referenced in our client-side script when we perform data validation.

We now set up the hidden field that will contain the step that should be processed next. Notice that we have set the value of this field to `Step2`, which is the next step to be processed when the user clicks the submit button.

After we have placed our hidden field in the form, we start building a table to help keep the layout of our fields consistent. Notice that the first column of data in the first row of the table contains the `HEIGHT` and `COLSPAN` properties. This is because we want to provide the appropriate spacing between the first row of data and the form fields, and we want the text to span across two columns.

```
<FORM ACTION=RegisterNewBoat.asp METHOD=post NAME=frmNewBoat>
<INPUT TYPE=hidden NAME=FormAction VALUE=Step2>
<TABLE>
  <TR>
  <TD HEIGHT=50 COLSPAN=2><FONT COLOR=navy>Boat Registration
    </FONT></TD>
  </TR>
```

We insert the text in the first column of the next row, and the text box for the boat name in the next column. Then we insert a column that contains no data. However, notice what we did for that column. We have inserted a blank column and have specified the WIDTH property of the TD tag. This will provide the appropriate spacing between the column that contains the text box and the next column that contains text for the next input field.

```
<TR>
<TD>Boat Name</TD>
<TD><INPUT TYPE=text NAME=txtBoatName SIZE=30></TD>
<TD WIDTH=50></TD>
<TD>Class</TD>
<TD><SELECT NAME=cboClass></SELECT></TD>
</TR>
```

The rest of the form contains the standard fields that we have discussed in previous examples.

```
<TR>
<TD>Launched</TD>
<TD><INPUT TYPE=text NAME=txtLaunched SIZE=8></TD>
<TD WIDTH=50></TD>
<TD>Certified</TD>
<TD><INPUT TYPE=checkbox NAME=chkCertified VALUE=1></TD>
</TR>
<TR>
<TD>Value</TD>
<TD><INPUT TYPE=text NAME=txtValue SIZE=10></TD>
</TR>
<TR>
<TD>Notes</TD>
<TD COLSPAN=4><INPUT TYPE=text NAME=txtNotes SIZE=60></TD>
</TR>
<TR>
<TD>  </TD>
</TR>
<TR>
<TD><INPUT TYPE=button NAME=btnSubmit VALUE=Submit></TD>
</TR>
</TABLE>
</FORM>
```

After we have completed building the form, we need to establish a database connection and check for errors. We do this by including the appropriate include file for establishing a connection and then calling the error handling function.

Next we create the Recordset object, set the SQL string and open the recordset. After we open the recordset we check for errors.

```
<!-- #include file="Connect.inc" -->

<%
'Check for database errors
Call CheckForErrors(objConn)

'Create the recordset object and open the recordset
Set objRS = Server.CreateObject("ADODB.Recordset")
strSQL = "qAllBoatClasses"
objRS.Open strSQL, objConn, adOpenForwardOnly, , adCmdStoredProc

'Check for database errors
Call CheckForErrors(objConn)
%>
```

Next we build the client-side script and code the `Window_OnLoad` event. Remember that this is the first event to fire when the page loads on the user's browser. We demonstrated in a previous example how we perform the code to load a combo box so we will only touch on the highlights here, as they are important to understand.

Remember that the `TEXT` property of the `Option` object contains the actual text that is displayed for the user and the `value` property is the value that will get submitted with the form. After all options have been loaded in the combo box, we include the file to close and de-reference our `Recordset` and `Connection` objects. This technique was demonstrated earlier in the case study.

```
<SCRIPT LANGUAGE=vbscript>
Sub Window_OnLoad()
<%
  Do While Not objRS.EOF
%>
    Set objOption = document.createElement("OPTION")
    objOption.text = "<%=objRS("ClassName")%>"
    objOption.value = "<%=objRS("ClassName")%>"
    document.all.cboClass.add objOption
<%
    objRS.MoveNext
  Loop
%>
  <!-- #include file="DisConnect.inc" -->

  Set objOption = Nothing
End Sub
```

Again we have used a standard button and given it a `value` of `Submit`, which is the text that the user will see on the button. The actual `name` of the button in our code is `btnSubmit`. We need to perform our client-side validations in the `OnClick` event of this button.

These validations are the same that we performed in an earlier example.

```
Sub btnSubmit_OnClick()
  'Verify required fields are complete
  If Len(frmNewBoat.txtBoatName.value) = 0 Then
    Alert "You must enter a boat name"
    frmNewBoat.txtBoatName.focus
    Exit Sub
  ElseIf frmNewBoat.cboClass.selectedIndex = -1 Then
    Alert "You must select your boat class"
    frmNewBoat.cboClass.focus
    Exit Sub
  ElseIf Len(frmNewBoat.txtLaunched.value) = 0 Then
    Alert "You must enter when your boat was launched"
    frmNewBoat.txtLaunched.focus
    Exit Sub
  ElseIf Len(frmNewBoat.txtValue.value) = 0 Then
    Alert "You must enter the value of your boat"
    frmNewBoat.txtValue.focus
    Exit Sub
  ElseIf Len(frmNewBoat.txtNotes.value) = 0 Then
    frmNewBoat.txtNotes.value = " "
  End If

  'If we get to this point all is OK, submit the form
  Call frmNewBoat.submit()
End Sub
</SCRIPT>
```

After the preceding section of code has executed, the code in Step 2 will be bypassed and the results you will see are shown below:

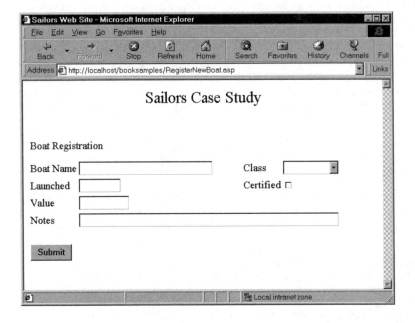

## Step Two

After the form in the previous step has been displayed and the user has entered all of their data, they will submit the form. This causes the page to be executed again but this time the field `FormAction` has a value of `Step2` and this section of the code will be executed.

The first thing that we need to do is to establish a connection to the database and check for errors. Again we do this by including the appropriate include file and calling the error handling function.

```
<%
'*****************************************************************
'* Step 2: Process the new boat form the user has submitted
'*****************************************************************
ElseIf Request.Form("FormAction") = "Step2" Then
%>

  <!-- #include file="Connect.inc" -->

<%
  'Check for database errors
  Call CheckForErrors(objConn)
```

Since we have a check box on the form that was submitted, we once again must examine the value to determine if the check box was checked. We covered this earlier so we won't go into the details again.

```
  'Set the certified variable
  If Request.Form("chkCertified") = 1 Then
    bytCertified = 1
  Else
    bytCertified = 0
  End If
```

Remember that we must enclose our string parameters in single quote marks. This could cause a problem if the string parameter being passed contains a single quote mark in the data. This would lead to an error because we would then have an un-terminated string. To get around this problem, we use the common function called `ConvertString`, which replaces all single quote marks with two consecutive single quote marks. This way we will not run into any problems with passing this parameter in the SQL string.

We call the `ConvertString` function by passing it the string to be converted, which in our case is the field, `txtBoatName`, from the request form. If you recall our discussion near the beginning of the case study when we set up this function, we stated that it will return a string that has been converted. We can then set our variable that contains the converted string. Notice that we can do all of this in just one line of code.

```
'Run the boat name through the string conversion routine
'just in case there are any single quotes
strBoatName = ConvertString(Request.Form("txtBoatName"))
```

We now can set the SQL string with the name of the stored procedure to execute and pass it the appropriate parameters. Once the SQL string has been built, we need to execute the SQL string to insert the new boat into our `Boats` table. Then we check for errors.

```
'Set the parameters for the insert stored procedure
strSQL = "qparmInsertBoat ('" & CStr(strBoatName) & _
  "','" & CStr(Request.Form("cboClass")) & _
  "','" & CStr(Request.Form("txtLaunched")) & _
  "'," & CByte(bytCertified) & _
  ",'" & CStr(Request.Form("txtNotes")) & _
  "'," & CCur(Request.Form("txtValue")) & ")"
'Insert the new boat
objConn.Execute strSQL,,adCmdStoredProc

'Check for database errors
Call CheckForErrors(objConn)
%>
```

Next, we close the database and de-reference the `Connection` object by using the appropriate include file.

```
<!-- #include file="DisConnect.inc" -->
```

The last part of this step is to inform the user that their boat has been registered, and we do this by writing the text on the page using a different font color, in this case teal. Next we give them a hyperlink back to the `Options` page.

```
<!--Display registration message-->
<FONT COLOR=teal>Your boat has been registered</FONT>
<BR><BR>
<A HREF="Options.asp"
  ONMOUSEOVER="window.status='Return to Options Page'; return true"
  ONMOUSEOUT="window.status=''">Return to Options Page</A>
```

After this section of code executes, your browser will show a screen similar to the following:

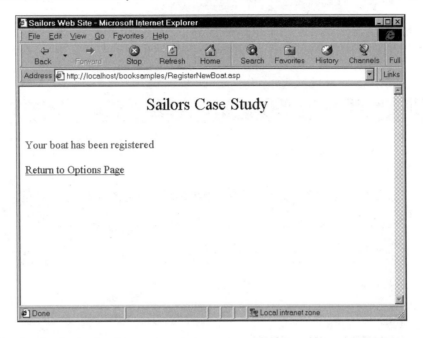

## Common Code (continued)

This is the last part of the common code. It contains the `End If` statement for our step processing and the standard HTML tags to end our page.

```
<%
End If
%>

</BODY>
</HTML>
```

This example has shown you how to use one Active Server Page to execute multiple steps. This is not limited to two steps as we have in this example. You are also not limited to just having one form in an Active Server Page. You can set up an Active Server Page to contain dozens of forms and steps to be executed. Before you set up a page that contains multiple forms and multiple steps, please review Chapter 12. This chapter lists some of the more common scripting errors that you will run into. By reviewing this chapter first, you will undoubtedly save yourself a lot of headaches when trying to debug your page.

# The Display Ranking Page

This is the last web page in our case study and this page selects all sailor rankings from the database, and displays the data in a table formatted with multiple table headers and rows. The Options menu lists this page as one of the options for the user to view, and this page accepts no user input.

This web page displays the sailor rankings by club. Every club is displayed in order and the sailors are displayed by ranking within each club, sorted by rank and date. The web page is shown in this next screenshot:

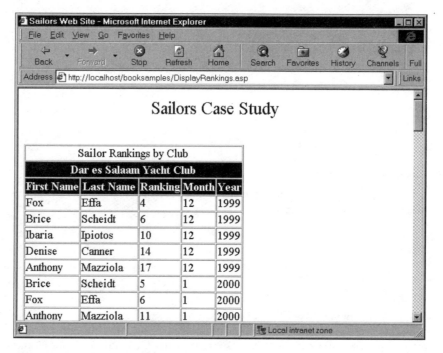

The stored procedure required here is `qAllRankings`.

```
SELECT People.PeopleID, People.PeopleNameLast, People.PeopleNameFirst, Clubs.ClubName,
Rank.Year, Rank.Month, Rank.Rank
FROM (Rank INNER JOIN People ON Rank.SailorID = People.PeopleID) INNER JOIN Clubs ON
People.PeopleClubCode = Clubs.ClubCode
ORDER BY Clubs.ClubName, Rank.Year, Rank.Month, Rank.Rank;
```

The code for the `DisplayRankings.asp` web page is shown here:

```
<!-- #include file="adovbs.inc" -->
<!-- #include file="AuthenticationCheck.inc" -->
<!-- #include file="ProductionErrorHandler.inc" -->
<HTML>
<HEAD>
<META NAME="GENERATOR" Content="Microsoft Visual Studio 6.0">
<TITLE>Sailors Web Site</TITLE>
</HEAD>
<BODY>

<!--Display the page data-->
<DIV ALIGN=CENTER>
  <BIG><BIG><FONT COLOR=navy>Sailors Case Study</FONT></BIG></BIG>
</DIV>
<BR><BR>

<!-- #include file="Connect.inc" -->

<%
'Check for database errors
Call CheckForErrors(objConn)

'Create the recordset object, set the SQL string and open the recordset
Set objRS = Server.CreateObject("ADODB.Recordset")
strSQL = "qAllRankings"
objRS.Open strSQL, objConn, adOpenForwardOnly, , adCmdStoredProc

'Check for database errors
Call CheckForErrors(objConn)
%>

<!--Build the table title row-->
<TABLE border=1 cellspacing=1>
  <TR>
  <TD COLSPAN=5 ALIGN=CENTER>Sailor Rankings by Club</TD>
  </TR>

<%
'Set a variable to hold the last boatclass
Dim strLastClub
strLastClub = Empty

'Loop through the recordset building the table
Do While Not objRS.EOF
  'If the current club is not equal to the last club
  'then build a new header row in the table
  If objRS("ClubName") <> strLastClub Then
%>
    <TR>
    <TH BGCOLOR=navy COLSPAN=5 ALIGN=CENTER>
      <FONT COLOR=white><%=objRS("ClubName")%></FONT></TH>
    </TR>
    <TR>
    <TH BGCOLOR=navy><FONT COLOR=white>First Name</FONT></TH>
    <TH BGCOLOR=navy><FONT COLOR=white>Last Name</FONT></TH>
    <TH BGCOLOR=navy><FONT COLOR=white>Ranking</FONT></TH>
    <TH BGCOLOR=navy><FONT COLOR=white>Month</FONT></TH>
    <TH BGCOLOR=navy><FONT COLOR=white>Year</FONT></TH>
    </TR>
<%
    strLastClub = objRS("ClubName")
  End If
%>
```

```
<!--Build a row of data in the table-->
<TR>
<TD><%=objRS("PeopleNameFirst")%></TD>
<TD><%=objRS("PeopleNameLast")%></TD>
<TD><%=objRS("Rank")%></TD>
<TD><%=objRS("Month")%></TD>
<TD><%=objRS("Year")%></TD>
</TR>
<%
  objRS.MoveNext
Loop
%>
<!--Build the last row in the table with a hyper link to the options page-->
<TR>
<TD COLSPAN=5>  </TD>
<TR>
<TR>
<TD COLSPAN=5><A HREF="Options.asp"
  ONMOUSEOVER="window.status='Return to Options Page'; return true"
  ONMOUSEOUT="window.status=''">Return to Options Page</A></TD>
</TR>
</TABLE>

<!-- #include file="DisConnect.inc" -->

</BODY>
</HTML>
```

### How It Works – DisplayRankings.asp – The Stored Procedure

The stored procedure that builds the recordset for this example is a little complex so we want to take a look at the relationships of the tables. Like the old adage says, *A Picture Is Worth A Thousand Words* and in this case it's true.

The three tables that make up this stored procedure are Rank, People and Clubs. The main table that we are concerned with is Rank since this is the main data we are going after. In order to get the details for the rest of the recordset we must join the People table to the Rank table using a relationship of Rank.SailorID = People.PeopleID. In order to get the clubs that the sailors belong to we must join the Clubs table to the People table using a relationship of People.PeopleClubCode = Clubs.ClubCode. This is illustrated in the adjacent figure:

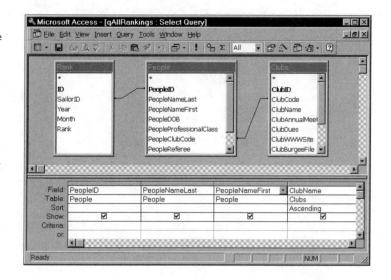

Now that we have explained the relationship and shown it to you, we want to take a look at the actual SQL code. Half the battle in coding this stored procedure is understanding and getting the relationships between the tables right. The other half is ordering the data to get the results expected.

The SELECT statement is pretty straightforward. Since we are selecting data from multiple tables, the table name is used along with the column names in the SELECT statement. This ensures you are selecting the correct data from the correct tables, just in case a column name is duplicated in one of the other tables.

```
SELECT People.PeopleID, People.PeopleNameLast, People.PeopleNameFirst, Clubs.ClubName,
Rank.Year, Rank.Month, Rank.Rank
```

Since we have already taken a look at the relationships of the tables, this FROM clause should be also be easy to understand. We select data from the Rank table and inner join the People table on Rank.SailorID = People.PeopleID. Next we inner join the Clubs table on People.PeopleClubCode = Clubs.ClubCode.

```
FROM (Rank INNER JOIN People ON Rank.SailorID = People.PeopleID) INNER JOIN Clubs ON
People.PeopleClubCode = Clubs.ClubCode
```

In order to get the expected results, we must order the data by ClubName first, which will return the data sorted by clubs. Next we want to sort the data by Year listing all the data for a particular year. Within the years we want to order the data by Month, which will list the months in order for a given year. Within a certain month, we want to sort the data by Rank, so we specify Rank last.

```
ORDER BY Clubs.ClubName, Rank.Year, Rank.Month, Rank.Rank;
```

That covers our stored procedure in detail and you should now have a good understanding of how we are joining the tables and ordering the data. So let's take a look at the code for the web page.

## The Web Page Code

This page starts off the same as most examples in this case study. We have an include file to include our ADO constants, one to check for authentication and one for our error handling function. We have the standard HTML headers and also write the first line of text on the page.

```
<!-- #include file="adovbs.inc" -->
<!-- #include file="AuthenticationCheck.inc" -->
<!-- #include file="ProductionErrorHandler.inc" -->
<HTML>
<HEAD>
<META NAME="GENERATOR" Content="Microsoft Visual Studio 6.0">
<TITLE>Sailors Web Site</TITLE>
</HEAD>
<BODY>

<!--Display the page data-->
<DIV ALIGN=center>
  <BIG><BIG><FONT COLOR=navy>Sailors Case Study</FONT></BIG></BIG>
</DIV>
<BR><BR>
```

We know that we are going to be opening a recordset so we need to establish a connection with the database and check for errors. Again, we do this by using our include file and calling our error handling function.

```
<!-- #include file="Connect.inc" -->

<%
'Check for database errors
Call CheckForErrors(objConn)
```

Since this stored procedure expects no parameters, setting the SQL string is really straightforward. We then open our recordset and check for errors by calling our error handling function.

```
<%
'Create the recordset object, set the SQL string and open the recordset
Set objRS = Server.CreateObject("ADODB.Recordset")
strSQL = "qAllRankings"
objRS.Open strSQL, objConn, adOpenForwardOnly, , adCmdStoredProc

'Check for database errors
Call CheckForErrors(objConn)
%>
```

We start building the table using a standard single row, which describes the data in the table. Once again, we are just using one column and have specified that this column should span across five normal columns, using the COLSPAN property of the TD tag.

```
<!--Build the table title row-->
<TABLE BORDER=1 CELLSPACING=1>
  <TR>
  <TD COLSPAN=5 ALIGN=center>Sailor Rankings by Club</TD>
  </TR>
```

Since we are displaying the data by club we need a means by which we can track when a club changes in the recordset, so we can create a new header row for each club. We are once again going to use a variable, but this time we set the variable to empty first instead of setting it to the recordset field, as we did in a previous example.

```
<%
'Set a variable to hold the last boatclass
Dim strLastClub
strLastClub = Empty
```

We start our loop to process the recordset. The first thing we want to do in the loop is to check to see if the ClubName in the recordset is different from our variable. If this is true, we want to write some header rows.

We start by writing one header row containing the club name. This header row provides a visual separation between one club and the next, and uses the TH tag and the BGCOLOR property to set the background color of the header column. We also use the COLSPAN property to specify that this column should span across five normal columns. We use the FONT tag to specify the color of the text that is being displayed.

The next header row contains five different columns, using text that describes the data in each of the columns. Again we are setting the background color and the font color of the text. After we write the last header row, we set our variable to the current club name.

```
'Loop through the recordset building the table
Do While Not objRS.EOF
  'If the current club is not equal to the last club
  'then build a new header row in the table
  If objRS("ClubName") <> strLastClub Then
%>
    <TR>
    <TH BGCOLOR=navy COLSPAN=5 ALIGN=center>
      <FONT COLOR=white><%=objRS("ClubName")%></FONT></TH>
    </TR>
    <TR>
    <TH BGCOLOR=navy><FONT COLOR=white>First Name</FONT></TH>
    <TH BGCOLOR=navy><FONT COLOR=white>Last Name</FONT></TH>
    <TH BGCOLOR=navy><FONT COLOR=white>Ranking</FONT></TH>
    <TH BGCOLOR=navy><FONT COLOR=white>Month</FONT></TH>
    <TH BGCOLOR=navy><FONT COLOR=white>Year</FONT></TH>
    </TR>

<%
    strLastClub = objRS("ClubName")
  End If
%>
```

We can now build the table row with the data in the current row of the recordset. Once again notice that the recordset fields are enclosed in the server-side script tags within our HTML data. We advance the recordset and go back to the beginning of our loop to process the next row of data.

```
  <!--Build a row of data in the table-->
  <TR>
  <TD><%=objRS("PeopleNameFirst")%></TD>
  <TD><%=objRS("PeopleNameLast")%></TD>
  <TD><%=objRS("Rank")%></TD>
  <TD><%=objRS("Month")%></TD>
  <TD><%=objRS("Year")%></TD>
  </TR>
<%
  objRS.MoveNext
Loop
%>
```

As in our previous example, we want to build a separator row at the end of the table, and then build a row that contains a hyperlink back to the options page. This example, however, does not use a silver separator row, just a plain one.

```
  <!--Build the last row in the table with a hyper link to the options page-->
  <TR>
  <TD COLSPAN=5>  </TD>
  <TR>
  <TR>
  <TD COLSPAN=5><A HREF="Options.asp"
    ONMOUSEOVER="window.status='Return to Options Page'; return true"
    ONMOUSEOUT="window.status=''">Return to Options Page</A></TD>
  </TR>
  </TABLE>
```

The end of our page includes the include file to close and de-reference our recordset and database objects. The last two lines of code are our standard HTML tags to end the page.

```
<!-- #include file="DisConnect.inc" -->

</BODY>
</HTML>
```

# Interesting Observations

There are some interesting observations to be made while working with this web site. All of these observations come after you have registered and have a cookie written on your machine.

## Not Authenticated

The first observation is when you open your browser and key in the URL of a specific page, let's say the Options.asp page. Since this page checks to see if you are authenticated before letting you view the page, your browser is redirected to the Default.asp page, which in turn finds a cookie and redirects you to the WelcomeBack.asp page.

## Session Timeouts

Another observation is when your session times out. Your session timeout value is set to 20 minutes by default, and your session will timeout after this time has elapsed if you have not requested a new page or refreshed the current page.

Let's say your current page is the sailor rankings and your session times out. When you click on the hyperlink at the bottom of the page to return to the options page, you actually go there. But here's the catch, you are no longer authenticated because your session has timed out, and you no longer have the Session variable Authenticated. Therefore your browser gets redirected from the Options.asp page to the Default.asp page, and this page finds a cookie and redirects your browser to the WelcomeBack.asp page.

Why does all of this happen? Because we set up the AuthenticationCheck.inc include file to redirect your browser if you have not been authenticated, and we have included this file in most of our web pages.

# Some Things To Try

We have intentionally left some code in these web pages that is common to all web pages in this case study. This is the first line of text that gets displayed on all pages. Having gone through the complete exercise you should now be ready to experiment a little.

Try removing this code and place it in an include file. Insert the code to call the new include file into your web pages.

Hint: the code to remove is shown below.

```
<!--Display the page data-->
<DIV ALIGN=center>
  <BIG><BIG><FONT COLOR=navy>Sailors Case Study</FONT></BIG></BIG>
</DIV>
<BR><BR>
```

If you feel up to the task, you could combine the `Register.asp` and the `RegistrationConfirmation.asp` into one web page. Use the `RegisterNewBoat.asp` page as a guideline. This page contains multiple steps that first displays a form for user input and then posts the data back to itself and then processes that data.

# Summary

After having used various methods to create web pages that use data from the database you should now have a firm grasp on database access using ADO. We have demonstrated how to read data using stored procedures, some of which accepted parameters and some of which did not. We have also looked at and demonstrated how to execute action-stored procedures that accept parameters, to insert data into the database.

Include files were used extensively to demonstrate how to create and use include files, and we have shown you how these files can be included before and after your HTTP headers are written. We have also shown you how to redirect the user's browser if a cookie was not found or the user was not authenticated.

The error handling include file that was created in Chapter 12 was used again here also. This include file was used to check for database errors after every connection to the database and after every stored procedure was executed. This is a very important part of database programming. You must check for database errors to help ensure data integrity.

Since we used tables in our web pages to display data, you should now be very familiar with the way tables are used and the various properties of the TH and TD tags. Tables were used to help format the data on our web pages in order to keep the appearance of the data concise.

To summarize, you should have revised how to:

❏ Use all kinds of stored procedures

❏ Use recordsets in server-side script and client-side script

❏ Create and use include files

❏ Create and use tables

❏ Know when and how to redirect a browser

Setup cannot install system files or update shared files if the files are in use. Before ~~~~ any open applications.

WARNING: This program is protected by copyright law and international treaties.

You may install Microsoft Data Access 2.1 on a single computer. Some Microsoft produc~ with additional rights, which are stated in the End User License Agreement included with ~~

Please take a moment to read the End User License Agreement now. It contains all of the t~ conditions that pertain to this software product. By choosing to continue, you indicate accep~ these terms.

Exit Setup

Continue

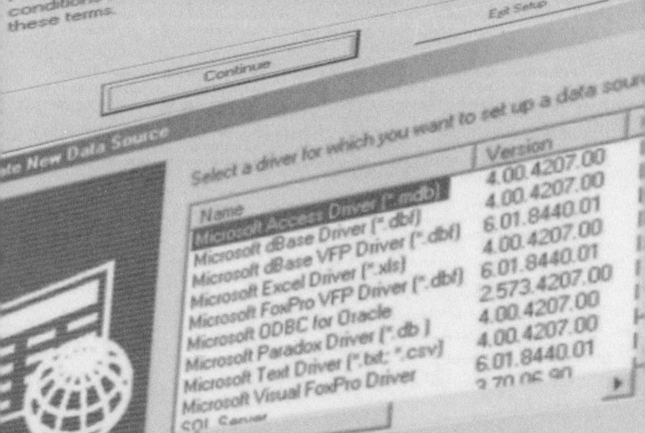

Create New Data Source

Select a driver for which you want to set up a data sour~

| Name | Version | |
|------|---------|---|
| Microsoft Access Driver (*.mdb) | 4.00.4207.00 | |
| Microsoft dBase Driver (*.dbf) | 4.00.4207.00 | |
| Microsoft dBase VFP Driver (*.dbf) | 6.01.8440.01 | |
| Microsoft Excel Driver (*.xls) | 4.00.4207.00 | |
| Microsoft FoxPro VFP Driver (*.dbf) | 6.01.8440.01 | |
| Microsoft ODBC for Oracle | 2.573.4207.00 | |
| Microsoft Paradox Driver (*.db ) | 4.00.4207.00 | |
| Microsoft Text Driver (*.txt; *.csv) | 4.00.4207.00 | |
| Microsoft Visual FoxPro Driver | 6.01.8440.01 | |
| SQL Server | 3.70.06.90 | |

Finish    Cancel

# Structure of Sailors.mdb

## Introduction and Objective

`Sailors.mdb` supports a hypothetical web site for competitive sailors. The web site includes pages to notify sailors of upcoming regattas, changes in rules, reports on past regattas, and personalized pages based on each sailor's interests. Additional features allow the posting and statistical analysis of regatta results and the ranking of sailors.

## Vocabulary and Business Rules

**Sailors**, in this database are people who race sailboats. These people have the normal personal information such as names and nationalities, as well as an assigned professional class, which reflects their commitment and accomplishment in the sport of yachting. The most skilled sailors, those of Olympic caliber, are rated Professional Class 1 while those who compete at an amateur level are class 3.

**Boats** are owned by Sailors. A boat has a name and an identifying sail number. Every boat is of a boat class.

A **Boat Class** is a group of boats of the same shape, sail area and hull size, thus ensuring an even competition among the sailors. Sailors generally race in one class only and thus are not interested in information for boats of other classes.

Sailors race under the aegis of **yacht clubs**, the organizations which typically sponsor regattas. Yacht clubs have an identifying flag called a club burgee, may have a web site, and each year a yacht club has a meeting at which time information for the season is disseminated. Larger boats are limited to sailing from clubs with a crane to hoist the boat from its trailer to the water.

**Competitions** generally consist of a series of races (typically 3 to 10), which together constitute a regatta. Based on the results of regattas, sailors are ranked each month from first (most skilled) to 20th (least skilled).

# Where to Download

This database, in Access format, is available from the Wrox site. The procedures to create the queries for Microsoft SQL Server are also available from the same site in the file `Sailors.sql`. The end of this appendix lists the information to create the structure of the database by hand.

# Structure and Relationships of Tables

The Sailors database contains five tables. There are no relationships permanently created, they are created in queries as needed.

### People Table

Sailors are listed in the `People` table; each person is a record. The `People` table can be related to the `Clubs` table and to the `boats` table, since each sailor is a member of a club and most sailors own boats. In addition, the `People` table can be related to the `Rank` table. As in all tables of this database there is an ID field with a data type of autonumber. To keep the database small for the download, there are only twenty sailors.

### Boats

Within the `Boat` table each record is a boat. The boats can be related to the `People` table by the PeopleID as well as the `BoatClass` table.

### BoatClass

This table has only a few records, each representing a class of boats. It can only be directly related to the `Boats` table. Since all the boats of a given class have the same length, weight and sail area, this information is kept only in the `BoatClass` table. In our simple example there are just three classes.

### Rank

Each record in the `Rank` table represents one sailor in one month of one year. Fields hold the sailor's ID as well as the rank number. This database covers the four months from December 1999 to March 2000.

### Clubs

Each yacht club holds a record in this table. In addition to contact information, this table holds data for the URL of the club's home page. An image of the club burgee (flag) is held in two places, a file on the server and in a BLOB field in this table.

# Overview of Queries

One group of queries, those beginning with qAll, merely list the records of the table. An exception is the qAllRankings query, which joins the `People`, `Clubs` and `Rank` tables to create a useful recordset for reporting the standings.

A second group of queries begins with qparm. These are for demonstrating the use of passing parameters through the ADO command object. This group includes the qparmInsert queries, which are called to append records to tables.

# Structure of Tables

| Table | Field Name | Field Type | Field Size | Notes |
|-------|-----------|-----------|-----------|-------|
| **BoatClass** | ClassID | AutoNumber<br>Number (Long) | 4 | Attributes: Fixed Size, Auto-Increment |
| | ClassName | Text | 50 | |
| | ClassLength | Number (Long) | 4 | |
| | ClassWeight | Number (Long) | 4 | |
| | ClassEntered | Date/Time | 8 | Format: Long Date |
| **Boats** | BoatsID | AutoNumber<br>Number (Long) | 4 | attributes: Fixed Size<br>Auto-Increment |
| | BoatName | Text | 50 | |
| | BoatClass | Text | 50 | |
| | BoatLaunched | Date/Time | 8 | |
| | BoatCertified | Yes/No | 1 | |
| | BoatNote | Memo | - | |
| | BoatPhoto | OLE Object | - | |
| | BoatValue | Currency | 8 | Decimal Places: Auto<br><br>Format: $#,##0.00;($#,##0.00) |

| Table | Field Name | Field Type | Field Size | Notes |
|-------|-----------|-----------|-----------|-------|
| **Clubs** | ClubID | AutoNumber Number (Long) | 4 | Attributes: Fixed Size Auto-Increment |
| | ClubCode | Text | 50 | |
| | ClubName | Text | 50 | |
| | ClubAnnualMeeting | Date/Time | 8 | |
| | ClubDues | Currency | 8 | Decimal Places: Auto Format: $#,##0.00;($#,##0.00) |
| | ClubWWWSite | Hyperlink | - | |
| | ClubBurgeeFile | Text | 50 | |
| | ClubBurgee | OLE Object | - | |
| | ClubHasCranes | Yes/No | 1 | |
| | ClubMembership | Number (Long) | 4 | |
| | ClubNote | Memo | - | |
| **People** | PeopleID | AutoNumber Number (Long) | 4 | |
| | PeopleNameLast | Text | 50 | |
| | PeopleNameFirst | Text | 50 | |
| | PeopleDOB | Date/Time | 8 | Format: Short Date |
| | PeopleProfessionalClass | Number (Long) | 4 | |
| | PeopleClubCode | Text | 50 | |
| | PeopleReferee | Yes/No | 1 | |
| | PeopleState | Text | 50 | |
| | PeopleView | Text | 50 | |

| Table | Field Name | Field Type | Field Size | Notes |
|---|---|---|---|---|
| Rank | ID | AutoNumber Number (Long) | 4 | Attributes: Fixed Size Auto-Increment |
| | SailorID | Number (Long) | 4 | |
| | Year | Number (Long) | 4 | |
| | Month | Number (Long) | 4 | |
| | Rank | Number (Long) | 4 | |

# Structure of Queries

| Query Name | Query Details |
|---|---|
| qAllBoatClasses | SELECT BoatClass.ClassName<br>FROM BoatClass<br>ORDER BY BoatClass.ClassName; |
| qAllBoatNames | SELECT Boats.BoatName<br>FROM Boats; |
| qAllBoats | SELECT Boats.BoatClass, Boats.BoatName<br>FROM Boats<br>ORDER BY Boats.BoatClass, Boats.BoatName; |
| qAllClubs | SELECT Clubs.ClubName, Clubs.ClubCode<br>FROM Clubs<br>ORDER BY Clubs.ClubName; |
| qAllRankings | SELECT People.PeopleID, People.PeopleNameLast, People.PeopleNameFirst, Clubs.ClubName, Rank.Year, Rank.Month, Rank.Rank<br>FROM (Rank INNER JOIN People ON Rank.SailorID = People.PeopleID)<br>INNER JOIN Clubs ON People.PeopleClubCode = Clubs.ClubCode<br>ORDER BY Clubs.ClubName, Rank.Year, Rank.Month, Rank.Rank; |

| Query Name | Query Details |
|---|---|
| qDemoQueryGrid | SELECT People.PeopleNameLast, People.PeopleNameFirst, People.PeopleProfessionalClass |
| | FROM People WHERE (((People.PeopleProfessionalClass)=2)) |
| | ORDER BY People.PeopleNameLast; |
| qparmBoats | PARAMETERS Class Text; SELECT Boats.BoatsID, Boats.BoatName |
| | FROM Boats |
| | WHERE (((Boats.BoatClass)=[Class])); |
| qparmInsertBoat | PARAMETERS Name Text, Class Text, Launched DateTime, Certified Bit, Notes LongText, [Value] Currency; |
| | INSERT INTO Boats ( BoatName, BoatClass, BoatLaunched, BoatCertified, BoatNote, BoatValue ) |
| | SELECT [Name] AS Expr1, [Class] AS Expr2, [Launched] AS Expr3, [Certified] AS Expr4, [Notes] AS Expr5,  [Value] AS Expr6; |
| qparmInsertBoatClass | INSERT INTO BoatClass ( ClassName, ClassBoatLength, ClassBoatWeight, ClassSailAreaMainJib,  ClassSailAreaSpinnaker, ClassAuthority ) |
| | SELECT [Name] AS Expr1, [Length] AS Expr2, [Weight] AS Expr3, [MainJib] AS Expr4, [Spinnaker] AS Expr5,  [Authority] AS Expr6; |
| qparmInsertPerson | PARAMETERS FirstName Text, LastName Text, DOB DateTime, ProfessionalClass Long, ClubCode Text,  Referee Bit, State Text; INSERT INTO People ( PeopleNameFirst, PeopleNameLast, PeopleDOB, PeopleProfessionalClass,  PeopleClubCode, PeopleReferee, PeopleState ) SELECT [FirstName] AS Expr1, [LastName] AS Expr2, [DOB] AS Expr3, [ProfessionalClass] AS Expr4,  [ClubCode] AS Expr5, [Referee] AS Expr6, [State] AS Expr7; |
| qParmSailorRanking | PARAMETERS ClubCode Text, Ranking Long; |
| | SELECT People.PeopleID, People.PeopleNameLast, People.PeopleNameFirst, People.PeopleProfessionalClass, People.PeopleClubCode, Rank.Year, Rank.Month, Rank.Rank |
| | FROM People INNER JOIN Rank ON People.PeopleID = Rank.SailorID WHERE (((People.PeopleClubCode)=[ClubCode]) AND ((Rank.Rank)<=[Ranking])) |
| | ORDER BY Rank.Year, Rank.Month, Rank.Rank; |

| Query Name | Query Details |
|------------|---------------|
| qparmVerifyLogin | PARAMETERS FirstName Text, LastName Text, ClubCode Text; SELECT People.PeopleNameFirst, People.PeopleNameLast, People.PeopleClubCode |
|  | FROM People |
|  | WHERE (((People.PeopleNameFirst)=[FirstName]) |
|  | AND ((People.PeopleNameLast)=[LastName]) |
|  | AND ((People.PeopleClubCode)=[ClubCode])); |
| qranktest | SELECT Rank.Rank, Rank.Year, Rank.Month, Rank.SailorID |
|  | FROM Rank |
|  | ORDER BY Rank.Rank, Rank.Year, Rank.Month, Rank.SailorID DESC; |
| qTestWhereIn | SELECT People.PeopleNameLast, People.PeopleNameFirst, People.PeopleClubCode |
|  | FROM People |
|  | WHERE (((People.PeopleClubCode) In ('scow','dsyc'))); |

Setup cannot install system files or update shared files if the files are in use. Before ... any open applications.

WARNING: This program is protected by copyright law and international treaties.

You may install Microsoft Data Access 2.1 on a single computer. Some Microsoft product... with additional rights, which are stated in the End User License Agreement included with ...

Please take a moment to read the End User License Agreement now. It contains all of the te... conditions that pertain to this software product. By choosing to continue, you indicate accep... these terms.

Exit Setup

Continue

New Data Source

Select a driver for which you want to set up a data sourc...

| Name | Version |
| --- | --- |
| Microsoft Access Driver (*.mdb) | 4.00.4207.00 |
| Microsoft dBase Driver (*.dbf) | 4.00.4207.00 |
| Microsoft dBase VFP Driver (*.dbf) | 6.01.8440.01 |
| Microsoft Excel Driver (*.xls) | 4.00.4207.00 |
| Microsoft FoxPro VFP Driver (*.dbf) | 6.01.8440.01 |
| Microsoft ODBC for Oracle | 2.573.4207.00 |
| Microsoft Paradox Driver (*.db ) | 4.00.4207.00 |
| Microsoft Text Driver (*.txt; *.csv) | 4.00.4207.00 |
| Microsoft Visual FoxPro Driver | 6.01.8440.01 |
| SQL Server | 3.70.06.90 |

Cancel

# Structure of Clothier.mdb

## Introduction and Objective

The Clothier database supports an Internet site to manage new items in the inventory of a clothing wholesaler. As the wholesaler contracts to buy clothing from manufacturers, the buyers post the items on the web site so they can be ordered by individual stores.

## Vocabulary and Business Rules

An item refers to a given model (design) of clothing. An item is not one piece of clothing, but rather one offering by the wholesaler such as the "Mountain Walker" hiking trousers. Every item belongs to a department, such as Women's Sportswear or Men's Formalwear. In addition, each item has a type such as trousers, shirts, or hats.

Items have a release date and since the wholesaler wants to show clothes as early as possible, they are frequently posted to the site prior to release. A quantity per box helps the sales staff since orders are made in full-box quantities. To make this database simpler we use only one price, the wholesaler's buying price.

This business buys from three vendors. Each vendor has a name and a vendor code.

## Where to Download

This database is available from the Wrox site. We make it available in Access97 format, which can also be read by Access 2000. The end of this Appendix also lists the information to create the structure of the database by hand.

# Structure of Tables and Queries

### Items Table

Each clothing item (design) gets its own record. However, for this site there is no need to differentiate among the sizes and colors. Fields for ordering are included, such as the price and quantity packed per box so the buyer can estimate delivery costs. A numeric code field identifies the vendor and can be used for joins to the `vendorID` field of the `vendors` table.

Note the clarification in the name of the price field. Many of my students start with fields named price, but most items have at least two prices (buy and sell) and can have many more (discount price, manufacturer's suggested retail price, etc). I suggest that a field named Price is always followed by one or more adjectives describing which price.

### Vendors Table

This wholesaler buys from several vendors, each of which has its own record in this table. The `VendorID` field can be joined to the `ItemVendor` field of the `Items` table.

In this simple database there are no stored queries.

# Table Data

If you are unable to download the tables (like when I lectured in Ulaan Batar in '94, although my friends in Mongolia now communicate by Email without problem), you can create the structure by hand from the data below.

| Table | Field Name | Field Type | Field Size | Notes |
|-------|-----------|-----------|-----------|-------|
| **Items** | ItemID | Number (Long) | 4 | Attributes: |
| | | | | Fixed Size, Auto-Increment |
| | ItemName | Text | 50 | |
| | ItemDepartment | Text | 50 | |
| | ItemType | Text | 50 | |
| | ItemPriceBuy | Currency | 8 | Decimal Places: Auto |
| | | | | Default Value: 0 |
| | | | | Format: $#,##0.00;($#,##0.00) |

| Table | Field Name | Field Type | Field Size | Notes |
|-------|-----------|-----------|-----------|-------|
| **Vendors** | ItemVendor | Number (Integer) | 2 | |
| | ItemQtyPerBox | Number (Long) | 4 | |
| | ItemDateRelease | Date/Time | 8 | |
| | VendorID | Number (Long) | 4 | Attributes: Fixed Size, Auto-Increment |
| | VendorName | Text | 50 | |
| | VendorCode | Text | 50 | |

Setup cannot install system files or update shared files if the files are in use. Before any open applications.

WARNING: This program is protected by copyright law and international treaties.

You may install Microsoft Data Access 2.1 on a single computer. Some Microsoft product with additional rights, which are stated in the End User License Agreement included with

Please take a moment to read the End User License Agreement now. It contains all of the t conditions that pertain to this software product. By choosing to continue, you indicate accep these terms.

Exit Setup

Continue

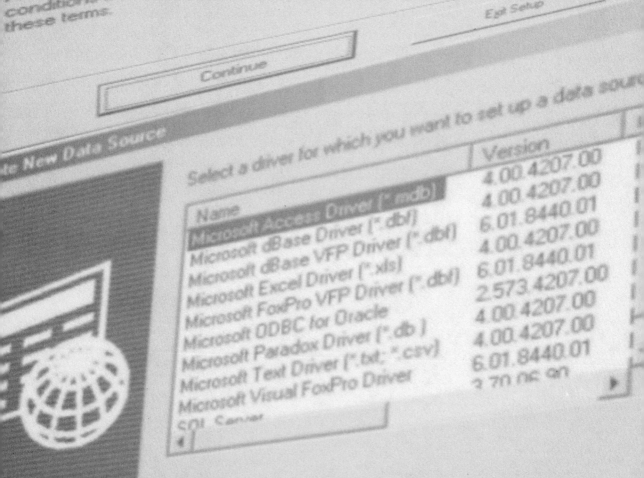

te New Data Source

Select a driver for which you want to set up a data sour

| Name | Version |
|------|---------|
| Microsoft Access Driver (*.mdb) | 4.00.4207.00 |
| Microsoft dBase Driver (*.dbf) | 4.00.4207.00 |
| Microsoft dBase VFP Driver (*.dbf) | 6.01.8440.01 |
| Microsoft Excel Driver (*.xls) | 4.00.4207.00 |
| Microsoft FoxPro VFP Driver (*.dbf) | 6.01.8440.01 |
| Microsoft ODBC for Oracle | 2.573.4207.00 |
| Microsoft Paradox Driver (*.db ) | 4.00.4207.00 |
| Microsoft Text Driver (*.txt; *.csv) | 4.00.4207.00 |
| Microsoft Visual FoxPro Driver | 6.01.8440.01 |
| SQL Server | 3.70.06.90 |

Cancel

# Profile.mdb Database Schema

The following tables describe the `profile.mdb` database.

## Tables

### *profile*

| Field Name | Data Type | Length | Indexed | Req. | 0 Len. | Description |
|---|---|---|---|---|---|---|
| fname | Text | 30 | No | Yes | Yes | First Name |
| mname | Text | 30 | No | No | Yes | Middle Name |
| lname | Text | 30 | No | No | Yes | Last Name |
| handle | Text | 75 | No | No | Yes | Nickname |
| usehandle | Yes/No | | No | No | | Use Handle instead of Name in profile |
| phone | Text | 20 | No | No | Yes | Phone Number |
| email | Text | 100 | Yes (dup) | No | Yes | Email Address |
| password | Text | 20 | Yes (dup) | No | Yes | Password to edit profile |
| address | Text | 100 | No | No | Yes | Address |
| city | Text | 50 | Yes (dup) | No | Yes | City |
| state | Text | 30 | Yes (dup) | No | Yes | State |

| Field Name | Data Type | Length | Indexed | Req. | 0 Len. | Description |
|---|---|---|---|---|---|---|
| zip | Text | 20 | Yes (dup) | No | Yes | Zip Code |
| country | Text | 20 | Yes (dup) | No | Yes | Country |
| image | Text | 50 | No | No | Yes | Image file name |
| template | Integer | | No | No | | Template Number to use in profile |
| fontstyle | Text | 75 | No | No | No | Font Style for Headings in page |
| fontsize | Integer | | No | No | | Font Size for Headings in page |
| fontcolor | Integer | | No | No | | Font Color for Headings in page |
| bgimage | Text | 50 | No | No | Yes | Background Image for page |
| bgcolor | Integer | | No | No | | Background Color for page |
| linkcolor | Integer | | No | No | | Hyperlink Color for page |
| vlinkcolor | Integer | | No | No | | Visited Hyperlink Color for page |
| alinkcolor | Integer | | No | No | | Active Hyperlink Color for page |
| tblbgimage | Text | 50 | No | No | Yes | Background Image for tables in page |
| tblbgcolor | Integer | | No | No | | Background Color for tables in page |

| Field Name | Data Type | Length | Indexed | Req. | 0 Len. | Description |
|---|---|---|---|---|---|---|
| textcolor | Integer | | No | No | | Font color for text in page |
| tblborder | Integer | | No | No | | Table Border width for tables in page |
| website | Text | 100 | No | No | Yes | Web Site Address |
| newsletter | Yes/No | | No | No | | Does User want to receive Newsletter? |
| job | Text | 255 | No | No | Yes | Job Description in profile |
| hobbies | Memo | | No | No | Yes | Hobbies in profile |
| bio | Memo | | No | No | Yes | Biography in profile |
| other | Memo | | No | No | Yes | Additional Comments in profile |

## BLOBs

| Field Name | Data Type | Length | Indexed | Req. | 0 Len. | Description |
|---|---|---|---|---|---|---|
| fname | Text | | | Yes | Yes | First Name |
| email | Text | 100 | No | No | Yes | Email Address from profile |
| picture | OLE Obj. | | No | No | | BLOB picture |
| sound | OLE Obj. | | No | No | | BLOB sound (.wav file) |

# Stored Queries

### *deletetest*

```
DELETE *
FROM profile
WHERE email LIKE 'takempis@whatever.net';
```

### *inserttest*

```
INSERT INTO profile ( fname, mname, lname, handle, usehandle, phone, email, password,
address, city, state, zip, country, website, newsletter, job, hobbies, bio, other,
[image], template, fontstyle, fontsize, fontcolor, bgimage, bgcolor, linkcolor,
vlinkcolor, alinkcolor, tblbgimage, tblbgcolor, textcolor, tblborder )
VALUES('Kevin', 'C', 'Spencer', 'Kevin', FALSE, '111-222-3333', 'takempis@aol.com',
'hello', 'address', 'city', 'state', '11111', 'USA', 'http://www.takempis.com', TRUE,
'Internet Database Programming', 'programming', 'I was born. I lived. I will die',
'whatever', 'none', 1, 'Arial', 2, 29, 'rosesbg.jpg', 30, 29, 30, 28, 'rosesbg.jpg',
18, 30, 0)
```

### *paramselecttest*

```
SELECT profile.*
FROM profile
WHERE email LIKE mystr;
```

### *selecttest*

```
SELECT profile.*
FROM profile;
```

### *updatetest*

```
UPDATE profile SET email = 'takempis@whatever.net'
WHERE email = 'takempis@aol.com';
```

Setup cannot install system files or update shared files if the files are in use. Before c
any open applications.

Exit Setup

Continue

e New Data Source

Select a driver for which you want to set up a data sourc

| Name | Version |
|------|---------|
| Microsoft Access Driver (*.mdb) | 4.00.4207.00 |
| Microsoft dBase Driver (*.dbf) | 4.00.4207.00 |
| Microsoft dBase VFP Driver (*.dbf) | 6.01.8440.01 |
| Microsoft Excel Driver (*.xls) | 4.00.4207.00 |
| Microsoft FoxPro VFP Driver (*.dbf) | 6.01.8440.01 |
| Microsoft ODBC for Oracle | 2.573.4207.00 |
| Microsoft Paradox Driver (*.db ) | 4.00.4207.00 |
| Microsoft Text Driver (*.txt; *.csv) | 4.00.4207.00 |
| Microsoft Visual FoxPro Driver | 6.01.8440.01 |
| SQL Server | 3.70.06.90 |

Finish

Cancel

# Creating a Sailors Database in SQL Server

This section covers the required steps to create the `Sailors` database in SQL Server and assumes you already have the Access `Sailors` database on your machine. You will need administrator rights to the SQL Server database that you use, and it is recommended that you have SQL Server installed on your workstation. These procedures have been tested with SQL Server 6.5 and SQL Server 7.0.

We will be *exporting* the tables and table data from the Access `Sailors` database to the SQL Server `Sailors` database. This is by far the easiest method to duplicate the Access database into SQL Server.

## Creating the Sailors Database

Start SQL Server Enterprise Manager and expand the databases folder. Right click on **Databases** and choose **New Database** from the popup menu. Enter the name of **Sailors** for the database name and select an initial database size of **5 MB,** which is more than enough for this database. Take the default for all other options and click on the **Create Now** button (or **OK** button if using version 7).

The database has now been created and we need to set up a DSN next.

## Creating the Data Source Name

Chapter 2 stepped you through creating a DSN in detail, so we'll just cover the highlights here with no illustrations. Select the **System DSN** tab in the ODBC Data Source Administrator dialog and click on the **Add** button.

In the next dialog, choose **Microsoft SQL Server** and click the **Finish** button. Give the DSN a name of **SQLSailor** and select the server where the version of SQL Server that you are using is installed.

On the next dialog select the option **With SQL Server authentication using a logon ID and password entered by the user.** Enter the **logon ID** and **password** of the account you are using to access the `Sailors` database on your SQL Server. Click **Next** to continue.

Once you receive the next dialog you may need to change the **default database** to Sailors, if the logon ID you are using has access to more than one database. Accept all other defaults on this dialog and click the **Next** button. Accept all defaults on the next dialog and click the **Finish** button.

The next dialog gives you the option of testing the DSN to ensure you are able to connect successfully. It is always recommended that you test the DSN. Once you have tested the DSN click **OK** to close the dialog and the new DSN will be set up.

# Exporting the Tables

Open the Access Sailors database and click on the **Tables** tab. Perform the following steps for each table listed. Select a table and right click on it, and choose **Save As/Export** from the popup menu (just **Export** for Access 2000). Click **OK** on the **Save As** dialog.

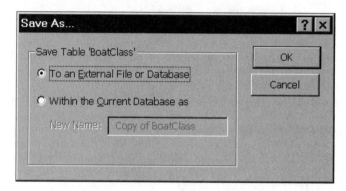

In the Save Table dialog choose ODBC Databases () in the Save As Type combo box.

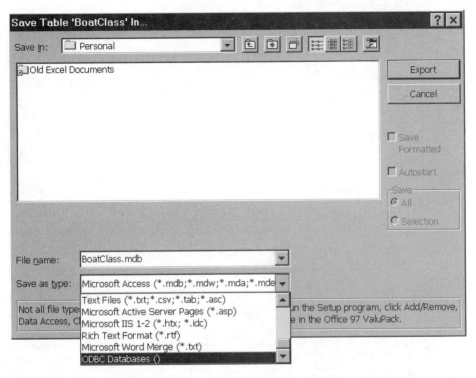

Once you click on ODBC Databases (), the Export dialog will appear. Click on OK here without changing the table name.

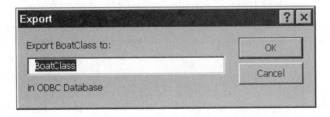

The Select Data Source dialog will appear and you need to click on the **Machine Data Source** tab and select the SQLSailor DSN as shown below.

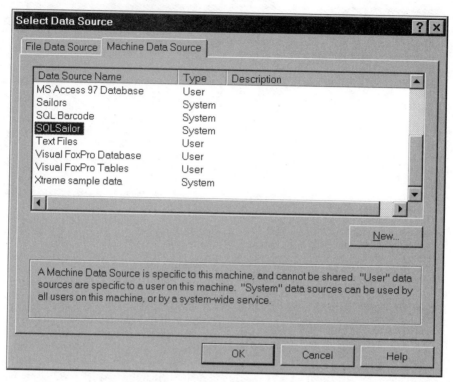

Once you click **OK** on the previous dialog you will be prompted with the **SQL Server Login** dialog asking for the password for the user id that was specified in the DSN, as shown here.

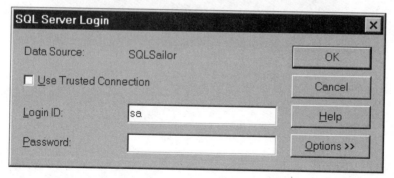

Once you have specified the correct password, click on **OK**. The table will be created in SQL Server, and the data that exists in the table in Access will be loaded into the new table in SQL Server.

Repeat this process for all tables in the Access `Sailors` database. Note that it is not possible to do all tables at once, without writing complex code. This code would need to extract the database schema, work out how to use this schema to build tables, and extract data, all within the code.

Setup cannot install system files or update shared files if the files are in use. Before
any open applications.

WARNING: This program is protected by copyright law and international treaties.

You may install Microsoft Data Access 2.1 on a single computer. Some Microsoft produc
with additional rights, which are stated in the End User License Agreement included with

Please take a moment to read the End User License Agreement now. It contains all of the t
conditions that pertain to this software product. By choosing to continue, you indicate accep
these terms.

Exit Setup

Continue

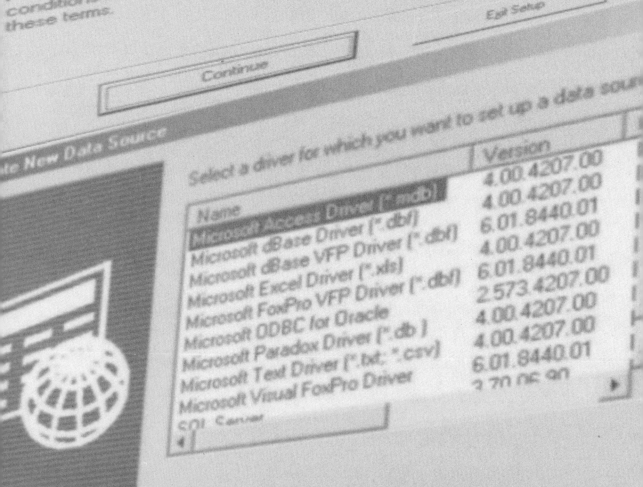

e New Data Source

Select a driver for which you want to set up a data sour

| Name | Version |
| --- | --- |
| Microsoft Access Driver (*.mdb) | 4.00.4207.00 |
| Microsoft dBase Driver (*.dbf) | 4.00.4207.00 |
| Microsoft dBase VFP Driver (*.dbf) | 6.01.8440.01 |
| Microsoft Excel Driver (*.xls) | 4.00.4207.00 |
| Microsoft FoxPro VFP Driver (*.dbf) | 6.01.8440.01 |
| Microsoft ODBC for Oracle | 2.573.4207.00 |
| Microsoft Paradox Driver (*.db ) | 4.00.4207.00 |
| Microsoft Text Driver (*.txt; *.csv) | 4.00.4207.00 |
| Microsoft Visual FoxPro Driver | 6.01.8440.01 |
| SQL Server | 3.70.06.90 |

Finish     Cancel

# Active Server Pages Object Model

This appendix offers a handy reference to the Active Server Pages **object model**, and in each case provides the properties, methods and events for the object, along with their collections.

## The Request Object

Together, the Request object and the Response object form the 'conversational mechanism' of ASP. The Request object is responsible for controlling how the user sends information to the server. Using the Request object, the server can obtain information about what the user wants – either explicitly (e.g. through programmed ASP code) or implicitly (e.g. through the HTTP headers).

| Collections | Description |
| --- | --- |
| ClientCertificate | Client certificate values sent from the browser. Read Only |
| Cookies | Values of cookies sent from the browser. Read Only |
| Form | Values of form elements sent from the browser. Read Only |
| QueryString | Values of variables in the HTTP query string. Read Only |
| ServerVariables | Values of the HTTP and environment variables. Read Only |

| Property | Description |
| --- | --- |
| TotalBytes | Specifies the number of bytes the client is sending in the body of the request. Read Only |

| Method | Description |
| --- | --- |
| BinaryRead | Used to retrieve data sent to the server as part of the POST request |

# The Response Object

The Response object is responsible for sending the server's output to the client. In this sense, the Response object is the counterpart to the Request object: the Request object gathers information from both the client and the server, and the Response object sends, or resends, the information to the client by writing to the HTTP data stream.

| Collection | Description |
|---|---|
| Cookies | Values of all the cookies to send to the browser. |

| Properties | Description |
|---|---|
| Buffer | Determines whether the page is to be buffered until complete |
| CacheControl | Determines whether proxy servers are allowed to cache the output generated by ASP |
| Charset | Appends the name of the character set to the content-type header |
| ContentType | HTTP content type (e.g. "Text/HTML") for the response |
| Expires | Number of minutes between caching and expiry, for a page cached on the browser |
| ExpiresAbsolute | Explicit date and/or time of expiry for a page cached on a browser |
| IsClientConnected | Indicates whether the client has disconnected from the server |
| PICS | Adds the value of a PICS label to the pics-label field of the response header |
| Status | Value of the HTTP status line returned by the server |

| Methods | Description |
|---|---|
| AddHeader | Adds or changes a value in the HTML header |
| AppendToLog | Adds text to the web server log entry for this request |
| BinaryWrite | Sends text to the browser without character-set conversion |
| Clear | Erases any buffered HTML output |
| End | Stops processing the page and returns the current result |
| Flush | Sends buffered output immediately |
| Redirect | Instructs the browser to connect to a different URL |
| Write | Writes variable values, strings etc. to the current page as a string |

The Response interface elements can be divided into groups, like this:

| Response Items | Description |
| --- | --- |
| Write, BinaryWrite | Inserts information into a page |
| Cookies | Sends cookies to the browser |
| Redirect | Redirects the browser |
| Buffer, Flush, Clear, End | Buffers the page as it is created |
| Expires, ExpiresAbsolute, ContentType, AddHeader, Status, CacheContol, PICS, Charset | Sets the properties of a page |
| IsClientConnected | Checks the client connection |

# The Application Object

Each application is represented by an instance of the Application object. This object stores variables and objects for application-scope usage. It also holds information about any currently-active sessions.

| Collections | Description |
| --- | --- |
| Contents | Contains all of the items added to the application through script commands |
| StaticObjects | Contains all of the objects added to the application with the <OBJECT> tag |

| Methods | Description |
| --- | --- |
| Lock | Prevents other clients from modifying application properties |
| Unlock | Allows other clients to modify application properties |

| Events | Description |
| --- | --- |
| OnStart | Occurs when a page in the application is first referenced |
| OnEnd | Occurs when the application ends, i.e. when the web server is stopped |

# The Session Object

The Session object is used to keep track of an individual browser as it navigates through the web site.

| Collections | Description |
| --- | --- |
| Contents | Contains all of the items added to the session through script commands |
| StaticObjects | Contains all of the objects added to the session with the <OBJECT> tag |

| Method | Description |
| --- | --- |
| Abandon | Destroys a Session object and releases its resources |

| Properties | Description |
| --- | --- |
| CodePage | Sets the codepage that will be used for symbol mapping |
| LCID | Sets the locale identifier |
| SessionID | Returns the session identification for this user |
| Timeout | Sets the timeout period for the session state for this application, in minutes |

| Events | Description |
| --- | --- |
| OnStart | Occurs when the server creates a new session |
| OnEnd | Occurs when a session is abandoned or times out |

# The Server Object

The main use of the Server object is to create components.

| Property | Description |
| --- | --- |
| ScriptTimeout | Length of time a script can run before an error occurs |

| Methods | Description |
| --- | --- |
| CreateObject | Creates an instance of an object or server component |
| HTMLEncode | Applies HTML encoding to the specified string |
| MapPath | Converts a virtual path into a physical path |
| URLEncode | Applies URL encoding including escape chars to a string |

# The ObjectContext Object

When we use MTS (Microsoft Transaction Server) to manage a transaction, we have the functionality within our script to commit (or to abort) the transaction. This functionality is provided by the ObjectContext object.

| Methods | Description |
|---------|-------------|
| SetComplete | Declares that the script knows no reason for the transaction not to complete. If all participating components call SetComplete, then the transaction will complete. SetComplete overrides any previous SetAbort method that has been called in the script |
| SetAbort | Aborts a transaction initiated by an ASP |

| Events | Description |
|--------|-------------|
| OnTransactionCommit | Occurs after a transacted script's transaction commits |
| OnTransactionAbort | Occurs if the transaction is aborted |

Setup cannot install system files or update shared files if the files are in use. Before
any open applications.

Please take a moment to read the End User License Agreement now. It contains all of the t
conditions that pertain to this software product. By choosing to continue, you indicate accep
these terms.

| Exit Setup |

| Continue |

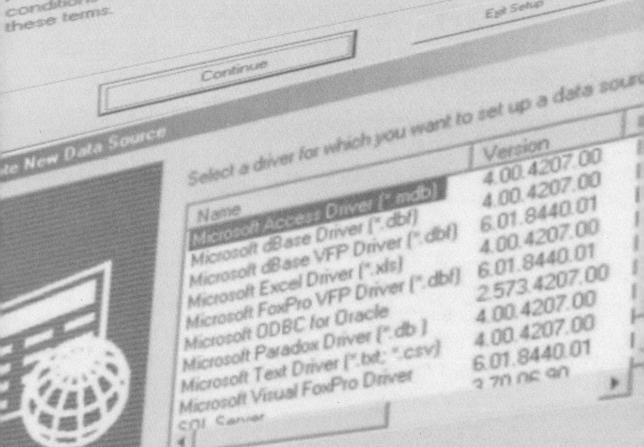

te New Data Source

Select a driver for which you want to set up a data sour

| Name | Version |
| --- | --- |
| Microsoft Access Driver (*.mdb) | 4.00.4207.00 |
| Microsoft dBase Driver (*.dbf) | 4.00.4207.00 |
| Microsoft dBase VFP Driver (*.dbf) | 6.01.8440.01 |
| Microsoft Excel Driver (*.xls) | 4.00.4207.00 |
| Microsoft FoxPro VFP Driver (*.dbf) | 6.01.8440.01 |
| Microsoft ODBC for Oracle | 2.573.4207.00 |
| Microsoft Paradox Driver (*.db ) | 4.00.4207.00 |
| Microsoft Text Driver (*.txt; *.csv) | 4.00.4207.00 |
| Microsoft Visual FoxPro Driver | 6.01.8440.01 |
| SQL Server | 3.70.06.90 |

| Cancel |

# Microsoft ActiveX Data Objects 2.0 Library Reference

In this section we will find the objects, methods, and properties necessary for ADO transactions using VB. This should aid the programmer when connections are to be made to a database from within a web application.

> **All properties are read/write unless otherwise stated.**

## Objects

| Name | Description |
|------|-------------|
| Command | A Command object is a definition of a specific command that you intend to execute against a data source. |
| Connection | A Connection object represents an open connection to a data store. |
| Error | An Error object contains the details about data access errors pertaining to a single operation involving the provider. |
| Errors | The Errors collection contains all of the Error objects created in response to a single failure involving the provider. |

| Name | Description |
|------|-------------|
| Field | A Field object represents a column of data within a common data type. |
| Fields | A Fields collection contains all of the Field objects of a Recordset object. |
| Parameter | A Parameter object represents a parameter or argument associated with a Command object based on a parameterized query or stored procedure. |
| Parameters | A Parameters collection contains all the Parameter objects of a Command object. |
| Properties | A Properties collection contains all the Property objects for a specific instance of an object. |
| Property | A Property object represents a dynamic characteristic of an ADO object that is defined by the provider. |
| Recordset | A Recordset object represents the entire set of records from a base table or the results of an executed command. At any time, the Recordset object only refers to a single record within the set as the current record. |

# Command Object

## Methods

| Name | Returns | Description |
|------|---------|-------------|
| Cancel | | Cancels execution of a pending `Execute` or `Open` call. |
| CreateParameter | Parameter | Creates a new `Parameter` object. |
| Execute | Recordset | Executes the query, SQL statement, or stored procedure specified in the `CommandText` property. |

## Properties

| Name | Returns | Description |
|------|---------|-------------|
| ActiveConnection | Variant | Indicates to which `Connection` object the command currently belongs. |
| CommandText | String | Contains the text of a command to be issued against a data provider. |

| Name | Returns | Description |
|------|---------|-------------|
| CommandTimeout | Long | Indicates how long to wait, in seconds, while executing a command before terminating the command and generating an error. Default is 30. |
| CommandType | CommandTypeEnum | Indicates the type of Command object. |
| Name | String | Indicates the name of the Command object. |
| Parameters | Parameters | Contains all of the Parameter objects for a Command object. |
| Prepared | Boolean | Indicates whether or not to save a compiled version of a command before execution. |
| Properties | Properties | Contains all of the Property objects for a Command object. |
| State | Long | Describes whether the Command object is open or closed. Read only. |

# Connection Object

## Methods

| Name | Returns | Description |
|------|---------|-------------|
| BeginTrans | Integer | Begins a new transaction. |
| Cancel | | Cancels the execution of a pending, asynchronous Execute or Open operation. |
| Close | | Closes an open connection and any dependant objects. |
| CommitTrans | | Saves any changes and ends the current transaction. |
| Execute | Recordset | Executes the query, SQL statement, stored procedure, or provider specific text. |
| Open | | Opens a connection to a data source, so that commands can be executed against it. |
| OpenSchema | Recordset | Obtains database schema information from the provider. |
| RollbackTrans | | Cancels any changes made during the current transaction and ends the transaction. |

# Properties

| Name | Returns | Description |
| --- | --- | --- |
| Attributes | Long | Indicates one or more characteristics of a `Connection` object. Default is 0. |
| CommandTimeout | Long | Indicates how long, in seconds, to wait while executing a command before terminating the command and generating an error. The default is 30. |
| ConnectionString | String | Contains the information used to establish a connection to a data source. |
| ConnectionTimeout | Long | Indicates how long, in seconds, to wait while establishing a connection before terminating the attempt and generating an error. Default is 15. |
| CursorLocation | CursorLocationEnum | Sets or returns the location of the cursor engine. |
| DefaultDatabase | String | Indicates the default database for a `Connection` object. |
| Errors | Errors | Contains all of the `Error` objects created in response to a single failure involving the provider. |
| IsolationLevel | IsolationLevelEnum | Indicates the level of transaction isolation for a `Connection` object. Write only. |
| Mode | ConnectModeEnum | Indicates the available permissions for modifying data in a `Connection`. |
| Properties | Properties | Contains all of the `Property` objects for a `Connection` object. |
| Provider | String | Indicates the name of the provider for a `Connection` object. |
| State | Long | Describes whether the `Connection` object is open or closed. Read only. |
| Version | String | Indicates the ADO version number. Read only. |

# Events

| Name | Description |
|------|-------------|
| BeginTransComplete | Fired after a `BeginTrans` operation finishes executing. |
| CommitTransComplete | Fired after a `CommitTrans` operation finishes executing. |
| ConnectComplete | Fired after a connection starts. |
| Disconnect | Fired after a connection ends. |
| ExecuteComplete | Fired after a command has finished executing. |
| InfoMessage | Fired whenever a `ConnectionEvent` operation completes successfully and additional information is returned by the provider. |
| RollbackTransComplete | Fired after a `RollbackTrans` operation finished executing. |
| WillConnect | Fired before a connection starts. |
| WillExecute | Fired before a pending command executes on the connection. |

# Error Object

## Properties

| Name | Returns | Description |
|------|---------|-------------|
| Description | String | A description string associated with the error. Read only. |
| HelpContext | Integer | Indicates the `ContextID` in the help file for the associated error. Read only. |
| HelpFile | String | Indicates the name of the help file. Read only. |
| NativeError | Long | Indicates the provider-specific error code for the associated error. Read only. |
| Number | Long | Indicates the number that uniquely identifies an `Error` object. Read only. |
| Source | String | Indicates the name of the object or application that originally generated the error. Read only. |
| SQLState | String | Indicates the SQL state for a given `Error` object. It is a five-character string that follows the ANSI SQL standard. Read only. |

# Errors Collection

## Methods

| Name | Returns | Description |
|------|---------|-------------|
| Clear | | Removes all of the Error objects from the Errors collection. |
| Refresh | | Updates the Error objects with information from the provider. |

## Properties

| Name | Returns | Description |
|------|---------|-------------|
| Count | Long | Indicates the number of Error objects in the Errors collection. Read only. |
| Item | Error | Allows indexing into the Errors collection to reference a specific Error object. Read only. |

# Field Object

## Methods

| Name | Returns | Description |
|------|---------|-------------|
| AppendChunk | | Appends data to a large or binary Field object. |
| GetChunk | Variant | Returns all or a portion of the contents of a large or binary Field object. |

## Properties

| Name | Returns | Description |
|------|---------|-------------|
| ActualSize | Long | Indicates the actual length of a field's value. Read only. |
| Attributes | Long | Indicates one or more characteristics of a Field object. |

| Name | Returns | Description |
|------|---------|-------------|
| DataFormat | Variant | Write only. |
| DefinedSize | Long | Indicates the defined size of the Field object. Write only. |
| Name | String | Indicates the name of the Field object. |
| NumericScale | Byte | Indicates the scale of numeric values for the Field object. Write only. |
| OriginalValue | Variant | Indicates the value of a Field object that existed in the record before any changes were made. Read only. |
| Precision | Byte | Indicates the degree of precision for numeric values in the Field object. Read only. |
| Properties | Properties | Contains all of the Property objects for a Field object. |
| Type | DataTypeEnum | Indicates the data type of the Field object. |
| UnderlyingValue | Variant | Indicates a Field object's current value in the database. Read only. |
| Value | Variant | Indicates the value assigned to the Field object. |

# Fields Collection

## Methods

| Name | Returns | Description |
|------|---------|-------------|
| Append | | Appends a Field object to the Fields collection. |
| Delete | | Deletes a Field object from the Fields collection. |
| Refresh | | Updates the Field objects in the Fields collection. |

## Properties

| Name | Returns | Description |
| --- | --- | --- |
| Count | Long | Indicates the number of Field objects in the Fields collection. Read only. |
| Item | Field | Allows indexing into the Fields collection to reference a specific Field object. Read only. |

# Parameter Object

## Methods

| Name | Returns | Description |
| --- | --- | --- |
| AppendChunk | | Appends data to a large or binary Parameter object. |

## Properties

| Name | Returns | Description |
| --- | --- | --- |
| Attributes | Long | Indicates one or more characteristics of a Parameter object. |
| Direction | ParameterDirectionEnum | Indicates whether the Parameter object represents an input parameter, an output parameter, or both, or if the parameter is a return value from a stored procedure. |
| Name | String | Indicates the name of the Parameter object. |
| NumericScale | Byte | Indicates the scale of numeric values for the Parameter object. |
| Precision | Byte | Indicates the degree of precision for numeric values in the Parameter object. |
| Properties | Properties | Contains all of the Property objects for a Parameter object. |
| Size | Long | Indicates the maximum size, in bytes or characters, of a Parameter object. |

| Name | Returns | Description |
|------|---------|-------------|
| Type | DataTypeEnum | Indicates the data type of the `Parameter` object. |
| Value | Variant | Indicates the value assigned to the `Parameter` object. |

# Parameters Collection

## Methods

| Name | Returns | Description |
|------|---------|-------------|
| Append | | Appends a `Parameter` object to the `Parameters` collection. |
| Delete | | Deletes a `Parameter` object from the `Parameters` collection. |
| Refresh | | Updates the `Parameter` objects in the `Parameters` collection. |

## Properties

| Name | Returns | Description |
|------|---------|-------------|
| Count | Long | Indicates the number of `Parameter` objects in the `Parameters` collection. Read only. |
| Item | Parameter | Allows indexing into the `Parameters` collection to reference a specific `Parameter` object. Read only. |

# Properties

## Methods

| Name | Returns | Description |
|------|---------|-------------|
| Refresh | | Updates the `Property` objects in the `Properties` collection with the details from the provider. |

## Properties

| Name | Returns | Description |
|------|---------|-------------|
| Count | Long | Indicates the number of `Property` objects in the `Properties` collection. Read only. |
| Item | Property | Allows indexing into the `Properties` collection to reference a specific `Property` object. Read only. |

# Property Object

## Properties

| Name | Returns | Description |
|------|---------|-------------|
| Attributes | Long | Indicates one or more characteristics of a `Property` object. |
| Name | String | Indicates the name of the `Property` object. Read only. |
| Type | DataTypeEnum | Indicates the data type of the `Property` object. |
| Value | Variant | Indicates the value assigned to the `Property` object. |

# Recordset Object

## Methods

| Name | Returns | Description |
|------|---------|-------------|
| AddNew | | Creates a new record for an updateable `Recordset` object. |
| Cancel | | Cancels execution of a pending asynchronous `Open` operation. |
| CancelBatch | | Cancels a pending batch update. |

| Name | Returns | Description |
| --- | --- | --- |
| CancelUpdate | | Cancels any changes made to the current record, or to a new record prior to calling the Update method. |
| Clone | Recordset | Creates a duplicate Recordset object from an existing Recordset object. |
| Close | | Closes the Recordset object and any dependent objects. |
| CompareBookmarks | CompareEnum | Compares two bookmarks and returns an indication of the relative values. |
| Delete | | Deletes the current record or group of records. |
| Find | | Searches the Recordset for a record that matches the specified criteria. |
| GetRows | Variant | Retrieves multiple records of a Recordset object into an array. |
| GetString | String | Returns a Recordset as a string. |
| Move | | Moves the position of the current record in a Recordset. |
| MoveFirst | | Moves the position of the current record to the first record in the Recordset. |
| MoveLast | | Moves the position of the current record to the last record in the Recordset. |
| MoveNext | | Moves the position of the current record to the next record in the Recordset. |
| MovePrevious | | Moves the position of the current record to the previous record in the Recordset. |
| NextRecordset | Recordset | Clears the current Recordset object and returns the next Recordset by advancing through a series of commands. |
| Open | | Opens a Recordset. |
| Requery | | Updates the data in a Recordset object by re-executing the query on which the object is based. |
| Resync | | Refreshes the data in the current Recordset object from the underlying database. |
| Save | | Saves the Recordset to a file. |

| Name | Returns | Description |
|---|---|---|
| Supports | Boolean | Determines whether a specified `Recordset` object supports particular functionality. |
| Update | | Saves any changes made to the current `Recordset` object. |
| UpdateBatch | | Writes all pending batch updates to disk. |

# Properties

| Name | Returns | Description |
|---|---|---|
| AbsolutePage | PositionEnum | Specifies in which page the current record resides. |
| AbsolutePosition | PositionEnum | Specifies the ordinal position of a `Recordset` object's current record. |
| ActiveCommand | Object | Indicates the `Command` object that created the associated `Recordset` object. Read only. |
| ActiveConnection | Variant | Indicates to which `Connection` object the specified `Recordset` object currently belongs. |
| BOF | Boolean | Indicates whether the current record is before the first record in a `Recordset` object. Read only. |
| Bookmark | Variant | Returns a bookmark that uniquely identifies the current record in a `Recordset` object, or sets the current record to the record identified by a valid bookmark. |
| CacheSize | Long | Indicates the number of records from a `Recordset` object that are cached locally in memory. |
| CursorLocation | CursorLocationEnum | Sets or returns the location of the cursor engine |
| CursorType | CursorTypeEnum | Indicates the type of cursor used in a `Recordset` object. |

| Name | Returns | Description |
|------|---------|-------------|
| DataMember | String | Specifies the name of the data member to retrieve from the object referenced by the `DataSource` property. Write only. |
| DataSource | Object | Specifies an object containing data to be represented as a `Recordset` object. Write only |
| EditMode | EditModeEnum | Indicates the editing status of the current record. Read only. |
| EOF | Boolean | Indicates whether the current record is after the last record in a `Recordset` object. Read only. |
| Fields | Fields | Contains all of the `Field` objects for the current `Recordset` object. |
| Filter | Variant | Indicates a filter for data in the `Recordset`. |
| LockType | LockTypeEnum | Indicates the type of locks placed on records during editing. |
| MarshalOptions | MarshalOptionsEnum | Indicates which records are to be marshaled back to the server. |
| MaxRecords | Long | Indicates the maximum number of records to return to a `Recordset` object from a query. Default is zero (no limit). |
| PageCount | Long | Indicates how many pages of data the Recordset object contains. Read only. |
| PageSize | Long | Indicates how many records constitute one page in the `Recordset`. |
| Properties | Properties | Contains all of the `Property` objects for the current `Recordset` object. |
| RecordCount | Long | Indicates the current number of records in the `Recordset` object. Read only. |
| Sort | String | Specifies one or more field names the `Recordset` is sorted on, and the direction of the sort. |
| Source | String | Indicates the source for the data in a `Recordset` object. |

| Name | Returns | Description |
|------|---------|-------------|
| State | Long | Indicates whether the recordset is open, closed, or whether it is executing an asynchronous operation. Read only. |
| Status | Integer | Indicates the status of the current record with respect to match updates or other bulk operations. Read only. |
| StayInSync | Boolean | Indicates, in a hierarchical `Recordset` object, whether the parent row should change when the set of underlying child records changes. Read only. |

# Events

| Name | Description |
|------|-------------|
| EndOfRecordset | Fired when there is an attempt to move to a row past the end of the `Recordset`. |
| FetchComplete | Fired after all the records in an asynchronous operation have been retrieved into the `Recordset`. |
| FetchProgress | Fired periodically during a length asynchronous operation, to report how many rows have currently been retrieved. |
| FieldChangeComplete | Fired after the value of one or more `Field` object has been changed. |
| MoveComplete | Fired after the current position in the `Recordset` changes. |
| RecordChangeComplete | Fired after one or more records change. |
| RecordsetChangeComplete | Fired after the `Recordset` has changed. |
| WillChangeField | Fired before a pending operation changes the value of one or more `Field` objects. |
| WillChangeRecord | Fired before one or more rows in the `Recordset` change. |
| WillChangeRecordset | Fired before a pending operation changes the `Recordset`. |
| WillMove | Fired before a pending operation changes the current position in the `Recordset`. |

# Method Calls Quick Reference

## Command

*Command*.Cancel
*Parameter = Command*.CreateParameter(*Name As String, Type As DataTypeEnum, Direction As ParameterDirectionEnum, Size As Integer, [Value As Variant]*)
*Recordset = Command*.Execute(*RecordsAffected As Variant, Parameters As Variant, Options As Integer*)

## Connection

*Integer = Connection*.BeginTrans
*Connection*.Cancel
*Connection*.Close
*Connection*.CommitTrans
*Recordset = Connection*.Execute(*CommandText As String, RecordsAffected As Variant, Options As Integer*)
*Connection*.Open(*ConnectionString As String, UserID As String, Password As String, Options As Integer*)
*Recordset = Connection*.OpenSchema(*Schema As SchemaEnum, [Restrictions As Variant], [SchemaID As Variant]*)
*Connection*.RollbackTrans

## Errors

*Errors*.Clear
*Errors*.Refresh

## Field

*Field*.AppendChunk(*Data As Variant*)
*Variant = Field*.GetChunk(*Length As Integer*)

## Fields

*Fields*.Append(*Name As String, Type As DataTypeEnum, DefinedSize As Integer, Attrib As FieldAttributeEnum*)
*Fields*.Delete(*Index As Variant*)
*Fields*.Refresh

## Parameter

*Parameter*.AppendChunk(*Val As Variant*)

# Parameters

*Parameters*.Append(*Object As Object*)
*Parameters*.Delete(*Index As Variant*)
*Parameters*.Refresh

# Properties

*Properties*.Refresh

# Recordset

*Recordset*.AddNew(*[FieldList As Variant], [Values As Variant]*)
*Recordset*.Cancel
*Recordset*.CancelBatch(*AffectRecords As AffectEnum*)
*Recordset*.CancelUpdate
*Recordset = Recordset*.Clone(*LockType As LockTypeEnum*)
*Recordset*.Close
*CompareEnum = Recordset*.CompareBookmarks(*Bookmark1 As Variant, Bookmark2 As Variant*)
*Recordset*.Delete(*AffectRecords As AffectEnum*)
*Recordset*.Find(*Criteria As String, SkipRecords As Integer, SearchDirection As SearchDirectionEnum, [Start As Variant]*)
*Variant = Recordset*.GetRows(*Rows As Integer, [Start As Variant], [Fields As Variant]*)
*String = Recordset*.GetString(*StringFormat As StringFormatEnum, NumRows As Integer, ColumnDelimeter As String, RowDelimeter As String, NullExpr As String*)
*Recordset*.Move(*NumRecords As Integer, [Start As Variant]*)
*Recordset*.MoveFirst
*Recordset*.MoveLast
*Recordset*.MoveNext
*Recordset*.MovePrevious
*Recordset = Recordset*.NextRecordset(*[RecordsAffected As Variant]*)
*Recordset*.Open(*Source As Variant, ActiveConnection As Variant, CursorType As CursorTypeEnum, LockType As LockTypeEnum, Options As Integer*)
*Recordset*.Requery(*Options As Integer*)
*Recordset*.Resync(*AffectRecords As AffectEnum, ResyncValues As ResyncEnum*)
*Recordset*.Save(*FileName As String, PersistFormat As PersistFormatEnum*)
*Boolean = Recordset*.Supports(*CursorOptions As CursorOptionEnum*)
*Recordset*.Update(*[Fields As Variant], [Values As Variant]*)
*Recordset*.UpdateBatch(*AffectRecords As AffectEnum*)

Setup cannot install system files or update shared files if the files are in use. Before
any open applications.

WARNING: This program is protected by copyright law and international treaties.

You may install Microsoft Data Access 2.1 on a single computer. Some Microsoft produc
with additional rights, which are stated in the End User License Agreement included with

Please take a moment to read the End User License Agreement now. It contains all of the t
conditions that pertain to this software product. By choosing to continue, you indicate acce
these terms.

| Exit Setup |

| Continue |

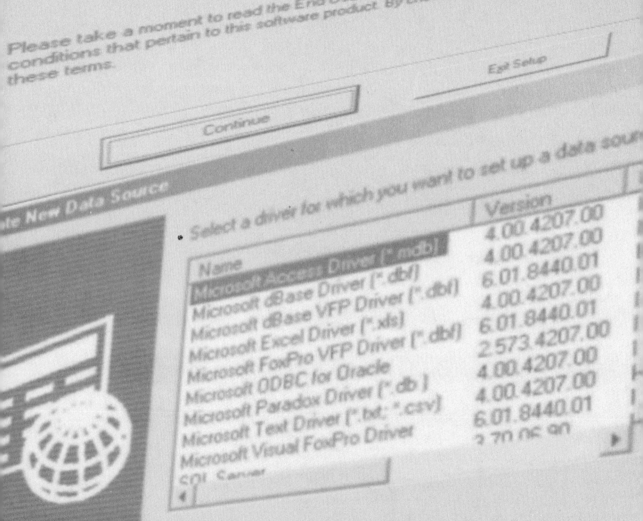

te New Data Source

Select a driver for which you want to set up a data sour

| Name | Version |
|---|---|
| Microsoft Access Driver (*.mdb) | 4.00.4207.00 |
| Microsoft dBase Driver (*.dbf) | 4.00.4207.00 |
| Microsoft dBase VFP Driver (*.dbf) | 6.01.8440.01 |
| Microsoft Excel Driver (*.xls) | 4.00.4207.00 |
| Microsoft FoxPro VFP Driver (*.dbf) | 6.01.8440.01 |
| Microsoft ODBC for Oracle | 2.573.4207.00 |
| Microsoft Paradox Driver (*.db ) | 4.00.4207.00 |
| Microsoft Text Driver (*.txt; *.csv) | 4.00.4207.00 |
| Microsoft Visual FoxPro Driver | 6.01.8440.01 |
| SQL Server | 2.70.06.90 |

| Finish | | Cance |

# VBScript Reference

## Array Handling

Dim – declares a variable. An array variable can be static, with a defined number of elements, or dynamic, and can have up to 60 dimensions.

ReDim – used to change the size of an array variable which has been declared as dynamic.

Preserve – keyword used to preserve the contents of an array being resized (otherwise data is lost when ReDim is used). If you need to use this then you can only re-dimension the rightmost index of the array.

Erase – reinitializes the elements of a fixed-size array or empties the contents of a dynamic array:

```
Dim arEmployees ()
ReDim arEmployees (9,1)

arEmployees (9,1) = "Phil"

ReDim arEmployees (9,2)              'loses the contents of element (9,1)
arEmployees (9,2) = "Paul"

ReDim Preserve arEmployees (9,3)    'preserves the contents of (9,2)
arEmployees (9,3) = "Smith"

Erase arEmployees                   'now we are back to where we started - empty array
```

LBound – returns the smallest subscript for the dimension of an array. Note that arrays always start from the subscript zero so this function will always return the value zero.

UBound – used to determine the size of an array:

```
Dim strCustomers (10, 5)
intSizeFirst = UBound (strCustomers, 1)     'returns SizeFirst = 10
intSizeSecond = UBound (strCustomers, 2)    'returns SizeSecond = 5
```

> The actual number of elements is always one greater than the value returned by UBound because the array starts from zero.

# Assignments

`Let` – used to assign values to variables (optional).
`Set` – used to assign an object reference to a variable.

```
Let intNumberOfDays = 365

Set txtMyTextBox = txtcontrol
txtMyTextBox.Value = "Hello World"
```

# Constants

`Empty` – an empty variable is one that has been created, but has not yet been assigned a value.
`Nothing` – used to remove an object reference:

```
Set txtMyTextBox = txtATextBox          'assigns object reference
Set txtMyTextBox = Nothing              'removes object reference
```

`Null` – indicates that a variable is not valid. Note that this isn't the same as `Empty`.
`True` – indicates that an expression is true. Has numerical value –1.
`False` – indicates that an expression is false. Has numerical value 0.

## Error constant

| Constant | Value |
|---|---|
| vbObjectError | &h80040000 |

## System Color constants

| Constant | Value | Description |
|---|---|---|
| vbBlack | &h000000 | Black |
| vbRed | &hFF0000 | Red |
| vbGreen | &h00FF00 | Green |
| vbYellow | &hFFFF00 | Yellow |
| vbBlue | &h0000FF | Blue |
| vbMagenta | &hFF00FF | Magenta |
| vbCyan | &h00FFFF | Cyan |
| vbWhite | &hFFFFFF | White |

# Comparison constants

| Constant | Value | Description |
|----------|-------|-------------|
| vbBinaryCompare | 0 | Perform a binary comparison. |
| vbTextCompare | 1 | Perform a textual comparison. |

# Date and Time constants

| Constant | Value | Description |
|----------|-------|-------------|
| vbSunday | 1 | Sunday |
| vbMonday | 2 | Monday |
| vbTuesday | 3 | Tuesday |
| vbWednesday | 4 | Wednesday |
| vbThursday | 5 | Thursday |
| vbFriday | 6 | Friday |
| vbSaturday | 7 | Saturday |
| vbFirstJan1 | 1 | Use the week in which January 1 occurs (default). |
| vbFirstFourDays | 2 | Use the first week that has at least four days in the new year. |
| vbFirstFullWeek | 3 | Use the first full week of the year. |
| vbUseSystem | 0 | Use the format in the regional settings for the computer. |
| vbUseSystemDayOfWeek | 0 | Use the day in the system settings for the first weekday. |

# Date Format constants

| Constant | Value | Description |
|----------|-------|-------------|
| vbGeneralDate | 0 | Display a date and/or time in the format set in the system settings. For real numbers display a date and time. For integer numbers display only a date. For numbers less than 1, display time only. |
| vbLongDate | 1 | Display a date using the long date format specified in the computer's regional settings. |

*Table Continued on Following Page*

| Constant | Value | Description |
|---|---|---|
| vbShortDate | 2 | Display a date using the short date format specified in the computer's regional settings. |
| vbLongTime | 3 | Display a time using the long time format specified in the computer's regional settings. |
| vbShortTime | 4 | Display a time using the short time format specified in the computer's regional settings. |

# Message Box Constants

| Constant | Value | Description |
|---|---|---|
| vbOKOnly | 0 | Display OK button only. |
| vbOKCancel | 1 | Display OK and Cancel buttons. |
| vbAbortRetryIgnore | 2 | Display Abort, Retry, and Ignore buttons. |
| vbYesNoCancel | 3 | Display Yes, No, and Cancel buttons. |
| vbYesNo | 4 | Display Yes and No buttons. |
| vbRetryCancel | 5 | Display Retry and Cancel buttons. |
| vbCritical | 16 | Display Critical Message icon. |
| vbQuestion | 32 | Display Warning Query icon. |
| vbExclamation | 48 | Display Warning Message icon. |
| vbInformation | 64 | Display Information Message icon. |
| vbDefaultButton1 | 0 | First button is the default. |
| vbDefaultButton2 | 256 | Second button is the default. |
| vbDefaultButton3 | 512 | Third button is the default. |
| vbDefaultButton4 | 768 | Fourth button is the default. |
| vbApplicationModal | 0 | Application modal. |
| vbSystemModal | 4096 | System modal. |

# String constants

| Constant | Value | Description |
|---|---|---|
| vbCr | Chr(13) | Carriage return only |
| vbCrLf | Chr(13) & Chr(10) | Carriage return and linefeed (Newline) |

| Constant | Value | Description |
|---|---|---|
| vbFormFeed | Chr(12) | Form feed only |
| vbLf | Chr(10) | Line feed only |
| vbNewLine | - | Newline character as appropriate to a specific platform |
| vbNullChar | Chr(0) | Character having the value 0 |
| vbNullString | - | String having the value zero (not just an empty string) |
| vbTab | Chr(9) | Horizontal tab |
| vbVerticalTab | Chr(11) | Vertical tab |

## Tristate constants

| Constant | Value | Description |
|---|---|---|
| TristateUseDefault | -2 | Use default setting |
| TristateTrue | -1 | True |
| TristateFalse | 0 | False |

## VarType constants

| Constant | Value | Description |
|---|---|---|
| vbEmpty | 0 | Uninitialized (default) |
| vbNull | 1 | Contains no valid data |
| vbInteger | 2 | Integer subtype |
| vbLong | 3 | Long subtype |
| vbSingle | 4 | Single subtype |
| vbDouble | 5 | Double subtype |
| vbCurrency | 6 | Currency subtype |
| vbDate | 7 | Date subtype |
| vbString | 8 | String subtype |
| vbObject | 9 | Object |
| vbError | 10 | Error subtype |
| vbBoolean | 11 | Boolean subtype |

*Table Continued on Following Page*

| Constant | Value | Description |
|---|---|---|
| vbVariant | 12 | Variant (used only for arrays of variants) |
| vbDataObject | 13 | Data access object |
| vbDecimal | 14 | Decimal subtype |
| vbByte | 17 | Byte subtype |
| vbArray | 8192 | Array |

# Control Flow

For...Next – executes a block of code a specified number of times:

```
Dim intSalary (10)
For intCounter = 0 to 10
   intSalary (intCounter) = 20000
Next
```

For Each...Next – repeats a block of code for each element in an array or collection:

```
For Each Item In Request.QueryString("MyControl")
   Response.Write Item & "<BR>"
Next
```

Do...Loop – executes a block of code while a condition is true or until a condition becomes true. Note that the condition can be checked either at the beginning or the end of the loop: the difference is that the code will be executed at least once if the condition is checked at the end.

```
Do While strDayOfWeek <> "Saturday" And strDayOfWeek <> "Sunday"
   MsgBox ("Get Up! Time for work")
   ...
Loop
```

```
Do
   MsgBox ("Get Up! Time for work")
   ...
Loop Until strDayOfWeek = "Saturday" Or strDayOfWeek = "Sunday"
```

We can also exit from a Do...Loop using Exit Do:

```
Do
   MsgBox ("Get Up! Time for work")
   ...
   If strDayOfWeek = "Sunday" Then
      Exit Do
   End If
Loop Until strDayOfWeek = "Saturday"
```

If...Then...Else – used to run various blocks of code depending on conditions:

```
If intAge < 20 Then
   MsgBox ("You're just a slip of a thing!")
ElseIf intAge < 40 Then
   MsgBox ("You're in your prime!")
Else
   MsgBox ("You're older and wiser")
End If
```

Select Case – used to replace If...Then...Else statements where there are many conditions:

```
Select Case intAge
Case 21,22,23,24,25,26
   MsgBox ("You're in your prime")
Case 40
   MsgBox ("You're fulfilling your dreams")
Case Else
   MsgBox ("Time for a new challenge")
End Select
```

While...Wend – executes a block of code while a condition is true:

```
While strDayOfWeek <> "Saturday" AND strDayOfWeek <> "Sunday"
   MsgBox ("Get Up! Time for work")
   ...
Wend
```

With – executes a series of statements for a single object:

```
With myDiv.style
   .posLeft = 200
   .posTop = 300
   .color = Red
End With
```

# Functions

VBScript contains several inbuilt functions that can be used to manipulate and examine variables. These have been subdivided into these general categories:

- ❑ Conversion functions
- ❑ Date/time functions
- ❑ Math functions
- ❑ Object management functions
- ❑ Script engine identification functions
- ❑ String functions
- ❑ Variable testing functions

For a full description of each function and the parameters it requires, see the Microsoft web site at http://msdn.microsoft.com/scripting/.

## Conversion Functions

These functions are used to convert values in variables between different types:

| Function | Description |
|----------|-------------|
| Abs | Returns the absolute value of a number. |
| Asc | Returns the numeric ANSI (or ASCII) code number of the first character in a string. |

*Table Continued on Following Page*

| Function | Description |
|----------|-------------|
| AscB | As above, but provided for use with byte data contained in a string. Returns result from the first byte only. |
| AscW | As above, but provided for Unicode characters. Returns the Wide character code, avoiding the conversion from Unicode to ANSI. |
| Chr | Returns a string made up of the ANSI character matching the number supplied. |
| ChrB | As above, but provided for use with byte data contained in a string. Always returns a single byte. |
| ChrW | As above, but provided for Unicode characters. Its argument is a Wide character code, thereby avoiding the conversion from ANSI to Unicode. |
| CBool | Returns the argument value converted to a Variant of subtype Boolean. |
| CByte | Returns the argument value converted to a Variant of subtype Byte. |
| CCur | Returns the argument value converted to a Variant of subtype Currency. |
| CDate | Returns the argument value converted to a Variant of subtype Date. |
| CDbl | Returns the argument value converted to a Variant of subtype Double. |
| CInt | Returns the argument value converted to a Variant of subtype Integer. |
| CLng | Returns the argument value converted to a Variant of subtype Long. |
| CSng | Returns the argument value converted to a Variant of subtype Single. |
| CStr | Returns the argument value converted to a Variant of subtype String. |
| Fix | Returns the integer (whole) part of a number. If the number is negative, Fix returns the first negative integer greater than or equal to the number |
| Hex | Returns a string representing the hexadecimal value of a number. |
| Int | Returns the integer (whole) portion of a number. If the number is negative, Int returns the first negative integer less than or equal to the number. |
| Oct | Returns a string representing the octal value of a number. |
| Round | Returns a number rounded to a specified number of decimal places. |
| Sgn | Returns an integer indicating the sign of a number. |

# Date/Time Functions

These functions return date or time values from the computer's system clock, or manipulate existing values:

| Function | Description |
|----------|-------------|
| Date | Returns the current system date. |
| DateAdd | Returns a date to which a specified time interval has been added. |

| Function | Description |
|---|---|
| DateDiff | Returns the number of days, weeks, or years between two dates. |
| DatePart | Returns just the day, month or year of a given date. |
| DateSerial | Returns a Variant of subtype Date for a specified year, month and day. |
| DateValue | Returns a Variant of subtype Date. |
| Day | Returns a number between 1 and 31 representing the day of the month. |
| Hour | Returns a number between 0 and 23 representing the hour of the day. |
| Minute | Returns a number between 0 and 59 representing the minute of the hour. |
| Month | Returns a number between 1 and 12 representing the month of the year. |
| MonthName | Returns the name of the specified month as a string. |
| Now | Returns the current date and time. |
| Second | Returns a number between 0 and 59 representing the second of the minute. |
| Time | Returns a Variant of subtype Date indicating the current system time. |
| TimeSerial | Returns a Variant of subtype Date for a specific hour, minute, and second. |
| TimeValue | Returns a Variant of subtype Date containing the time. |
| Weekday | Returns a number representing the day of the week. |
| WeekdayName | Returns the name of the specified day of the week as a string. |
| Year | Returns a number representing the year. |

# Math Functions

These functions perform mathematical operations on variables containing numerical values:

| Function | Description |
|---|---|
| Atn | Returns the arctangent of a number. |
| Cos | Returns the cosine of an angle. |
| Exp | Returns e (the base of natural logarithms) raised to a power. |

*Table Continued on Following Page*

| Function | Description |
|---|---|
| Log | Returns the natural logarithm of a number. |
| Randomize | Initializes the random-number generator. |
| Rnd | Returns a random number. |
| Sin | Returns the sine of an angle. |
| Sqr | Returns the square root of a number. |
| Tan | Returns the tangent of an angle. |

# Miscellaneous Functions

| Function | Description |
|---|---|
| Eval | Evaluates an expression and returns a boolean result (e.g. treats x=y as an *expression* which is either true or false). |
| Execute | Executes one or more statements (e.g. treats x=y as a *statement* which assigns the value of y to x). |
| RGB | Returns a number representing an RGB color value |

# Object Management Functions

These functions are used to manipulate objects, where applicable:

| Function | Description |
|---|---|
| CreateObject | Creates and returns a reference to an ActiveX or OLE Automation object. |
| GetObject | Returns a reference to an ActiveX or OLE Automation object. |
| LoadPicture | Returns a picture object. |

# Script Engine Identification

These functions return the version of the scripting engine:

| Function | Description |
|---|---|
| ScriptEngine | A string containing the major, minor, and build version numbers of the scripting engine. |
| ScriptEngineMajorVersion | The major version of the scripting engine, as a number. |
| ScriptEngineMinorVersion | The minor version of the scripting engine, as a number. |
| ScriptEngineBuildVersion | The build version of the scripting engine, as a number. |

# String Functions

These functions are used to manipulate string values in variables:

| Function | Description |
| --- | --- |
| Filter | Returns an array from a string array, based on specified filter criteria. |
| FormatCurrency | Returns a string formatted as currency value. |
| FormatDateTime | Returns a string formatted as a date or time. |
| FormatNumber | Returns a string formatted as a number. |
| FormatPercent | Returns a string formatted as a percentage. |
| InStr | Returns the position of the first occurrence of one string within another. |
| InStrB | As above, but provided for use with byte data contained in a string. Returns the byte position instead of the character position. |
| InstrRev | As InStr, but starts from the end of the string. |
| Join | Returns a string created by joining the strings contained in an array. |
| LCase | Returns a string that has been converted to lowercase. |
| Left | Returns a specified number of characters from the left end of a string. |
| LeftB | As above, but provided for use with byte data contained in a string. Uses that number of bytes instead of that number of characters. |
| Len | Returns the length of a string or the number of bytes needed for a variable. |
| LenB | As above, but is provided for use with byte data contained in a string. Returns the number of bytes in the string instead of characters. |
| LTrim | Returns a copy of a string without leading spaces. |
| Mid | Returns a specified number of characters from a string. |
| MidB | As above, but provided for use with byte data contained in a string. Uses that numbers of bytes instead of that number of characters. |
| Replace | Returns a string in which a specified substring has been replaced with another substring a specified number of times. |
| Right | Returns a specified number of characters from the right end of a string. |
| RightB | As above, but provided for use with byte data contained in a string. Uses that number of bytes instead of that number of characters. |
| RTrim | Returns a copy of a string without trailing spaces. |
| Space | Returns a string consisting of the specified number of spaces. |

*Table Continued on Following Page*

| Function | Description |
|----------|-------------|
| Split | Returns a one-dimensional array of a specified number of substrings. |
| StrComp | Returns a value indicating the result of a string comparison. |
| String | Returns a string of the length specified made up of a repeating character. |
| StrReverse | Returns a string in which the character order of a string is reversed. |
| Trim | Returns a copy of a string without leading or trailing spaces. |
| UCase | Returns a string that has been converted to uppercase. |

## Variable Testing Functions

These functions are used to determine the type of information stored in a variable:

| Function | Description |
|----------|-------------|
| IsArray | Returns a Boolean value indicating whether a variable is an array. |
| IsDate | Returns a Boolean value indicating whether an expression can be converted to a date. |
| IsEmpty | Returns a Boolean value indicating whether a variable has been initialized. |
| IsNull | Returns a Boolean value indicating whether an expression contains no valid data |
| IsNumeric | Returns a Boolean value indicating whether an expression can be evaluated as a number. |
| IsObject | Returns a Boolean value indicating whether an expression references a valid ActiveX or OLE Automation object. |
| TypeName | Returns a string that provides Variant subtype information about a variable. |
| VarType | Returns a number indicating the subtype of a variable. |

# Variable Declarations

Class – Declares the name of a class, as well as the variables, properties, and methods that comprise the class.
Const – Declares a constant to be used in place of literal values.
Dim – declares a variable.

# Error Handling

On Error Resume Next – indicates that if an error occurs, control should continue at the next statement.
Err – this is the error object that provides information about run-time errors.

Error handling is very limited in VBScript and the Err object must be tested explicitly to determine if an error has occurred.

# Input/Output

This consists of `Msgbox` for output and `InputBox` for input:

## MsgBox

This displays a message, and can return a value indicating which button was clicked.

```
MsgBox "Hello There",20,"Hello Message","c:\windows\MyHelp.hlp",123
```

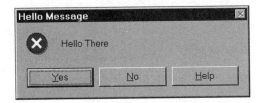

The parameters are:

`"Hello There"` – this contains the text of the message (the only obligatory parameter).

`20` – this determines which icon and buttons appear on the message box.

`"Hello Message"` – this contains the text that will appear as the title of the message box.

`"c:\windows\MyHelp.hlp"` – this adds a **Help** button to the message box and determines the help file that is opened if the button is clicked.

`123` – this is a reference to the particular help topic that will be displayed if the **Help** button is clicked.

The value of the icon and buttons parameter is determined using the following tables:

| Constant | Value | Buttons |
|---|---|---|
| vbOKOnly | 0 | OK |
| vbOKCancel | 1 | OK Cancel |
| vbAbortRetryIngnore | 2 | Abort Retry Ignore |
| vbYesNoCancel | 3 | Yes No Cancel |
| vbYesNo | 4 | Yes No |
| vbRetryCancel | 5 | Retry Cancel |

| Constant | Value | Buttons |
|----------|-------|---------|
| vbDefaultButton1 | 0 | The first button from the left is the default. |
| vbDefaultButton2 | 256 | The second button from the left is the default. |
| vbDefaultButton3 | 512 | The third button from the left is the default. |
| vbDefaultButton4 | 768 | The fourth button from the left is the default. |

| Constant | Value | Description | Icon |
|----------|-------|-------------|------|
| vbCritical | 16 | Critical Message | |
| vbQuestion | 32 | Questioning Message | |
| vbExclamation | 48 | Warning Message | |
| vbInformation | 64 | Informational Message | |

| Constant | Value | Description |
|----------|-------|-------------|
| vbApplicationModal | 0 | Just the application stops until user clicks a button. |
| vbSystemModal | 4096 | On Win16 systems the whole system stops until user clicks a button. On Win32 systems the message box remains on top of any other programs. |

To specify which buttons and icon are displayed you simply add the relevant values. So, in our example we add together 4 + 0+ 16 to display the Yes and No buttons, with Yes as the default, and the Critical icon. If we used 4 + 256 + 16 we could display the same buttons and icon, but have No as the default.

You can determine which button the user clicked by assigning the return code of the MsgBox function to a variable:

```
intButtonClicked = MsgBox ("Hello There",35,"Hello Message")
```

Notice that brackets enclose the MsgBox parameters when used in this format. The following table determines the value assigned to the variable intButtonClicked:

| Constant | Value | Button Clicked |
|----------|-------|----------------|
| vbOK | 1 | OK |
| vbCancel | 2 | Cancel |
| vbAbort | 3 | Abort |
| vbRetry | 4 | Retry |

| Constant | Value | Button Clicked |
|----------|-------|----------------|
| vbIgnore | 5 | Ignore |
| vbYes | 6 | Yes |
| vbNo | 7 | No |

# InputBox

This accepts text entry from the user and returns it as a string.

```
strName = InputBox ("Please enter your name","Login","John Smith",500,500)
```

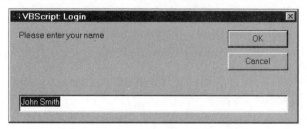

The parameters are:

"Please enter your name" – this is the prompt displayed in the input box.

"Login" – this is the text displayed as the title of the input box.

"John Smith" – this is the default value displayed in the input box.

500 – specifies the x position of the input box in relation to the screen.

500 – specifies the y position of the input box in relation to the screen.

As with the MsgBox function, you can also specify a help file and topic to add a Help button to the input box.

# Procedures

Call – optional method of calling a subroutine.

Function – used to declare a function.

Sub – used to declare a subroutine.

# Other Keywords

Rem – old style method of adding comments to code (it's now more usual to use an apostrophe (').)

Option Explicit – forces you to declare a variable before it can be used (if used, it must appear before any other statements in a script).

# Visual Basic Run-time Error Codes

The following error codes also apply to VBA code and many will not be appropriate to an application built completely around VBScript. However, if you have built your own components then these error codes may well be brought up when such components are used.

| Code | Description | Code | Description |
|------|-------------|------|-------------|
| 3 | Return without `GoSub` | 502 | Object not safe for scripting |
| 5 | Invalid procedure call | 503 | Object not safe for initializing |
| 6 | Overflow | 504 | Object not safe for creating |
| 7 | Out of memory | 505 | Invalid or unqualified reference |
| 9 | Subscript out of range | 506 | Class not defined |
| 10 | This array is fixed or temporarily locked | 1001 | Out of memory |
| 11 | Division by zero | 1002 | Syntax error |
| 13 | Type mismatch | 1003 | Expected ':' |
| 14 | Out of string space | 1004 | Expected ';' |
| 16 | Expression too complex | 1005 | Expected '(' |
| 17 | Can't perform requested operation | 1006 | Expected ')' |
| 18 | User interrupt occurred | 1007 | Expected ']' |
| 20 | Resume without error | 1008 | Expected '{' |
| 28 | Out of stack space | 1009 | Expected '}' |
| 35 | Sub or Function not defined | 1010 | Expected identifier |
| 47 | Too many DLL application clients | 1011 | Expected '=' |
| 48 | Error in loading DLL | 1012 | Expected 'If' |
| 49 | Bad DLL calling convention | 1013 | Expected 'To' |
| 51 | Internal error | 1014 | Expected 'End' |
| 52 | Bad file name or number | 1015 | Expected 'Function' |
| 53 | File not found | 1016 | Expected 'Sub' |
| 54 | Bad file mode | 1017 | Expected 'Then' |
| 55 | File already open | 1018 | Expected 'Wend' |
| 57 | Device I/O error | 1019 | Expected 'Loop' |
| 58 | File already exists | 1020 | Expected 'Next' |

*Table Continued on Following Page*

| Code | Description | Code | Description |
|------|-------------|------|-------------|
| 59 | Bad record length | 1021 | Expected 'Case' |
| 61 | Disk full | 1022 | Expected 'Select' |
| 62 | Input past end of file | 1023 | Expected expression |
| 63 | Bad record number | 1024 | Expected statement |
| 67 | Too many files | 1025 | Expected end of statement |
| 68 | Device unavailable | 1026 | Expected integer constant |
| 70 | Permission denied | 1027 | Expected 'While' or 'Until' |
| 71 | Disk not ready | 1028 | Expected 'While', 'Until' or end of statement |
| 74 | Can't rename with different drive | 1029 | Too many locals or arguments |
| 75 | Path/File access error | 1030 | Identifier too long |
| 76 | Path not found | 1031 | Invalid number |
| 91 | Object variable not set | 1032 | Invalid character |
| 92 | For loop not initialized | 1033 | Un-terminated string constant |
| 93 | Invalid pattern string | 1034 | Un-terminated comment |
| 94 | Invalid use of Null | 1035 | Nested comment |
| 322 | Can't create necessary temporary file | 1036 | 'Me' cannot be used outside of a procedure |
| 325 | Invalid format in resource file | 1037 | Invalid use of 'Me' keyword |
| 380 | Invalid property value | 1038 | 'loop' without 'do' |
| 423 | Property or method not found | 1039 | Invalid 'exit' statement |
| 424 | Object required | 1040 | Invalid 'for' loop control variable |
| 429 | OLE Automation server can't create object | 1041 | Variable redefinition |
| 430 | Class doesn't support OLE Automation | 1042 | Must be first statement on the line |
| 432 | File name or class name not found during OLE Automation operation | 1043 | Cannot assign to non-ByVal argument |

| Code | Description | Code | Description |
|------|-------------|------|-------------|
| 438 | Object doesn't support this property or method | 1044 | Cannot use parentheses when calling a Sub |
| 440 | OLE Automation error | 1045 | Expected literal constant |
| 442 | Connection to type library or object library for remote process has been lost. Press OK for dialog to remove reference | 1046 | Expected 'In' |
| 443 | OLE Automation object does not have a default value | 1047 | Expected 'Class' |
| 445 | Object doesn't support this action | 1048 | Must be defined inside a Class |
| 446 | Object doesn't support named arguments | 1049 | Expected Let or Set or Get in property declaration |
| 447 | Object doesn't support current locale setting | 1050 | Expected 'Property' |
| 448 | Named argument not found | 1051 | Number of arguments must be consistent across properties specification |
| 449 | Argument not optional | 1052 | Cannot have multiple default property/method in a Class |
| 450 | Wrong number of arguments or invalid property assignment | 1053 | Class initialize or terminate do not have arguments |
| 451 | Object not a collection | 1054 | Property set or let must have at least one argument |
| 452 | Invalid ordinal | 1055 | Unexpected 'Next' |
| 453 | Specified DLL function not found | 1056 | 'Default' can be specified only on 'Property' or 'Function' or 'Sub' |
| 454 | Code resource not found | 1057 | 'Default' specification must also specify 'Public' |
| 455 | Code resource lock error | 1058 | 'Default' specification can only be on Property Get |

*Table Continued on Following Page*

| Code | Description | Code | Description |
|------|-------------|------|-------------|
| 457 | This key is already associated with an element of this collection | 5016 | Regular Expression object expected |
| 458 | Variable uses an OLE Automation type not supported in Visual Basic | 5017 | Syntax error in regular expression |
| 462 | The remote server machine does not exist or is unavailable | 5018 | Unexpected quantifier |
| 481 | Invalid picture | 5019 | Expected ']' in regular expression |
| 500 | Variable is undefined | 5020 | Expected ')' in regular expression |
| 501 | Cannot assign to variable | 5021 | Invalid range in character set |
| | | 32811 | Element not found |

*For more information about VBScript, visit Microsoft's VBScript site, at*
http://msdn.microsoft.com/scripting.

Setup cannot install system files or update shared files if the files are in use. Before any open applications.

WARNING: This program is protected by copyright law and international treaties.

You may install Microsoft Data Access 2.1 on a single computer. Some Microsoft produc with additional rights, which are stated in the End User License Agreement included with

Please take a moment to read the End User License Agreement now. It contains all of the conditions that pertain to this software product. By choosing to continue, you indicate acce these terms.

| Continue | Exit Setup |

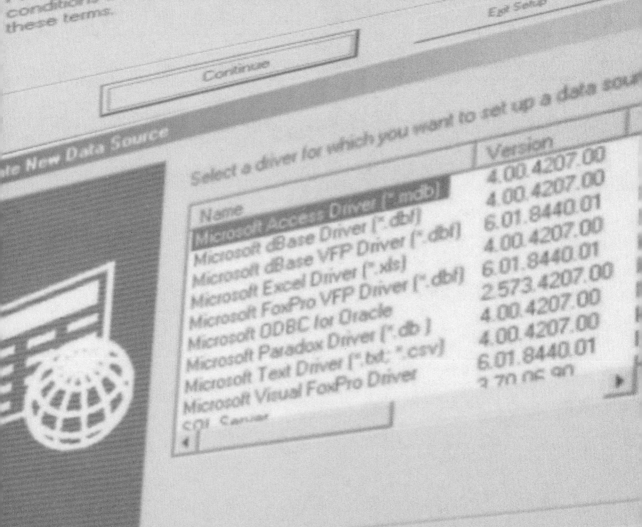

to New Data Source

Select a driver for which you want to set up a data sour

| Name | Version |
| --- | --- |
| Microsoft Access Driver (*.mdb) | 4.00.4207.00 |
| Microsoft dBase Driver (*.dbf) | 4.00.4207.00 |
| Microsoft dBase VFP Driver (*.dbf) | 6.01.8440.01 |
| Microsoft Excel Driver (*.xls) | 4.00.4207.00 |
| Microsoft FoxPro VFP Driver (*.dbf) | 6.01.8440.01 |
| Microsoft ODBC for Oracle | 2.573.4207.00 |
| Microsoft Paradox Driver (*.db ) | 4.00.4207.00 |
| Microsoft Text Driver (*.txt; *.csv) | 4.00.4207.00 |
| Microsoft Visual FoxPro Driver | 6.01.8440.01 |
| SQL Server | 3.70.06.90 |

| Finish | Cancel |

# Index

stuffing data from recordsets, 85
viewing values, 247
**variants, 559**
stuffing fields, 519
**VB script**
Alert function, 348
Len function, 348
Response.Write
*common mistakes, 85*
**VB Script**
common errors, 467
error object
*error syntax, 452*
*properties and methods, 436*
*run-time errors, 451*
InStr function, 628
IsNull function, 626
Timer () function, 662
**Visual Interdev**
Personal Web Server (PWS), 47

# W

**WAM**
see Web Application Manager (WAM)
**Wcat**
see Web capacity analysis tool (Wcat)
**Web Application Manager (WAM)**
processor time, 652
**Web capacity analysis tool (Wcat), 655**
**web site URLs**

displaying text only, 365
**WHERE clause, 119, 512**
BETWEEN...AND keywords, 121
common mistakes, 234
cookies, 415, 419
Delete method, recordsets, 320
DELETE statement, 373, 380
IN keyword, 122
IS NOT operator, 121
LIKE/NOT LIKE comparison operators, 121
logical operators, 124
login verification, 712
numeric comparison operators, 120
simple, 120
to find specific record, 121
UPDATE statement, 356
values, types, 120
**Windows 2000**
ADO, installing, 61
ASP, 36
*installing, 43*
Internet Information Server (IIS), installing, 43
Personal Web Server (PWS), 48
**Windows 98**
Personal Web Server (PWS), 47
*installation, 48*
**Windows 9x**
ADO, installing, 61
**Windows NT**
see NT

Setup cannot install system files or update shared files if the files are in use. Before any open applications.

WARNING: This program is protected by copyright law and international treaties.

You may install Microsoft Data Access 2.1 on a single computer. Some Microsoft produc with additional rights, which are stated in the End User License Agreement included with

Please take a moment to read the End User License Agreement now. It contains all of the conditions that pertain to this software product. By choosing to continue, you indicate accep these terms.

Exit Setup

Continue

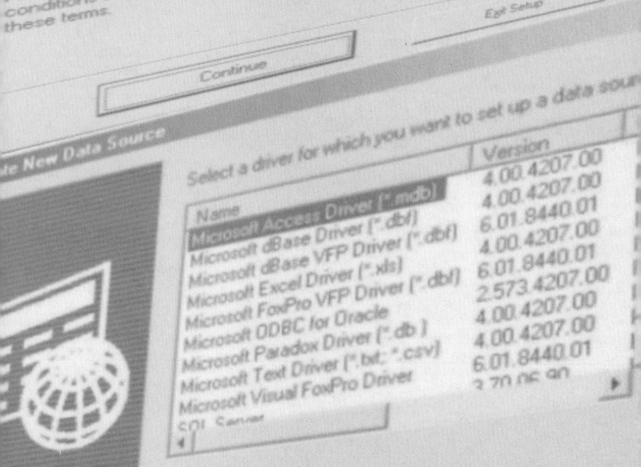

te New Data Source

Select a driver for which you want to set up a data sour

| Name | Version |
|---|---|
| Microsoft Access Driver (*.mdb) | 4.00.4207.00 |
| Microsoft dBase Driver (*.dbf) | 4.00.4207.00 |
| Microsoft dBase VFP Driver (*.dbf) | 6.01.8440.01 |
| Microsoft Excel Driver (*.xls) | 4.00.4207.00 |
| Microsoft FoxPro VFP Driver (*.dbf) | 6.01.8440.01 |
| Microsoft ODBC for Oracle | 2.573.4207.00 |
| Microsoft Paradox Driver (*.db ) | 4.00.4207.00 |
| Microsoft Text Driver (*.txt; *.csv) | 4.00.4207.00 |
| Microsoft Visual FoxPro Driver | 6.01.8440.01 |
| SQL Server | 3.70.06.90 |

Finish

Cance